One Eye Closed

The Other Red

The California Bootlegging Years

To Ron Logo
Hope you enjoy
this desert heritage &
California memories
Clifford Riddell
December 1999

One Eye Closed
The Other Red

The California Bootlegging Years

By Clifford James Walker

Back Door Publishing

Barstow, CA.

BACK DOOR PUBLISHING
1204 GEN COURT
BARSTOW, CALIFORNIA 92311

©1999 by Clifford James Walker
and Back Door Publishing

Set in 11 point Roman type
Designed by Ron McKinley
Southwest Savvy, Apple Valley
Cover design by Maggie Heyn
Manufactured in the United States of America

Library of Congress Catalog Card Number: 99.96454
Walker, Clifford James, 1930-

One Eye Closed, the Other Red: the California
Bootlegging Years

A Back Door Publishing Book
Includes index.

California History—1917-1940. 2. Prohibition—1917-1935. 3. Roaring Twenties.
4. California Bootlegging. California Moonshining. 5. California in World War I,
1917-18. 6. California Society, Social 7. California Rumrunning.

ISBN 0-9673141-1-9

Table of Contents

LIST OF MAPS

PREFACE

As a little girl, my mother went with the Simpson girl in Venice to deliver pints of alcohol for Simpson's bootlegging father, who later changed his name to Simson, dropping the "p" because of trouble he had while bootlegging. My grandfather, Alexander Walker, in Menlo Park, used his small basement to distill alcohol which he turned into scotch and bathtub gin. According to my cousins Bill Ator and Alison Ryerson, Grandfather Walker and Harry Shotten opened a speakeasy in a big wooden house on Alameda de las Pulgas, known during bootlegging years as Whiskey Row. Alison said her young uncles, Dave and Bill Walker, talked her into siphoning off a bit of Grandfather Walker's basement stash because she would not get into as much trouble if she were caught. My sister, Alexandria Planting, said when Walker ran for mayor of Menlo Park, he brought pints over to St. Patrick's Seminary in order to win over 12 votes at the seminary. He won that election but in the next a "clean government" slate of candidates won. Perhaps there was a connection between his elections and his bootlegging.

Uncle Fred Ator "made fine fig wine" in his basement, and he was practically a non-drinker. Uncles Dave and Bill got into that too. Once they drank so much that when changing clothes for a date, they took off their work clothes and put on each other's dirty clothes. Story goes, they didn't know the difference.

Jim Walker, my father, was a mechanic in San Francisco in the late 1920s, and several times repaired bullet holes in federal prohibition cars, metallic scars from gun fights with rumrunners. He patched the same cars more than once. These bootlegging stories peaked my interest in this period of California history.

As a history teacher I looked forward to teaching a most fascinating period of American history—the Roaring Twenties. Lectures brought chuckles to the class and insights to the students' own behaviors as they learned about changes occurring in the first twenty-five years of our 20th century: Out went corsets, up went skirts, on went bras, teddies, flappers, off went long hair. For men, off came most mustaches; on came double-breasted suits.

Soldiers came back home after spending time in England or France, back to a country where women could now vote in most states. By 1920 women's suffrage would be the law of the land. Back came the soldiers to a country where they could not legally buy a cold beer or a highball. Saloons *per se* were gone, but a whole culture evolved around sneaking drinks into nightclubs or into Cal-Stanford games or restaurants, or taking a lady to a speakeasy—those were the things to do.

The automobile made a more mobile country. Cars and a network of national roads replaced trains and buggies as the family mode of transportation. Entire industries evolved around the automobile: factories, accessories, filling stations, auto courts, tourist camps and automobile clubs. Courtship patterns changed with the advent of "tin lizzies" and "Model A's" and rumble seats. Inventions like electric appliances, movies, radio altered family life. The stock market, college and professional sports, sex and Freud were common discussions—even in mixed company. Women even smoked in public.

I had many reasons for studying the prohibition period in California. History books barely covered the Roaring Twenties—a little about bootlegging in Chicago, New York and Appalachia, but nothing of this time in California. Even California history books ignored this colorful era. As I researched Mojave Desert history, I found more about prohibition activities. I found that desert springs and mine tunnels were once used for making moonshine. Some of my students said their grandparents made moonshine in the desert, in Oklahoma or both.

In the late 1970s I interviewed older Californians for their bootlegging stories. I wanted to record their recollections, their words, their feelings. Up and down the state I traveled, looking for their dramas. I walked into a bar in Gualala along the north coast and asked the bartender if he knew of a 70-year-old prostitute *(I was less than 50 years old then.)*. The word went around town and that night and the next day I had some great interviews about bootlegging—but not with any old prostitutes, sorry to say.

I did not want to write a history book as such. I wanted the bootleggers' account so readers could feel the history of that period. I wanted readers to experience U. S. Customs patrolmen's stories of trying to stop smuggling along the Mexican border. I wanted wives' and children's perceptions as they remembered living through those times. Since I wanted the flavor of the people, the differences in speech in the various regions of California, the expressions of the times, I edited their stories as little as possible. For example, the words *gat, big shot* and *lay low* are not just cliches out of James Cagney and Edward G. Robinson movies; they were words used by bootleggers or prohibition agents (known as "prohis" in California).

In some cases photos are poor. Though they may be old or fuzzy or taken by amateurs 60-80 years ago, they convey part of the bootlegging story. Newspapers and even governments are not always accurate. Names are sometimes spelled wrong—a few even have three spellings. I tried to use the names as I found them and as informants told me. Errors, however, are still my responsibility.

Because I also wanted to cover the entire state, I sought writings from local historians. Therefore, *One Eye Closed, the Other Red: The California Bootlegging Years* is told by over a hundred people. A story with "as told by" means the person gave me the story orally, usually tape recorded; "by" means the person wrote the article. Most informants and authors are included in the text, and therefore not in the endnotes. Full reference is in Works Cited.

These tales are sometimes sad, filled with pathos, sometimes humorous, often exaggerated, often warm, often brutal, but always *human*. My regrets are that I could not cover each community, could not include all participants, all the stories. Further regrets are for not finishing this book in time for some participants to read their stories. Descendants of the participants deserve to have their ancestors mentioned in history. History should not just be about wars, governors and presidents, but about common folk. Death took most wives, rumrunners and federal agents before their stories could be told. To the millions of living Californians descended from participants of this era, I have tried to capture the times of your ancestors.

Besides the decade of the 1920s the bootlegging years also included the late 1910s with local option laws and "War Time Prohibition," which ironically went into effect eight months **after** World War I ended. Of course the "dry years" overlapped early depression years of 1930-33. Even after prohibition ended on December 5, 1933, bootlegging and moonshining continued. The main bootlegging era lasted from 1919-1933—14 years.

Let's go back with these Californians and revisit the *California Bootlegging Years.*

ACKNOWLEDGMENTS

For over 20 years, people have helped with this book. They have been encouraging, urging me to finish and have been patient when it took so long. Generous folks at historical societies, archives (national, state and local), museums, libraries and newspaper offices—thank you for being gracious and helpful.

Thanks to so many who found a bed for me, enabling me to afford covering most of California: Bill and Celia Ator, Bob and Cecily Bundy, Pat and Heather Davitt, Shirley DeLucci, Wally Eshleman, Mike and Robin Iten, Frank and Shirley Moreno, Sandy and John Planting, Bill and Yvonne Plate, Pam and Maurice Pelletier, Dorothy Dallara Reed, Mary Walker Valdez, Ethel Walker and Peggy Prater.

How can I thank the writers who so generously gave me their works, their stories, their time? Some of these important contributors were Lee Echols, Chula Vista; Ralph "Swede" and Pat Pedersen, Sausalito; Carl Eifler, Salinas; Norton Steenfott, Eureka; Herbert Hughes, Holtville; Gladys Ferguson, Holtville; G. William Puccinelli, San Mateo; William Cullen, San Mateo; Nellie Hyman for Frank Hyman, Fort Bragg; Richard Mason, Inverness; Margaret Brush, Trona, for generously allowing me to use her father's writing; Ralph and Barbara Oswald, Menlo Park; Ernie Wichels, Vallejo; Allen Lehman, Crescent City. Special acknowledgment to Larry Williams of Bakersfield for his efforts in preserving prohibition history. To all those others who gave me their stories, this book belongs to you too and your descendants.

For proofreading, Larry Cady, Myrtie Keddy, Adrienne Knute, Kandee McKinley, Barbara Walker and others who read parts, thanks for catching many errors I missed. I am totally responsible for any errors in this book, whether in content or usage, and welcome any corrections to improve the next edition.

To Ron McKinley of Southwest Savvy, Apple Valley, for his organizing and computer skills and Dave Tisthammer of Adelanto Printing & Graphics for his technical assistance.

And finally, thanks to my wife Barbara for allowing me to pursue my dreams and patiently waiting for me in some basement archive or waiting until I read another year of a California newspaper. To my children, Leslie, Dian, Lane, Scott, Randy, Heather, thanks for understanding when I was researching or hiding away writing.

INTRODUCTION

By 1913 the united forces of the Anti-Saloon League, Prohibition Party, Woman's Christian Temperance Union (WCTU), dozens of churches, World League Against Alcoholism, National Temperance Council, Templars of Honor and Temperance, Citizens' Committee of One Thousand and a score more had so much clout they could determine who would be elected. Prohibitionists passed important bills at the local and state level and a few at the federal level. The Webb-Kenyon Bill, for example, prohibiting the transportation of any alcohol into dry states, was passed over President Taft's veto in 1913, despite fierce resistance from the alcohol beverage industries.

At the end of 1914, the House of Representatives voted for a resolution to submit a prohibition amendment to the states, a vote of 197 to 190, not enough for the two-thirds vote required. Coming close, however, charged the prohibition coalition like no other defeat ever stimulated any cause. Before the 1916 election, dry forces asked every House and Senate candidate to pledge to vote submission of a national prohibition amendment to the states. Then drys organized a vigorous campaign to elect men who so pledged. Before the country knew whether Wilson or Hughes won California's electoral votes, drys knew they had won. Said Wayne B. Wheeler, the driving force behind the movement: "Dry workers throughout the nation were celebrating our victory. We knew the prohibition amendment would be submitted to the states by the Congress just elected." By the time the United States entered the Great War on April 6, 1917, prohibition became law in 26 of the 48 states. California was not one of these but most California counties were dry or partially dry. Nationwide, local option laws enabled 2,235 counties to vote themselves dry, with only 305 counties wet."[1] Prohibitionists were high with spirit and momentum.

Working the amendment through Congress started in June 1917 with the Judiciary Committee of the House recommending passage of the amendment. "There is probably no other constitutional amendment that has been submitted to the states in the past that has been petitioned for so largely, and it would seem that whatever may be the individual views of the members upon the merits of the moral question involved, the legislative duty to submit is plain," reported the committee.

Even anti-prohibitionist representatives, signing the pledge, honored their pledges by voting to submit the amendment to the states for ratification. Shrugging their shoulders, congressmen said, "Let the states and the people decide." Both Senate and House voted to do just that in December, 65-20 and 282-128 respectively.

Fighting then shifted to states for or against ratification. Local and state officials knew if they wanted to be re-elected, they should vote for the Eighteenth Amendment. Money poured into prohibition campaigns from all over the country, dimes and dollars from church offerings, pennies and nickels from Sunday school children and huge sums from businessmen who believed strongly in prohibition, and from those who found it advantageous to donate to the cause.

Wets fought back. But they had some disadvantages. The wine industry, liquor companies and breweries did not organize as they could have. Individually, each struck sorties at the temperance enemy, wrote pamphlets, articles and gave money to campaigns. An example: the California Grape Growers Association collected $1,500 in December 1917, for their anti-prohibition fight in California. Their plan, in the hands of Frank P. Swett of Martinez, was basic: fight ratification of the 18th Amendment and take the contest to the courts. Wine growers planned to challenge pre-election pledges as a violation of the state penal code, Section 85. The wets did not have the power to determine who would be elected or who would go down to defeat, but organized prohibitionists did.

Reformers used every appeal possible: pity, shame, style, bandwagon, celebrity, family, home, the noble workingman who faithfully brought his check home to his family versus a man who cashed his in the saloon while an undernourished waif of a daughter looked into the saloon to see if her daddy were inside. Other appeals to emotion came from American sympathies for the allies and against the German-Austrian-Hungarian side. Patriotism became a weapon for the drys. Since Germans drank beer and Germans were ruthless in Belgium, America should eliminate beer. Despite poor logic the propaganda had its effect.

Seventy-five to 85 percent of the state legislators voted for change in the Constitution. All states passed it except Connecticut and Rhode Island. In 21 states not a single vote was cast against it.[2] New York, Pennsylvania and Illinois made the prohibition amendment an issue in the 1918 election. Drys won in those states. As Fletcher Dobyns said in *The Amazing Story of Repeal*, "There can be no question that...the overwhelming majority of the people were determined that the nation should be purged of the liquor traffic and the adoption of the amendment was the result of irresistible pressure of the public sentiment."

As 1918 ended, thirty-three states had legislated themselves dry and voted for the amendment. Other states allowed local option, which meant cities and counties could vote themselves dry. Many had done so in California. The country voted dry. The Eighteenth Amendment became part of the Constitution of the United States, the law of the land.

Amendment XVIII

Section 1. After one year from the ratification of this article the manufacture, sale, or transportation of intoxicating liquors within, the importation thereof into, or the exportation thereof from the United States and all territory subject to the jurisdiction thereof for beverage purposes is hereby prohibited.

Section 2. The Congress and the several states shall have the concurrent power to enforce this article by appropriate legislation.

This new law of the land was proposed on December 18, 1917, ratified January 16, 1919, certified January 29, 1919, and became effective January 16, 1920.

The battle was over. Drys won and wets lost. Drys celebrated and wets wept, got drunk, moped, despaired, and some prepared to hunker down for the long dry spell.

Political and moral reformers changed the Constitution. Legislative morality caused millions of moral dilemmas. *In One Eye Closed, the Other Red: The California Bootlegging Years,* Californians tell their stories about facing political and moral conflicts during the next fourteen years—the bootlegging years of California.

Pages of hymns and prohibition fight songs sung by Woman's Christian Temperance Union and prohibition groups from the late 1910s to the end of prohibition. Many songs used tunes of famous battle, church and popular songs of the day.

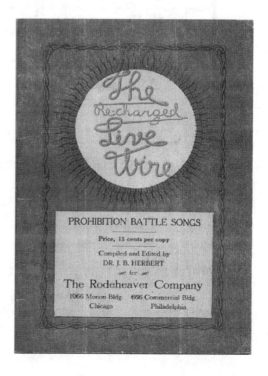

1944 - 115

To Carry Forward the W—— of the

Anti-Saloon League of Pennsylvania

"THE CHURCH IN ACTION AGAINST THE SALOON"

For one year I will pay toward the support of the Anti-Saloon League of Pennsylvania the sum per month indicated by my (X) mark, payable quarterly, in advance.

Name ....

....

Church .... Date ....

	$20.00 per month		$1.00	per month
	10.00 per month		.75	per month
	15.00 per month		.50	per month
	3.00 per month		.41⅔	per month
	2.50 per month		.33⅓	per month
	2.00 per month			per month

Fifty cents of the above subscription of 33⅓ cents per month, or more, is intended to pay my annual subscription to The American Issue, Pennsylvania Edition. Subscription entered when first quarter is paid.

STATE HEADQUARTERS, 1014-1022 Stock Exchange Bldg., Phila.

Typical drive of Anti-Saloon League for membership and monetary support. Each state had a branch of the Anti-Saloon League. Thousands of dollars and hard work made the prohibition movement the most powerful political force in the country.

FOR THE INFORMATION OF THE SIGNER.

House Joint Resolution 168 was introduced by Congressman Hobson, of Alabama; Senate Joint Resolution 88 was introduced by Senator Sheppard, of Texas. These two resolutions provide for the submission by Congress for ratification by the legislatures of three-fourths of the States of an amendment to the United States Constitution, *providing for nation-wide prohibition of the manufacture and sale of Wine, Beer, Whiskey, and other fermented and distilled liquors,* except for mechanical, scientific and medicinal purposes. Senate Joint Resolution 50 is offered by Senator Works, of California, for like prohibition of "DISTILLED liquor containing alcohol." All are measures supported by the Anti-Saloon League and other "dry" organizations who are flooding Congress with letters and telegrams urging their passage. No State denies to the individual the right to use liquors. The right to use, necessarily implies the right to purchase. The right to purchase is of small avail if this attempted national legislation, by prohibiting manufacture and sale, should make it impossible to purchase.

We urge you to protest against this sumptuary legislation which affects the right of each individual to regulate his own conduct.

DETACH THE SLIP BELOW. SIGN, ADDRESS AND MAIL IT TO THE CONGRESSMAN FROM YOUR DISTRICT. Also send similar protests to the two SENATORS from your State. DO THIS AT ONCE. It is the duty of your Congressman and Senators to file your protest.

Your Postmaster can give you the name of the Congressman from your district and of the two Senators from your State.

(City)————————————————1914

Hon.————————————————————————————

Washington, D. C.

Dear Sir:

I, the undersigned, a voter in

County,

State of————————————, protest most earnestly against the adoption of House Joint Resolution 168, Senate Joint Resolutions 88 and 50, and all similar prohibition measures introduced in Congress as an unwarranted interference with the rights of all American citizens and a usurpation by the Federal Government of a domestic question belonging to the several States.

These attempts to bring about such legislation would deny to me that full freedom of choice in personal conduct now accorded in all the States of the Union in the purchase of Wine, Beer, Whiskey, and other fermented and distilled liquors.

1914 anti-prohibition campaign to stop the dry momentum in the country and to prevent Congress from submitting a prohibition amendment to the states. It did not work.

MAP OF CALIFORNIA

California Counties
and
Selected Cities
and
Place Names

CHAPTER 1

THE BOOZE IS BEHIND THE TOILET

W hen he heard the knock on the door of his fashionable home in Palm Springs, the movie actor host opened the door for the guests, a local politician and his lovely girlfriend. A talking parrot greeted visitors with: "The booze is behind the toilet! The booze is behind the toilet!"

Each time a new guest arrived, the parrot squawked, "The booze is behind the toilet!" Later, a guest looked out the window and saw the local constable drive up. The host threw a towel over the parrot and welcomed the constable at the door. He entered, walked over to the covered parrot cage, pulled off the cover. "The booze is behind the toilet! The booze is behind the toilet!"

Armilda Jane James, a former chorus girl who went to Palm Springs as a maid, told the above incident about the bootlegging days, only one of millions of stories occurring in the fourteen years of prohibition, 1919-1933.[1] Up and down the state, from small villages to large cities, people reacted to a law that prohibited selling, transporting and making alcoholic beverages. Not just a law—it was now part of the Constitution, Amendment 18, the law of the land. Thousands of Californians responded to the law by violating it: they sold, transported or made booze. Hundreds of thousands drank liquor, creating a demand that never seemed to be satisfied. Adding to this demand were thousands of tourists and immigrants entering California in the 1920s. Moonshiners and bootleggers helped satisfy this increasing market. A sophisticated smuggling operation evolved in California from land, sea and air providing more affluent drinkers with the finest liquor from Europe and Canada. Attempts to stop this flood of liquor created a California Rum War.

Most Californians kept one eye closed to violations. Of course those who drank appreciated their sources and ignored other lawbreakers. Supporters of the prohibition amendment and supporters of law and order reported these violations, but became discouraged when the same bootleggers kept selling or when new bootleggers took the places of old ones. Eventually concerned citizens just gave up and looked the other way.

For the most part, Californians faced prohibition with **one eye closed, the other red.**[2]

The following pages are some of their stories, Californian stories during the **Bootlegging Years.**

In a quiet, respectable Italian restaurant in Los Angeles early in November, 1929, five men, two from Los Angeles and three Italians from Chicago, were having their wine and antipasto. They discussed the fate of Austrian-born Frank Baumgarteker should he refuse to accept the ultimatum of relinquishing control of his distillery and winery.

The Los Angeles distillery had the capacity of producing $50,000 worth of alcohol a day. The Cucamonga winery could produce more thousands of dollars worth. Both operated under government permits and had thousands of gallons of bonded wine, brandy and alcohol stored.

The "request" was reasonable: relinquish control of the distillery and winery and be a rich man; refuse and be eliminated. Frank Baumgarteker had refused so far. They decided to make one more offer.[3]

∅

The steamer *Washington* delivered to Eureka thirty big metal drums labeled "Coffee," consigned to Northland Coffee Company of Arcata. Since there was no such company, federal prohibition agents, "prohis," investigated the July 1926 shipment. The huge drums each contained 50 gallons of whiskey. Agents subsequently arrested Hans Stittmatter for his importing activities.

During the investigation, the government had the "coffee" securely stored. All 30 drums disappeared—1500 gallons of whiskey, taken from under the noses of the federal guards!

Even though all the evidence vanished, state officials held Stittmatter because he was one of eighteen wanted on warrants for a state-wide rumrunning ring, and because of his possible involvement in the Moss Landing gun battle near Salinas.[4]

∅

The angry wife of prohibition agent Kerrigan sued him during their divorce. She wanted a bigger share of his assets: a town house, a country house, two cars, a speedboat and money in the bank under assumed names—all saved in a few years while working as a Prohi. His weekly wages as a prohibition agent: $35.00![5]

∅

"I was delivering booze for my father before I was ten year old," stated William Genini of San Francisco. "Once I was pushing a baby carriage up Vallejo Street. In the baby carriage were bottles of booze wrapped in a blanket. I got three-four houses up the hill, when a policeman came around the corner. I became nervous and afraid. I didn't want to be arrested so I let go of the baby buggy and ran across the street.

"Thinking there was a baby in the carriage, the policeman ran after it. When it crashed against a light pole, the concerned policeman examined the contents under the blanket. He called me over. I was afraid but I went to the policeman. He picked out a bottle, put it under his jacket and said, 'Be a good boy now and go about your business.'"6

⌀

A young couple who had walked off the San Francisco-Sausalito ferry, went over to two fishermen on a pier in Sausalito who had just finished lunch.

"Where can we get a drink?" the young man asked.

"See that cross sticking out of the trees on the side of the hill?" answered the fisherman, pointing to the church steeple.

"Yes," nodded the couple.

"Well, that's the only place in Sausalito where you can't get booze."7

⌀

In the middle 1920s, the San Anselmo Rotary International conducted its luncheon meeting at Pastori's Roadhouse near San Anselmo. Reverend Ernest Bradley, Rector and Dean of the Episcopal Church of San Rafael and Secretary of the Rotary Club, presented a lecture for the luncheon program.

Toward the end of the lecture the law raided the restaurant. The "dry squad" agents confiscated a large stock of liquor, "stronger than the 18th Amendment allowed," hidden in a false basement. No liquor was found in possession of the club members. Bradley's lecture: "Law Enforcement." "Action suited to the word," wrote the *Sausalito News*.

Sweet Wine
as told by William Cullen, San Mateo

Late in 1932, in South San Francisco, Joe Pucci and I made wine with a ton of late grapes. We both worked at Swift and Company. Body textly one ton of grapes will make 150 gallons of fine dry wine, but these grapes were so late they were too sweet. After Christmas, Joe let me have what was left of his share because of its sweetness—too sweet for that Italian. I sold much of it for 35¢ a gallon, but people kept coming over to my house at all times of the day, even at four o'clock in the morning. Old Baldwin Butte always came over to my house in San Mateo, banging at my door. Oh, no, 3:00 a.m. It's Baldwin Butte wanting wine.

I finally got rid of those three fifty-gallon barrels, gave most of it away. Just as I got rid of the wine, the country went wet. I was able to sleep better after prohibition ended—no more waking up to help one man's problem with National Prohibition.

⌀

The Madden shipworks in Sausalito started fulfilling a new government contract remodeling the first of ten federal launches, making them faster and more modern, able to compete in an unequal war with speedy, sleek rumrunners.

On the other dock several of Madden's workers tested a high-powered motor boat which mechanics tuned with precision, checked the greased gears and pulled the emergency dump-shoot lever to make sure it released perfectly.

Madden specialized in remodeling rum-running launches too.

The emergency lever was specially designed to pull if a Coast Guard ship trapped the boat. The load of alcohol, wrapped in canvas, slid smoothly into the water and a float marked the spot, while the lightened rumrunner sped away pursued by the Coast Guard boat.

Madden was satisfied with his workers' job—remodeling a rum-running launch at the same time he worked on the federal boats.

Well respected by all his constituents, Mayor J. Herbert Madden, of Sausalito, later spent 15 months as a guest of McNeil Island federal prison in Washington state, because of his involvement with a northern California rum-running ring.[9]

The Prohibition Border
excerpts from *The Deadliest Colonel*
by Thomas N. Moon and Carl F. Eifler

The Mexican border was alive with problems and characters. One bootlegger and smuggler named "Koot" Davis crossed over from Mexico and was arrested for the knifing of another man. He remarked to U. S. Customs agent Lee Echols, "Hell, Lee, I just stuck my knife in his guts and walked around him."

The little walk around him cost the other man his life and the charge was amended to murder. This incident caused an international problem. Davis stabbed him in Mexicali, Mexico, but the man died in El Centro, California. Both countries wanted to prosecute Davis.

One of the big problems was rumrunning from Mexico. Then, as now, U. S. Customs relied heavily on informants in Mexico. One group in particular was being watched, and the information came that they were going to make a run over the border at a certain point on a certain night (east of Tijuana). Eifler and fellow officer Rusty Russel lay in ambush. Suddenly the truck came in view, loaded with booze. As the customs men moved in to make the arrest, a gun battle broke out. Firing came down on Eifler and Russel from another direction. They feared a pincer movement. Finally the smugglers broke contact and fled back over the border, leaving the evidence behind.

Several days later Eifler and Russel sat in a small cafe in Tijuana with the men they had tried to arrest, discussing the gun battle as one might discuss a game of checkers.

"Who was up the hill using that .45?" Eifler asked.

The other men looked at each other, then looked back at Eifler. "It wasn't one of our men. It must have been one of yours," they replied.

"No, we weren't using .45's. All we had was shotguns," Eifler replied. By piecing the action together, both sides suddenly realized there was a third party at the battle. Some hijackers had been waiting to pick up the load after it crossed the border and the customs men had inadvertently stepped in between two groups.

"Well, anyway, it's good no one was hit," Eifler finally said.

One of the other men quickly replied, "You are wrong, Señor. You hit my brother and he lay on the hill for two days."

Eifler had instinctively fired at a flash and had no idea he had hit anyone.

Attempts to Crash into San Quentin

Fred E. Clements could see the big gray walls of San Quentin projecting out of the November 1929, San Francisco Bay fog. The bus parked in front by the visitors' parking lot. Clements pulled his coat around his neck, climbed down the bus steps and walked over to guards at the main gate. The walls looked even higher up close. Maybe it was just the fog.

"I'm Fred Clements from San Bernardino," he told the guards. "I've been sentenced to San Quentin and I'm here to turn myself in."

"You're here by yourself? Where's your commitment order?" asked the huge guard.

"I guess it's down in San Bernardino," he answered, "but I have to serve one to three years for moonshining and I'm here to start my sentence."

"We can't let anyone in unless it's official. That's the rules."

"I have been sentenced and the Supreme Court of California turned down my appeal. I'm out on $10,000 bond and need to turn myself in. Just take me in, okay?" pleaded Clements.

"I'll call the warden," said the puzzled guard.

"Warden, I have a man here, a Mr. Clements, who insists on being admitted," the guard said into the phone.

Warden James B. Holohan talked to Clements in the admittance office.

"I have to serve one to three years and I'm here to start my sentence," Clements explained again.

"I'm sorry, we can't let you in without a court commitment. I'll wire the San Bernardino Court and tell them you're here. You can wait outside, go over to the town and wait if you want."

Deputy Sheriff W. L. Shay of San Bernardino wired back with instructions. Deputy Sheriff Tom Mulligan would be arriving that afternoon or in the morning to incarcerate two more county prisoners and he would take custody of Clements.[10]

When Mulligan found the willing prisoner "hanging around," Clements asked if he could ride back to San Bernardino with him. After they arrived in San Bernardino, Clements turned himself over to Jailer R. A. Bright.

In a couple of days Clements and a deputy made the 470-mile trip back up to San Quentin. This time the guards received him and Warden Holohan welcomed Clements to the "big gray house."

His almost two years of playing with the San Bernardino Sheriff's Department and the courts had ended.

San Bernardino "Dry Squad" had arrested Clements and his wife early in 1928 for possessing and operating a still. The court found them both guilty under the new law which made operating a still a felony. Jesse Clements started serving her year sentence while Fred got out on a $10,000 bond when he asked for a re-trial.

The judge turned down the re-trial but his lawyer appealed to the Supreme Court on grounds that one cannot be sentenced for "possessing" a still as a separate crime from "operating" a still. The Supreme Court agreed, dismissed the "possession" charge but upheld the "operation of a still" conviction.

In the meantime, Jesse had served her time, was released and filed for a divorce under desertion charges.

The county sheriffs could not find Clements. His bondsman stated he was in contact with Clements, could not reveal where he was, but assured the court he would turn himself in. Clements had vacationed his way up to San Francisco when he heard about the State Supreme Court ruling.

After a couple more days of freedom, Clements bought a one-way ticket to San Quentin and went to turn himself in. Unlike most prisoners who wanted out, he wanted in.

Bull Creek Moonshine
as told by Norton Steenfott, Eureka

There was a story of Bill out at Bull Creek who came into Eureka every two weeks with a ten-gallon keg. He took his mash, got his still going, let it run off into one of his kegs. Then he'd have another barrel of mash starting and in two weeks that would be ready.

Then he'd come back into town, to me first and I'd buy a gallon off him. That was right after repeal, we'd still have bootleg whiskey, $3.50 a gallon. I'd get him two or three more customers so he'd drive up and look for me when he'd come in. I'd go get a goddamn jug. We'd go into the alley and siphon it out. My friends bought some and then he'd go around to other customers he had.

Later he'd go out to a cuttin' area [lumber cutting] where he left the barrel with a friend. His friend could finish off any contents still in it. He'd pick up the empty barrel the next trip. Out there, a bunch of men were drinking. One of the fellows who already had bought a gallon and had taken it home, came back that next night to help clean that barrel up (drink it clean). They were all sitting around drinking, draining the goddamned thing out. They didn't want me to get any back. They had a funnel back there and this goddarn jug. Two guys held the barrel up to pour it into the funnel. Out came this goddamn gray squirrel, all the hairs off it, and it was just as slick and slimy as can be.

Most of those guys got sicker than hell right there. Here they were drinking this goddamn whiskey. This one guy got hold of Bill and made him give him his money back. He didn't give the whiskey back but made Bill give the money back.

Bill told me, "Jesus, I left the bung out of the barrel out there and the gray squirrel got down there, couldn't get out and drowned before I got back. I didn't know the goddamn thing was in there."

He told me about the slimy squirrel after my whiskey was already gone. I didn't notice any different taste however.

CHAPTER 2

BONE DRY OR DAMP: THE WAR YEARS AND PROHIBITION

A s the Great War progressed, from 1914 to 1917, American sentiment turned more against Germany and for England and France. Three years of English and French propaganda against the Germans and Austrians, three years of reading about German atrocities (according to the propaganda) and three years of dreaded submarines sinking ships with civilians aboard caused Americans to lose their neutrality. The Great War was in its third year when the Americans declared war on April 6, 1917.

Although sadly unprepared for war, the nation committed itself to whipping the Kaiser, "making the world safe for democracy" and "fighting the war to end all wars." America mobilized as fast as it could, establishing training camps, such as Camp Fremont in Menlo Park. North of San Diego the government established Camp Kearny, between Linda Vista and what is now Miramar Naval Air Station. Los Angeles tried to locate the camp close to the City of the Angels, protesting that San Diego had too much crime. The government chose San Diego and created a camp from a dry desolate area. Citizens donated land. Civilians worked hard in the war effort, building roads, rails, sewer, water, gas and electric systems, built so fast a motor division and a cavalry unit with 20,000 horses and mules moved in by June. In August, California National Guard outfits came on board. Ellen B. Scripps of La Jolla donated $15,000 for library books; YMCA set up a hostess house at the New Southern Hotel, 6th and B, where owner J. M. Anderson and the Rotary Club remodeled the first floor for enlisted men. When General Hunter Liggett inspected the camp in September, he called for more activated national guard units from California and other western states. These units formed the which served honorably in France. Besides 30,000 to 40,000 troops, the camp had airplane hangars, a huge hospital, trenches for trench-warfare practice, 1,162 buildings, including 10 warehouses and 140 mess halls. The brush and sand mesas were so out in the country that long after taps, soldiers were serenaded with coyotes. One night the coyotes were loud and close. Hearing the horrible sound, a sentry gave the alarm to the corporal of the guard and they inspected the imposing danger. They formed a small skirmish line and moved carefully toward the sound, surrounded it and closed in and found it came from one tent—a soldier was playing his bagpipes! As early as September 11, 1917, some units of the 40th National Guard struck their tents and headed for France. More guard units and draftees arrived in October.

With high morale, units trained hard. An Arizona national guard group came in with the slogan "From Linda Vista to France!" They also played hard with baseball and boxing. A San Francisco unit did especially well since it had members of the San Francisco Olympic Club.[1]

Californians volunteered for the war effort. Knitting clubs formed with Thursday night becoming knitting night. Ladies knitted warm socks and mittens to be used in the trenches of France and afghans for veterans hospitals. The Sonoma Eastern Star decorated Red Cross packages to be sent overseas and to training camps. Miners, ladies of the night, bootleggers and ranchers, according to the *Barstow Printer,* helped the Red Cross Fund by putting on a big barbecue for miners from Atolia, Trona, Johannesburg and Randsburg. The next month, May 1918, Barstow area earned $160 for the Red Cross with a barbecue at Waterman Ranch.[2]

Local vigilantes promised to ferret out enemies, urging people to turn in names to the American Defense League and to check out Germans, Austrians, Bulgarians and Turks"—everyone a potential enemy." One of these vigilantes, Senator Edward Grant, accused Henry J. Widenmann, a member of the State Highway Commission and a Supervisor of Solano County of disloyal German sentiment and "menacing the navy-yard city of Vallejo for propaganda purposes." The Solano County Council of Defense defended the Solano-born citizen as being totally loyal to America. He was loyal, of course, but Widenmann was a brewer and Grant was a radical prohibitionist.[3]

But perhaps nowhere did any Council of Defense do a better job in rooting out suspicious foreigners than did the Inyo County Council of Defense. It investigated A. O. Barnekow, supposedly from Sweden, after he drank a bit too much in Lone Pine and made anti-American speeches. He was given 60 days in the county jail. The Council would later decide whether to turn him over to the federal authorities as a dangerous alien.[4]

Before that the Council met in Independence on Tuesday, October 30, 1917, to hear charges about John H. Lubken. Lubken admitted he had "given voice to disloyal thoughts...(but) his future conduct would prove his loyalty to his Government." Although the council had affidavits to substantiate a few actions, others were not verified. He expressed his sorrow and resigned. For Lubken was himself a member of the Council of Defense for Inyo County. Members of the council accepted his resignation and believed he would be a good and loyal citizen of this Republic. The rancher Lubken also resigned his other job: Member of the Board of Supervisors of Inyo County—Chairman of the Board of Supervisors!

Every six months or so, the nation had a Liberty Bond Drive. During the fall drive of 1917, the 40th Division in Camp Kearny bought almost $100,000 worth of bonds in one day. As a result the soldiers were bombed on October 21, 1917, bombed into redoubling their efforts when the army squadron at North Island flew over Camp Kearny and bombed the camp with leaflets touting the foot soldiers with the amount of bonds North Island bought. Kearny doughboys then bought almost a million dollars worth. In May 1918, Druids (a club) withdrew $1,200 out of a German bank in San Francisco and bought Liberty Bonds. Small towns all over the state did their share. Barstow, for example, raised $5,230 in the May 1918 Liberty War Stamp Drive. Again in October 1918, another drive pushed the bonds with slogans like "Bonds Win Battles—Buy More Bonds." War Stamp Chairman for the city of Martinez, the last half of 1918, thanked citizens for buying 11,245 War Stamps at $5.00 each and 22,079 Thrift Stamps for 23 cents each, totaling $61,789. In the spring of 1919, after the war, the government ended its fifth and last Victory Loan with the cry "We have got to finish the job."[5]

TWO BIRDS -- ONE STONE

—Adapted from Dwig, in Des Moines Register.

The Kaiser could make no shrewder move than to subsidize every grog shop in America to keep on at full blast ladling out the stuff that takes the stamina out of this great people. Dr. Frank Crane

Prohibition movement poster using the Great War to create a stronger prohibition sentiment. Courtesy of the Warshaw Collection of Business Americana, Smithsonian.

May 1918, the *Sonoma Index-Tribune* took pledges for "Our boys in France Tobacco Fund." Inyo County was as patriotic as any other part of the state. Citizens gave a dance for all servicemen and newly-drafted young men in Bishop, providing all food and transportation and non-alcoholic drinks.

Up and down the state, newspapers such as the *Sonoma Index-Tribune*, pushed the war effort with recipes using meat and wheat substitutes, such as "Victory Mix Flour," urging all to make every day a "wheatless meal," using potatoes, fresh vegetables and fruit. Save four cups of flour a week per family and save 22 million pounds a year. Californians made many loaves of yeast potato bread during the war years.[6]

The U. S. Food Administration of California announced in the spring of 1918, that Californians would no longer need to have meatless days, but Golden Staters needed to conserve wheat as well as grains of all kinds. "You may eat all the meat you need, but be sure to save all the wheat and wheat products you can...." The announcement asked civilians to act like a military unit and in this campaign do their share three times a day. Along with this plea came several recipes: Wheatless Pie Crust, Barley Pone with Corn Meal and Egg-less Rye Muffins.[7]

In the summer of 1918, the government urged Americans to save even more food. Donate to Belgian Relief, clothing for Belgians, pleaded the government. Dr. Ray Lyman Wilbur, Vice President of Stanford, wrote "Fighting with Food," an article appearing in dozens of California newspapers. "The Key Notes of the 1918 California State Fair: Patriotism—Profit—Pleasure," ran the ad for the fair. "Exhibit your best to help solve the Nation's Food Problem." Prohibitionists used the war to push for conservation of food, especially barley, wheat, corn and sugar, by prohibiting these foods from being used for making alcohol. It was not right for foods to be taken away from feeding our soldiers and allies and used for alcohol, said the drys. Even Kaiser Wilhelm closed saloons and curtailed breweries in his war economy.[8] Congress passed a law prohibiting liquors and beers being sold to servicemen in 1917, supposedly making servicemen better soldiers.[9] In August and December of the same year, the Senate and House voted to send the 18th Amendment, the liquor prohibition amendment, to the states for ratification. Patriotism and prohibition seemed interwoven.

Inyo Independent, in the fall of 1917, ran a summary of William T. Borah's analysis of liquor use in the U. S., costing $2.4 billion, compared to $2.0 billion for the second Liberty Bond drive and $2.1 billion for Red Cross subscriptions. From the standpoint of food conservation, food waste and manufacturing energy wasted, versus good citizenship and good war effort, liquor should be prohibited, said Borah.

With the added pressure of prohibitionists and desire to save food for the war effort, President Wilson proclaimed that after October 1, 1918, no sugar, glucose, grains and fruits could be used to produce malt liquors, including near beer. On March 4, 1919, after the war, another proclamation allowed near beer to be produced but continued the prohibition of these products for making alcohol.

A TOAST

—Apologies to Minor and New York World

THE ALCOHOLIC UNFIT--"Here's to the Guy that went in My Place!"

"SEVENTY-SIX PER CENT of the young men who applied for enlistment were rejected because unfit to serve -- from their own drink habits, or their parents"--COL. MAUS

Does Your Boy Fill the Place of a DRINKING SLACKER?

A hyperbolic war-time ad appealing to patriotism and unfairness as thousands of American men were rejected from joining the military or discharged after being drafted because of alcoholism. Courtesy of the Warshaw Collection of Business Americana, Smithsonian.

War, obviously always in the news, pushed patriotic themes in every way possible. A serial book appeared weekly in the newspapers: *Outwitting the Hun*, by Lt. Pat O'Brien. Patriotism stirred the hearts and minds of Americans, made them volunteer, buy bonds, save bread, enlist in the service. Prohibition leadership used this patriotism to put pressure on legislators to vote for ratification of Amendment 18 and to pass local prohibition in cities and counties. Prohibition propaganda linked beer with the dreaded Germans. The drys made the most of war-time sentiment and tried to confuse prohibition with patriotism. German atrocities in the war fed prohibitionists with anti-beer propaganda. Basically, the Germans drank beer and look at the barbaric behavior of the Germans in the rape of Belgium. Therefore, beer caused this type of behavior. The non-sequitur went further to point out that prohibiting beer drinking would help the morals of Americans. Notice this excerpt from an Anti-Saloon League publication used for voters to choose pro-ratification legislators:[10]

The Dry Candidate Believes in: 1. The Conservation of Food, 2. The Conservation of Coal, 3. The Conservation of Man Power, 4. The Protection of Women and Children, 5. The Fostering of Patriotism, 6. The Defense of Liberty.

The Wet Candidate Believes in: 1. Brewery Politics, 2. Brewery Slush Fund, 3. The Purchasable Vote, 4. The Politically Negligent Churchman, 5. Liquor Politicians, 6. The Pro-German Vote.

Countering the prohibition high tide was an awesome task. *The Liberal Leader, The Official Organ of the Bartenders' Union,* Local 41, spoke out vehemently during 1916-18 period.[11] One article spoke of the inhumane massacres of Armenians and Georgians by the Turks. Yet Turkey banned alcohol and intoxicants. The French, on the other hand, served wine to its valiant soldiers fighting against the Germans. The English served rum to its soldiers in the trenches and the sailors on the ships, "but the world has heard nothing of atrocities committed by them." The slanted argument above was obvious with the use of "valiant soldiers" for the good guys and "massacres" for the bad ones. Both sides used fallacies. It is a wonder the wets did not use the fact the Kaiser prohibited saloons and breweries during the war and that made the German soldiers so ruthless. People may get mean without their beer.

The Manufacturing Chemists and Pharmacists published a 24-page pamphlet by William Eslers Von Krakou using fallacies. China, stated Von Krakou, stopped alcohol, then had a drug problem, now is receptive to allowing breweries. The Arabian reformers caused the downfall of a great empire and culture. "When the non-usage of alcohol took effect, intellectual stagnation and decay set in, they began to weaken and were driven out of every country previously conquered by them: their civilization became almost extinct for today they are a semi-savage tribe." Indians of the U. S. declined when they were put on reservations and not allowed to drink. People needed alcohol to fight off diseases, especially when old age set in with high blood pressure. Older people should worry about the "evils of water." The French, for example, had only one appendicitis out of 200 wine drinkers and 20 for the water drinkers. People needed alcohol, given to man by nature, to fight pathogenic microorganisms. If the country obeyed the law it might cause the "elimination of our race." He urged all to confront legislators because of the "right to overthrow such laws. It is not disloyalty to advocate their repeal when this Union is threatened by moral code, predigested by pious reformers and enforced by clubs, handcuffs and bullets." We must keep this country from being the "land of the free and home of the slave."[12]

The wine industry had an air of confidence. Because of their influence in key parts of the state, namely San Francisco, northern California, the central valleys, and some southern California grape growing areas, the industry had many supporters, and voters knew the economic importance of wine. California Grape Protective Association had campaigned hard and won the November

Nurses and "Corps Men" at Camp Kearny, North of San Diego, and overseas convalescents taking a sunbath at Camp Hospital. From 1917 through 1918, Californians supported the war effort, while prohibitionists used the war to end the manufacture and sale of liquor. Photos courtesy of Charlie Mitchell Collection, Mojave River Valley Museum, Barstow.

1916, election against California Proposition 1 and 2 to stop the selling of liquor by 1918, in saloons, stores, hotels and restaurants, and prohibit wine production by January 1920. Voters supported the wine industry. The legislature voted down the Rominger bill to prohibit saloons and sale of wine and liquor in the spring of 1917.[13] Again voters defeated liquor regulation Initiative

Proposition 1 and 2, on November 5, 1918. Despite state after state ratifying Amendment 18 and prohibitionists proposing numerous plans to destroy the wine industry, vineyardists had confidence. Sam Sebastiani went to New York in 1918 to sell his wines because that year would be a banner year for wines.

The wine industry countered arguments for plans to turn wine vineyards into raisin-grape fields or into orchards. Four years to replace wine grapes with eating or raisin grapes was impractical since the country did not need 170,000 more acres of raisin grapes and they could not plant fruit trees because Californians already pulled out over four million fruit trees since 1900. How unfair for a wine maker to be fined $1,000 for offering a glass of wine in his own house. The jobs of 150,000 people would be threatened, grape and wine export ruined, and the country hurt economically.

A local soldier Oscar A. Studley had his censored letter from the 822 Aero Repair Squadron, France, published in the *Sonoran-Index*. He commented on his duties, the price of items, 65 francs being worth 17.5 cents and how hard franc change was to count. The farmer in Studley remained as he observed great vineyards in France: "they sure look fine." He planned to find out what the French sprayed with and [censor...censor].

Ironically the same paper had an editorial about some prohibitionists' idea of buying vineyards and giving the land to soldiers when they come home from France. Confiscating vineyards and rescinding the right to raise grapes and wresting their lands by sumptuary legislation, the article stated, "is absurd—like legislation to regulate the size of bedsheets! When it becomes a crime to grow grapes, something is wrong with the world....Call it a crime to drink wine, but when it is a crime to possess a vineyard, make wine and have it in your possession, there is something disjointed with the point of view of those who come to think that way and something fundamentally unbalanced about this line of reasoning out of the problem of sobriety."[14]

"You cannot compensate a man for the passage of arbitrary laws whereby his life's work, the life he loves, is suddenly branded as illegitimate and a criminal calling."

The suggestion of raising chickens on vineyards was summarily dismissed as the poultry growers were having a difficult time "to make ends meet." As to giving the land to the returning soldiers "now fighting the fight of fights over there," they will return and turn the tide of justice, honesty and the temperate consideration of questions that now shake the foundations of our democracy. These soldiers will perhaps open the eyes of the politicians.

Other news appeared in California newspapers besides war news and prohibition propaganda. From October 1917 on, the flu epidemic was big news. In Marin County those without masks could be subject to arrests. Influenza started again in the fall of 1918, continuing until the spring of 1919. The year 1919 started with warnings to wear masks or stay out of school. Los Angeles announced on January 2, it had 487 new cases and 17 deaths, the next week 659 new cases and 21 deaths, San Francisco, 608 cases and 27 deaths.[15] The *News-Leader* of San Mateo recommended schools and movies be closed. It featured an article on "Spanish Influenza—What It Is and How It Should Be Treated." By the end of January, Richmond citizens had a mask-burning ceremony as the epidemic receded. Out of the 2,148 Richmond flu cases, 105 died in 1918; sighs of relief exuded as scores of people threw their masks into a pyre, watched carefully by the Richmond Fire Department. For them the flu season was over for another year.[16] The hysteria and the impact of the flu epidemic decreased until it was not a threat by the summer of 1919.

The OVERSHADOWING CuRSE
THE LEGALIZED SALOON

HAS SHE A FAIR CHANCE ?

"Our religion demands that every child should have a fair chance for citizenship in the coming kingdom. Our patriotism demands a saloonless country and a stainless flag."—P. A. Baker, General Superintendent Anti-Saloon League of America.

A Curse—is what the Anti-Saloon League called the legalized saloon. Notice the appeal to religion, fear and patriotism with "a stainless flag." Courtesy of the Warshaw Collection of Business Americana, Smithsonian.

The Internal Revenue Service extended the newly established income tax March deadline to April 1, 1918. A new profession started with income tax preparers—only $3.50 for one's tax preparation. Citizens had to pay 6% on the first $4,000 net income. Single earners of $1,000 and married couples earning $2,000 had to file.

Californians could buy a Hot Point stove and conserve fuel to help win the war. One button union suits cost $1.50-$3.50. The nine-button long underwear was not necessary. The company saved eight buttons—thus helping the war effort in a small way.

Along with omnipresent slogans like "Save a loaf a week, help win the war," the papers listed events at local theaters. Fetters Springs advertised its movies in the March 9, 1918, *Sonoma Index-Tribune*: "Nuf Sed." Patrons could hear the Original Ragtime Orchestra. Other theaters featured Mary Pickford starring in "A Romance of the Redwood" and Sessue Hayakawa in "Call of the East." For 15¢, plus 2¢ war tax for adults, 10¢, plus 1¢ tax for children, people could see the shows and help finance the war. A big musical comedy, "The Original Katzen-Jammer Kids—Hans and Fritz" appeared at Hill Opera House in Petaluma.

Vacationers could help the war effort by going to resorts. Customers at Fetters Springs Resort, "the only big resort in the valley where intoxicating liquors are not sold," paid 11 ¢ war tax in July 1918. "Stick by Fetters," was their motto.[18]

Price of ice cream: 50 ¢ a quart. Radiolite Waterbury watches cost $2.25-$4.00. A Ford Runabout cost $435 in the middle of 1918, plus $11.45 war tax added on.

All during the war the Woman's Christian Temperance Union (WCTU), Anti-Saloon League, Prohibition Party and various church organizations had been pushing on three fronts: Have California cities and counties pass local option laws prohibiting the sale of liquor, have Congress pass War Prohibition and have states ratify Amendment 18. The World War ended almost too soon for the prohibitionists, but this attack was successful on all three fronts. Since California adopted the local option law, half the counties and cities voted themselves dry in 1917 and 1918.

San Bernardino County was nearly dry in the summer of 1918. The *Victor Valley News-Herald* of July 6 reported local option elections in San Bernardino and Colton:[19]

San Bernardino Dry—Saloons at the County Seat are a thing of the past—At 12 o'clock last Saturday night the saloons in San Bernardino closed their doors to remain closed forever so far as the sale of intoxicants are concerned. Crowds from nearby towns (who came) to take part in the closing scenes augmented those of the county seat and the various emporiums resembled the closing hour of a stock exchange. Everything passed off quietly, however, the blotter of the desk sergeant at police headquarters the following morning showing only the usual Saturday night grist of arrests.

Many of the places were entirely sold out before the closing hour arrived and in one or two instances the thirsty crowds were served non-alcoholic beer. Before twelve o'clock practically every house in town had exhausted its supply of goods.

Thirty-four liquor establishments were affected by the new law as follows: Retail, 20; wholesale, 7; restaurants, 5; wholesale beer, 2.

Colton also voted itself dry. The Hub City will have no saloons after July 14.

ALCOHOL---The Great Enemy

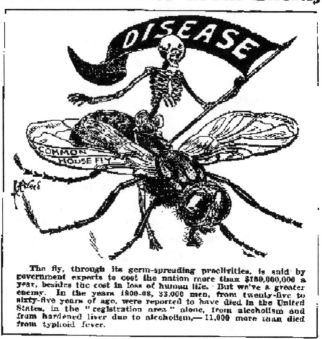

The fly, through its germ-spreading proclivities, is said by government experts to cost the nation more than $150,000,000 a year, besides the cost in loss of human life. But we've a greater enemy. In the years 1800-08, 33,000 men, from twenty-five to sixty-five years of age, were reported to have died in the United States, in the "registration area" alone, from alcoholism and from hardened liver due to alcoholism,—11,000 more than died from typhoid fever.

Thirty-Six States Can Stop It By Constitutional Amendment

Typical prohibition propaganda using appeal to fear had great impact in helping pass the 18th Amendment in January 1919.
Courtesy of the Warshaw Collection of Business Americana.

At the election held in Colton last Thursday on the saloon question a victory of substantial proportions was won by the uplift workers and good citizens who have been laboring for a closed town. The vote resulted in a majority of 316 in favor of a dry town, and on Saturday night, July 14, the five retail and two wholesale establishments will turn the keys in the doors and go out of business. The above date was agreed upon by the two factions and will give the saloon men time to dispose of the stocks now on hand.

The election leaves Needles as the only wet territory in San Bernardino County.

Oakdale

Louise Gilbert, Henrietta Holoway and Bernice Ferguson manned the phones in the 1917 election in Oakdale. These ladies called and sent drivers to pick up voters in favor of a dry town. The drys won—won by only three votes out of a total vote of about 650. Earlier that afternoon rumors spread through Oakdale that the drys would win by about 50 votes. "It was whispered around for the effect that if the saloons won, the trustees intended to raise their license to $600 a year. This $5,400 a year in high license revenue was quite a sneaky trick and many voted for the saloons who otherwise would have voted dry." Drys celebrated with an impromptu automobile parade, bells clanging and horns blowing, especially clanging cow bells loud on D Street, the wettest part of town, rubbing salt (not alcohol) in the wound. Another town dried up with local option, forcing nine saloons out of business within ten days.

Bone-Dry Modesto

Previous votes to make Modesto dry failed and wets felt they would win again. But with war hysteria, patriotism and better dry organization, Modesto's council voted to allow the citizens to decide whether saloons should be closed in October 1917. The plebiscite occurred in August. Those WCTU ladies did it again. Women took an active role, driving voters to the polls. Over fifty women came back from vacations long enough to vote. They watched polls, even offering $1000 reward for anyone catching someone casting an illegal vote. Unfortunately for the wets, many drunks must have anticipated the death knell of the saloons and tried to fill up for the last time before the election. The citizenry showed revulsion at local drunks bouncing off the buildings downtown. This repugnance accounted for a few more dry votes. Hundreds of dollars of ads for a week did not work for the wets this election. Modesto went dry with a vote of 1,156 for, 944 against. And at midnight October 21, 1917, another city closed the swinging doors of its saloons.[20]

Newman waited until forced to go dry on July 1, 1919, closing bars for the first time after 30 years, seven days a week. Citizens took several last-chance drinks during June 30 up until midnight. They tried to store up for the long drought.[21] The next morning, Newman citizens realized their stomachs would not store the booze for the dry spell, and their headaches made the first dry day doubly painful.

Stockton City Council voted without an opposing vote in June 1918 to close the 75 saloons in town. The farm bureau especially supported the ordinance to close saloons during harvest time. When it was put to popular vote, the measure won by 400 votes. After that hotels and restaurants would be permitted to serve intoxicating liquors with meals costing not less that 20 cents, and only between the hours of 11 a.m. and 9 p.m. In October 1919, Ordinance No. 699 made it unlawful to have liquor in hotels, offices, stores, restaurants, soft drink parlors or any place frequented by the public. Stockton publicly became dry.

When historic El Pinal Winery voluntarily closed it doors on May 1, 1919, government agents put on the padlocks. Carl Rothenbush, President of El Dorado Brewery Co., however, went another direction. He prepared for prohibition because he knew it was coming as sure as "2 + 2 = 4." He found a recipe for near beer, therefore becoming the first brewer in California to turn out non-alcoholic beer. He also made root beer and other soft drinks.[22]

Congress, being overpowered by the collective dry forces, passed the War Prohibition Act, often called War Time Prohibition, on November 21, 1918, ten days after the Armistice was signed on November 11. Charles H. Randall, the only California Prohibition Party Congressman, cleverly attached the war time prohibition rule onto the 1918 Agricultural Bill as a rider. The law was to go into effect on July 1, 1919—six months and 20 days after the war ended. Nevertheless, dry forces succeeded on the second front.

When the war ended, the country celebrated. The country prepared to get back to a peacetime living. Meat was off rationing right after the armistice and sugar was off by December 1, 1918. "Peace war bread" was no longer necessary as wheat was off rationing and could be used freely, but leaders recommended limiting wheat-use. Europe was devastated, soldiers and civilians needed to be fed, winter had set in. Herbert Hoover declared World Relief Week December 1-7, 1918. On December 20, Hoover prepared new food-saving programs. He reported 200,000 people in Vienna would perish of cold and exposure unless supplies were sent. Hoover had maps printed in California newspapers, showing which countries had the most famine. All during 1919, food and clothing had been shipped to Europe. Contra Costa County, for example, went over the top for their subscriptions to the Armenian-Syrian Relief fund in January 1919.[23]

After the war, Americans tried to return to a prewar life but the world had changed. Minimum wage for Ford Motor Company went up to $6 per day. Eggs dropped from 60 cents per dozen to 50 cents. Tong War activities broke out again in San Mateo County. News topics came up showing a beginning fear of communism, starting anti-Red scares. *Bolsheviks* became known to every California newspaper reader.

In the movies, Geraldine Farrar starred in Goldwyn's film "The Hell Cat." Tom Mix had two hits: "Law North of 65" and "Master of the Plains,"

Harold Lloyd appeared in "Nothing But Trouble" and A.L.KO Comedy produced "Nuts and Bolts." Jack Dempsey trained for his fight with Jess Willard.[24]

The government started paving highways across the desert: National Old Trails and Arrowhead Highway, forerunners of Highway 66 and 91.[25] Optimists predicted not only post-war prosperity but the greatest California road-building effort yet. On July 1, 1919, the state voted for a $40,000,000 bond issue, starting new roads, paving dozens of dirt roads, and improving others to make them all-winter roads: Skyline Boulevard from San Francisco to Santa Cruz, Oxnard to San Juan Capistrano, Barstow to Mojave, Ukiah to Tahoe City, Crescent City to the Oregon line and Placerville to Lake Tahoe. Some of these were primarily for tourists and vacationers, others for easier access for agriculture and industry.[26] Congress also voted $20,000,000 for California road building. To travel on these roads, cars had improved. Studebaker, for example, came out with a light six in 1919.

American dress designers incorporated ideas from history and the world, from Cromwell's England to the modern orient. Corset-less styles appeared in California newspapers portending what was to follow in the 1920s. Battlemented hems, wide linen collars and cuffs, sweet-gum of crepe under square bodice were features started in 1919. Some skirts were hobble type. "Sedateness" entered into the fashions, sinuous hips "from the orient" (along with silks), "waist-lines [were] capricious," and some sleeveless blouses started what evolved into the Roaring Twenties look.[27]

In the meantime states continued to ratify the 18th Amendment. By December 1918, 27 states voted themselves dry and voted for prohibition. California ratified the amendment in Joint Senate Resolution No. 4, January 1919. Sara J. Dorr, President of the Northern California WCTU and Stella B. Irvine, President of the Southern California group, sent the following letter to the legislators thanking them for their support for the "Dry Bill": "On behalf of the Woman's Christian Temperance Union of North and South California, we express heartfelt appreciation of the support given by the California legislature to the cause for which we have labored nearly half a century, and which resulted in the satisfaction of the amendment for national Constitution prohibition." The WCTU and anti-Saloon League accomplished their third objective for both the state and the nation.

When Nebraska became the 36th state to ratify the 18th Amendment on January 16, 1919, the amendment passed, ready to be the law of the land "After one year from the ratification..." on January 16, 1920. *Contra County Gazette* used only small headlines and an even smaller article to announce "37 States Ratify: U. S. to Be Dry." Missouri was the 37th state. Two weeks later, however, the editor derisively wrote that prohibition forces were not going to let people vote on being bone dry or not: But the American people while patient to a fault, and charitable even to criminal politicians and crazy people,

In WAR or PEACE

WHICH NEEDS IT MOST?

For the Money Represented by

Three Ten Cent Drinks a
Day For a Year

Even at "War Prices"

Any Grocer in Your Town Will Give You the Following Groceries:

10 Fifty pound Sacks of Flour
10 Bushels Potatoes
100 Pounds Granulated Sugar
5 Pounds Salt
20 Pounds Butter
10 Pounds Rice
10 Pounds Oat Flakes
10 Pounds Coffee
5 Pounds Tea

25 Cans Tomatoes
10 Dozen Oranges
10 Dozen Bananas
30 Cans Corn
10 Pounds Beans
100 Cakes Soap
1 Pound Pepper
4 Gallons Molasses
20 Gallons Oil

And There Would Be ENOUGH MONEY LEFT To Buy a Good Present For Your Wife and Babies

A war-time ad using logic to show the waste of money three drinks a day would cause. Notice the appeal to emotions with the word "babies" at the end. Courtesy of the Warshaw Collection of Business Americana, Smithsonian.

come with an irresistible kick when they do turn upon their tormentors. One of these days the majority will have something to say again."[28]

He Wants the Revenue

Is the Game Worth the Bait?

THE GREEDY BEAST NOW GETS ONE BOY OUT OF EVERY FIVE.

"A Saloon can no more run without boys than a grist mill without wheat." FRANCES WILLARD

Another emotional appeal aimed at counties and city councils that allow saloons. The logic is simple: a vote for saloons (and profit) is a vote against young boys. Courtesy of the Warshaw Collection of Business Americana, Smithsonian.

Twenty-five National Prohibition and Anti-Saloon League leaders asked Congress to make laws to ensure the states were "bone dry," that is, regulate the sale, manufacture, search and seizure laws, safeguard the sale of medicinal and religious liquors so they would not get out into the market, insure that "intoxicating liquor" would include distilled, malted, fermented, vinous alcohol. Congress, said Wayne B. Wheeler, should make sure the "beverage liquor traffic will never be legalized in this nation again as it will take two-thirds of Congress and three-fourths of the States to repeal (the amendment)."[29]

Congress must have harmony with the states in carrying out prohibition and making "Such other provisions as will destroy every vestige of the beverage liquor traffic throughout the U. S. and its territories." When Acting Secretary of State Frank L. Polk proclaimed the dry law will go into effect on January 16, 1920, representatives from the Anti-Saloon League, WCTU and Representative Randall from California helped celebrate the victory of the long struggle.

Ironically after Congress passed War Prohibition and the country ratified Amendment 18, Californians defeated two more liquor prohibition initiatives in May 1919: Proposition 1, by 256,778 to 341,897 and Proposition 2 by about 40,000 votes. Judging by the results of the popular votes, Californians were not sold on prohibition. Californians voted against prohibition, but elected officials voted for it.

Arrests were made in local option laws, portending what was to follow. A. Pezutti and his brother Frank saw the wrath of complaining prohibitionists when federal agents arrested them for selling liquor too close to a naval facility in Crockett. Bail of $1,000 hit these owners of a soft drink parlor, a movie theatre and a bowling alley. Government officers also set a bail of $1,000 on W. Barrett for the same charge at his soft drink parlor next door to Pezutti's.[30]

In the meantime the country waited for July 1, 1919, the day War Time Prohibition took effect. A young black veteran, William Cullen of San Mateo, returning from the war remembered a popular song of 1919, sung in clubs and by black entertainers in California. He remembered the words in 1980, 60 years after:

America, I must say, I love you.
You've been more than a mother to me
And although I must say as I'm going away
Still my home you will always be.
So good bye, I am leaving you soon.
I must sail with the last day of June.
I must go over there, I can't stay over here
If I do I'll surely die.
For I am a-man-who-must-have
A little liquor when I'm dry-dry-dry.
America, have you thought it over
Why should you make the whole country dry?
There are millions like me who drink more than tea
In that hot burning month called July.
So good-bye I'll be seeing you soon
I must sail with the last day of June

I must go over there, I can't stay over here
If I do I'll surely die.
For I am a-man-who-must-have
A little liquor when I'm dry-dry-dry.

And when I die, and when I die
Don't bury me at all, don't bury me at all
Just pickle my bones in alcohol
Put a bottle of booze at my head and feet
So that I know that I will keep
For I'm a man-who-must-have
A little liquor when I'm dry-dry-dry.

Another song sung by William Cullen from the 1919 play *Ladies First*,
"Prohibition Blues":
What ails you brown man—
What makes you frown man?
I ask my man...

I got the blues, I got the blues
I got those alcoholic blues
Lordy, Lordy, all is well
You know I don't have to tell
Oh, I've got those alcoholic blues, some blues.

When Mr. Hoover said to cut my dinner down
I never even hesitate, I didn't frown
I cut my sugar, I cut my coal
But now they're dug deep in my soul
I've got the blues, I've got the blues
I've got those alcoholic blues.

No more beer, my poor heart to cheer.
Good bye, whiskey; you used to make me frisky,
So long, high ball, so long, gin
Tell me when you come in, back again.
I've got the blues, I've got the blues
I've got the alcoholic blues.

Prohibition, that's the name
Prohibition drives me insane.
I'm so thirsty, soon I'll die

I'm certainly going to evaporate.
I'm just that dry.
I wouldn't mind the liquor ever in my drink
If only my daily work would only let me think
But not Bevo, nor ginger ale
I want real stuff by the pail
I've got the blues
I've got those alcoholic blues.
Lordy, Lordy, all is well
You know I don't have to tell...

This song, "Prohibition Blues," was sung from the early part of the dry years 1919, during War Prohibition and later after regular prohibition started. The reference to Hoover is his food conservation to feed the starving people in war-ravaged France and Belgium. The reference to Bevo is to the non-alcoholic beer made by Pabst Blue Ribbon in 1919.

The editor of The Mountain Democrat[31] said the American people will accept War Prohibition. They will "give sufficient time to enable them to give expression in a dignified way to their real sentiments. In a republic the will of the majority must prevail."

The California Republic accepted War Prohibition. Orland, Glenn County, had traffic jams with celebrants, enjoying the last wet night before War Prohibition took effect:"...the town was lighted like the Milky Way—without the milk—and looked like the Fourth of July, New Years Eve, the Declaration of War, the signing of the Armistice, the Orland Fair, and the Sunday School Picnic all in one."[32]

Redding had a more formal reaction with an impromptu funeral led by the Redding band playing the death march leading a rented hearse with John Barleycorn inside and the town mourned his death as he passed by. Vallejo-Benecia marched with a Barleycorn hearse in a parade. Santa Monica citizens marched it all the way off the Santa Monica pier!

By the summer of 1919, almost all bar and saloon owners had applied to the city and county to turn their establishments into soft drink parlors. Many were hoping Congress would allow 2 ¾ percent beer and light wines. Court cases around the country had to be fought out as the country muddled through War Prohibition. Contra Costa Gazette commented with a bit of levity on a woman's fashion fad calling for grapes to trim ladies' hats. Prohibition or no, said the Gazette, it's the same old grape—goes right to the head.[33]

Famous San Franciscan night clubs, Tait's At The Beach and Tait's Down Town, sent a notice to its patrons on June 30, 1919, that Tait's could have drink setups (ginger ale, lime rickey, soda) and serve liquor out of the patron's bottle, providing he brought in his own liquor. A set-up fee and corkage fee, storing opened bottles for the client, could be charged. John Tait promised to serve the best ice drinks and "Fancy Cream Dishes" that had ever been served in the city. Thus the first loophole of War Time Prohibition.

Congress voted down a bill allowing indiscriminate search of private homes. But the Supreme Court defended challenges to the War Prohibition Act; for example 2.75 percent beer was not allowed. Ads testing legality of selling homebrew-making material appeared in newspapers. In the fall one ad in California sold ingredients for making homebrew: "You should worry—Make your own Beer at home" for only 20 cents a gallon. One dollar could buy a booklet of recipes for making whiskeys and brandies.

Thirsty citizens did not have to wait to make homebrew. Within three weeks of War Prohibition, there were 25 blind pigs in Stockton.[34]

The wording of the new part of the Constitution, Amendment 18, had the seeds of its own destruction.

By January 16, 1920, a person would not be able to sell, make or transport intoxicating beverages. But it said nothing of possessing or buying. Owning a case of Jim Beam was not illegal. Neither was buying a case of Old Crow. The middle class Americans who wanted a little emergency snakebite medicine or a couple extra pints for medicinal reasons had all of 1917 to stock up while Congress discussed the proposal. Grandma too had all of 1918, while the states debated ratification, just to put away a little extra cooking sherry for security. After ratification on January 16, 1919, the Constitution allowed a year before prohibition went into effect in January, 1920. A year was plenty of time for Pop or Uncle Hiram to buy a small stock in case the family failed to see what was happening the previous two years. One would have had too much California sun beat on his brain for too long not to be able to provide a little extra for the forthcoming dry years.

Ah, but the rich! They not only had time, but money besides. The wealthy could order cases of liquor to store in their basements or wine cellars and thousands did. Businessmen and the upper social class knew the value of a well-stocked liquor cabinet. They planned ahead. In dry states and dry local option counties, smuggling and bootlegging had already occurred with little interference from the law. The people in Holtville, for example, and other dry towns could not buy in the town but they went up the highway to wet Imperial, Mexicali or over to San Diego and brought back what they needed. Soon, bootleggers brought booze for them. Three years were enough for those with foresight and money to store up.

The change in the Constitution created a legal monster when it did not specify what indeed was "intoxicating." Since 1917, the government used the definition of intoxicating liquor as containing "one-half of 1 percentum" alcohol. Case after case defendants challenged courts to prove they were selling intoxicating liquor—clogging the court system. Clever lawyers created a reasonable doubt in the minds of some jurors, who thus let defendants off.

To clarify this amendment and to provide the enforcement laws, Andrew Volstead, Chairman of the House Judiciary Committee, wrote the National Prohibition Act, NPA, a law designed to implement the War Prohibition Act and the 18th Amendment when it went into effect in January 1920.[35] President Wilson vetoed this National Prohibition Act, the Volstead Act. The House and Senate almost immediately passed it over his veto by the necessary two thirds margins on October 27 and 28, 1919. The new amendment would take effect in just a couple of months. The NPA used one-half of one percentum as the definition of alcohol; regulated scientific, religious, industrial and medical uses of alcohol; limited physicians' liquor prescriptions to one pint per 10 days with refills—only after an exam; and specified pharmacists' use and dispensation of alcohol. As a concession to California and New England, NPA allowed each family to make 200 gallons of wine or hard apple cider for home use. Though beer was not permitted, wine and cider use made the country "Not bone dry!"[36]

Punishments included closing (abating) premises where liquor was sold, fining not less than $100 nor more than $1000 or imprisoning for not less than 30 days nor more than one year and confiscating property (houses, boats, cars) used in liquor dealings.

What a decade! The Great War. The reforms of anti-trust, referendum, recall, initiative, California woman suffrage in 1911, 8-hour working day for women in 1911, cross-filing for candidates, nonpartisan candidates for judges, city and county offices 1911-13, public utility and railroad regulations 1911, Red Light Abatement Act 1913, Wylie Local Option prohibition 1911, income tax, direct election of U. S. senators, and the Armistice. So many innovations came to the country and the world: People were playing with and building crystal sets, the new toy called "radio" and electrical appliances of all sorts entered the market. Autos and trucks had essentially replaced the horse and wagon: a network of paved roads had been started, and new businesses centered around the automobile, such as the auto court, tourist industry, filling stations, the Automobile Club of Southern California. The movie industry, telephones and airplanes had gone beyond the novelty stage. A dirigible spanned the Atlantic from Scotland to Long Island in 108 hours. Sadly Californians still displayed much discrimination against Negroes, Filipinos and especially the Japanese. Nations developed better and more efficient ways of killing people: mustard and chlorine gas, Big Bertha (a gun that could send a shell into Paris from 75 miles away), machine guns, tanks and airplanes. Wilson, however, gave the world a little hope with his Fourteen Points, plans for a just peace and a League of Nations—thus truly trying to make the late war a war to end all wars, truly giving the world hope for permanent peace. But by the end of 1919, the world found that France, England and Italy had their own agendas and a just peace was not obtained. America, in turn, took a turn toward isolationism.

The reform movements had soared so high that progressives knew reforms of the next decade would make America a liquor-less country, a more moral country, with prosperity and peace and orderliness to be fulfilled. Californians had decisions to make in the dry years ahead: obey the law, drink anyway, report violators, or look the other way and mind their own business. Californians looked forward to the new era of the 1920s, wondering what kind of decade it would be. They would soon find out.

California Grape Protective
Association published this 24-page
plea to vote against National
Prohibition, ca. 1918. Notice this
side also used appeals to emotions.
Courtesy of California Historical
Society, # 2572, San Marino.

CHAPTER 3

ROBBIN' HOODS

L ike Robin Hood of old, who stole from the rich to give to the poor, prohibition "robbin' hoods" stole from the alcohol rich and made it possible for the alcohol poor to obtain the wet wealth. It seemed the patriotic thing to do, because some thieves felt the government oppressive, tyrannical, despotic or unrealistic. To them the United States government was as unfair as King John. Besides these robbin' hoods could be noble and make a little profit too.

Maybe it was a socialist thing to do: redistribute the wealth. The rich had two years to store up alcohol. And store they did—they filled their wine cellars, basements, summer or winter homes (or both) and their yachts. They vaulted away some of the best booze in the world.

Rich estates of San Mateo and Marin counties, vacation homes, wherever they were, became targets of robbin' hoods of new. Their arrows and spears struck swiftly and thoroughly, and they carried their liberated booty to their hideouts and garages in modern Sherwood Forest.

The natural contempt commoners had for a law they did not believe in was nothing compared to the contempt they had for the rich who were able to buy whatever they wanted before and during prohibition. It wasn't fair for one man to have eighty or more cases of scotch, English gin, French liqueurs. Commoners showed little sympathy for moneyed gentry who lost their alcoholic stash. When 1920 newspaper readers read about the tragic losses of the wealthy, more than a few commoners said or thought, "Serves 'em right," or maybe, "It serves 'em right, the bastards!"

The week before National Prohibition became the law of the land on January 16, 1920, the home of A. P. Giannini, founder of Bank of Italy (later to become Bank of America), felt the sting of the robbin' hoods. Thieves ransacked his home looking for liquor, searched his wine cellar, but found only wine. After wine tasting, the hoods left a note: "We're looking for booze. We don't like your vino."

Not all hoods were as selective as these. Just a few days after National Prohibition started, three drinkers evidently with alcoholic withdrawal, William Treber, Samuel Treber, William Sullivan went into the home of Steve Garbarino in San Bruno on a Sunday night. They demanded Garbarino unlock his wine cellar and "the three men proceeded to taste the liquor." The host was surprised when they left. He called the local reserve officer Frank L. Foppiano, who turned the matter over to the federal authorities in San

Francisco. Prohibition had just started and already these three men felt deprived.[1]

A. Baradat, a resident of South San Francisco, had his San Francisco warehouse hit by the robbin' hoods. Thieves took $4,000-5,000 worth of wet goods. He offered a $200 reward for the name of the person who broke in. Baradat's loss was great, considering he opened up a string of soft drink parlors on the Peninsula—and sometimes hard liquor found its way in amongst the soda pops.

The amendment was a little over a month old when the *San Mateo News-Leader* of February 25, 1920, had a catchy alliterated headline: "Luscious Liquor Loss." Nectar of the gods was stolen from the Portola Valley home of S. W. Morsehead, Union Oil official. The private stock of the "joy of life" made Morsehead "well fixed up for the long dry spell...up until last night!"

Liberated from Morehead for recirculation: two cases of gin, two cases of whiskey, a 38-gallon barrel of whiskey and ten gallons of wine.

In one and one-half months of prohibition, thieves stole $20,000 worth of liquor from Marin and San Mateo counties. The two sheriffs had a strategy meeting, declaring war on the liquor robbers, warning citizens that robbin' hoods used such guises as laundry men and gas meter readers, after obtaining information about their prospective victim first, then striking. San Mateo County Sheriff said: "This gang is by far the best organized crowd of thieves that has ever operated in San Mateo County."

In Marin County so many homes were hit that Sheriff John J. Keating warned residents to watch for strange persons who have come into Marin County, resulting "in depredation upon nearly every summer home in the vicinity of Ross, San Anselmo and Mill Valley." Keating planned to stop vehicles going to San Francisco at the Sausalito ferry and hoped to arrest these thieves for theft and transportation.

But thieves had just begun to strike. They came out of their forest hideouts again and again. Suffering a tragic loss at the hands of the robbin' hoods was W. M. Fitzhugh, a wealthy San Franciscan. On March 5, 1920, the *San Mateo News-Leader* reported, according to the caretaker in Portola Valley: "Entrance was gained by breaking open the iron doors of a vault in which the liquor was kept." When the gardener found 8" solid rubber tire tracks the next morning, investigators realized the crooks used a huge truck to take away $30,000 worth of liquor—only about half the stash he was keeping for the long liquor drought. Fitzhugh offered $1,000 reward leading to the arrest of the robbin' hoods. Next day, March 6, Fitzhugh raised the reward to $3,000, or $10 a case for each case returned. Thieves took 141 cases of imported whiskey, 68 cases of wines and brandies, and 34 cases of miscellaneous whiskey, brandy and champagne. Missing liquor from

Fitzhugh's inventory illustrated the magnitude of this raid: 10 cases of Roderick Scotch, 24 of Andrew Usher Scotch, 59 John Dewar Scotch, 46 Old Crow Whiskey, 4 bottles Old Hermitage, 1 case Bushnell Irish, 10 cases of brandy, 5 cases of cognac and on and on.

The editor of the *News-Leader* posed an interesting question: Can the liquor be returned? Under the new amendment to the Constitution, liquor could not be transported. The editor commented on how Fitzhugh was "making a desperate effort to run the robbers to earth."

D. C. McDonald rented the basement of his Eureka store to a mysterious man for $100 a month. The next month several trucks of alcohol came and were unloaded and stored. He said to McDonald, "Keep this locked up until I come for it." Months passed. Checks came regularly. McDonald became apprehensive because of the now illegal booze and federal raids in the area. After a year, a man with several trucks told McDonald, "We came to pick up our booze." Relieved, McDonald opened the basement. The next month another check came, surprising McDonald, then another came and a third. The renter finally appeared with two large trucks. He found McDonald in his store and said, "I came to pick up the supplies I left in the basement." Robbin' hoods had struck! Photo and story courtesy of Norton Steenfott.

Any place with liquor was a target for those anxious to redistribute liquid wealth. Four days in March, thieves hit the upper Peninsula, taking 75 bottles from M. A. Hirschman of Hillsborough and liquor from Mr. and Mrs. Peters of Burlingame who had gone to call on friends and came back to an empty liquor closet. The next night bandits hit four other Burlingame homes.

Out of the live oak forest of the Peninsula came a gang to right the wrongs of the times. This gang robbed the McNear mansion in Menlo Park and freed $24,000 worth of the best liquor. These liberators of locked-up booze then struck with fury at the Hart Estate in Menlo Park in March 1922. Seven men, including Clifford J. Rollins and John Arthur Walsh, raided Hart and liberated thousands of bottles of liquor.[2]

Justice came quickly for Rollins and Walsh, however. San Mateo County Court, on April 27, 1922, had no sense of humor as it sent these two robbin' hoods to San Quentin for an "indeterminate time." Three witnesses, Julian Hart, a chauffeur and a governess, saw and identified the men from San Mateo County's Sherwood Forest. Rollins confessed and implicated the rest of his gang.

In May, Hart went to San Quentin to try to obtain early parole for one of the thieves, Arnold Thompson, a Redwood City man and ex-soldier from Camp Fremont. Thompson kept the rest of the hoods from harming any of the Harts.

Other places robbin' hoods struck were government storage warehouses, city and county jails, or perhaps the closet behind the sheriff's desk. Crooks seemed to be around after raids to find where liquor was temporarily stored for inventory or for shipment to a government warehouse for safekeeping. After federal agents raided Belmont Casino, near Belmont, they arrested proprietors Joe and Tony Berolucci [probably Bertolucci]. Several thousand dollars worth of liquor was taken by the dry squad, sealed and locked by the agents. The next morning, some robbin' hoods liberated the liquor"—removed by persons unknown." Said the *Redwood City Standard:* "recent raids on truckloads of confiscated liquor stocks in transit to prohibition headquarters, attempted by alleged bootleg bandits...the Belmont stock was stolen by an organized gang of men."

Caught for burglarizing the liquor vault of Louis Balati, 310 [319?] Spruce Street, Redwood City, were Sam Placker, Robert Murray, Joseph Palalin, William Cuneo and Frank Crye—all of San Francisco. While San Mateo District Attorney Franklin Swart was examining witnesses at the trial, a five-gallon demijohn of wine exploded with a large bang. "Fragments of demijohn and its precious content scattered all over the ceiling and the walls of the court room..." So much for exhibit # 5!

Despite dispersing five gallons of the evidence, the court held the men anyway. The trial finished with the court room smelling a little like Balati's wine cellar.

The government allowed several loopholes, such as liquor for religious, industrial and medicinal uses. These were all places where some enterprising thieves could strike a blow for more equality, thus strike a blow for democracy and against tyranny.

Eureka Paid to Store Wine

Four hogsheads of wine, taken from the Pomona House bar at C and First streets in Eureka, were saved by the police because the police did not spill confiscated wine. It was stored in the Schmeder warehouse at the foot of E Street. The officers rolled the hogsheads, each containing 150 gallons of wine, next to the wall. They were still there several months later, but one was empty.[3]

The dry squad looked for hidden wine in the Popular saloon at First and E streets. They found the wine behind a false wall. Investigating further, officers went into a narrow alley between the Popular and the Schmeder

Mason's Malt Whiskey Distillery Company in Sausalito, one of the biggest in the U. S., where robbin' hoods such as Joe Campanelli, sometimes with help from the inside, diverted legal alcohol by stealing or bribing. Clint Mason lost control of the plant and it was later became the American Distillery. The plant burned in 1963, and became a condominium project, aptly named "Whiskey Springs," according to Jack Tracy's Sausalito Moments in Time: A Pictorial History of Sausalito's First One Hundred Years: 1850-1950. *Photo courtesy of Jack Tracy and Sausalito Historical Society.*

warehouse. They found a small hole drilled through the warehouse and into the hogsheads lying against the wall on the other side. Robbin' hoods siphoned 150 gallons into containers in the narrow passageway and happily went on their merry way. The frugal city fathers evidently were not the only people who did not want to waste precious wine. Waste not, want not.

Booze from the U. S. Customs Warehouse

San Bernardino Sun, September 13, 1929

Ship captains could procure alcohol for medicinal purposes at naval facilities in California: San Francisco, Los Angeles, Eureka, San Diego and San Pedro. According to Prohibition Circular 210, June 11, 1923, medical officers of the Public Health Service at these cities could authorize Form 1539 granting certificates of need for medicinal alcohol for ships.[4]

Four clever San Franciscan white-collar robbin' hoods found a source of liquor to be the bonded alcohol in the U. S. Customs warehouse. The government required five copies of the application to withdraw alcohol from warehouses to use aboard ship. One copy went to the ship's master, one each to the liquor seller, prohibition administrator, prohibition officer in Washington, D. C., and the U. S. Health Service.

U. S. Attorney George Hatfield declared that Mrs. Agnes A. Cress engineered a plot that extracted "enough bonded liquor to flood San Francisco." Someone slipped one extra copy of the application into the stack of five forms. When the ship's master filled out the application form, there were six copies instead of five. This merryman or merrywoman removed the extra copy to withdraw any amount of bonded liquor desired.

Federal agents arrested for conspiracy Cress, Daniel J. Tottrell, former acting cashier of U. S. Customs in San Francisco, Charles Smiltz, customs broker and R. N. MacWilliams, owner of a drugstore near the Customs house. Mrs. Cress, for 12 years a confidential secretary for a wholesale liquor firm, attempted suicide after she was exposed, recovered, escaped from the hospital and was captured by the authorities. The court set the bail for each at $10,000.

Social Shortages

Captured boat Ray Roberts loaded with 1,050 cases of smuggled liquor, was seized "improperly" outside San Diego, and the court forced the government to return the boat and its illegal cargo. When lawyer Harold C. Faulkner, formerly the defense lawyer in the *Coal Harbor* case, took inventory of the released liquor, he reported "social shortages"—a euphemism for 33 cases missing in the government- secured warehouse. Robbin' hoods had struck again.[5]

Conspiracy with the Robbin' Hoods

John and DeWitt Clint Mason owned American Distillery, outside Sausalito. DeWitt Clint Mason helped the wet cause by conspiring with others to hijack his own liquor shipment. He also set up an elaborate plumbing system to evade watchful eyes of federal inspectors assigned to monitor

American Distillery. According to Millie Robbins, in her article "Sausalito's Salty Days": "All he had to do was to go to a certain spigot and drain off a few gallons when the need arose." Investigators uncovered Clint's conspiracy, arrested him, the court found him guilty, and he lost his ownership in the company.[6]

When the Coast Guard seized *Federalship* in 1927, towed it into San Francisco, and charged it with smuggling, it confiscated 12,500 cases of scotch whiskey. Federal officials removed the cargo to the U.S. appraiser's store for safekeeping. The U.S. Federal Court disagreed with the seizure and ordered the Coast Guard to return the cargo, to "tow *Federalship* out to the point of capture" in the Pacific and release her to the owners. But the entire cargo of 12,500 cases, 250 tons, had disappeared while under guard by federal authorities![7]

Truly, arrows of robbin' hoods hit the bull's eye this time. Northern Californian merry yeomen and fair maidens had some mighty good scotch whiskey for many months in 1927-28.

During the whole fourteen years of prohibition, robbin' hoods did their duty as they saw it, and did it well. Some of these gangs became highwaymen who preyed upon bootleggers, moonshiners and rumrunners. Therefore, in the early 1920s entered the hijackers! A different type of robbin' hood, a more dangerous type.

CHAPTER 4

ADD THREE DROPS OF CREOSOTE AND LET IT AGE THREE HOURS

The cleverness of Americans never ceases to amaze the world. Inventiveness, ingenuity and resourcefulness helped struggling colonies survive, eventually out-creating, out-inventing and out-producing the mother country. Isolation of little settlements as the frontier moved westward necessitated a self-reliance that made the westerners second to none. This self-reliance mothered creativity from colonial days to the last frontiers in the west. Then came prohibition! Americans answered the challenge of "no beverages of more than one-half of one percent alcohol." Californians epitomized the best in cleverness, as creatively as their fathers and mothers had solved problems before the turn of the century. With a mastered skill of ingenuity, California had an adequate supply of intoxicating beverages all 14 years of the "Noble Experiment." In some years manufacturers created a surplus of fine-drinking refreshments—some not-so-fine stuff too.

The biggest challenge was to turn moonshine, straight alcohol, into a reasonable facsimile of old-time "likker." To make the famous bathtub gin, the home consumer or the enterprising part-time businessman bought five gallons of white lightning. Depending on the desired strength (or the desired return on his investment), he diluted the moonshine with five gallons of water in the bathtub or crock, then added glycerin, oil of juniper and let it age thoroughly for a few hours.

Added to alcohol, crushed juniper berries with a little sugar made a facsimile of gin. A nearby park or garden could provide enough junipers, or family picnics to the mountains or deserts could net a year's supply of juniper berries (even branches could serve the cause).

For international drinkers, shrewd Californians made the finest scotch, imported all the way from Salinas, Oakland or West Los Angeles, by adding caramel coloring, prune juice and creosote oil to raw alcohol. A cheaper "quality" could be made by using burnt sugar for color and flavor. Wood shavings, burned redwood sticks, or oak barrels burned on the inside helped create the "imported" scotch flavor. Mother's liquid smoke, used for cooking, often disappeared into dad's homemade whiskey which tasted and smelled somewhat like aged-in-burned-oak-barrels-Glasgow-made whiskey. Five gallons of grain or corn liquor costing $6.00 to $10.00 made ten gallons of homemade scotch in the best American inventive tradition.

Making bourbon out of 180 proof "alky" produced more finished liquor for local palates. Individualism that Herbert Hoover so admired manifested itself to the pinnacle as bootleggers cut raw alcohol 1 ½ times with water to turn 10 gallons into 25 gallons of bourbon. By diluting so much, the bootlegger helped his customers by making sure they didn't over-indulge. Kitchen Bouquet flavoring, food coloring and red peppers created the illusion of liquor as good as that from Bourbon County, Kentucky, especially if the consumer drank enough of it. The pre-prohibition recipe of nailing a couple plugs of chewing tobacco to the bottom of an oak barrel to help color and flavor whiskey while being shipped from Kentucky was too lengthy a process for thirsty clients of the 1920s. More ethical moonshiners used a combination of burned barrels, chewing tobacco, caramel coloring and creosote, to age the liquor by rotating the barrel round and round for a couple days. Variations of this technique allowed the moonshiners in the San Gabriel Mountains to suggest they dried their grain slowly over a peat-moss fire—scotch, just as in the Highlands of Scotland.

Rectifying moonshine or straight alcohol into pre-prohibition type liquors and drinks became a popular topic at barbershop and friendly gatherings. People shared their recipes and their experiments. U. S. Senator David A. Reed, for example, gave his friends his recipe for pumpkin gin and apple jack. In his little way he helped people survive the liquor drought of the dry years with a bit of variety.

A popular book, *Home Made Wine and Beer: A Neatly Compiled and Arranged Collection of Formula*,[1] compiled by Howard Williams, appeared on the California market in 1919. This useful book contained recipes for cider and fruit brandies, the art of distilling and rectifying spirituous liquors and recipes for making wine and liquors without aid of distillation. The following samples enabled bootleggers, middlemen and bathtub-gin makers to take raw alcohol and rectify it into popular drinks:

Scotch Whiskey

Neutral spirits, four gallons; alcoholic solution of starch, one gallon; creosote, five drops; cochineal tincture, four wine glasses full; burnt sugar coloring, quarter of a pint.

Tuscaloosa Whiskey

Neutral spirits, four pints; honey, three pints dissolved in water, four pints; solution of starch, five pints; oil of wintergreen, four drops, dissolved in half an ounce of acetic ether; color with four ounces of burnt sugar.

Irish Whiskey

Neutral spirits, four gallons; refined sugar, three pounds in water, four quarts; creosote, four drops; color with four ounces burnt sugar.

Old Rye Whiskey

Neutral spirits, four gallons; alcohol solution of starch, one gallon; decoction of tea, one pint; infusion of almonds, one pint; color with one ounce of the tincture of cochineal, and of burnt sugar, four ounces; flavor with oil of wintergreen, three drops, dissolved in one ounce of alcohol. By some, rye whiskey is colored only to a slight brownish tinge, with burnt sugar alone.

Jamaica Rum

Neutral spirits, four gallons; Jamaica rum, one gallon; sulfuric acid, half an ounce; acetic ether, four ounces; burnt sugar coloring, eight ounces.

Bathtub Gin

Aromatic Schiedam Schnapps—Neutral spirits, four gallons; water, four pints; dissolved honey, four pints; oil of juniper, fifteen drops, dissolved in citric ether, one ounce.

Peach Brandy

Neutral spirits, four gallons; three pints honey, dissolved in two pints of water; mix infusion of bitter almonds, one pint; sulfuric acid, eighty drops; porter, one pint; tincture of saffron, half a pint; and flavor with oil of pears, one ounce dissolved in two ounces of alcohol, and acetic ether, half an ounce.

The formulas are examples of the variety of methods Californians had at their disposal to metamorphose straight alcohol and moonshine. Californians had their eyes on another source of alcohol to make beverages: industrial alcohol. Several years before prohibition, the federal government denatured industrial alcohol to make sure it never reached the beverage state. Federal scientists employed 76 denaturing recipes to make alcohol undrinkable, e.g., lavender coloring, soft coal, iodine, sulfuric acid and wood alcohol. An admixture of five to ten percent wood alcohol was a common denaturant for such uses as dye, cleaning solvents, paints, varnishes, films, artificial leathers, antifreeze, inks and explosives. Bonded distilleries made denatured alcohol for these industrial uses. Here then were two potential sources for drinking alcohol. First, alcohol could be stolen or smuggled out of the distillery before denaturing. A few distilleries risked their bonds by producing for this illegal trade. The second source was to re-work the legal denatured products. And Californians created methods to do that over the years, keeping a step or so ahead of the federal scientists and inspectors. Once Californians skimmed off alcohol designed for industry or ameliorated the denatured alcohol, all they had to do was follow the above recipes to turn it into scotch or gin. According to Ernie Wichels of the *Vallejo Herald Times*, sailors and others drained alcohol from many compasses and used torpedo alcohol. They strained this and wood alcohol through French bread. And some died.

One of the biggest loopholes of the 18th Amendment was the right of people to make 200 gallons of wine a year. Italians, Greeks, Spaniards, Serbians, Austrians—all felt they had a right to make wine as part of their heritage. The Volstead Act also gave them the legal right to make 200 gallons of wine or hard apple cider a year for family use. This law, placating California and New England, created problems of control, too much for the prohibition agents. Wine, of course, served to the family and to *bona fide* guests caused no problem.

Anyone visiting an Italian family had a social routine that was beautiful. While women talked in the kitchen, men made their way to the wine cellar and tapped the wine, savoring and commenting, comparing as if they were professional wine tasters, and many were qualified by years of experience. As they breathed aromatic wine-cellar smells they exchanged opinions on world affairs, news items, jokes, family events—bonding these men while passing quality time. Young boys too bonded as they watched the camaraderie of the men and were given small samples to sip. It was beautiful quality time.

But extra wine made, sold or transported was a felony. To distill a little "grappa," hard liquor, from wine was a felony. Families obeyed or fudged on the law as their consciences dictated.

Common Recipe for Homebrew Beer

The Volstead Act did not allow homebrew for family use and certainly not for selling. Yet for just a few dollars the family could make its own beer. With a little more effort, a farmer could make some to sell. As early as March 1921, making suds was prevalent enough for the *Plumas National Bulletin* to write: "Now that home-brewing is very popular, we want to suggest that most any kind of hops can be used in brewing trouble."[2] Beer was easily made. Hard-to-catch fathers in their garages or basements generally caused few problems. When served to family guests—still no problem. But when a few bottles ended up in the back seat of an automobile which had been in an accident or when chilled bottles appeared on the evidence inventory in a raided soft drink parlor, then federals concerned themselves with finding the mini-brewery.

The following is a typical prohibition beer recipe. Grandma's pickle crock served as a fine container to make homebrew.

Beer

1 can Blue Ribbon Malt   1 cake yeast
8 lbs. sugar   1 handful rice or grain
15 gallons water

In large pot, dissolve sugar, malt with some water. Dissolve yeast in lukewarm water.

Mix in crock and fill with lukewarm water. Put hydrometer in mixture which should read 1.050-1.060, and skim foam from top every day until it stopped "boiling," i.e., working. When the hydrometer read from 1.010 to 1.000 and did not change for a day or so, it was time to bottle. The formula was 1.060 - 1.010=.050 X 105 =5.25 per cent alcohol by weight. Because alcohol weighs less than water, one multiplied 5.25% X 1.25=6.56% by volume. The above figures indicated strong beer.

Some brewmasters were not careful and bottled it too soon because of demand or greed or both. Seasoned beer drinkers knew that green beer could give drinkers the "green-apple trots," but over the years many did not know what real beer was supposed to taste like. And they drank whatever was sold or given to them—green-apple trots or not. To obtain a good foam and bubbly beer, the brewer added ½ to 2/3 teaspoon of sugar to each bottle just before the bottle was capped. This priming often was too much, and many a Sunday afternoon gathering of church ladies had their meetings interrupted with the loud explosions of dad's beer bottles blowing up in the basement. Sometimes the explosion was strong enough that the bottles flew in the air leaving the base of the bottle in the bottom of the case or on the floor.[3]

The natural phenomena of fermenting (working) is that yeast will turn the starch in barley or corn or wheat or you name it, into sugar and then yeast devours the sugar, turning it into carbon dioxide and alcohol. The beer stops working when the sugar is used up or when the alcoholic content becomes high enough to kill the surviving yeast.

The process is a magic of nature, an act of God—with man helping out. What joy, what excitement it is to see the bubbles, the boiling, of these living yeast cells multiplying and naturally turning sugars into CO_2 and alcohol. For some brewers it was the pride of creation, like creating a cake, a loaf of sourdough bread, a painting. Most never knew much of the chemistry involved, but they knew it was good, magical and godly, and an accomplishment.

Unfortunately sometimes wild yeast took over and created vinegar. Peaches that should have been peach wine ended up as peach vinegar—awful stuff! When brewers or wine makers were not careful with cleanliness, they often created rot and foul-smelling, non-drinkable brew that often found itself in the marketplace anyway. California had all kinds of brewers and vintners. Most artistic brewers kept their integrity and pride throughout the prohibition period. Others made liquor for profit only.

Homebrew in Ontario

Fredkin's store, on B and Laurel in Ontario, sold several cases each month in 1928 of two kinds of malt extract, Puritan from Chicago and Tacoma from San Francisco. All grocery stores in Ontario with the exception of Olinger's, according to the editor of the *Ontario Weekly Herald,* sold malt extracts which were advertised for use in cooking but were nearly exclusively used for making beer of 5 to 6 percent alcohol content.[4]

Moore's grocery did a fine business selling malt extracts, Puritan and Blue Ribbon from Peoria, Illinois. Walter [Moore?] showed the editor of the *Herald* the page advertisement in the *Los Angeles Examiner:* "Free can of malt with one case paid for." Moore bought ten cases (24 cans each) of the malt and received one case free from the company. Malt sold for 65 ¢ a quart can which could make five gallons of beer with 5-6 percent alcohol. Malt displays at Daley's store and Safeway were as prominent as peaches and melons. No recipe for making beer appeared on the can but one salesman offered Moore a lot of recipes for making beer from malt and the recipe for "ginger snaps." If the Inland Empire inhabitants did not make beer, they must have made millions of ginger snaps.

Typical Italian Families
by Lou Dallara, Marin County

As far as I know Italian families stuck to the 200 gallons of wine a year. It took a ton and one half of grapes to make 200 gallons. Several families and my relatives would work together on the wine. My brother got a ton-and-a-half and usually so did my father and I. We'd take the crusher over to my dad's house and do his grapes. And soon after they were fermented, we'd use the presser, pressing the juice out of the fermented grape mixture. We aged it, then bottled some of it.

Even after the grapes were pressed once, we would add more water, let them ferment again to make "Picola" or "Vinetta," weak wine. We'd drink that too.

My father made grappa each year in the basement. He had a little gas stove and a copper cooker where we distilled the wine. Grappa was strong, clear alcohol. Depending on the person's preferences, he could use grappa as a shot for himself and his friends, or some used it for highballs, others for coffee royals. Our family also put some cherries in it for dessert.

Grappa was so strong, according to Vallejoan Ernie Wichels, that it would take the varnish off the table

Mula
as told by Mike Rodriquez, Barstow

During prohibition, my father, Eugenio Rodriquez, made a distilled liquor called *mula* in New Mexico and Arizona and later in Barstow, California, in the mid 1930s. He boiled raisins, prunes and potatoes, put the mixture in a large crock with sugar, let cool some and added yeast and let it sit and ferment.

After it had fermented, he distilled it to make the *mula*. He and a friend sometimes sold it for $1.00 a gallon. It was strong clear alcohol, gave quite a kick. That's why it was called *mula*, the Spanish word for mule.

A Curling Iron to Mellow the Whiskey
as told by William Genini, San Francisco

When I was born I was baptized by rubbing two fingers that had been dipped in wine across my lips. Wine and spirits were always around our home ever since I was born in 1917, and being of Italian-Swiss descent and living in an Italian-Swiss-French-Mexican ethnic neighborhood where everyone used wine, it was very difficult to realize that my parents and other people were manufacturing much more wine than was used or allowed by law for family consumption.

I was perhaps six or seven years old when I began to realize that these people coming to the door at all times of the day and night paying my father money and slipping out furtively with a bag under their long coats were doing something not quite right. Later, I was recruited by my father to push a baby buggy that had two or three gallons of wine in it camouflaged as a baby wrapped in a blanket to make deliveries.

Something that stands out vividly in my mind is that every time the prohibition agents invaded someone's home, arrested the owner and busted in the bungholes on the oak casks, wine would flow down the gutters from the hills in North Beach and all the winos, bums and many soldiers stationed at the Presidio or Fort Mason would be down on hands and knees sucking up the old nectar from the gutter. When it [prohibition] ended, there was rejoicing by some people, more because I believe the great promise of all the jobs this would create during the Depression, than because of the idea of legally being able to get booze, because booze of every sort was always available during prohibition.

Liquor was also distributed by car. A bootblack with a little shop stand in North Beach did a lively business. Stevedores, or dock workers (mostly of Italian origin), used to bring an auto load of bottles to work and distribute them to the rest of the workers at perhaps 50 cents per bottle. Others had contracts with speakeasies to deliver wine, whiskey, cognac, etc.

All families were allowed approximately one ton of grapes per year to make wine for family use. The grapes came from the surrounding wine grape growing areas. Some people hired a truck to go to the location or to boxcars that were parked on the spur rails by the Embarcadero. Every boxcar was loaded with lugs of grapes, mostly zinfandel, carignan, muscat and malaga. Each boxcar had its hawker out in front extolling the grapes he had for sale.

Usually from six to ten tons of grapes were taken home, delivered in box lugs where each family had a crusher for crushing the grapes, an oak or redwood tank for the fermentation and a press to press out all the wine after fermentation. First the grapes were crushed, then placed in the tank to ferment; after about 15 days the liquid was drawn off and remaining pulp was placed in the press to squeeze out the remaining wine. Wine was placed in 50-55 gallon oak casks and these were left open for a period of time, because to place the large wooden stopper in the hole on the barrel could cause the barrel to burst because some fermentation was still going on.

The best, purest wine was taken for family use; to the other, water and sugar were added to make it go farther on sales. From the sediment on the bottom of the barrel after filtering, the Italian who had a copper still with a

46

serpentine [coil] going through a bucket of cold water would make what they called grappa—a type of Italian brandy that used to run about 110 proof. This grappa was sometimes run through the still again, this time coming out as straight alcohol of about 195 proof, which, when cut with distilled water, would be about 90 proof.

Then Dad would go down to the drug store on the corner of Powell and Broadway, get all the necessary extract flavors to make such things as rum, brandy, whiskey, cognac, etc. When a customer came to the house desiring one of these, Dad would go to the basement, fill a bottle with 90 proof alky, put the necessary flavor in, put in a little coloring also, hit it with a red-hot, old-fashioned curling iron to give it that mellow flavor, cork it with the corking machine he imported from Italy, bring it upstairs to the customer and announce: "This is good five-year-old stuff." I'll add that the bottles had been kept out in the backyard in the dirt; this dirty exterior on the bottle helped to convince the customer that it was aged.

Using a still was very dangerous, sometimes developing a leak and the escaping alcohol fumes would ignite. One time up on the corner of Wayne and Pacific Streets someone was brewing a batch of grappa in his still and evidently not paying too much attention to what was going on. The still blew and the building, being made of bricks, dispersed bricks in an area of two blocks. A small-type A-bomb.

The cost of grapes during this period was from $18 to $25 per ton and was sold at various places such as 45 Wayne Place, formerly known as Scott Place, between Broadway and Pacific Street and 965 Vallejo Street, between Powell and Mason, also on Filbert Street.

There was one speakeasy on Pacific Street Dad did business with. It was an old house way back on a lot. There they entertained with eating, gambling and girls. It was on Pacific between Powell and Wayne.

My cousins in the country, around Stockton, used to make wine, too. They had a dairy and when my uncle would make wine for sale, he'd cover the barrels with straw and cow shit to mask the wine smell and to keep away the prohibition agents.

Here is a copy of a letter from one of my uncles to another one of them:

Dear Brother,

I am not working now. If you want to Come up be fore Sinday I got to tanks of wine to take off. And then I am going to fill one up again. The one I filled when you was up I pressed that one We are all well and hope The same with youse all. From your brother [signed, Genini]

Making the Best Moonshine
by Jay Baker, Mendocino County

I learned how to make good stuff from my father in Arkansas. There, everybody had a still. Out here I made it out of corn or barley. I'd do the same with either one. I'd lay the corn out between wool blankets, leave it there until it sprouted three or four inches long. It would sprout quickly between the wool blankets because wool holds the heat. Lay it about an inch thick between the damp blankets. In six to eight days the corn germinated, depending on how the weather was—wool blankets were quicker than gunny sacks because they held the heat better, especially at night keeping a steady heat.

I'd take that and grind it, put it in a wooden vat with plenty of water and let it turn sour, six to eight days. "Sour mash" it was called. Usually I'd put a few yeast cakes in it to keep it "boiling." I added some sugar, maybe five pounds in about 50 gallons of mash. When that got good and sour, I'd put it in a cooker, a copper still, and let it simmer, regulating the heat so it would stay simmering.

Alcohol came off in steam. The cooker was pressured so the steam would be pushed out into the coil. There you had a cooling vat to put the coil in. The steam goes though this coil cooling off with water running over it. That's why they had stills in the woods along a creek bed letting the water run across the coils. Then it would liquefy back into clear alcohol. Usually you ran the coil down and then up a little so it would drip out. From a big hundred-gallon cooker, a small stream of liquor would come out. In a pressure cooker, two to three gallons, it would drip out.

Then to get the fusel oil out, you'd run it through French bread, cutting the top and bottom out. The bread absorbs all the fusel oil, but you'd lose some of your alcohol. Fusel oil is a poisonous oily substance that comes out of anything you use to make alcohol. It's what gave you a hangover if you drank too much bonded whiskey. Bonded whiskey is nowhere near pure. Besides the hangover, it can make you sick, burn your throat, can even affect your eyesight and blind you. We'd make alcohol mostly out of corn and barley here but I could make alcohol out of everything. During prohibition days some people drank too much bum stuff. It affected their nerves, giving them jake leg. I never knew anyone in California who had it, but in Arkansas my granddad and dad pointed out people who had been affected by bad booze. A number of people went blind. A few bootleggers would use lye to speed up and slip the skin off the corn quicker, start it to swell quicker, and some never washed all the lye out. Others used lye from hard wood ashes which didn't affect you as much if they didn't get it washed thoroughly. Some bootleggers made it so fast, it was so hot you could hardly drink it with all the lye and impurities in it.

We used a rope for aging purposes. We'd take a 25 foot, one-inch manila rope out in the barn, hang it up, put a small hole in the lid of the liquor and let it drip out and drip down the rope. It would travel all the way down to the bottom of the rope and drip into a container by one strand. It aged and purified the liquor quite a bit. You'd lose some alcohol but not very much. It took the sharp edges off the alcohol and it went down smoother when you drank it.

In order to color it, we used tan oak bark chips off a tan oak tree between the outer and the inside of the tree. One chip as big as your hand would color two to three gallons. It was slightly reddish and looked like bonded bourbon. It put some taste to it like it was shipped or aged in barrels.

I drank a lot of gin made out of alcohol and junipers but I didn't make it.

Bootlegging was more popular in Mendocino County during the 40s than anyone thought. It didn't end with the repeal of prohibition. A still was way out, near a creek bed or someplace. There would be a long wooden trough where the moonshiners ran their water through wooden barrels where they'd keep their mash. There was a furnace built usually out of brick where they did their heating. The cooker (copper still) and coils were protected because they were valuable. Anything else would be left if there were a raid. There was usually some kind of shed where they kept the sugar and corn or barley.

We built up a pretty good still once. We often ran off a batch. We didn't know what we made. When we ran off a gallon, we'd go around the country and give everybody some. If nobody died it was good enough to drink ourselves.

We took a batch to Healdsburg, bought some groceries, got drunk for a week, started home, had a big truck loaded with groceries and stopped to dig out some more booze for the long ride home—that's a long back road through the country. By this time all the groceries started stinking like hell, all the meat, milk and everything spoiled. We backed up to a bank and shoveled off the groceries, canned goods—everything. We had a bunch of barley with us, hog feed. It rained all the time we were there; we was soaking wet.

When we got home we dumped this barley in barrels. We'd catch wild hogs in those days and we'd fatten them up and take them and sell them, making a few bucks. After being drunk for a week, ruining all the groceries and everybody mad at us, we went to the cabin. We could smell that sucker—the fermenting barley. What could we do with that? So we got busy and built us a still. We ran off a bunch of it, used every trick I ever heard of to get it working. Started with a gallon and a half, gave some to everybody we could think of. The old man who stayed in the cabin at that place there, normally stayed drunk all the time, drink all he could get of anything he could get. We got there and he was drunker than hell already. We got to drinking, were half drunk ourselves, gave him some shots of our stuff but forgot and left a half gallon sitting there. About ten or eleven o'clock we came back, checked to see if he was doing all right. Here he was, couldn't tell if he was dead or alive, out cold, hardly any pulse or anything.

Midnight we checked on him again; he was the same way. We said, "Hey, we'd better do something." We run back and got the cat (bulldozer) and dug a big hole. We covered everything ten-foot deep.

We went back there and here he was, this old guy, staggering around. "All right, you dirty devils, you got me drunk, now give me something to sober up on."

"Christ!" we said. "That must have been damn good stuff. He drank a half gallon of that and didn't die." That would have to be awfully good booze or it'd killed him.

Around here they would make grappa. It was also called "apple jack" or "jackass," but in this country the Italians called it grappa. It was run-off wine; if you ran it off three times you'd get about a fifth of alcohol to a gallon of good wine. You'd get that down to 180 proof. You buy good wine, go to the wineries and get good wine, cheap by the gallon, one dollar a gallon, take a pressure cooker. It takes about an hour to a gallon to cook it off. You put it on your stove, take the pop valve out of the pressure cooker and screw a copper tube into it. That's where you run it off three times. No more fermenting, just boil off the pure alcohol. That's what they call jackass in this country.

I go to the winery and get 180 proof grappa and pour over cherries or grapes with the stems on. Nothing but pure alcohol goes through the peel. The juice that's left contains no alcohol. Store-bought liquor leaves a black scum on the lid, but the 180 proof I buy is absolutely clear. Prunes will get awfully strong in grappa. Dried prunes will swell and absorb so much alcohol that you could hardly eat them. Put alcohol in a jar of prunes twice and it would be like five shots a prune.

In prohibition days small guys made the stuff along the coast or in the hills between here and Healdsburg. But mostly it was made around Healdsburg and in the winery itself. There's where the big volume went out. The other stuff made back in the hills in Mendocino was made by small guys, made mostly for their own use. They let a little of it out to recover their own expenses. All the bigger stuff was handled through the wineries—illegally.

The old-timers who are died out now were into bootlegging heavy in those days. They used to bring it into the dog holes from ships. They'd take wagon loads of it over the hills inland.

Gualala was the center for that. There was an old man up the river here. I knew him well. He used to be a teamster who hauled it over the hill. There was a big gun battle here at the Gualala Bridge. One time the Internal Revenue came to raid a wagon shipment. They fought a gun battle here until the wagons got over the mountains. There were quite a few killed at Gualala Bridge south of town, but a large shipment came in and they held the government off until the wagons scattered over the hills. There were quite a few killed along the coast here, one killed up the riverbed. He was a bull whacker. Old Charlie

Dagoss was there at the time it happened, showed us the spot where the cabin was. He was killed over a card game, killed with a shovel, but they was all teamsters and bull whackers pushing alcohol wagons over the hills. They fought amongst themselves.

Gualala is small now but it was a boom town. There's a lot of history here, unwritten history.

A fern picker came up to pick ferns to sell in San Francisco. He found an old case of booze in an old redwood stump. All the labels were corroded off. Evidently some teamster threw it in there and forgot about it. The fern picker reported it to the Internal Revenue that he found a still but all he found was a case that had been hidden there during prohibition. These federal guys who came out laughed about it. We got a bottle of it and sampled it right there and it tasted very good yet. But I took it and re-boiled it off and we drank it—damn good stuff. The age wouldn't have hurt it but we didn't know where it was from, who made it and what it was made of. It was damn near pure alcohol, not much left after I boiled it off.

℘

Leonard Brock, near Santa Rosa, decided he would not be without his beer when prohibition came in. He used brewers yeast and made beer in 24 hours. Later, he said, "When my friends got to drinking it faster than I could make it, I stopped." If he wanted some during the dry spell, he bought it from individuals, not over the counters. There was plenty of it around Santa Rosa. "If I had a nickel for every dollar paid off to the Santa Rosa officials during those days, I'd be a rich man."[5]

I Wanted Brown Likker
as told by Bat Falcone, San Pedro

Besides imported alcohol filtered off from the rumrunners, the San Pedro citizens had their choices of liquor. Nick Papadakis, a Greek who started with a small restaurant, with the help of prohibition, expanded his assets to several million. He sold grapes for wine, bought fields of grapes, took orders from door to door and delivered at 15th and Center. He rented out crushers and pressers to local Italians and Slavs who made their 200 gallons. Papadakis made more than his allotted 200 gallons, stored it in several rented garages. He sold it. After prohibition he opened a string of liquor stores.

Our family would get together, buy several tons, crush the wine, ferment it and then divide it up. My father and uncles made seven barrels of wine. Everyone liked to lift it up (drink it). We'd even squeeze the grapes a second time to get more.

We bought some wine grapes one time from Papadakis that were too green. It tasted sweet at first then tasted bitter. It was ruined; some of my uncles wouldn't drink much of it, it was so bad. From then on, we watched to make sure the stems were half dried.

Demeglio also made a lot of money by selling wine at the Ocean Fish Company.

Bootleggers lived at the Mission Hotel and the Lasalle Hotel, but kept their stashes elsewhere. A thirsty Pedroite could make contact there and the boot brought him liquor. Some made contacts at the poolhall across the street. When one thirsty pool player wanted a bottle, his contact left and returned in a few minutes with a pint of white mule.

"Hey, I wanted brown stuff, not this fresh alcohol," he said.

"This is the same stuff only clear, not brown," said the bootlegger.

"Oh, no. I know this. This is just moonshine. I want the real stuff."

"All right, I'll be right back with the kind you want. "A couple men in the poolhall snickered.

In a few minutes he returned, "How's this, nice brown whiskey?"

"Yea. That's what I wanted. That's good." He took a drink, showing his pleasure, and a couple men laughed, others smiled and nudged each other. They knew what the bootlegger had done. He went outside on 7th Street, spit some of his chewing tobacco juice into the bottle, shook it, looked at the color, chewed some more and again spit into the bottle. Ah, just right!

Original drawing by John Behnke

CHAPTER 5

PICKLED PIGS

A desert duck hunter approached a reservoir in Hinkley, northwest of Barstow, in the Mojave Desert. When he fired his first shot, the frightened ducks took flight. However, some ducks never raised off the water; a few lifted off the water but crashed into the pond or on the desert. The ducks were drunk. The rancher-moonshiner used grain mash in his still, and after he boiled off the alcohol, dumped the mash into the reservoir, allowing ducks to destroy the evidence. The fermented mash contained high-proof booze and the ducks enjoyed their debauchery until the hunter shot at them.[1]

The moonshiners, large and small, had a constant problem: They had to dispose of the leftover fermented mash, which called for clever solutions, depending on the proximity of neighbors' sight, and especially smell. One can imagine the logistical problems in a city even with just a few gallons of waste mash a week or the mash from several 3,000-gallon tanks of the larger moonshine operators.

During the early part of the Depression in 1932, Harry Jennings Sr. finished his job for the day at the gas station on Lincoln Boulevard in Venice, and headed his car home to Bundy Drive in Santa Monica. On the side of the road near a vacant lot he saw a full gunnysack. He stopped and found it contained moist grain, put it on the front bumper of his car and took it home.[2]

His chickens loved it. But they soon began acting strangely, even tripping. They were drunk! They had eaten leftover mash from a bootlegger's still. One bootlegger was solving his refuse problem in a crowded city by dumping it along the side of the road.

Though Jennings reported entertaining and happy chickens, he did not report the quality and quantity of the eggs for the next few days. Pickled eggs? The Jennings family story gives the reader no more information.

One bootlegger-rancher, high on the northern side of the San Bernardino Mountains by upper Deep Creek, had his still well-hidden. He had further protection with his clear desert view and he could see the visitors climbing up the winding dusty road. The sounds of the struggling Fords could be heard for miles, giving him enough time to hide evidence of his clandestine activities.

After each run of alcohol, he threw out his cooked mash for his few cattle. He had happy mountain cows. Several times he saw intoxicated mule deer staggering around the piñon and oak forest indicating they could not hold their liquor. The venison might have been more tender and perhaps tastier.

Tahoe Jackass
as told by Ralph Kerr, Mendocino County

When I was ten years old, a school friend of mine outside Lake Tahoe had chores to do each weekend. I'd take the bus to his house on Friday and spend the weekend. I helped him shovel the used mash to dispose of the residue from the still. We'd dump it around. My friend's father had chickens to use up the mash, 200-300 of them. The chickens were drunk all the time. Most happy chickens I ever saw. The jackasses around sometimes got into the mash. They'd eat until they fell. They couldn't get up, their legs crossing like a human's except there were four of them. They sat and brayed, like they were crying for help. Finally they'd roll over and sleep it off.[3]

The ranch was in Butterfly Valley. After years of moonshining in the valley, the name was changed to Jackass Valley. Jackass is the same as moonshine (hell of a bite, hell of a kick)—got its name because it kicked like a horse and bit like a mule.

The stuff they made was so strong, it took the enamel off your teeth.

Every Friday that I was at the ranch, I helped load a Mack truck with hundreds of one-gallon cans, headed for Emeryville—Oakland, the destination point.

Happy Flyers

Two boys in the center of Los Angeles found sport in feeding their father's used mash to pigeons that came to the second story windowsill. The pigeons flew off, but when they landed on nearby telephone wires, they often missed the wires with one or both feet. The feathered alcoholics always came back when another batch was ready. They were happy flyers![4]

Another moonshiner-rancher had the fattest hogs in the San Joaquin Valley as his mash repeatedly went into his pigpen. A friend commented, "Don't think those hogs ever sobered up before they went to market. They were well-marinated hogs, those were."

They were pickled pigs.

Young Swede Pederson of Sausalito and his friends increased their hunting take by soaking grain in bootleg alcohol, then throwing it out in their quail hunting area in Marin County the night before the hunt.[5]

When Swede and the boys arrived the next morning the quail had feasted on the grain but they could not fly. Since they became numb to the potential danger sounds, their disoriented running (sometimes staggering) made them easy hits for the boys' guns.

In Humboldt County, Norton Steenfott learned from an old Italian family how to catch birds live. Before dawn the Italian threw on the lawn grain that had been soaked in grappa for a few days. By morning the robins and blackbirds were sprawled out all over the yard. The Italians picked up the passed-out birds they wanted, wrung their necks and cooked them for a favorite Sunday dinner, polenta and wild game. Years after prohibition, Steenfott used a similar method to catch pigeons that were overrunning one of his buildings in Old Town Eureka. He took the sack full of pigeons to a friend of his out of town who raised pigeons.[6]

"Why, these birds aren't any good," the friend said. "They're all dead."

"No," answered Steenfott, "you put them in the cage with the rest—they'll be fine in the morning."

Sure enough after they slept off their drunk, you couldn't tell the difference between the pigeons. It looked, however, as if some of the pigeons rubbed their heads a lot with their wing feathers.

According to Constable Penny Morrow of Oro Grande, sheriffs had a unique way of knowing whether a still was operating as they investigated the ranches up and down the Mojave River: They watched the flies. If a fly landed on their arms and the sheriffs were able to swat it without much speed and effort, they knew the fly's motor-sensory reactions were deadened by the sweet run-off of the stills. A moonshiner was in the immediate area.

The strangest case of animal intoxication occurred in Holtville in 1924. Headlines in the August 8, 1924, *Holtville Tribune* read: "Apple Jack Whiskey Kills 80,000 Rumrunners," subheaded, "Bootlegging bees. A new kink for the Volstead Sherlocks."

David James Sr., nicknamed "Honey James," and his son David Jr. went to extract honey from one of their apiaries. They discovered "what may prove to be a link in the purported rum-running ring said to be operating in the Imperial Valley."

When James smelled the pleasant aroma of whiskey, he and his son explored the area but couldn't discover any. They started to extract the honey from a three-story hive and found smuggled contraband, 30 pounds of apple jack brandy with a small quantity of honey mixed in, eight combs filled to the top with liquor. Alcohol so diluted the honey it could not be extracted. The bees also stored grape wine and corn whiskey in some compartments. Bees imbibed too freely and died as a result of the orgy. The three-story hives contained 80,000 bees—all dead.

All around James's hives were farmers, Swiss dairymen, cotton growers, and without a doubt some moonshiners. The bees were probably attracted to the sugary smell of a new brand of apple jack that came off the barrel of mash and they started transporting it—transporting liquor certainly violated the Volstead Act.

The *Tribune* article continued, "...since the reign of Volstead, rum running has been developed to a point of perfection, but nowhere not even by the cleverest sleuths have evaders of the Eighteenth Amendment proved to be owners of bootlegging bees."

The *Chico Enterprise* of June 8, 1928, also reported wayward bees coming home drunk. A farmer in the Sacramento Valley, near Paradise, could not trust his bees out alone because they kept coming back home drunk and flavored his honey with corn mash. Chico and Oroville authorities found John Van Horn preparing to go into the business of manufacturing liquor. Even though the agents suspected him of corrupting the young bees, he could not be arrested for selling, nor manufacturing. Although officers could not find the still or the fermenting mash, they arrested Van Horn for possession and confiscated 12 sacks of sugar and a quantity of corn.

They probably could not get any of the wayward bees to confess where they obtained the contraband. They kept their code of silence. They were bees, after all, not stool pigeons.

In the small San Joaquin Valley farming town of Dos Palos, the farmers and deputy constable knew when Cardoza finished his batch. His pigs would be "a' squealing and carrying on and one could hear them for blocks."[7]

Cardoza and other moonshiners, large and small, found ways to dispose of the leftover mash, and in the process several generations of California animals became pickled animals.

Original drawing by John Behnke.

CHAPTER 6

DRYING UP THE STATE

The country quickly turned the war economy to a peacetime economy in 1919-20. The dry 1920s began what became known as the "Roaring Twenties," began with hope that came from 75 years of struggling to make the country dry, hope of continuing progressive reforms, making the country a more moral place, and hope resulting from winning the Great War and having a secure peace. Californians, and the country as a whole, were ready to enjoy the fruits of prohibition, peace, progress and prosperity.

Wets had lost the political war over prohibition, but felt so strongly about their cause and prohibition injustice that anti-dry forces were not convinced. Even though Amendment 18 was etched in stone as part of the Constitution, 200,000 people enrolled for $1 a year in the Association Against the Prohibition Amendment (AAPA). This start of the wet crusade had three main goals: repeal the Volstead Act, permit states to decide to be wet or dry and repeal the 18th Amendment. Wet Californians had begun the long fight against the drys. Prohibitionists soon realized the war was not over.

Federal dry squads in California, receiving thousands of tips in 1920, made a flurry of raids the first two years of prohibition, closed stills and bootleg joints, arrested and convicted several thousand violators. Newspapers recorded victories as it had in the late war: small salients taken here, such and such roadhouse closed for selling liquor, biggest haul of moonshine in this or that county so far. Many trenches were overrun: bars closed, thousands of gallons of booze dumped down street gutters, buildings abated, bootleggers sent to county jails and evidence stored in basements of court houses. Prohibitionists knew they were winning the war.

Since the radio was still just a toy, people found out about the world by reading and then by word of mouth. "They got ol' so and so, yesterday, didja hear?" If one were to read the *San Francisco Chronicle* of October 4, 1921, he would be impressed with the dry squad in stopping liquor violations: 18 "Dry Law Violations" said the paper. In San Francisco: 401 and 47 Sixth Street, 200 and 311 Third, Seventh and Stevenson, 232 Fifth, 842 Kearny, 246 Leavensworth, 643 Montgomery, 614 Broadway; in Oakland: 2225 Brush Street, 1435 Thirty-fourth, 803, 200, 101 Broadway.

The same day, the *Chronicle* reported the breakup of a smuggling ring and confession of one leader, Giovanni Patroni of Granada at Princeton, Half Moon Bay. He admitted to authorities his involvement with one of the two Vancouver firms sending ships to the Pacific Coast, landing liquor, then transporting it to San Francisco. "Patroni's information will put a stop to booze smuggling along the Pacific Coast," said the *Chronicle*. With this one day's news reporting, Californians might be convinced prohibition would be effective.

Raids into and environs, for example, lulled drys into thinking the war was almost over—just a little mopping-up to do.

49er Days in

State dry leaders helped prepare for the annual 49er Days in in May 1922. Californians would see they could have fun without the disgrace of liquor and without drunks falling around ruining this historic event and family outing. Since numerous blind pigs had been shut down in and around , visitors would have to celebrate with soft drinks and milk. Drys were pleased and hopeful.

Confident as could be, Prohibition Agent C. H. Wheeler said, "The Mojave Desert will have nothing on this week for aridness. The WCTU picnic will spread out saloon tablecloths, serve sandwiches and pop and (visitors will) see not one drop (of alcohol)."

The *Chronicle* editor was a better sage than the prohibition agent or he knew the people better. Said the *Chronicle:* Wheeler "is wrong on the Mojave Desert stuff," and wrong about what kind of celebration the California capitol would have during this year's Days of the 49ers.[1] The *Chronicle* predicted "likker" would be like the original bootleggers, hiding liquor in their boots and selling it to the Indians. There would be lots of boots and lots of whiskey and much of it will find its way to the customers. Maybe blind pigs will be closed but the newspaper was not "banking" on a dry holiday. The newspaper was correct and Wheeler wrong. Celebrants found a watering hole in, then another and another. Visitors and modern 49ers survived the predicted dry trek as did their ancestors.

Liquor was available to Californians who wanted it. And hundreds of thousands wanted it. The United States Government organized the country into prohibition districts, dividing California into Northern California and Nevada as one district and Southern California as another. Federal agents (Prohis), hit most counties and all cities, relying on enthusiastic prohibitionists to turn in usurpers of the law. Informers kept prohis busy. It looked as if drys would consolidate their victory and they would dry up the state in just a few years.

The state passed the Wright Act, called Little Volstead Act, May 7, 1921. Score one for the drys, but wets obtained enough signatures to put it on a referendum ballot in 1922—a clever way to delay the bill almost two years. Score one for the wets. Many communities passed their own Little Volstead Acts, making federal laws local laws. Another for the drys. Each local and state official took an oath of office to obey the Constitution of the United States and uphold its laws. Local officials in most areas, but not San Francisco, did enforce laws if they wanted to or if they had to. In November 1922, the Wright Act narrowly survived the referendum, 445,076 yes to 411,133 no, and became law. Another score for the drys. The state bound itself to the Constitution, promising to enforce prohibition since the Volstead Act was also an official state law under the Wright Act.

Within the first two years, the bone-dry Volstead law showed signs of leakage. Volstead provision, Section 29, written in 1919 to placate New England and California legislators by enabling families, who had a cultural tradition of making hard apple cider and wine, to continue making 200 gallons for personal use. Each head of a family, so culturally inclined, could make 200 gallons of either, not to be sold, transported or bartered. A 22-year-old Greek son, an adult living at home, could therefore make his own. Thus the family could have 400 gallons of wine to last until the next harvest. If the family fudged and made a little more than allowed, there were more chances of some leaking out to a local bootleg joint or sold to neighbors to buy the kids "Sunday-best" shoes. A little wine distilled on the family stove made clear grappa, family moonshine—usually for family use but illegal nevertheless. Thousands of gallons of grappa spilled over to the public.

Some wineries called it quits. That was it. Others kept trying to survive in a more hostile environment. Lodi-area vineyards, as an example, produced 139,944 tons of grapes in the last harvest before prohibition, 1919 according to "Wineries in the Greater Lodi Area."[2]

Most of this crop was sold to private parties, shipped east as juice, or boiled down and shipped as "syrup." Boiling down into syrup saved money on freight charges; and the syrup when diluted again to normal strength could be set aside, like fresh juice, in a basement, cellar or attic and allowed to ferment in anticipation of the coming prohibition drought.

Wineries spent the last few months of 1919 trying to sell and ship out their existing bottling before "Black Friday," January 16, 1920. The wine that could not be exported before the deadline was sold to private parties, given to investors as dividends, or sold to patent medicine groups. Wineries would be able to continue to function on a limited basis, producing wine vinegar and wine for medicinal and sacramental purposes.

In 1920 there were 8,071 freight carloads of grapes shipped out of the Greater Lodi area while the local wineries and dehydrators handled another

18,000 tons. During prohibition prices rose to $100 a ton for Tokays and $185 a ton for juice grapes. With the coming of prohibition, prices for dehydrated wine grapes jumped from eight cents a pound to twenty-one cents to twenty-five cents a pound.

Raisins made from wine grapes can be used only for wine making; they are not suitable for table use. Properly dried grapes, when reconstituted, can be made into as good a wine as could have been made from the original grapes. Dried grapes, pressed into "wine bricks," sold from the early 1920s with directions on how to make wine, disclaiming that if one followed these directions he would make wine and that was illegal. Another wine brick label had reverse directions to the effect "Do not let this wine brick soak in a gallon of water at room temperature for 80 hours..." Thus if the "do not" directions, were followed, the bricks would turn into wine and that would be illegal. Obviously much wine came from wine bricks. Wine juices, syrup, and grapes themselves permeated the state for wine making purposes— helping vineyardists, but hardly

Prohibition bottles sold legally for sacramental wine to help Concannon Vineyards. Although many wineries closed, numerous survived prohibition by making vinegar, alcohol for industry and sacramental (religious) wine. Photo courtesy of Concannon Vineyards.

keeping California bone dry. Loopholes of various kinds derived from the concessions given to the grape and apple growers.

The Wine Growers Association pushed on legal fronts too. One example was its lawsuit against the United States to regain personal property. Madelena Carattini of Winthrop had her liquor property destroyed in a 1923 raid at the Carattini Hotel in Delmar and the Mt. Shasta Hotel in Kennet. She won, forcing the government into compensating her for the lost wine, but more important, making the government more cautious in its actions against the wine industry.[3]

Rabbi Tovil exploited another leak in the bone dry ship of state. A truism: If you can do something, you don't need to brag about it. That lesson was not learned by Rabbi Jacob Tovil until it was too late. Tovil bragged about how he could sell any amount of wine he wanted, that he had federal protection "in return for having knocked over two federal protection men." Word came to Agent H. W. Barnes about his boast and about people buying sacramental wine from him at 1024 S. Maple Avenue . Barnes arranged a buyer while agents F. F. English, A. S. Rinckel and J. C. Cooper watched from a distance. Buyer Jimmie Belk planned to purchase 10 gallons of sacramental wine at $6 per gallon, but he had to drive into the garage in the alley for the wine to be loaded into the car. The rabbi's son Morris Tovil brought the wine from the house and loaded it into the car. Since Belk was a gentile, it showed how magnanimous the 71-year-old rabbi was as he helped people outside his congregation. Along with confiscated wine, officers also took a 38 caliber revolver from the good rabbi. Records showed that in six months of 1923 he received about 1,100 gallons of wine and sold to his "congregation" 1,541 gallons, disposing of about 500 gallons of wine more than he had permits for. He was, indeed, a gifted man of God. Bonds of $25,000 held both Tovils in jail until their trial. Tovil was denied more permits for sacramental wine.[4]

Major loophole in the "Dry" laws. A January 16, 1926, prescription for a man living at Hotel Sequoia for liquor. Signed by the doctor, filled by the druggist, enjoyed by the "patient"—making the liquor law less effective and making a couple professionals a little richer. Property of the author.

Medical Loopholes

Exposing another loophole, the Grand Jury of Santa Rosa brought charges against four doctors for falsifying names on prescriptions to obtain liquor. They or a friend would be able to go to a drugstore to fill the prescription of whiskey. They pleaded guilty and the court fined them $50 each. These professional violators were Drs. Cuthbert Fleissner, Clifford M. Carlson, David J. Mahan and Paul T. Quarry.[5]

Throughout the state this loophole leaked much liquor to the populace, some by one-pint prescriptions, given only after examination and then no more than a pint every 10 days with no refills without another exam. Stolen prescription pads became a valuable commodity as these forged forms could be used to obtain pints from druggists. Some doctors were in collusion with druggists, a few may have sold prescription pads to druggists and other doctors were just caring professionals helping their patients.

Michieli's Cold and Influenza Remedy

"An Old and Reliable Remedy for Colds and Influenza"

In 1924, John P. Michieli, Chemist, 3276 Mission St. in San Francisco, proposed Michieli's Cold and Influenza Remedy for sale and filled out Form 1404 to obtain a permit to produce and sell this medicine which had 50 percent whiskey. On his application he included directions for use: "For adults, two

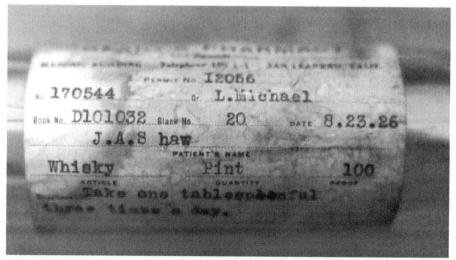

Prescription label for medicinal alcohol, Old Forrester Whiskey, prescribed by Dr. L. Michael, San Leandro on August 23, 1926, for a J. A. Shaw. "One tablespoon three times a day of 100 proof whisky." Permits like #12056 allowed thousands of pharmacies like Geary's in San Leandro to have liquor—creating one of the many loopholes in the Volstead Act. Photo by author.

tablespoons in cup of hot water with a little sugar at bed-time. When necessary to be taken oftener, one tablespoonful three times a day will be found beneficial."[6]

The application was marked "**DISAPPROVED**."

Federal Prohibition Director in San Francisco, S. F. Rutter, forwarded Washington's rejection to Michieli, who immediately wrote to the Department of Justice asking for "full protection of my rights under the Constitution." He said the remedy contained "four (4) grains of quinine to each fluid ounce of whiskey (making it) unfit for beverage use." Michieli stipulated, "It is doubtful if Congress is permitted to legislate in the field of medicine at all."

Mabel Walker Willebrandt, U. S. Assistant District Attorney, fired back a response that this was clearly a matter for the Federal Prohibition Commissioner of the IRS. Although Michieli was denied, other medicines were approved.

We Were Just Trying to Put Out the Fire, Your Honor

Americans were their own worst enemy when it came to punishing someone for violating a law these same Americans or their representatives made. Juries often sided with liquor violators, despite the preponderance of evidence. Case N 16812 in the Federal Court in San Francisco must have been frustrating to the prosecution. Prohis charged Hugh Twomey, Carsten Allworden and Mrs. C. Taylor, at 1095 Rhode Island Street, San Francisco, on four counts: possession of a still, possession of alcohol, manufacturing, and another count of possession. The evidence: 80 gallons of jackass brandy, 100 gallons of mash, a 50-gallon still, two pressure tanks, two triple burners, grain and various bottles and jugs of liquors. During the raid, the accused hurriedly dumped the mash to get rid of evidence. The mash they were dumping was to help put out an impending fire, they said at the trial. In 1925 Twomey and Allworden were found by the jury to be not guilty, and the government dropped the case against Taylor.[7]

Besides juries siding with violators, technicalities hurt the dry cause. The government dismissed the case against John Francis Broska in 1925 because agent D. W. Rinckel made the search warrant for John Francis—therefore making it an invalid search warrant, almost like no search warrant.

Judge Frank Kerrigan threw out hundreds of cases because of search warrant and other technicalities. Judge Partridge dismissed 1,500 cases where agents used bogus names for informants. Partridge said that good results cannot be justified by bad methods.[8]

And when prosecutors did go after a violator and the court upheld the procedures, usually Californian juries, especially San Franciscan juries, did not convict. One bootlegger boasted that he was indicted 80 times without one conviction.

Strange things happened even in high priority cases like the U. S. Government versus Peter McDonough, where undercover agent Maurice O'Callahan Jr. bought five gallons of whiskey from McDonough. O'Callahan, the son of a police officer, had been threatened if he testified, and someone threatened to have his father discharged from the police force. Witnesses had been moved to Fresno for protection. "The five-gallons of whiskey which were brought to court as evidence unfortunately disappeared from the clerk's office." In McDonough's case, however, there was enough evidence to convict, but dozens of other cases were dismissed after evidence or witnesses disappeared.[9]

By 1925, the prohibition agency became more thorough in its investigations. Too many cases had been thrown out of court, too many not-guilty verdicts or too many hung juries. In 1925 the case against Fred Jacobs and Ivor Armstrong illustrated the thoroughness of the preparation of its case. Armstrong hired Jacobs to help set up his distillery at 1143 Post Street, San Francisco. The prohis raided the city moonshine operation and confiscated four stills from 30 to 125 gallons, two 10-gallon copper buckets, one gas stove with two triple burners, nine sacks sugar, two pressure tanks, 49 barrels of mash, sacks of corn and barley, electric fan, gallon of coloring, funnels, electric pump, hydrometers, test tubes, one hand hoist pump and 100 feet of hose and rope. The government had a separate charge for the 395 gallons of jackass brandy, another for manufacturing and a fourth for possession. The trial for Jacobs ended in the jury finding him not guilty six months after the arrest. In May 1926, a year after the arrest, the prosecution was well prepared for Armstrong: obtaining gas consumption records for the last two years, records of Spring Valley Water Co., garage and auto repair receipts, building lease agreements, maps of the building and the mezzanine trapdoor leading to the basement, and shipment records of sugar from the supply house. Agent F. A. Lea testified about his smelling fermenting mash when he investigated the suspected distillery. On May 13, jury foreman George F. Sand read the judgment: "We, the Jury, find Ivor C. Armstrong the defendant at the bar, guilty as charged on all counts." Armstrong received a $1,000 fine and a year in jail, plus six months on the last charge to start as soon as the year sentence was completed.[10]

"Every sweet has its sour," said Ralph W. Emerson, and that quotation applied to prohibition enforcement. The sweet success of California prohis caused problems. Ninety percent of federal cases in northern California were prohibition cases. San Francisco, in 1924-25, had as many federal cases as New York and Chicago and had more jury trials than either of the two notorious cities. In 1924 the courts in the Northern District were behind 5,000 cases. Bootlegging charges added 50 cases a day. Successful raids produced more cases than could be handled. When first-offender fine limits rose from $150-400 to $600, more defenders threatened to go to trial rather than plea-bargain

64

or plead guilty. Since the City and County of San Francisco refused to seek out their bootleggers, it was beneficial to the legal system. Therefore, Emerson, every sour also had its sweet.[11]

Thirty-two agents in the mid-1920s could not adequately enforce regulations in the Northern District of California and Nevada with a population of 1,500,000. Yet the courts could handle no more. In 1925, there were 12,000 permit holders who used alcohol legally, including 2,500 druggists, 7,000 physicians, a dozen breweries, 30 vinegar manufacturers using cider, 100 transportation companies permitted to carry liquor and 750 manufacturers—all regulated by 30 clerks and 20 agents. Congress authorized too little manpower to prevent leakage and too few courts to unclog the court system. Officers attempted to make California bone dry even though Californians wanted to be wet or didn't care.

Nothing Left to Chance

The *Sausalito News* of December 10, 1926, reported that thieves raided alcohol out of a sealed and guarded railroad car at Pittsburg. The industrial alcohol, 6,300 gallons, came from Mason By Products in Sausalito consigned to Great Western Chemical Company in Pittsburg, California. John Mason showed the investigators receipts for all the alcohol and affirmed that the car had been thoroughly sealed. The railroad always sent a guard when pure alcohol was shipped, but nothing was placed on the car to give a clue of its contents. Yet only 5,100-5,200 gallons arrived in Pittsburg. Missing: 1,100-1,200 gallons, enough to make 2,400 gallons of bathtub gin, enough for 307,000 shots.

Great Western Company produced Zanthile, a chemical for the floatation of copper, gold and silver ores and had permits to use industrial alcohol.

Mason manufactured one tenth of all the alcohol for industry in the United States, employing 150 people at that time. The biggest customer was the United States Government. Mason Malt Distillery in June 1921 sent 100,000 gallons to New York and then to Greece. The exporter, American Products Sales Co., filed a $250,000 bond with the government. With this kind of volume, the Mason company was likely to be a target and a temptation to filter off some alcohol for other than industrial uses. The *Independent* of San Rafael reported federal agents had been investigating Mason in June 1930. Chief Inspector James Robb from San Francisco accused the company of "short comings and practices which render it liable to revocation of its permit." Three complaints were as follows:

1. Commercial alcohol being vended was insufficiently denatured—ready to permit a simple redistillation into alcohol fit for beverage.

2. Insufficient precaution to prevent "disappearance" of alcohol.

3. Charges made several years ago may entitle the company to lose its permit.

Theodore Robb, Mason's attorney, defended the company: "We are satisfied—absolutely nothing is left to chance." Here then was another leak of alcohol, making a bone dry California an impossibility.

∅

The Mexican border was another source of liquor. Freedom to travel across the "linea," freedom to walk from Calexico to Mexicali in a few minutes, drink as much as one wanted, and sometimes sneak a bottle back. As a result of complaints, the federal agents closed the border at nine in the evening and opened at six in the morning. "ABW Club dropped girls from daily programs in response to an attempt to cleanup border conditions."[12] But still the liquor came across, either inside the person or on his body.

Poison Booze

Federal reports for the year 1923 showed a 30 percent rise in deaths from bad alcohol over 1922. Deaths of 2,467 for the year represented 2.6 per 100,000. Of these, 20 were reported in California, with Pennsylvania leading the states with 1,000, New York 400, and Illinois 200.[13]

Ned M. Green, Prohibition Administrator in San Francisco, collected and displayed prohibition material to warn bootleg buyers. "Some of the things we are seizing nowadays could not be better poison makers. More stills are poison breeders." Alcohol making requires cleanliness. "Amateur moonshiners make their still out of milk cans, oil cans, garbage cans or any thing else. They use decayed fruit for the mash. No wonder the stuff they turn out blinds and kills the drinkers," said Green.

How dry was the state capital after three years of winning battles against the bootleggers? In a report from Law Enforcement League, President Edwin E. Grant wrote to Prohibition Director Rutter, detailing successes of a year's work in cleaning up Sacramento. So many places had been hit again and again, the Law Enforcement League used abatement proceedings to close the buildings for good—at least for one year. Agents filed 23 liquor and red-light abatement cases in superior court, of which 14 were completed, winning 13 of 14 of these completed cases. Here were the addresses of these cases involving liquor and other liquor cases pending or with evidence of selling and ready for padlocks: Second Street, 901, 905, 911, 917, 924, 925 1/2, 929 1/2, 1024; Third Street, 1116; I Street, 220; J Street, 412, 526; K Street, 130, 221, 228, 231, 304, 308, 500; L Street, 218, 231. Grant ended his letter thanking Rutter for the cooperation and hoping that information would help in the successful prosecution in that most difficult field at . "Better finances," he said, "would help drive the bootleggers to cover."

After several major attempts to clean up the state capital, drys still hadn't driven the bootleggers (and prostitutes) to cover. Streets like the 900 block of Second and 200 block of K must have been something after state employees got off work and later at night. Perhaps some customers were assemblymen just secretly meeting with their wet constituents.[14]

Analysis From Within

After Agent H. W. Hess resigned as prohibition agent in 1926, he agreed to answer questions from George L. Horner, Special Agent, U. S. Dept. of Justice at San Francisco. Hess's candid statements reveal much of what was wrong with the first six years of prohibition and enforcement thereof. Hess resigned so that "Mr. Beasley and Mr. Green could carry on their department to suit themselves..."[15]

Hess asserted the department hired people who should never been appointed. For example, "...they would put on a man as a so-called 'undercover buyer,' who were very low types, from the underworld or the fringes of it. These men would make buys for a certain time and then be appointed as agents...Never properly instructed, they didn't have the proper mentality, they had no investigating experience, and they were totally unfit..."

When asked if Colonel Green had any staff on the payroll of the bootleggers, Hess answered in the best government doublespeak: "Well I would state this, that there has been, and I believe there are at the present time, men on the payroll who are living under circumstances such as would cause a reasonable man to believe they had a large income from some other source than that of the salary of a prohibition agent. For instance, I believe you will find one agent who claims to have purchased an apartment house, his statement being that his mother has gotten rich. I think that by reasonable investigation you can determine who these agents are. Another agent maintains an expensive apartment and covers his post of duty with an automobile which is valued at more than $3,000; I think its price is about $4,500. The upkeep of that machine alone amounts to practically as much as his salary is. There are a lot of instances of that sort. For instance, there is a man who has just been sent to the penitentiary for impersonating an officer. Mr. Bohner, of your Department of Justice, can tell you all about him...the Prohibition Department...insisted on having him around the office, being friendly with him, even after Mr. Bohner had told them that that practice should be discontinued."

The liquor is landed, "to some extent, through the connivance of agents and the agents draw down a commission on that which is landed." Two years ago they would arrange for a small "knockout" in one part of town and then they would land a big load in another part of town. They would take credit for the knockout. The bootleggers' attorneys told Hess these things. "Two years ago there was the so-called Monterey Raid...involving the seizure of one thousand cases of whiskey on the beach. [The gang was comprised] of 25 men, ten automobiles, men and women of scattered localities." Hess said that as far as he knew no effort was made to determine the connection between the various groups.

There are two big rumrunning operations units in San Francisco—the "Consolidated" and the "Exporters." These are both Vancouver men. Another group is called the "Independents," headed by Tom Murphy and Paul Pane. This group operates two boats.

The Consolidated and the Exporters have about five boats. Connected with the Exporters is "Black Tony," an Italian named Pagamassino. Now he is operating in the south.

Under Rutter's "machine" the Prohibition Department was constantly under turmoil, under investigation. The Chief Clerk John R. Smith was dismissed for supposed graft over the wine affair. When Hess offered his services to Rutter and made suggestions about coordination of effort and investigation, Rutter was not "very friendly about it so I made it my business to stay out of the investigative work entirely." Hess said that Rutter was conscientiously trying to enforce the law, but he was using the "shotgun" approach. Dr. Briggs of the Anti-Saloon League practically dictated which places would be raided. They raided some sixty to seventy places enough times to get almost the evidence needed to shut the places down under #5, the abatement law, the padlock law. Instead of concentrating on those places and closing them for good, they would raid others and go after the $250 fine and "never get the old offenders closed up." Hess said it took over a year to close those places on Columbus Avenue. There was no method or system followed at all, simply a shotgun enforcement.

"Sacramento was the most flagrant and San Francisco very bad," said Hess. One can get what he wants in Sacramento. They are operating with bars. San Francisco is openly wet. The reason these places are so open is that the Prohibition Department has no real plan, has poor personnel and Colonel Green gave unfavorable publicity to the newspapers. He said he was not interested in the little man, the man with a flask, had no intention of disturbing the restaurants, and no intention of interfering with the "jollification at the football games." Therefore the Cal-Stanford big games went on as usual. The cafe owners and the roadhouses opened up again and operated as usual.

Federal authorities arrested San Francisco's District Attorney Brady two times, once on Silver Avenue at the Niomo Grill and once in Half Moon Bay. Both times he was "pretty well lit." He is wet, said Hess. The Chief of Police [O'Brien] is wet, admits he is wet and that he will never put on a dry squad and is not in favor of the law. The sheriff [Tom Finn] is wet and had never made a raid in that county. Since it's the County and City of San Francisco and the limits are the same, the chief of police and the sheriff can put the blame on each other and not do much of anything. Primarily "Finn is wet to begin with." The majority of people are wet. However enforcement is possible and feasible. As with all the history of enforcement in California, Hess summarized, it has been the result of misdirection, improper personnel, and lack of organization and plan.

Another insider expressed the views of thousands of Californians as they saw absurdities in the enforcement of and attitude toward the prohibition law. The judge was six years ahead of the expressions voiced in the Wickersham Commission under President Herbert Hoover [see Chapter 26].

Judge Jesse Olney Speaks Out

"Do away with needless technicalities, obtain speedy justice, give jail time, not just fines and urge officials to enforce it conscientiously, without fear or favor," said Judge Jesse Olney to the St. Paul M. E. Church in San Bernardino, on April 11, 1924. Already bootleggers had become a great power.

"The large amount of money at the command of the bootleggers makes them a distinct menace in any community." They control many officials in the country. Bootleggers need to be sent to jail, at least to dry out for awhile. We must

uphold the Constitution and its statutes, said the Judge. "If our people don't like the law, let them change it, but so long as it stands, enforce it.... Lawbreakers in high places who are encouraging the vendors of this illicit traffic are responsible for this vastly increasing disrespect for the law."[16]

Yet the election of 1924 evinced a strong support for prohibition. Coolidge won handily, being elected as president in his own right. Wayne Wheeler, Anti-Saloon League leader, announced on November 8, that only one of the 33 senators elected was an open wet. In 1925, the new congress would be a dry majority: 72 dry senators with only 24 wet; 319 dry congressmen, 105 wet. Those attempting to win elections as a wet, in state after state, went down to defeat, sending a clear message to candidates: run as a dry or you won't be elected. The dry political forces not only suppressed but soundly defeated their political opponents. Strongly backed by an influential voting machine, it appeared that prohibition was there to stay.[17] Yet the attempt to make California bone dry had failed. With all the loopholes, the exceptions to the law, the advantages of the wets and the blind eye to violations, California was more wet than dry. By 1926 agents knew all the tricks of smuggling, bootlegging and moonshining, but these violators knew the tricks of the agents and knew the loopholes that had not been stopped during the first six years of prohibition and they discovered more clever ways of keeping the state wet.

Woman's tea or dinner
Pajama, 1926 (bobbed haircut)

Cloth day vest, 1920

Knitted swimsuit, 1928

One piece man's combination,
1920s

Dance set
brassiere
and panties,
1927

Man's swim suit, 1920s

Original sketches by Paul Salopek, Barstow

CHAPTER 7

THE DRY DESERT MOISTENS LOS ANGELES

Profits in desert agriculture, railroading and mining kept thousands of families with good incomes from the 1900s to the end of the first World War. But as the wartime demand for agricultural products to feed starving people in Europe declined, prices fell, and many farmers had trouble making mortgage payments in the 1920s, especially on marginal farmland. After the war, demand for copper, lead and tungsten fell, prices fell, mines closed and smaller desert railroads suffered. Therefore, with some "rails" (railroad workers), homesteaders, farmers and miners struggling to make a living in the postwar recession and the "farmers' depression" of the 1920s, desert residents did not realize they were in what would later be called "The Roaring Twenties."

Upon this background came prohibition and a demand for another product—alcohol. The desert had water, springs and ranch wells all over the place. Flowing underground much of its course across the Mojave Desert, the Mojave River held a great aquifer of what seemed like an endless supply of fine water just below the surface of the dry riverbed. Ranchers and miners who turned to moonshining knew the desert had the advantage of distance and isolation from the dry squads' sorties coming out of San Bernardino, Riverside and Independence, county seats of three inland counties. Water, isolation and labor created the three ingredients for favorable moonshine operations.

As with every area of California local moonshiners set up small operations, big enough to supply local demand; other booze makers supplied family needs and needs of their neighbors making a little profit to pay expenses.

Large liquor wholesalers in Los Angeles paid for stills to be built or encouraged ranchers to make moonshine and bought it from them. The syndicate, for lack of a better word, often had a conspirator lease a ranch, then set up a liquor operation. For fourteen years liquor flowed from the Mojave Desert into the Los Angeles basin, an endless supply of liquid wealth. Such a supply existed that if a few stills were not knocked over, the price of moonshine would drop and it did drop in 1929 and the early 1930s.

"If the desert gets any wetter, Noah will have to build another ark."— these words were uttered in frustration and with a little jest about the deserts of Riverside and San Bernardino counties.

Local constables, charged with enforcement in their townships, had the unenviable duty to stop violators who were usually their friends or neighbors, often people they grew up with. Moonshiners were decent folks, struggling to make a living and if they made some moon on their homesteads or at an abandoned mine or desert spring, the constable generally looked the other way. Walt Wilhelm, pioneer gas station owner east of Yermo who started his station when the road to Las Vegas was sand and gravel, had respect for the desert bootlegger: "All decent men." Wilhelm assisted Constable Tom Williams and later, in the 1930s, became constable himself.

Penny Morrow, constable of Oro Grande, born in Barstow in 1885, said the same thing: "I didn't go out looking for them or I would have had to arrest all my friends and neighbors."

If someone made bad booze, Constable Melvin "Red" Butler of Victorville searched out the culprit to put him out of business. He frowned on unscrupulous moonshiners who used five-gallon metal cans for their stills or

Later photo of Constable Penny Morrow, Oro Grande, showing how he looked when he joined county sheriffs or "dry squads" searching for stills along the Mojave River. Photo courtesy of Penny Morrow.

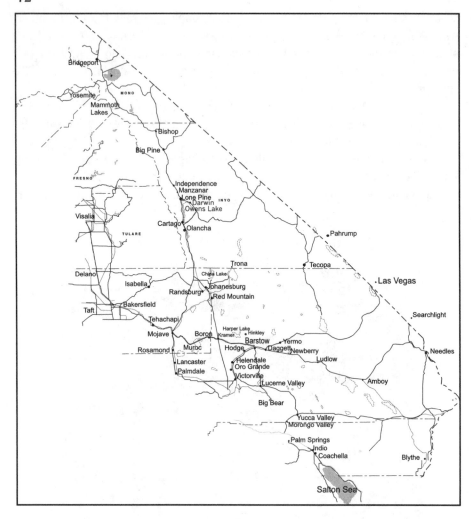

California High Desert Area

old car radiators for the coils—creating poison. He did not molest makers of quality liquor. Other constables basically felt the same way: J. W. Everett of Ludlow, Jim Lucas of Daggett and Ed Harris of Barstow.

Constables solved community problems such as drunkenness, drunk driving and disturbing the peace, especially if the culprits were from big cities. If someone issued a complaint of selling intoxicating liquors, constables investigated and made arrests if appropriate and if expedient. Since the WCTU, Anti-Saloon League and vociferous church groups weren't the force in the desert they were other places, there were few complaints about miners coming into town Saturday night to play pool, drink a little moonshine and kick some tailings off their boots. If they kicked too much, the constable acted.

Gates Ajar for J. H. Gates
from *Victor Valley News Herald*, April 11, 1924

J. H. Gates explained that he had that gallon jug of vile-smelling hootch for his own behalf, but he had a party in his house helping to drink it, and there was evidence he was peddling it. When Special Santa Fe Officer H. W. Johnson and Constable Edward Dolch rudely and suddenly butted into the hilarious party, Gates tried to break the jug over a cook stove. The earthen jug rebelled at the abuse, remained intact, and demolished the stove. Gates had been in Victorville from Texas some weeks with the construction crew and lived down by the sausalitos *(little willows)*. Presently Gates was before Justice Hoffman who said $250 would be about the right price for dispensing such stuff. Not having the $250, Gates had 125 days to think over the matter while keeping step with the chain gang on county highway work.

Barstow Printer editor, in 1932, reported a few county dry squad officers with their six shooters shot a few holes in the ceiling of one bootleg establishment and a few holes in the floor of another. They wanted to let in a little fresh air, the editor said. But the tone of the article was that desert citizens did not take liquor violations seriously.

Occasionally serious events happened. In Randsburg a drinking spree ended in the death of Amos Leese. John Fleming accused Leese, a local miner, of making advances toward his woman. Leese denied it but Fleming shot him three times with a .45.

Tom Kimbro struck Kirkendal with a beer bottle in a Barstow poolroom brawl. Both had been drinking according to the *Printer* of June 9, 1932.

Ed Harris put Natividad Hernandez and Ysidro Sanchez in jail after they indulged in part of a gallon of bootleg whiskey east of Newberry in 1930. When they had their fill, they planted the whiskey in the desert, drove to Barstow where they ran into a Cadillac heading for Los Angeles. Dr. John Graham attended to their injuries before Harris placed them in jail. Harris found the cache of bootleg. These were the types of incidents local constables and justices of the peace handled.

If a complaint reached San Bernardino, the sheriff could direct the constable to check it out or county dry squad officials to investigate. In 1930, Deputy Sheriff J. E. "Pop" Farley arrested William Fisher of Barstow, charging him with selling liquor. When he pleaded guilty as charged, Justice of the Peace Hoffman fined him $250. In 1930 Farley arrested one old Hinkley farmer, who had his place searched for booze several times. Barstow's Ed Harris had to escort the sheriff to search for a still rumored to be in Hinkley. They searched all over, with Harris leading the officers on a wild goose chase. The dry squad finally used one of its old tricks: It followed a truckload of sugar across Highway 66, over Hinkley Road to the Sandoz Ranch in Hinkley. Since the agents had formed a posse and had a warrant, Harris could not divert the dry squad anymore. They knocked over the still, a large 1,000-gallon still with several 1,000-gallon redwood mash-fermenting tanks. An underground excavation enabled trucks to drive in one end of the barn and out the other side. Loading ramps at the truck-bed level expedited unloading grain, sugar, cans and yeast and loading five-gallon cans of fresh moonshine ready for the all-night trip to Los Angeles. Pumps discharged spent mash into the ranch reservoir, causing drunk ducks and tipsy wild birds and desert critters—easy for duck hunters to shoot. It took all afternoon to dismantle the still and carry truckloads of copper stills and coils away. The sheriff hired young Ray Conaway to work through the day.

A Los Angeles lawyer paid the bail for workers caught at the still, one of the biggest hauls by the Southern California Dry Squad. Sandoz had leased the ranch to moonshiners. The Sandoz family was embarrassed, saying they rented to a couple of men who planned to make a dairy. The L. A. men dug the big excavation which can still be seen today and built a huge barn around the hole. They let all the fruit trees die out and trashed the house. There were, of course, no cows for the dairy.[1]

Desert rats devised clever ways of disguising their surreptitious activities. The Oro Grande Market on Route 66, east of Victorville, had its saloon in the back of the store when it was a blind pig. But for further protection the owner had a trap door in the dirt behind the market to hide his extra alcohol; trapdoors, common in those days, hid another Oro Grande businessman's stash, but his trapdoor was under the chicken coop. A little dirt, hay and a day or so of chicken droppings disguised his extra business.

Maggie Langley moved into her newly-purchased home in Oro Grande in the 1960s, just a couple doors south of Constable Penny Morrow's house and found a hole in the ceiling of the pantry that led up to the attic. Here she found evidence of a former bootlegger's paraphernalia.[2]

In Hodge, a rancher had a false floor in his barn. In Lucerne Valley, a rancher had his stash buried in the driveway, covered over with a few tire tracks. When the bootlegger had a fight with his wife, she informed on him. Prohis came, showed the warrant and asked to borrow a pitchfork from the farmer. They then pitchforked everything, the hay stacks, the bales, the grain, the ground all over the driveway. They gave up, returned the farmer's pitchfork and left. They had parked right over the part of the driveway that hid the booty. History did not leave enough information to ascertain if the couple divorced or reconciled after this incident.

Camouflaged tunnels lined the Mojave River bed, reported in Hodge, Helendale, Minneola Road east of Yermo and near historic Camp Cady. Workers at the present community of Silver Lakes by Helendale reported finding a tunnel one-quarter mile long during one of its excavations for a new school built in the 1970s. This tunnel may have been from a reported distillery in the area.

In Hinkley and Harper Lake, sand dunes easily hid stashes of alcohol and also kept the moonshine cool while the nearby hills hid the stills. An uncle of Thelma Depue Gwin reprimanded his niece because she took the cute little flags off the sand dunes that marked the location of her uncle's hidden reserve in Harper Lake. The uncle evidently did not appreciate the game of hide and seek he had to play. Gwin remembered telling a classmate about life on the homestead with "Pop" Moore and other bootleggers. One day she came from school so excited. Her girlfriend asked if she could spend a night at her house. Mrs. Depue said that would be okay. "Oh, I am going to have a girlfriend over," thought eight-year-old Thelma. She couldn't wait. After playing, then eating supper, the friend said, "Let's go outside and watch the lights at night." They went out and played. After dark they could see headlights on the dry lake bed, then blinking off and on, then lights answered from the hills near Black Canyon. Then as if on cue a plane landed on the lake bed. A few minutes later, the plane took off, the car lights disappeared and the night show was over. The girls went back into the house and slept, ending an exciting day.

The next week, the Feds raided the area. A bachelor uncle took the blame, allowing the married culprits to continue supporting their families.

Thelma's little friend retold the stories, probably to her father, who sent her to spend the night and she, perhaps unknowingly, became an informant. Thelma never forgot the pain and the betrayal.[3]

Where the riverbed of the Mojave River widened, sometimes to a mile wide, moonshiners hid their stills in thickets of willow, mesquite, cottonwood and catalpa trees. At the present golf course resort of Silver Lakes the stills were in the open among the thickets. One could walk within a few yards of a small still and not know it was there; only the smell and occasional smoke would give it away. An informer said as a young kid he would follow the main path across the riverbed, knowing it was not wise to go off on side trails. At Silver River Ranch in Helendale, a moonshiner kept his still under the manger. A fierce bull protected the manger. This "watch bull" never allowed anyone but the owner and his worker to enter. "We went to raid it," said Constable Morrow, "but the bull wouldn't let us in there."

The western part of the Mojave Desert sloping upward to the dry side of the San Bernardino Mountains had at least a dozen stills. One clever moonshiner had a large still in a horizontal "L"-shaped mine tunnel, one of countless abandoned mines in this part of the desert. Wooden doors at the entrance could barely be seen by the few travelers who took this steep back road to Holcomb Valley. Thirty feet inside the shaft, at the elbow of the "L", the moonshiners put another heavy door. To protect themselves more, they had a trap door escape hatch with a ladder straight up through the air vent to the top of the granite hill. The distillers diverted the mining pipe from an old mine shack to the escape hatch down into the still.

Inside, the right angle of the "L" contained a bin for barrels on their sides used for fermenting mash; on the left side of the six-foot-wide tunnel, shelves contained buckets, Fleishman's Yeast, coffee and food. At the end of the "L" was the storage for the liquor or for extra barrels. The still itself was in the center with a white-gas burner under a homemade metal stove. Ventilation came from the escape hatch and from the small part of the "L" that went to the first door. The date on the box of dynamite indicated the mine was used in 1926 or that in 1926 the moonshiners widened and improved the shaft for its new role in the world. In 1980 when the mine was rediscovered, every can, barrel and bucket had one to three axe holes, evidence of a federal raid. The copper still was missing, probably taken to San Bernardino for evidence along with the alcohol. But in 1980 everything had remained as it had been when it was raided. Since the MJB coffee cans had dates of 1932, the raid probably occurred somewhere between 1932 and the end of 1933. Whether the moonshiners escaped out of the trapdoor or were captured is not known.

The Monahan brothers were rumored to be suspected moonshiners at Arrastre Springs in Hesperia where the 1860s Van Duesen Road wound up the north slope of the San Bernardino Mountains. Further up Arrastre Creek, someone had a big operation. Desert historian Ellsworth Sylvester pointed out the site that old-timers involved in it had shown him. Moonshiners dammed up the slow-moving creek to have water year round. Several tons of grain were heaped in huge piles on top of large canvases on level ground in the mountain foothills. Even after 50 years, pieces of canvas could be found on the flat ground.

A deep-rooted mesquite tree shaded the distillers on their off-hours. A cabin, the fermentation tank and the still have long since been removed. Supposedly an armed 24-hour sentry guarded the only entrance to the fortress-like canyon, just above the Monahan place.

Deep Creek had several stills, one at Hanna Flats and one at Squint's Ranch [see Deasy, Chapter 16].

Most desert bootleggers made a little and sold it. They were small operations. One old man sold to the thirsty travelers on Highway 66 at Newberry Springs, ironically called Water at the time. Another man, a cobbler in Yermo, repaired shoes, but made trips to his still on Coyote Dry Lake and sold to special customers.

Redman, a farmer and bootlegger, sold to people at the Saturday night dances held at the Hinkley School and paid off his ranch with his profits. At some Saturday night dances in California there were so many bootleggers they had to wear badges to keep from selling to each other, according to an old timer.

Others bought liquor from someone, then retailed it. Victorville had a blind pig at the corner of 7th and D Streets where a bootlegger sold moon. At times one could obtain liquor at the hotel on D Street, according to informant Lackyard who grew up in the area. He felt prohibition worked because he bought only four or five bottles all during those years. Most of his friends did not drink either.

The following is an excerpt from former state senator Edwin E. Grant's 1925 letter to the Grand Jury of San Bernardino County. Grant was President of the State Enforcement League.[4]

Victorville

"Then our party of investigators went out in the desert and investigated the town of Victorville. This town we found to be wide open with no visible effort to enforce the law. Booze, redlight houses, nickle [sic]-in-the-slot machines, everything goes in Victorville. In Victorville, there seems to be a well defined scheme to restore redlight houses on the old segregated district plan, now outlawed in every state of the Union except Nevada. In fact Nevada redlight women are harbored in Victorville. Booze is sold without any question and there seems to be not a semblance of interference with this wholesale system of crime. We even found out who tips off the raids in Victorville; a hanger-out at the booze and redlight dives in San Bernardino." Said Grant: "There is no law in Victorville."

Another old-timer from Barstow told a story of a deputy sheriff named Brown. He raided many desert places in and around Barstow. His nephew sold booze in Red Mountain. Brown hijacked others' loads of booze or sugar. He even sold back the sugar to the moonshiners. One day his nephew's place blew up in Red Mountain. No building was damaged on either side as the explosion went inward—a professional mining job, no accident.

Newspaper articles of the time illustrate the life of the prohibition violators and some of the people involved in curtailing them. Officer Stanley Snedegar brought Rose Winkley before Judge Lubin Henderson for possessing a still near her property in the Needles district. Henderson dismissed the charge because of "lack of evidence." However, R. H. Morton, L. H. Sowell and L. C. Thomason were charged for possession in the same district. When Thomason admitted his guilt, the Superior Court fined him $500. Morton and Sowell received dismissals. C. H. Smith of Needles came up for possession. When the judge asked him if he were guilty and to make a statement, Smith said, "Whatever the officer says is alright." He wouldn't deny or confess. When the judge fined him $500, he had no money and went to the county jail. Near dawn on a September 1929 morning, Deputy Sheriff J. E. Farley caught Bob Brewer and Oscar Tampian with wet goods on them at Harper Lake. They were taken before Judge J. D. Huey at Oro Grande. After both pleaded guilty to possession, Huey fined them $200 each, which they promptly paid. Farley confiscated 18 gallons at their place. How ironic that Harper Lake always had several moonshiners, yet it was probably the driest voting precinct in the county.[5]

The *Victor Valley News-Herald* of 1926 reported two more of Farley's arrests. "Seven disturbers in Little Chihuahua," on a Sunday in May, were caught drinking some "very low grade concoctions of liquor." They were fined $25 each, and on the promise of better behavior in the future, the judge suspended the jail time. Farley destroyed their supply. In the eastern part of the county in November of that year, Farley and others arrested three bootleggers at Milligan. Judge Dix Van Dyke of Daggett fined John McIntire $500 which was paid and fined S. L. Carr $300. Van Dyke fined G. B. Morrison, known for his "operation" around Victorville, $500 each for two counts. He went to jail for 1000 days, "unless somebody comes to his rescue with money to pay the fine," said the *Victorville News-Herald.*

The constable had the authority in his own district. As soon as he left his district, he became a deputy sheriff. For example, in October 13, 1932, in the raid on the Fisher ranch (now the Mitchell ranch) on Minneola Road, six miles east of Yermo, the federal officials from L. A. and San Bernardino County Sheriff's Departments and Yermo Constable Tom Williams had jurisdiction. Jim Lucas of Daggett, Charley Poe of Barstow and Stanley Snedegar assisted as deputies. They arrested John Fisher and two workers, Peter Enriques and Frank Galli. Fisher's wife (Davis?) and child were both in Los Angeles at the time. Fisher and his workers denied knowing anything about the new operation. The deputies destroyed the equipment not needed for evidence. The only liquor found was in the process of being made. The elaborate still was secreted in two hundred feet of tunnels and rooms, hollowed out of the hard-packed ancient sand dunes, the entrance hidden by desert brush, only 100 feet from the ranch house. The hapless venture, machinery and excavation cost at least $10,000. Just as Fisher was ready to distill the first batch, the dry squad raided him.

Another time when federal officials planned a raid on a known still on what they thought was eastern San Bernardino County in 1929, they enlisted the help of county deputy sheriffs Ira B. Castro and J. E. Farley. When they arrived at the still site, Castor and Farley could not participate since the still was in Clark County, Nevada.

According to J. A. Larson, San Bernardino County dry chief, this 300-gallon still supplied much of the liquor for the county. The Feds arrested Tom Foster, alleged owner, as he was driving away from the still. They confiscated his car with 45 gallons of moonshine, taking Foster and his car to Las Vegas.

"I'd Have to Arrest Half the Town"
as told by Penny Morrow, Constable
Oro Grande, 1920-1940

My last prohibition arrest occurred the day liquor became legal in December 1933. A Los Angeles man had a minor hit and run accident in Victorville. When he came through Oro Grande, I gave chase. I caught him going up the grade east of Helendale. I arrested him for hit-and-run and when I saw he had a gallon of booze in the back seat, I charged him with possession.

"That's not fair. You can't do that. Tomorrow likker will be legal," he protested.

"I've got 12 more hours," I said as I put the booze into my patrol car.

Some of the desert towns had ten times more bars than grocery stores. One bar sold a lot of strawberry soda but one could buy a shot of moonshine whiskey for 25¢.

Most desert towns had prostitutes and most helped their incomes by selling liquor. Victorville expelled one lady of the evening and put her on the train heading east. I was told she might try to get off the train in Oro Grande so I met the train and sure enough, she tried to get off, but I wouldn't let her. She was so bad you could smell her over the telephone. I made sure she headed east. I assume some desert train stop had a new desert resident, a new business woman.

To hunt bootleggers in the Mojave Riverbed area, the raiding parties often rode horses. I carried a .38 rifle. I'd get a call from the sheriff in San Bernardino that we were going to make a raid or search an area. The word would get out. It was up to the bootlegger or moonshiner to hide his wares.

I had authority in Oro Grande but as soon as I left this township I became a deputy sheriff. So a sheriff from the county and several of us constables were on most raids in the desert.

My next door neighbor made liquor and hid his still and liquor in his back yard under a trapdoor concealed by a bale of hay. Rumors went out that the sheriff would be making a raid the next day. Evidently the sheriff suspected my neighbor of being a moonshiner. The neighbor piled more bales of hay on top of the trapdoor.

After the sheriff searched the house and store and didn't find anything, he went directly to the bales of hay and started moving all the bales. Another deputy and I helped him. He kicked around the ground looking for signs of wood or for hollow sounds. Finally the sheriff sat down on the last bale and said, "I thought sure there was some hooch hidden back here."

It was there, hidden under the bale on which he was sitting!

There were no payoffs as far as I know. One man throwed a twenty at me and I throwed it back. The judge gave him seven days for attempted bribery.

There was, however, a deputy sheriff who made $85 a month. After seven years of his working with prohibition, he paid $1,700 cash for a rooming house and $13,000 worth of furnishing. He has a bank account of $45,000. Supposedly he double crossed a bootlegger named Angelo Fontana. When Fontana was up for sentencing he lived at the deputy's house.

Although most law enforcers were honest, every time confiscated liquor changed hands leaving the desert and heading down to San Bernardino Courthouse there would be less of it and less of it, and it changed hands perhaps five times before the little that was left was used for evidence in the court.

Obtaining a conviction was difficult. I remember on one jury there were three bootleggers. The case? Trying a rancher for bootlegging. He was not convicted. In another case the lawyer dismissed everyone who did not drink.

Much of the time, rather than go through the trouble of arrests and trials, I'd just put them on the train. They seldom came back to Oro Grande.

I didn't bother with local citizens who made a little, drank a little or sold some; otherwise I'd have to arrest half the town.

Bootlegging In Antelope Valley
by Carl Bergman, Lancaster

Remembrances of the good days when I first came to Antelope Valley. At the time I was operating the Union Oil Station Number 773 at the corner of Antelope Highway and the old 10th Street, we had a customer come in for fuel. In talking to him, he would complain that the stock market was off and that the cow and calf did not sell as he had hoped. It seemed odd, that same cow and calf made that same trip to Los Angeles at least two times a week. Dan Murphy was a good customer so who cares?

Some time after we became better acquainted, he had us put the old one-and-half-ton truck on the grease rack for service, I couldn't help but notice that there was a planked section between the truck frame or rails—a secret compartment. This was used to haul 100-pound sacks of sugar on the trip coming north. On the trip going south, that same compartment was used to haul five-gallon tin cans, loaded with liquor. The cans were lying flat in order to fit.

This old Chevrolet truck would smell quite cow (barny) from all those trips. Perhaps the cow litter etch did not do much damage to the sugar and it surely could not penetrate the tin cans so the hooch must have made it to the speakeasies in Hollywood O.K. It was reported that some of the liquor made it to Chicago. Who knows?

Dan Murphy had quite an operation going. Glen Settle remembers that Dan would buy sugar by the truckload. Also when coming back from L. A. he would bring a few sacks of sugar on that little old truck with the same old cow and calf going both ways. Once when prohibition officers raided the liquor establishment there at the Rosamond Dry Lake underground operation, they smashed his copper still as well as destroying the supplies on hand. Dan was clever enough not to be anywheres near the property at the time of those raids and no one can remember of him doing time for bootlegging.

Pat Pedias used to tell of a time that he went through the underground bootleg factory in Rosamond Dry Lake right after there had been a raid. He said it was a very large operation, that there was a storage room for the barley, sugar and hops, etc. The copper still and five-gallon cans were all smashed and ruined, all unusable.

After prohibition Dan Murphy became a gold miner hanging around Las Vegas. He had several large gold nuggets to show to prospects. How his mining operation turned out is anybody's guess as we here in Antelope Valley lost track of him at that time.

When Alta and I first moved to the Antelope Valley there was a shortage of rental homes, not like it is today 69 years later. So we were desperate to find living quarters. Mr. Howard Bland owned and operated the Palmdale Inn just across the street from the newly erected Union Station that I managed. Mr. Bland and his wife put us up in their hotel for a few weeks. This was a bit expensive for us; we were getting $80 per month. Alta talked Mrs. Bland into fixing up a glass-fronted storeroom as our living quarters which was just across the street from the station. We scrounged furniture from the hotel in order to get by. I recall using orange boxes as cupboards, a kerosene stove, no sink or water in the building. We used the hotel bathroom or the one at the station just across the Antelope Valley Highway, now known as the Sierra Highway.

Living so close to the old Palmdale Inn we knew about some of the parties that went on. We were not in with the locals but we could hear and see some of the good times they had.

There was a Richfield service station kitty-cornered across the street from my station. It was alleged that this station was the drop-off for liquor, Jamaica gin, and perhaps some of Dan Murphy's good stuff. I recall a couple of old fellows who had "Jake Leg," no doubt from the Jamaica gin. I never got to try it, thank gosh.

The Palmdale Inn had two bars, one upstairs and one in the cellar. I was told that there was a tunnel across the street connecting that cellar with the service station. No doubt a good place to hide and store the surplus liquor, as well as to get to the hotel unseen.

I wonder if that old tunnel is gone. If it is still there it surely is full of spider webs. The Richfield station location is now occupied by Palmdale's new Civic Center buildings on Palmdale Boulevard.

Effects of Desert Moonshine
from *The Barstow Printer*

The duties of a policeman or constable in a small town are not as easy as they appear. A simple disturbing of the peace call to Barstow's Ed Harris, 1:30 a.m., Thursday, April 25, 1929, ended in a three rounder with an ex-fighter. On Wednesday evening Jim Sullivan, an ex-pug, and a few other road construction workers, improving the road east of Barstow, drank a little too much moonshine. When Ed went over to the Melrose Hotel on Main Street, half a dozen drunks stopped their noise making which was disturbing the guests at the hotel. All the drunks ran except one, Jim Sullivan. He was placed under arrest. The fighter had other intentions and started practicing on Ed. The first round had to go to the officer as Sullivan was brought to the jail but not before damaging Harris's face.

The start of the second round went to Sullivan as he swung on Ed's nose, then grabbed Ed by the throat. Harris retaliated by gripping Sullivan's wind pipe, and drawing his service revolver he fired into the floor a couple of times.

Sullivan stopped his training immediately and went into his corner at the jail.

The last round went to Harris as a sobered Sullivan was taken to Judge D. Van Dyke in Daggett where he received 180 days.

Ed took his disfigured face to Dr. Graham who set Ed's broken nose and closed the cut over the left eye. His face was a little worse for wear.

Nine months later Ed Harris resigned his job as Santa Fe Special Agent after twenty years. He wanted to devote more time to the Barstow Township and the people who elected him constable.

Late one hot summer night in August, 1931, Ed Harris was awakened by the frantic owner of Smith & Smith Pool Hall. "Hurry, please, Ed, there's a riot here, fighting. They're tearing up the place!"

Ed quickly dressed, headed right for the pool hall to execute his duty, assuming he'd be stopping a fight by himself. When he burst into Smith's, he was stopped by a blow—all his deputy friends and nearby constables cheered him. Constable Jim Lucas of Daggett (and County Deputy Sheriff) gave him a gold badge, to replace the tin badge he had used for 21 years of desert law enforcement service. Instead of a fight, Ed had a celebration in his honor.

Around Victorville
by Arlene Kallenberger, Hesperia

Bob Angel, a former deputy sheriff before being drafted in WW II, chuckled as he recalled an episode involving his father-in-law, Deputy M. M. Black, a "dollar a year" sheriff. It seems in order to avoid apprehension some bootleggers tossed whiskey bottles in a pit. Unfortunately the bottle smashed into smithereens when they hit bottom. What a shame!

Deputy Black came up with an idea. In the darkness, he would position himself at the bottom of the pit (just before a raid) and would grab a bottle before it hit bottom. Victorville must really have been dry!

Veronica (Taylor) Cook, who grew up in Oro Grande and environs, remembers one Guy Wadsworth, who was quite famous for his rock houses. Some of which may be seen off National Old Trails Highway (Old Route 66) between Oro Grande and Helendale. One rock house was built in such a manner that his bootleg whiskey could be concealed among the rocks. They were so cleverly concealed that the local sheriffs, even after numerous attempts, were unable to learn his secret and his bootlegging operation was never discovered. The remains of his house on Old Route 66 has the exposed trapdoor that went from the kitchen down to the secret basement, next to his garage. After Guy Wadsworth's bootlegging days were over, he settled down with his second wife, Mary Kinney. Veronica believes that after his death he was buried in the Victorville cemetery [see Chapter 8].

Mirl Orebaugh of Helendale said the old Helendale Ranch included apple orchards. A storage tunnel was dug, large enough to accommodate even trucks. Eventually it became an ideal location for a bootlegging operation. Part of the tunnel remains, and little do people realize it runs beneath the Helendale Elementary School!

On Old Route 66
as told by Henry Jay, Helendale

We called deputy sheriff Farley "Pops." Even older men called him that because he was liked and respected. He was an honest lawman as far as we knew. But he did not go out of his way to arrest the local desert businessman or rancher.

At the Hodge Station on old Route 66, my father had a gas station in the late 1920s and during the 1930s. It had no running water, no ice—we made trips to Barstow for ice—but we had a filling station, a little store and a shade-covered area for people to rest and picnic. My father made homebrew beer and people would come over and enjoy a glass or so. The moonshiner Guy Wadsworth sold whiskey to my father. My father paid him at the station. Then at night my father went out to the greasewood bushes and found a can or small keg of whiskey. He poured whiskey into skinny half-pint bottles and sold these to special customers.

He always got word a day or so before there was going to be a raid. We did not have a phone, or even electricity for that matter, all during this time. I am not sure how he found out there was going to be a raid but he did.

When Farley came down the hill in his big black touring car, he would put his sirens on, we'd know Farley would be here in a few minutes. To hide some bottles of liquor, my father one time put them in the drain around the roof of the station. Some bottles got so hot the cork popped out and the liquor drained out the rain spout onto the ground.

Farley was there then and said to my father, "You got any alcohol here?"

"Why no," he answered.

"It smells like a distillery around here."

Whole Hotel for $35 a Month

by Dr. Edmund C. Jaeger, excerpt from *Desert Magazine*, August 1954

On a windy winter day in 1925, Dr. Edmund C. Jaeger, the famous desert botanist and naturalist from Stanford, was on one of his jaunts in the desert:

The Hesperia Hotel [38 rooms] was unoccupied, and a man posed as an owner of the place tried to persuade me that it would be a mighty profitable business to use the upper floor for a bootlegging establishment.

"I would tell nobody you was up there," he promised, "and a pretty profit you could make of it."

I had two students with me and these the man took to be my sons. "Why if I had two sons like that I'd sure make a go of it. One could be hauling in grain and taking out the booze while you and the other boy could stay home and tend to the distilling."

"But what if I got in trouble with the law?" I asked.

To that question he had a ready answer. "If you got caught, mister, perhaps you might go to jail for six months, but your time wouldn't be wasted; for you could use all those long days thinking up a way to do your booze-making better next time. Mister, you'd better rent my hotel. There is no place like it for making good money quick."

Needless to say, the offer was turned down.

Around Early Barstow

from *Barstow Printer*, January 29, 1925

Ed Pitcher and Deputy Sheriffs Jack Brown and Amaries raided W. C. Lester's room at the Barstow Hotel. He had a keg at Osdick (Red Mountain), but left before the raid. Judge Henderson gave him a choice of $500 or 500 days. He chose to "visit Walter Shay's (San Bernardino County Sheriff) hotel at the expense of the county for awhile. Of course he might earn his board doing road work."[6]

Steve White pleaded "NG" [not guilty] for violating the Wright Act for having a small jug...let out on $200 bond. Loraine Worth pleaded not guilty and was let out on a $300 bond in1923, before Judge Henderson.

Officers made a raid on a still at Goldstone. Constable Ed Pitcher had a warrant for John Bish but passed him on the way. Bish didn't waste any time disposing of his "stuff" and departed to "parts unknown." At Goldstone mine camp the officers found 14 barrels of mash, 250 gallon still and corks and bottles. Monday the officers went out again, finding two more stills and found Ben Redfield's house burned to the ground Sunday.

We Always Had Our Stories
as told by Ralph Wilkins, Boron

Ralph Wilkins came to the Mojave Desert around 1912, eighteen years old at the time. He drilled most of the wells for Dan Murphy's stills around Muroc, California (now Boron and Edwards Air Force Base), east of Lancaster. "They kept me busy," he recalled in 1980. Wilkins lit his pipe again and went on with his recollections:

Sometimes there were as many as six stills at one time. Sometimes they'd work on the well and dig out the excavations for the underground still at the same time—they were in such a hurry. If one got knocked over, they'd have another ready to start up.

Dan (Murphy) was my grubstake. He paid me well. He'd give me whiskey if I needed it. I didn't drink that much but my mother-in-law did. Cold whiskey and warm water made medicine. I could get some for her—but I'd have to bring my own gallon jug.

We'd always have to have a story made up ahead of time in case a prohi checked on what we're doing. The Feds came up once when I was drilling a well for Dan.

"What are you doing?"

"Drilling a well for this cattle ranch. The cows need water; they're gonna put the corral right thar."

"See any stills around?"

"Liquor stills?"

"Yes."

"No, I haven't. Are there any around here? Do you have any business cards? Give me one and I'll call you if I run across any stills."

They'd give me their cards and I'd give them to Dan Murphy to check out.

"If you have a bottle in the car, don't throw it out if you're being chased. Break it and empty it. They need to have evidence," Dan would tell us workers. "If you can't outrun them, break your goddam jug," he'd say.

If anyone got caught, he'd be paid for every day he was in jail and Dan would pay the fine. Dan did too. He'd take the pay right over to the family.

The sugar trucks were to come in and out of the stills at night. They'd come to a certain point, get picked up and brought in. Once I followed two sugar trucks that came in too early. I thought I'd give them a scare. I started chasing them. They had five tons of sugar but they lit out and out ran me. My car could go 70 too (70 MPH). They had three gears, one just for out running the Feds. If these truck drivers get in the third gear, no one would catch them.

The next morning Dan asked me, "Ralph, see any Feds around?"

"No, why?"

"One chased two of my trucks across the lakes all the way to Antelope School. The trucks lost 'em but one truck got stuck where they hid out."

"Ha, Dan, that was me who chased them. They were comin' in too early so I thought I'd scare 'em."

"You sure as hell did! Good, I'm glad it was you."

"Come on, I'll help pull 'em out," I said.

Most drivers knew me and my truck or my car. But one night I ran straight into a big truck filled with liquor. I didn't know the driver; he didn't know me. I had a new car. He sat in his and I sat in mine. We got out and talked around. He couldn't get past me and he blocked my way also.

"What are you doing out here?" he asked.

"I'm just looking around. What about you? What do you have in the truck?"

"Water." he answered quickly. "Going to take it over to a rancher on the other side of the lake." He had his story all ready.

Large illicit alcohol distillery seized by Federal officers at Muroc, Rogers Dry Lake. Mash vat at left, new five-gallon cans center and still at right. NRA sign, referring to a Roosevelt's depression recovery plan, was a joke, as was the "Tea" sign on part of the still. Photo courtesy Pomona City Library.

I looked at the truckbed—filled with five-gallon cans.

"I think I'll just strike a match and see if it's water or not," I threatened. He got scared. We sparred around for a few minutes, then I identified myself. "Ah, get out of here; I'm just going into the same place you're coming out of. I drilled the well for the still." We shook hands. I backed down on the lake and let him pass.

One night I was heading across the lake by a cattle pen. My truck suddenly fell into the sand, got stuck. My friend and I started to dig out. We kept banging into barrels buried in the sand and couldn't get out. "There's something hidden here. Let's hurry and get the hell out of here," I said. We got some brush, tore down new redwood fence posts to put under the wheels when we jacked up the car. We practically built a road to the solid dirt.

"Hey, Dan," I said the next day, "I ran into one of your stashes yesterday. Got my truck stuck."

"Did you cover it up?"

"Sure did," I answered. "But you're gonna have to get new fence posts for the corral."

"That's okay," was all Dan said.

If that still ran one day, it'd pay all the expenses.

"Those were the good ol' days," Ralph said, chewing on the end of his cold pipe, long since gone out. "Yes, sir, those were good days—most everybody's gone now."

A Little Bullshit
as told by Donna Fairchild, Boron Historian

Only one worker was in Dan Murphy's still in the middle of the night, when a large bull was grazing for blades of desert grass and forage. He wandered up a little sandy knoll where Murphy's crew had put corrugated tin roofing to cover the still and placed sand and a few desert shrubs on the sand to disguise the still from aerial observation.

Well the bull crushed through the roofing, fell right in one of the huge 3000 to 9000 gallon vats full of fermenting moonshine about ready to be run off.

The lone worker did the best he could to save the bull by lassooing his horns and tying the rope to a 4x4 post. Then he did the same again and tied that rope to another 4x4. Thus the bull was saved from drowning. After the initial panic, he probably enjoyed the fumes of the alcohol until he had no feelings.

When workers arrived the next morning to distill the fermentation, they could not figure how to extricate the drunken animal. They called well-digger Ralph Wilkins to bring his heavy equipment over and he pulled out the numb bovine. The mash was covered with feces from the night's stay in the barrel.

Looking at the polluted mash, the foreman asked Murphy, "What do we do with this batch?"

"Run it off; a little bullshit never hurt anyone!"

Big Shots
as told by Phil Raymond, Los Angeles

My father was a short, stocky, kind, gentle Italian who married a Jewish woman and lived in the Jewish neighborhood of Boyle Heights, in L. A., which was between State and Brooklyn and Boyle streets. Most of Boyle Avenue was predominately Italian. My mother-in-law was Jewish. She bootlegged by selling shots of whiskey. People came over to the house after work, sometimes buying her delicious pastry or cookies and bought a shot or so of whiskey. She bought the whiskey and resold it.

When I was in my last year at Roosevelt High School, about 1932-33, Vito Gruppi and I delivered sugar for a bootlegging organization operating in our neighborhood. We picked up approximately five tons sugar from a warehouse in San Pedro with a large Chevrolet truck with two-axle back wheels, we carried the load to Boyle Heights. Vito and I each received $100 a trip to drive out into the Mojave Desert, deliver the sugar to stills and bring back loads of five-gallon cans of alcohol. We also used huge Mack trucks, single axle rear end with double tires, that could carry eight tons. We enjoyed the adventure, thinking we were "big shots" delivering to the stills. We didn't realize the dan-

Dan Murphy operated this underground still in Rogers Dry Lake for two or three syndicates in Los Angeles. Dewey Holden was caught in one raid and served a year in McNeil Island, Washington. Notice the camouflage with bushes tied in the sand that covers the corrugated iron roof. Photo courtesy Pomona City Library.

*Federal agent in moonshiner's lookout Joshua tree at Rogers Dry Lake,
now Edwards Air Force Base. Dan Murphy ran as many as seven stills in
this area. Although the agents captured this and a couple other stills, they
did not catch Dan Murphy. Photo courtesy of Pomona City Library.*

ger. We could have been arrested and were often followed. At the desert town of Mojave, prohibition agents often watched for trucks loaded with sugar or alcohol. I always felt the agents were paid off by the hoods. We then headed out across the desert roads, losing anyone tailing us before we headed out to the still [probably to Dan Murphy's stills at Muroc Dry Lake]. We were all mechanics of sorts and had souped up the trucks to have a lot of power and could out run most vehicles despite our weight. From San Pedro we had fewer problems with the law because we were just delivering sugar to someone in Boyle Heights. That was not against the law. When a still got knocked over, we delivered a new still and equipment to another location in the desert.

We had fun driving, 17-18 year-old big shots. We talked, joked and sometimes sang. We bought an Atwater Kent radio, changing it from ac to dc and let it blast while driving in the desert.

We had rules we had to follow and since we respected the men we worked for we obeyed the rules: drive carefully, obey the laws, don't mess with girls and don't touch the alcohol. We didn't. We were expected to keep the values of the community like respect for our mothers. Our bosses were great people, helping out problems in the neighborhood, such as paying for funerals for the poor and building a baseball field for the kids. Behind these men were gangsters like Benjamin Segal and Mickey Cohen, connected with Meyer Lansky who made arrangements for the sugar to come from Cuba. I never saw these men but knew they were involved. Once there was a meeting of the "gang" involved in one of the basements of the Italian's house—you know they all had basements with concrete floors—and a uniformed policeman was there. The police were bought off and the "government was in their pocket."

I didn't drink much except we always had Dago red wine. My mother sometimes complained that my father put too much wine in our glasses at dinner. "It won't hurt 'em!" my father exclaimed. "Look at me; it didn't hurt me, did it?" My father made 400 gallons a year, and then made enough kosher wine for the family. Even though my father made 200 more gallons than the law allowed, my folks would not have permitted my involvement with running sugar if they had known what the sugar was used for.
Once at a party of Jewish kids, I drank too much wine. I got sick and threw up everything including my balls.

When prohibition ended on December 5, 1933, my father celebrated too much, and he couldn't walk up the stairs. He apologized for being drunk: "I'ma sorry you see me lika this."

I said, "That's okay, we'll just go up and go to bed."

Las Vegas

In Nevada, near Las Vegas, a bootlegger had buildings covered with sand. Prohis raided it, chopped holes in each 5-gallon can and threw them over the cliff. Paiute Indians found the liquor and found enough firewater left in the cans to make the Indians wild.

When prohis raided in Las Vegas and Clark County, Sheriff Sam Gay of Las Vegas cooperated but usually looked the other way, allowing the back doors opened when the Feds locked the front door. Sheriff Sam reportedly tipped off bootleggers and moonshiners when the prohis planned a raid. He controlled the city. Ironically, in one respect, he controlled Clark County— keeping it free from graft! Vegas, therefore, was wet. Springs and ranches, like in Pahrump, supplied moonshine to southern Nevada and southern California, via Arrowhead and National Old Trails Highway, later Route 91 and 66. Nevada dry lakes made fine runways for liquor planes from Mexico to provide those visiting Nevada for quick marriages and divorces with finer Mexican and Canadian liquor.

Early Times in Las Vegas and Searchlight, Nevada
by Robert E. Ames

In covering the Nevada territory before booze became legal, I had a number of experiences with the old-time businessmen who never paid their bills by check, always in cash. They all had a jug or two of good White Mule or bootleg whiskey on hand.

One place in Searchlight ran a small eating house on the east side of the main road which ran between Las Vegas and Needles. This eating house furnished a good meal, and if you were known to them you could also get a good drink of hootch (hooch).

One day I left Needles in a storm for Las Vegas, and it started to snow before I arrived in Searchlight. It was very cold. I pulled into this eating house for a meal and drink. I was wearing a heavy brown overcoat and hat pulled down all around to ward off the snow. As I entered the place I heard a glass jug hit the sink and shatter, and the booze went down the drain. I was the only customer there at that time. When I walked up to the service window the owner said to me, "By God, Ames, I thought you were a prohibition officer because of your heavy coat and hat, I got rid of my whiskey in the sink. Just wait about 15 minutes and I will get another gallon." When he returned he told me the officers had been after him. He served me a good steak from local beef slaughtered at one of the cattle ranches and a good drink of Searchlight whiskey—my cost $1.00.

Desert Whiskey Stills
by Robert E. Ames, San Bernardino

Another time in Las Vegas one evening I was asked to take a ride with one of the "Big Brothers." I got in the car with him. It was a big black sedan which was bullet-proof and very fast. The windshield and all glass on this car was at least ½ inch thick, and the windows cranked up and down very hard.

We headed Northeast, and he told me to put a large bandana over my eyes and face as he did not want me to see where we were going. We traveled for about an hour, and the last mile or two was very rough. When we stopped he told me to take off the blindfold, and we were in darkness except for one small light at the entrance of an old mine tunnel.

We went in the tunnel about 20 yards to a large room about 30 feet square. Three men were running a large whiskey still which was all copper. A number of vats were full, and the odor of mash was very strong. Also there were many sacks of sugar, corn, and other stuff used for making desert bootleg whiskey.

He told me they were producing more than 50 gallons each day. We had a sample and it was the best I had ever tasted. This was the largest still I had ever seen, and in those days there were lots of them—both large and small.

This man was a local Vegas businessman and a straight man to do business with. We were there about one hour, and when we came out and got in the car he had me put on the mask again and I didn't take it off till we got back to Las Vegas. He asked me to say nothing about the trip to the stills. It was an exciting experience.

My Story of Whiskey Pete and Death Valley Jack
by Robert E. Ames, San Bernardino

This story is about Whiskey Pete and Death Valley Jack. They were tough characters in Southern Nevada in prohibition times and during the construction of Boulder Dam. They operated a few whiskey stills and as far as I know were never caught. They made very good bootleg and sold it for $10 per gallon. They could never catch up in their orders.

They finally quit the partnership as they suspected each other of chiseling. They each had a large still, so went into competition with each other. Bad blood soon existed. Whiskey Pete drank very little, but Death Valley Jack seemed to be drunk all the time. Large loads of sugar and corn were unloaded at "Windmill Service Station" on the California side a few miles west of the Nevada line where it was picked up by them and hauled to their stills.

As time went on, Whiskey Pete built a service station just inside the Nevada line and named it State Line Service. He made a deal with a woman from Las Vegas to operate the cafe end of the station, and she did a good business. Water was hauled about 30 miles for domestic and car service so he put a sign "No free water unless you purchase something from the station."

Pete always had a 30-30 rifle just behind the door in the front of the cafe and also a bed next to the glass window so he could see all comers. He was a sick man himself as he had miner's consumption caused from working in the mines and not waiting for the dynamite fumes to clear out before going to work again.

One late afternoon he was alone in the station as the woman was shopping for supplies in Las Vegas. Two Chicago tough hoodlums drove into the station. Pete came out to see what they wanted. They told him they wanted water in their radiator, and he told them to read the sign. Both of them pulled out six shooters and pointed them at him and told him to fill the radiator. Pete filled the radiator and they told him to dump the barrel of water out and made him dance in the water as they shot their guns off near his feet as he danced.

They soon left and headed south for Barstow. Pete got his 30-30 rifle and shot at them several times but did not know if he had hit them or not as he shot at their backs and the back of their car which was going fast and some distance from the station when Pete started shooting. Pete shot to kill.

These men arrived in Barstow several hours later. They went to the doctor as one was shot through the shoulder. The doctor called the local law who arrested them at once. They told the lawmen someone shot them near the Nevada state line but they did not tell the whole story. The sheriff took the one who was not injured to see Pete at the state line the next morning and Pete identified him as one of the two men who made him dance in his own water from the barrel. Pete was not arrested and he was very happy with himself and told everybody about his shooting ability at long range at a moving target. The two hoodlums were sent back to Chicago, as they were wanted criminals.

As stated in starting this story Pete and Death Valley Jack were competitors in the booze business and hated each other. One day Jack got overly drunk with a tough truck driver and they decided to go to Pete's station and give him a beating. Pete saw them coming. When they staggered up to his door Pete opened the door and hit each one in the guts with the barrel of his 30-30 knocking them out cold. Both layed out in front of the door on their backs. Pete pissed in their faces then finally threw water on them to bring them to their senses. He then kicked both of their butts and sent them on their way.

As time went on Pete's lung trouble got worse so he was taken to a Banning T.B. sanitarium. I called on him several times at Banning and the last time I saw him he was very weak and only skin and bones, but he knew me and we talked some and he told me, "It won't be long now, Ames." He died soon after and his body was taken back to the state line for burial.

Pete had made all arrangements for his burial, and it was told to me as follows. First, two of his worst enemies, one being Death Valley Jack and the other I don't know, were to attend an all night party with others and drink at least 5 gallons of Pete's whiskey.

The next day they were to dig a grave on a small rise at the rear of the station where the coyotes howled at night. They started digging and found it a hard rock formation with a soft center about 3 feet wide. They did their best but digging was very difficult and they could not make a hole large enough for the casket to lay flat in the bottom of the grave so they buried him standing up with about three feet of sand and gravel on top. On Pete's instructions they planted a large barrel cactus on top of the mound.

Whiskey Pete's name was Pete McIntire and in his younger life he followed the sea and was a captain of a sea-going vessel. [Whiskey Pete's Casino at State Line, now Primm, Nevada, is named after Pete McIntire. His grave overlooks the casino.]

Some of these stories were told to me and some were actual happenings that I saw happen myself.

Rich the Barber Found Dead
Barstow Printer, April 1, 1926

Clyde E. Richardson is dead, a victim of John BARLEYCORN. "Rich" had many friends and for years a number of these friends have taken care of him during his periodicals. He would close up his business for a month at a time and then when the drinking session was over would return to his barber shop and pool hall and attend strictly to business for months, sometimes running close to a year between drinks. When he was drinking he would go away alone and for weeks would stay in his room while bootleggers or others would supply him with liquor.

Rich was found dead this Thursday morning after officers and friends had searched for him. He had been gone from home nine days and his mother, with whom he lived, had asked the officers to make a search for him.

Chic Warner had joined in the hunt and located Rich in one of the rooms of a cement house owned by Engineer Poole and located opposite the Harvey House.

Deputy Coroner Emmett Waters of San Bernardino was notified and came to Barstow to hold an inquest. Acute alcoholism was given as the cause of death.

Twenty three pint bottles mostly empty were mute evidence that some bootlegger was busy.

Rich had been a resident of Barstow the past twenty years following the barber trade and for many years manager for the Postal Telegraph Company.

The deceased was 41 years eight months and five days being born July 23, 1885 in Illinois. The date of his death was given as March 30th. The body was taken to the local funeral parlors where it was prepared for burial.

Mrs. Richardson, mother of the deceased is 84 years old. [Copied as is] [Rich was one of early advertisers in Barstow   High School yearbook "El Desierto."]

Surviving Needles Weather

Local newspapers are beautiful in the way they bring back the thoughts and events of the times. Business leaders, the right church people and the more affluent have their names in the paper because they hosted a visitor from San Bernardino, went on vacation to Lake Tahoe or had a birthday party. Papers revealed concerns of the times. Will Rogers had a weekly column in dozens of California newspapers between 1930-32. Often, he started each article with "I only know what I read in the papers," then proceeded to discuss what was of interest to him at the time, usually putting humorous twists on it, exposing absurdities of certain human behavior or the silliness of a politician's actions. More and more he reported the weaknesses of prohibition and its humor. For example, when Rogers heard about a "Bootleggers' Convention," he thought that would be a popular convention and a money-maker for some city. Free samples would be popular. Later he said the wets were gaining so much strength that Roosevelt, a wet Democratic candidate, would beat the dry candidate for the democratic nomination. These items appeared in the *Needles Nugget* along with the news of the week. From 1928 on, the *Needles Nugget* talked about building Boulder Dam (now Hoover Dam but always Boulder Dam to Democrats), paving of Route 66, the "Shortest route from coast to coast," and putting a bridge right over the Colorado River from Needles instead of going south to Topoc to cross. These economic concerns reflected thoughts of Needles businessmen. They took interest in the writer Arthur Brisbane's report of his experiments with growing alfalfa on his Hodge ranch west of Barstow. Needles citizens followed Secretary of Interior Ray Lyman Wilbur and Dr. Edward Mead's plans for the dam, the railroad to the dam site, the first tents that started Boulder City and they cheered when the paving was complete on Route 66. The editor of the *Needles Nugget* pointed out absurdities when he saw them. When Lakeport Police Chief N. A. Wilcox started his new campaign against drunken driving, the first arrest he made was L. O. McKelley of Lake County, the County Sheriff of Lake County.

The depression hadn't set in yet in the first part of 1930, so with much hope and promise, local car dealers advertised new Chevrolets for $495 to $625 and introduced Studebaker's "New Erskine." The Needles Theater opened with stars and a week of celebration and the movie talkie "Chasing Rainbows" starting a new era of entertainment in the "Gateway to California" town. "Tomato Cocktails Clicks," an ad read pushing to sell tomato juice because "It clicks."

Evidently not enough people drank it because the State of California declared warfare on drunk driving since 2,000 Californians died in accidents in 1929, mostly involving drunk drivers.

Although much is learned from newspapers, much more was missing from the papers. Minorities and the little guy who worked for a living seldom made the news—unless he was on the wrong side of the law. Then he made the paper. Mark Barnett and his wife on I Street in Needles for example, weren't just drinking tomato cocktails one night at 2:00 a.m. They were arrested for having a drunken party with too many fights.

Joe Collins finally lost one of his many battles in court, this one stemming from a liquor raid in the spring of 1929. A federal court convicted him and sentenced him to serve four months for his North Side liquor sales. Whenever Joe Collins was sent up for a jail sentence, his two children were told his father was away on a business trip. Another time they were told that Collins had gone to Europe.

"Joe Collins paid my grandmother's fine when she was arrested, " said Ehrma Watkins. "My grandmother made it for Joe. He was the distributor. When someone was caught with the liquor, Joe paid the fine." Authorities caught her grandmother, Henrietta Jackson, for having an "aging plant" in the house next door to her. She had some electrical apparatus to place in the white lightning to age it. She delayed her trial for several months and then asked for a jury trial. When the jury found her guilty, Judge Marks fined her $200. "Joe paid it," said Ehrma Watkins. "I remember one time Joe came over with some friends and went to the house next door with my grandmother. A couple of us kids peeked in the window to see what they were doing. They moved the rug back and we saw the whole floor come clear up. It was on hinges. And underneath were all these bottles of liquor."

In another raid in 1931, as the county dry squad attempted to dry up the North Side of Needles, Deputy Sheriff J. E. Farley, aided by Santa Fe police and Needles police, netted much liquor and a "Crowd of Offenders." Caught were George Hart, Charles Galligan, John Lako, Bert McDonald, Lucy McDonald, Effie Kear, C. Hernandez, J. G. Martin, and E. Dillenbeck. Judge Marks released all on bonds. Hart assumed the blame for Galligan and paid $300, Lako pleaded guilty, Bert McDonald paid $200, assuming *mea culpa* for his wife Lucy. But Lucy had a previous charge of resisting arrest in a house the McDonalds operated.

Kear, Martin, Hernandez and Dillenbeck pleaded not guilty. On February the court fined Martin $100 for operating a club, Hernandez pleaded guilty, was fined $250 of which $150 was suspended, Effie Kear was fined and then it was suspended. Judge Marks suspended $100 of Dillenbeck's $250 fine. In another case Marks suspended half of Frank Brodigan's $100 fine.

Ehrma Watkins didn't remember the time when her mother, Effie Kear, was busted. Sometimes Ehrma lived out of town and she was also busy with school and her friends. "Maybe some of this was kept from us kids. Times were tough and my mother and grandmother survived any way they could."

She did remember one time when she was a little younger: "My mother had this beautiful glass liquor decanter and set of small glasses which she used to serve drinks. After one raid I remember going to the court for the trial. I did not know it but my mother just finished denying knowing anything about the decanter or the glasses. She hadn't seen them before, didn't know who owned them, she swore.

"I came in and saw them and yelled, 'Mother, they got your glasses!' "

The *Needles Nugget* reported in April 1931 that 70 cases of home-brew beer had been seized. Norman Lako and Joe McIntyre pleaded guilty for possession and transportation. They each paid half their $100 fine and Marks gave them 30 days to pay the other half. The same paper said two prisoners at the city hall, under the direction of Chief Brown, emptied 1,680 bottles of liquor into the sewer.

A local historian, Maggie McShan, in 1994 said the chief of Needles police "always saved half the liquor he confiscated, buried it for a few months, then shared it with the judge."

Watkins remembered Hasty Jones, called the "Mint Julep King," and his wife "Lady Jones." He had a place on West Broadway, with a shady, cool yard with tables and booths. He served mint juleps and all the dignitaries in town came and relaxed there. One can imagine the pleasure in Jones's yard on a hot summer day and warm Needles evenings. Everybody knew Hasty Jones and his Ford delivery truck and his famous mint juleps.

Another bootlegger Watkins remembered was Joe Fisher. Fisher had a big dark gray heavy coat, never took it off, even in the heat of summer. Inside the coat were dozens of pockets in the liner. Each pocket had pints or half pints of liquor that Fisher sold.

A few people remember some of those wild bootlegging years in Needles. Needles was such a small town with so many people related to each other. Rumor was that Constable Frank Bland often looked the other way, had selective eyesight and even let the word out on impending raids. Most people did not mind the bars and the bootleggers or the small but busy red light district in North Town. These desert lovers knew where they could obtain relief from the hot, sultry summers or the cold winters. A cold beer or a shot of moonshine helped these desert dwellers endure the weather.[7]

Turtle Juice
Reminiscences by E. Q. Sullivan, Former District Engineer

In the early period of District VIII, there were numerous moonshine stills throughout the desert. The product was usually referred to as "turtle juice." Turtle juice was said to be made of cactus [probably just desert moonshine]. It would be distilled in a hidden canyon, a little distance from the moonshiner's cabin.

The moonshiner's shack would be near a spring or well and it was always alongside of a desert trail that passed for a road. The moonshiner's dwelling would consist of perhaps a lean-to but sometimes only a tent.

Soon after the formation of District VIII, headquarters office sent me an engineer (from out of state) to go over my district with me. I was trained as a child and as a young man, in the moral theory that strong drink was sinful, so I was well-fortified ...I was "on the wagon." However, this out-of-state engineer had no such scruples. He sampled the goods of several moonshiners we passed. He enjoyed the turtle juice and partook generously. At the end of the trip he was barely able to stand and put himself to bed. He called the next morning about 10:00, called for some help. He said he had gone blind. I got this man dressed and into the hospital; blindness was a common complaint in those days. After a few weeks of intense medical attention, his sight came back (that is, fairly well).

In the early days there were some "Road Associations." The Road Associations were promoting different routes with the idea of benefiting their communities. At frequent intervals these groups would want to make a trip over some desert trail to promote a particular route which they felt would benefit their communities. Usually the younger, more vigorous and adventurous of the group would go on the more dangerous trips, but there were sometimes a few mature men who went.

The Automobile Club would cooperate with these groups and helped on these trips. I would always go. Before the group got to the moonshiner's shack, I made it a point to tell about the incident of the young engineer who was temporarily blinded by turtle juice. This would warn more mature men, but the story only served to whet the thirst and add spice and excitement to the desire of the more adventurous young men in longing to try out the turtle juice.

I recall on one memorable occasion that one of the leaders of the group said that if you really wanted to enjoy turtle juice you should not drink it from a glass, because, if you did, you might look through the glass and see the blue "fusel oil" floating around in the turtle juice. On the other hand, he said you should not drink it out of a tin cup because if you did this and it tasted tinny, it was hard to tell whether the tinny taste was from the moonshiner's still or the tin cup. In view of this, he said he always carried along a supply of paper cups for the group to drink from. On this particular memorable occasion nearly all of the more rugged members of the party, but not me, joyously accepted a sample of the turtle juice. It was served in paper cups.

The group undertook to wait until everyone was served, before drinking to the success of the expedition. Suddenly, one of those first served noticed that his paper cup was leaking. He called for a new cup, but then everyone else also noticed their respective cups were leaking too.

The turtle juice had eaten holes right through the paper cups. This was the end of the joyous sampling of this particular turtle juice.

Owens Valley

It was isolated, it had water, even after Los Angeles took most of it, and it had little population—it was Owens Valley, a valley that had widespread bootlegging and a divided population. All mines needed supplies, especially the liquid necessities of life. And when miners, freighters and ranchers came to town, they were covered with fine dust from the mines, powdery alkali dust from the trails and blowing dust off Owens Lake, and no little bit of this dust had to be washed out of their throats. Usually around each mining camp, some moonshiner, like Sam Ball of Skidoo, provided those thirsty miners with a drop or so of moonshine made at an isolated desert spring. In the small towns from Bridgeport down to Lone Pine, the WCTU was strong and the voters made most of Mono and Inyo counties dry several years before prohibition. Liquor was, of course, still available and drunk. According to the editor of *Inyo Independent* from Independence, rival Bishop had "over 12" bootleg establishments, serving countless clients. The editor satirically poked fun of Editor Parcher of Bishop's *Owens Valley Herald* who said he knew *one place* in west Bishop selling liquor to 25 booze-loving customers on a Wednesday evening. *The Independent* editor said the sheriff and the Bishop constable needed jurors to do their duty and find bootleggers guilty. A few months before, Bishop spent $2000 obtaining evidence and trying cases, with the result of no convictions and Bishop being open to bootlegging as was no other part of the county. At that time *Herald's* Editor Parcher was also Recorder Parcher of the justice court who let some of these men go without bail. When the cases came to trial, defendants often skipped the county. Judging from the evidence of the latest prosecution, the conclusion was that a majority of the "so-called respectable people want bootleggers—or why do they nearly always fail to convict?" The dry editor from Independence ridiculed the hypocrisy of the wet-leaning editor from Bishop. The county wanted Bishop cleaned up "so the conditions there would not be a disgrace, which they are now."[8]

An Owens Valley couple started celebrating the holidays early on December 14, 1917, even under dry local-option laws. William Gallagher and Jessie Russell had too much to drink and were openly happy with bootleg cheer. After a sheriff let them continue celebrating in the county jail, Gallagher was given 60 days, Russell 90 days, suspended as long as she stayed away from liquor.

The editor of the *Independent* seemed to be for prohibition, quoting *Woman's Home Companion* how dry laws were "sweeping the country" and how even the navy wouldn't take drinkers. But the editor warned that an opinion held by thousands was that stopping a man from buying liquor curtailed his "liberties and interfered with his freedom."

"We must not delude ourselves that if we have national prohibition," said the editor, "all drinking will stop." The law must have the people behind it to enforce it.

How perceptive of the editor.

Showing his partiality for the dry cause, the editor said in April 1918 that since it looked as if Nevada would vote for the dry amendment, even in wet-leaning Reno, "it behooves the electors to get men into office who will enforce the 'bone dry' provisions of the law, and it would be a travesty on the law to elect men who are wet leaning and who would wink at the violations."[9]

By that time the editor had already seen evidence of widespread county bootlegging with just a few people caught and punished. One habitual criminal, Bill Worley, entered Inyo County about seven years previously. A good carpenter who paid his debts as promised, Worley moved to the Bishop area and changed. He raised hogs and had a herd of horses and entered into every nefarious activity he could: bootlegging, running a suspicious house with lots of drunkards and prostitutes, assaulting a Mexican, putting him in a hospital for three months and assaulting another person with a gun. Once Justice Eugley of Big Pine fined him only $90 for bootlegging. When his house was raided by Sheriff Logan, two prostitutes pleaded guilty, yet he was freed after demanding a jury trial. His defiance of the law and his experience of seemingly being immune to the law gave him a contempt for officers, the court and his neighbors. Finally in February 1918, he was charged with assault with a deadly weapon in Darwin. He pleaded guilty. This time the court gave him a minimum of one year in San Quentin. When his neighbors in Bishop recommended he not receive probation, probation was denied. His probation officer could find no redeeming qualities except that he was a good carpenter and paid his debts. The court made sure he went to San Quentin to pay his debt for all the grief he had given Inyo County.[10]

Sheriff Logan went to Lone Pine and picked up Samuel Fletcher, sometimes known as "the Kaiser." This well-known "character" was known to be a bootlegger and his occupation was supposed to be a "peddler of beer." He pleaded guilty. The same day Deputy Sheriff McAfee trekked to Keeler and brought back accused bootlegger L. W. McCarty.

The first woman's jury (eight women, four men) saw its duty in Inyo County and found J. C. Cuddebach guilty in the justice court in Independence of selling liquor in Darwin. Another jury, a few days before, was hung with nine-three jurors in favor of guilty. DF. McDewitt, president of the Miners' Union, testified he had taken drinks in Cuddebach's place. He remembered with whom he drank, but he did not know whether the beverage he drank was ginger ale, grape juice or whiskey. "The climate, or something else, is responsible for a man's taster getting in such a condition," said the editor. Other witnesses had the same problem of not remembering what they drank. Perhaps these men had too much sun or had gotten too close to too many blasts with short fuses.

Immediately after his conviction by a jury with women on it, Cuddebach pleaded guilty to another charge of keeping a place where alcoholic beverages were sold. The judge gave him a fine of $500 or six months in jail, the second charge being suspended on condition he "lead the straight and narrow path" in Inyo County.[11]

Like many isolated places, Inyo County did not go along with the push for prohibition. Though the Wright Act passed in the state by a majority of 24,517 out of over 1,770,000 votes cast, Inyo County voted against the measure 551 to 531 for, and voted down a county dry ordinance 934 for, 983 against. Perhaps the valley already had too much experience with War Time Prohibition.[12]

Cartago had its bootleggers especially on paydays of the Soda Works. Their stashes were hard to locate, as these boots moved around from thicket to thicket and sand dune to sand dune. The resulting drunkenness often led to violence. One night in January 1917, Francisco Martinez called Flumentino Falcon out of his tent and cut him up with a knife. The next morning Falcon sought out Martinez and beat his head so bad, Martinez was in too serious a condition to be moved. Under Sheriff McAfee arrested both, however.[13]

Finally Caught Casey Jones

Deputy Sheriff Hazard and Sheriff Collins caught a much-sought-after bootlegger who had been operating in the southern part of Owens Valley and in Kern County. They caught Casey Lloyd Davidson Jones a few miles south of Lone Pine with 20 gallons in his car. Justice Probasco of Lone Pine found him guilty of possession and transportation, sentencing him $500 or 1000 days. He sold his Buick to pay part of the fine, but served some jail time. "We were after him for a long time," said the sheriff [see Chapter 8].[14]

Sometimes compassion permeated the system. When Collins and Hazard caught 69-year-old Dan M. Driscoll on a Saturday night in May 1923, about one mile south of Olancha with a still and a gallon of whiskey, the judge gave him a continuance of two years on the condition he doesn't drink or violate any law and he go to the county farm at Big Pine. A similar suspended sentence went to GeorgeE. Hoagland of Tecopa after he was fined $500 for driving drunk.[15]

For minorities, courts in Inyo and most counties were not as generous as they were with whites. A Japanese named Y. Suzuki and a Mexican Leonardo Rico were caught by Sheriff Collins and Deputy S. King for having a barrel of mash, four quarts of booze, and a still near Aberdeen. When Justice King gave

Suzuki $300 or 300 days, a friend paid the fine. Rico wasn't as lucky, for when he could not pay $180, he had to choose the 180 days.

Topics in the papers, at barbershops, Saturday night dances and at picnics were about the town's baseball team, ranching, water, Los Angeles Department of Water and Power, closing and moving out of Skidoo or some other mining town; they talked sadly about the tragedy in July 1922 of the Keough family whose boy Jack died in an accident at Keough Hot Springs. He was such a delightful boy and Keough was one family who resisted Los Angeles Department of Water and Power. They talked about social events like the Go Getters Club dance in the Valley on Saturday nights. One popular location for dances was at Manzanar, where in November 1922 12,500 boxes of apples were shipped and where the folks built a new church near the grammar school.

The Owl, Silver Dollar and Monkey House
by George Pipkin, Trona

The Owl is not a bird. The Silver Dollar was not money and the Monkey House was not a zoo; [In Red Mountain] they were houses of pleasure for many and houses of tragedy for some. They proffered the nearest social services for the many single men employed in Searles Valley and a few married ones too, as well as the miners who worked the Rand Mining District.

The casinos flourished illegally during the days of prohibition when the country was supposed to be dry. In its heyday the town had many names. Take your pick: Hampton, Osdick, Inn City, Sin City, Gin Town and finally Red Mountain, coming from a landmark, the big red mountain against which it nestles.

The Monkey House has been gone for many years. It was destroyed late one night after everyone had gone home by a dynamite blast set off by a disgruntled miner who claimed he'd been gypped in the place by a blackjack dealer, given knockout drops by the bartender and rolled by one of the girls.

The Silver Dollar which was owned and operated for many years by Jimmie Holcomb burned. When rebuilt, the place was changed to The Palace.

Only the old Owl remains intact as it was originally built and enlarged back in the early 20s by C. H. "Slim" Riffle. My friend, Slim, made a fortune out of the Owl; part of which was used to finance a Dodge-Plymouth dealership which was located in a big building across the highway from the Owl. The business was not insured and when it burned, Slim lost $175,000. Why wasn't it insured? Because of the scarcity of water. What little there was sold for 3/4 cent a gallon and there was hardly enough to drink, let alone waste on fires.

The writer must tell you his introduction to Red Mountain. At the age of 22, he was a member of the Cartago baseball team which had played and beat the Trona Tigers, 19-18 (sounds like a football score) on Sunday afternoon, September 8,1925. Seven of us players were riding in John Marshall's new Dodge touring car. We had heard so much about "wild Red Mountain" that we were curious. So, as it wasn't much out of our way, we swung around that way. Arriving just after sundown, the thing which impressed us most was a giant Santa Fe steam locomotive parked in the middle of town. Across the railroad track to the left there was a blue building with a high false front labeled the Monkey House. So that was where we went, to see the monkeys. Apparently we were ahead of the happy hour as the place was deserted except for the help: a bartender, a blackjack dealer, a piano player, and a couple of girls. Being strangers we were greeted with cold stares. Bellying up to the bar, the bartender gave us the old fish eye as he asked: "What will you boys have?" "Beer," we cried in unison. He went down under the bar, so that we couldn't see what he was pouring and came up with seven, eight ounces of beer. Till this day, I still swear that it was near-beer, "Bevo," a brand that was popular at the time. When asked how much we owed, he said $3.50. Wow! That was a lot of money for young working men in those days. The 50¢ for a 5¢ glass of beer was too rich for our pocketbooks. Paying the bill, and downing the beer we silently filed out of the Monkey House, climbed into the Dodge and headed north on 395 for home.

After the writer moved to Trona in 1928, he got better acquainted with Red Mountain, as he had a car for hire and drove some young blades over occasionally. Some of the tales about Red Mountain are printable, some are not.

Bill "Baldy" Baker was a Trona pipe fitter. He had a crush on June, a girl at the Owl. One night while drinking at the bar, they got into a beef and she whacked him on the head with an empty beer bottle. Staggering around until his eyes focused, he said, "Hit me again, honey." She obliged with a full bottle, splitting his bald scalp wide open.

A unique saloon was the Dugout. It was located in a cellar between Red Mountain and Johannesburg astride the county line. Half was in San Bernardino County and half in Kern County. Whenever the owner received a tip that a raid was coming from one county, he would move the liquor stock across the room into the other county. This worked real well until someone got their wires crossed and both counties raided simultaneously.

In the Argus fire station, there's a valuable antique, an old Stutz fire truck, vintage about the year 1926. The Stutz was Trona's first fire truck and W. E. Tripp the first fire chief. The truck was purchased from the city of Colton and while being driven to Trona by the late Charles "Pee Wee" Cameron, it created quite a commotion in Red Mountain. It was during prohibition and after dark Pee Wee drove through the town with red lights flashing and the siren going full blast. Thinking that an unexpected raid by the law was about to take place, the girls and gamblers scattered into the darkness while the bartenders, trying to get rid of the evidence, dumped a lot of booze down the drain. We know for sure that for a long time Pee Wee wasn't welcomed in Red Mountain.

Many people lost their lives in automobile wrecks on the old Trona-Red Mountain dirt road. Most of the accidents happened coming down the three and nine-mile grades. They were attributed to booze, fatigue and speed. In a span of 20 years, 38 people were killed.

Trona Liked Its Beer

"Ho! Hum! How much did you say the fine was, Judge?" asked Mrs. Ella Clay as she flipped open a stuffed and choking pocketbook. She had just been found guilty of the possession of beer.[16]

"Two hundred and fifty dollars? Ho, Hum. Count those and make sure that I haven't short-changed you. This pocketbook was getting a little crowded anyway."

Mrs. Clay, according to *The Trona Pot-Ash*, was "out-Caponing" Al Capone himself in setting up beer parlors on both sides of Trona.

Arthur Johnson started in the beer bottling business around Trona—it was a hot summer in the Searles Valley, near Death Valley. But he decided to close shop when things, besides the weather, were getting hot. He waited around Trona for a few debts to be paid him when the dry squad arrested him and liberated $250 from him. In that one series of raids, the judge earned money for the local government: Walter Yarberry paid $200 in fines, F. J. Hardy a mere $150—altogether $850 from the dispensers of beer.

Two summers before, the federal agents swooped out of Bakersfield and raided several beer gardens in Trona. The arrested men pleaded guilty before Justice R. K. Obereuffer. When Charles Engstrom was unable to pay his fine of $300, Constable Reilly escorted him to San Bernardino. The Bakersfield newspaper said these men were hauled into a desert court "pitched amid the sand dunes and presided over by a wandering Trona justice of peace." William Patterson pleaded guilty before this wandering justice and fined $300 for sale and possession. Christ Gfeller and George Hall, partners, paid $250 and $50 respectively; Harry R. Smith was assessed $150. Randsburg liquor operator Charlie Adcock was taken to Atolia and assessed $150 for possession.

The beer gardens lined the county road, while the breweries were located in the sand dunes. "Two clearing houses" or middlemen were near retail parlors.

The pass through the ancient ice age lake sediment southwest of Trona was Poison Canyon. This pass had its beer garden in a little shack and under the shade of a couple salt cedars. It was run by Ma and Hill Batterson. In the middle of the room sat galvanized tubs containing bottles of homemade beer covered with ice from the Trona plant. Under a trap door were more beer. One Sunday Battersons sold 780 bottles, 25¢ each for a great income of $195 in

1928. The tunnel he used to obtain potable water served as a brewery since it was warm in the winter and cool in the summer.

On rare occasions when one of these places was raided, the boot would pay his $50 fine, replace the broken glass and be up and running again in days. Butch Glixinor and his wife sold out of their home in Pioneer Point and even got robbed and had a shootout with the bandits. After repeal, Batterson sold out to Jack Hawkins who remodeled it into a legitimate beer joint with live music and dancing on the weekends.

Trona liked its beer, whether legal or not, and has continued to enjoy foamy froth, winter or summer, to this day.

℘

The Argus Range was noted for a few springs of fresh, non-salty water, from which the citizens of Trona assuaged their thirst. The Department of Public Health certified as to its great purity for both drinking and for culinary purposes. But the Argus—the name meaning seeing with 1000 eyes—served another important function during the dry years of prohibition. Visitors to the unpopulated area had been obtaining a different type of thirst quencher. J. M. Jacobs used the water to mix an illegal concoction of, according to *The Trona Pot-Ash,* formaldehyde, wood alcohol and burnt sugar for a potentially dangerous drink that sold as whiskey. Judge Burke gave him a $100 plus 30 days in the San Bernardino County jail—free room and board.

Two Bootleggers in One Canyon
by George Pipkin
from Trona Memories, Chapter XLIV

I first met Doug Graham, Co-owner of the Graham-Jones mine (Ruth Mine) in the late summer of 1928. The mine was in the upper reaches of Homewood Canyon. Doug had lost his partner Jones and at the advanced age of 72 was getting too old to mine. The country was dry at the time, so he had turned to an easier way of making a living—bootlegging. There were two bootleggers in the canyon at the time. Bob Weir, who lived near the mouth of the canyon (now Crabtrees's place), was the other one. Although the two men were competitors, Weir kept Doug supplied with moonshine whiskey (wholesale) which was purchased from Ash Meadows, Nevada. Weir ran the whiskey across Death Valley and Panamint Valley under cover of darkness to avoid the law and hijackers, mostly the latter. Ash Meadows whiskey, which sold for $12 a gallon, was much better than the $10 Randsburg whiskey. Doug sold out of his home at the mine which was a long way from the Inyo County law. Sunday was the big day sales-wise. Trona and Westend men would go up the canyon to replenish their stock.

∅

No matter what part of the desert or what prohibition year it was, bootlegging and moonshining flourished unabatedly. Because of the vastness of the desert, chauvinistic constables and sheriffs leaving locals alone to handle liquor problems, and the role large operators had in supplying Los Angeles, the dry desert perhaps was not wet enough for Noah to start building another ark, but the desert was by no means dry.

CHAPTER 8

BOOTLEGGERS

T hey were just plain folks, the kind that would get up in the middle of the night and help pull you out of the sand," said Walt Wilhelm about the desert bootleggers. Some bootleggers were small-timers, just family members making a little extra to pay the mortgage or buy the wife a new dress. While these humble operators were the majority of bootleggers, rumrunners and moonshiners in California, the others were big-time syndicates, backed by hundreds of thousands of dollars.

My Bootlegging Years
as told by William S. Cullen, San Mateo

William S. Cullen came to San Francisco after his discharge from the U. S. Army. He was black, struggling in the early days of prohibition to make a living.

In South San Francisco at 1622 Commercial Avenue in 1922, my first wife and I rented a room to Henry Whitfield who knew how to make corn liquor. He obtained his barrel and distilling equipment and set up his operation. I wouldn't allow him to make it at night but only in the daytime so the afternoon breeze would blow the smell out the window toward the salty bay. My wife was a strange mean one. She always raised hell with Whitfield with his moonshining yet she enjoyed the money, keeping it for herself. She took trips to Weed and Woodland, sold liquor to the lumbermen. When she returned she wouldn't give Whitfield any of the money.

One day he met her at the center of town and they had a screaming fight all the way to our house. The police followed, putting me in an embarrassing position. The police gave Whitfield fifty cents to catch the ferry and stay out of town. When my wife left

William Cullen, World War veteran, worked in San Francisco brothels and speakeasies, made liquor and wine, worked at Swift meat packing plant and settled down in San Mateo, raising a fine family. Photo by author.

one day I buried the stuff and kicked the wife out of the house, just the first of several times.

Another boarder, Willie King, lived with us. My wife and Willie stayed in South City whenever I went to San Francisco. I decided to sell some five gallon cans of liquor and Italian wine at Potrero and 10th Street in San Francisco. The police were waiting for me.

"What do you have in the truck, coal oil?" asked the policeman.

"Now what would I be doing bringing coal oil from South San Francisco to the City? You know very well what's here—hooch!"

"Got $40?" asked the policeman.

"No, but I have a watch worth $40," I said.

"We can't take watches. I'll have to arrest you."

That night in jail, I had a dream that if I made the judge laugh, he'd let me go.

The judge asked the next day if I made the stuff and I said, "Yes."

A woman attorney said, "Not the wine!"

"I made all of it," taking the blame for all of it, and the court laughed.

"$10 or 10 days!" said the judge.

"Do I have time to get the ten dollars?"

"A professional bootlegger like yourself should always have $50 in his pocket."

"Well, you see, Judge, I'm not a professional bootlegger." The judge laughed.

"Ninety days," the judge said. "Suspended."

I found out my wife was messing around with Willie King and King was the one who turned me in to have it [sex] whenever he wanted. I went over to where he was staying in San Francisco. I beat him up on the porch. That afternoon I was across the bay in Oakland. I kept thinking about King and my wife and him turning me in. I got madder and madder so I took the ferry back to San Francisco and beat him up again.

My next brother-in-law took me to San Jose one day. We bought a half-gallon of white wine made from grappa and prunes for $1.50. This cured my kidney trouble, never had it since.

Generally a quart of wine cost 65¢.

The night of June 30, 1919, was a night to remember. North Beach went wild with drinking and dancing the night before war-time prohibition went in effect.

Later, on Pacific Street between New Montgomery and Stockton, there must have been 25-30 speakeasies and whorehouses. I lived in a whorehouse. It had rooms in the back so it could be called a rooming house. But in front, the owner Benjamin Collins, nicknamed "Bright Eyes," and his wife—we called her Mrs. Collins, but I'm sure she wasn't—and three other girls operated the cat house. The room cost me $2 a week.

The police were taking money "hand over hand" at the houses of prostitution. One of the biggest cheap houses was Fairfield Hotel, 1325 Stockton Street. Pansy Burr, a black woman, ran it. Her husband ran a gambling place and a farm in Stockton. I worked cleaning up the rooms about 1923-24. The street floor was a furniture store. The same with the next floor. The third floor had the main cheaper prostitution, $2 and up. The top had the high class ladies, $10 and up all night.

Pansy had one or two black girls, one or two white and the rest in between—usually Mexicans. When the fleet came in, sailors took over the hotel. When it was time for Alaskan fishing, Mexicans took over. When they left, I could pick up two bushels of marijuana seeds. I didn't know anything about that then. Booze was available anytime.

When the Shriners' Convention came each year, especially the Diamond Jubilee year in 1923 or 1924, the Fairfield Hotel became the Shriners' center. Some Shriners didn't even march in their parade. They just spent their time in the hotel. Kate Wiley, a 300-pound cook, directed the gourmet chef. The meals cost $1.50 but we made extra money by selling them for $3 and up at the rooms.

In San Mateo, the hills to the west hid many moonshiners. If one went west from 36th Avenue to the Alameda [Alameda de las Pulgas], he could find hidden stills.

Noel Williams operated Noel's Ark in San Mateo with the city's agreement not to allow another restaurant within four blocks. The city didn't honor this and in about 1932 Noel went bankrupt. I and my brother worked for Noel for several years. He did not serve bootleg but he made a specialty of white of eggs called Noel's Silver Fizz. The workers and customers brought in their own grappa and gin. That made a popular drink in San Mateo. Grappa is soured wine that is distilled. This could be purchased in South San Francisco.

At the Ben Franklin Garage, William "Slim" Gurraman was the biggest bootlegger in San Mateo. He was an excellent pilot and later when World War II started, the army used him to train pilots. My brothers-in-law, Luis "Grafter" Guidroy and Ben Guidroy delivered for him. Ben found out that there was going to be a raid on Slim's cache in the hills. Slim told the Guidroys to bring the stuff down and hide it in the garage.

The first legal beer I liked was Aztec from San Diego. It sold for 10¢ a bottle in the store and 15¢ in the bar. The Negroes drove up the price of beer. Whenever there was a black store the price was higher. The beer that sold for 15¢ in a white bar sold for 20¢ in a Negro bar. We were happy to obtain beer in 1933. We didn't like Bevo, the prohibition near beer.

"Pinched Him Many a Time"

Some people just seem to step over the line no matter whether it's to violate the prohibition law or a traffic law. Guy Wadsworth, a desert "rancher" at Bryman Road between Oro Grande and Helendale, was such a person. He had the natural proclivity to be on the other side of the law, the person who would rather make one dollar illegally than two dollars legally. He stole everything in the country, said Constable Penny Morrow of Oro Grande. He made homebrew and sold it, hiding his bootleg in the floor of his two-story rock house. His still was up at the chalk mines, four-five miles up the hill. "I pinched him many a time," recalled Morrow.

Wadsworth made sure Morrow earned his constable's pay. Once Wadsworth nearly killed Deputy Sheriff J. A. Larson, Chief of San Bernardino's "dry squad." According to Larson, he was trying to search Wadsworth's car when Wadsworth struck him with a monkey wrench. The first blow knocked Larson down, but Wadsworth continued to beat him.

"Okay, enough, enough! I've had enough!" shouted Larson. Wadsworth hit some more until neighbors heard the shouts and ran to the scene. Wadsworth ran off across the desert on foot.

County authorities arrested Wadsworth and brought him before Justice George W. Holbrook. After listening to Larson's side of the incident, the judge heard Wadsworth's testimony: he didn't know that Larson was an officer, that Larson was not wearing a badge, that Larson had struck him in the face with a flashlight before Wadsworth hit him. "I was fighting for my life," pleaded Wadsworth.

Justice Holbrook dismissed the charges, stating that he "didn't believe there is a jury in the land" which would have convicted the rancher.
County officials did not feel the same way. Upon hearing of Wadsworth's dismissal. Deputy Attorney Wardell D. Evans brought the case before the San Bernardino grand jury where an indictment was issued. Upon the returning of the indictment, Superior Judge Charles L. Allison issued a bench warrant for Wadsworth's arrest, setting bail at $2,000. Wadsworth's attorney Trent Penland telegraphed his client about the incident, urging him to surrender to San Bernardino County Sheriff Walter Shay.[1]
For the next six months Wadsworth had been a part-time resident at the county jail at county expense. It was quiet along that strip of Route 66 for a few months anyway.

Another time, Larson, this time with the help of Deputy Sheriff J. E. Farley, arrested Wadsworth for two counts of selling, filed at the Colton court, and one charge of selling and one of possession filed at the Victorville court. Thus, this doubled the chance of obtaining a conviction.
While waiting for these two trials, Wadsworth had to start a 30-day sentence for disturbing the peace because of an early December argument on the Mojave

River bridge with transcontinental bus driver Bill Knight. On January 13, 1929, at Colton, Wadsworth pleaded guilty to bootlegging. Justice C. F. Healey gave him six months in jail. On the 14th, he pleaded guilty to possession before Justice F. F. Hoffman of Victorville. His lawyer Penland had the other charges dismissed.

For another six months things were a little dull along the Mojave River east of Victorville as Guy Wadsworth vacationed in San Bernardino.

The Desert Fox
based on information by David Gunn and Ralph Wilkins, Boron

After midnight two high-powered Buicks with lights off sped westward over the dirt road heading toward Lancaster, California. When they came to the paved road north of Lancaster, they stopped and waited. Seeing no cars on the road, they turned their lights on and headed toward Palmdale and then south-west to Los Angeles. This routine, a nightly occurrence, varied only with different routes, and sometimes with different vehicles, Cadillacs, Packards or trucks. For almost ten years the Muroc area and around Rogers Dry Lake and Rosamond Dry Lake supplied dry southern California with wet goods—180-190 proof alcohol.

The cars had no back seats enabling them to hold two layers of five-gallon cans, up to 120 cans that would not show above the bottom of the window. One inventive driver obtained a mannequin, set her in the front seat with him so it would just look like a couple driving to L. A. It sure fooled the boys at the still. "Hey, who's the blonde you have in the car with you?" a loader asked the driver.

"That's my girl. Leave her alone," said the driver. But when one of the boys went to the front of the car to check her out, he yelled back to the others loaders, "Shit, that's a goddamned dummy!"

Prohibition agents knew the general area of the source of illicit alcohol. They even caught a few drivers, busted a few distilleries, but for ten years they could not stop the distilleries in the Muroc region.

Perhaps no region produced more moonshine than this little isolated desert area radiating 15 or so miles from Muroc. Muroc was homesteaded by a rancher named Corum. The railroad stop would have been called Corum, but California already had a Corum so the railroad spelled the stop backwards—Muroc. In the 1920s Muroc had a school, small store, tiny station and a few houses. Gutsy desert ranchers struggled to make a living in the desert.

The Feds swarmed around Muroc looking for the stills they knew were there. The three L. A. owners of the stills had several advantages over the law enforcers: isolation, knowledge of local terrain, distance, but most important, they had hired Dan Murphy to run the distilleries around Rogers Dry Lake and Rosamond Dry Lake, up to seven stills at one time. Dan Murphy was a desert fox—15 years before Rommel. He owned or leased the old Cohen Ranch, hired an old bachelor named Hanson to run it. Murphy was a big Irishman, heavy-set, black-haired with a medium-dark complexion. He was serious, yet had a great sense of humor. This affable, clever desert lover knew the desert like a coyote. He knew mining roads left by the little gold rush of the early 1920s and the oil-exploration roads of the 1910s near Kramer Junction (Four Corners). He knew each ranch and homestead, occupied or abandoned. When the depression hit Los Angeles, more homesteaders moved to the desert. He developed a symbiotic relationship with the ranchers. They minded their own business, did not know anything, did not talk. Murphy employed quite a few men at the stills on eight-hour shifts, thus helping families survive the early years of the depression without being on the dole. He paid them well and received their loyalty in return. If a family were in a bad situation, a car might pull up in front of the homestead and unload groceries—that's Dan Murphy [see Chapter 7].

He started some homesteaders in the cattle business as a front for a still, the well dug by Ralph Wilkins, paid for by Murphy, the corral built with moonshiner labor. A rancher could survive, especially with some part-time work. Murphy's roads to stills ran right through the cattle pens, allowing the cattle to cover the tracks of sugar trucks and booze cars.

Dan Murphy was quite a guy. He had a slick operation. Most stills were located on government land, usually right behind private land. Surveyors worked it out. Murphy located one distillery behind Mud Camp, a spot at the edge of the lake where miners dug lake soil to be used for "rotary mud" for drilling and other industrial purposes. The road led to the Mud Camp and stopped. Though the miners knew nothing about the liquor operation just over the hill, no one talked. Gifts of moonshine and Dan's persuasion kept miners silent.

A typical Muroc still was like the one near Rich section house. The road ran up toward the cattle pen where the cows stayed for the night. A prohi coming up the road at night would just see a dead-end road at the cattle pens. In the daytime, the wife, Mrs. Norma Rich, a cowgirl by nature, took the cows out grazing, covering the moonshiner's night truck tracks. Husband Max Rich kept guard on the little hill with a ladder up to a platform in a Joshua tree. He could see for miles.

Another distillery eluded the prohis because it was only 75 yards from the main dirt road heading across the lake. Agents drove by the still dozens of times. Ralph Wilkins drilled a well for cattle to the left of the road. A pipe ran underground from the well, under the road and around a knoll where the still lay hidden. A moonshine road walked on daily by cattle forked off the main road to the right around the knoll. Workers dug the distillery site in a depression next to the hillock so trucks could drive right underground. The ceiling, supported by 4x4 posts and beams, was plank wood or corrugated steel, covered with dirt. Murphy tied wire to sagebrush and other desert plants and anchored them to the roof so the still could avoid being spotted easily from the air. Inside, white gas stoves heated the fermented mash, thus avoiding smoke. Smoke stacks and vents exited the still so vents were hidden by bushes. One stack went right up through a Joshua tree which camouflaged the pipe. Huge fermentation tanks 10-15 feet across occupied one side of the cavern.

The best method of catching moonshiners was to follow sugar trucks to the still. Sugar and grain came up the long drive from Los Angeles or more efficiently unloaded from a train boxcar brought within a few miles from the still. Train tracks to Bakersfield cut across the dry lakes quite a few miles west of the present tracks. Local switchman unhooked boxcars at sidings. Workers unloaded trucks with five tons of sugar and drivers headed for the center of the dry lake. At a designated spot the truck stopped, waited for the flashing lights of the all-clear signal and waited also to make sure he was not followed. Being sure of his safety the driver drove directly to the still. If the prohis pursued the truck, the driver just took off on one of the numerous desert side roads, losing the prohis.

During the later years of prohibition a couple of stills had been knocked over, but the number of distilleries and the years of operation made Murphy's success rate incredible. One trick Murphy employed was to play the fox. Sugar trucks heading for the dry lake after dark went to a designated point on the lake where another truck, similar to the sugar truck but empty—at least of sugar—was stationed. If the sugar truck were being followed by the prohis, it raced to the dummy truck, signaled with its lights, then turned off its own lights as it came next to the dummy truck. The sugar truck veered off behind a hillock or off into another part of the lake. The dummy truck took off with its lights blazing, followed by the Feds, and if caught it had to be let go since there was no evidence and no still in sight. Murphy used dummy cars to distract the Feds who might be following his cars heading for the still or heading out with a batch of five-gallon cans of moonshine.

Murphy had picnics for workers and local farmers once in awhile. Celebrating the Fourth of July was certainly the patriotic thing to do. He invited families to come over to swim in his reservoir. Dinner at Murphy's usually started with Hanson digging up a bottle to relax the guests.

In return for his generosity, Murphy had a score or so of loyal ranchers, miners and informers to tip him off if someone were around asking questions. No one said "Boo" to his nefarious activities.

An old timer from Boron, David Gunn, told the following story: I was single during the late 1920s, had a good-paying job at the Borax plant. I bought me a 'hot shot' car, a Chrysler convertible. Once I took a girlfriend, Grace Viets, for a long drive. We reached Muroc Dry Lake and parked in the aloneness of the desert. Silent under the clear stars. We talked and later necked. Suddenly lights flared in front of us as a car charged at my new car. It was Murphy, but he saw my Chrysler and circled, honked, and sped away, leaving us lovers alone to romance in the warm desert air. It took a few minutes for our heartbeats to slow down. This place was no place for strangers to be. I was glad I knew Dan Murphy. Grace was nervous; we chose other spots to romance. She later became my wife for 48 years.

Although Dan was friendly and neighborly, he played rough. One man complained about someone he really disliked. Murphy listened to his friend's complaint for a few minutes and finally said, "For two hundred dollars I could have that son-of-a-bitch hanging from a Joshua tree in the morning."

"What? Oh, I'm not that mad at him," Murphy's friend answered.

"A lot of people disappeared in those days," stated Gunn. These three main suppliers from L. A. organized the stills in the area. Although they were separate operators, they formed a loose association. They elected one of the three as leader. All worked fine until the leader said, "We'll have to shut down for awhile. The prohis are really coming close."

They did shut down two-thirds of the operations in the Muroc area but the leader kept one of his plants going, selling his liquor at a higher price because of the newly-created scarcity. Soon the other two associates found out about it. The leader disappeared, never to be heard of again.

One night a prohi stepped into the road, his gun drawn. He had been waiting for the moonshiners for several hours. The moonshiners stopped and the prohi thrust the gun in the open window, ordering the two men in the car to put their hands up. "You're under arrest!" he shouted. The driver pulled the prohi's hand down, trapping it and the gun on the inside of the door. The partner then shot the defenseless prohi between the eyes. According to Dewey Holden, a moonshine employee, the agent was never heard of again and never found.

One worker, weakened to temptation or threat, it's not known which, led the prohis to a hidden still. Feds knocked it over. Revenge came swiftly and permanently. When goons caught him they took him out into a remote part of the desert, castrated him and left him to die. He didn't die. He survived but left the area with haste [Maybe he left slowly.].

The Los Angeles owners of the stills undermined Dan Murphy's effective operations. The government put pressure on syndicate operations, pressure that taxed Murphy's logistics skill. Guards and drivers had been caught on the long drive to L. A. But overall this was a profitable operation. Since distillery owners throughout California had been successful with payoffs, L. A. owners decided to pay off key prohi agents. It worked for awhile. Then defections, leaks and double-crossing resulted in the prohis knocking over several stills in 1932 to 1933, curtailing the liquor output and challenging Murphy's ingenuity. At the clay mines, agents surprised the still and caught Dewey Holden and two others running out across the desert. The agents agreed that if one confessed, they'd let the others go. Since Holden was single, he confessed. The others went back to their desert work. The Feds wrecked the still and added a conviction to their record. Holden served a year on McNeil Island, Washington, a federal penitentiary. Murphy paid Holden's salary for the year and offered Holden his job back when the year was over.

"I don't want any more of that life in prison. No more for me," Holden told Murphy. He hired on at the Borax plant and worked for years. He had some wild tales to tell. "He told me them for years," said Gunn.

"God darn, those days were exciting, adventurous days. Murphy was great to me, paid me well but I wanted no more of that prison stuff."
With repeal in December 1933, the stills went into disarray. The government locked up a couple of the stills; they dynamited a few. Curious desert rats explored the abandoned or dynamited sites. Depression homesteaders and ranchers appropriated usable items: wood, corrugated steel, hinges, shovels, dismantling the stills. Ranchers and miners lost their grubstakes. Dan Murphy went into the liquor business for awhile at Rosamond and later went into mining, some old-timers said, but eventually disappeared from the area he had been so much a part of for so many years. He disappeared as did those prohibition times, as did hundreds of L. A. basin speakeasies that Dan Murphy supplied with a steady flow of alcohol for almost 10 years.

During World War II, the government built Edwards Air Force Base, moved the railroad to the east and the prohibition period was lost to all but a few old-timers.

Artifacts remain within the boundaries of the Air Base and Kramer Hills. But sixty years of parched desert, wind and sand are reclaiming the site of the greatest moonshine distilleries in California.

David Gunn related: "Want another beer?" I asked old Dewey during one of our get-togethers in the 1950s.

"Sure, thanks," said Dewey.

"God, Dave, you remember that whiskey we used to get from ol' Dan Murphy?"

"Yeah, sure do," I answered.

"That was good stuff, better than a lot of liquor you buy now in the store."

"That's true, Dewey."

"I remember one time when I was working for Dan and...."

"Wad" Oates
as told by Carl Eifler, Salinas

Wad Oates [Walter C.] was a former customs officer who turned smuggler. He and I and Lee Echols were very good friends. Wad was a border patrolman in the Calexico area. We had a deputy collector down on the border that Wad Oates just didn't get along with. After Wad turned smuggler he said he would show him how smuggling was really done.

He had a little Model A in those days, had a piece of inner tube tied on a type of trap that he could pull over his muffler and the car would "'wheuwp pleep' like it was fartin' at you.

He'd see an officer and pull that lever and he'd fart at him. When he drove past the Customs Office in Calexico, he'd fart at it.

He put the word out that he wasn't going to be taken alive by anyone with the exception of perhaps [Lee] Echols or me. He still liked us.

[Later, when] He was under warrant and he couldn't get back into the United States. So he'd get a load of alcohol across there once in a while and we'd knock it off. I'd call him up and say, "Hey, Wad, got your load today."

Wad sent his load of alcohol across by his gang. He had a lieutenant, one I knocked off. Anyway I called him up and said, "I got your load today, Wad."

"Okay, dinner's on me, Carl."

So I'd go over to Mexico and we'd have dinner.

And sometimes he'd call me up and say, "Okay, I put one through on you, Carl."

I'd say, "Okay, dinner's on me." I'd go over and buy his dinner.

So one night we were having dinner together. I bid him good-bye and shook hands. I knew he was putting a load across that night and of all things in the darn book, he carried the load himself.

He came across the border and I stopped him. He got out and I looked at him and said, "Okay, Wad, what are we going to do, fight it out here or fight it out in court?"

He took a few minutes thinking it over, and then he said, "Ah, let's fight it out in court." He submitted to arrest. I caught him right on the border, just after he got across in his car.

There was a lot of the border that wasn't fenced where you could drive across. That was the part of being an officer of that particular type in those days. You had to find out where they were going to cross it and be there and get them. One time we were on a stake-out for two weeks waiting for Wad. Two of us would bring as much water as we could carry, throw a canvas over some bushes for shade and wait it out where smugglers had come across before.

A couple of days after I caught Wad, he was out of jail. He made bond and was on his way back. I knew about it and I had gone and got a couple more warrants for his arrest naming him for every darn thing he did. Anyway, even though he was on his way back, having just made bond, I arrested him and took him back.

He said, "What the heck is this anyway? Who's doing this, Carl?"

"No, I thought it up. I'm doing it, Wad. I made it up."

This friendship might seem odd but this was a game we played, you see. He was on his side and I was on mine. I liked him and I still like him.

So he went up to the penitentiary again and it was about four years or so when he finally got out. I was in Heber, California, when this incident happened so the time was 1928 and the court trial would be between '28 and '32. All of a sudden a car came shooting off the highway, coming right straight at me. I had to jump or I'da been hit. He comes to the side laughing, "How are you, kid?"

It was old Wad. We had dinner again that night. It wasn't too long after that that he was back in the racket again. He was smuggling again.

We were having dinner in Mexico and he said, "Who's working on me, Carl?"

I said, "I don't know but I'll tell you this much, I'm not."

He didn't get caught again. Afterwards he went down to Texas and I heard he got a ranch in Texas and went straight. I haven't heard from him since [see Chapter 12 and Appendix F].

The Greatest Law There Ever Was
as told by G. William Puccinelli, San Mateo

I was a "land shark"! I picked up loads of liquor off the beach and delivered them to my storage places in the City (San Francisco), then to my customers. I used to run booze into Nevada. Nobody else could. If you had a California license, they'd knock you over in a minute. All the booze in Nevada during this time of prohibition came from San Francisco. I wasn't stopped 'cause it was all set up. Never got caught. One time the prohibition department went up to Nevada to clean out the fucking town because it was running rampant, never had been knocked over.

I went up there with two loads of booze, two big loads of booze, me and one of the Swedes. We parked our trucks right there in front of the office of internal revenue, right in front of the sons of bitches. They went into the raids, took a week before they knocked everybody over. Then we unloaded our booze. A high price—$80 a case. We paid $25 (a case) after it landed.

When things were hot at one landing area, like Half Moon Bay, we'd be notified that they would land someplace else. The people who brought it in, like the Swedes, told us. They brought it in from the mother ships outside the sea boundary. Two ships were the *Federalship* and the *Quadra*, which carried 35,000-40,000 cases of booze. I was out on a boat one time, but I'd never go again. We sometimes picked up loads in Eureka, Oregon or down Santa Monica by Los Angeles. Sometimes we'd take our big sedans, La Salles or Cadillacs, like we were going on a fishing expedition, fishing poles tied to the top. Once we were coming down from the northern coast with a load. A prohi tailed us, took the same ferryboat from Sausalito to San Francisco. When the ferry ramp dropped down at the San Francisco side, we started to pull out in line to go down the ramp. Just as we took off, one of the agents ran up, jumped on the running board of the driver's side, but he hit a cable, almost decapitating him. We didn't stop or know what happened to him until later.

It's all according to the Coast Guard. The Coast Guard let them know where to land it. The rumrunners would straighten it out with the Coast Guard—five thousand, ten thousand, twenty thousand—big money! They got rich: those in charge of the Coast Guard ships.

They paid off at the Palace Hotel, Market and Montgomery streets. All those guys who brought in the booze would meet every day at the Palace Hotel, in the outside room, the Tudor Room they call it now. Stained glass windows of Henry the Eighth and Queen Elizabeth and other leaders of the Tudor times—symbolic of leaders who defied authority and customs, charted their own destinies and destinies of their country. When distributors from Canada came in, they liked the bigger, plusher place. We'd meet in the back room for awhile and then adjourn to the Tudor Room for lunch. Hotel workers liked it when we came in, spent lots of money. I've left $100 tips lots of times. That's when it would be announced when the booze would come in, where it would be landed. They knew everything. The whole country was based on graft—like now.

Another place where liquor deals were made was Hoffman's Bar (Grill), 619 Market Street, established in 1891. Millions of dollars worth of Canadian alcohol—paid for over the tables of Hoffman's. What a place for three-hour afternoon business luncheons: $100 tips, silver and brass, old-fashioned mirrors in the "Gentlemen" and "Ladies" rooms, four large fans on each side hanging from the ceiling, brass chandeliers, the east wall filled with old original paintings.

Every rancher on the coast was paid to stash this whiskey. They weren't making anything on the goddamned artichokes at that time, so they'd get money from the guys who brought in the booze. They'd hide it in their barns or some place on the farm. They had to hide it. They'd bring it in, hundred cases at a time, sometimes a couple hundred cases at a crack. The Filipinos would do all the heavy work, loading and unloading. One time five Filipinos got machine-gunned in Moss Beach. [The author could find no documentation for this.]

I had two fellows working for me (when picking up a load at the beach). I paid these two big Italian boys over $100 a day depending on the load. I always went along with them, see, tail behind in another car when we were driving back to the city.

We picked up Canadian Club, Coon Hollow, Peter Dawson, Glen More, Hospitality and Log Cabin. A bottle of Canadian Club cost about $10, a case of twelve, $80-90, depending on how much was brought in. If we brought it all in, it would be cheaper. I sold it by cases, not many bottles. I had all the best trade on Montgomery Street, bankers, officers of Crocker Bank. They'd buy it by the case. Then the Swedes brought in wines and vermouth from Europe and my customers would buy it. My office was in the Russ Building.

G. William Puccinelli, the Land Shark, holding his daughter Barbara in 1926. Dapper young man, this smuggler brought the booze from the shore to San Francisco and Reno. Photo courtesy of Barbara Puccinelli Osborne.

Only ten percent of alcohol used during prohibition came from Europe or Canada. Ninety percent was made in California. Millions of gallons—some good, some bad. You could tell by the smell. Five-gallon cans of 180 proof cost $25, made ten gallons of 90 proof gin by adding water and juniper berries. Sonoran farmers from the valley made 6-7 thousand gallons a day. It's 180 proof alcohol, see, and they'd sell it that way. The buyers, local bootleggers who sold it by the pints, would cut it right in half with water, make it 90 proof.

The American Distillery of Sausalito sold alcohol, sneaked it out the back door, millions of gallons, for Christ sake! That's where the Buck family got rich. [Buck owned it after John Mason.]

Good houses of prostitution sold liquor, like Sally Stanford's couple of houses. She'd give you a drink, no charge. If a customer stayed overnight, she'd give him a bottle, charge him plenty, you know. We got along pretty well. She was a son-of-a-bitch in her day. I was the one who turned her out, helped her get started in San Francisco and later in Sausalito. She came down the coast from Portland, Oregon (or Seattle?), got run out, 1922.

In San Francisco the cops were the boss, I tell you. I told you the chief of police got a load of (hijacked) booze back for me. Pete and Joe Campanelli sold me a load, which I picked up from Half Moon Bay and parked it in front of my apartment on Marine Boulevard. I was tired from the night drive.
The next morning it was gone. I told Captain Dulaney about it. He traced the tires and he said, "Son-of-a-bitch, Pooch, I know who this is." He went there, checked the tires on the suspect's truck and son-of-a-bitch it was the same tires. It was Pete Campanelli. They sold it to me and hijacked it back. That's the kind of son-of-a-bitch he was. That happened before but I couldn't prove it. At least I got this load back, thanks to the police captain. I should have killed Campanelli. I don't want murder on my hands. I had nothing to do with killing, nothing, nothing. I'm even afraid of guns to be honest with you. I like to fight but not that way.
Campanelli did the same trick to Canizzario. I was there when Canizzario was going to shoot him with a pistol. Campanelli was on his knees pleading, "I didn't do it. I didn't know it was you—" whimpering. Canizzario was going to shoot and I knocked the goddamn gun out of his hand.
So the police chief helped me get that load back. So did the editor of the *Chronicle,* Howard Welch, help me get it back, about 1927. He and the chief of police were both my friends.

Mayor Rolph, later Governor Rolph, was not in charge. He was a hell of a guy, never lost an election. He was a good person. People loved him, gallant, good looking son-of-a-bitch, kiss women's hands and they'd melt. Every Dago in North Beach voted for him, ha ha.

The police department was the gangster. And Tom Finn ran the police and the mayor. Period! The gangsters here never had a chance, like Capone in Chicago. The cops were the fucking gangsters in San Francisco, tough cops too. They'd take on the goddamn bad men. The cops were the boss—no outsiders here. I was very good to them. Capone came out here once, the police met him at Mills Field [present San Francisco airport] when he got off the plane and sent him back.

Capone did control the labels. No labels were sold without his cut in it. They were made back east and shipped out here. They made the labels, any kind, Gordon's Gin, any kind of scotch. They call them set-ups. Third and Townsend was a set-up place where they'd make the booze, dilute Canadian whiskey, make five bottles out of two or three and put the labels on them.

The "Rum-running Swedes" were the first big smuggling operators. Harold Hansen was one of these. Johnny Moreno was one of the biggest operators out of San Francisco. Supposedly made 13 million dollars. Harry Reifel and a Jew, worked out of Canada, had B. C. Distributors. I often bought from Reifel and Ben Silva. We worked together like peanut butter and bread. Dutch Baker with United Distributors of Canada. "Blind Baker" he was called because of his thick glasses. Joe Parente, Bill Nard and Paul Madden were three other smugglers.

Lawyers took their clients to Judge George M. Bourquin who kept throwing bootlegging cases out of court. If my daughter wanted to marry a lawyer, I'd shoot him.

Patronis House, Half Moon Bay, Patroni smuggled, made a lot of money. He smuggled some in the earlier days, was arrested but still stored it and bootlegged.

Another famous bootlegger was Henry Dolger. His brother was in real estate. Used his money to build houses in San Francisco and Daly City.

Two Italians conceived the boldest plot during the fourteen years of prohibition. Vince Quattaro and Sila Liva. They bought off every important official from the Coast Guard, key harbor federal agents, Customs men, the police—everybody who was anyone. The rum-running ship *Quadra* sailed from Canada with maybe 50,000 cases of liquor, but instead of hovering 12 miles out, the captain brought it right through the Golden Gate, boldly docking at Pier 35. Everything was cleared and the crew and longshoremen started unloading. People came from San Francisco to watch the audacious move. Liquor being unloaded in broad daylight in the open at Pier 35. Beautiful move.

But a stupid watchman, curiously examined the cargo. Contraband liquor! He called the authorities who came and halted the importation. After a long legal fight, the liquor was confiscated and Quattaro ended up in prison.

Alioto's father was a bootlegger during prohibition. He dealt mostly in wine though. All I had exclusively was Canadian whiskey, beautiful whiskey. I had stashes of it. I paid to have it hidden and left alone. I paid plenty—cash. In the restaurant I paid off. One policeman would come in, get the money and distribute to the heads of their cops. One week, I'd give $1,000, lots of weeks, $500.

The small places, whorehouses, paid off to the cops on the beat. Sometimes I think the cities are better off having a strong, strong big shot. Tom Finn was the Joe Gaws out here, the main guy, and he ran the city for 20 fucking years. He got tough; when there was going to be a raid, he notified his people where they were going to be. Nowadays you never know who to trust. Entirely different today. I like the old style better.

The greatest period in my life was during prohibition—I had guts. Sometimes I made $10,000 a week. I was a millionaire by the time I was 25 (in 1925), invested it in the stock market. Went bankrupt in the stock market crash of 1929. I had an eighth-grade education and made five million dollars in my life.

I opened the e across from the Hall of Justice, where the Holiday Inn is today. It was the finest restaurant in San Francisco, the highest class and one of the most expensive in America. No cops, no patrolmen came in, just lieutenants, captains, judges, mayor, coroners and Tom Finn. I did a couple of thousand a day, today worth $10,000 a day.

One day we got knocked over (by the Feds). Governor Rolph, the chief of police, the coroner, a captain of the police were there. We had a big son-of-a-bitchen business that day. Since we ran out of French bread, I went up Broadway to pick up more. I was coming back down this alley with an armload of bread when a friend saw me, ran up waving his arms, "Get away, Pooch, get away! The place is raided! The Feds raided you."

The agents let the celebrities go, but they arrested my two waiters and were looking for me. They closed it right down, used the abatement law, put a big goddamn padlock on the front door, four-inch thick padlock.

Valuable liquor was in the restaurant. I got the idea of going in through the building across from the park, up to the roof on the next building and then down to the roof of mine. I broke in from the roof and took my liquor out, case by case. Two policemen helped me. They were taking a chance, stealing liquor out of a federally locked-up restaurant. I gave each a case of the best.

I took a vacation for a month or so until my lawyer worked it out. I went up to Canada. This raid cost me about $10,000 in payoffs so I could come back. But the Blue Fox stayed closed for the year. I opened it up again, ran it to the end of prohibition, bought a liquor license and ran it for years, till I sold it.

My brother was a bail bond broker; I had two nephews who were cops. I saw more cops go to jail during that time; a few committed suicide. One girl prohibition agent was named Daisy Simpson. She eventually committed suicide in jail. She would sleep with anyone to get a conviction.

I had just bought a new Marmon car, a big bastard for about $3,500. The back end was remodeled to hold 75 cases of liquor. Heavy-duty springs made the load ride in a normal way. No one would be suspicious because the back end wasn't dragging. I had a large order for Oakland loaded in my Marmon but before taking the Oakland ferry, I stopped off at the Federal Building to watch two federal agents go to jail. Curiosity, perhaps a little ironic devil in me, maybe a little revenge, but I enjoyed the sentencing.

When I came out of the trial, my car was gone—never seen it again.

One time there was a warrant out for my arrest. I went to Juarez for about 40 days until I could've killed that charge. I was lucky: I never hit the can. I paid $12,000 one time to beat the competition. I stopped smuggling in 1934, after repeal, smuggled it in to avoid taxes. Repeal came in 1933 but we smuggled for another year. Then I sold 16 restaurants and bars. I made another million dollars, later bought some property down the Peninsula here.

Prohibition was the greatest law there ever was.[2]

The Water Shark

Napoleon Jack Hale, usually operating out of Sausalito, considered himself a "water shark" since he coursed his way to the mothership floating out in the Pacific and brought Canadian liquor back to the "land sharks," like his friend G. William Puccinelli. Fun-loving Hale, a dare-devil rumrunner, operated two notorious 'fire boats," fast shore boats, named *It* and *Zeitgist* [see Chapter 11]. Once he almost lost his boat in the Pacific off Point Reyes. Logs and trees traveling down the Japanese Current from the north create a serious hazard for fast speedboats. While speeding toward a mothership, he took a log through the keel. He shoved a mattress from one of the bunks trough the hole and pulled full throttle which lifted the bow out of the water so he could run her back through the Golden Gate and onto the beach in Sausalito. He made it safely.

A Deal's a Deal
by George Pipkin
from *"Pete Aguereberry: Death Valley Prospector"*

Sam Adams wasn't long in Death Valley country until he began to dabble in politics. He got himself appointed deputy sheriff and then began to give the boys a bad time. Sam had brought to Harrisburg and Skidoo, the petty, chiseling crookedness of the Los Angeles political era of the 80s and 90s, which was a mistake on his part. He just didn't understand the desert men and their code of ethics. A desert man was as good as his word and ninety-eight percent of them lived up to the expectation.

Sam Ball's trouble with Sam Adams happened after prohibition came into being and the country was legally dry. Ball was the moonshiner and town bootlegger at Skidoo, and Adams, the deputy sheriff, was his best customer; that is his best non-paying customer. Before embarking upon the illicit profession, Ball made a deal with Adams. If the latter would let him operate, he would keep him supplied with free liquor.

Adams was short, stocky and barrel-chested, weighing in the neighborhood of two-hundred pounds. He consumed a lot of liquor. He was a silent drinker and he could drink as much as the average two men without visible effect. This, Ball knew since he was furnishing the liquor.

It must be said that during the period of prohibition, the sheriff's office at Independence was tolerant about the flow of booze in the far out-of-the-way places, such as Death Valley country. Wise in the ways of hard working men, they knew that the hardy miners who manned the mines had to have some kind of diversion and drinking hard liquor was one of them. If they couldn't go on a spree occasionally, they were liable to brain each other.

The sheriff's office knew that trying to stop a miner from drinking or procuring liquor would be as ineffectual as trying to stop the flow of time. So, they merely winked at what was going on in the isolated mining camps. Normally they only intervened when violence occurred, such as murder.

This was the case in Skidoo when Sam Ball almost killed Sam Adams by whacking him on the back of the neck with a length of tool steel. It happened when Adams committed the unpardonable sin of the desert. He broke his word with Ball. Ball was faithfully keeping his word by giving Adams whiskey in return for protection, when one day "Ornery Adams" strode into Ball's cabin and declared, "You are under arrest."

Startled, Ball asked, "What for?"

"Bootlegging," Adams replied.

Adams didn't have to look for the evidence. He knew where it was, for hadn't he helped himself many times to the cache of liquor concealed under a trapdoor in the floor of the cabin? When Adams stooped over to lift the trapdoor, Ball let him have it. Adams went down like a poled hog and shuddered like one in the agony of death. Ball thought that he had killed him, but no such luck, as Adams was too rugged an individual. However, he was unable to walk for a week, much less make an arrest.

Eventually, Ball was arrested and taken to Independence. When he told his story at the preliminary hearing, the judge fined him thirty dollars and turned him loose. Shortly afterwards, Adams' deputyship terminated suddenly. Then, when an election was held in Skidoo to fill the office of constable, by popular choice Sam Ball was elected.

Sam K. Adams

Sam K. Adams, in Skidoo in July 1923, faced charges of malicious use of explosives—to injure and blow up a tank structure, belonging to Carl Suksdorf and Frank "Shorty" Harris and for trying to destroy lumber to be used for a mill by Harris and Suksdorf. He went before Justice Margaret Lee at Darwin after he furnished a bond of $500. It wasn't Ball who arrested Adams, it was Deputy Sheriff Al Belin on July 4th. Adams started his fireworks early on June 30.[4]

Selling Whiskey Weren't No Crime, Just Happened to Be Against the Law
from "This Week's Snappy" in *Imperial Enterprise*

"It was 1902 when I first got into the whiskey business," said bootlegger M. B. "Bob" Davis of Imperial County. "There was local option until 1912 when Imperial (city) voted wet. All the towns were organized with charter clauses prohibiting liquor. But this country wouldn't have developed if it weren't for whiskey." Davis did his best to help all of Imperial County develop. He operated pool halls, sold bootleg, and even ran or owned the ABW Bar (the Owl) in Mexicali during the prohibition period.

Once he was arrested when the county was first formed. The militant WCTU was after him. Davis hired an aspiring law student, who was picking cantaloupes in the valley, to go around the county to have the moral folks donate money and sign a petition "to get rid of Bob Davis."

"Well," said Davis, "the lawyer went around to just about everyone, declaiming the evils of Davis, and collecting donations of $1 to $5 from everyone who would sign the petition. He got $600 in all, and I gave him 25 percent, so he left for the coast."

"They thought they had the jury box filled when I brought out the petition of those who donated." Davis laughed. That disqualified them. "The rest were my friends." Since only two qualified anti-Davis people could be found, the judge dismissed the case.

Davis' attitude was that investigators were "stool pigeons in those days and juries always decide against them." Years later his favorite saying was "Selling whiskey weren't never a crime, just happened to be against the law."

Joe Campanelli
as told by Joe Campanelli (son), Redwood City

Joe started as a very young man. He kept pestering someone at the Mason Distillery in Sausalito. He begged, bribed to get some alcohol out of the distillery. He finally succeeded, sold the stuff and was on his way to a career in bootlegging and smuggling. "My father persisted and got started."

He eventually had a front on Powell Street in San Francisco, a bottle company. He was helped by having an uncle on the police force, who would "take care of him."

He went deep into smuggling. He made trips to British Nassau in the Caribbean to bring back imported liquor for his California trade. He operated the boat *Julia* [*Guilia*], which was captured or scuttled off Pismo Beach.[5]

Rival Syndicates

In 1924, the *San Francisco Examiner* exposed the rival smuggling syndicates. Campanelli was a member of the "Hell Ship" syndicate, of which their boat "Guilia" surrendered and captain released on $2500 bail. This gang flooded San Francisco and the state with liquor, realizing millions of dollars in profit. The liquor came from England, through the West Indies and through Canada.

Banks financed the operations and often advanced the funds to "Black Dan" Henderson's syndicate of which Campanelli is accused of being a member." Two former officials of the Fish and Game Commission were founders of this gang. These men are said to facilitate landing of booze on "rum coast" off Monterey. Juan de Maria surrendered and warrants were out for Henderson and a woman, who posed as his wife, and two associates.[6]

When the smugglers were caught, sometimes the cases dragged on for years. A few of the witnesses left town, or made themselves scarce, some died and eventually the case got closed out. In case 15828-S, involving the boat *Julia*, also known as *Guilia* in 1925, the grand jury indicted 24 smugglers. The court found Guiseppe Companelli, i.e., Joe Campanelli, and J. O'Hagan guilty, and thirteen were found not guilty. In 1929 the case was still open as eight had not been apprehended: Henderson left the United States and was operating a restaurant in Cuba; McMillion and Holmes went back to their homes in England; two, P. J. Walsh and Ricardo Canpanelli (Campanelli) were around San Francisco but evidence would not support a conviction. Finally the Intelligence Unit of the IRS had no information on three of the defendants. The U. S. Attorney General George J. Hatfield of the Northern District of California asked the U. S. Attorney General if he could *nolle prosequi* these defendants. Therefore four years after the "Julia" case opened, it was off the court calendar.[7]

Casey Lloyd Davidson Jones—Indian Wells Bootlegger
by Ken Wortley
excerpts from *Adventures With the Misfits*
Ken Wortley not only found himself in the Southern Sierras after getting out of the Marines in 1919, but he found crusty desert old-timers he dubbed "misfits." Wortley, "green as grass," learned to survive by his wits from these mustangs, especially his moonshining partner, Casey Lloyd Davidson Jones, a prospector, musician, entertainer and moonshiner:

The era of prohibition which bred gangsterism, corruption, and wholesale disregard for the law is not a chapter of our history to be proud. People who never touched liquor before in their lives drank to excess, not because they liked bootleg brew and moonshine whiskey, but because of resentment toward being told they could not drink whatever they wished. This feeling was so well developed toward the end of prohibition that it was almost considered impolite to refuse to take a swig of rot-gut regardless from whence it came or what poison it might contain.

During prohibition this area was not without its quota of bootleggers, moonshiners and customers who were willing to buy any type of poisonous concoction manufactured—as long as it contained alcohol.

Casey Lloyd Davidson Jones and I spent the winter of 1921 trapping in Sand Canyon in the foothills of Indian Wells Valley. When spring arrived and fur became no longer saleable, we began to ponder some method of livelihood without going to work for someone else, a prospect extremely distasteful to both of us. (Casey went to Randsburg to dispose of the furs, which should have brought several hundred dollars.)

Three days later, Casey drove our Model-T into camp with a load as high as a haystack. Casey informed me he had had the good fortune while in town of securing a secret formula for making fig brandy, in view of the tremendous profits to be derived from the sale of such, he had taken the liberty of investing all our money to purchase the necessary materials and equipment to get into production ($400 down on $700 worth of moonshine equipment).

The load consisted of five fifty-gallon barrels, a dozen five-gallon oak kegs, a huge copper kettle, fifteen feet of copper tubing, a thousand pounds of figs, an equal amount of sugar, and small items including a meat grinder and a case of dynamite...the latter being to blow the other stuff to smithereens in case of an impending raid by revenue officers. They owed the first three kegs of brandy to compensate for the $300 they were short.

We assembled our still in an army tent well hidden in a pile of rocks a short distance from camp and set our first batch of brew. As a security measure according to plan, we buried the case of dynamite beneath the still with the cap and fuse attached. All there was to do now, so we thought, was to wait until the brew settled, draw it off and run it through the still. There was one detail, however, Casey's friend in Randsburg had neglected in his instructions, namely that it was necessary to keep the brew warm and at an even temperature or it would not ferment. After waiting patiently for ten days with no results we decided to make a trip to Randsburg to find out what the trouble was.

Soon after arriving in town we learned that Casey's bootlegger friend had been arrested and lodged in jail in Bakersfield. It seemed that a number of people had suddenly become violently ill after drinking moonshine and this man was accused of putting it in circulation. We found another friend who advised us to purchase a kerosene stove and keep it burning in the tent. The friend agreed to sell us a stove, a grub supply, and enough gasoline to get back to camp in exchange for two kegs of brandy. At that time moonshine was selling at $40.00 a gallon, so we were now $600 in debt.

Keeping the brew warm did the trick and we ran off eight kegs of fig brandy. Another thing Casey failed to ask was how to test the stuff for alcoholic content but he invented his own method. If a spoonful from the still would burn dry he estimated that the brandy was ready for human consumption.

We delivered three kegs of brandy, as agreed, which temporally cleared our books, but we were forced to contract another five kegs in order to get refinanced. I was beginning to wonder if moonshining was as lucrative a business as Casey believed it to be.

Our main worry meanwhile was whether or not prohibition agents had learned of our operation. At that time various agencies of the law were playing hide-and-seek with several hundred moonshiners in the hills. Deputies and stool pigeons were everywhere, either looking for stills and making arrests, or collecting revenue on the side and seeing to it that no arrests were made. Here in Kern County, like everywhere else in the country during the era of prohibition, corrupt officials were having a heyday. If a moonshiner knew the right people and was willing to pay the price, he could become rich; if he didn't know the right people or was unwilling to pay the price, he went broke or to jail.

News travels fast in the desert country. It wasn't long until Casey and I were paid a visit. Two quail hunters dropped by to see us one day, but they were not hunters at all. From the looks and from the questions they asked we knew that they were stool pigeons. The two finally left without discovering our distillery. Two days later we were awakened at dawn by two deputy sheriffs in uniform; and they meant business. It didn't take these two boys long to find our still and confiscate a keg partly filled with brandy which was all the evidence they needed. Naturally I supposed they intended to destroy our still, so I suggested to Casey that we save them a lot of work by setting off the dynamite, but he didn't agree. Since there was no danger of the dynamite going off unless the fuse was lit, Casey argued in all fairness to the taxpayers the deputies should be made to earn their pay. As it turned out the officers had no intention of destroying the still. The work was usually reserved for another detail to follow, or if the still was a good one it would be removed intact and turned over to an operator in good standing.

After being formally placed under arrest, we were loaded in the back seat of the officers' sedan along with the keg of brandy as evidence and were on our way to Bakersfield.

For the time being it seemed that we were to be treated like just an ordinary pair of prisoners on a routine trip to jail, but Casey Jones was by no means a man to remain an underdog for long. By the time we reached the mouth of the canyon he had managed to engage our captors in pleasant conversation. At Indian Wells everybody was quite friendly and when we reached Walker Pass, Casey convinced the officers that there would be no harm in all of us having a few drinks of the evidence. The method Casey had devised for testing the alcoholic content of our brandy had apparently been a good one, because when we finally reached Onyx, Casey was driving and the rest of us were out cold, piled up in the rear seat of the sedan.

The next thing I remember was awakening with a terrific hangover. I was lying on a cot in a strange shack and Casey was nearby preparing a meal over an old wood stove. After expressing his disgust in no uncertain terms at allowing himself to become associated with a tenderfoot unable to consume a pint or two of brandy without passing out, he explained as follows:

After leaving Onyx, he had driven on to Weldon where he had spent several hours enjoying a dance that was in progress there. He had then driven to Isabella where he found shelter for us and also for the two deputies when he made them comfortable at the town jail. He also explained that while at the Weldon dance, he had disposed of the keg of brandy at $40.00 a gallon. We were now as good as free men since there was no longer any convicting evidence.

After Casey had consumed a hearty breakfast and I had several cups of black coffee to settle my nerves, we went over to the jail to see if the two deputies had survived. We found the officers still in a daze, but awake. Casey explained what had transpired, only departing from the facts in regard to the evidence which he said had disappeared in some manner unknown to him. After hearing this and in view of an embarrassing situation, the two officers were more than willing to forget the whole thing. We then shook hands all around and agreed to let bygones be bygones. The deputies left for Bakersfield to report an unsuccessful raid and Casey and I went to our shack to await a lift back to camp.

[Casey and Ken Wortley signed for a grubstake and bought a Model-T converted into a truck from Gus Suhre, who owned a store at Isabella.] Suhre, also a deputy constable, said Isabella had so many bootleggers, "they had to buy each other's moonshine to keep the money in circulation."

[When Casey and Ken got back to Sand Canyon, they borrowed an extra Model-T from Howard Gill at Brown and loaded their bootlegging gear and headed toward Wilson Canyon in the Argus Range, now on the Naval Air Warfare Center, China Lake Naval Weapons base.]

It was one of those beautiful, still nights that are so rare in the desert. A full moon illuminated the canyon road so there was no need to use the car lights, for which we were thankful, because we intended to keep our new quarters a deep secret. In this we might have been successful had not an unforeseen calamity occurred at exactly the wrong place and exactly the wrong time.

We were about past the aqueduct station near the mouth of Sand Canyon with both throttles wide open. Casey was in the lead with the largest load, and I right behind like a dog on the tail of a Brahma steer. Unfortunately at this point, there was a huge boulder alongside of the road. There was a resounding crash and a split second later a louder crash as the car I was driving plowed into Casey's truck, which had swung sideways off the road. Another crash followed as both vehicles tumbled off the roadbank into the sandy wash.

All this would not have been so bad had not this been Saturday night and the fact that a meeting of the valley's anti-bootleggers' association was in session at the station. Practically every long-hair and good prohibitionist between Independence and Mojave were on hand to discuss ways and means to cope with the moonshiner problem. Even so, it was fortunate for us that they had heard the above-mentioned series of crashes and came running en masse with lanterns and torches. When these good people realized, however, that they were about to aid two moonshiners engaged in the very business they were trying so hard to exterminate, there were several in the group who suggested that the rescue be abandoned. Fortunately for us, these were in the minority, for both Casey and I were hopelessly pinned under the wreckage. Casey on the very bottom did not help much because there were ladies present. In those days, more women frowned on profane language than they do today, especially of the variety and type which Casey Jones was capable of emitting under such circumstances.

After all the people left and things quieted down, Shorty, caretaker at the station who was a friend of ours as well as a good customer, volunteered to hitch up some mules and help get the vehicles back on the road. This was accomplished by daylight.

[Up Wilson Canyon] we found just the tunnel we were looking for. It had a winze [an inclined or vertical shaft or passage between levels in a mine] in which we were delighted to find water. The water was full of dead rats and mice, so we could not use it for domestic purposes, but decided that a little contamination should in no way affect the quality of our brew. Besides two sacks of sugar had been well saturated with kerosene at the mishap in Sand Canyon and Casey decided that the kerosene should offset any other noticeable flavor discovered in our brands.

[They ran off another five-gallon keg and had friends visit them by accident. When asked if authorities knew about them, the friend answered, the sheriffs and their deputies of three counties were looking for them, but did not know where they were.]

An old prospector died at Mountain Spring a few days before and bad liquor was believed to be the cause. It was traced to an Inyo County bootlegger who had used a tin can to distill corn whiskey. [Ken decided to break up the partnership, traded his two kegs to the friend for a horse. They ran off two more kegs because they owed that for debts. These were not bad, but the last two had a kerosene flavor from the spoiled sugar.]

It burned with a peculiar glow, indicating the presence of some foreign substance. In view of the death of the prospector who had so recently died from the effects of drinking poison liquor, neither Casey nor I was inclined to be the first to take a drink of the stuff, in order to discover what effect it would have on the human system. In time this proved to be a Godsend, because it caused an argument which broke the monotony of talking to ourselves. Casey's argument was based on the theory that I should be the one to do the sampling because I was youngest, possessed a good constitution, and therefore, would stand a better chance to survive should the stuff contain poison. It was my contention that Casey should be the sampler, since I was still young with a future before me, while he had already practically outlived his usefulness.

Finally, after an hour or two, we agreed to both be guinea pigs. We drank a half-cup of the stuff at the same time. Fortunately, outside of a terrible taste resembling a mixture of castor oil and kerosene, no bad effects resulted.

We divided the four kegs of brandy, each accepting one keg of good quality and one keg flavored with kerosene. The matter of who should have the truck was decided by a hand of draw poker. Of course, Casey won, because he had been a dealer at Goldfield, and was quite adept at dealing off the bottom of the deck.

[They both buried their caches, but Casey got up in the middle of the night and switched his kerosene tainted brandy for Ken's good one. Later in the wee hours Ken discovered this, then switched both bad for the two good ones, reburied them and brushed away his tracks. Before light Casey sneaked off with his truck and headed out. Ken returned the car to Gill and got a job driving cattle for Eaton, former mayor of L. A. and owner of Long Valley where Crowley Lake is now.]

After leaving Wilson Canyon, Casey headed for Inyo County with the two kegs of tainted brandy. At Independence he negotiated a sale with a bootlegging establishment across from the county jail. With four hundred dollars in his pocket resulting from this transaction, he then proceeded to put as much distance between himself and Inyo County as a Model-T over rough roads would permit. Unfortunately for Casey, the proprietor of the place decided to sample the stuff, an act which he had neglected to do before Casey left with the cash. The purchaser took one swallow, and, believing that Casey had sold him two kegs of pure kerosene in place of brandy, became infuriated...told the sheriff, who when finding the kegs did contain alcohol promptly lodged the bootlegger in jail. [The *Inyo Independent*, May 19, 1923, reported he was caught with 20 gallons in his Buick. A roadblock at Lone Pine caught Casey, who was given six months in jail. Judge Probasco of Lone Pine fined Jones $500 or 1,000 days. "We finally got Jones; we were after him for a long time," said a county officer. The paper said Jones sold his Buick. Wortley said he had a truck. Casey made such a nuisance of himself in the county jail, he was let out early...before everyone went crazy. It was like "caging a grizzly."]

[He always needed money and in 1927 $1,000 had been paid to him by Inyoites to blow up the Los Angeles Aqueduct siphon at Noname Canyon. His old friends, Indian Tom and Ken Wortley, refused to help him and Jones huffed off. The following day the evening papers reported 350 feet of heavy steel siphon of the Los Angeles Agueduct torn apart in a canyon south of the Inyo County line. Someone as notorious as Casey Jones would have been a suspect had he not been the first to accept a well-paid job as one of several hundred guards hired by Los Angeles to protect the aqueduct from those "damned dynamiters."]

[After his protection was no longer needed, he went back into the bootleg business. Then having enough money for payoffs, he manufactured wine from wild grapes in Grapevine Canyon. Wortley said he had three stills hidden in the hills.]

The last time Wortley saw Jones was one night in Hoppie's Bar along Highway 14, just south of Brown. He was drunk and refused to go to bed and sober up. The next day when Wortley stopped at Hoppie's, he was told Casey was dead, a victim of drinking too much of his own bootleg whiskey. Aqueduct workers found his body pinned beneath his car in the bottom of Grapevine Wash. So ended the life of a musician, miner, trapper, moonshiner, bootlegger and con-artist.

Perhaps some consolations may be found in this free-spirited 19th century man finishing his life at the end of the Roaring Twenties, a life spent uninhibited by social mores and legal restrictions. One can only imagine how he would have operated in the mid-twentieth century.

CHAPTER 9

THOSE MINERS WILL TAKE ANYTHING—PROSTITUTION

Red Mountain Pros

Miners from Boron, Indian Wells (by Ridgecrest) and Trona went to wide-open Red Mountain. In Red Mountain, the hustle was on.

Sell the miners cheap expensive moonshine, or was it expensive cheap moonshine? Get them to buy a meal, do some gambling and buy a whore for a quickie. One can still see several sets of cribs that prostitutes used in the 1920s up to the end of the 1940s. Tunnels ran from the Owl and the Silver Dollar and other clubs of the day. These escape and hiding tunnels remain in town but most are sealed off. The Owl, now preserved as a bed and breakfast, takes pride in ringing its buzzer, used in the old days in case of surprise raids and as signals to the girls out in back at the cribs. The Owl in Red Mountain in 1995 obtained its call light back after it had disappeared. It was electrically operated with eight marks and one arrow that moved and could be lit up when crib four was ready or when Suzie in crib seven was available. A man would buy a few drinks (moonshine usually) and wait for the next girl available or for Suzie. When the arrow pointed to seven and lit up, he got to occupy crib seven for a few minutes.

San Bernardino County made few raids and federal agents made even fewer. The tunnels were really not needed. Gambling, drinking and prostitution became synonymous with Red Mountain.

During the early part of the depression, when things were bad all over, things were bad in this small mining town along the Barstow-Lone Pine Road. One former miner used to see a normally cheerful prostitute almost every morning, doing her shopping, having her breakfast before she went to bed to rest during the day. One morning she was gloomy, no exuberance emanating from her. "What's the matter with you this morning, Rose?" he asked her.

"Things are rough all over. For me too. See this body, I got a million dollars worth of assets and I can't get ten cents for it!"

David Gunn, a retired borax miner, said some of these girls were as pretty as could be, young girls from fine families, it looked like, beautiful girls from Utah, sweet-looking young girls from northern California and Oregon. He wondered how they could have gotten into that business.

Some, however, were not too "good looking" because they had been around the circuit. They worked in Los Angeles, Gunn said, then spent time in the San Bernardino area, then maybe Bakersfield. Finally they would come out to Red Mountain 'cause "Those miners would take anything."

Boomers at Red Mountain
as told by David Gunn, Boron

The three towns in the Red Mountain area were Red Mountain, Randsburg and Johannesburg. By agreement, almost miner's common law, Johannesburg was the family town, a church, store, school, family homes—very peaceful. Randsburg had families and some saloons but few ladies of the street.

Red Mountain had open house to all and to anything. The Red Mountain miners were called "boomers" because Red Mountain was a boom town. It was called Inn City at one time, changed to "Sin City." At the height of prohibition the miners frequently said, "Let's go to 'Gin Town'" after work. Anything went. The only reason someone might be locked up was for damaging a bar. Then the constable, paid by the saloon and brothel owners, took a prisoner over to Randsburg and locked him up in the cement jail. He'd be questioned: "Where do you work?"

"At the borax plant."

"When is your next shift?"

"Seven a.m."

"Okay, we'll lock you up and wake you up at 5:00 a.m., plenty of time to get back to work."

And they did.

Saloons lined the main street of Red Mountain, all wide open during prohibition. Each had three-four girls working for them. It was an island by itself. None was ever knocked over as far as I know. You could do anything you wanted as long as you were big enough.

Imagine my astonishment as I saw Red Mountain for the first time. I came from a strict Scotch Presbyterian town in Canada. On Sunday we couldn't even play baseball. The drug stores weren't even open on Sunday. Then to come into Red Mountain off the swing shift and see it wide open all night long, Sundays too—that was something.

You could buy a couple drinks of liquor, moonshine wholesaled up there by Dan Murphy, maybe 50 cents a shot, buy the girls a couple and take them to the little rooms in the back. They were good-looking girls—from 18-24 wasting their lives at $3.00 a trick, dropping down to $2.00 during the depression. These girls were mostly white, a few Mexicans, no blacks. A lot came from Utah strangely enough.

Miners could also buy gallons or half gallons of whiskey at Red Mountain (½ gallon for $5, gallon $8). Almost all the miners had a bottle. It was moonshine but cut, flavored and colored. It was good stuff. One group of miners in a bunkhouse at the borax mine chipped in to buy a 15-gallon keg of whiskey. After work, they'd take a drink or two. If somebody else needed a drink, he'd just come in and help himself. No one would steal anything. A man could leave his pay on the table, no one would touch it.

The Saturday night dances, held at the Muroc school house, showed the same type of trust. They'd dance and then go out to the car and have a drink. I had a gallon setting on the running board all night. Anyone could take a swig of it but no one would steal the bottle.

Those boomers worked hard, seven days a week, no days off, and they played hard. They often had fights in Red Mountain with the miners from Searles Lake, Trona.

The miners were big-hearted too. One family was down and out. A miner passed around the hat at the chow line and in just a few minutes collected over $200. With pay in those days $4.50 a day, $200 was a lot of money.

A boomer could come into a mining camp and have room and board for a day or so. He usually knew someone he had worked with at some other mine. Even during the depression when wages were cut, a wandering miner was welcomed. If there was a job, he could start working. If not or if he was just traveling through, he could count on free meals and a bunk.

Since there were no vacations or days off, a miner might want to move on after working for a few months or even years. He'd just say to the foreman or owner, "Well, she's deep enough!" The boomer drew his pay and moved on.

Down the Line
as told by Allen Lehman, Crescent City

In Crescent City, during prohibition, we had seven houses of prostitution, lower class. They were located in little shanties south of town, over the bridge, where Del Norte Ice Plant is. They were right there. We used to call them "across the bridge" or "down the line."

They all sold whiskey. The madam would have two or three little shot glasses inside her apron or down in the pocket of her dress on one side and a pint of whiskey, jackass, on the other side. So you'd go in there and she'd give you a glass, pour you a drink. You'd drink it and give her back the glass. I never saw a sanitary problem. I think that stuff was so damn strong that it would kill any bugs that might be transmitted from one person to another.

The price then for the girls was $2.00. I'm not kidding you one bit; they had some of the prettiest damn little girls. I never could understand, some of those kids getting involved in that racket. But they did. I remember one incident: Two blonde sisters that came down from Coos Bay, called Marshfield at that time. They were pretty, pretty little girls. Well, I used to deliver ice there for my father. We always delivered ice in the day time, naturally and the girls never worked much in the day time, usually at night. I remember going to house number one. The madam was Mildred, her pimp Curt. Curt is still living in Crescent City, Frank Curtis, but he went by Curt. He admits it today.

Anyway I went down there delivering ice this day and one of the sisters was lying on a cot on a pad in the kitchen. It was wintertime and it was cold. Crescent City can have some awful rough weather, you know, rain, 115 inches of rain. Blow! The houses were right on the beach, getting the full force of the southwesters.

I don't remember her name. I said, "What's the matter?"

"I'm not feeling well," she said.

Each time I'd deliver ice she'd be there. I said to Mildred, "What's the matter?"

She said, "She's going to have an operation tomorrow."

We had a doctor there, name of Dr. Fine. The Fine Bridge in Crescent City over Smith River is named after him, wonderful old fellow. He was our only surgeon for years here. He operated on her. I happen to know the nurse. The hospital here was just a little old house, hardly anything. I delivered ice there too.

This nurse told me that Dr. Fine opened this girl, removed everything she had. She was so sick with gonorrhea that it was a mass of puss.

It took her time to recuperate, but she went back into the business.

The girls in those days worked the circuit. There wasn't any organized crime deal involved like there is in prostitution today. They're kinda in a circuit: Coos Bay, Eureka, Astoria, up and down the coast here. They'd stay in a place three-four months and move on.

About a year and a half later, I saw her and I couldn't even recognize her. I don't know how she ever did any business in a house of prostitution. She was probably then only 23-24 years old. That racket is awfully damn hard on a woman. She deteriorated—she looked like hell!

I'll tell you another experience in Eureka. They had lots of houses there because those were the days of loggin' in Eureka. Loggers lived well out in the woods and they never came to town in the week. They got to town on the loggin' trains, usually on Saturday and Sunday. In the beginning there was only one day off. They worked six days, ten hours a day in the loggin' racket when I was a kid.

There was a traveling salesman, Cal Overy, sold Morrill Meat products. He was a good friend of mine. I had to go to Eureka to buy a bunch of groceries and stuff and I ran into him. He wasn't married either. He said, "Al, let's go to the whorehouse and have a drink."

I said, "Okay, Cal." We went down an alley right between Second Avenue and Third Street. Every other door was a girlie house; most of them you had to go upstairs. Anyway, the madam in this place was a very striking person about 36-38 years old. I'm 10-11-12 years younger than her. Even at my young age, she looked great. In that time of life somebody 10-15 years older than you seemed like they're older than Methuselah.

We went up in a little parlor which was not a high-class place at all. Saturday, Eureka was full of loggers, tough guys that came in on the train. They came in from Blue Lake, Bell, all those places. They came in for a Saturday night of whoopie.

Anyway we were sitting in the parlor having a drink. Pretty soon we heard the God damndest scream, four-five doors down a little hall to the rooms the girls took the fellows. Scream! Scream!

The madam got up and went down and a great big logger that couldn't handle his booze was beating the hell out of this little whore. She finally got out of that room and came down the hallway, with the madam and blood running out of her.

Cal said, "We'd better get out of here. There's going to be trouble here."

We left. About a couple three months later, why, I was in the same place with a couple other friends having a drink or two. I asked the madam what transpired.

She said, "He was a prince, a prince of a fellow sober, but a son of a bitch drunk." He's got full of that wild "red eye," rot gut, rotten bootleg whiskey and he'd [gone] berserk.

We had seven houses in Crescent City and I can tell you this: If characters ever was, the madams in those places were characters. Some of them were the finest people, the most kind-hearted people you ever met. I knew them through business. My father and I ran a little butcher shop and a few groceries. Five out of the seven traded with us. In those days everything was delivery, you know. My father built a small ice plant in Crescent City. It wasn't the first one, but it was the first of any consequence 'cause we could make enough ice to sell a couple thousands pounds a day. We did that in conjunction with our refrigeration. It didn't take any more processing or anything. We just made it. We got a penny a pound which was unheard of. In San Francisco you could get 1000 pounds for a dollar. Here with such a small volume, we couldn't do it. All the madams bought little oak ice chests, ice boxes. So as a young fellow, I delivered about twice a week to the girls "on the line." I knew them; I frequented them mainly only under that condition.

Disease was very prevalent here in those days; gonorrhea and syphilis and I didn't want any of that, so I stayed away from these places. In that respect I noticed some of my friends, or people I knew, they weren't necessarily my friends, had contracted some diseases down there.

The problems we went through those days. There wasn't any penicillin; there was hardly any effective medicine. Therefore I never got involved. I was friends with them all, patted them on the fanny and said what a nice girl and all that, but as far as going to bed with them—No!

The little houses in Crescent City were small; the little cubby hole that you went in with the girls was small, a little cot in it, about all it was. I remember the names of some of the madams: Gerry, in house number three. She had her house full of monkeys and parrots. She was quite a character. Her pimp was—I can't think of his name but I knew him well. He's still living in Nevada City. The next house was Florence, a very charming looking dark-haired woman. She was on dope. Finally she just disintegrated. She just went. When she came here and took over house number four, she was fine looking. I remember in a period of two years or so this Florence—she didn't work herself; she had two or three girls; course she started out working in her younger days—you could see something change in her mentally and physically and everything. She left here and I did hear she passed away shortly afterwards.

Prostitution was never a bother. There was a lot of it. Fact of the matter was, it existed until we entered the war with Japan. Japan floated some balloon bombs and they landed around the mountains here at night. I heard some of them. That scare of Japan invading the west coast made us realize we were very vulnerable to the landing. We patrolled the beach ourselves on foot for 14 miles, six or seven months, a group of us civilian guerrillas. Then the government sent in about 80 Coast Guard boys and horses. They patrolled on horses. When they sent the boys here, we had seven girlie houses and the Coast Guard came and closed them all up. So it would be 1942 that they closed the whorehouses here in Crescent City.

The Girls of Eureka
as told by Norton Steenfott, Eureka

The girls who came to Eureka to work had to report to the police station. Police took down a description of where they came from and if they had a record. Then the girls had to have a slide [physical] every 30 days. They had to have a blood test every 60 days. If a girl didn't get it, she couldn't work. She had to report to the police station before she went from one place to another. The madams went along with it, went along with all the regulations of the city. The prostitutes in those days cost $2.00, a good woman, better than what you have around here now.

When Eureka was founded, one section belonged to two brothers. They divided the section. In these days the houses of prostitution were called on the old maps "female boarding houses." It seemed that all the female boarding houses were in one half of one section downtown, owned by one brother. He was in the land business, of course. That was the only business we could ever find him in but all the female boarding houses were in his section.

There has always been a state law against prostitution but it was semi-legal in Eureka. The laws were more lax. In Eureka there probably weren't laws on the books regulating prostitution, but there were rules the police department used to regulate the business. They operated well up until the time of World War II, when the government moved in stopping all houses of prostitution or Eureka would be put out of bounds. After the war it came back but the state attorney general's office started enforcing state laws.

In the early days in the lower part of town, one house had good quality clientele, politicians for examples. The madam had everyone sign a book. Nobody bothered her. They couldn't do anything to her because she had their names. There was an emergency where she had to go to the hospital. When she came back from the hospital, she found out someone broke into her house and stole the book. Shortly after she was closed down. As long as she had "that black book," she was left alone.

Rio Dell Fights for Its Ladies

For the second time raiders hit the old Scatena place in Wildwood (Rio Dell). They arrested Mabel LaRue and Mary Davis, "inmates of the house of ill fame," for selling wine and jackass. They locked the place up but did not catch the men who escaped in the back, some leaving barefooted and hatless. A few of these might have had some explaining to do to the little women when they returned home sans part of their clothing.

After the first raid on this property, San Francisco detectives [probably prohibition agents] Clarence Stitt and Ernest Hendricks received some rough treatment in the pool hall in Rio Dell. Several men "mobbed" them. V. Peccia, an ex-con, and A. Giorgia (Croigia ?) were charged with assault to murder. It seemed as if the local boys felt emotionally protective over their own. These ladies may be prostitutes but they were their whores, and big city officers should leave them alone and mind their own business.[1]

Scarlet Row
excerpts from "A History of Prostitution in Jackson, California"
by Linzy Hudson[2]

Mami said she sold her business years ago to men who bootlegged and ran girls. "Her buyers became involved in gambling and bootlegging and Jackson was a big bootlegging town in the prohibition days." Mami married a blacksmith in Missouri. He came to California to find a good job and then send for his wife. He sent for his wife Mami, but the home he bought was in the center of the redlight district on Poverty Hill in Jackson. He had a house, not a home. She was shocked, but accepted the business and later ran the place after her husband died.

Most of the business came from ranchers and in the earlier days from miners. From Nevada came the idea of tokens and all the houses started using them. Mami sold "her coins for $10 which included a bath, shave, drink, and company for the night." Mami said, "The shave and bath was for the girl as much as for the customer." Sam's Place, down the street from hers, was the first to use the coins.

Poverty Hill was like another town. Wooden buildings, across the creek, usually with liquor served downstairs and women upstairs. A sign hung on the front with a red lantern hanging near the sign—making the street glow red at night. Another former girl said, "In those days they were more affectionately known as Scarlet Row."

Poker City—Tracy, California
by Pat Craig
excerpts from *Tracy Centennial Edition*, September 6, 1978

When Tracy was called "Poker City and a man's pleasure was limited only by the bankroll in his wallet, "every night was like New Year's Eve; the lights, the noise the crowds—24 hours a day. It was like the beach at Santa Cruz. Trains pulled into the center of town day and night. And the action-craving rails [railroad workers] hit the streets, with a pocketful of cash and a craving for adventure.

They'd head over to Charlie Clark's Terminal Grill or to the Central Club for poker and pan. There were slot machines in just about every place in town—"common as weeds." Other places featured games for those who wanted action with dice, the roulette wheel, or the Chinese lottery [keno]. And south of the high iron, those with a taste for something more than gambling could stop in any of a half-dozen Southside bordellos for an evening of adventure.

A little booze with your fun? No problem, even during prohibition, booze flowed like water around Poker City. It was available from bootleggers and across the counter—most of it was swill, old-timers recall.

"Jackass, we used to call it. It wasn't more than sugar alcohol that you could buy for five bucks a gallon," an old-timer says. "That was most of it, but then there was the stuff made by Arch Brown. I don't think I ever tasted anything as smooth as that then or since then. It was made out of spring water."

Strangely, Tracy's major card club didn't serve booze at the tables.

Hooch, jackass or not, was available at most of the local bordellos. Old-timers say Hazel's was the top place. Her house on First Street had "the best girls—really first class." Hazel Price is what she called herself but her legal name was Amelia Broedel. She was a "whore with a heart of gold," giving cash to the scouts, building funds, Christmas food drives, pregnant women, and hard luck guys. "A lot of people on the Southside would have gone hungry if it hadn't been for Hazel. Christmastime she'd take a bunch of turkeys and give 'em away."

Hazel earned most of her money a buck at a time, according to old-timers. The price of a Poker City bordello adventure was $3.00, a dollar for Hazel and two for the girls. "Hazel would have as many as 16 girls in the heyday. These girls would be here 30-60 days, and then they'd be gone," the old-timer says. "I think the madams kind of had a union, the girls would go from one place to another. [If changes were not made] the merchandise would begin to get, not faded but kind of stale, because the same 200 or so rails would be coming from the Bay area..."

"There was no hurry, no pressure. You could go into Hazel's and spend some time," the man says. "The girls would come up to you and ask you to buy them a drink."

Quite often, the visitors to Hazel's could listen to music in the parlor room. The ragtime tunes were supplied by Paul Nutting, a big fat guy from Oakland. Sometimes, there would be a three-piece band to entertain visitors to Hazel's. But the real action took place downstairs in little bedrooms called cribs.

Throughout the state prostitution was tied in with bootlegging and sometimes with gambling. The hustle was always on, the drive to get that extra dollar or change or tip from the customer, the sale of a cold beer or shot of whiskey [or tea] for the lady. Variations of the theme played slightly differently but the basic theme was the same: Sell the product or the service and don't get caught.

Sally's Place
as told by anonymous

I was in Sally Stanford's house in San Francisco about 1927-28. It was the most parlor looking thing I've ever seen in my life, plush. It was between Nob Hill and Van Ness Avenues. I don't remember the exact street. That's once I did frankly get tangled up in a whorehouse, but fortunately I never had any ill effect from it.

It was a big Victorian-type house, about three stories. I went to San Francisco one time and had a Buick Master. I tore the transmission out getting off the ferry from Sausalito. You had to go down and up the ramp and I rammed it too much. I turned it in on a Pierce Arrow Roadster. If I had that car today, it would be worth 25,000-30,000 bucks.

The fellow who sold it to me was so elated, think I paid $2,200 or so for it. So after I made the deal with him on this car he said, "Would you like a drink?" and I had sampled drinks a little bit, not very much but some.

I said, "Okay."

He took me in his car in an alley, two or three blocks off Van Ness in San Francisco. That's why they called them blind pigs: so many of them were in seedy areas. We had a drink or two and finally he said, "Let's go to the Embassy!"

I didn't know anything about the Embassy. We looked through the little peep hole. The guy knew him. We went in. It was just like modern cabaret only not so large. There were quite a lot of people in there, bands playing away and

I had a couple-three more drinks, probably the first time I really felt the extreme effects of alcohol, not drunk but I felt it.

"Let's go to the whorehouse?" he asked.

"Okay with me," I answered.

He had too much to drink so he left the car and called a cab. We went down and up those hills and around. I didn't know where we were, not knowing San Francisco at the time.

We finally came to a big house and parked at the bottom of it. We got out, knocked on a nice door. It was one story down from the street. A very large colored lady came to the door, with a little white apron and a black satinish dress. She said, "Hello there, Ted. How are you?"

"Oh, I'm fine."

"Come right in, Ted, and who's this gentleman you have with you?"

He said, "This is Mr. _____."

We walked in, up a stairway, into quite a large room, living room of a well-to-do guy, with a grand piano, nice furniture, real nice furniture.

"Gentlemen, will you all just 'cuse me for a minute or two?"

"Okay," Ted said.

Maybe in 20 seconds in came two of the prettiest, good looking ladies you *ever* saw in your life. And they were well dressed, nicely dressed, well groomed.

The colored lady came back, "Gentlemen, would you all like something nice to drink?"

"Sure," said Ted, "set it up for us."

She brought in the traditional four glasses on a tray. They were brown, but I noticed that two of them were sitting on that side and two were sitting on this side. She gave Ted and I the two on this side and the girls the two on the other side. And I know damn well that, I found out later, it was just colored tea. That's all the girls could take, all they were allowed to take.

After a little time—these girls carried on a sensible conversation, there was nothing rough about them, no nasty talk. I, by golly, bought a drink, one dollar a drink, and four bits was most at speakeasies, fifty cents a shot. In this place it cost $4.00 a crack and of course you had to tip the girls.

Pretty soon this very striking lady came in, a little on the heavy side. She knew Ted. He introduced me to her. And it was Sally Stanford but I didn't know Sally Stanford from Adam's old fox. He told me later.

In about three or four minutes the girls got up and excused themselves and left and not over 10 seconds came two more equally as nice looking. I don't think either of them was over 20-21 years old. We had another round of drinks. So that made four drinks after maybe three or four before and I can almost truthfully say that was the first intoxication situation I'd ever been into. But I wasn't bad. I mean I could still walk. After that drink Ted took this little girl and said, "Come on, honey."

"Okay,' she said.

They left, went through a nice big tall mahogany door.

So I said to this one girl, "Well, I guess we'd better follow suit."

On the way up the stairs she said, "What's your name?"

I said, "Jimmy."

So we get up into a very clean, well-groomed, put-together room.

"Jimmy, is this going to be a trick or an all-night piece?"

By this time it was probably ten or eleven o'clock at night, you see.

"Well, what about it? I'm not too familiar with this thing."

"Well," she said, "a trick is five dollars; all night is $20. I wish you would stay all night."

"Well, okay."

It would be $20 for the madam; anything I would give her beyond that she'd get. That's the assumption I got.

I stayed all night. We got into the goddamn shower and had a hell of a nice shower. She said, "You know, Jimmy, I have three days off. I work four days and get three off." Her name was Thelma, she told me.

"I have a date in San Jose tomorrow, a dinner with a friend, nice restaurant. Why don't you go with me?"

I had told her information about myself, about not being married.

I didn't feel quite as good in the morning as I did the last night with that moonshine—didn't feel too good.

She rang a cord. I couldn't hear anything but apparently it made a noise some place. In came another black lady, not the same one as the night before. Thelma told her something and soon she brought me an eggnog thing and I noticed there was booze in it. After I drank that I felt better. So I consented that night that I would go to San Jose with her with this brand new beautiful desert sand Pierce Arrow Roadster. I wanted to try that damn thing out.

San Jose at that time was quite a bit further than it is now. You went through every town. Anyway we went to a house. There were two or three fellows, three or four girls. She introduced me to all of them. Then some guy was celebrating something, I don't remember what. He invited all of us to a dinner in a restaurant in a banquet room that was exclusive, not open to the public. I think he was a bootlegger or a high class pimp. I don't know which. They served a drink or two more and that mellowed me again a little bit. I accepted. We went to this place and had dinner. It turned out to be maybe six or seven women and six or seven men. Thelma told me later every fellow there was a pimp and every girl there was a whore, prostitute. Anyway it was quite a time. By golly they had a little jazz band, everybody danced. There wasn't any vulgarity no place. No vulgarity involved in it, you know. They danced the Charleston. I remember the girls kicking their legs—they were very attractive.

I had occasion then to go down to San Francisco for business deals every two months. Of course I'd always look up Thelma. The second time down she wanted to get out of that racket, get married and have a family. I enjoyed her a lot but I couldn't give her that. So anyway I came back home after about the third time and became associated with a girl in town here.

I'd go to these places but I was always scared. I had friends who had been infected with syphilis and gonorrhea. In those days there were damn few cures for it.

In San Francisco, I would go there [whorehouses] 'cause you could have a drink or two there.

Down on Mission Street there was a place during prohibition times. I'm sure there were 50-60 girls there. A trick was two bucks. They'd give you 10-15 minutes. They'd be 10-15 girls, you take your pick. I would stay in the bigger room where the bar was, where they served the drinks. Some of my friends would go with the girls, a couple of them regretting it very much and ended their _____[?] [inaudible on the tape.] Two bucks.

Doubling Profits
as told by anonymous

There was a fellow on Green Street in San Francisco who was a few years older than me. That was on the north side of Green, between Stockton and Powell. He was said to be quite a handsome fellow. His father had a speak-easy there on Green in his basement.

Well, the old man would send his son out to pick up the prettiest blond he could find. She'd be brought back, given all the free drinks she wanted until she passed out.

Then she'd be hauled to a cot in the backroom and when men came in for a drink, they could screw her for two bits or half a dollar—which the old man got, anyway. So she got screwed and the old man made a double profit off the whole thing.

Save Your Nickels and Dimes
as told by William Cullen, San Mateo

If a john or customer wanted a drink, the whorehouse in San Francisco provided him with one. The cost of the girls was two dollars during most of the prohibition days. The famous Mae West saying, "Save your nickels and dimes, get $2.00 and come up and see me sometime," came from those days.

After the first World War, there started a small depression. From the 30th of June, 1919, things began to peter out. There wasn't any money to be made. That's when the $2.00 prostitutes came along. From then to Hoover's time that was the going rate for lower-level women. When Hoover came in and the real depression began, prices went for whatever they could get. During all this early time (January 1920 to about June 1921) when things got worse, the whorehouses would always get raided, always get put away.

They practically closed up the North Beach district in San Francisco. The old Bella Donna, on Pacific between Montgomery and Kearney, the prostitutes used to sit in the window showing their wares. But when prohibition really came on, the people complained about being robbed. If a customer laid down a $20.00 bill, I don't care what he was buying, a drink or a girl, he'd get a dollar change. The people who patronized those houses complained.

These were practically closed until they became more "honest"—about 1922. Then there was a Chinese restaurant on the corner of Montgomery, not new Montgomery, and Pacific on the northwest corner called Fing Fat and here's what was going on. This had to be dope. It couldn't be anything else. A guy would come out of one of the those red light houses and come in and get a saucer with a potato in it and take it back to the houses. The restaurant was legitimate but anytime you would see a number of people come out with a boiled potato (I'd say a boiled potato.) and carry it back in a salad bowl. This was how they got that dope from the Chinese to the house of prostitution.

One night I was sitting in the restaurant and the Chinese were going every which way. We were playing keno, only it was called "Chinese Lottery." That's where I learned how to play it and learned to like the game. You could play a ten spot ticket for a dime or more. If you caught all the ten spots you could win $386.00. A ticket known as a nine spot cost 35 cents. If you caught all nine, $772 for only 35 cents. You could double it for 70 cents or triple it for $1.05. There were 80 numbers on a ticket. It was later called "horse race" and later keno in Nevada but it came from the Chinese.

No Chinese that I know of bootlegged.

The Italians sold the wine. When a sailor or soldier wanted wine, we could buy a quart bottle of wine for 65 cents and sell it to the soldiers for $1.00. The house made the extra money on alcohol if a john wanted a drink. The madam usually sent out for the alcohol.

On 1325 Stockton Street, Pansy Burr at the Fairfield Hotel sent out (for booze) but she didn't sell it herself. The police wouldn't shake them down. Everybody in the North Beach district who ran prostitution or bootlegged had to pay off the patrolman. Patrolmen in my district would meet each night on the corner of Grand Avenue and Pacific where they changed the guard and divided the money. Every night! Between 12:30 and 1:00 o'clock.

They collected by the night or the week, not by the month because if anything happened the department would shuffle the police around, put a new captain in the precinct, but they all knew what was going on.

The shake-down ran from $2.00 to $10.00 a night, depending on the kind of place. Perhaps that's why some houses didn't sell booze. They would have been shaken-down for two vices instead of one.

Drew Straws to Go to Flora's

Perhaps the most famous California prostitute was Flora—the lady in John Steinbeck's *Cannery Row* and *Sweet Thursday.* Flora was the noted lady in Monterey. She was of Portuguese descent, according to Salinas historian George Robinson who interviewed old-timers. Flora married Texas cowboy Joe Woods. When Woods disappeared, Flora had to make a living for herself and her daughter, first as a call girl and then as a madam. She eventually had the best house in Cannery Row, The Lone Star, and owned a second house, the Golden Stairs, which was across from Jock's Ball Park, that ironically has the motto "Clean sports make a clean town." Her third house was in east side of town called Seaside. Jimmy Costello told Robinson the following: "I worked at a Coca-Cola place in high school and college. When a call came in from the Lone Star, we'd fight over it. We even drew straws to see which of us delivers. One day I won and went down there and one of the girls was behind a long bar that was in front of the restaurant part of the place. She said, 'I'll sign for it.'"

"'No, Flora always pays cash.' I went back out of this main room. Flora was wearing some lacy negligee. When she got the money, she asked questions like how's your family, how's your uncle?"

George Sparkie, in 1928, was also in high school, but had a job that paid $25-30 to catch squid. On his first try to get into the Lone Star, he was turned down because Flora was a midwife and told Sparkie that she helped deliver him. Later he grew a beard for two days and got to charge what he wanted, girls or booze. Sparkie said Flora at that time weighed about 300 pounds. He said the Lone Star was changed to the Bear Flag and was right across Dr. Rickett's lab, Steinbeck's friend and character Doc in *Cannery Row* and *Sweet Thursday.*

One girl interviewed by Robinson was "Mary" because she did not want her real name used. She also said Flora entertained gentlemen across from Ed Rickett's lab on Ocean Front Street. "Flora sat on the left side of the bar, could hardly fit on the stool, 300 pounds, but a wonderful person to work for. They sold drinks. A lot of fellows just came in to drink and chat with us.

"She had a side door. Quite a few gentlemen came in the side door, not feeling they should enter the front door. If they made an appointment, we'd meet at the side door. They didn't want their wives to know. There was no disrespect. Flora was free with her donations, generous with us gals. I came from a big family, never had good clothes. For the first time I could buy fancy clothes.

"The building was one story, the front bar being the reception area. The back bar was the entrance to several small bedrooms, neat and clean, but nothing fancy. She never had less than five girls, sometimes ten when the fish were running or a convention going on. We moved around, King City, Salinas—customers wanted a change. We always had one or two of us on duty. In the day we walked the beach. If we met a john, we never recognized him in public."

As with so many brothels in California, when World War II came along, the government threatened to put cities off limits if they did not close their houses. Since the army established Fort Ord nearby, Monterey cleaned up the image of the city, and a little history started to fade.

Trenary's Place
as told by David Gunn, Boron

When girls were well used in one town, they were what we would call now "recycled." They were sent to San Bernardino or Fresno or Bakersfield. They made a circuit so there would always be fresh (so to speak) women in a brothel. And when they were really used or used up, they were sent to the mining camps—for those desert miners, being isolated, working under extreme heat in the summer and cold in the winter, being away from large supplies of water and perhaps just plain being desperate—many miners were not too fussy.

Actually even miners drew the line sometimes. They didn't always just "take anything." Many considered Charlie Trenary, the founder of Boron, as having less than admirable qualities. About 35 miles from the Atolia-Red Mountain-Randsburg-Johannesburg mining center, Trenary had his little desert store, gas station and whorehouse. He had so little respect and trust that the miners preferred to travel to Red Mountain. His bootleg liquor could not be counted upon as being pure. Some claimed he adulterated it, i.e., watered it. He sold it but not usually much to miners who knew him.

Behind his frame building, home and store, where the present Security Bank is now in Boron (1980), he had a couple rooms for his girls, two cubby holes each—four cribs. He cheated the girls, took money from them. If they left, he'd obtain more from Los Angeles and exploit them. One example of his endless list of nefarious activities is his use of the punch board chance for one of his girls. The punch board was a rectangular board with 100 little holes. For 25¢, a miner or traveler chose to punch out a round depression. Out the other side came a paper. The miner unrolled the paper to see if he won 50¢ up to $10.00 for his 25¢ investment. Usually nothing. This form of gambling was illegal in California, but was a popular way for a business to earn extra money and a chance to obtain a little extra from the workingman's paycheck or an extra 25¢ from a traveler who just wanted a cup of coffee and a sandwich.

Trenary used the punch board for a chance on one of his girls—no cash outlay for prizes. It didn't take the girls too long to see that he was making 90 percent profit and the girls nothing. They objected to this scheme.

Trenary never was convicted during the prohibition days of selling his questionable and watered-down moonshine. Yet, after repeal and selling of liquor was legal, Trenary continued to sell moonshine without a license, thus avoiding taxes. He was caught.

Despite losing most of his mining trade, he had plenty of tourist and business travelers on this long stretch of dry desert from Barstow to Mojave. He bought some property, subdivided and sold Boron lots.

The Father of Boron—some old timer said as he shook his head.

Well, as other old miners said, "She's deep enough!" at least for this chapter.

CHAPTER 10

DRY HUMOR

Not only did Californians face prohibition with one eye closed, the her red, but people from the Golden State maintained a sense of humor, humor that exaggerated the silliness and the seriousness of those on one side or the other (wet or dry). Californians smiled through these confusing days of prohibition, smiled through exciting days of the "Roaring Twenties" and even laughed through the frustrating days of the early depression years.

Since humor of any age reflects that age, alludes to incidents of the times, creates metaphors and hyperbole out of its context, humor helps readers understand the bootlegging years. Several jokes have to be read a few times to catch double meanings of words, innuendoes and allusions. A few have some meanings hidden by the ages. Consequently this chapter can be savored for several readings.

A New Sensation

"Well after next July we won't be able to take a drink except on the sly."

"That's no hardship. I've led an open life so long now under government inspection that it will be a pleasure to practice deceit in any form."

—January 4, 1919, *San Rafael* Weekly *Independent*

A woman in 1919 entered a drug store. "I'ze wants five pounds of Vaseline," she said.

"Five pounds! How come?" asked the druggist.

"Haven't you heard?" she answered. "The country's goin' bone dry."

—Anonymous

Now that the states have voted the country dry, *water* you going to do about it?

January 25, 1919, *San Mateo News-Leader*

A drunk longshoreman, Paddy Hogan, with too much overflow in the bilge, wandered around Daly City. John Basskey, a Daly City teamster, found him in his chicken coop with a dead chicken and rabbit in his hands. Dressed in a nightshirt, holding a shotgun, Basskey kept Hogan until officer A. L. Hilton arrived.

"You got no evidence against me," Hogan said to the policeman.

"How about the chicken in your hand with his head off?"
After spending the rest of the night in jail, Justice of Peace Ellis C. Johnson gave him 24 hours to replace the animals. Hogan complied.
—January 29, 1919, *San Mateo News-Leader*

The Prohibitionists are spending money like a drunken sailor on shore.
—October 7, 1921, Letter from T. M. Wright

There are two reasons for a man to have a line across his nose: He wears glasses or he drinks whiskey out of a fruit jar.
—Henry James, Barstow

10,000 Jews are making booze
With government permission
To fill the needs of a million Swedes
That voted for prohibition.
—Mike Pollard, Dos Palos

The constable may not be dishonest, but there was a lot he didn't see.
—Artie Williams, Deputy Constable, Dos Palos

The police chief wasn't crooked; he just had bad eyesight.
—Artie Williams, Deputy Constable, Dos Palos

"Water is only good to wash your feet"—quotation from a man on his death bed after receiving communion.
—Father Richard Prendiville, Fairfax

Many a secret has come out
As many a secret will
But where de moonshine cometh
Is sho'a secret still.
—Verse on the window of Totter's Pool Room
January 24, 1924, *Oceanside Blade*

The lingering sunset across the plain,
Kissed the rear end of the Trona train
And shone on the Ford that was bound in
With two flat tires and load of gin.
—February 28, 1925, *The Trona Pot-Ash*

Pome [sic]
>   Out here in dear old Trona,
>   Where everybody has the blues,
>   Where Austin and Jamieson write poems,
>   And the officers steal the booze.
>   The bunk house full of synthetic gin,
>   The populace keeps well juiced;
>   And the Pan Room keeps a panning
>   Up where the pigeons roost.

—April 25, 1925, *The Trona Pot-Ash*

"K. O. Drops"
"Even on the Arid Desert"
by Bella Donna
The first business of those who investigate an automobile accident is to look for the bottle.

—May 9, 1925, *The Trona Pot-Ash*

"K. O. Drops"
>   Little smells of cigarettes,
>   Little smells of gin,
>   Tell a nosey Daddy
>   Where his girl has been.

—July 11, 1925, *The Trona Pot-Ash*

"K. O. Drops"
"Hot Blasts from the Mojave"
by Bella Donna
Chicken Liquor—Four drinks and don't care where you lay.

One thing that can't be preserved in alcohol is a secret.

"Going to the dance tonight?"
"Naw, I'm gonna get drunk at home."

—August 1, 1925, *The Trona Pot-Ash*

You will never take Prohibition out of politics so long as the Anti-Saloon League remains in.

—August 6, 1927, *The Trona Pot-Ash*

If publishing anti-Communistic articles encouraged Communism, why does not publishing anti-religious articles encourage religion?

—August 6, 1927, *The Trona Pot-Ash*

A dozen empty bottles is a sad case.
—January 2, 1928, *The Corona Daily Independent*

A drunk passing a subway excavation said to the men in the pit, "Shay, watcha doin' down there?"
"We're building a subway."
"How log is it goin't to built tha' subway?"
"Eight years," came the answer.
"Eight years! (Hic.) To 'ell with it. I'll take a taxicab."
—August 4, 192?, *Barstow Printer*

A typesetter took a snifter from an ice cold jug.
Drunk editor-wobbly on feet but head clear as a bell: Twenty-five cows, broke to work; 41 head of cultivators; 10 head of shoveling boars with scoops by side; 3 piano mares; 120 rods of canvas belting; better than new, De Laval cows with ice cream attachment; McCormick binder, in foul; Poland China, bobsled due to farrow in April; 14 head of chickens with grass seed attachment in good working order; 2 J. I. case riding heifers, good as new; spraying outfit can be ridden by children; 15 Billy goats, 70 bushel capacity, with spraying nozzle and other articles too numerous to mention.
—January 19, 1928, *Ontario Herald*

Prohibition may have made a few millionaires, but it has kept a few million from feeling like one.
—February 16, 1928, *Ontario Herald*

The Plutocrat
How times have changed. Today one of our fellow citizens regards himself as an employer of labor, merely because he has a lot of elderberries working for him in his cellar.
—February 16, 1928, *Ontario Herald*

"Don't Seem Genuine: There is something wrong when a lawyer advises you to avoid litigation or a doctor drinks to your good health."
—February 17,1928, *Tracy Press*

Frank Mariana had to pay off so many times for their bootlegging, Frank told Mrs. Helen Pollard of Dos Palos: "I wish they'd hurry and knock us off so I wouldn't have to worry about it."
—Helen Pollard, Dos Palos

They joked so much about the flivvers that Henry Ford brought out a new and better car. Apropos, they're joking a good deal about Prohibition.

—September 4, 1928, *Ontario Herald*

Among the supplies carried along on the Byrd expedition to the South Pole were listed: 1,000 gallons of grain alcohol, 400 gallons of rum, 100 gallons of port wine, 100 gallons of sherry, 100 quarts of champagne, 400 gallons of whiskey and say, did you read that thousands of volunteers had to be turned down?

—September 27,1928, *Ontario Herald*

Christmas shouldn't have anything to do with booze, but it brings out either the best or the worst in a fellow just the same.

—December 1928, *Ontario Herald*

After Hearst Publishers offered $25,000 for a solution to the prohibition problem, besides repeal, two editors of the *Sausalito News*, Stu Dunbar in a column called "Moonshine" and C. M. Bailey in "Letters of Bill Bailey" satirized prohibition, giving facts along with humor. The reader could tell they enjoyed their profession. Said Dunbar: "Some day some rich guy is going to offer a prize for the best way to find out if there is such an animal as prohibition."

"Now that the holidays are over, there is an empty gin bottle problem added to the used safety razor blade problem."

King of Afghanistan said if women should go with faces uncovered, it would cause a riot. "We have seen a woman like that in Sausalito." [This joke has nothing to do with prohibition but the author thought the citizens of Sausalito would appreciate the humor of their ancestors—or at least about one them.]

"Remember, Louie, if this [booze] kills me, tell the wife I died making the noble experiment."

—December 1928, *Sausalito News*

From "Letters from Bill Bailey:

"San Quentin and the 'Noble Experiment' grew up together."
Nine years ago they passed prohibition, telling the end of Demon Rum would mean no more use for prisons, they would fall or crumble. "Not to worry, the new east wing is built" with 570 new cells—all spoken for. Governor C. C. Young said the population of San Quentin and Folsom is the largest in history, increasing two years ago from 5,343 inmates to 6,227 in December 1928. Also the prediction that poverty would end, yet San Francisco's Community Chest

is larger than ever. Los Angeles crime was not much nine years ago, now in 1928, there were more murders than in London, a wet city nine times the size.

"More noble experiments—"the bridge they are planning [Golden Gate Bridge] will be sort of "a Bridge of Sighs between San Francisco and the jail-house [San Quentin].

Americans will stand for total prohibition as long as they can get all they want to drink—as at present."

And: "...prohibition is getting to be the most pestiferous thing that the USA ever had to contend with since George Washington crossed the Delaware."

Efforts to pass prohibition "overran the bag" as they say in baseball. In 1917 "true" temperance unwittingly became allies with "political" temperance workers. "In the meantime wets have their liquor and drys have their law."

"Moonshine: A San Francisco woman was imprisoned for two days in a rum den. The women get all the breaks nowadays!"

In Chicago, police "rounded up 3,000 more crooks, soon there will be no more bankers to take bootleggers' money."

—January 4, 11, 18, 25, 1929, Sausalito News

Instead of a curse, liquor ought to be considered a blessing by the drys. It gives them an issue and helps elect their candidates.

—January 1929, Ontario Herald

Who Did the Buying?

When the Jew and the Scotsman were haled into court, the judge asked the arresting officer:

"And what are they charged with, Murphy?"

"Drunkenness, your honor."

"Well, where's the other fellow?"

—Trona Pot-Ash

"His comments last night were bitter."

"Yes, I know it. He's not very good with a cocktail shaker."

—3 November 1929, San Bernardino Daily Sun

Reformer: Young man, do you realize that you will never get anywhere drinking?

Stewed: Ain't it th' truthf? I've started home from 'ish corner five times already.

—November 3, 1929, San Bernardino Daily Sun

Will Rogers Remarks about:

Booze Expose
Beverly Hills, Nov. 7
To the Editors of the Sun

It wasn't drinking that Senator Brookhart wanted to show at that dinner. It was the fact that an Iowa Senator sat next to Mr. Kahn, a wet representative from San Francisco, also excused Mr. Kahn for going to the flask.

Progressive Senators relating all the ingredients of social functions might have been why Hiram Johnson's invitation went astray. But Mr. Johnson's health is better by it, for no matter how tasty a dinner the Hoovers might have served, it would have disagreed with Senator Johnson. Mr. Hoover's alibi as to why the invitation miscarried should have (been): "I mailed it to the Republican side of the Senate."

Yours,
Will Rogers

—November 8, 1929, *San Bernardino Daily Sun*

"What are those holes in your diploma?"
"Oh, I graduated from Chicago U."
—November 24, 1929, *Notre Dame Juggler,San BernardinoDaily Sun*

A Scotsman, not feeling as well as usual, called on his family doctor, who looked him over and gave him some pills to be taken at bedtime. Whisky also was prescribed for his stomach's sake, a small glass to be taken after each meal.

Four days later, Sandy again called on the doctor, stating he was feeling no better.

"Have you taken the medicine exactly as I instructed?" the doctor inquired.

"Well, doctor," replied the patient, "I may be a wee behind with the pills, but I'm six weeks ahead on the whisky."
—November 24, 1929, *Iowa Weslayan Woofus,*
San Bernardino Daily Sun

"The Saga of Tony the Bootlegger"
Listen my children and I'll tell you
Of the midnight ride of Tony Balou.
Tony, you see, was a bootlegger bold.
If he didn't like you, he'd knock you cold.
The hooch was to come from a boat at sea,
Where no one knew, not you or me.

But Tony was there with his crew of men,
In hopes to gather in a few more yen.

By hook or by crook, the law had devised
A plan that called for Tony's demise.
But Tony you see, was a smart old rat,
And couldn't be caught in that kind of trap.

The chase started there in the land by the sea,
From bush to bush, and tree to tree.
Till Tony got his hopped up car,
That was built to go fast and travel far.

Thru hamlet after hamlet and town after town,
The chase went on till almost dawn.
The Fed's car was not built for this sort of race.
And just before dawn it gave up the chase.

And Tony went on for the time scot- free
And returned to his gang in the land by the sea.

—Rolan Lyttle, Barstow

Intoxicated with Love

"Jerry smashed his car yesterday and was taken to court."
"Really! What was the charge?"
"Driving while under the influence of woman."

—February 6, 1930, *Barstow Printer*

A much inebriated individual flopped into a seat in the lobby beside a clergyman.

"Nysh day," he began.

"Yes, I find it very comfortable."

"Will you have a drink?"

That was too much. The clergyman's face set severely and intoned sternly, "No, thank you. I don't indulge."

"Shay, whattaya given' us feller? You're drunk now. You gotsha collar on backwards."

—March 8, 1930, *The Trona Pot-ash*

Prohibition is becoming quite serious but with a few thousand exceptions no place is violating the law now except by the quart or pint.

—March 22, 1930,
The Trona Pot-ash

He doesn't smoke, he doesn't swear, he doesn't drink AND HE DOESN'T LIVE IN TRONA.

—April 19, 1930, *The Trona Pot-Ash*

The latest thing in foresight is the bootlegger who wraps his bottles with instructions on how to learn the Braille system.

—*Stanford Chaparral,* May 10, 1930, *The Trona Pot-Ash*

Trona, with its air no money can buy,
With pure, clear hue of cloudless sky,
Where men will live and women will cry,
For the town is **wet** and the lake all dry.

—June 14, 1930, *The Trona
Pot-Ash*

If you take a drink in your host's home and don't report it, you're a felon under the Jones law, says a court. New toast: "For he's a jolly good felon!"
—*Los Angeles Record,* August 30, 1930, *The Trona Potash*

"According to a press report, several dry agents were recently poisoned by hootch."
"They ought to have stuck to the places they know."

—December 11, 1930, *Ontario Herald*

If the mother-in-law jokes were not taboo, we'd venture the remark that prohibition is like a mother-in-law come to stay. Or prohibition is like women: We can't get along with it and we can't get along without it.

—December 18, 1930, *Ontario Herald*

It might be appropriate to the prohibition investigating committee to report that nobody knows how dry we are.

—December 25, 1930, *Ontario Herald*

A new hat is like wine to a woman: It goes to her head very quickly.

—From a London Humorist, October 7, 1932, *Dos Palos Star*

Some cities built Hoover Bridges, dry above and wet below and straddles both sides.

—Election time 1932

There's gold in them there mountains
There's gold in them there hills

The natives there are getting it
By operating stills.

—Anonymous

An amphibious ichthyosaurs—equally comfortable whether wet or dry.

—Anonymous

"Small Town Stuff"

Hi Wells said, "I never took a drink of intoxicatin' liquor in my life, but if the government goes to makin' it I guess I'll try a shot—why not?"

Everybody that didn't drink before prohibition's doin' it now—that is, except a few of us labeled "long-hairs." Everybody has their turn, don't they?

Joe Jackson looked Hi over with suspicion and a bit of cynicism on his unrefined mug. "Never took a drink—you? I thought you wuz one of them good guys in your old age that had tried out everything in your youth. Never took a drink in your whole life, hey?"

Hi blushed and the old boys laughed.

"Take it back," said Hi, "Mother gave it to me when I had pneumonia."

And when I left they wuz sure razzin' Hi lest he had forgotten some other time.

—by Don O'Brien, July 1932, *Dos Palos Star*

Prohi: Son, where's your pa?
Boy: Pa, he's up at the still.
Prohi: Where's your ma?
Boy: Oh, Ma? She's up at the still too.
Prohi: I'll give you a dollar if you take me to the still.
Boy: Okay, give me the dollar.
Prohi: I'll give it to you when we get back.
Boy: No, give it to me now. You ain't comin' back.

—Anonymous

In the desert a horse rancher supplemented his income by making what the locals called "Horse Blanket Whiskey" because he strained out some of the dangerous fusel oil by pouring the liquor through horse blankets.

One old desert rat talked about this whiskey: It wasn't too bad. I kinda' got used to it. In fact, I drank so much of it that I could tell if it was run through the blanket of a Morgan, Arabian or quarterhorse.

—Anonymous

The justice of peace of Venice, California, offered Mack McNeil a drink of confiscated Canadian whiskey.

"We're required to throw away this liquor," said the decider of the law with a smile, "but there's nothing that says we can't pass it through our kidneys first."

—Henry "Mack" McNeil, Santa Monica

"I want something tall, cold and full of gin," said a man at the speakeasy.

"Say, you're talking about my wife," said a drunk at the bar.

—Unknown

In Bisbee, Arizona, the sunshine is 330 days a year, but the moonshine every night.

—May 31, 1933
Fort Bragg Advocate and News, from *Brewery Gulch Gazette*

In Arizona, a bootlegger got caught and sent to the county jail. He raised bail money by selling treasure maps to his buried stash of liquor.

—Anonymous

At the country Saturday night dances, there were so many bootleggers that they started wearing badges to keep from selling to each other.

—Anonymous

At one country dance, two young men saw a local bootlegger coming toward them.

"Hey, George, got any *drinking* whiskey?" asked one of the men and all three laughed.

—Anonymous

The prim old lady was given the first glass of beer she ever had. After sipping it for a moment she looked up with a puzzled air.

"How odd!" she murmured. "It tastes just like the medicine my husband has been taking for the past twelve years."

—October 20, 1934, *The Trona Pot-Ash*

CHAPTER 11

RUMRUNNING WAR

The long coast of California, one thousand miles long, perhaps two thou sand including islands, inlets, bays and rivers, enabled rum smugglers to choose their places to land liquor. The few Customs agents, prohibition agents and local officials who tried to stop this flow of illegal booze could not possibly eliminate the landings from motorboats, fishing boats, sailboats, rowboats with outboard motors and dories that could come right through the waves.

Ships from Mexico, the Caribbean, Tahiti, and from Europe joined in the lucrative adventure of supplying the needs of thirsty West Coast drinkers. Vancouver, British Columbia, supplied the bulk of imported alcohol. Big supply ships, called "mother ships," hovered off the coast, at first three miles, then 12 miles and later "one hour's steaming time" from the coast. They waited for fishing boats, speed launches, private yachts to rendezvous and pick up their consigned order.

After these shore boats loaded their liquor, the race to the shore was on: to slip by Coast Guard boats, navigate to the right dog hole on the coast of northern California, chug the fishing boat into San Francisco or San Pedro bays or speed to beaches where they could anchor outside the surf and unload into dory boats—flat bottomed rowboats with high sides, sharp bow and a deep "vee" transom that could go through the surf and land high on the beach.

Men awaited these landings, loaded the cargo onto Reo trucks and big Packards and raced for San Francisco, Sacramento or Los Angeles.

United States Coast Guard failed to stop the flow of illegal liquor from the sea. They succeeded in stopping hundreds of ships and boats over fourteen years of prohibition, but lost the Rum War. The flow of booze into California never stopped.

In any war, one side usually had the benefit of better intelligence. Rumrunners knew more about the movements of the Coast Guard than the reverse. In most wars one antagonist had the benefit of numbers, so a war of attrition favored that antagonist, in this case the smuggling side. The supply of liquor never ceased, neither did the supply of smugglers willing to chance capture.

Both protagonist and antagonist evoked help from the gods, help of the law for the legal authority and from citizens for support or at least to keep one eye closed, thus being neutral. Both sides claimed a moral right. Although government claimed the legal right, ironically rumrunners used the law to their advantage. The law gave rumrunners the edge. It was a great Rum War, both sides deserving credit for the way it was fought—fought for fourteen long years.

You Keep Quiet and You'll Be Fine
as told by BC[1]

When I was about 20 years old, I was on my boat from Richmond heading for Ft. Bragg. Usually fishing boats traveled in pairs, or at least two men on a boat, but this time I was alone and tired. I pulled into a cove just south of Fish Rock, north of Gualala River. I anchored at night to rest. Shortly after I had fallen asleep, I was awakened by men on my boat. They had guns. "You leave your boat here and come with me. We need your help," one said.

With many guns pointed in my direction, I had no hesitation or thought of saying no.

They took me out to sea to a mother ship, the rum ship from Canada. We pulled along side and they lowered a net. We worked hard, handing the cases into the hold of the smaller boat (we were on) where another man stored it.

When we finished loading the boat, we headed for the cove where my ship was anchored. We ate huge sandwiches, expensive ones, and drank coffee. When we landed on the beach, we unloaded the cases of booze and carried them to a big Mack truck.

Then we headed out for more. We ate well but worked hard. When we finished for the night, one said, "You keep quiet and you'll be fine. Here's $100 for your work and two bottles of Canadian whiskey."

I kept quiet. I used the money to help my mother who was in the hospital very sick.

For a couple of years later (1930-1933), a man walked up to me in Ft. Bragg or wherever I was working and whispered close to me: "We want you. You got something to do." It was always a different man, but I knew what it was for. I made maybe 8-9 trips. On a couple of trips Baby Face Nelson was one of the men with a gun. They would bring loads in up and down the coast, Noya River, Vitalez Dock, Little River, Russian Gulch, Point Arena. There was always plenty of coffee to keep you awake and these great sandwiches!

American-British Treaty

To help counter illegal liquor importation into the United States from Canada, West Indies and Great Britain, the United States and Great Britain agreed to a treaty, January 1924, to prevent importation of liquor. Both parties agreed to uphold the principle of the three-marine-mile extension from the low-water line as proper limit to territorial waters, but His Britannic Majesty raised no objection to the U. S. authorities boarding British vessels suspected of smuggling liquors outside this limit and to seize and take into port such vessels. However, these rights cannot take place if said ship was beyond one-hour traversing time of that ship from shore. If a rumrunner used a speedboat to

162

Coleman Beach, on Bodega Bay, shows the rugged Northern California Coast. Fast speedboats used coves and beaches like this to land liquor from the Canadian "mother ship," 20-40 miles out in international water.

unload from the British vessel, the one-hour traversing time is the time of the speedboat from shore; thus a British ship could be 12-25 miles off shore and be seized. Sea-store liquor (boat and medicinal liquor) and liquor cargo going to a foreign port shall not be confiscated. While in the territorial waters of the United States, these liquors must be locked or secured. Therefore when a British or Canadian ship came into the port of San Francisco, Customs sealed the liquor storage and this seal could only be opened by a Customs official or when out of territorial waters.[2]

Cooperation with Mexico

Since the capture of several rum ships off the coast of California, large mother rum vessels stationed themselves off Ensenada, Santo Tomas or Guadalupe Island in Mexican waters and received supplies of liquor from Canada or Tahiti, then discharged 1,000-2,000 cases to smaller boats that either went directly to California beaches or stayed far off the coast to await smaller fishing boats or speedboats which would take from 200- 500 cases to shore.

Mexico signed a treaty with the U.S. to help prevent smuggling activities within Mexico and her waters. Consequently Special Agent Alf Oftedal in San Francisco assigned Agent W. E. Dresser to seek cooperation with Mexico to perhaps arrest mother ships *Prince Albert* and *Hurry On,* reportedly off Guadalupe Island. It was not expedient to contact officials in Ensenada, "not expedient" being a euphemism for Ensenada officials not being trusted. With permission from Baja's Governor Rodriques, Dresser arranged with Captain Angulo to proceed to Guadalupe with Dresser and catch the two rum ships violating Mexico's maritime rules.

However, of the three Mexican ships, only two worked, the better one, *S.A.S. No. 1*, was being repaired in San Diego and waiting parts from Oakland, and the other working one, *Tecate*, was too bad to travel the seas alone. When both ships were repaired and supplied with soldiers, they sailed for Guadalupe Island, but found no ships, only signs of a lookout and signs of camping on the island a week or so earlier. Perhaps word got out to the more efficient rumrunners. Later *Tecate* had to be towed 200 miles by *S.A.S. No. 1*.[3]

This failure was the first of many attempts to stop illegal smuggling and transferring liquor within Mexican waters.

The Capture of the *Diatome*

It is fortunate when the spoils of war are used so readily against the antagonist, as when Stonewall Jackson turned the better Union cannons around and, using Union powder and shell, fired at retreating Union forces. The capture of the rum-runner gas screw *Diatome* became a covetous prize in 1931, a prize the Coast Guard officers could not wait to get their hands on and use against the rumrunners.

Planning to land near Ventura on the night of June 1, 1931, the *Diatome* came upon U. S. C.G. Cutter *Arrow*, with her engines and lights off just waiting and watching for rumrunners. As soon as the *Diatome* spotted *Arrow* 200 yards away, she turned and sped away.

Arrow Commander, Boatswain K. C. Tharp, ordered pursuit. Motor Machinist's Mate A. C. Peterson turned on running lights and searchlights, shining them on the *Diatome*, sirens blasting. C.H. Williams, Boatswain's Mate, fired five warning shots over her bow, but the *Diatome* refused to stop and "zig zag[ed]" a course to get away. Motor Machinist's Mate Ralph R. Ellis fired six rifle shots over the *Diatome*, then fired several machine gun bursts in the air as a further warning. *Diatome* still would not stop. Ellis lowered the sights of the machine gun and let loose several bursts into the engine room to disable her. The chase lasted an hour and a half, until Master of the boat David J. Clark stopped the motors and waved a white handkerchief out of the pilot house, yelling "We quit!"

Besides Clark, who was wounded, the boarding party found Walter C. Moore, unhurt, and found the body of William K. Milligin, shot in the head from the machine gun burst. The cutter took *Diatome* to San Pedro Section Base 17, confiscated 289 sacks of liquor and ten jugs of rum, arraigned Clark and Moore, releasing them on $2,500 bond each.

Investigators found D. E. Seward, 2661 Flower St., Walnut Park, owned *Diatome*. Seward was foreman of Greer Robbins Co., Chrysler Distributors in

Smugglers Cove, south of Anchor Bay, formerly St. Orres Cove. Deep enough for speedboats to beach. A popular rum-running cove, renamed for Canadian whiskey being landed there and for one payoff man killed in a rum battle.

southern California. The "highly respected" Seward paid Fellows and Stewart of Long Beach to build the hull and outfit her with three Liberty motors, with a capacity of 1,200 horse power. Seward said he charted the boat to Clark for $250 a month for fishing. Repairs at Fellows and Stewart, from November 25, 1930, to May 25, 1931, showed on the books with no record of who ordered or paid for the work.

When the defense lawyers, Simpson and Simpson, pleaded his clients Clark and Moore guilty for four charges, the district attorney lowered the fine to only $500 each and no jail time in return for not contesting the condemning of the *Diatome.*

The plea bargain made both sides happy. Since one of the crew died and another was wounded, a sympathetic jury might be too lenient to come up with a "guilty." The conspirators, perhaps Seward, Clark and Moore, lost $9,000 worth of liquor, a great boat and a dead comrade, but an easy fine and no jail time made them go "whew!" Simpson agreed: "no claim will be filed by owners or master of the vessel in answer to the libel." The "moral effect to the rumrunners interested has perhaps already 'gone home.'" The boat was appraised for $12,000.

*Captured **Diatome**, 1200 horsepower rumrunner that could go twice as fast as most Coast Guard ships, confiscated and given to the Coast Guard to become CG 827, assigned to Section Base 17, San Pedro. Boatswain K. C. Tharp, on U. S. CG Cutter **Arrow**, captured her with 289 cases of imported liquor after a running battle where crewman William K. Milligin was killed. Notice the windows shot out by Coast Guard machine gun. Photo courtesy of National Archives, # 26-X-9.*

166

Perhaps Coast Guard officers could hardly keep from drooling as they thought how *Diatome* could augment their outclassed, out-sped, out-maneuvered patrol boats and cutters. A letter to Washington said, "...[we are] very desirous of our securing this boat under customs laws so that she may be...a great addition to their [our] fleet because of her speed." Commander M. S. Hay and Executive Officer Lt. Fletcher, of Section Base 17, were anxious to have *Diatome* before deterioration set in.

Assistant U. S. Attorney condemned the boat and ordered it to be delivered the Commander of Section Base 17 on August 3, 1931, just two months after its capture: "The Gas Screw *Diatome* # 230255, her motors, tackle, apparel, furniture, etc.—condemned and forfeited to the United States of America." Section Base 17 had a new speedboat, now called CG 827, a Coast Guard boat faster than most rumrunning vessels.[4]

Spectators watch with interest as captured rum-running barge **Redwood City***, behind the* **Elcisco***, is brought into San Francisco wharf. Coast Guard Patrol Boat 282 captured* **Redwood City** *with cases of smuggled liquors. Photo courtesy National Archives # 25-G-27-02-24 (XI).*

The Gas Screw *Tornado*

The gas screw *Tornado* with 250 cases of imported liquor from Canada, ran without legal boat lights in Santa Monica Bay, near Palisades Del Rey.

When Coast Guard boat 827, the old *Diatome*, spotted it, *Tornado* refused to stop or slow down even with a few shots across its bow. During the chase Nels Larson opened the stern gate and kept throwing out its cargo. When Coast Guard Officer K. C. Tharp, now commander of 827, spotted the cargo being dumped, he marked the spots. As Tharp boarded *Tornado*, Larson was sweeping broken bottles and straw. The dory on top of *Tornado* had broken loose and smashed some of the cases, making it smell like the rum boat it was. Tharp arrested Herbert L. Johnstone and Nels Larson, taking the boat and the two men to Section Base 17 (San Pedro).

The *Tornado*, valued at $7,500, was not returned to the owner. The next day Tharp dragged areas where the cargo was jettisoned and recovered many sacks and cases of liquor. Larson never showed up for his trial. In May 1933, charges against Johnstone were dropped. Since all but a few diehard drys knew prohibition would end soon, the prohibition department felt $350 fine (bail) each, plus approximately $12,000 loss in investment, $7,500 for the boat and $4,500 for the loss of liquor at $18 per case wholesale, this was enough punishment. The government paid $5.00 per day to keep the *Tornado*, $455 for the 91 days before the court sold the boat.[5]

Humboldt Bay

It would seem that Humboldt Bay with its small entrance, would be an easy place to stop the smuggling, but it was not. Rumrunners knew when the Coast Guard went out to sea, where it was going, when it would be back. Lookouts informed gangs on the whereabouts of Coast Guard boats—what few they had. A fishing boat or a motorboat could enter the harbor on the south part of the bay opening, half a mile from the Coast Guard station lookout north of the entrance. At night if a boat entered with no running lights, watchmen could not see it and could not hear it especially if the boat's exhaust were muffled.

Once a smuggler entered the bay, he could head north for Eureka, going past the small Coast Guard Station in North Bay. A smuggler with local knowledge could follow the east side of the bay keeping three-quarters of a mile from the station. Most smuggling boats, however, entered the harbor, heading south for Fields Landing in South Bay where they unloaded contraband on the beach or the pier and transferred it by truck to Eureka or San Francisco on the Redwood Highway. Boats entering South Bay were a mile from the station, and had only two miles to Fields Landing.

This Coast Guard facility lacked adequate boats and ships to do the job. They needed fast picketboats to patrol the bay at irregular intervals and to catch boats entering the harbor and heading south. Officer in charge repeatedly requested additional boats. Cutter *Cahokia*, docked in the North Bay, was usually out along the coast. Sophisticated smugglers, with a network of spies and informants, knew when *Cahokia* was out for its ten days and whether it would be heading north or south along the coast.

The two Coast Guard motorboats could not handle duties especially during the summer and fall fishing season. One motored dory, used as a supply and boarding boat, was too slow to catch fishing boats if they didn't want to stop, too small to use around the entrance to Humboldt Bay at night and the engine "would not stand up" if run at full speed for many minutes. The other boat, the motor lifeboat, was not equipped for patrolling as it had no accommodations for the crew, it was too slow to catch fast boats, and if the engine or boat were damaged, it would endanger its lifesaving mission.

Charles Walker, Commander of Coast Guard Station, Humboldt Bay, in November 1924, received word from Deputy Collector of Customs in Eureka, H. F. McGrath, that Italian steamer *Piave II* of Trieste might try to unload some of its alcoholic cargo, while loading legitimate cargo at Fields Landing. Walker posted a sentry on Light House Wharf and used the motor lifeboat to patrol the bay, watching for boats coming up from South Bay. The Coast Guard got outrun by one boat and stopped a few fishing boats but found no liquor boats. The next night, the Guard heard a motor launch coming from the North Bay. It seemed to have trouble and landed on the sand island. Charles D. Padias,

British twin-screw steamship rum-running "mother ship" Quadra tied up in San Francisco after being captured by the Coast Guard Cutter Shawnee in 1925 with 12,000 cases of whiskey and champagne. The Quadra was within the 12-mile zone off San Francisco and loading fishing boat C-55 with 50 cases of whiskey. Although the runners appealed to the Supreme Court, they lost the case and the ship lay in San Francisco harbor for several years.

the lookout at 7:30 a.m., reported the boat aground. Coast Guardsmen went over in skiffs and pulled the boat loose with a kedge anchor. The boat, gas fishing boat *#2980* owned by Francis Reeves of South Bay, had a two-man crew, William Nye of South Bay and an unidentified man, soaked and huddled in a blanket in the front of the boat. At Light House Wharf, workmen repaired a jammed rudder by 10:00 a.m. and the boat was allowed to go.

Later, officers sent two men over to check the area where the boat went aground and they found 20 cases and one sack of smuggled liquor hidden between two logs and covered by weeds and trash. The Coast Guard felt it could not arrest the fisherman until they found more evidence. They did not. *Piave II* went to Samoa in North Bay, then headed toward Aberdeen, Washington. Walker sent warnings to watch the Italian ship as she made her way north. Even though Reeves lost his contraband, he lucked out avoiding arrest. And the mysterious wet man huddled in the boat—might even have been Reeves.[6]

In 1926, Walker made another request for help. "Last summer there were fifty to seventy boats running out of Eureka, besides...probably twenty-five out of Trinidad, seventeen miles north."[7] He wanted another boat that could travel 15-20 miles and could sleep two men. He needed two more men so he would not take away from the crew he had at this station.

The Coast Guard Knew

Each week in 1932, John W. Smith, Customs Agent, Bureau of Customs, San Francisco, sent a report showing the location and movement of ships and motorboats off the West Coast. Weekly "Customs Information Bulletins" illustrated details of Coast Guard intelligence about ships along the coast. The Pacific Ocean along the Oregon and California coasts was dangerous; yet these ships and large motor boats were hovering 20-40 miles out in the Pacific, and smaller motorboats, skiffs, launches and fishing boats ventured out to load up. "Customs Information Bulletin No. 127," December 23, 1932:[8]

The information herein given is confidential and for the official use of Federal Government officers, and is furnished with the understanding that secondary distribution in any form is prohibited.

Algie-Canadian Vessel. –Has been hovering off coast for the past week, contact position 40 miles west of Point Sur. December 18th unloaded 500 cases to shore boat. December 21st unloaded 500 cases to shore boat. December 23rd, 60 miles south magnetic of Point Sur bound for San Ysidro Point empty.

Arwyco-British Steamer.—Cleared Vancouver December 17th in command of Captain F. Coe with the following liquor on board: "United Distillers, Ltd., to Consolidated Exporters, Nassau Bermuda, 4715 cases liquor." "United Distillers, Ltd., to Consolidated Exporters, St. Pierre, Miquelon, 16530 cases liquor."

Audrey B-British Motor Ship.—December 15th released 500 cases to American motorboat latitude of Pigeon Point. December 18th placed under picket and at present time is 35 miles west southwest from Point Anonuevo. Still under Picket.

Amigo-Canadian Gas Screw.—Hovering off coast in vicinity of Medicino [Mendocino] City, where she intends to land direct to the beach. Was expected to land night of December 22nd. Located and picketed by the Coast Guard December 18th, escaped picket night of December 21st.

Brompton Manor-British Boat.—Small American motorboats have been making contact and carrying from 100 to 200 cases at a time. See *Hurry Home.*

Chief Skugaid-British Motor Schooner.—Active off Washington coast.

Colnett-Canadian Motor Vessel.—Active in the Los Angeles area.

Hickey-Canadian Motor Schooner.—Arrived at Vancouver December 17th in command of Captain George Hann for overhauling.

Hurry Home-British Motor Boat.—December 19th cleared Ensenada for San Quentin. December 19th received 700 cases from *Brompton Manor* and 550 from *Lillihorn* and is presumed to be enroute to position in the San Luis Obispo area, where she may unload direct to the beach.

Kagome-British Motor Boat.—Is at the *Old Maid II* and will take on a load of less than 500 cases as soon as weather permits and expects to land direct to the beach in vicinity of Crescent City of False Klamath Bay.

Lillihorn-Canadian Motor Ship.—December 16th gave *Ragan* 1810 cases. See *Hurry Home.*

Old Maid II-British Auxiliary Schooner.—Hovering off coast 85 miles west of Mendicino City [sic]. Has been slowly unloading by *Kagome* and *Temixcouda*. See *Kagome*. Now has orders to proceed to position 30 miles southwest of some point believed to be Trinidad Head to contact American shore boats, as the unloading by British boats has been unsatisfactory.

Prince Albert-British Boat.—Correction Bulletin No.. 125 (Dec. 9, 1932) Was reported at Ensenada, should be Seattle.

Ragna-British Vessel.—December 16th took 1810 cases from the *Lillihorn* and is now believed to be on position vicinity of Point Conception.

Ruth B-British Motor Boat.—Hovering off Washington coast with a load.

Ryou II-Canadian Schooner.—December 16th delivered load to *Ruth B* off Washington coast and is returning to the *Lillehorn* light.

Skeezix-British Motor Boat.—Hovering off Washington with load.

Tapawingo-British Triple Screw.—In Vancouver.

Temiscouda-Canadian registry.—Hovering vicinity Point Arena with load.

Taiheyo-British Motor Vessel.—Active in Los Angeles area.

Tooya-British Motor Vessel.—Enroute from Tahiti to *Malahat*, was expected to arrive Dec. 22nd.

Yurinohana-British Motor Boat.—December 17th entered Ensenada from Vancouver. This boat has not been in Vancouver since November 2, 1931, and for more than a year has been actively engaged in smuggling liquor from the mother-ships to the California coast. During this time has twice been in Ensenada.

Zip-Canadian Motor Vessel.—Hovering in vicinity of Point Arena with load of about 1,500 cases on board.

Byrnje-Norwegian Steamer.—Cleared Vancouver December 13th for Belize, British Honduras, with 500 cases of Uncle Sam Whiskey and 272 cases of Coon Hallow shipped from the British Columbia Distillers to Melhada and Sons. This liquor is ex *M. V. Nordhval* which returned to Vancouver after meeting with an accident.

American Shore Contact Boats, San Francisco Bay.

Delta—Out

General Pershing—Location unknown

It (3876)—Refer to Bulletin 125. Dec. 20th Customs records showed this boat sold by W. J. Dunn to N. K. Hale, Sausalito

Jericho—December 21st after paying fine of $700 and is now in Seimers Ways.

Mizpah Out and active, believed to have been contacting the *Algie* and *Aubry B*, is probably landing in the Monterey section.

Panazone—Location unknown.

Ricomer—Believed to be going in legitimate business since having been sold by the Marshall.

Thor—At Bodega Bay last report. Was reported for not displaying anchor lights and is believed to be contacting the *Zip* and *Temiscouda*.

Zeitgeist—Was in Bodega Bay December 18, 19 and 29th. Believed to be contacting the *Zip* and T*emiscouda*.

On "Bulletin No. 128," Smith reported the *Ragna* hovering in the vicinity of Point Conception. He also noted the seizure of 275 cases on the beach 30 miles north of Santa Barbara on December 27 where Pico Conero [Cornero] and Joe Lavino were arrested. The liquor was believed to have come from the *Ragna*.

The *Shoshone* caught American Motor Boat *6495* six miles off the shore of Point Arena after leaving the side of *Ryuo II* of Vancouver on June 9, 1932. The Coast Guard arrested Sven Adolfson and Nils Nelson of Noyo, California, and towed the boat to San Francisco for inspection and investigation. H. Anderson owned the boat and lived at 272 9th St., San Francisco, registering the boat out of Benicia.[9]

An insight as to how smugglers coordinated ship movements, made their payments, organized pickup locations, chose landing sites and alternate sites, coordinated with local sheriffs, coordinated with Coast Guard move-

172

ments—came from a bust in San Francisco, 1887 19th Avenue, in 1930, where Canadian Harry Bruce Mowatt ran an unlicensed radio station. Federal Radio expert C. E. Reeves found the radio transmitter by triangulation, taking his receiver by 20th Avenue, strong signals between Ortega and Noriega. Then he went east and west and found the location and the tower in back. Commissioner Williams issued complaints against Mowatt, George McDonald, and Tony Picetti.

Found at the scene were messages to and from the *Ragna*, *XL* and *Hurry Home*. Sample messages appeared as follows:[10]

November 30, to *Ragna*: "Go to own mother ship and pick up order."
December 1, to *Ragna*: "Come inside Point Banda tonight and meet chance."
December 1, to *Ragna*: "What do you mean refuse to make another trip explain what reason wish one trip before holidays please do not worry about pay if any other reason answer."
December 1, from *Ragna*: "Ship poorly provisioned have no water and you have failed to send monies home to the crew as you promised please understand we have families depending on us."
December 1, to *Hurry Home*: "Have you doryman. Steam south to Point Buchon and be ready to come in at oil well tonight about 8 p.m. If any further changes will advise 5 p.m."
December 1, from *Hurry Home*: "One dory and one doryman, also have one small dory carry twenty sacks, can you supply doryman?"

Lt. Commander F. L. Austin, Coast Guard, reported *Hurry Home* took 1200 cases from Dorin, on November 27; and *Ragna* loaded from *Lilliehorn*, November 1, both off the Mexican coast.

The Doryman
as told by Denton "Buster" Hyder, New Cayumas

"Don't buy fancy new cars, live a normal life, don't show you're making a lot of money," Tony Cornero told me. He paid me $100 a trip, sometimes up to $250 a night. I was getting 32¢ an hour working at the ship yards, so with rumrunning I made me a lot of money.

I was the doryman, the one who took 40 cases of smuggled liquor through the surf to the beach. Often my 16' Hollister dory carried three 20-gallon barrels back out to the shore boat so the boat could load up with gas or diesel and rendezvous again with a mothership, a liquor tender, 40 miles off the coast of California. We operated from San Pedro north, mostly north of Santa Barbara: at Arroyo Borruel, where the light house is between Santa Barbara and Golita at a clump of eucalyptus trees, we brought in loads.

Another landing place was Spooner's Landing at Point Bashon by San Luis Obispo. The loading crew waited in the barn at Spooner's Landing. I took an azimuth from Point Bashon 45 degrees SW where tender would be waiting.

You see it was always dark and I didn't get to see much. If you [the author] didn't see a barn then it could've been the warehouse that I thought was a barn. The boats unloaded at the small sandy beach next to the big solid rock that was used for a dock years before. If they could not go through the surf, I would use my dory to bring the load to the beach.

[Signed] Old Rum Runner Buster

Eureka Smuggling
as told by Norton Steenfott, Eureka

In the later part of prohibition federal agents made sugar companies give records of large sugar sales and destinations of the sugar. Agents caught a carload of whiskey in Ogden, Utah, checked it back and found it came from Fields Landing south of Eureka. Federal agents checked and also found that several months before a bunch of loads of sugar went to Biaatrix, two miles

Coast Guard radioman at Point Vicente, monitoring rum-running radios to break codes and locate "mother ships." The rum war helped make the Coast Guard proficient with the new wireless radio, giving them at least one advantage in an otherwise losing cause. Photo courtesy of National Archives, # 26G-34-9-30 (1).

from Fields Landing. The Feds thought they had them. On a big ranch, where the College of the Redwoods is now, they found a large still that had just produced 1,000 gallons of alcohol. Mash was cooking for another batch. When agents went in, distillers had been eating, the food still warm on the table. No one was caught.

But what they caught in Utah was bottled whiskey. This was alcohol. They knew they did not get what they came for but another operation by accident.

Agents checked more, checked boats that had come into Fields Landing when that shipment was to have been loaded.

A Coast Guard ship was here in Eureka, in ten days, out ten days looking for rumrunners. Anyway, this one ship *Bertie Hamlon,* always came in just prior to the Coast Guard ship going out to sea. If the Coast Guard ship went out that night, *Bertie Hamlon* came in that morning, tied up to a dock in the bay. The Coast Guard boat went south, went by Fields Landing, then usually out to sea. When it left Fields Landing, *Bertie Hamlon* went south to Fields landing and unloaded unmolested.

This time, however, the Coast Guard ship came back into the harbor the same night and went right to Fields Landing. Federal agents boarded *Bertie Hamlon* and found it loaded with whiskey from Canada. That's all that boat had been doing: running booze out of Canada and dropping it off. That's where the load came from that was found in Utah.

There was a wharf in Fields Landing, eight miles south of Eureka where the crab market is now, Boccis Place. Booze went along with the crabs during prohibition.

Outboard motors were invented down at Bodega Bay because of rumrunning. The Coast Guard was catching so damn many rumrunners down there because they were using the same type boats. There's a lot of shallow water in the lowland and marshes. This fellow came up with the idea of a boat that can run in one to three feet of water. When the Coast Guard boats came after the small outboard motor boats, these boats kept going in the shallow water as the Coast Guard had to stop.

Inland Rumrunning
by Ernest D. Wichels, Vallejo

Despite the supply of "barafoota" wine and "raisin wine," much good liquor came in through the rumrunning operations from foreign ports.

Many ports, such as Half Moon Bay, Bodega, and the North Coast fishing resorts, were entry points without benefit of customs officials—except when caught. But it wasn't all from the ocean side. Solano County had its "import" districts, too, especially near Collinsville and on points along Montezuma Slough—the duck hunters' paradise.

Wood Young, noted County historian, wrote the "Saga of the *Hawk*," which was published in the *Fairfield Daily Republic on April 3, 1962.*

That fascinating story is typical of the rumrunning boats throughout the Delta region.

The *Hawk* was a sturdy 50-foot craft with two Hall-Scott engines and 800 horsepower, capable of plying the waters outside the Golden Gate and meeting, presumably, "mother" ships.

That saga began outside Birds Landing when local Constable and Deputy Sheriff Talbert observed a strange craft mooring on the north levee of Montezuma Slough near the mouth of the Sacramento River.

He notified Sheriff Jack Thorton and customs officials. Deputy Olsen was stationed atop an old farm windmill, and from his observation post he saw a smaller boat, the *Elma*, pull along side, load some bulky sacks and take off for Pittsburg.

Two federal boats were dispatched, but were too deep for the shallow waters of the slough. A local posse was then organized by the deputies. They were fully armed, but among the lot, there were only two handcuffs.

Crawling through the pickle weed, they reached the levee bank, told the crew of the *Hawk* to hold up their hands (which they did), and then wondered what to do next. The skipper of the *Hawk* broke the ice with "What's your price, officer?"

The posse leader gave the order to fire shots into the hull of the *Hawk* and sink it to prevent escape and make the crew come ashore.

The crew, under arrest, finally was taken to the Fairfield jail; the next day federal officials came up from San Francisco. Scotch and champagne were aboard when the evidence was finally taken, but there was some local skepticism as to whether it was real or if the labels had been placed on local moonshine. In all, perhaps 30 sacks were aboard.

The *Hawk* was raised, confiscated and an offer of $5,000 made for its purchase. On September 17, 1928, a federal jury tried the three defendants in Sacramento. They were found guilty of rumrunning and each given six months in the Fairfield County Jail.

It was then the prisoners confided the labels were from foreign bottles and the contraband aboard the *Hawk* came from "factories" along the California coast—perhaps San Mateo County or north of the Golden Gate.

Wood Young's "Saga of the *Hawk*" should be published in entirety—it is 5000 words of intrigue, attempted bribery and humor. But it is only one of the hundreds that could be written about the 14 years of national prohibition.[11]

West Basin, San Pedro
as told by Mr. Duckett, Timber Cove

The rumrunning boats docked at West Basin in San Pedro. Almost daily the Coast Guard checked which rum-running launches were docked and which were out to sea. When smugglers wanted to land booze on the beach, they sent a dory to the shore with a cable from the launch. They pulled the booze under water to the dory. If a Coast Guard boat came up, the runner dropped the cable; the booze stayed on the bottom and later they dragged for it.

The Coast Guard knew what they were doing but couldn't arrest either the man or the dory or the launch unless they had the contraband in their possession.

℗

Catalina Island served as a frequent stop for rumrunners. Constable Finch of Avalon called Coast Guard Base 17 about a discovery of a cache of 32 assorted liquor cases in Silver Canyon on the west side of Catalina. Officer Gabe Zimmerman, CG-255, proceeded to Avalon, picked up the constable and a Mr. Smith, engineer of a rock quarry who found the cache. They traveled to the west side and confiscated the load and turned it into Customs, San Pedro.[12]

Capturing the Yukantravel
by Lee E. Echols, Chula Vista

My partner was Harry "Bud" Bump and one day Rae Vader came to San Diego. He was Special Agent with the Customs Service, stationed in Los Angeles, and he had come to talk to Bud and me.

"There's a rum boat operating out of Ensenada," he told us. "It's called the *Yukantravel* [*Yukatrivol*, according to Miles *Slow Boat on Rum Row*] and it damn sure can. It's powered with three big Liberty engines, has a bottom covered with sheet copper to keep the barnacles from accumulating on it and this makes it even faster. It clears Ensenada with about six hundred five gallon cans of alcohol about once a month, ostensibly for Bamfield, Canada, but actually for places like Half Moon Bay and other sites along the coast between Los Angeles and San Francisco.

Rae was tall and hawk-like. He looked like he should be teaching anthropology at Stanford and most of the time he was deadly serious. I learned later though that he could be one of the funniest men on earth.

"Now we haven't got a boat on the coast, including Coast Guard boats, which can outrun the damn thing, but I've got a plan to make them beach her right on the strand between Imperial Beach and Coronado, and here's how you boys can fit into the schemes.

"The owner of *Yukantravel* is Walter Welliver, a Canadian, and he's always on board when they leave Ensenada with sugar cane alcohol. The skipper is 'Doc' Boarland. Now they've got a Mexican man who is their cook and he too accompanies them and he lives in Ensenada.

"My plan is for you two boys to go to Ensenada and by some manner of operation, get in good with the cook and learn when they are leaving. I'll leave it up to you how you go about it but when you learn this, we'll be waiting for them off the Coronado Islands with three of the fastest boats the Coast Guard has available. I feel that if they are going to land alcohol north of Los Angeles, they will need to save all the fuel they can. This means they must come up between the mainland and the Coronado Islands. If they go out around those islands, they will be outside the twelve mile limit and we can't touch them, but I'm betting they'll come up inside them.

"We'll put a fan-shaped whamydoodle on them with the three boats and herd them right in to the Coronado Islands. When they try to get out of it, we'll lay some tracer bullets across their bow and they'll have to get back in the net."

The deal sounded valid enough and Bud and I left the next morning for Ensenada, which lies on the Baja California coast in Mexico, about sixty miles south of the Mexican border. We were dressed in civilian clothes as typical tourists and had driven Bud's personal automobile.

On arrival at this quaint little city, we bought ourselves a bottle of Berreteaga, which is a cheap, sugar-cane brandy, and, carrying it in my hip pocket and taking a swig out of it every once in a while, we proceeded to the wharf where the *Yukantravel* was tied.

Sure enough the cook was aboard and busy as he could be swabbing the deck of the beautiful and powerful craft.

We pretended to be drunk as a tin miner's dog and I asked him in Spanish what was the name of his boat.

He replied it was the *Yukantravel* under Canadian registry, and that it plied between Ensenada and Bamford, Canada, with various types of cargo.

We offered him a drink of the Berreteaga bottle but he politely refused. He said, however, that he would be through with his chores on board in a couple of hours and would meet us at Hussong's Bar.

We agreed to this and as we left, Bud said, "My God, Lee, this looks like it's going to be easier than we thought."

And it was, too. When we met him at Hussong's Bar we bought him a couple of rounds of drinks and Bud told him we were going to be in the area about two weeks and wanted to know if he'd like to go with us further down the coast to Santo Tomas as a sort of guide.

The cook said he'd sure like to do that, but he was leaving with the owners of the *Yukantravel* the following night for Canada and that was the reason he had been on board that afternoon to get her shipshape for the voyage.

We had a couple more drinks with him, wished him well and told him we were going to the big hotel which had been built a couple of years before by Jack Dempsey and others.

Of course, Bud Bump and I didn't go anywhere but straight back to San Diego, where we furnished Rae Vader with this intelligence.

"Good," he said. "I'll get in touch with the Coast Guard and we'll string out the ambush. Would you boys like to come along?"

Of course we would, and as it grew dusk the three sleek patrol boats moved out of San Diego Harbor, Rae Vader on one, Bud Bump on another and I on the third. After we'd cleared Point Loma Lighthouse, we set a south-westerly course toward the Coronado Islands which lie about ten miles west of the coast. They set up the trap by putting one of the boats about six miles from the shore, directly abreast the Coronados. The second was straight west of the first one and almost to the Coronados. The third one, on which I was located, anchored about two nautical miles straight north of the second boat.

And about two o'clock in the morning we could hear the powerful Liberty engines of the *Yukantravel* throbbing between Boat Number 1 and Boat Number 2. She was running north with so much alcohol aboard, the decks were almost awash.

Our boat radioed the other two, telling them that when the *Yukantravel* proceeded far enough north as to be beyond them, to put the big lights on her and move up fast. They did and the *Yukantravel* almost jumped out of the water as the skipper poured on the coal. He couldn't see Boat Number 3 and he headed right toward us. The lieutenant in charge of our boat turned on his big spotlight and fired a fifty caliber machinegun across the bow of the *Yukantravel*. The tracer bullets made him turn toward the shore and the three boats closed in on him.

He saw he was trapped and tried to make a run for the Mexican waters. Boat Number 2 put a salvo of tracers across his bow and he had to turn back.

Finally as the *Yukantravel* headed straight for the Coronado Strand, it became clear that they were going to beach her. They did, and when she plowed in through the breakers, she went so far up on the sand that Rae Vader said later the city of Imperial Beach should put a house number on her.

The three occupants of the boat jumped out and went flying up the strand like stake horses on the Caliente straightway. Coast Guardsmen were after them quickly and they ran down the captain, "Doc" Boarland, as well as the Mexican cook. They were no match for Walter Welliver, however. He "joined the bird gang" and got away. The boat carried 612 five-gallon cans of alcohol.

"Doc" Boarland told us they intended putting it ashore north of San Francisco and that was why they were running inside the Coronados instead of around behind them. He said they were trying to save fuel for the long trip. If they'd stayed behind the Coronados they'd have been outside the 12-mile limit and could have thumbed their noses at us.

Rae Vader put out an all points bulletin for the arrest of Walter Welliver but it was no use. The next we heard of him he was at his home in Vancouver, British Columbia.

Rae tried to extradite him but got nowhere with it. The Canadian government would have none of that.

Bud and I saw Rae again in San Diego a few weeks later.

"I've got a scheme to get him out of there," he told us. "It'll be lots of fun, too."

"How're you gonna manage it?" I asked him.

When he told us I thought he was crazy, but it worked. And here's what he did: He went to San Francisco from where he sent Walter Welliver a telegram. It read: "MEET ME IN LOBBY OF HOTEL MONARCH IN SEATTLE AT NOON NEXT WEDNESDAY," and it was signed "DOC."

Although Walter Welliver had no way of knowing this, his friend "Doc" was still in *durance vile* in San Diego, having not been able to raise the $25,000 bond which Vader had insisted the U. S. Commissioner place him under.

Accordingly, Welliver crossed the border at Bellingham and drove to Seattle. He went to the Monarch Hotel and at exactly twelve noon he entered the lobby.

Rae Vader was waiting for him. He walked up to him with a friendly smile. "Are you Walter Welliver?" he asked.   When Welliver agreed that he was, Rae replied, "Well, Walter, I'm 'Doc'!" and he put a pair of Peerless handcuffs on him.

Ø

After ten years of the Rum War off the California coast, the Coast Guard evolved better intelligence but no better luck in stopping the flood of liquor. From the "Report of a Customs Official on the West Coast," July 21, 1930, to the Wickersham Commission[13] came startling realities: This official estimated 46,040 cases entered the coast in the year ending June 30, 1930, not counting over 7,000 cases coming from Canada in Puget Sound. The estimate was undoubtedly understated, considering the amount of liquor on the mother ships each year and the number of shore boats daily running liquor. The report continued: A number of large seagoing vessels have been and are at the present time hovering off the coast of California and Lower California, acting in cooperation with contact vessel and fast motorboats. The recent change in clearance regulations by the Dominion of Canada, it is generally believed, will result in increased high seas activities. The method recently adopted by Consolidated Exporters, Ltd., will in all likelihood, be used. This method comprehends the clearance of liquor from Canada for Antwerp, a free port, where it is actually landed and reloaded, and returned from Antwerp to positions off the Pacific Coast of the United States.

As an indication of the extent of some of the organized smuggling operations, it is reported the German M/S *Peryneas* cleared Rotterdam on January 25, 1930, with the following cargo, owned by Ben Silver [Ben Silva] and Frank Cornero: 100,000 gallons alcohol, 1,000 kegs malt and 8,000 cases scotch whiskey.

She cleared Balboa on March 17, 1930, for Shanghai and was sighted by the U. S. C.G. *Alert* on May 21, 1930 off Cape Colnett, Mexico. She was later seen at anchor in San Ramon Bay, known to have discharged cargo on the high seas into other vessels. Ben Silver is believed to be a notorious character from New York, who has been extensively engaged in smuggling narcotics.

The report concluded that the installation of a radio message interception station has been successful [probably Point Vicente at Palo Verdes]. Most intercepted messages were in code, and nearly all codes were broken by Coast Guard experts.

My Father
as told by Charley E. Petersen

I was born in 1920 and I went on fishing and smuggling boats from the time I was five years old. My father, Charley W. Petersen, was a fisherman and a smuggler who ran several boats. His main rumrunning boat was the *Admiral*, a 65' launch with two Liberty engines and a smaller engine for cruising.

His and other fishing boats often came in to the cannery and unloaded the fish they caught, then I am sure many of them delivered smuggled cases of liquor. Sardine or bait boats were ideal for smuggling because there was less suspicion as they were constantly coming in and out every day or so. Sardines were very plentiful in those days. About six miles west of Los Angeles Harbor, floating cages of bait tanks held live bait and fishermen went out and dipped out the fresh sardines they needed. Sardine boats kept up a steady supply of fresh bait in the tanks. But they also kept some cases of liquor in the tanks— ready to dip out with the big fish scoop nets. Cases could easily be brought to shore for thirsty California customers.

The *Admiral* and other boats brought smuggled liquor in at the cove at White's Point, near Point Fermin, on the Palos Verdes Peninsula. Dory boats took the loads from the *Admiral* to a secluded beach. My father was so skilled with the dory that he could bring it in high and dry and launch his dory out into the ocean the same way. He sat off shore with his loaded dory, waited for the right wave, hit it and rode it all the way up on the sand. On shore he picked out the right time and rowed the dory back out to sea.

Once I was with my father when the smugglers put on a party on a Coast Guard boat. The Coast Guard enjoyed the party on their boat, drinking the best imported liquor. They seem to have drifted into another territory and some shooting started between two Coast Guard boats. This was when I was about eight or nine years old, about 1928-29.

Once my father was caught with 50 cases. The confiscated contraband was taken to Los Angeles. When it came time for his court appearance, one of my father's workers told him not to worry.

"What do you mean not to worry? They caught us with 50 cases."

"Don't worry, don't worry."

At the courthouse Petersen's attorney told the officials that there was no liquor in those cases. It was all tea. They checked and sure enough the evidence contained tea. They checked all 50 cases: **It was all tea!**

Some policeman, or property room cop, was probably in on substituting tea for the liquor [an inside job for some robbin' hoods no doubt].

Case dismissed.

The *Mizpah*

After four years of dodging Coast Guard cutters and patrol boats, landing at harbors and on beaches, supplying California with good Canadian and European liquor, American motor boat *Mizpah* finally met her demise while under the command of Louis E. Askelund, well-known smuggler with three prior arrests and two convictions. A crewman, E. Nelson, a.k.a. Axel Bjork, arrested on the *Emma S* in 1924 with 450 cases of smuggled liquor, was another known rumrunner. *Mispah*, previously known as *Rethalulu* running booze off southern California, was registered as a pleasure boat, yet the boat was never designed or used for pleasure, except for the recipients of pleasure liquor. She carried a large dory used by rumrunners to row the booze through the surf. With her two converted Liberty airplane engines, she had speed inconsistent for a pleasure boat. The registered owner, Samuel C. Levin, harbored her in San Francisco. A Coast Guard vessel seized her 50 yards off Soquel Cove, Monterey Bay, and ironically charged her with trading without a license and for fraudulent registry. The government won its case and sold the *Mizpah*.[14]

$\wp$

Some boats just were not able to be seized. They were not captured with the goods said J. P. Pryor, Customs Collector at Monterey. "...it seems strange that we are impotent to do anything about detaining or seizing this boat." In 1926 he was complaining about Antonio Castagnolia's Motor Boat 3817, blatantly smuggling on the coast by Monterey.[15]

Seasick Rumrunner: Johnnny Schnarr
information from Marion Parker and Robert Tyrrell, *Rumrunner—The Life and Times of Johnny Schnarr,* Orca Press.

Johnny Schnarr, an American from Washington, working in Canada for several years, fought in France in the World War in the American army. He only weighed 135 pounds, was an amateur boxer, fast and strong. He made 400 rum-running trips from 1920 to 1933. Coast Guard had offered a $25,000 reward for the capture of his boat. No one collected. Most of his trips were from Canada to Puget Sound.

Schnarr picked up loads from Consolidated Exporters, Inc., which had two offices, Vancouver and Victoria. Charles Hudson was the shore captain for the corporation, directing operations with a wireless radio from Vancouver. He directed the mother ships, the liquor warehouse ships such as the *Malahat* and *Cold Harbour* that stayed 40 miles off the coast of California. Boats like *Chief Skugaid, 90'* purse seiners, picked up about 3000 cases from the mother ship and rendezvoused with shoreboats that came a few miles out to pick up 200-500 cases. The company guaranteed the liquor, even if got hijacked or confiscated by the law on the way to the shore or stolen while cached.

Payment was seldom made on the high seas. The speedboat captain presented his half of the torn dollar bill that matched one of those on the purse seiner. Possession of the right torn bill meant the load had been paid for. Later, mother ships hovered off the three-mile coast line of Baja California.

*Redwood of San Francisco, captured by the Coast Guard. In book **Rum War at Sea**, author Malcolm F. Willoughby stated the **Redwood** later became a Coast Guard vessel, CG-9272, and eventually sold. Photo by author from Admiralty Case Files 1850—1934, U. S. District Court, Northern District, RG 21, National Archives, San Bruno.*

Another company operating out of Canada was owned by the Reifel Brothers. They owned a distillery in New Westminister. Some of their shipments went to Tahiti, where they were reloaded tax free to a mother ship or a supplier ship that sailed back to the California coast.

By the end of the decade rumrunning changed again. The Canadian government made more of an attempt to catch Canadian smugglers by enforcing a ruling that no ships would sail for ports like Vera Cruz, where there was no intention of unloading. Much liquor went to Bowen Island, British Columbia, and from there was transferred to ships sitting off Rum Row. Schnarr's smuggling stayed mostly in the Straits of Georgia and San Juan de Fuca, smuggling into Washington's Puget Sound. He designed several ocean-going boats. One was *Revuocnav*, Vancouver spelled backwards, with two 860 horsepower Packard airplane engines in it. The motors cost $7,000 each, making his boat $23,000. A low profile boat, it was 56' long, 12' wide with a deeper V than earlier boats. He designed it for carrying 250 cases and still outracing Coast Guard boats, by going as fast as 40 knots. In other boats he built he used Fiat and Liberty airplane motors, even inventing a way to modify the engines to keep the oil pressure down, a constant problem with airplane engines.

Early in the 1930s increased competition created hard times. Too many Americans became involved off the California coast. The price for handling a case of liquor dropped from $11 to $5 at the end of 1933. The split was one-third to the boat (and debts), one-third to the crew and one-third to Schnarr. His two helpers were Joe Fleming and Tom Colley. Once his boat hit a fir tree floating in the Pacific, causing $2,400 in repairs.

Charles Hudson designed the *Kagome* for which Schnarr helped install the two 400 horsepower Liberty engines. The sleek rumrunner carried 2,500 cases of liquor and 2,000 gallons of fuel in fifty 45-gallon drums on the stern deck.

Consolidated Exporters had 20,000 cases stored in a warehouse in Ensenada, Mexico, about 1932. Since Hudson wanted boats to unload 2,500 cases from the warehouse, delivering them to California, he hired Schnarr as engineer and Colley to run the *Kagome* with a crew of eight, half of them Mexicans.

Schnarr became horribly seasick 200 miles north of Los Angeles. He almost died or said he did or perhaps was afraid he wouldn't die.

As they sat 40 miles off the coast, messages on the wireless radio told them where to meet the speedboats. One speedboat smuggler talked Hudson into bringing *Kagome* to the shore and unloading with two dories.

Though Schnarr felt better, Hudson ordered a speedboat to take him to shore where a car took him to Sugarman's, a kingpin of the rum trade, living in a fine house in Hollywood. Schnarr recovered in Hollywood and spent five days seeing the sights of southern California. Sugarman paid for his air flight to San Francisco.

Sugarman was involved in many businesses. He had a boat built for him with two 860 horsepower Packard airplane engines in Canada, a fast boat like the *Kagome*. He had all kinds of oil pressure and valve spring problems with the boat, having to go in for repairs every one or two trips. Reportedly he lost $125,000 on that venture.

Out in the ocean, Colley took over as engineer on the *Kagome*, but mangled his foot in the engine. After gangrene set in he was taken by a shoreboat to San Francisco where to save his life, doctors amputated his foot. For awhile he was under police guard, but since he couldn't run away, he recovered as guest of the country he was smuggling liquor into. He went back to Canada, but left his foot in San Francisco.

A $2,500 reward was offered for the capture of Captain Hudson, of the *Kagome,* the new fastest boat on the coast. After returning to Canada, Schnarr stuck to smuggling inside Puget Sound.[16]

A Rumrunning Kid

Fraser Miles dropped out of high school, knocked around Vancouver with odd jobs, finally worked his way through Spott-Shaw Wireless School. But he could find no radio operator jobs in the fall of 1931.

When one of his schoolmates did not want a one-day job loading the fish packer *Ruth B.*, Miles took the job, then was asked to watch the boat while the cook went shopping, then asked to watch the boat overnight. So here he was with a little one-day job, going into the second day. When the radio operator did not show, Miles finally had a job: wireless radio operator, crewman and second engineer on a fish packer—clean and fresh smelling because it carried Canadian whiskey to rum row off the coasts of Washington, Oregon and California. He was a teenage apprentice rumrunner, earning about $75 a month or 16 cents for every case sent to the beach. The crew of the *Ruth B* loaded the California "fireboats," shoreboats that took "firewater" to landing spots on the coast, all working hard in "dedicated service [to] American drought relief."

Later he went out on *Ryou II* for owner Henry Reifel and Pacific Navigation Co. until the summer of 1933. *Ryou II* took aboard 1200 cases of liquor from large mother ships like the *Lillehorn*, *Ragna* and *Malahat*, then loaded 250-500 cases on each shoreboat. The mother ships stayed about 40 miles off shore, and in the later years, they stayed off the coast of Mexico, having *Ryou II* going down to Mexican waters to load. Ships came from Tahiti and Canada to re-supply mother ships.

In a beautiful book, *Slow Boat on Rum Row,* Miles narrated his life off the coast of California.[17]

Excerpts from *Slow Boat on Rum Row*
by Fraser Miles

An American shore boat appeared after lunch, circled the *Ryou II* once, and pulled alongside, fifty feet away. Hot Pants [Skipper Lind of *Ryou II*] recognized her skipper.

"He's okay, Jack, put the fenders over," he said. "Come alongside, Truscott you old rummy, and have a drink."

The speedboat tied along our starboard side. Hot Pants and his old buddy Truscott disappeared into the wheelhouse, with the small flat bottle of firewater from the galley. We hadn't received a release by radio as far as I knew, but maybe they had a different system down here. They were in the wheelhouse half an hour or more.

"Okay Jack, transfer two hundred and twenty-five off the deckload," Hot Pants said, throwing an empty brown bottle overboard.

Transferring alongside from a deckload is fast and easy; Truscott and his no-name speedboat were away in less than half an hour.

On the seven o'clock schedule we received a message from Vancouver, and Hot Pants gave me one to send. The next day, November eighteenth, we loaded two American shoreboats in succession, in late afternoon, over two hundred cases each, leaving us with about eight hundred cases. We moved offshore thirty or forty miles and drifted.

We drifted from November eighteenth to December tenth. Quite ignored by all, until the tenth, when one of the larger size cutters picked us up and stayed close by [called "cutterized"], even after we traded a case of firewater for a crate of fresh fruit and vegetables. We received a message on the noon radio schedule, and met the *Ragna* on position December eleventh.

We stopped our run to the northwest December twenty-ninth, somewhere off San Francisco again, we guessed, and we received a message from Vancouver.

Each of the next two days we loaded a fast American shore boat, missed the third day in bad weather, and met the *Zip* Monday morning in calm weather. *Zip* was going in, after twelve months at sea. Charlie went north with her. She had a spare fifty-watt tube for me. We also transferred five hundred cases to the *Zip*, probably for the *Ruth B* up north.

Several days of bad weather took us to Wednesday, January eleventh, which broke clear and smooth. We received a signal on the eight-thirty radio schedule but no shore boat arrived. On the seven o'clock schedule we received a message for immediate answer. Hot Pants handed me the answers for Vancouver and our Jimmy came back with another, also for immediate answer.

Hot Pants called Jack into the cabin, and there was a subdued discussion in there for some time, and then another message for Vancouver, and Jack came into the galley.

"He couldn't navigate a rubber ducky in a bathtub," he said. "We are a hundred miles away from position."

On the twenty-fourth, we loaded twelve hundred cases, but then tied astern of the mother ship for the night. The next morning we left right after breakfast, ran northwest for five days against a strong head-wind and were on position forty miles off Eureka.... Early on February first, in a rising northwest wind, a big fishing boat pulled up—all names covered as usual—hollered our name, and Hot Pants waved him alongside.

"Weather's gonna blow up," the fishing boat skipper said, "but we got everything arranged ashore for tonight. We want seven hundred, like in the release, and will load it all this trip if the wind will hold off a while."

At first, the two ships were comfortable enough together, with tire fenders on each, but later the short, steep seas of those wretched Frisco northwesters rolled the ships so that the pipe rails around the wheelhouse roof were knocked off, then the *Ryou II* took a hard pitch, and smashed the port window of the fishing boat cabin.

Footing was treacherous, the ships at times several feet apart, but we kept throwing cases across, and a good few landed on the fishing boat deck in a crunch of glass.

[later]"Well," Jack said while we ate lunch, "I hope there is a good market in Eureka for broken glass."

[later][When a shore boat came alongside without a release, the two crewmen, Clyde and Walt, wanted a load even though the paperwork hadn't cleared yet.]

"No way at all, Clyde. Sorry, but I did that about a month ago, and they raised hell with me—I'll be on the beach for sure if I do it again."

They were back on the twenty-eighth with good numbers, and a crate of fresh vegetables for us. They took two hundred and fifty cases a load, some five tons dry.

[Clyde and Walt told them about the hard times, with Roosevelt closing the banks the day before.]

[Later, the *Ryou II* was sent only *14 miles south*west of Santa Catalina Island—dangerously close to the one hour's steaming time from shore. In the morning *CG 827,* one of the fastest coast guard boats, the old rumrunner *Diatome,* headed right straight for them, perhaps to *"cutterize"* the *Ryou II.* The skipper thought they were captured since *CG 827* called for a tugboat.]

A blob of smoke came up in no time, and turned out to be three ships, a three-hundred-foot passenger ship, the *City of Panama,* another Coast Guard cutter, and a third boat, a tugboat, that was sightseeing. The *Panama* stopped near us, and a cargo door opened on her port side, a few feet above the water-line.

"Pull alongside under the door," a great loudhailer voice boomed down from her bridge. We moved alongside and took the bow and stern lines. From the stage rigged outside the cargo door a ship's officer dropped down to the *Ryou II* and went into our cabin with Hot Pants.

"Okay, get the hatch off," Hot Pants said when the officer climbed back aboard *Panama*. They're taking three hundred cases, Old Colonel and Coon Hollow, half each. And get to it—we want to get the hell back to San Clemente." The upper deck of the *Panama* was lined with men and women, all fairly young, half of them with cameras snapping away at us. The two cutters came in close and took pictures, and the sightseeing boat did the same. The *Panama* steamed slowly ahead all the while, making a couple of knots....Both cutters stayed with the *Panama*.

[In the summer of 1933, some of the skippers had a farewell party on the *Shuchona*.]

Brother Joe Keegan, here in spirit only but still on active service, is therefore nominated to Great Elder Brother for his long dedicated service in American drought relief work, from November 1922, to sometime soon in 1933. As runner-up, Brother Lind is asked to accept this award for second place, a whole case of Coon Hollow Bourbon, with one hundred percent breakage." Cap Harwood handed Hot Pants a case of Coon Hollow, with a great rattle of broken glass, to much applause.

"In our kiddies corner," Cap went on, "an honourable mention goes jointly to those two refugees from the kindergarten Small Brother Hoodspith and Small Brother Miles, who, after years of loyal and spirited service, are almost old enough to vote." Applause.

"Our last award goes to Brother [Harry] Slattery, the Honourable Surviving Brother. One night while drifting off San Diego in the schooner *Jessie*, he hit something big and sunk with the loss of all cargo. Later off San Francisco, he burned the *Fleetwood*, again with loss of all cargo. Good job there weren't many like him around, or we would have run out of ships years ago." Lengthy applause.

"...Brethren of the Row [rum row]...we wish to introduce our kindergarten to one of the finer things in life, Apricot Brandy, my contribution to this final meeting of the Brethren—Smokey ,the glasses please.

"We toast ourselves, Brethren of the row, *Lillehorn* Chapter, and all our absent Brethren of the *Malahat* Chapter, high type fellas all, and also the unknown organizers of the international drought relief project, who through their initiative, spirit and enterprise, have kept us in funds these many years; and others from thirst.

"Rum-running is finished—we are all on our last trip but will do our duty to the end, buoyed up by those fat paycheques and the thought that we

188

shall soon be fondly embraced by our loved one, the cuddly kittens at Celestine's [a cat house in Vancouver], who surely love us for ourselves alone."

Cries of, "Yeah, love those cuddly kittens."

"And finally," Cap Harwood went on, "we must never forget the Brethren's motto 'Don't tell nothin' to nobody nohow.'"

[They sing their song, John Thomas's 'Farewell to Celestine,'" a risque men's song]

We ask that you, John Thomas, our joy, our pride,
Our single delight in time of great need,
Please find strength for another Miss Deed,
Just once more 'fore we sail on salty tide.
First chorus please—
Oh my darling, oh my darling, oh my darling Thomas mine
You are limp and down forever, dreadful sorrow, Celestine.
We *thank you John, for joy on many a night,*
But John, we need you again for our pleasure.
To comfort, to charm our beloved, our treasure,
The second chorus please.
Oh my darling, oh my darling, oh my darling Thomas mine
Stand firm and serve your master, faithful soldier, Thomas mine.

Last verse.

You wake, you rise you come up strong,
You feel the touch of loving, soft white hand,
Of the lovely Celestine, and rise on command,
To please your master for all the night long.

[Miles wrote about how much money earned from rumrunning was filtered off to places like Celestine's and spent instead of saved or invested.]

A Roaring 20s roadhouse, Willoby's, which specialized in artichokes—artichokes every which way. Located northwest of Moss Landing on Monterey Bay, the roadhouse overlooked a key beach for landing smuggled liquor. The lookout "crow's nest" allowed signals to give the all clear to the rumrunning shore boats. Photo by author.

A case of liquor caught in mid-air being thrown from a mother ship to the shore boat Zeitgeist, taken by movie camera by smuggler/ owner Jack Hale, and then videotaped in the 1990s. Another shot of the Zeitgeist, loaded with whiskey and ready to come ashore; notice the arm of the rumrunner and the sharp-pointed dory on the back of Hale's boat. Party and picnic for Jack Hale and his friends on an island in San Francisco Bay. Video courtesy of Ralph and Barbara Osborne, Menlo Park.

CHAPTER 12

BY LAND—THE BORDER WAR

The second act passed by the new Congress under the Constitution organized the Customs Service in 1789, even before the first Secretary of Treasury, Alexander Hamilton, took office—thus being the oldest federal agency. The Service was incorporated as a division of the Treasury Department. It continued as a division until 1927 when it was given the status of bureau, directed by a commissioner appointed by the president, thus becoming the Bureau of .[1]

Collecting tax revenue, prohibiting smuggling and regulating withdraws of alcohol were the main missions of . Prohibiting the smuggling of alcohol was not a main function except as it pertained to avoiding taxes. Obviously since few smugglers reported their contraband to , liquor smuggling came under ' jurisdiction as tax offenders.

With headquarters in San Francisco and regional offices at each port, including Stockton, the Service had a prodigious job. Los Angeles office was in charge of protecting the border between Mexico and the United States and along the coast of southern California. It soon became clear could not handle the job with the few men it had. They recruited "Mounted Patrolmen" who found ways to become mounted on fast cars and even airplanes to help in this border war.

Badge, Pistol, Clock and Dagger
by Lee E. Echols

"Dammit, Echols , you wouldn't make a wart of the fore-gut of a Border Patrolman. I'm looking for men with some size and age on them."

It was the Collector of Schwabe, of Los Angeles, talking and he was talking right at me. Still at ease, I was standing before him—he didn't ask me to sit down—and when he raised up from behind his desk and towered over me, I didn't think he'd ever quit unfolding. He must have weighed well over 300 pounds and he was tall like a Colorado River cottonwood.

It was early February, 1928 and although I wasn't yet 20 and weighed about 140 pounds with the Sunday *Examiner* under my arm, I was up there in Los Angeles from my home in Calexico on the Mexican border, and I was looking for a job. This was the third time I'd confronted him, and I could see he was getting mighty sick of me.

I knew Collector Schwabe was building up the Patrol after it had been out of business for several years, but I couldn't understand why he'd want them 35 years old and as big as he was.

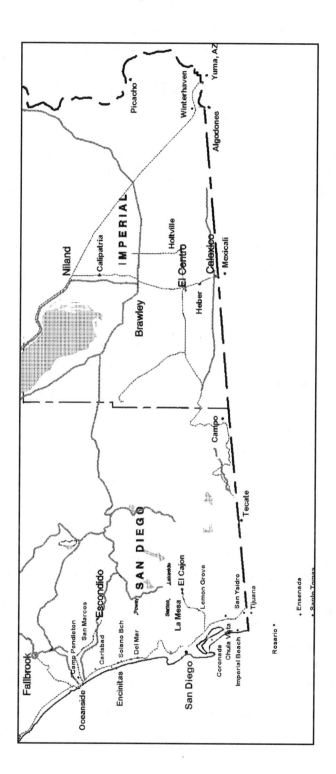

California Border

He went at me again, "You're not big enough, you're not old enough, and you certainly could have had no experience in any type of gun-carrying job."

"Oh, yes, I have!" I lied to him. "I'm older than I look, and I've been a deputy sheriff in Imperial County and a police officer in Calexico, off and on for a couple of years."

"You get out of here!" he said, scowling at me. "I want men, but in my wildest thoughts I never conjured up anybody that looked like you do."

I left, but I didn't remain idle. I went back to Imperial County to see the sheriff, Charlie Gillett. I didn't have much hope he'd help me in my scheme, but I was desperate. He had gone to San Quentin with a prisoner, but his son was there. He was Harold Gillett and he was a kindred soul, in that he'd gone to work for his father when he was about 16 years old as a deputy sheriff.

I told him my problem and he said, "Lee, let's write you a real humdinger of a letter of recommendation on Dad's official paper. I'll sign his name to it and if that big German won't hire you then, we'll sue him for slandering my dad."

We wrote one that was so glowing it scared me. Not enough though to keep me from going right back up there to Los Angeles with it. I broke in on one of Schwabe's private conferences again, waving my letter at him. He excused himself from the man he was conferring with and walked over to where I was standing by the door. "What the hell are you doing back up here?" he demanded.

"Here," I said triumphantly, "read this!"

He took it, with a curious look on his face. It took him about five minutes to read it, as he went over it two or three times, scowling at parts of it in disbelief, and finally nodding his head sagely, he asked, "When can you come to work?"

"Now," I told him.

"You show up down in the basement garage tonight at eleven," he said. "They'll be a couple of great big bastards down there waiting for you named Richard Bell and Paul Shadell. Maybe they can keep you from getting killed until you grow a little more."

As I started to leave, he asked me, "Have you got a gun?"

"Certainly," I replied. I'd borrowed a big .45 single action Army Colt from my father who was a captain on the Calexico Police Force.

"Have it with you," he said, and he handed me a round gold-plated badge from his desk.

"Don't I fill out papers, and sign in, all that fol-der-ol?" I asked him.

"You can do that tomorrow," he bellowed at me, "get the hell out of here!" I was gone.

I met Bell and Shadell that night. Shadell was the driver and we were to operate in a huge Packard automobile, seized by with a load of smuggled liquor from .

Shadell was built like a first mate on a coal tender and he reeked of cheap whiskey. Bell also was well up in the air and must have hit the scales at about 260. He didn't seem to have been drinking, but after talking with him a few minutes, I decided he was crazy. I never saw anything about him later which made me change my mind, either.

I was riding in the front seat with Shadell and Bell was humped up in the back. "We're going to check out some inlet up north," Shadell said. "Lots of boats are comin' in from the rum ships." He was driving out Sunset Boulevard and was soon hitting 70. "If any of these city, county or state cops stop you for anything," he yelled at me, "jist stick your head out the window and say 'United'?"

"I guess that'll put them in their place," I said trying to keep up my part of the conversation.

Bell broke in from the rear seat, "I always carry a lot of money on me," he said smugly. "Nobody'll try to rob me of it, either. I'm too well known in the underworld." Then he seemed to feel that this put him in a bad light, "Damn 'em!" he finished.

Nothing of any consequence happened that night except Shadell almost got us killed a few times with his race-track driving.

The next day I filled out a lot of papers, boosting my age up a couple of years, and my weight about fifteen pounds.

That night Shadell said we'd go south along the beaches and inlets toward Laguna Beach. He still smelled of whiskey and I learned that night he always had a pint of it in his heavy coat, which he'd take a quick draught from every time he thought Bell and I weren't looking.

We pulled into a dark lagoon near Newport Beach about two in the morning, with Shadell covering the inlet with his huge spotlight, looking for suspicious boats on the water or at the shore, when a Hudson roadster pulled up on us, with its red light turned on.

We identified ourselves to the lone driver and he said he was Carl Eifler, a Newport Beach police officer. I couldn't see much of him, as he sat slumped down in his car, but he appeared to be 20 or 21 years old.

"How do you get a job like you've got?" he asked me.

"Well," I told him looking him over in my great wisdom, "it ain't easy! There's a great big hulk of a man named Schwabe, and he wants them to be at least 35 years old."

He looked me over then, "Jesus, how'd you make it?" he asked.

"Well, I made such a nuisance of myself, breaking in on conferences and things, he finally hired me to get me out of his way."

Eifler said, "Well, I'm nowhere near 35 years old, but I'm fairly good sized." He got out of the car and he had the altitude and tonnage, all right. He looked like a great cinnamon bear, standing on its hind legs. And his jaw jutted out like he had a railroad lantern hung on it.

"What about experience?" Bell asked, feeling 's leg muscle. "You've got to have that!" I learned the next day that Bell's experience was as chauffeur for a rich friend of Collector Schwabe.

"I've been with this department a year, and I was on the Los Angeles Police Force three years before that," replied Eifler.

"Come off it, Eifler," I said, "you can't be that old."

Eifler grinned, "I'm not. I went with the LAPD when I was 17 years old. I worked three years before they found me out. I still wasn't 21, so they had to boot me out.

"I'll go up there and take a fall out of him," said. "I'm a convincing talker when I'm looking for a job."

In the meantime, Schwabe hired Lou Flammery, a tall, straight, part-Indian who had been in the patrol before; he'd gone with the California Highway Patrol, didn't like it and was to be the Officer in Charge at the station in Calexico.

Meantime, Schwabe fired Shadell and Bell. He fired Shadell for drinking all the time and Bell for being crazy, so I guess I wasn't too far wrong on Bell.

He sent Flammery and me down to Calexico to open the station there and he gave us a fairly new Buick to do our patrolling in. It too had been seized loaded with whiskey. We hadn't been there but about a week, when Schwabe sent Flammery a telegram. It said: "Report in my office day-after-tomorrow for conference. Use Buick for transportation. Leave in charge."

So there I was, nineteen years of age, and already in charge! It took me some time to realize that I was in charge of myself—and afoot.

Flammery came back in a few days. Schwabe had called him up there to pass on several prospective patrolmen. He approved several of them and they began showing up to go to work. They too were assigned seized automobiles, and about two weeks later, Schwabe wired Flammery again. "Two men hired today. They'll report to you day-after-tomorrow." He seemed to like that phrase "day-after-tomorrow" in his telegrams.

Well one of the two men who showed up was another big German, almost as big as Schwabe himself, named Berthold Belkie and the second one— I was surprised to learn—was Carl Eifler, whom I'd met at Newport Beach.

"How'd you make it?" I asked him. "You're fifteen years short of the minimum age limit set up by that gargantuan monstrosity up there in Los Angeles."

Eifler grinned, "I figured nothing was impossible after seeing he'd hired you," he said.

We hit it off well together, and although we each worked with different partners for some time, in 1930 we both transferred to San Diego, and were soon assigned to work together.

I'd been appraising for some time, and although I thought the world of him, I had about come to the conclusion he was damn near as crazy as Richard Bell, who was so well known in the underworld. He didn't seem to be crazy in the same way as Bell; it was a quirk he had about moving right into danger. I think I've known about three or four men in my entire life who were absolutely fearless, and Carl has to be the bellwether of this small cluster. I had noticed it indirectly on several occasions along the border near Calexico, but when it first dawned on me that fear and Carl were complete strangers was one night in the River bottom, west of the border crossing at San Ysidro.

We were concealed along one of the trails leading from Mexico, when we heard the clunk-clunk of alcohol cans coming up the trail. There were ten carriers, each with a newspapers-bag over his shoulders, with two five-gallon cans in front and two in back. Two hundred gallons of sugar-cane alcohol from Los Mochis, Sinaloa, on its way to become bathtub gin in California. We stepped out on them and "handsed them up" as the saying goes, with drawn pistols. They obliged readily enough, and after we'd gone over all ten of them for weapons and found none, we were preparing to march them into San Ysidro, where we could place them in the little jail there until the following day, when we'd take them into San Diego for arraignment before a United States Commissioner.

About this time, we had holstered our revolvers, and we heard a sharp command in Spanish from a flanker, who had been hidden in the brush on the right side of the caravan. "Arriba los manos!" he demanded. "Get your hands up!"

He was about fifteen yards from us and he had a big, fierce looking pistol in his hand. Well, instead of putting his hands up, Carl walked right toward the flanker. When he reached him, he grabbed the barrel of the revolver with his left hand, pushing it away from his face. He swung a mighty blow from his right shoulder and connected with the flanker's jaw. I saw the jaw go completely around to where the center of the man's mouth was directly under his right ear. He went down like a pole-axed hog, completely out of business, with broken teeth falling out of his mouth like popcorn. When he came to, we felt him over and found that had broken his jaw on both sides. He was in the hospital, under guard, for ten days before he was even able to get up before the U. S. Commissioner for arraignment.

In 1931 while I was working out of San Diego, there were about fifty of us working in pairs on the Mexican Border and along the coast to the Orange

County line. We were Patrol Inspectors and our means of transportation were automobiles which we had seized transporting illegal liquor or drugs. We even had an immense Cadillac which we used as a squad car. We had seized it from the old-time movie star, Alma Rubens, who got herself hooked on morphine and made the mistake of bringing almost a half pound of it through the border at .

With an Empty Gun
as told by Carl Eifler, Salinas

While working under cover at one time, I was called in the office by the boss, Leo Stanley. "Carl," he asked, "do you speak German?"

"No," I said, "I've had a background in German and studied German the first six years of my life but you have to keep up with the language in order to speak it. I still understand quite a bit of it."

"Jack here says if I can give him anybody who can understand it, he can give us some cases," said Stanley. Jack was a smuggler and he was kinda' proud of it. He said if he could take someone down and crawl under the floor of Johnson Distillery in Tijuana, he could listen to some of this conversation in German and find out where and when loads were going and handle it ourselves.

So we did and that started the deal. Jack was telling the truth. I worked with Rusty Russel but this was a one man job. I had to do it alone. Rusty was staying at a hotel in central San Diego. We'd check into the office; then I'd tell Rusty to go to the Grant Hotel and stay there until I got back from . Then we'd go out and catch the smugglers as they came across the border.

I was sitting in the court room on a case one day when Jack gave me information that the smugglers were going to pull a load that afternoon. I headed toward the border with Jack, went into Mexico but found the load had already gone out. We took after it. I tracked the tire marks and found where the truck turned down toward the border. On the way down to the border we ran into the car coming back that had taken the load down. They had already unloaded on the American side. When I got to the fence, we left my car on the Mexican side. Jack and I jumped over the fence and we began tracking on the American side. Here's a broken twig, here's something else broken—just as a tracker does. We got fairly well across the line when this man jumped up and ran so I took off after him. He wouldn't stop and we had a running gun battle. He jumped over a tree trunk, a fallen tree, and I jumped over after him but when I landed I felt my leg go. And with what strength I had with the other one, I took one more step and dove at him. He jumped down a little ravine and so I landed with my hand right on his shoulders, but I couldn't get a grip on him. As we went on down, one of my hands went into his hip pocket. This tripped him and he fell. I over-powered him and handcuffed his hands behind his back. We were right on the edge of a cliff then, eight feet from the top and one hundred feet down to the bottom. There was a tree right there that I could get a hold of. When Jack came up, I gave him my keys, handcuff keys too.

"Jack, I think my leg is broken. Now you get back to the border and get hold of some of the boys and get them back up here to relieve me. You tell them I think my leg is broken."

He took off. I laid there, making the guy face away from me. I didn't want him to see me if I couldn't hide the pain I was in. This was just at dusk.

After we had laid there for a couple of hours we heard somebody coming up the trail. It wouldn't have been my men because they'd be hollering. It had to be his. I told him to keep quiet for a moment. I took his hat and pulled it down along side his head. He asked, "What are you going to do?"

"Well," I said, "I'm going to put you out. I'm going to rap you along side your head with the .45 and put you out and go after your friends."

He begged me not to.

I said, "All right, you keep your mouth shut, don't make a whimper of any kind."

I reached up, caught hold of this tree, pulled myself up. I reached down and pulled him up. I crawled toward the bank on my knees.

His partner came up the trail. As he gets close enough to me, I stood up and walked a couple steps toward him, had my .45 out and placed him under arrest and put him alongside his partner. That attempt of walking without showing I was injured was just excruciating. I was afraid I was going to pass out. So I made them sit with their face away from me. I was behind them and told them not to say a word, not to talk. When one coughed, I reached over and grabbed him, pulled out my gun and said, "That's your last time. The next time you make a sound of any kind, I'm gonna let you have it."

My gun was empty. I had two prisoners there. I was injured. They could have got up and stomped me to death and I knew it. I didn't know what type of prisoners I had, whether they were petty guys or big guys or what the score was. Anyway the point was my fight to keep conscious as much as I could and if I passed out for them not to know it. I had no more shells for my gun.

I'd been really tough with these two. It had gotten cold. They wanted a fire. By that time I figured I could use a fire too, basically because I knew the men had been looking for me for hours and they hadn't found me. I could gamble that these two didn't have any more men who were coming up to help them with the alcohol. The alcohol was stashed. He had run from the stash which he just brought across the border.

I didn't know what the score was. Perhaps the first man was to walk out to say the load's safely hid away and when he didn't show up the second man came out looking for him.

It was about eleven that night when finally I heard Mike calling for me and Richardson was the first one to get up there.

Anyway Richardson walked up and I said, "Richie, you got any extra shells with you?"

We carry some in our .45 and extra shells in clips of three.

Richie said, "Yeah."

"Well, give me a load."

After I took the load, I took the gun over to the prisoners and I said, "You two can take it easy now. My leg's busted and my gun was empty—that's why I was tough."

One man was a third time loser for felonies. That would have been life in prison. Of course life in prison doesn't mean they stay in there for the rest of their lives.

When this case was tried, I was in the San Diego Naval Hospital. What had actually happened was my leg hadn't been broken. The bones on the inside of my ankle tore apart. I had landed a little bit too hard and it just kicked out the inside.

When any point came up to the jury, the prosecutor had to say. "Well, the officer who can testify to this particular case is in the hospital." Anyway the case was won.

"Chinese Aliens and Booze Had Priority of First Patrol"
anonymous[2]
Valley Grove

In 1927, the local border areas were a "river of liquor" flowing north and Chinese nationals used San Diego as an illegal gateway to San Francisco.

Ralph Armstrong, of the Sweetwater Mobile Lodge in Spring Valley, was on duty here as a border patrolman then. He is a charter member of the border patrol, having received his appointment on July 1, 1924, the day after the patrol was founded.

Before becoming a border patrolman he turned down a job as an instructor in the maintenance and use of machineguns for the Mexican contemporary of Poncho Villa named Dellahuerta.

Methods of catching illegal aliens and booze smugglers were about the same then as now, Armstrong said, adding, "They're really the only ones that will work."

"We used to spend about 75 percent of our time stopping cars on roads, in operations similar to present border patrol roadblocks, both near the border and further north," he recalled.

Although traffic sometimes amounted to only one car per hour at the road checks, occasionally the action got rather wild.

"Once we were using a theatrical log to stop cars. We'd put it on the road and people would think it was a real log and stop. Actually, of course, it was made of wire and plaster.

One night a big smuggler got drunk in and vowed he was going to run right through the checkpoint because he knew the log was fake.

We heard about this and substituted a real log for the phony one.

Well, the smuggler came barreling through and didn't even slow down for the officers trying to stop him. He hit the log and the running gears of the car stopped—but the rest kept on going.

The whole area beyond the roadblock was decorated with three Chinese and the smuggler."

Various forms of wildlife made waiting in the brush for aliens (and booze runners) on Otay Mesa more interesting than it is now. "The place was lousy with rattlesnakes," Armstrong recalled. "We used to have to beat the brush for a diameter of about 10 feet around where we were going to sit to chase them away."

"Once I was sitting on the mesa at night and suddenly I was knocked over by a terrific blow. I knew what it was when I hit the ground and saw two coyotes, the female in the lead, streaking across the flat land."

Instead of the mix of Mexicans and central Americans apprehended by modern border patrolmen, the first border guards dealt mainly with Chinese and southern European aliens.

Mexican immigration laws were then far more liberal than U. S. regulations, so many persons denied legal entry into the United States tried to come illegally through Mexico.

Chinese paid as much as $1,000 for the trip to San Francisco and Armstrong said that some had to work for 10 years to repay the debt.

Alien smugglers in those days were considered "more ruthless than booze smugglers" by the *Herald-Examiner*. In those days the border patrol made 90 to 150 arrests per week, about two days' total for today's borders guards.

An able assistant of Armstrong's for many years was a German shepherd name Berkie van Erlandgurnd. A graduate of the German police academy, Berkie was a gift of a wealthy La Jolla woman.

"Whenever I had Berkie I never needed a partner," Armstrong said. "Once a group of Chinese escaped from a roadblock near Warner Springs near daybreak, and Berkie had flushed them all out of the brush by noon.

"Berkie could catch up with a running man, throw him to the ground in a cloud of dust and keep him there and the prisoner wouldn't be scratched.

"Once I left a Mexican prisoner sitting in the back seat of my car, and Berkie in front. My partner felt sure the prisoner would escape, but when we returned he was laying in the back with Berkie atop him."

Report to the Wickersham Commission, 1929

The Border Patrol was under supervision of Collectors in the Department of Treasury.[3] The agents technically had nothing to do with the enforcement of the prohibition act. They investigated smuggling of liquor, as they did smuggling of Chinese, narcotics and jewelry, for violations of tariff acts, tariff tax evasion, not necessarily prohibition acts.

During the 1920s, eight agents were killed along the border, six of them in Texas, the other two by Canada, none in California.

The agents themselves did their job with little violence. In the first ten years of prohibition, the officers killed 26 men, most of whom lost their lives on the Texas border. A. H. Hendricks, however, was shot and killed at the official crossing at . The only California victim was shot by officers in self-defense.

The job across the country was overwhelming. Washington, Oregon and California had 2,730 miles of coastline to protect and 1,035 miles of island shoreline. Nearly three hundred miles of California frontier with Mexico, most of it uninhabited and hostile desert, gave clever smugglers an advantage.

Because of the prodigious job across the country, the Canadian border, the oceans, the Gulf of Mexico and the Mexican border, expanded the border patrol by 717 men, of which 135 were already working for . In November 1929, San Francisco district # 28 had 410 permanent employees, Los Angeles

U. S. Customs Patrol Office at Heber. Notice the patrol cars behind the men: Most cars were confiscated vehicles, taken from liquor and alien (Chinese) smugglers. From L-R: Frank Goodell, Lee Echols, Clarence Griffith, Vern Williams, Bud Bump, Fred Brafford, Bert Belkie, Reid Cunningham, Carl Eifler, Charley Johnson, Oliver Freeman and Ralph Armstrong, ca. 1929-1930. Photo courtesy Lee Echols.

district #27 had 210, of which 34 were "Mounted Inspectors" (like and) along the Mexican border stationed at , San Diego and other locations; another 52 were inspectors and 3 "inspectresses" along the southern coast, up as far as Santa Barbara and Ventura, and inland from Imperial County to Fresno. At the ports were 22 Guards and 18 Collectors and Deputy Collectors.

Under the Treasury Department, the Prohibition Bureau worked directly and indirectly with the Coast Guard, Bureau, Internal Revenue Bureau, Public Health and Department Committee on Coordination. The latter tried to solve problems created because of disjointed efforts and duplicated work.[4]

The Coast Guard took care of the coast of California and had an Intelligence Section for prohibition and smuggling rings. controlled land borders between Mexico and United States and along some beaches in southern California, coordinated with the Prohibition Bureau in San Francisco for Mexican and Canadian information, maintained special agents to investigate liquor and narcotic smuggling, and governed exports and imports of lawful liquor. Internal Revenue Bureau collected lawful taxes on alcohol and granted permits dealing with alcohol. Public Health controlled permits for medicinal alcohol for ships.

War with the MacClemmy Gang

MacClemmy's gang in Mexico and San Diego County operated Red Top Distillery just across the border in Tijuana with a capacity of 3,000 gallons

Early Condley, Clarence Griffith and Lee Echols in customs office in either Heber receiving a "hot tip" from informer. Probably a posed picture. Photo courtesy Lee Echols.

per week, the largest of four distilleries. Hugh G. MacClemmy also transported liquor into San Diego and Los Angeles counties.

Taking a page from the Standard Oil vertical monopoly, where Standard controlled the product from raw material to the retail outlet, MacClemmy
controlled manufacturing in Mexico, sneaking and bribing his liquor across the
line by truck, by Hudson sedans (even his own Hudson) carrying 20 five-gallon
cans and by cars with secret 15-20-gallon liquor tanks. Across the border, his
drivers had a race to San Diego and Los Angeles. He also flew it over the
border, using as many as three airplanes. One of these was caught in Mexico
and then used by Mexican authorities. He transported by boat to San Diego
Bay and San Pedro, where drivers met the boats and raced to the city, delivering it to retail and wholesale distributors.

From 1913 on, when Los Angeles County sent him to two years at
Folsom for burglary, MacClemmy had a proclivity toward making money by
smuggling. In 1923 he paid a $300 fine for transporting booze in Alhambra.
Arrested by San Diego County sheriffs when he and his wife delivered liquor,
they paid their $500 each and were apprehended again in 1925. He acquired
the Red Top, delivering much of his own liquor at first. Four more arrests in
1926: he and his wife smuggled in separate Hudson coaches paying fines of
$1,200; smuggled Red Top alcohol and A.B.C. beer from Mexicali, and finally
smuggled 1,000 gallons on a Moreland truck.

Despite being fined frequently, he expanded with more cars, trucks,
planes and boats. His distillery cans were unique and recognizable with red on
top of the 5-gallon cans and his liquor preferred because of high quality. From
Jacumba to Tijuana, 75 miles, his drivers sneaked through the border. More
accurately, they drove across the border right through the lanes. They were not
checked if they went in the right line at the right time. For 18 months (about
1925-6) almost no smuggler had been caught at the border by . MacClemmy
had corrupted the Customs Service.

Then the Treasury Department sent the good guys down, Special Agents
Charles Cass and O. C. Macumber. Their job was to clean up the mess and
corruption in San Diego County. These honest men were appalled at the situation. They waged war against two forces, the MacClemmy Gang and the corrupt men on the border crossings. Cass and Macumber had an intelligence task
force, kept good records, stopped suspicious vehicles a mile or so after they
had crossed the border, making numerous arrests. One driver caught was Francisco Cuevas who admitted he had "come through the Gate at " every day in
1926, making a round trip to Los Angeles, filled with 25 gallons of Red Top
liquor in concealed tanks in his car. Soon 2,700 gallons of confiscated Red Top
liquor sat in its own section of the federal warehouse in San Diego.

This elaborate operation involved many gang members, including
former federal agents: his right-hand man, C. K. Aiken, a dangerous character,

assisted in beating up informer Victor Carusso in the Red Top Distillery; Mrs. Nora MacClemmy, convicted of transporting liquor in San Diego; Pete Badillo Jr., trucker who hauled from Red Top to Hermosillo Cove, below Rosarita Beach; Carlos Cuervo, transporter across the border, indicted by the Feds, and owner of much property in bought from his proceeds; Francisco Cuervo [Cuevas], arrested for smuggling but jumped bond; Clyde Hupp, aliases Clyde Hudson and A. B. Figueroa, arrested for smuggling; Homer Eads, of National City, alias Homer Hearst, having made 63 long-distance calls in two months to the Red Top, transporting liquor for two years, over 100 trips; Mrs. Harry L. Baldwin, mother-in-law of Homer Eads, whose house at 1105 Seventh Street, National City, contained gallons of smuggled liquor; Fred Buck, former Agent and deputy sheriff of San Diego County, later employed by MacClemmy to pilot airplanes to deliver alcohol into the U.S.; William Long, former Agent, discharged lookout man for MacClemmy for landings in San Diego Bay, partner of Leon Cesmat, former Inspector discharged; Pasadena bootlegger and boat operator Albert Moynier, 1360 Wesley Drive, Pasadena; Nick Zorn, Hollywood bootlegger, Los Angeles agent for MacClemmy liquor; a firm of Herbert Jaffe and E. P. Baker, owners of bars in and the Aztec Brewery, whose beer was shipped with Red Top liquor to Hermosillo Cove, then to California by boats *Hawk* and *Titicaca*.

The gang's San Diego representatives were the "Diehl Boys" (Deal, Diel?) who acted as middlemen, taking orders and delivering. However in 1926, the "boys" sold 600 gallons at $40 per gallon and disappeared. Hugh MacClemmy offered anyone $1,000 for knowledge of their whereabouts.

S. L. Coatza, owner of a resort at Suncrest by La Mesa, was an informer and knew the inside of the gang because he was a Spanish bookkeeper at the Foreign Club in . William Pruett, alias M. M. Martin and Happy Martin, became another informer after he had been caught smuggling several times and was on MacClemmy's boat when it overturned on the beach at Imperial Beach in June 1927.

MacClemmy corrupted agents at the border, one being Fred A. Markley, in charge of at San Ysidro, who for two years allowed smuggling cars through his line at the border. He said he was told from higher up to lay off MacClemmy. No one believed that. Markley objected to Cass making arrests about a mile from the border, after supposedly being inspected at the border. He felt it was embarrassing and demeaning. It was of course, 'cause Markley was crooked. Markley's co-workers learned not to turn information over to him because it got back to the person being investigated. Officer Bill Evans in Tecate closed the gate, went to a Mexican bar and drank himself drunk. Several Americans in Tecate wrapped up packages of liquor to carry across because old Bill was drunk. Investigative agents later stopped cars after they had gone through inspection at Tecate. Of the 14 stopped, none had been searched, four had booze, some in plain sight. Cass confiscated a Hudson car which he later drove for the Intelligence branch of . Another informant said he could buy liquor from Agent Cesmat; another said three agents were under the pay of MacClemmy. One was Agent Bishop who allowed loads to go through. A recruiter for smugglers told the informant that a smuggler won't get caught because "there was no chance at certain hours when certain officers were on duty, the road is clear." Smuggler Tichner, when caught north of the border, admitted that was his 42nd trip for MacClemmy. Frank Cuevas made a trip everyday for six months. He was caught when each day he bought five dollars worth of gas. That was all the tank held. The rest of the tank held liquor. The attendant reported him to the right agents.

Notorious Hollywood bootlegger and smuggler Nick Zorn was caught at the border because he made a mistake and lined up in the wrong line. After the arrest, the corrupt agent phoned MacClemmy who later put up bail for Zorn.

Cass and Macumber collected evidence and plea bargained to obtain witnesses against the gang. One of those given a break to testify was Eads, who moved to Los Angeles to go straight and avoid agents and the gang. Once MacClemmy and Aiken came to see Eads and offered him $1,000 to bring one load of liquor across. Eads told agents he didn't take the offer of $1,000 because "I was convinced these men came to Los Angeles for the purpose of giving me a 'Chicago ride,' " i.e., to be killed. When the gang found out from former undercover agent W. A. Brockway that bootlegger Jack Rogers was really Agent C. J. Garner, obtaining information on the gang, MacClemmy became white with anger and threatened to kill anyone associated with Garner. It was a risky business, like spying on the spyers. Brockway, betraying the government, told MacClemmy that he "could clear the road to land alcohol in Los Angeles" for $4,000. MacClemmy accepted. Eads said that information given to the prohibition office got to MacClemmy in the next day. The gang used money, fear and intimidation to keep in power. Eads did not keep his promises to the agents, conning the agents for almost a year. They believed Eads lied on parts of the interview, but assured them he was planning on going straight as a used-car salesman at 4257 South Vermont and invited the agents to come to the car lot anytime—apparently his lying proficiency helping him in his new profession.

A Federal Grand Jury, finally hearing the evidence against MacClemmy, said they did not want to hear any more witnesses and voted for a no-bill. Brazenly MacClemmy bragged about his immunity with having jurors and federal officials in his pocket. He said he bought the U. S. Attorney and the Grand Jury for $6,500. In fact, two files of this case disappeared from the office of the U. S. Attorney in San Diego during the summer of 1927.

Agents, however, kept pushing with other arrests and presenting the case to a new Grand Jury. The prosecution told the jury of his bragging of owning this jury too; in fact, one new juror affirmed he had already been offered a bribe. This new Grand Jury came up with a true bill.

Hugh G. MacClemmy was convicted July 15, 1927, on smuggling conspiracy. He was sentenced to two years and fined $5,000 by the U. S. District Court in San Diego. He had also been in the jail for attacking Immigration Inspector Ashton, who had testified against him. MacClemmy evidently could not corrupt all agents, so he tried to frame Agents Cass and O. C. Macumber, witnesses against his smugglers.

These years of investigations and arrests, with a successful trial, put this gang in disarray. But as with the bootlegger arrested at a Saturday night dance, another took his place the next week, and another gang filled the vacuum in the San Diego area.[5]

With a new breed of men being recruited, like Lee and Carl , and with the discharge and arrest of dishonest ones, the United States border with Mexico became respectable again. However, smuggling continued, by land, sea and air, but not right through the Gate with agents looking the other way.

Jiggers, The Cops
by Lee E. Echols , Chula Vista

I was born dead. Not literally, I kicked as hard and yelled as loud as any baby in the Indian Territory. It is an old Oklahoma expression, meaning I didn't have a chance. That is, a chance of being anything but a policeman of some sort when I reached my majority.

My paternal grandfather, Flemon , was a United States Deputy Marshall in that sink of lawlessness that was the Choctaw Nation and he worked under Judge Isaac C. Parker, who held forth as United States District Judge at Fort Smith, Arkansas, and had outlaws, murderers, bank robbers and horse thieves hung in bunches like Thompson seedless grapes.

My maternal grandfather, Scipio Hughes, was a Texas Ranger when their sole excuse for being was to shoot Kiowa Indians through their gall bladders when they came whooping and hollering down from the *boi d'arc* thickets of the Indian Territory, stealing horses and cattle from the Texas ranchers.

Both these fine old relatives of mine were half-breed Cherokee Indians. Now my father, Guy Echols, tried to beat the system. He became a cattle rancher in western Oklahoma, right in the heart of Kiowa Nation and among the mean old blanket Indians that Granpa Hughes helped shoot the living be-Jesus out of right after the Civil War.

My early life was spent in Oklahoma and California. It didn't take hardly any time for Pa to go flat busted in Kiowa Country and he wound up with a Model T Ford and we headed west. He made a little money contracting in Imperial Valley and went back to the Kiowa Nation where he got back in the cow business. He blew it again and from then until my 14th year, my life was spent either in Imperial Valley, California, Gotebo, Oklahoma, or the road between the two. We beat out a buffalo trail with model T Fords that was later known as Highway 80.

Finally, Pa decided that either he wasn't a cattleman, or western Oklahoma wasn't the place for one. We settled in Calexico, California, on the Mexican border and he reverted to type.

He went to work on the police force and it wasn't too long until he became Chief of Police and he held that position for 20 years.

By the time I was 20 years old, I was a Border Patrolman and stationed at Calexico.

Most of our work at that time was running down liquor smugglers and we got most of the big ones through infiltration of their organization with informants. Of course, they used informants in their nefarious methods of eluding us and one of these was a big colored man, Rufe Reddings, who lived in New River bottom, just west of Calexico. This was a major site of operation for the liquor smugglers as it was well covered with weeds and brush and Rufe's cardboard shack was about 30 yards from the Mexican border. There was a great thicket of arrowweeds, tumbleweeds and milkweeds growing between his shack and the road which ran parallel to the Mexican border, about a hundred yards to the north.

Through informants we had in Mexicali we learned that this man would watch closely for or immigration officers and if any showed up in the area for a stake-out, he would immediately put a sheet on his clothes-line. Then the smugglers—most of whom were paying him a weekly stipend—wouldn't cross the border until the sheet was down. Through our informant we learned that when the sheet was down, pack trains of Mexican alcohol carriers would cross the border Indian-file and make it to the border road where they'd be picked up by all manner of vehicles.

I talked this over with my partner, Harry "Bud" Bump. Bud was as big as a Belgium Congo gorilla and played fullback on our Calexico High School football team when I was playing end. We were good friends as well as partners and Bud could come up with some mighty ingenious schemes.

"Let's burn ol' Rufe out of there, Lee," he said. "We'll wait until there's a good wind blowing from the road toward his shack. Then we'll drive down the road and I'll fire a Very signal pistol into the big clump of dry weeds on the edge of the road. When that big ball of fire hits those dry weeds ol' Rufe will be taking it on the heel and toe and by the time he gets slowed down enough to look back, he'll see his shack and his sheet burning up like the Brooklyn Theater!"

About four nights later a good enough wind came up that Bud Bump decided it would carry the fire from the big clump of weeds to Rufe Redding's shack, so I drove the car quietly along the border road, without lights, until we reached the dry weeds. Bud Bump aimed the Very pistol into the middle of the clump and pulled the trigger. The great ball of fire went right into the clump of weeds and hit an immigration border patrolman right square in the lumbar region of his crupper. He yowled like a crotch-kicked warlock and took off toward the river, throwing a tail of fire behind him as he went. Oh! It was lively! Lively!

I laid the throttle back in the sand box, as the railroaders would say, and Bud Bump and I left there in the opposite direction from that taken by the bottom-shot border patrolman and we were "making the Memphis time," which on the road, connotes the highest possible rate of speed.

The following day our office received a notice from the Chief of the Immigration Border Patrol, advising our units to be extremely cautious in working stakeouts in the New River bottom as an assassination attempt had been made against one of their men the night before and the would-be-murderer used a sawed-off shotgun.

Bud Bump and I kept our mouths buttoned up about our part in the little escapade and we hid that Very signal pistol so deep you couldn't have found it with a metal detector.

The Border Patrolman Wins a Coast Guard Boat
as told by Carl Eifler, Salinas[6]

The border patrolmen always pulled tricks on each other. I can remember Lee Echols and Aaron Quick coming off the pier at Oceanside. They were eating salted peanuts. Lee had just given Aaron Quick some salted peanuts. Aaron had them in his hand and says, "Say, have you ever mixed these little Mexican hot peppers with salted peanuts and given them to anybody? That's really a dirty trick to do." Aaron just threw them in his mouth. Lee had already put peppers in them. With a hot mouth and burning throat, Aaron looked for revenge. He put a fish in Lee's pocket. It wasn't till some days later when the fish was rather putrid that the wife discovered it.

Lee and I would do a little magic. We had a little bottle and we could lay it down and it would lay there. If we handed it to you and you laid it down, it would pop right back up. We won a Coast Guard boat on that trick one night at Lee's house. The Coast Guard captain was so darn sure he could make that darn bottle lie flat, he bet his boat.

He lost.

When he was ready to leave to go back to the boat, we said, "What boat?"

We worked closely with the Coast Guard; we were often on the boats with them. In those days most of the Coast Guard's boats were also captured rumrunners' boats. I remember a lot of the boats had Liberty airplane engines. During World War I they had Liberty 12 cylinder aircraft engines which were converted to rumrunners. We'd go out on the Coast Guard boats because they were on our cases and we'd get the Guard in on it. They were in the Treasury Department and so were we. We were practically one unit.

The Service is the most honest I've been in. If anybody ever went crooked, the boys in the Service got him. The pay was fairly good in those days. We received $2,100 a year.

At Newport Beach there was some conversation and evidence that our youngest recruit, Hodger, who afterwards was chief of police for many years, was on the take but I don't think he was when he was a policeman.

Right where the Ex-President Nixon lives there was a ravine just north of his home in San Clemente; next to that was a beach, a state park in there now. The old road used to go along there. That was a smuggling spot in there. I used to get in there with my shotgun. I came down the cliffs, this side (north) of where the immigration stop station is. I'd get down the beach and walk in. I'd lay there or I'd come in from this ravine. One night I jumped 'em in there. I thought I had them but I didn't. But they knew me and knew that I was coming in there. They knew I was after them. The smugglers were sneaky. There were so many false beds, false gas tanks and false tires. Almost anything you can think of on a car where you could hide stuff they would use.

Smuggling Across the Border
by Lee E.Echols, Chula Vista

There were two methods of apprehending the liquor smugglers. The best was through informants and we used them as much as possible. The second was to "stakeout" known border crossings for several nights, hoping violators would choose that particular place to attempt their skullduggery. An excellent informer, whom we used for several years, was a hare-lipped Arkansawyer we called "Koots" Davis. "Koots" was so named because the Mexicans called him "El Cucho." This word, in Spanish, means fertilizer or manure, but it is also a Mexican slang word for a hare-lipped person. Koots was a smuggler himself. He was also a turkey and chicken thief and he was a man who would trade you blackbirds for turkeys. That is, he would send us over on the east side of Calexico along the border, while he slipped out on the west side and brought over his own little shipment. We realized this, but figured if we caught him, we'd lose him for an informer and the smuggling he was doing was so minuscule compared to some of the huge loads he was turning over to us. We didn't want to stop his flow of information.

It was hard for a stranger to come to Mexicali—which was the Mexican town directly across the border from Calexico—for liquor smuggling operation, without Koots hearing of him from his Mexican connections, and he would invariably break right into the smuggler's plans. On one such occasion, he came by my house to see me about four in the afternoon, and I could tell by the way his rabbit-like lip was quivering that he was the bearer of important news.

"Stiffy Billings is in town!" he said, licking his upper lip.

"Go on with it," I told him. "I never heard of Stiffy Billings."

"Well," he said, "Stiffy Billings got his name because his head stickin' away off up in the air like he was a well digger lookin' for his lunch. He's down here from Pomona and he's after twelve cases of Waterfill and Frasier whiskey. I've already took him out by the golf course and showed him right whur it come to up through the big draw."

The Calexico Municipal Golf Course was built along the border, about a mile west of Calexico and there were two draws about five feet deep which ran from the border proper to the border road, a distance of about two hundred

On informer's tip, Customs agents Lou Flammery and Lee Echols caught a well-known Los Angeles bootlegger with 300 gallons of Mexican alcohol in his "empty" truck. He was "always the first one to cross when the border opened at Calexico at 6:00 a.m. Monday morning," said the tipster. He had a 300-gallon copper tank hidden in a false bed. Photo courtesy of Lee Echols.

yards. "Stiffy'll pick it up whur the big draw ends at the border road. You fellers can be awaitin' fer him on west a half a mile, at the road which comes out of Steven's Beach."

Steven's Beach was a large pond with a small sort of night club built on it, where gamblers and their girls came for a little fun after the border closed at 9:00 p.m.

"Now, looky here," Koots went on, "why don't you fellers crawl in there and git them four Mexicans who'll be a-bringin' it to him. They're my boys, and they're square shooters!"

"Where is this 'Stiffy' Billings now?" I asked him.

"He's over there right across the border in the Gambrinus bar, drinkin' pussy cafes like he's jist a-darin' himself to git sick," Koots said. "Wanta go over there and see him?"

I agreed and we drove down to the border. "I'll go across the line and into the Gambrinus and git him out," Koots told me. "You cross behind me and wait on the corner down toward the Southern Club."

There were two big gambling clubs in Mexicali at that time. The Southern Club and the A.B.W. Club, known as "The Owl." It was the larger of the two and was owned by Allen, Byers, and Withington. Both clubs had excellent jazz bands and all sorts of entertainment which came down from the coast, with a new act every couple of weeks or so. Jack Tenney, a piano player, headed the band at the A.B.W. Club, later becoming a California State Senator. He wrote the famous old song "Mexicali Rose."

Unknown Customs Officer at border stakeout, drinking coffee, waiting to catch liquor smugglers. According to Lee Echols, who took this picture around 1929, they would make an improvised tent and stay out for as long as two weeks—as long as the water held out. Photo courtesy Lee Echols.

Prior to entering the Service, I had been a jazz drummer, and had played with Jack Tenney and his band on assignment throughout Imperial Valley. During those days he and his wife used to come visit me and my wife and while the gals talked, Jack and I would sit at the piano and write songs. We wrote enough of them to play an entire dance without playing a song that was ever published.

Jack had got off to an early start with the popularity of "Mexicali Rose," and made the mistake of selling it outright to a song publisher in Los Angeles named Ray Quinkley, for three thousand dollars. It rose in popularity to where it became the third most popular song ever published, from sheet-music sales. Quinkley made several million dollars on it. There has been quite a bit of controversy as to who "Mexicali Rose" actually was. Well, she wasn't anybody. She was a figment of the imagination of Jack Tenney and the gal who helped him with the lyrics.

But to get back to Koots Davis and "Stiffy" Billings, I crossed the border after I saw Koots enter the Gambrinus bar, and walked toward the Southern Club. I stopped on the corner where I waited for Koots to come out. I didn't have to wait long. He came out the front door of the Gambrinus, arm in arm with Stiffy Billings, and I don't believe in all my life I've seen a more incongruous pair. Both of them were over six feet tall. Koots had a small, round head about the size of a pumpkin grown outside the irrigation area. His right arm, due to an elbow break early in life, was set akimbo, while his left arm was hooked into the right arm of Stiffy Billings. Koots had legs which reached well up past where his navel should have been and they looked like well-starched flamingo necks. Stiffy, as Koots had described him, had his head set off at an angle and aimed skyward. He had to roll his eyes down to where the whites showed to see dead ahead of him. They passed me, in earnest conversation with each other, heading for the Southern Club and as they got by me, Koots stuck his wingy right arm around behind him and began pointing at Stiffy's back, as if to say, "Here he is! This is Stiffy Billings!"

Customs patrolman named Early Condley and I waited at the road from Steven's Beach that evening and about 10 p.m., saw a car driving slowly by, toward Calexico. When it passed a big draw in the golf course, it turned around, pulled back to the draw and stopped. We saw some feverish activities then which were skylighted by the lights from the car: men running back and forth to the car and putting heavy sacks into it.

Within a couple of minutes, the men drifted back toward Mexico and the automobile started toward us. We saw it was a fairly new sheriff's model Studebaker touring car with side curtains concealing the load. We let it get down the road about a half mile before we came out of our hiding place and began tailing it without lights. We allowed him to get to the first road going north away from the border and then we turned the lights on our powerful

Buick, seized from another unfortunate rumrunner who had made the acquaintance of Koots Davis, and overhauled him. We turned the red light on, opened up the siren, and Stiffy Billings was out of the smuggling business for a couple of years.

Koots came up to my apartment one night about two in the morning. "Have you seen Bob?" was his opening salvo when I opened the door.

"Bob who?" I sleepily asked him.

"Bob Davis, my brother," he said, and I could see he was excited.

"No," I replied. "How would I have seen him?" His brother ran a small bar in Mexicali.

"Well," he said, "I was in a little splatterin' tonight."

"What the hell are you talking about?" I asked him, still fighting sleep.

"I jist stuck a knife in a feller over at Bob's bar and walked half-way around him," he said. "I don't know if he's dead or not. He fell like a pole-axed hog and I lit a shuck."

It turned out that the man wasn't dead, and he was brought to the United States side of the border and put in the hospital in Calexico. Koots was around town for the next few days, but the man finally died of his stab wound and Koots Davis disappeared. The sheriff's office got a warrant out for him, and a few nights later, while Border Patrol Officers Carl and "Bud" Bump were stopping traffic on a road from the border, who should drive up but Koots Davis. He was all packed up and leaving the country.

They brought him in and placed him in the county jail at El Centro, and then the diplomatic and political feathers began to fly. Mexico wanted to try him because the man had been stabbed in Mexico. Imperial County wanted to try him because the man had died in the United States. After two or three months of haggling, it was finally decided by all hands that neither country had any case.[5] Although the stabbing took place in Mexico, he didn't die there, and although he died in the United States, he wasn't stabbed over here. The sheriff's office finally had to turn him loose. I think the district attorney, the district judge and the Mexican judicial officers all got drunk together that night and Koots Davis walked out of the jail with his right elbow akimbo and the hare-lip quivering.

In those days I had a good friend on the Mexican side of the line who was a Mexican Rurale. He was stationed on the border at ten-foot drop, about four miles east of Calexico one day and I went over to talk with him. His name was Anacleto Nava, and he had a bottle of Bereteaga, a strong brandy made of sugar cane. We both took a satisfying draught from it.

"There's an empty truck crossing the border at least once a week," he told me in Spanish, "and it has about three hundred gallons of sugar-cane alcohol."

"How can that be?" I asked him. "If it's empty, how can it have a load like that?"

He laughed and took another short pull on the bottle. "It just looks empty," he said. "It has a copper tank about three inches deep, just below the bed of the truck, and then six-inch side boards around the bed to hide it. It also has the bottom all boarded up too, where you can't see anything underneath it."

He had the last three numbers of the license written down on a piece of a paper sack and he gave it to me. "It's always the first thing that crosses the border when the inspectors take down the chain at six in the morning," he said. "I found out about it from my uncle, who helped build the big tank and fit it in the bed of the truck. He works in a welding shop in Mexicali."

The next morning Lou Flammery and I were down at the crossing when the gate was opened, and I'll be damned if it wasn't the first vehicle across the border. We walked over to it while the inspector was questioning the driver, and felt the thickness of the bed. It was thicker than the boards would have made it, all right, and we also noticed it had huge, overload springs, to keep it from appearing to have a load.

Before we even found the screw-cap which covered the loading pipe, we had the driver out of the cab and handcuffed. He turned out to be a well-known Los Angeles bootlegger and he had 300 gallons of alcohol in his "empty" truck.

He grinned at Flammery and me, "Damn you fellers, anyway," he said. "I could have made a thousand gallons of bath-tub gin with that!"

Hole in the Fence

A saying in many California families is that what one does the first day of the year, he will do the rest of the year. New Year's Eve, 1931, the word was out: The Mexican border will be open. Not open exactly but someone had cut a huge hole in the fence across from the Climax Bar in Mexicali, just a short ways east of the regular border crossing. The U. S. Government closed the border at 9:00 p.m. and immigration guards check Americans coming back across the line up to closing. Checking, of course, for aliens and smuggled liquor. Officials prevented anyone from using the hole—up to 9:00 p.m.

But after nine no one checked except at places known for illegal smuggling. No one checked "the hole." Guards watched it from the regular crossing but did not stop anyone.

Then came New Year's. An estimated 7,000-8,000 people crossed back over the line, through the hole, after a night of celebrating the last few hours of 1931 and the first couple of 1932. "Thousands of New Year's Merrymakers sneaked back through the hole in the fence as Border Patrol idly turns its official back," wrote an editor from *Imperial Valley Farmer*, January 7, 1932. They came back plastered, a little fried and polluted. They came back with bottles of liquor to help tide them over until they elected Roosevelt and passed repeal. It was so crowded in Mexicali that one had to use a shoe horn to squeeze into the Owl.

When prohibitionists complained and asked guards why these violators were not stopped, one guard said he couldn't detain 6,000 Americans and keep them from going home, and said, "I got a cold sore on my lip so don't make me laugh!"

Week after week local papers talked about the hole. Back to Washington and from government agency to agency, blame, responsibility, costs and solutions were tossed back and forth. On January 21, the *Imperial Valley Farmer,* wrote "The Hole Is Still There." At 9:00 p.m. Uncle Sam yawns, puts the cat out and watches you cross the border. Then, the paper said, at 6:00 a.m. Uncle Sam yawns, opens the gate and checks you in and out. In February a reporter counted 2,000 crossers from nine to midnight. The Owl put up a new sign: "Dine and Dance Till Midnight." With gambling, women and drinking, workers could forget the depression and prohibition for a few hours. Unemployed could enjoy a legal cheap drink in Mexico. By the end of February U. S. Attorney General Mitchell ordered the fence repaired and Americans had to be more discrete in sneaking back into his country. Hoover, ironically, ordered the border to stay open to midnight, just in time for the Fourth of July—an American birthday present to the thirsty souls of this Southland desert. For the rest of the year drinkers could at least drink their fill and walk across the border (until midnight anyway) through the gate.

The border went back to the way it was before. Smuggling. In July, charged A. L. Rains, 19, Joseph Privo, 22, Harry Marsh (March), 19, and C. M. Blackford, 35, of El Centro, for smuggling 100 bottles of liquor across the border. They were too late for the open-fence policy.[7]

CHAPTER 13

BY AIR—SMUGGLERS FLY IT IN

America learned much from the World War, especially about the use of the "aeroplane." In the clear skies of southern California, Californians improved the effectiveness of the airplane in the 1920s. The air hobby, ubiquitous local landing fields in every town of note, barnstorming events, air shows, monthly headlines of someone breaking an aviation record—all propelled the interest of aviation. Amateur flying became almost as popular as playing the stock market, tinkering with crystal radio sets and taking automobile excursions.

It did not take long for the rumrunners to see the value of flight in their war against the Treasury Department's Coast Guard and Customs Service. Enterprising runners flew cargoes of smuggled alcohol from Mexico. Besides Mexican liquors, Mexicans exported liquor that came from Canada, Europe and the West Indies. Shiploads came to Mexico, trucked to Baja California, then flown into the United States. The modern rumrunner flew his cargo to California or southern Nevada, landing on local landing strips, newly-built airports, and numerous dry lakes in the California deserts: Rosamond, Lanfair, Fairview and Harper. Courageous pilots maneuvered joy sticks of heavily-laden planes—crammed with joy juice for dry Californians.

Pilots increased their skills, planes improved yearly, logistics became more sophisticated, especially with the use of radio and telephone communication. On the other side, the government was again always playing catch-up, always a take-off behind the smugglers.

Capturing the Sister Ship of *The Spirit of St. Louis*
as told by Carl Eifler, Salinas

Our informants told us a plane would land liquor at Santa Margarita Ranch, now the present Camp Pendleton. Two of us Customs men disguised ourselves as ranchers, wore old clothes. We camped out for a couple days in a bunch of trees near where the plane was supposed to land. When it came in we nabbed the pilot, took his clothes off him. Since we were laying in wait for three days, we were really dirty, hadn't had our clothes off in all that time. Oh, he was mad when I tossed him my old Levi's and shirt and overalls and took his clothes.

I saw a shotgun in the plane and laid it inside the wheel of the plane. My idea was to find out which was the best weapon, the machinegun or the sawed-off shotgun. When the pick-up crew came on up I was to grab the shotgun and if they wanted to shoot it out, okay, we'd find out which was the best weapon. But evidently when the pick-up crew came up they became suspicious or maybe the pilot was supposed to unload and take off or maybe this or that; anyway they knew something was wrong and didn't come up on the pick up.

We confiscated that plane and put it into use as a border patrol plane. I flew it as a border patrol plane. The plane was the sister ship of Charles Lindbergh's *The Spirit of St. Louis*. The two planes were built by Ryan in San Diego. One was used for Lindbergh's famous trans-Atlantic flight, the other for rumrunning, then later by Customs.

I got a call about another plane that crashed on the mesa by the old Torrey Pine grade between Oceanside and San Diego. A plane, loaded with champagne, had crashed there on the big old flats. An immigration officer had gotten to it and I was told to go on up there and take over as Customs officer. I called up another Customs officer, Lee Echols, to go with me. He had a young visitor from Texas at his house. "Okay to bring him along?" asked Echols.

"Sure," I said.

We drove up in a big black Cadillac, confiscated from a rumrunner we had put out of business for awhile. When we arrived at the scene, the guys were sweating carrying the champagne cases from down in the valley where the plane had crashed up to the road. The champagne was chilled just right from the air coming over from Mexico. Beautiful shape! So when I got there I took over from the border patrol officer who was an individual right down the line. This is it, you know, the way an officer should be. He wouldn't let the work crew drink any of the chilled champagne. So the immigration boys came to me and said, "Hey, Carl, can't we take a drink?"

I said, "Well sure, I don't care."

They began to sample the champagne on the way up the hill. We got all of it loaded up to the top. A lot of cases were broken, some full. The immigration officer said to me, "Well, let's take an inventory and sign for the inventory?"

I said, "No, I'm not going to take an inventory of this stuff up here. We'll take it in the Custom's garage and if you want to come tomorrow and get the inventory, you can take it tomorrow."

We drove home on one of the first two-way highways coming up that Torrey Pine grade. This friend from Texas was sipping and drinking champagne like soda pop, you know. "Wait till I get back to Texas and tell the boys about going down the two-way highway drinking champagne and tossing the bottles out the window!"

When we got into San Diego, Lee and I put the stuff in the garage. By the time we got away from the patrol headquarters, it was daylight. Lee's friend slept until afternoon, got up and went into the bathroom. He was a little rocky from getting tight. He drank a little water, sat down on the toilet and all of a sudden the room began to sway. He thought, Gee, I heard about this darn stuff, this champagne. You take a drink of water the next day and it hits you all over again. Anyway, he sat shaking on the toilet all through the Long Beach earthquake, thinking it was the champagne!

Only and Simply a Game
as told by Carl Eifler, Salinas

I can tell you another case. We had a smuggler down on the border in San Diego; I can't remember his name now. This was police work in those days. As far as I was concerned, it was good honest police work but we didn't play a boy scout game and you didn't have these ideas of personal rights and so forth. Between the crooks, the type of crooks I worked with, the smugglers, and us, there was a code of ethics: You didn't bother our wives and children and we didn't bother yours. Now this is a game, only and simply a game, all the way through.

It was a game we played. They were on one side of the fence and we were on the other side. There wasn't too much difference between us, except they were functioning from the standpoint of personal gain and we were functioning from the standpoint of law enforcement. We believed in our side; they believed in their side of the game. If you want to compare it, figure us as a football team. Instead of eleven men, they had 24 with all the padding and clothing and everything they could possibly have to protect themselves. Instead of us having eleven we had four. Instead of us having all the padding, we had shorts and tennis shoes. The game says: "We have to catch you in the act." It wasn't the game to come back after them afterwards. Basically, they performed the act and we caught them in doing it. That's what the game was.

My boss, Leo Stanley, said his wife had been threatened by one guy living by the San Diego Airport. That time it was part of my territory. I was flying border patrol. Because Patrolman Crawford had some fortune teller tell him he was going to die by drowning, he wouldn't fly a plane over the ocean. The smugglers, therefore, were flying out over the ocean to avoid us. Somebody had to go out there so I became the border patrol pilot.

I was at the airport taking care of our smugglers around the airport. We knew everybody who was smuggling. They knew us. We were all friends. It was basically a game, as I said. Walking into the restaurant in the airport, I saw him sitting there and tapped him on the shoulder and said, "Come on."

Well to him that meant an arrest. I got him out in the car and took off, but instead of going to town where the jail was, I went the other way. He says, "What's up?"

"Just wait awhile," and I went in behind the Marine Barracks, the only building that was in that particular area. The bay came in between the airport and the back of the Marine Barracks. So there was a section of land pretty isolated where I took him.

218

"Get out!" I pulled on my gloves and said, "Now you broke the rules. There is a rule that says you don't threaten, you don't molest, you don't touch one of the family. Now I'm going to give you the damnedest beating you ever had in your life and if you ever violate it again I'll kill you."

That was the way we played the game. I beat him up. He could have beaten me up if he were capable. If you check the border patrol you'll find a number of patrolmen were killed on the Mexican border but I defy you to find any place where any one of them was ever tried for murder. I don't think any one who killed a border patrolman ever got away with it.

Law enforcement in those days was an entirely different thing. It was a game. Violate the game. That was it. Shoot one of our guys....

This plane, loaded with champagne from Mexico, crashed in 1932 near Mira Mesa, north of San Diego. Lee Echols and Carl Eifler took a truckload of champagne to the Customs warehouse in San Diego. Photo courtesy of Lee Echols.

For a week after I had a gun battle on the hill and I was in the hospital, the word was out to all smugglers: Border patrolmen armed themselves with shot guns. There were no arrests made that time. If there had been there would be another gun battle, in my opinion. You had to protect yourself. The boys had to protect themselves.

Canadian Whiskey
by Robert Ames, San Bernardino

Another time this same man [see Chapter 7] took me for a ride in the same car at about eight o'clock in the evening. We went east on Fremont Avenue and traveled about half way to Mountain Pass on the road to Boulder City. He turned out his lights and took a dirt road to the left in total darkness. He drove very slowly for a mile or two and stopped. He flashed on his dome lights three times and about eight or ten small lights flashed around the area of about one acre or so. He would check his watch with a small flashlight he had in the car in a box. In about 15 minutes we heard a plane coming in from the northeast. It blinked its light, and the whole field in front of us lit up and the plane made a good landing. Ten or 12 men unloaded the plane in three or four minutes and it took off again and headed out. The plane was loaded with many cases of Canadian whiskey. It was loaded into cars and pick-up trucks, and as soon as they were loaded all the lights went out and they drove out in total darkness in a number of directions.

The bars and honky-tonks served you anything you wanted in drinks from bootleg to the best of Canadian whiskey. No matter what you asked for, you got it and it was good stuff.

The owner of the still and other businessmen always told the truth; but never in dealing with these men on refrigerating equipment did they pay me by check—always in cash and mostly in silver. I kept a canvas sack in my car at all times for this purpose.

I was offered many times $100 to bring into San Bernardino ten one-gallon jugs of bootleg whiskey. I was never a bootlegger and did not want that kind of money. Other salesmen did, and a number were caught and convicted and paid stiff fines. The way they were caught was when they stopped for plant and fruit inspection at Yermo inspection station coming from Nevada, and the Daggett inspection station coming from Needles, the inspectors would look for fruit and plants, and if they saw jugs of whiskey, they would phone the Barstow deputy sheriff station, and they would pick them up in Barstow. I was told that in the Barstow area the law enforcement officers always had good whiskey to drink.

With her tail dragging the water....
by Lee Echols, Chula Vista

As border Customs Officers, Carl Eifler and I were working on a group of Mexican alcohol traffickers who were loading airplanes below Tijuana on a flat mesa near Rosarita Beach.

Eifler said, "It'll be easy, Lee. We'll drive down there, hide our automobile, blacken our faces with burnt cork, and work our way within thirty yards of the loading operation. We'll take a pair of field glasses, and we'll look

Two booze-smuggling planes in the California desert in the late 1920s. Notice the man in the plane to the left with a gun. Courtesy of National Archives, # 26 G-35-12-05 (1).

up their home airports in the registration book and stake them out. The next trip they make, we'll be there as a reception committee when they land." This sounded very simple, but when we got our car concealed in a mesquite grove in a small draw, our faces blackened with burnt cork until we looked like Al Jolson, and began crawling up there to where a big Ford Tri-motor plane had just landed, I saw a tall, mean-looking Mexican, making the rounds with a shotgun in the crook of his arm. He was prodding around in the bushes where Eifler and I intended to be soon in order to read the numbers on the big plane.

"My God, Carl!" I whispered to him. "Let's get the hell out of here! That man's got a goose-hunting gun in his hands! He'll shoot out our gall bladders with it and will be completely justified in doing it. We're down here in Mexico, twenty miles below the border, where we have no legal right to be, and he would know that! Let's crawl back to the car and try something else. Maybe we can meet one of the loading crew and recruit him for an informer or something!"

"No, Lee," Carl said, "this is the luckiest thing that has happened to us. Can't you see that we'll be perfectly safe up there for sure, as he's already checked it out. It'll only take a few minutes to crawl up there and then I'll get the numbers off that Ford airplane and we'll find out where he's anchoring." I have none of that enviable firmness that enables a man to look calmly into the eyes of a madman and tell him "no go!"

I could think of no way of getting out of it, without frankly admitting I was scared to death, so we belly-crawled on up to the clump of bushes and it was just like Carl said. The shotgun guard didn't come back and Carl read the numbers off to me while I wrote them down.

We learned from the registration book that he was based at an airport in San Fernando Valley, north of Los Angeles, so we drove up there and staked it out.

We only had to wait four nights when we saw him coming in to land. He'd gone on up the coast past the San Fernando Valley, so that when he turned back and came in, he appeared to be coming in from San Francisco instead of Mexico. This didn't fool us, however, and we watched him set her down and taxi to the hangar, where we had learned he kept the plane.

As he entered it, he turned the plane around, heading back out, with the engine still running. Eifler ran our car right up to the center propeller which boxed him in. He could barely get out of the plane, what with alcohol stacked up around him.

"How did she ride?" Eifler asked him as he showed the pilot his badge.

"With her tail dragging the water all the way from Rosarita Beach," the pilot said with a big grin. He was carrying six hundred gallons of sugarcane alcohol.

A December 1932 *San Francisco Chronicle* reported Customs captured a plane at Van Nuys with 140 gallons of smuggled liquor.

Smuggler Jay Tabot aided Chief Patrol Inspector Leo Stanley by informing on air smugglers which helped capture a plane from Tijuana filled with Johnson Distillery whiskey. When Tabot's case came up, the court dismissed charges against Tabot.[1]

Special Prohibition Agents D. R. Lawrence and W. E. Dresser cracked a complicated case in June of 1933 by tapping phones. For almost three years Thurm Mankin, William Mankin, Carl Bell, John Burns, Kenneth Boyd, Clyde Phillips, Jack Murray had a syndicate that smuggled.[2] Like the U. S. Marines, these smugglers came by land, sea and air. At their main office on 1255 N. Orange Grove in Los Angeles, agents tapped phone numbers Gladstone 2606 and Hemstead 8023 by using "Viaphone interception." Phillips brought liquor in by speedboat *A-1772*; Murray did the bookkeeping; William Mankin, on February 15, 1933, landed 100 cases by air near Corona and was arrested. This gang brought in an auto load of beer in February; purchased a bar at 11293 Ventura Boulevard in North Hollywood, which the Feds busted in April of 1933, and the gang stored its contraband at 645 N. Martel Avenue at a place called the Trading Post. When the gang changed their office to 400 N. Maple Drive, it set up two more phones, and the agents tapped those too—which led to more arrests, including Dick Scott, "another big liquor dealer." Fifty pages of evidence mounted up against the defendants.

From big syndicates to small-fry flyers, men used airplanes to smuggle booze into California. *The San Diego Union,* August 13, 1929, reported a small air-travel smuggler using the newly opened Ryan air flights from San Diego to Los Angeles. Harry McNeil and Gene Normoyle at Ryan Field bought their tickets for a flight to L.A. Before boarding the airline, both men asked the airline official not to say they booked passage. The local dry agents already

"The Latest Method of Bootlegging—'Pinched' Near San Diego"—read the caption of this Underwood and Underwood, New York photo in 1921. With one of the first airplanes caught smuggling liquor across the border, Customs Officer W. B. Evans shown here with plane and auto he captured nearby. In this "flying saloon" were six kegs of whiskey. Evans also captured the aviator, chauffeur and lookout, December 16, 1921. Photo courtesy of National Archives.

knew them and suspected both men had liquor in their possession. They were arrested for transporting and possessing.[3]

Arrest of "Flying Bootleggers"

Another San Diego man, M. M. "Happy" Martin, with eleven years of liquor arrests and alien smuggling violations [see Chapter 12], had been released two months earlier from an 18-month sentence to McNeil Island. Customs confiscated a load of 325 gallons of high-grade alcohol. The plane had already flown away from the rendezvous point one mile from the main highway. Agents were leaving when in comes the plane again with another 150

After a three-day stakeout at Santa Margarita Ranch, now Camp Pendleton, where Customs Patrol Officers Carl Eifler and Crawford, pretending to be ranch hands, captured this Ryan-built plane (supposedly a sister ship of **The Spirit of St. Louis** according to Eifler) containing a load of liquor flown in from Mexico. The pilot's new clothes were liberated in exchange for Eifler's smelly ones. Photo courtesy Carl Eifler.

gallons. This time Customs caught the not-so-happy "Happy" Martin with the second batch of loot. After his arraignment, U. S. Marshall Sam Williams drove Martin through San Diego. Suddenly Martin jumped from Williams' car into a crowd at 6th Avenue and C. On a tip, the embarrassed Williams and a U. S. Mounted Patrol raided a house on 13th Street between Fern and Date, finding Happy in bed. This time Martin only had four hours freedom. His bail had been set at $10,000.[4] Williams also arrested Earl Beebe, 49, and John Phelps, alias John Glore, 26. Investigators sought the owners of the plane who were suspected of owning several planes involved in smuggling.

America's fascination with airplanes stemmed from the romance of glorious air skirmishes in the World War, from constant development of technology during the 1920s, from publicity given to records set in the air frontier, air novels, comics like "Tailspin Tommy," and from local air shows promoting cities and progress. In the process dawned another aspect of the air frontier: air smuggling in the United States.

CHAPTER 14

RACE TO THE CITY

Wherever rumrunners brought the booze ashore, along the long coast of California or in an inlet of some bay, they had to truck the liquor to the city, the larger markets in the state. Whether the liquor came across the border from Mexicali or El Paso, Texas, it had to be rushed to markets at Los Angeles, San Francisco or Sacramento. Drivers raced, raced to avoid hijackers, county sheriffs, local speed cops, small-town policemen and ubiquitous prohis (federal agents).

Depending on local police policy or policies of their officials, a smuggler might be able to pass through the town with no problem. Often policemen closed their eyes, or at least one eye, as these big mysterious Packards and Cadillacs and canvas-covered trucks sped by at 3:00 a.m.

A truck from Moss Landing on Monterey Bay had to come through Watsonville, Gilroy, Morgan Hill, San Jose, Santa Clara, Mountain View, Palo Alto, Menlo Park, Redwood City, San Carlos, Belmont, San Mateo, Burlingame, South San Francisco (or Daly City) and finally into the "City" (San Francisco).

One town could have a night policeman who might be daring enough or diligent enough to challenge a shipment. Redwood City Police Officer James Snider was such an officer. Redwood City's policy was to apprehend suspicious vehicles. Snider had an exciting chase through Redwood City early Saturday morning in February 1929. He saw a suspicious vehicle coming from the south on Middlefield Road, not on the State Highway, El Camino Real. As he followed the truck to Main Street, it sped up and the "protection" car, a big Cadillac Touring Car with three men, tried several times to cut Snider off and run him into the curb. Snider kept up the pursuit and as the truck suddenly turned north on Arguello Street, Snider was able to drive in front of it, forcing it to the curb. The protection car, realizing the "gig [jig] was up," sped away north on Arguello Street. Snider arrested Robert Jackson, 31, for having 65 cases, mostly Grannie Taylor whiskey valued at $6,500. When he pleaded guilty of possession, Judge Albert Mansfield fined him $500. Snider took the liquor to the warehouse.

Another officer from Redwood City, Ed McAuliffe, arrested Louis Ricci for illegal possession of liquor, 200 gallons on his truck. McAuliffe called Judge Mansfield at his home in the wee hours of the morning in March 1927. When told of Ricci's charge, the judge, holding court over the phone, said, "The fine will be $500."

Driver Fran Sibrian, 26, tried unsuccessfully to sneak through Redwood City with 2,280 pints of beer, "somewhat stronger than one-half of one per cent," said the *Redwood City Standard* in June 1927. Tony Mullinario, the passenger, and Sibrian posted $1,000 bonds, but the court dismissed Mullinario and fined Sibrian $100.

Officers Sylvester Douglass and Joe Roza followed a heavily loaded truck from "Five Points," south of Redwood City, in 1924. Upon inspection, they found 50 cases of good old scotch, worth $4,000. They arrested San Franciscans Joe Balsell, a chauffeur, and L. Pinkley, auto mechanic. Redwood City Chief of Police C. L. Collins caught a truck in 1923 on State Highway, El Camino Real, loaded with 49 cases of high-priced scotch, worth $4,000. It was Astor Hotel stock that never reached the city. Driver Owen Albert Raymon pleaded guilty of possession and transportation and was fined $500. Scotch evidently wholesaled at about $81 a case in 1923-24.[1]

Local policemen, Rolly Sommers of Atherton and Tom Kearney of Menlo Park, could recognize the heavily-ladened trucks and huge cars. Small-town police duty on the 12-hour night shift consisted of patrolling safe quiet neighborhoods, checking closed businesses and taking drunks home safely. Sometimes on a day off, Kearney or Sommers rode around together for company.[2] On Saturday night Kearney supervised dances at Blue Moon Dance Hall on Live Oak Avenue, where no drinks were sold, but men beat a well-trodden path over to Al Kelly's place on the east side of El Camino. Kelly had a trap door behind his bar where he kept his secret stash. The state allowed the city of

In the race to the city, Sausalito, with its 24-hour ferryboats, became a funnel through which smuggled liquor and northern California moonshine poured into San Francisco—thousands of gallons a day! Photo courtesy of "Swede" Pedersen.

Menlo Park to put its only stop signal on El Camino and Santa Cruz. "The council was afraid that if we worked it automatically, the state would deny us the right to use it. So every morning, after working all night, from 7:30 to 8:00 a.m., you had to work it by hand after freezing all night...the old Ford we had, had no side curtains in it or anything. Then from 8:30 to 9:00, I had to go down to the school zone with the kids coming across the highway," said Kearney. Quiet town, quiet 12-13-hour shifts.

Kearney perhaps summed up the attitude of most local policemen when hijackers and rumrunners came through: "The rumors were that you didn't stop smuggling trucks on the highway or you'd get shot. But at night you could tell what trucks were what."

Ralph Douglass remembered a high-speed chase of a hijacker who hijacked a load from Oakland and was coming through San Jose when a deputy sheriff of San Jose started pursuit that ended up in Burlingame with the death of the deputy.[3] Douglass said, "I was coming off California (Avenue) in South Palo Alto when they went speeding through on El Camino." This was in 1928 or 29.

Even when the liquor reached the big city, it was not safe from detection. Informants worked on both sides of the booze war. Agents learned tricks of rumrunners: The booze might be hidden behind boxes of artichokes from the coast or among chickens from Petaluma. And they learned to check on docks, warehouses, the S.F.-Sausalito Ferry and suspicious trucks early in the morning.

On a tip from Seattle, the Feds seized 41 barrels of alcohol labeled "dry herring" that came from Seattle to San Francisco by train. The contents were not dried fish at Terminal Warehouse, 631 Second Street, waiting to be picked up by Olsen Fish Company. Prohibition Administrator S. F. Rutter and Agent C. H. Wheeler hoped in vain someone would claim the fish. But this time the runners were tipped off.

Another seizure occurred the same day at 3rd and Mission streets when prohis caught a truck with 107 cases of second-grade scotch from two Canadian rumrunners.[4]

More to the south, in Ventura, Santa Barbara and San Luis Obispo counties, the Feds caught numerous smugglers trying to make it to the cities. The last two months of 1930 agents seized $60,000 worth of liquor at wholesale prices, 15 autos, five trucks, three stills and arrested 28 major Volstead violators.

A Smuggler's Wife
as told by May Hinds, Quincy

Most places were tipped off ahead of time. I know. In 1926 I married a bootlegger.[5] Since he was already in the business, it became a part of my life for a number of years. My husband was Al Campbell who was urged by Hugo Mack and Ed Begley, my two brothers-in-law, to join him in the rum-running business. Our home had three phones to take orders. The entire family operated the business. We'd pick up a load at Pismo Beach or Half Moon Bay. We paid workers on the beach as high as $100 a load, a handsome pay for one night's work. Several loads landed at the Hearst Castle wharf. The superintendent of the Hearst's property received $1.00 a case, the general price of anyone's land

Flapper May Hinds [pseud.], 26-year-old, married Al Campbell, a smuggler along with her two brothers-in-law, Hugo Mack and Ed Begley, making her part of a San Francisco family that raced "imported" liquors from the landing sites to the cities. Photo made from photograph in the Plumas County Museum.

used. Another $1.00 per case went to the highway patrol and another to the county sheriff of whatever county we landed in. That method protected us fairly well from legal intervention.

We did fear the hijackers, however. One night I answered the phone. It was my husband, Al, in a frantic but firm voice.

"May, open the garage door; keep all lights out. As soon as I drive in the garage, close the door quickly, lock it and keep all the lights out. Understand?"

"Okay, but what's wrong?" I asked.

"I'm being followed," Al said. "I think it's hijackers. I'll be there in less than an hour."

I did as he directed and we weren't hijacked that night.

We stored our liquor in various places in the city. Our two messengers delivered orders, a bottle here, a case there—all good Canadian liquor, all the best clientele, wealthy businessmen on Montgomery Street, a few restaurants, hotels, and estates down Burlingame. We kept the messengers busy.

Other groups of bootleggers were operated by Joe Gaviota around North Beach and Joe Vanessi. There's still the fashionable Vanessi Restaurant in San Francisco today.

One of our first suppliers was a fisherman named George. He'd take his fishing boat out to the Canadian supply ships off the coast, fill her up with liquor and go straight through the gates. The Coast Guard or prohis caught him once. He was obviously guilty and had to be sentenced but the law allowed him to choose which jail to serve in.

The authorities assigned him to his first choice: Martinez, California. He served his time there with lots of freedom. He'd go out on weekend cruises on the sheriff's boat, supposedly to help as a crewman but it was party time with booze and broads.

Later George died, drowned, maybe accidentally, knocked off the rum launch or fell off coming into the bay. No one would claim his body. All the bootleggers knew him. He had a star tattooed on his hand but no one would take the risk and identify him. We felt bad about that and we three wives complained to our husbands that George should be claimed. They talked the three of us girls into claiming him. We claimed the body and the city bootleggers chipped in for a fine funeral.

We had two large losses, one around 1930. Our messengers were followed and so was my husband, and an agent obtained a warrant and raided one of the garages we rented for storage. The Feds confiscated forty thousand dollars worth. They didn't get any of us but we kept low for a while.

The other loss occurred when we had a new Marmon sedan, with the back hollowed out, filled with liquor for across the bay. The driver sped out off the ferry and was caught and given a citation. We bailed the driver out for $50 but lost our new car and our valuable load.

"Rumrunner Gives Details
of Ring's Business in Confession"
by Jack Lawrence, *S. F. Chronicle*, October 5, 1921

My name is Jack Lawrence. I came to San Francisco from Sydney, Australia, in April of this year, to seek employment as a shipping clerk. After three weeks of unsuccessful search I was in the Neptune Dance Palace, Kearney Street, and got into a conversation with a man whom I afterward found to be James T. Wall. After some conversation in which I said I was from Australia, he asked me if I should like to earn some easy money. I inquired the nature of the work, and learned that I would be expected to carry liquor from various depots to hotels in San Francisco, the remuneration to be at the rate of $1 per bottle. The idea attracted me and I agreed.

On the 15th of May I was given my first job, taking a parcel of liquor, which I obtained from a saloon at Duboce Avenue and Sanchez Street. This liquor was packed between two pieces of cardboard and tied to represent a shoe box. The parcels were always handed to me tied in the same way, always containing four bottles. The deliveries were invariably made to James T. Wall in the lobby of the hotel to which I was sent. To avoid any suspicion I always obtained his signature as if I was a messenger from some firm of merchants.

The hotels I delivered to during my time with Wall were the St. Francis, Clift, Bellevue, Kensington, Manx, Techau Tavern, Ripperdan's Dance Pavilion, Pergola Dance Hall, Elks Cafe, Palace Hotel and Panama Theater, Market Street, where cocaine was sold, which I strongly suspect came from my employer.

On one occasion in August I was ordered to deliver 120 bottles of gin, whiskey, beer and wine to the Bellevue Hotel, room 731. On calling for the empty bottles a week later I learned from the manager that my client had drank so much that he had run into the corridor undressed, and broken his leg. He is now recuperating at Lake Tahoe.

The reason for wanting the empty bottles was for refilling, as we had a system whereby we could draw off the high-grade liquor from the original bottles without disturbing the seals and would then refill with moonshine whiskey. The operation was a tedious one. We would get a red-hot wire and make a hole in the bottom of the bottle, draw off the liquor and after refilling, seal the hole with a piece of glass rod held over a flame. This method took some time but we were fully paid because we drew off liquor worth anything up to $24 and substituting liquor worth $4, making a profit of $20.

After I had been working at this job three weeks I was sent to Plumas County to the still maintained by my employer at Clio. Clio was an ideal place for illicit stills. It was eight miles from Blairsden railroad station on the Western Pacific, and had been a lumber camp, but had been abandoned for years. There are only about a dozen shacks standing, and one, an old-time hotel, is occupied by Al Michomach for manufacturing moonshine.

In my country, Australia, I had never seen moonshine being made, and I was astonished at the magnitude of the operation. A huge still of fifty-gallon capacity was in operation and there were stacks of sugar in sacks, corn and empty barrels waiting to be filled. On this occasion I took 150 gallons to San Francisco in a motor truck and delivered it to Duboce Avenue and Sanchez Street saloon.

When I saw Wall I expressed my astonishment at what I had seen. He laughed and said, "That's nothing; wait till you see Seattle." I asked if he was not afraid of federal agents, and he told me that prohibition was a joke as far as San Francisco was concerned, and, indeed, this was the opinion of everyone with whom I was connected, and from what I saw myself San Francisco was no more dry than my home town, Sydney.

The next insight I got into the operation of my employer was when I went to Seattle with him in July. We stayed at Hotel Seattle, and there met all the Canadian booze runners. For my benefit I was told how the liquor was got into America. At Victoria an agent buys the quantity of liquor desired and loads it in power launches which run up Puget Sound. The price paid for best whiskey is $2 a quart and sold to buyers at Seattle at $5 so the agent and boatmen can make $3 on each quart of whiskey they carry.

After boats are loaded they proceed at night up the sound to land their cargo into trucks, which take it to Seattle for distribution. The funny part of it is that a government vessel, the *Viking*, which carries supplies up Puget Sound, the *Viking*, as often towed a string of booze runners when the tide was strong and received presents of liquor in exchange. The estimated amount paid for protection and rake-offs in Seattle alone by all operations is around $3,000 per week.

Only the best grade of liquor comes from Canada, and my employer always stipulated for the best, which he stored at Gobey's Cafe, 140 Manila Street, San Francisco. At one time he had a consignment of four shipping cases labeled merchandise from Seattle by the steamship *Admiral Schley*. This was delivered at Gobey's and contained Bass ale and stout.

Whenever a consignment arrived at Gobey's guards were always posted at each end of Manila Street and a prohibition agent stood no chance of getting by. All this liquor was sold to the best class of trade only, and some wild scenes have occurred at Gobey's in consequence. The cheapest drink was sold for $1 per glass.

Another source of supply, and the biggest, was the steamship *Sonoma*, which carries passengers from here to Australia. The liquor is shipped at

Wellington, New Zealand, and before it reaches here is packed in laundry bags and sent ashore after the vessel docks.

On August 10 the *Sonoma* arrived here with a large consignment, too much to pack in the bags, so the men on the ship hit on a scheme to beat the customs searchers. They hung the liquor on hooks under the pier, more than 600 bottles, and arranged for a boat to take it at night. Unfortunately, they were caught, and the customs officers got the whole 600 bottles, but another 700 were got ashore in safety.

On Saturday, September 3, I delivered four bottles of whiskey to Wall at the St. Francis, and on Monday, September 5, I delivered twelve more bottles to him. He came down to me at 11:30 a.m., when I delivered the first parcel and told me to hurry for another two. I brought the next parcel at 12:45 p.m. He came down drunk. I remarked: "You are having a fine time up there," and he said, "Fatty is having a fine old booze-up." I said, "He can afford it." Wall replied, "I'll say he can." [Fatty Arbuckle, popular comic in 1920, ruined his career when his drunk lady companion died and rumors flew about rape and orgies.]

I had carried nothing since Fatty's arrest, and when I saw Wall, he said to me: "Things are damned tough. Mitchell is getting busy. I am going to be quiet for a time." I asked what I should do and he sent me to Los Angeles and promised to send me money so I could live until he needed me again. Within a week of my arrival in Los Angeles I had to sell everything I possessed to get money, as I had no reply to my repeated requests to Wall.

On Friday, September 23, I told my story to Attorney Camarillo at Los Angeles, and was sent to San Francisco under care of Agent Wheeler. I was examined by McCormack, and after my statement had been checked by Mitchell, the prohibition agents proposed that I should get in touch with Wall again and secure my old job once more. This I did, and Wall promised to help me out. On Friday I got a letter from Wall instructing me to go to Plumas County, enclosing a letter I was to deliver. I turned this letter over to McCormack, who opened the envelope, which contained a clipping from a newspaper which the day before had mentioned a "booze ring," and a letter which read: "Dear Al: I am sending Jack up to you for you to fix up. I do not know whether he is on the square or not. I leave you to find out. Will come to see you soon. [signed] JAY"

This letter McCormack interpreted as a scheme to get me put out of the way, so the original idea of sending me to Plumas County was stopped. This James T. Wall is connected with the Association Boxing Hall on Sixteenth Street and other sporting interests, and is also a co-partner of Pete McDonough in the Neptune Palace, Kearney Street.

The plain facts of my work for this "booze" concern do not sound very exciting, but during my three and a half months of booze running in San Francisco I had funny experiences which did not seem funny at the time. On one occasion I was taking two bottles of liquor to the Palace Hotel. I had one bottle in each pocket of my overcoat, coming down Market Street on a street car. The driver applied the brakes pretty quickly and I was thrown against the rail of the platform, smashing one of the bottles. The whiskey soaked into my clothes, and the fine aroma of "Johnny Walker" filled the street car.

I did not dare to move, as I feared a policeman would get wise to me. The car was pretty full, and I could see the people sniffing up free shots of $24 scotch. They sure seemed tickled to death. I was thankful to get off and change my clothes. If the Prohibition agents used bloodhounds they could have tracked me. I was a walking distillery for days.

I was taking four bottles of whiskey one night to the Manx Hotel and got a jitney at the top of Valencia. Inside were three fellows who had more than was good for them. I had to sit on the edge of the car and in the jolting I broke the paper wrapping of my parcel and exposed the necks of the "medicine." Those fellows were sure staggered. They grabbed that parcel and in reply to my protests told me they would put me "overboard." I realized my position and compromised by making up a "party." I managed to get away in a traffic block at Third Street minus one bottle, leaving behind three men full of 100 per cent proof "moonshine." They got more kick out of it than I did.

The task of taking liquor from Seattle to San Francisco by machine was always difficult and if the machine stalled anywhere on the road, there would be all sorts of distress signals sent out to get the liquor home safely.

I went to Plumas County to fetch a load of "moonshine" and packed it in the back of the truck and covered it with cloths and rugs. Just outside of Sacramento a speed cop asked me to take him and his motorcycle, which had stalled, into town. We could not refuse, so put the motorcycle on top of the load. The cop sat on top of that and off we went. I wonder what his thoughts would have been if he had only known.

The greatest difficulty of all was getting liquor from the docks off the *Sonoma*. The payment for protection to customs and prohibition agents was always $500 or $600 per trip, so the high price of liquor in San Francisco was justified. There is one bootleg ring in Oakland and Alameda that supplies all the saloons on Park and Webster streets and Broadway.

After Landing in Ventura County
from *Me, Detective* by Leslie T. White

Rumrunning offered an alluring prospect and with fifty miles of lonely shoreline, there was plenty of material on which to work.[6] The rumrunners were high-powered professionals who were well organized and tough. Our office was so small that no real offensive could be launched against them; we were busy enough with other work. Once in a long period, somebody would tip off the sheriff and we would swoop down and capture a load of incoming stuff, but this was like blocking a waterfall with your hands.

Still, I was fascinated, and whenever Bill Suytar would agree to stay in the city for the evening, I took a sawed-off shotgun and prowled off down the coast by myself.

Most of the big loads came in below Point Mugu, near the Los Angeles County line. This was a lonely, fog-swept jetty of land reached only by a dismal little ribbon of asphalt. Subsequently this road became part of the new Roosevelt Highway that stretches from Santa Monica to Oxnard, but in those days it terminated at the county line. I would park the big car and work my way along the bluffs under cover of darkness.

My first sight of this spectacular performance is seared on my mind. I was lying on my stomach just over the crest of a sand-dune, my hands moist around the savage little shotgun. There was a huge truck parked just over the border in Los Angeles County. Figures flitted restlessly along the water line. There was no sound save the eerie swoosh of the swells dying on the sandy shore.

Vaguely the muffled throb of an engine filtered into my consciousness; at first a murmur quieter than the pounding of my heart, then it swelled in volume until the outline of a sleek boat loomed out of the mist. For a moment it paused a hundred yards off shore, poised for instant flight like a timid deer.

A man on the beach wigwagged a flashlight...a guarded glow appeared on the throbbing craft, then a black blob detached itself from the hull and approached the shore. It was a dory loaded with sacks of booze. Shadows evolved into the shapes of men; the beach teemed with them. They worked swiftly, efficiently, furtively. Load after load of liquor was rowed ashore from the swift rumrunner. While part of the men handled the sacks of liquor, a certain number of grim figures stood on guard, flashlights stuck in the sand illumined the scene and reflected the blued-steel of gun barrels. They were taking no chances on losing their cargo.

Discovery would have been fatal. The way their guards were spread out, it was impossible to cover them with one gun. So I merely watched. I thought of knocking over the truck when the boat crew left, but it was out of my jurisdiction for one thing, and suppose I did succeed in arresting them—it would have been impossible to march a half-dozen men through darkness for some twenty-odd miles of coastline!

The following day I bubbled with enthusiasm over my experience. I was sure the office would rush out in a body that night and make a pinch. As a matter of fact, the sheriff did have me drive him over to the spot where the landing had been. He pointed out what I already knew—that the truck, if not the actual landing place, was in Los Angeles County. When I suggested that we get in touch with Los Angeles County officers, he merely shrugged without comment.

We returned to Ventura. I was puzzled. The other officers soon straightened me out as to why the sheriff had ignored my simple suggestion regarding the Los Angeles officers.

"Why, you damned fool! Don't you know the L. A. boys are in on the racket? Probably half those guys you saw guarding the load were officers. We'd get hell blasted out of us if we monkeyed with those apes!"

So it was not only the small-town constables who were "cutting themselves in on the gravy."

The lure was irresistible, however, and I continued my nightly soirées along the coast. I imagine Bob Clark did far more worrying over me than my efforts warranted. Although he did not forbid these expeditions of mine, he insisted that I take along another man. By that Bob meant another officer, but since I could not find another officer with time to waste on his hands, I took a literal translation of the order and picked up any youngster my age who cared to accompany me.

These forays were fruitless. But perhaps they served a purpose, because the constant visits of the big police car bothered the rumrunners and after a few minor skirmishes, they kept over the line. They had several tricks to fool us. One that succeeded for a time was rather clever, though simple. They had an informer tip us off that a load was going to be landed up the coast towards Santa Barbara limits. Then, while we were shivering along the beach awaiting this fictitious load, they would bring in the real load at the other end of the county.

Eventually I wearied of this futile sport. I was beginning to doubt the sincerity of the men who made laws without making it possible to enforce them.

Rumrunning in Del Norte County
as told by Allen Lehman, Crescent City

We did not have any gangster battles in the Crescent City area but I did know two or three gangsters run out of the east that took up bootlegging here. About 38 miles up the coast above Brookings, Oregon, there was a cove there (to this day I can't remember the name of that cove) that was a popular place to run in their boats, fast boats from Canada. Some rumrunners even brought their stuff into Portland and Astoria and the smaller boats would run just from there. I remember these bootleggers telling me that. They had these fast boats and they didn't have a great deal of trouble here because the government did not have the speedboats to catch these rumrunners. I don't doubt there were a lot of pay-offs because the law enforcement people did not seem to make an attempt to catch them.

Well, anyway, they would land it at this cove in Oregon. Then with fast cars, I remember Pierce Arrows, big Cadillacs, Packards, with compartments in them, they'd run down to San Francisco.

One year there was an epidemic from Mexico called hoof and mouth disease. On this road here about 20 miles up Highway 199, the state made every car from Oregon drive through these two troughs of creosote to kill the disease because they thought it spread from the tires of cars. This was the start of our bug stations (State Agricultural Inspection Stations). This time they put one a mile south of Crescent City which caught anyone heading south from Highways 101 and 199. They stopped anybody with grapefruit or oranges. They'd go through you in those days. I mean they didn't just ask you if you had grapefruit, oranges or cherries. They searched the cars and trucks carefully.

Course the first thing rumrunners did was work it out with some of the guys on the bug station. Runners come through when those guys they were able to what you call "buy off" with whiskey and booze were on duty. That's how they got through that inspection station without being searched because some cars were loaded with booze—you know there'd be a lot of it.

I became acquainted with a couple of the rumrunners. One called Slim Kelsey, I remember him well, a great big, tough-looking guy with battered ears. He'd been a wrestler somewhere back east and he skipped out. I guess he became in disfavor back east and got out of there—the gang killings and all that stuff. So he became quite a well-known rumrunner in Crescent City. He went through that bug station at times when he knew the men he had made arrangements with were on duty. He would give them a case of whiskey or something like that, not so much money.

Anyway to this day for all these years, I still have some bottles of Three Star Hennessy with the wire still on it, champagne with 1916 vintage, Bacardi Rum in the old, old bottles, never been opened at all. I got them from Slim Kelsey, this big rumrunner.

I remember the last batch we bought. I and three or four other fellows might have bought ten cases. They didn't come in cases in those days. They come in burlap. The champagne came in burlap with straw around the bottles. Each of the twelve bottles slid into a little pockets sown into the burlap. These burlap cases took not more than half the space of modern cases. In those days cartons were not prevalent like today. They were mostly wood, you know, and wood was heavier and burlap was light and if handled properly there wasn't much breakage. We bought ten cases, wasn't very expensive because the last of the bootlegging years was the early depression years, you know. You could do a lot with a dollar that you can't do today. We bought them cases of mixed champagne, Hennessy, Whiskey, Canadian, was very hard to get hold of, cost more. Champagne was cheaper than whiskey.

At cocktail parties we became kinda accustomed to drinking Three Star Hennessy or rum or some of that imported liquor.

Moss Landing Gun Battle
as told by William Lehman, Moss Landing

Once the booze had landed, the race to the city began. But sometimes fate or happenstance took a turn in the wrong direction.

I was born in 1895, August 8, lived on the beach here at Moss Landing. My father sold the house before the earthquake (1906) to a man named Johnny Gomez, with a family of six or seven girls and one boy. My dad and Johnny Gomez were commercial fisherman, used to fish up at Elk Pond, along the beach, holding seines and nets along the beach. When the earthquake came it shook the house down. In the meantime my dad bought the property where the little marine store is now, where the post office is all the way to the corner. My dad added on to the house that was there. That's where we lived all the time.

Everything's changed. I'm the oldest one around here now.

We all knew and the law knew for a long time that they were running booze here, which they were. I and a couple of other kids, two brothers-we were just kids then-[would talk to the speed cop Henry Livingston]. There used to be a speed cop named Livingston who lived at the bottom of Springfield Hill. In those days the speed cops had motorcycles, wasn't in automobiles. Everyday why he'd come by there on his way home from Salinas. And stop and talk with us. We'd always be hanging out there by the store, by the marine store, where the post office used to be.

We were sitting by the porch one day and Livingston came by. Naturally he'd stop and talk, and after we were talking for about 20-25 minutes, a Standard Oil truck backed in an old Santos warehouse that used to be across the road from us. I told Manuel, sitting next to me, "Manuel, they're going to run booze tonight."

Then Manuel's brother Albert spoke up. "Yeah," he says, "you see the truck is bringing the gasoline for 'em."

And when Livingston got ready to go home, instead of going home he went back to Salinas and I suppose he told the sheriff just what us kids were talking about. Well, we weren't exactly kids, I was 24-around there.

Anyhow it was a beautiful moonlit night. They were going to gas the boat when it landed. The rumrunners were staying up there on the hill about half a mile back from Kaiser. Used to be a house up there, you can see where the trees are way back there. They could signal from there to the ocean. When the boat came in closer, why then the rumrunners were up and around and then, of course, officers were laying for them 'cause the rumrunners they parked their cars under the hill where those gum trees are, three cars.

That's when the shooting started when these bootleggers got over here with the sheriffs. The boat turned and went back to San Francisco.

But before that, a couple days before that there was a fellow by the name of Walter Johnson who had a dairy on the other side of Castorville and Johnny Gomez who had a dairy over there but lived here in one of the houses, just the other side of that boat [he pointed a few doors south]. They had that place leased where Kaiser is today, raising hay for their stock. Of course it was haying time then and they'd be shocks of hay.

Johnson and Gomez went up to the house, opened the door and here were these rumrunners. They pointed the gun at Johnson and Gomez and said, "Where the hell are you guys going?"

Johnson and Gomez were scared, naturally it scared them. They said, "Well, we have this place leased and it's ours."

They didn't have any liquor stored there then but these guys told them to keep their mouths shut. They gave them each a case of whiskey. Of course that all came out in the trial and, ha, they got involved.

I belonged to the Forresters in Watsonville and that night we went to a Forresters' dinner.

So we were coming back about midnight, maybe a little after. Right there on the hill between Kaiser and PGE, there was someone in the middle of the highway with a flashlight, whirling it. I slowed down.

"Don't stop! Don't stop! Keep going!" my wife yelled.

"No," I said, "we'd better stop." We stopped and it was the sheriff and he wanted to know where we were going and where we came from.

"We were in Watsonville and we're going home."

"No," he said, "there's a rum battle going on. There's a lot of shooting. Go back to Watsonville."

My wife spoke up, "No, we can't go back to Watsonville; we've got our two little children." Her mother was babysitting for the children back over the house there.

We argued for a little while, when he finally said, "All right, we'll let you go through. But you go slow and if anyone tells you to stop, you stop!"

I said, "All right."

We went slow and the shooting kinda' quieted down. Just as we came around the turn there, right at the corner there where this road makes a turn (near the present post office at Moss Landing), there was this guy sprawled out on the highway, we didn't know who it was. He was dead. We had to get around him 'cause I didn't want to run over him.

And just at that time when I was getting around him, they up and start shooting again and there was a deputy a little further back and they hit him in the kneecap. You could hear that guy scream for ten miles.

We put the car in the garage, came in the house and locked the door. We didn't turn on the light. We started looking out the window. We could hear the shooting all right, but pretty soon it quieted down and we could see them running right out there in the field, beautiful moonlight.

About a half hour later, after it quieted down, why I heard a knock at the door. My wife said, "Don't open the door. Don't open the door!"

Then a yell came through the door: "Bill, what's going on?"

I recognized his voice and I opened the door. It was Louie Gomez; he lived back under the hill there. He once again said, "Bill, what's going on?"

I told him what I thought and he said, "Let's take a walk down there."

Then we thought it was all over. We got about half way down (100 yards) to the post office and they opened up again. (Laughter)

Did we ever get back here in the house! You could play checkers on our shirt tails [ran so fast]!

When they stopped us, we could look across the road there 'cause it wasn't very far; they had one of these rumrunners already handcuffed with his arms around the tree.

Earlier they had their big cars, Cadillacs, parked at Louie Gomez's. "Gee, if I had known that I could have fixed their cars so they couldn't have started them."

"I could have fixed those cars," he said again. Course he never dreamed all those big Cadillacs parked in his yard were the rumrunners.

Of course, the next day, you know how it is: We were looking over the scene. My wife she was one of them and she picked up a German Luger. The deputy saw her when she picked it up (laughter). He went over to her. He knew her and he said, "Mrs. Lehman, would you hand that to me?"

Of course, she didn't want the damn thing and she gave it to him and she was called to the trial in San Francisco. She was in San Francisco for about three weeks, having a good time—and my sister too.

That was the time in '26, you know, they had quite an earthquake. I couldn't go because I was field man for a big produce company. I wanted to go but I couldn't. They didn't have to pay nothing, didn't cost them anything. They had a good time. My sister's husband he was there too, he was in it [earthquake], it scared my wife. It shook pretty hard. She went to my sister's room and said, "Come on, let's get out of here, go to the park," the park there in San Francisco.

My brother-in-law said, "Ah, go on, get the hell out of here and go back to bed." But she didn't go to bed. She went to the park. She had lots of company there.

Phil Ohler was the one wounded in the knee. He was a fish and game commissioner but they used everybody they could get as far as the law was concerned. They had them all down. That was the biggest rum battle.

They brought the booze in all the time. Go down in Giberson Road off Highway 1, near the beach, where Willoby now lives. A big concrete building. It was built as a roadhouse. A man had a place in Salinas, then built the road-house. He made artichokes as the main course but that wasn't the main course—it was booze. They were landing because they had a tower up on top of this so they could look out over the ocean and signal.

They caught him and closed his place up. I don't know what they done to him but it wasn't very much.

They could float the booze ashore there. Cardboard cases could even been waterproofed and floated ashore or rowed ashore by Willoby's.

They landed it by the King Ranch two or three miles south of us. They used small boats. If it's too rough they floated it ashore. They came to the breaker line and floated it with buoys and ropes. Here (Moss Landing) they were landing it on the pier. The night watchman was in on it. He never got caught.

The night before they made the raid, they took out 500 cases off to San Francisco.

There weren't places here where you could buy liquor retail. We made homebrew. My dad used to make homebrew. One day it was like the Fourth of July, 'cause he bottled it too soon or something and it exploded.

Some young people would get a hold of this bootleg whiskey. You'd take a drink of it you wasn't sure if you'd go die or blind, one or the other. Myself I never was one for drinking. I like a drink, a can of beer or a highball.

Mountain Accident

From one of the isolated beaches on the southern coast of San Mateo County, Pescadero or Martins perhaps, came $15,000 worth of imported liquor, up through the curvy La Honda Road, to reach San Francisco for the holidays. But the driver ran off the road and could not extricate his truck. Traffic Officer Chester Kreiss saw the large truck in November 1924, abandoned with 231 cases of scotch. Four cases had been hidden behind bushes before the driver gave up his cause. He left the scene, undoubtedly wondering how he was going to explain this to the boss. Kreiss reported it to Undersheriff Pete Larrecou, who along with Deputy Julius Harris took possession and brought it to the county jail. The truck belonged to David Shurin, 1406 Buchanan, San Francisco. Shurin lost his truck and cargo when Judge George H. Buck ordered a "judicial declaration of the forfeiture" and ordered the sale of the liquor, according to the *Redwood City Standard.* That would be an interesting story since even the government was not allowed to sell liquor for drinking. Maybe it was sold to a bonded warehouse, which could be resold as medicinal liquor. In which case a bottle of medicine would have an interesting tale to tell about its long journey from Scotland.[7]

At the Golden Gate Ferry, at 3:30 a.m., 1929, federal agents seized a truck with a still on it and arrested George M. Bettencourt, the driver. An hour later they caught 27-year-old Thomas Lovullo on the same ferry transporting 110 gallons of alcohol in a touring car registered to Frank Martini.[8]

Move the Rum North

In 1925 when pressure from the Coast Guard and prohibition agents became so formidable in San Francisco Bay, Half Moon Bay and southern "smuggler's nests," rumrunners moved to the north. Captain Charles Goff, in charge of enforcement in northern California, announced in 1925, that since the capture of a dozen rum boats off the coast south of San Francisco, ships have stationed north of the bay city. Agents George Eldridge and George Hard captured three men in cars transporting 100 cases on Tomales Road: Frank Hanley, W. K. Stiles and Ray Nolan.[9]

Just as a caravan of five touring cars and two trucks was about to pull out of a barn two miles from Noyo River on the coast of Mendocino, Goff's men struck, arresting four men (Frankie Maloney, an Oakland boxer, Roy Moleer and J. W. Mott also of Oakland and F. A. Barrett of San Francisco), confiscating the five vehicles and $50,000 worth of liquor: 800 cases of scotch whiskey, four barrels of bourbon and several cases of champagne. The convoy was heading for Sausalito where they were meeting launches to cross the bay to San Francisco instead of using the Golden Gate Ferry. Goff felt these men were part of a larger smuggling ring.[10]

Into California Via Back Door

Constable J. W. Everett of Ludlow, on Route 66 in the center of the Mojave Desert, confiscated 120 quarts of Old Taylor whiskey and champagne. A few bottles had been broken and a few were taken by passing tourists when the fancy Auburn car wrecked, injuring George Hallock and J. W. Covington. The car was similar to the one found abandoned in 1930. Both had a concealed compartment back of the seat. A tiny secret spring opened the compartment.

Covington exonerated Hallock who worked for the Harvey House in Needles for two years, and had just been given a ride to Barstow. Covington may have been a part of a powerful ring of smugglers with Canadian whiskey brought into Mexico, to Juarez, then by fast car to Los Angeles—a five thousand mile trip for those Old Taylor bottles, all for those thirsty Angelinos.[11]

Roll Out the Barrel
Rumrunners Roll Kegs Along Van Ness

Transporting liquor to safe storage places within the city was often challenging to smuggling organizations. Sometimes men showed cleverness beyond belief; other times things just didn't work out right despite best efforts.

242

Three unidentified men rolled three kegs of wine from Bay Street to almost the water's edge below Fort Mason after an automobile accident.[12] Their small truck, registered to Archilla Bianchi, 221 Bay Street, hit a tow car of the California State Automobile Association at Van Ness and Bay Street. Paying no attention to the driver of the tow car, William Cate, the three men inspected their truck, found it wrecked, unloaded the kegs and started a slow-motion marathon to the bay. San Franciscans probably never gave the three men more than just a passing glance—after all, this was San Francisco, one could expect anything—but the spectacle attracted the attention of policeman W. P. Pullen who gave chase. These smugglers stopped rolling out the barrels and outdistanced the policeman, escaping with only three sacks believed to be bottled alcohol. Pullen confiscated the three kegs. Here, smugglers successfully completed the race to the city, but not quite to the storage location.

Rumrunner landed on Avila Pier but their race to the city with 272 cases of alcohol ended abruptly with a mishap when the truck crushed through the county wharf. Even though a police officer's cap was found on the passenger seat, Sheriff Jess Lowery never found the runners. Photo by author from 1972 newspaper about 1932 "Doings in Avila."

East of San Diego in Dehesa Valley, the Reeses display a copper smuggling tank, once covered with upholstery and mounted as the back upright portion of a seat of a huge 1 ½ ton truck for smuggling liquor from Tijuana, Mexico. Notice ax hole made by revenuers after arrest of smuggler. Carsten Reese, a dapper man with money, bought the tank from a government auction and patched the ax hole and used it for kerosene on his ranch. Carsten had a still across the creek south of the old homesite. He concealed his still in a cut into the side of the mountain undercover of oak trees. Their son Ted, while hiking between 1930 and 1933, found shacks, with copper tubing and tanks for distilling, throughout the mountains surrounding Dehesa Valley. Tank donated by Theodore A. Reese and photo by Larry L. Reese, Victorville.

CHAPTER 15

THE WET IMPERIAL COUNTY

Moonshine in Picacho
by Herbert Hughes, 7th Sheriff of Imperial County

Shortly after peace was made with the Quechan Indians in 1852, thousands of Sonorans coming from Mexico to the California gold fields stopped at the Yuma crossing and found gold in the gravel on the west bank of the Colorado River, 25 miles north of Yuma. The settlement, named Picacho, was the first town in what is now Imperial County. At its peak, Picacho had 2,500 inhabitants with a mining payroll of $40,000 per month. In its brawling and lusty life it flourished in the style of Tombstone, Goldfield and Deadwood. In 1910, the mines ceased operations and the old mining camp just became one of the Old West's historic ghost towns. Zane Grey, the greatest of western novelists, made Picacho the setting of the first part of the novel *Wanderer of the Wasteland.* By the mid 1920s the old Picacho township had about 15 voters who elected their own justice of peace and constable.

Bill Quick, a big rawboned special deputy sheriff in charge of the Agricultural Inspection Station at Winterhaven, brought an Arizona cattleman to El Centro to see Charles L. Gillett, 3rd Sheriff of Imperial County. The cattleman, who ran a herd on both sides of the river in the Picacho vicinity, said he was tired of the judge and constable rustling his cattle, butchering them, selling the beef. "What can I do?" he asked. "They are the law." He continued, stating that they were also operating a still in the wash about a quarter of a mile south of the Picacho Landing. The judge peddled the moonshine in Yuma and Winterhaven and threatened to shoot the hell out of anyone who interfered with his operation. The sheriff told the cattleman to go home, say nothing to anyone, and he would take care of the situation.

Sheriff Charles Gillett and Deputy Charlie Nice met Bill Quick at the Inspection Station in Winterhaven the next day. With Quick as guide, they proceeded northward on Picacho Road. Within a short distance of Picacho, concealing the auto in the brush beside the road, they walked up the river in the darkness to a little wash toward the light of a fire. They quietly slipped up to higher ground. The fire made enough light to show the constable and another fellow tending the fire under the still and running off a batch of liquor into a five-gallon can.

The sheriff said they would wait, that the judge would show up. Gillett stationed himself in the footpath leading to the river and placed his deputies on the banks of the wash about 75 feet from the still.

The constable started down the path, possibly heading for home, a short distance away, and stumbled over the sheriff who had dozed off but awakened quickly enough to put his gun against the stomach of the constable saying, "You are under arrest. Hands up!"

The constable said in a loud voice in order to warn his partner at the still, "I can't raise my hands or I'll drop the whiskey I'm carrying!"

The partner dove into the brush and darkness, Deputies Nice and Quick began pouring rifle fire into the rocks and brush. The moonshiner yelled, "Don't shoot! I'll come out!"

Collecting eight rifles, pistols and shotguns lying around, officers destroyed quite a quantity of smelly souring mash.

The still consisted of a fifty-gallon drum that the constable had seen floating down the river, towed to the shore, and converted into a distillery with attached worms of one-fourth inch galvanized tubing coiled round and round in which vaporized fumes of alcohol from the heated mash would condense, dropping into various containers.

The prisoners were made to dig up several five-gallon cans which had been standing up so the rust could settle. The judge who did most of the peddling told his customers the liquor was run through copper. The only copper was a copper funnel used when it was finally bottled.

Both prisoners received an eight-month sentence in the county jail. The constable escaped from the chain gang and was never heard of again. The judge, who could not be charged, then spent most of his time in Winterhaven, across the river from Yuma, Arizona.

Our story continues with William Keating, a big moustached Texan, father of Hugh, Bill and Curt, who in time became noted peace officers in Imperial County. Keating wore a six-gun in an open holster on a filled cartridge belt and looked like pictures of an old time marshal in Indian Territory, Dodge City or Tombstone. He was Chief of Police of Imperial City, after serving as an Imperial County deputy sheriff but most of his life was spent as a peace officer in Texas.

He told Sheriff Gillett in Imperial that there was open gambling on a big scale in the King Cotton Hotel, saying that it might mean his job or much trouble if he ignored the situation. The sheriff's office was preparing to move in. For some reason the gambling equipment was moved over to Mike Mueller's saloon and gambling place in Winterhaven.

Mueller's place was raided by the sheriff but the lookout, the Picacho judge, dove through a glass window and escaped. Officers seized thousands of dollars in cash on the tables and a big haul of expensive gambling equipment of wheels, tables, cards and dice as evidence. The judge again escaped arrest, and in time became a Yuma wino, on the streets, selling liquor to Indians.

Brawley Dungeon Distillery

On the banks of the Alamo River near Brawley, J. D. Cass established one of the most complete distilleries found in the Imperial Valley. Confounding detectives for some time, the clever engineering served its purpose until finally discovered. Taking advantage of a small hole in the embankment beneath shrubbery and a connecting canyon, Cass built a moonshine den. He even timbered it with huge logs and wooden reinforcements to prevent cave-ins. Piped water entered the cavern from an irrigation ditch half a mile away, a second pipe taking away the mash and debris, dumping it into the Alamo River below water level.

When breached by Sheriff Charles L. Gillett, Under-sheriff A. R. Underwood, Brawley Chief of Police Charles Verge and Brawley Constable William O'Brien, they found a 50-gallon still equipped with three burners, some 380 gallons of mash and other contraband—all seized. The court convicted Cass for manufacturing and possession. But after serving only part of his 500-day sentence, he escaped from custody and fled the county, taking off like a jackrabbit who had just come upon a coyote resting in the shade of some arrowweed.[1]

The first two years of being sheriff of Imperial County, Charles Gillett confiscated over 100 stills and put them to the ax in one afternoon. The stills ranged in sophistication from home-made quality to $250 commercial caliber. One was a wash-boiler converted into distilling potent drink for the county folks. When he was finished putting holes in the estimated $8,000 of equipment he sold it to a junkman for $150, helping the county exchequer.

A compilation of figures showed that county dry squad was most active in 1923-24. "After one particularly successful week, a roundup of the prisoners taken in the raids practically all entering pleas of guilty in one morning. Before noon on that day $3,250 was taken in fines."[2] The article stated the sheriff's force stamped out much of the illicit liquor traffic in the valley.

Imperial County Bootlegging
as told by Paul Gillett, El Centro

"Blackie" Bell [F. D. Bell] was extremely active in the Brawley area. There was even a murder at his place. He served booze, ran a brothel and a gambling house.

In Calexico, Feds planned a raid at an establishment called Steven's Beach. They stationed young 19 year-old Customs Patrolman Lee Echols outside the back exit by the canal that separated Calexico and Mexicali. The sheriff and other deputies were stationed on the side and the front. As they entered the front door, several culprits ran out the back door. One man, running with a gun, pointed it at Echols. When the escapee didn't stop, Echols fired and the man fell dead by the canal. In the investigations which followed, Echols insisted the man had a gun. Authorities ordered the canal water shut off. The next day, in the mud, they found a gun, and it was linked to the dead man. Echols was exonerated, continuing his career in law enforcement. He later helped develop the OSS in World War II, then was sheriff at Yuma, and later retired from the CIA.

When one Swiss rancher was arrested for bootlegging, he asked permission to go in to tell his wife before going to county jail. After he went inside there were screams. Then the young wife came out with a gun in one hand dragging her two children in the other. She began shooting, hysterically. During her erratic firing, she chased the deputies from the ranch.

The county had some bad booze. One man drank some poisoned alcohol, becoming crippled for life with "Jake's leg." Later the man worked as a poolhall shill in the valley. One person I knew died of contaminated liquor.

A man named Tunstol of Brawley had a sophisticated operation. He had his own plane. Once, when he used the landing strip at Westmoreland, he let word out that the plane was going to be used for a rum run. The federal prohis watched it all day and night, while Tunstol partied at a Brawley picnic. His plane was protected for free while he enjoyed the picnic.

Unofficially, the county sheriff of Imperial County let repeated drug and alcohol offenders run off. The prisoners were put on public work projects like road building. If they were given enough freedom, they would run off, thus freeing the sheriff of the bother of arresting them next month. Fifty percent of the drug violator trustees eventually ran off, saving Imperial County considerable money. After the crooked constable from the old mining town of Picacho served several months for moonshining, the sheriff made him a trustee. Of course he escaped, never returning to the county.

One repeat offender was a pretty woman named Rose Erskine. She was caught for drunkenness, drugs and solicitation—on both sides of the border. Rose came to the Imperial Valley with her young husband but the environment and circumstances ruined her marriage, hooking Rose on drugs, alcohol and prostitution. Rose bummed around the border for years. One time she was confined to the county jail in El Centro, the upstairs being the women's section. Thirsty one night, she tied her bed-clothes together, escaping to Mexicali. After drinking with her friends most of the night, she returned to the jail. Since she was too drunk to climb up her home-made rope, she knocked at the front door for re-admittance. The night jailer and I, the youngest son of Imperial County Sheriff Charles Gillett, let her in and returned her to her upstairs cell, neither reporting the incident. Many people in the valley associate her with the song written by Senator Tenney, later of Long Beach. The Song—*Mexicali Rose* [see Echols, Chapter 12].

Right across the park in the center of Holtville was a speakeasy. It was raided once and closed. Years later as a city crew cleaned out the small ditch next to the speakeasy, they found a body. Speculation was that he was a gambler who disappeared while the place was used for drinking and gambling. Perhaps he was a drinker who really got "dead drunk."

Usually if a person wanted a drink he knew where to quench his thirst. A convenient bootleg place in Holtville was in the alley behind the "picture show" and the poolhall, which serviced customers from both establishments. Holtville was chartered dry: by law no liquor could be drunk in the township; it stated that on the deeds to the individual pieces of property.

A Saturday night dance was a tradition in this rural valley. At Heber Dance Hall, various bootleggers hid their bottles in the grass by the fence. After a customer agreed to the financial arrangement, usually in the dance, a walk for fresh air ended by the cache of a hidden pint. That way the boot was not caught selling with bottles on his person. Calipatria North End School also had Saturday night dances with bootlegging similar to Heber.

At the Barbara Worth Hotel in El Centro and the new De Anza Hotel at Calexico, a few dollars to the bellboy could obtain the desired refreshments. De Anza was so close to the border that one could obtain quick "imported" beverages.

The town of Imperial, one of the few formerly wet communities in the valley, had a difficult time going dry. A Mexican family in Imperial couldn't break its habit of enjoying a cold beer or so with their friends. They served fine homebrew at a large wooden two-door home on the main street east of the rail tracks. Customers sat at an oilcloth covered table and their desires were served family style. The family hid the beer in the cistern tied by ropes, keeping the homebrew cool and out of sight. The management threw me and my friends out one time when they found out that my father was the county sheriff and my older brother Harold Gillett was an energetic deputy. The building of this former speakeasy is still in the city of Imperial.

The Swiss Club members, traditionally law abiding ranchers, had conflicts, as many Americans had, with their heritage of celebrating events with beer and fine wine. Consequently, enterprising concessionaires set up booths at the Annual Swiss Picnic where clear alcohol could be obtained, to be mixed with orange juice. A successful Swiss rancher named Vogel paid for his nephew's transportation from the old country. The hard work at the ranch and the desert sun didn't appeal to the young immigrant. Temptation of easy money getting the best of him, he set up a still in the basement of his uncle's ranch. Authorities raided the ranch just as a batch was ready to bottle. Since the nephew was not home, prohis arrested the uncle and fined him $55. His nephew ran away, leaving the hot Imperial Valley sun and an equally hot and embarrassed uncle.

One of my friends and I bought from the county a confiscated Model T Ford for $13. Despite filling it up with gas, we ran out of gas. We refilled the tank and to our surprise, we ran out of gas again. We examined the gas tank under the seat. Under one strap that secured the tank, we found a loose seam. We pulled the tank and a sleeve came out holding 15-16 pints of whiskey, packed tightly in paper. The gas tank that remained held only three gallons of gas. When we told my father, he reconfiscated the car, refunding our bargain price.

I remember one elaborate still containing two barrels hidden in the center of a haystack. The condensing coils wound out of the hay stack into the pond and back to the hay dugout.

Charles Gillett ran for county sheriff on the dry ticket, easily being elected. But the unpopularity of prohibition became so strong that in the last few years the unofficial policy was to raid or make an arrest only when there was an official complaint or when there were rumors of a bootlegger using galvanized metal for his still instead of copper—a dangerous health hazard.

Hey, You're Losing Some
as told by Francis Rice, Holtville

I went to Holtville after being discharged from the army about 1921. I became owner of Sunset Auto Court and numerous gas stations in the 20s and early 30s.

The most common recipe for whiskey was made from ground corn mixed with honey. Mason jars were used for most drinking. Distilled wine was one of the best liquors of the southern desert.

Monty Haynes was a volunteer fire department driver for Holtville. Once I visited him in his basement home across from the park. Handing me an almost empty bottle of Palo Verde liquor he said, "Go ahead, I can get more." When we finished it off, Haynes went across the street and brought back another bottle from the Holtville Fire Department. Haynes and I were drinking one time, perhaps too long, when the fire alarm rang. We got on the truck, both taking turns driving around and finally returning after not being able to find the fire. The mill burned down.

Entering Holtville one day, I dropped by Newt Gray's behind the trailer court, picked up a bottle from Newt Gray, good quality booze. At the beginning of the Plank Road across the sand dunes on the road to Yuma, Gray also had a garage—Gray's Well. The two government workers there were supposedly alcoholics.

Anyone could buy booze at the Barbara Worth Hotel. I rented a room there for $90 a month, which included maid service and two meals daily. "Harry" was head bellhop. The bellhops provided booze the customers needed. The same was true in the De Anza Hotel which had service from Mexicali—a few hundred yards away.

"Waterfill and Frazer," brewed in Mexico, was popular whiskey on both sides of the border. Businessmen often took their clients across the border.

After lunch they went to the free bar at one of the breweries. A man named Foreman, with a plush car, high-padded seats, joined me in a business trip to Mexicali. After returning to Calexico, Foreman noticed an extra bulge in the back seat. He discovered four quarts of Waterfill and Frazier. Foreman was worried and asked me what to do. "Go tell Shepherd," the officer in charge of the line [border], I said.

Shepherd checked the corks, replaced them, saying he would find the culprits who used Foreman's car to smuggle. Marks on the corks told the brewer and the distributor. Foreman then asked Shepherd, "What do we do with the whiskey?"

"Goddamn, don't you know?" Shepherd asked.

Once a friend named Bates and I gambled at the Owl in Mexicali. The roulette table occupied our minds and money so much that we hadn't noticed the time. It was after midnight when we looked at our watches. The border closed at nine. Occasionally an American could bang at the steel gate and the awakened Customs agent would let him into the United States. Bates and I, however, decided to use the hole behind the Calexico Police Department. We walked through without notice. But we saw a policeman sleeping on an old wooden cotton wagon. Bates said, "Wait. Let's go back."

We went back into Mexicali, bought a pint, set it on the wagon beside the sleeping officer. "Now when he wakes up," Bates said, "he'll have an eye opener."

My future father-in-law, way out on an isolated ranch, asked me, "Do you ever drink?"

When I said I did occasionally, we went to a haystack. The old man reached in between two bales, pulled out a bottle. He always kept his stash hidden, not from the prohis but from his wife who was a prohibitionist. He feared her more than the agents.

Frequently I visited the garages I supplied. On one occasion the Holtville garage owner said, "Hey, Rice, want a drink?"

"Sure," I replied. The owner proceeded to search each Model T Ford, looking under the seats. When he found the right car, he pulled out a bottle of clear liquor. "Drinks on the farmer!" said the owner as he tilted the bottle. He gasped, put the bottle down, and tears flowed out his eyes.

The mechanic standing there looked at the tears and said: "Hey, you're losing some."

Flour Dough Convicts Them
as told by Harold Gillett, Citrus Heights

I started as a deputy sheriff of Imperial County under my father, Sheriff Charles Gillett, 3rd Sheriff of Imperial County. I was only 17 at the time, 1923, worked for him and George L. Campbell who beat my father in the election of 1931 and later Bob Ware who beat him. I often worked the 7 p.m. to 7 a.m. shift, 12 hours a day, not one day off for a year and a half, for $120 a month. One year I went to Sacramento and became a fingerprint expert, later returned to become Special Investigator of the State, eventually becoming Chief of State Bureau of Criminal Identification and Investigation. I retired in 1962 with 39 years in law enforcement, counting the years as an MP in World War II.

As a young boy, I worked for Mr. J. B. Baker, a fine man, owner of the *Holtville Tribune*. I was a helper, the "Devil's Advocate." One of my jobs was to hide the printer's booze from Mr. Baker.

In those old days of prohibition we cooperated with the Arizona authorities in the Yuma area. There was a strip of land on both sides of the Colorado River in dispute between California and Arizona. Often we'd go out on raids with officers from both states so a moonshiner could not claim immunity by saying to Arizona sheriffs, "No, you can't arrest me; this is California." The strip of the disputed area we called no man's land. We cooperated to avoid legal technicalities. I remember even at the bug station, State Agricultural Inspection Station, we stopped a car thief who came from Arizona. We called their sheriff to come to California. So we didn't have to waste time extraditing him back to Arizona, we declared this part of California rightfully Arizona in our judgment. They often did same for us. In some cases other counties cooperated with each other. The long border between Riverside and San Bernardino counties had disputed areas. Many times officers flipped a coin over who had jurisdiction.

I set up the Yuma fingerprint lab and file. I did the same thing for Mexicali Police Department. But I had to do that twice. They changed police chiefs in Mexicali as often as we change shirts. We were looking for Ruth Judd [later in Gillett's career], a murderess whom we thought might be in Mexicali at the time. The police chief said, "I'll get her before morning."

Frank Godell, who spoke Spanish, said, "You'd better, Chief. You probably won't be chief the day after tomorrow!" We all laughed.

We used fingerprints successfully on moonshining cases. Shiners' fingerprints would be baked in the flour dough that's used to seal the still. They pat it around to seal the still, let it dry, then cook off the mash. Their fingerprints were cooked in. We raided one spot, made too much noise and so the moonshiners left. But we had their fingerprints on the stills. When we caught the owners of the stills, they thought they would surely be acquitted since we hadn't caught them with evidence. We shocked them when we produced their fingerprints that were on the stills. The court found them guilty.

We had tips that a Negro near Calipatria at Long Green Place sold booze. We arrested a drunk Hindu once, called Step and a Half—that's what he was called because of a limp leg. Since he wanted to be turned loose, we agreed to let him go if he'd buy liquor from the Long Green Place. We were outside the bar, listening through the screened windows.

"I want a drink," said Step and a Half to the Negro.

Step took the drink, drank it all the way down. Realizing he drank all the evidence in the glass, Step yelled, "No good, no good, no good. I want another."

"You have to pay for this drink first," said the black bootlegger.

"I want another one. No good, no good!" Step shouted louder so we would hear him and come in. He had no money.

"You must pay for the other drink."

Step turned his head toward the screened window, "If you guys don't come in pretty soon, I'll have to pay for this damn whiskey!" he shouted. Before we could get in and rescue our buyer, he almost got beat up.

We had a bird dog with Phoenix tags that was lost. It hung around the Imperial County Sheriff's Department for a couple of years. I wrote to Phoenix—never could find the owner so it became our dog, really my dog as it went everywhere with me. We named it Hypo after the term hypo—drug addict. We deputized him by putting a star on his collar: Imperial County Deputy Sheriff. Near the present roadside rest on Highway 111, between Calipatria and Brawley, we were looking for a still. Hypo went with us as we looked around the river brush. He disappeared. I couldn't find him or the still. I went back again a couple of times, called and looked—never did find him. Several months later a prisoner told me that the dog ran right up to the still. Seeing the dog with a sheriff collar, the moonshiners panicked. They thought that Hypo was trained to seek out shiners and would go back and report the location. They tied him up and later shot him. We all felt as if we lost one of our family to the moonshiners—we were so attached to Hypo.

Hijacked liquor had no value. One could not be arrested for stealing something that was unlawful to have. We'd have to arrest him for stealing bottles and caps. Some hijackers pretended to be cops. Gene Hudson, a black poolhall owner and bootlegger, across the tracks in El Centro, was hijacked a couple times. Once the bandit shot him in the chest. He carried a dollar in his vest pocket. That's what the bullet hit. He carried it around, bragging, showing the dollar with the round indentation.

Prohibition agent Bob Knight and I went to make a raid in Palo Verde. We took the long road then by Beale Well and Wiley Well where our axle broke. It was August and we had only a gallon and a half of water with us. Knight had a crippled leg so he couldn't walk much. He slept on top of the car while I slept on the ground. Since he was so afraid of snakes, he slept on the car.

Our county tried, probably more than most, to enforce the law. When we received tips we checked them out. Tips came from odd places. A grocer sold ten sacks of sugar to a moonshiner, then phoned up. A handyman built a still for a man, then called us up.

Prohis came in from L. A., would hire stoolies to go in and buy, then issue warrants to raid. Those were discouraging times for enforcing the laws. I brought fellows to San Quentin. Afterwards I went to a restaurant near San Quentin. "You want a drink?" the waiter asked—only about a mile and a half away from San Quentin! At the ferry by San Quentin, another bootlegger approached me.

Most of us officers didn't drink much. We were on 12 hours a day, and on call any time. We might go over to the San Diego Cafe in Mexicali, have a chicken dinner and a beer but that was all. I couldn't arrest someone for something I was guilty of—just couldn't do it.

The Bootlegger Down the Road
as told by Joe Anderholt, Imperial

"The water here in Holtville is so bad that I had to distill it to make it fit to drink," said Jack Roche to the court when explaining why he should not be convicted for possessing a still. Roche was an Italian who bootlegged and moonshined. He lived down the same road my family had its ranch, just north of Norrish Road, 1 ½ miles west of Highway 115. For years Roche made various kinds of liquor. As far as I know he never did any jail time. Two of his workers did, Andy Rossi and Phillip Fornasera, serving some county jail time.

When we'd see the constable or deputy sheriff go down the road, we would know what was happening. If he stayed down at the Roche Ranch for a couple of hours, we knew it was a social call. If he were down there just a couple minutes, we knew there was going to be a raid. Officers tipped off Roche.

One time in the middle of the night, we heard a loud commotion by the barn. We kids could not go out there, but the next morning, we noticed the ladder was moved. We climbed up to the loft and saw loose hay piled up over Roche's stash of liquor. He was tipped off and used our hay stack to hide his liquor. He had chickens and hid half pints under his chicken nests. But the bulk of his stash was hidden out in the bushes.

Every Friday afternoon, almost every Friday, my grade school teacher drove down our road to Roche's. She had a yellow convertible and I'd wave at her. She was an alcoholic and her husband was just as bad. They did not drink during the week because they both had good jobs, but on the weekend they partied. He drank so much that at work Monday, a coworker said, he would drink a glass of water and still be drunk all day Monday. My teacher had such a hangover that on Monday she was meaner than hell. We did not take any chances to make her madder. On Wednesday through Friday, she was an excellent teacher. We learned a lot from her, but on Friday we'd see her car going down our road again.

My father was a good customer of Roche, but down the street we also had the Whitney family. Mrs. Whitney was a worker in the WCTU, but may have been naive not knowing for sure what was happening. At night we could hear the Italians playing their games at the Roche Ranch, yelling and cheering. In fact I became a customer when I was a teenager. I'd go over there at age 15 or so and buy some liquor. He knew me and knew I wouldn't turn him in. We kids would have a party.

Most people, especially foreigners, made wine. We had Portuguese and Greeks here and Swiss. The Swiss made their allotment of wine, then added more water to the leftovers and let it ferment again. Over a very low heat, they distilled just the liquor and none of the water. Would come out 180-90 proof. The Swiss called that schnapps or brandy. Almost everybody made beer. My mother made beer, sold it to the Swiss Club for their gatherings. The club bought five cases from her and more from other families. The grocery stores sold hundreds of cases of malt.

Another bootlegger around Holtville was "Slick" Coppenger, who later opened "Slick's Pool Hall." The most notorious was Newt Gray. He owned a station in the east on the road to Yuma, called Gray's Well. He and another bootlegger, Bob Davis, had a trick they'd pull. They took an unbranded mule across the border to Mexico, loaded it up with whiskey and let it wander across to the California side. If the Customs men caught the mule, all the smugglers lost was the liquor, and of course the mule. Gray or Davis picked up the mule on the California side.

Sometimes, Newt Gray took his grandson Jack across into Mexicali when he would do his buying and make his arrangements. He left Jack at this house and the lady there took care of him as he played and sometimes spent the night. He found out later that the house was a house of prostitution and the madam was supposedly "Mexicali Rose" [see Echols, Chapter 12].

Bob Davis was very political. He helped obtain votes in one election— before prohibition. So the story goes: When Davis was in Winterhaven, a politician asked him how many votes did their side have in Winterhaven.

"How many do you need?" asked Davis.

"How many do you have?" he asked again.

"How many do you need?"

Finally he said, "Forty."

Davis said, "We have forty."

Davis had some clout in the valley and was pretty much left alone. The county official did not bother the locals very much. Once the federal agents were out searching a ranch and the sheriff (maybe Charles Gillett) found some whiskey hidden in a milk can next to the pig pen. Often the farmers let milk sour in the cans and fed the curdled milk to the pigs. The officer saw the alcohol inside the milk can, closed the lid again, sat on the can and said something to the effect, "I'm tired, you guys keep on looking" [see Davis, Chapter 8].

And Still the Raids Continued

As the depression sank the country into a morass, so did the intensity of bootlegging and moonshining. In the second full year of the depression, 1931, Imperial County became a prohibition quagmire, like the mud in New River: violations, arrests, violations, arrests. An Imperial Valley bootlegger, A. Piazzi, residing on the Roche Ranch, was hit again by Harold Gillett, Ernest Clay and Fred Elliott, who confiscated cases of beer, gallons of wine and bottles of whiskey. Piazzi put up a $250 cashier's check, went to court on June 5 and pleaded not guilty, asking for a jury trial. In July Lee Nuffer of El Centro defended him, arguing that the alcohol was not his, but was left by the officers from the April raid at his place. Since the officers failed to destroy all of Piazzi's whiskey in April, the whiskey was technically the property of Imperial County, not Piazzi's.

The jury freed him.[3]

In the middle of July, agents from southern California, concentrated on the wet Imperial County. For weeks prohi informants and undercover men reported and bought from the sellers.

Then for almost 12 hours straight raids continued, one city after the next: El Centro, Brawley, Westmoreland, Meloland, Calexico, Calipatria, Imperial, Heber and Kane Springs. They destroyed thousands of gallons of liquor, wine, beer, whiskey, gin—all except samples from each bust went into the gutters and the fields of the hot dry desert. In drying up Brawley—for a few days anyway—prohis arrested F. D. "Blackie" Bell, 40, George Merrian, 33, Kent White, 24, Wiley Bird, 24, Jim Ryan, 47, W. H. Modum, 23, Joe Hood, 29 and J. L. McDonald, 27.

From El Centro: W. S. Murphree, 28, Thelma Kessler, 28, Allen Brown, 31, William Jones, 23, Angelos Buglitsis, 33, and Albert Doar, 34. From Meloland, H. R. Fulton; Kane Springs, Joe Lorasco, 27; Heber, Alex Thompson, 37; Calexico, James Woodbury, 38; Westmoreland, Leon Gonzales, 27 and E. M. Bosby, 27.

Agents also arrested Norman Cole, 26, and M. L. Null, 42 of Calipatria, and R. L. Maloney, 63, and John England of Imperial.

The judge dismissed Murphree's case but hit Thelma Kessler for $400 or 200 days. Six went to the federal court in San Diego. Most the others received fines from $100 to $500. The seven who pleaded not guilty were fined heavily after being found guilty. Generally the $300 fine for selling and $200 for possession worked off at a rate of $3 per day for selling and $5 per day for possession—all helping the county pay bills or do needed road work.

The year ended with caring citizens of Holtville and other towns pre-paring Christmas baskets for the poor. Others planned their holiday—with less liquor. For example, Bob Carson, one-half mile west of Holtville, had a half gallon of alcohol to celebrate with friends. When raided, the judge cheerfully gave him $200 or 100 days, which sobered his holidays.

Even though most Imperial Valley communities were chartered dry, they were wet through prohibition. A dry desert, served by irrigation canals, allowed these desert pioneers to create fine towns and year-round crops. With the canals and irrigation systems creating high humidity, these pioneers and their descendants seemed to need a little beer or whiskey to handle the heat and the humidity.

CHAPTER 16

A PEANUT EXPOSES THE LAPD

Crooked Cops—LAPD and the Southland

Carl Eifler dropped out of junior high school so he could join the army. At the age of 15 years he became Private Eifler. While attending cooking school in the Philippine Islands, he tried to be reassigned to the Aerial Photography unit. His junior status was too much to buck until fate gave a hand.

While returning to the barracks Eifler saved a sergeant from being beaten up by a group of natives. The drunk sergeant was in the much-sought-after aerial photo unit. In a few days the army transferred Eifler to that unit. He gained valuable experience in photography and aircraft knowledge, used later in his career as a Customs Agent and an organizer of the Office of Secret Service (OSS) in World War II.

The following is an excerpt from *The Deadliest Colonel* by Thomas N. Moon and Carl F Eifler:[1]

Eighteen months had passed since Eifler had entered the service. A serious illness of his father arose. His mother went to the Red Cross and revealed his true age—just seventeen then. It was the end of his short-lived military career.

As he stood before the captain after confessing, he lowered his head. Asked why, he replied he was ashamed of having lied about his age. "Don't be ashamed of that, son. I'd have done the same thing," replied the understanding officer.

Now it was back to the job of searching for something that was both challenging and had a future. He headed for Mexico to look things over. He followed rumors and promises but found nothing to satisfy him. Back in Los Angeles he secured a job with the private Los Angeles City Fire Prevention Control. He and his partner would patrol certain areas of security. He also made extra money with a magazine firm. In reality, he worked two jobs which necessitated him leaving the fire prevention job and racing down Wilshire Boulevard to his other job. One morning while doing this he was arrested for speeding. At that time there were no fines for this offense—only jail. He spent five days in jail. "It taught me something," he said later. "I learned how valuable a man's freedom is, and I was always over-cautious in making an arrest."

A short time later he decided to go into law enforcement and entered the Los Angeles Police Academy. In 1926, he graduated in the LAPD sixth class, along with well-known former police chief of detectives Thad Brown. Brown was later to become acting chief of police with the death of Chief Parker.

The country was now in the throes of prohibition. When Los Angeles annexed Venice, Eifler was assigned there as a patrolman. Rumrunning was heavy in the Venice area, which lent itself to such activity because of the terrain. Eifler worked his beat with a zeal unknown to most other policemen. He became known as the one sure to make an arrest when he went out. "Get the wagon ready, there goes Eifler," they would say as he headed out the door.

In an attempt to look older, he grew a mustache and sported a pair of pince-nez glasses. He was encouraged by his superiors. He also became known for his ability to find stolen cars and was commended by his superiors. Several years later Eifler learned his superiors were getting $25.00 for each recovered car.

While on the beat one day he noticed a car parked at the curb. It appeared to have been there for some time. He placed a peanut under the wheel. The next day it was crushed, but the car was in the same place. Something was odd. A check with the police headquarters did not reveal the car was stolen or abandoned. In pondering this, Eifler noticed a man nearby walking into a large garage. He followed him to ask if he knew the owner of the car. On entering the door, he came face to face with the largest bootlegging operation ever uncovered in the Los Angeles basin. Out went the call for paddy wagons, and in rolled police by the score. The detectives from Los Angeles were alerted and also moved in. As case after case of evidence was loaded into police vehicles, one of the Los Angeles detectives asked if he should take over. Eifler said that to his knowledge this was the customary thing and to go ahead. Then he overheard a detective talking to someone on the phone saying: "Honest, I had nothing to do with it. The cop on the beat did it, the cop on the beat did it."

Eifler returned to the station house to find less than one wagonload of the confiscated booze. Four loads had been sent. "Where is the rest of the stuff?" he asked. The desk sergeant said: "This is it. If there was any more sent, I don't want to know about it." Eifler decided to think about it. He walked outside the door where he was greeted by the banker next door. "Hey, Carl, that was great stuff you sent back," he said. The light began to dawn. "Oh, you got some of it?" Eifler replied.

"Hell, all of us did," the banker told him.

To the young idealist it came as rather a bitter blow. He just walked over to the street and sat down on the curb to give it some more thought. But an even crueler blow awaited him. His superiors were not all pleased with the action of the cop on the beat. They decided he had to go.

A thorough check of his records indicated he had falsified his age. He was called in and told of the severity of giving false information on civil service records. He had the choice of resigning or being put on trial for record falsification. He took the obvious choice.

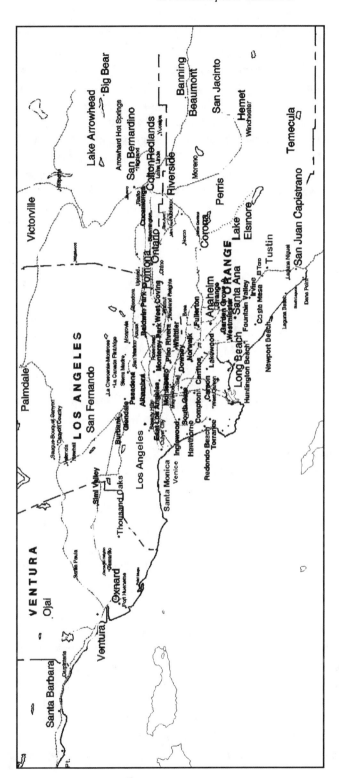

The Southland

Crushed by this chain of events, Eifler sat down to talk things over with his family. A boyfriend of his sister was now his brother-in-law and doing some contracting. He asked Eifler to join him, which he did. For about a year he worked with hammer and saw but found it unfulfilling and left for a new job. He returned to being a cop—this time on the Newport Beach Police Department. The small force consisted of less than ten men. Because he had precious experience Eifler commanded a prowl car and was assigned some of the more remote areas. One night he stopped a car on a lonely back road. Eifler was alone. The car contained four men. Eifler asked what they were doing and demanded identification. They turned out to be U.S. Customs agents. One asked Eifler if he was not worried about stopping a car with four men on a lonely road.

Obviously he was not.

Before leaving, one of the men, obviously impressed by Eifler, gave him his card. He was Lee Echols, the youngest and the smallest of the four. He was destined to play a big role in Eifler's life.

"Look me up if you ever want to come to work for customs," he said. Eifler pocketed the card and wisely kept it. Less than a year later a new police chief was elected. He asked Eifler to stay on but he elected to move on and resigned.

He was not quite twenty-two when he went to work for the U.S. Customs and was assigned the Calexico area with Lee Echols. He later worked under the coordinator of smuggling, which included southern California and Arizona.

In May 1928 he enlisted in the army reserves as a private. Six months later he was commissioned a second lieutenant under the command of Major Isaacs.

The years 1928 to 1934 saw him serving as a U.S. border patrolman on the Mexican border. There were numerous confrontations and gun battles. Eifler determined to become a crack shot and practiced continually. He had the advantage of being able to do both with his regular job and also with the army reserves.

Crooked Cops?
as told by Carl Eifler, Salinas

During the prohi days there wasn't anything out in the open unless you got into a speakeasy. Let's take an honest cop, honest from the word go as far as bribery or anything like that is concerned, John Edwards. Now I'm a Federal officer and John used to come down to Mexico and we'd hunt and whenever I went into Los Angeles, I visited him. I went in to talk to John one day and he said come and have a bite of lunch. We went to a speakeasy. In other words we went into a bootlegging joint right in his district. Course he went to the door and they checked him, opened the door and let him on in. We had a couple drinks and some sandwiches.

Then I looked at him and said , "John, tell me. Now damnit, you're the Chief of Detectives in this area and you have a vice squad. This place here is one of the places where your vice squad is operating. What are you doing here?"

"Well, Carl, I also have a burglary squad and a robbery squad. I have a lot of other squads. Now where are my boys going to get information, in the church? If the vice squad picked this place and knocked it off, okay, but my other detectives are not going to tell them as long as they're using this place to get information. This here is where they meet stoolies and their prostitutes, so on and so forth."

Only the vice squad is interested in that. John is ahead of all of them. Now is he crooked for that? Okay, then he's crooked. This is police work.

Unbridled Booze Debauch[2]
January 31, 1925
REPORT TO SAN BERNARDINO COUNTY GRAND JURY
ON VICE AND LIQUOR SITUATION
BY
EDWIN E. GRANT
PRESIDENT, STATE LAW ENFORCEMENT LEAGUE
San Francisco
July 12, 1924Grant

Mr. George W. Loring
Foreman, San Bernardino County Grand Jury

At the request of a group of citizens of your county the writer has been conducting, for the past several weeks, investigations into the liquor and vice situation in San Bernardino County and begs leave to submit herewith the findings of our investigations, the detailed evidence concerning which is now available to the courts.

After we had gotten our lines of investigation firmly established and worked our way into the good graces of the gang, we sought and secured the hearty co-operation of the Federal Prohibition Department. Accordingly, the raids were made today. Criminal liquor cases are going into the Federal Courts. We are asking the District Attorney of the San Bernardino County to institute abatement proceedings closing these dives for one year, which procedure is in fact the most effective of all.

FEDERAL RAIDS

The jails were filled today, as a result of these raids, with bootleggers, jackass brandy, narcotics, stills, wine, bonded goods, beer and home brew outfits. One case of conspiracy, a felony, was completed in the arrest of a local doctor and a druggist for operating a fake medical permit scheme. This calls for a penitentiary sentence. Fake bonded goods were also uncovered also carrying a serious penalty. One hotel proprietor told of making $300 per month bootlegging. He must tell the income tax collector about it in addition to the penalty for sale. At one still at Devore Station, the raiders destroyed 1,600 gallons of mash, 60 gallons of whiskey and 30 gallons of wine. At a place in San Bernardino, we destroyed a home brew outfit and siezed [sic] a large quantity of beer. In one hotel a large cache of narcotics was captured. Even as this letter is being written, prisoners and contraband booze are pouring into the jail.

SAN BERNARDINO

The early part of May, [we found] a system of Law Enforcement quite capable of dealing with the liquor and vice problems. We did manage to buy liquor and to gather together evidence of redlight violations, but the illegal business was done under such restrictions as to make its continuance unprofitable and hazardous.

THE EAGLES

And then the Eagles came. [State Convention of Eagles, May 26, 27 and 28, 1924]

When the Eagles arrived, the keys of the city were turned over to them, the lid flew off, and the sky was the limit. A veritable carnival of drunken debauchery was permitted such as would make the ancient booze orgies of the San Francisco Democratic Convention of 1920 blush for shame.

This booze lawlessness was headed up more particularly at the Eagles' dance held both at the Eagles Hall and the Civic Auditorium. There booze was sold at the very doors of the dance, bottles were passed from one hip pocket to another and men and women left the dance together, and strolled to secluded benches and shadows of trees in the park and there guzzled down whole flasks of jackass brandy. Even acts of immorality in the park were witnessed by our operatives.

Men yelled and shrieked and screamed and went staggering over the grounds and along the side portico and steps and then back into the dance hall. Even little children in the dance hall and playing out on the steps were compelled to witness this drunken orgy. Bottles were strewn all over the park. We picked up a basketful for your observation.

The writer has been in every one of the fifty-eight counties of the State in connection with Law Enforcement work, but never since the passage of the Eighteenth Amendment has he witnessed such unbridled debauch as he saw in conjunction with the Eagles dance in San Bernardino.

The general understanding seemed to be that word had been passed down from some place higher up that "the lid was off" during the celebration. But whatever may be the situation there, the facts are that uniformed police officers were present in and about the dance in positions where they could not help but see the law violations that were going on, and made no visible effort to

Citizens gather around L.A. distillery when raided. Agents smashed all the barrels of whiskey. Notice wet footprints on pavement from whiskey. Photo courtesy CA State Library, California Section Photograph Collection.

stop them. I witnessed one hip pocket artist pass a drink to another man within ten feet of a police officer.

A thorough investigation...might reveal sufficient information to indict for conspiracy through some kind of "gentleman's agreement." On occasion the Eagles were heard to make the remark that they had the keys to the city and they were going to use them. And use them they did. Who gave them the keys?"

[Grant went on to tell of drunken driving, alleged criminal assault on two women, auto crash where a whiskey flask fell out of the driver's pocket which "littered and stenched the street with broken glass and booze," and fights. Grant said that even "Slim" Davis came out of lying low waiting for two state witnesses to get out of the court's jurisdiction so his case would be dismissed. He sent for his car down by the Mexican border and came back to San Bernardino to sell booze to help the Eagles celebrate. All this information gathered at this carnival of drunkenness was made available the county grand jury.] Grant continued:

San Bernardino has not yet recovered from the effects of this unprecedented let-down of lawlessness. While the lid was theoretically put back after the Eagle convention, yet booze has since been sold more openly, except when word was passed along to lay low, and redlight women have been known to hail men even on the streets as they passed their houses.

COLTON

Our investigations disclosed the fact that the vice system of San Bernardino County is centered in Colton. In a rooming house known as the Harvard Hotel in Colton we uncovered a white slave ring operating to several points in the county. In this house we found that a girl named Thelma, one named Helen and another were harbored, while skulking around the hallways were their male parasites waiting to grab the blood money earned by these unfortunate victims of the white slave traffic.

On one occasion, one of these girls chased her male parasite around with a knife. Perhaps she had good reason to. Then after she was disarmed I saw this male parasite rush back into the room shouting that he was going to kill her. But the riot later subsided without any bloodshed, and the next night these strange lovers were cooing like turtledoves.

CUCAMONGA

At Cucamonga, we gathered evidence of one redlight and two booze violations, a rather bad showing for a place of its size. Cucamonga seems to harbor the redlight and bootlegging business supplying Ontario and Upland. Even narcotics were found there in a recent county raid.

REDLANDS

A survey of Redlands was made and while rumors of law infractions were heard, yet we did not find anything there that might be in any sense called a real problem, except for a booze cache and possible still at Redlands Junction.

ONTARIO

At Ontario, we found the law enforcement situation in very good shape, law violators generally being compelled to go to Cucamonga, and other outside points when in quest of debauch, a situation over which Ontario officials have no control.

UPLAND

The situation at Upland was also found generally to be in good shape, except for a Thursday night dance there which attracts patrons for many miles around, and where evidence of booze were found. This booze business seemed to connect to Cucamonga. It seems the bootleggers in San Bernardino follow very closely these unsupervised public dances. A police blockade of bootleggers at these dances would cut off a vast portion of the bootleggers' trade in San Bernardino County. In fact this very thing has since been inaugurated at the Upland dance, where police officers were seen to rout couples out of machines in shaded spots where they had hidden away "between dances." This new form of vigilance also made bootlegging at the dance a rather hazardous business.

CHINO

A survey was made in Chino. In and about this city is a situation that would bear watching, though vice is intermittent and bootlegging is not flagrant as far as surface indications are concerned. A recent county raid of a still near Chino has had the effect, temporarily at least, of quieting things down considerably there.

RIALTO

The situation in Rialto as judged by surface indications does not seem to be bad, except for the menace of outlying territory.

We have gathered evidence of not less than forty-five liquor and vice violations, also partial evidence involving numerous other places.

For raids a posse of sixteen Federal men was brought from Los Angeles. The Sheriff's office here co-operated with us splendidly in the raids.

Very respectfully yours,
Edwin E. Grant (Signature)

San Bernardino County Loses Booze

When the results of these raids in San Bernardino County did not achieve many convictions, Edwin E. Grant, of the State Law Enforcement League, a private organization formed in 1917 to help local, state and federal agencies enforce the law, investigated complaints of violations of laws, especially liquor, drugs, gambling and prostitution violations. In 1925, in utter frustration, Grant wrote numerous letters to Washington, D.C. and to state officials to help with enforcement. On January 30, 1925, he wrote to Alf Oftedal, Special Agent, Intelligence Department, wanting an investigation of the U. S. Attorney Joseph Burke in Los Angeles. San Bernardino County had problems stopping vice, said Grant. Federal agents Cole and Tyson, with Sheriff Shay and Deputy Sheriffs Brown, Richardson and Young raided the Bartlett Hotel and the Augustine Hotel in San Bernardino. They confiscated liquor and arrested Frank Walby, Laura Milligan, Dollie Fisher and Peterson, the owner of the Augustine Hotel. The U. S. Attorney produced no liquor evidence even though it was obtained under a search warrant after purchasing liquor from those hotels. Some of the evidence "disappeared" and some evidently was not admissible. Grant wanted Oltedal to investigate the U. S. Attorney in Los Angeles. Even if the liquor disappeared, why weren't any of the officers involved in the raids called to be a witness? Grant wanted to know. Grant was furious because the government dismissed the cases against Dollie Fisher and others.[3]

Grant wanted charges brought up against Joe Burke, U. S. District Attorney, who just resigned; Mark Herron, his chief deputy; and Judge W. P. James, in whose court irregular dismissals occurred.

All types of rumors of disappearing evidence occurred during the prohibition period 1919-1933. A San Francisco jury found a defendant not guilty after they drank all the evidence. A charge in Eureka was dismissed after a friend drilled a hole through the courthouse storage floor and through the wooden keg, draining the alcohol (evidence). Constable Penny Morrow of Oro Grande said that every time alcohol was moved, some of the evidence disappeared. When he arrested someone in Oro Grande, some booze disappeared when it was moved to Victorville. When it was sent to the Sheriff's office in San Bernardino, the government lost some more and even more when it was sent over to the court.[4]

Consistent disappearing of liquor frustrated Detective Leslie T. White of the Ventura County Sheriff's Department, as explained in his book *Me, Detective*:

"It is natural that in the light of altered perspective, I should lose interest in bootlegging and other forms of vice. Since it was obvious the business men desired it and the disinterested portion of the public were apathetic, I could see small point in becoming a 'collector' of graft—for that is exactly what it amounted to as far as I could reason it out. On top of that, we had in jail a farcical situation which irritated me.

"It was the standard procedure, when making liquor violation arrests at night, to leave all evidence, which, obviously, was mostly liquid, in custody of the jailer. This worthy was something of a human sponge and we used to figure out what his maximum consumption was likely to be between the time of arrest, when the evidence was placed in his custody, and the arraignment when the evidence would be turned over to the clerk of the court. For example: if we arrested a violator in a Saturday evening, we knew the jailer would be good for at least two quarts before court on Monday, and it was always advisable to allow a margin of another quart in case he entertained any cronies during the interim. Therefore, if we planned to use one quart of liquor as legal evidence, we had to deposit four quarts on a Saturday night. This griped me so much that...I focused my attention on more serious crime." No wonder someone said, "Californians faced the prohibition period with one eye closed, the other one red."[5]

Making Spirits Bright
by Veronica Deasy, Crestline

Once again the holiday season is upon us, accompanied by the chill blasts of winter in the San Bernardino Mountains. Entertainment takes place indoors and festively decorated homes become the setting for fun-filled parties featuring traditional food and drink. These gatherings reflect the pleasure of sharing season's joys with one another. Alcoholic beverages are frequently part of the celebration, with a variety from which to choose.

This wasn't always the case. During prohibition, when the 18th Amendment made the manufacture and sale of alcoholic beverages illegal, choice was strictly limited. Although consumption of alcohol declined, some hearty souls resorted to making their own bootleg liquor or purchasing it at illegal bars called speakeasies. Mountain residents were no exception.

Many enterprising mountaineers saw the profit to be gained by making illegal booze and selling it to residents and tourists. According to a local pioneer, the late John Adams, fine apple brandy was brewed in Crestline's Dart Canyon area, where several orchards were located. A majority of the "whiskey" shipped down the hill was this same apple brandy laced with pan-fried brown sugar to make it like the real thing. One ingenious Dart Canyon resident even raised "high priced" chickens which could be purchased conveniently stuffed with bottles of moonshine liquor.

Squint's Ranch, along Deep Creek north of Lake Arrowhead, was a center of clandestine operations during the 20s and 30s. William "Squint" Worthington augmented his ranch activities by supplying bootleg liquor to local residents, workers at Lake Arrowhead dam and the mountain nightspots that catered to tourists. Over the years, Ranger Bert Switzer made several frustrating, unsuccessful attempts to discover Worthington's still and put him out of business.

Prohibition was difficult to enforce, so local law agencies did little to interfere with illegal liquor traffic, aside from cooperating with Federal Revenue agents in roundups of bootleggers or raids on suspected establishments. Unfortunately the San Bernardino County Sheriff's Department, which was responsible for organizing the raids, had the odds stacked against it, since several informers were on their payroll.

One successful Big Bear raid in 1923 relied on an undercover team of a man and his wife who were supposedly making their first visit to the area. Claiming to know all the bootleggers at their regular drinking haunts in Lake Arrowhead, they were ready to finance unlimited rounds of drinks in Big Bear, providing they could make connections with local suppliers.

In this instance, greed overcame caution and the man had no difficulty getting names and addresses of bootleggers in the vicinity. The raid the next morning, on July 6, 1923, came as a complete surprise. By nightfall, according to eyewitness reports, "the Feds had made a good start towards depopulating the valley." From then on, people were a little more careful about talking to "flatlanders."

The effects of mountain brew were also in evidence at Crestline's Pioneer Days—raucous celebrations held annually in the Valley of the Moon. The late John Dexter, who operated a lumber mill at Twin Peaks, also served as town constable and recalled some of the free-for-alls that resulted from imbibing too much liquor. "The only way we could stop one brawl was to cut off the outdoor lights. Then at least nobody could see who they were hitting. But while the lights were out, some crook stole 20 hams that were intended for raffle prizes."

No history of prohibition days in the mountains would be complete without some mention of the infamous "Club Arrowhead" in Arrowhead Villas, known today as the Tudor House. Built about 1926, it was a meeting place for underworld figures and high-rolling thrill seekers, each profiting from the illicit gambling, prostitution, and sale of bootleg liquor that went on.

John and Donna Traband, Tudor House owners for the past 20 years, found evidence of the speakeasy during extensive remodeling. "We discovered a complete still, with a 500-gallon tank, while investigating a space that was unaccounted for on the second floor. It wasn't too surprising, considering the club's reputation and its location near one of the purest water sources in the mountains, an essential for making fine whiskey."

Horses were stabled at the Club, providing a good cover for the grain needed to operate a still. There was talk of a gas station out back, while actually whiskey was being pumped into false tanks under the chassis of specially fitted cars. Bootleg liquor also traveled across Lake Arrowhead, via Fleming Creek and Bourbon Gulch, to supply North Shore Tavern, the boat docking at Tavern Bay.

An uneasy truce existed between law enforcement agencies and the Club, with mutual tolerance the rule. Mirror signals, flashed "up the hill" by Sheriff's Station informers, warned of imminent raids. Children on the rim watching for signals would relay the messages to the Club and be rewarded with special treats. This gave ample time to either hide the evidence or set up dummy slot machines that could be smashed to make the raid look authentic.

By the time national prohibition ended in December, 1933, the mountaineers settled down to legal beer and liquor to celebrate the holidays. They had to temper their celebrations surviving the depression that engulfed the nation and the San Bernardino Mountains as well.

L. A. Hotels
from *Ontario Weekly Herald,* July 26, 1928

Hotels in larger cities sell liquor openly and aboveboard. Recently at a big celebration in a Los Angeles hotel, a party in a large room ran short of liquor. A man ordered a case of liquor over the phone from a bootlegger. The bootlegger promptly brought it over. Soon a second case was ordered and brought up to the room. But the bootlegger said he could not bring any more as the house detective was watching him.

After the bootlegger left, there was a knock at the door. The detective came into the room. The host told him they were entertaining men from outside Los Angeles and had to have some booze. He replied: "We do not care how much liquor you have, but after this, order it from me. The hotel sells it and if you buy from me you will get good liquor and also there will be no bootleggers running in and out to give us a black eye."

ω

Although law enforcers often looked the other way to avoid arresting men with small amounts of liquor, each officer had his standard code where he drew the line. Generally he left the local people alone, his neighbors, and of course his constituents. Local officers had few qualms, however, about arresting drunk big city boys or out-of-town drivers who wandered on the wrong side of the town's road. San Bernardino County Deputy Sheriff J. A. Larson arrested Norman Baldwin, an L.A. salesman, for passing a highball to a young girl in an auto. Said Larson: "I am not attempting to arrest every man on a bootleg charge because he has a small amount of liquor in his possession. But I am going to halt the furnishing of liquor to young girls if there is any possible way to do it." Judge C. F. Healey of Colton fined Baldwin $50 for having less than a pint.[6]

More LAPD Corruption

Two plainclothes policemen followed the Reo truck up U.S. Highway 101, Pacific Coast Highway. When the truck reached the L. A. city limits, police pulled it over, arresting two men with a load of smuggled alcohol, containing thirty sacks of Canadian whiskey, scotch, West Indian rum, 12 bottles per sack.

The police knew the load came in that night in a cove north of Laguna Beach and had been following it for over sixty miles.

Putting handcuffs on the men, the police called another police car to take the men in and book them for violating the Volstead Act, i.e., transporting liquor.

After the police car left with the defendants, one plainclothed policemen climbed into the cab of the Reo and followed the car of the other, both vehicles heading up Harbor Boulevard, then turning left on Main Street until it reached a closed theater in central L. A. The Reo stopped in the alley at the back door of the theater. Four hard knocks and it opened.

Two men came out, unloaded twelve sacks, mostly Canadian. The driver of the truck signed a slip, put some green bills in his pocket, hopped back in the truck, heading for the central police department, followed by his partner.

At the L.A. Police Department, the two men received the receipt for inventory of the prohibition confiscation: one Reo truck, 1927, five Canadian Club Whiskey sacks, six Bacardi Rum, four White Label Scotch, and two Gordon's Gin. The sergeant and two dry squad detectives certified this as being the stipulated alcohol confiscated by the two officers.

J. B. Westman, alias Harry D. MacDonald, Whittier bootlegger, exposed police corruption in Los Angeles. After MacDonald was caught transporting smuggled liquor, not by the L.A. police but by un-bribable federal agents, he confessed and agreed to turn state's evidence against this kind of corruption.

He listed 24 Los Angeles police officers, ranging from captains down to patrolmen, as members of an asserted "shake-down" ring exacting tribute from bootleggers. According to the *San Bernardino Sun*, MacDonald made a 42-page statement to District Attorney Buron Fitts. The federal prohibition office announced it had a list of 62 L. A. law officers involved in similar corruption.

Deputy District Attorney David Clark revealed that MacDonald had declared that a empty Main Street movie theater was the liquor storage and "pay-off" station used by the police. MacDonald confessed he was "tired of the continued tribute" exacted by the police. Instead of turning in confiscated liquor, police withheld the majority of it and then sold it to bootleggers from whom they demanded protection money.

"They even resorted to hijacking my Whittier or Compton bound liquor. Then they phoned to tell me it was locked up. For a certain price, I could buy it back," MacDonald said. He decided to quit the business and come clean because now there wasn't any profit in it.

L. A. District Attorney Buron Fitts placed a guard at the MacDonald home in Whittier because his wife received threatening phone calls.

Fitts refused to name the "alleged" grafting officers but called for a conference of investigation to determine if a special grand jury should be called.

J. B. Westman received immunity for five years for running a bootleg place. He also exposed L. A. police selling photograph and fingerprints to criminals for $1,000 to $3,000. In other words, key evidence could disappear for a price [see Appendix D].[7]

In another case, Col. Leo A. Stromee, former San Bernardino councilman and a federal enforcement officer, had charges dropped by S. W. McNabb, U. S. District Attorney. Stromee was removed as federal agent because he was accused of looking the other way when attempts were being made to land contraband. When Ralph Morley, self-styled payoff man for a rum ring was sick in the hospital and could not be a witness, W. R. Gallagher Deputy U. S. District Attorney took the case off the calendar.

Just Let Him Out of Jail for a Few Hours

Ray Wallace approached jailer Joe Irvine about making some easy money. All he had to do was let Claude Williams out of Santa Ana jail for a few hours on Sunday, June 10, 1925, and Irvine would receive a proportionate share of liquor that was to be removed from the Orange County liquor storage room at the Old Courthouse in Santa Ana.

Where would there be an easier place to obtain liquor than a courthouse storage room? The booze had already come all the way over from Europe, to Vancouver in Canada, down the coast, bouncing for weeks outside the 12-mile limit, sneaked into some beach in southern California, and finally captured by the dry squad and stored right here behind this door—and all this confiscated liquor unguarded!

Irvine let Williams out of jail Sunday morning, wherein Williams, Wallace and Herbert L. Eldred kicked in a "panel and removed the door" and liberated 80 cases of intoxicating liquor, to an awaiting truck, then to Ora Hobbs' ranch near Santa Ana where they buried 50 cases and took 30 cases to Wallace's home in Orange. In the meantime Williams went back to his jail cell to enjoy the quietness of that Sabbath afternoon and evening.

"...on or about the 16th day of June, 1925, defendant Walter South, alias Walter Southard, alias Walter Oats, met the defendant W. E. Knowlton, alias Jerry Knowland, at Santa Ana..." These two bootleggers evidently bought Wallace's 30 cases and hired Charles B. Ross to deliver them to Huntington Park in a Graham truck.

The complicated conspiracy was broken up by Agent Botka in the spring of 1927, but the trials ended in dismissal of most of the conspirators in May and in August, 1928.[8]

Venice—Wet Resort
from Eric Grimm,
"Rum-running in Venice: History or Fiction," *Evening Outlook*
(Santa Monica), March 22-23, 1980

In January 1920, a group celebrated the death of John Barleycorn by pushing a "dilapidated cart," with a paper machè bottle off the Santa Monica pier to symbolize the demise of demon rum.

Although Santa Monica passed local option prohibition in December 1917 and Los Angeles in November, their neighbor Venice stayed as wet as its European namesake. Venice, a popular resort and getaway for thirsty southern Californians, had several speakeasies and a series of tunnels that ran under streets and buildings. One tunnel came in from the ocean "under Ocean Front Walk, south to Zephyr Court (the alley south of Windward Street), crossing beneath Speedway, Pacific and ending somewhere under the Bank of American building, now Ace Gallery." Grimm stated that Frank and Anne Bennett owned the Town House saloon on the southside of Windward in 1980, but the basement was used as a speakeasy in the roaring twenties. It had high ornate tin ceilings typical of the 1920s. Some of the tunnels evidently came up in hotels and could have been used as escape routes in case of raids. Since most beaches and coves were used at one time or another during the bootlegging days, dories could have been rowed to the beach and booze loaded into the tunnel under Ocean Front Walk.

George Heap remembered seeing a garbage cart, pulled by mules, heading for Venice late at night in 1929. He followed it and found the driver loading alcohol in the cart. When Heap reported this to the city engineer, the city chief

Los Angeles street scene during raid of a speakeasy. Courtesy of National Archives, # 306-NT-727-1.

told him to stop his investigations. "He was scared," Heap said. "This was during prohibition; they killed people. They didn't mess around."

A Boy's View of the Roaring Twenties in Culver City
by Jiggs Triepke, Barstow

Culver City was a pretty loose place during prohibition. I remember from 1927 until 1931 all the clubs starting at Fairfax and Washington Boulevard out toward Venice. I suspect they were setup houses, where a couple brought in their own liquor and the club furnished the set-ups of ginger ale, lime rickey and soda. There was Danceland at Fairfax that had an outside dance floor with a band, but around the outside perimeter there were dart games and the milk bottles you threw balls at—plenty things to do. It later became Pete's 101 Ranch. My oldest brother found a hole in the roof where we could watch the dancing girls change costumes. The next club was the Lighthouse Gardens, and the building is still there, a laundry. The next was King's Tropical Inn, which was decorated with real palm fronds. That burned up early one Sunday morning— man what a fire! This was rebuilt immediately and finally torn down because of the January 1994 earthquake.

Across the street was the Chicken Shack owned by the Guze family. Going down the boulevard, La Cienega and Washington, there was a farm owned by John Jensen. On Sunday I was sure to be there because he always had boxes to take from his house and put in his car, which was a brand-new Moon. I was always paid 50¢ for my labor. I was moving booze, my dad said. I could get a pineapple malt at Chris's Market three blocks away for 20¢, made with real ice cream. So 50¢ was a lot of money.

The next club was Cherryland—I believe oriental. Then came Picadilly Circus that was where Helms Bakery is now. My brother worked in a poultry market across the street. When the Picadilly was abandoned, my brother and I would throw eggs and watch them slide down the wall. Across the street at the building two blocks away was Frank Sebastian's Cotton Club. It was an enormous building built out of wood. They had a sepia or Creole revue there in those years. It later became Mama Guka's [Madame Zuka] with Andy Russell the main attraction. It also burned up (or down). Before it burned, the big bands appeared there. I recall seeing Charlie Barnett there.

For probably two miles there was nothing as I recall. Then came the Plantation that I recall looked to me like Mount Vernon. I remember the celebrities such as Walter Winchell went there.

After that it was Venice beach which was a real fun place! Canals with their blue and green lights, the fun house and real good hamburgers and hot dogs for ten cents and that super merry-go-round. Always trying to get the brass ring, we learned how to get one with our left hand and another with our right as we passed by. I think I got the brass ring twice. And the indoor plunge was really neat.

As I remember there apparently was no real problem getting booze. We had a Spanish neighbor who made his own wine. We would go to a grape vineyard owned by a Mr. Casserina, get horse-drawn wagons full of grapes. They had the barrel in the chicken coop. Us kids would get in the barrel as they dumped the grapes in (unwashed yuk!) and us kids would stomp them with our bare feet. That would leave our feet purple the rest of the summer. When it was a certain state, they put it in 50 gallon barrels and put in the basement on the dirt. We could sneak some by putting our thumb over the end of the funnel, but we got the whole works at once; that kind of took your breath.

My mom and dad made their own beer. Boy, they had I guess about a 12-gallon crock. She always put some potatoes in the beer. Mom and Dad did their grocery shopping at the Grand Central Market that was in downtown L. A. They bought a 3-gallon wooden barrel of kippered herring they kept out by the beer since no one had a refrigerator then. So I would sneak some fish and half made beer. But when it was done, you took the crock, put it on the table, had the bottles on the floor, then someone would start the siphon. You just pinched the hose until the next bottle.

A Swedish man named Johnson was in the hardwood floor business. He had a big tin barn, 300 feet from our house, that he kept his wood in. But one Sunday morning the street was full of bottles and hundreds of labels. The revenue people raided the basement that no one knew was there and confiscated the booze. Needless to say he and his three daughters left for Canada. Seventeen or 18 years later my brother and I were in the process of going in business on the very lot where they lived. Since there was a lien on the property we were delayed six months as we had to advertise in a paper. When no one came forward we received a clear title.

I remember going to the mine fields in 1929 which is now LAX to watch the Graf Zepplin take off for Germany. We stayed till 2:00 a.m. before it left. It was breathtaking to see that giant take off with no noise. In 1927 after Lindy flew the Atlantic he came west. He came down West Adams in a motorcade going to where downtown L. A. was at the time. He was the first celebrity I saw.

My father was doing carpentry work in Palos Verde for Mr. Doheny of Doheny Oil Company. He also allowed us to picnic at his home on Doheny Boulevard in Beverly Hills on Sundays. He had a tremendous covered duck pond. He built Doheny Park at West Adams and Figuero and built the beautiful Catholic Church on Adams and Figuero. When the stock market crashed in October 1929, someone came out to where my father was working and told him to quit in the afternoon.

It got pretty rough to make a living. My father met a Mr. Johnson whose wife was making pies and selling them. My father made some fly-proof pie carrying cases, holding five pies. He got a job delivering pies up the coast as far as Malibu. We got to keep all the day-old pies. Dad received $12.00 a week and furnished his own car. Then on Saturday and Sunday we delivered the L. A. *Examiner* to drug stores and grocery stores, also for $12.00 per weekend and using our car too. I was my dad's helper when I was ten years old. My older brothers had their own paper corners. Everyone of us kids bought our own clothes and had our own spending money. But through the bad years we always had a new house and plenty to eat. I remember my dad made a deal in a market to get the box of bad apples each Wednesday for 25¢. He would take them home, dump them on the table and everyone would take a paring knife and cut out the good part of each apple. Mother then made pies, apple butter, etc.

A Tub Full of Iced Gin
by Nan Hauser Colton, Paradise

My father, Frank M. Hauser, manager of Hauser Packing house on 9th and Mateo in Los Angeles, his four brothers and wives all were indulgers in scotch and bourbon. They hosted many social gathering that included friends, business associates, and Los Angeles and state public officials, appointed and elected. Law enforcement personnel often were invited. Alcohol was always served. I recall booze in a bathtub of ice when we resided at the Georgian Apartments in Santa Monica and the Rosalin Apartments in Los Angeles in the 1920s and '30s. In spite of prohibition liquor was always available to those who could afford the price.

My dad had sources for obtaining the cases needed for personal consumption and for his guests; however, what they were I don't recall. This shows how readily available was alcohol and the lack of respect for enforcement of prohibition. We can't legislate social behavior and those that were good law abiding citizens didn't inhibit their desire for a good shot.

Me, Detective
by Leslie T. White

The district attorney had a Bureau of Investigation—another group of officers known as the Enforcement Detail, whose duties were to enforce liquor laws, raid gambling joints and curtail prostitutes. "We called them the Booze Squad," said Detective Leslie White.

The Booze Squad was not too popular: They sometimes encroached on other law-enforcement agencies, such as the police or sheriff's vice squads, but perhaps more important they interfered with the system of "graft and corruption" that was an integral part of the vice work.

White helped Captain O'Brien and the Booze Squad out of a bad hole. The squad arrested a "big-shot liquor dealer" on a possession charge, with many bottles found in his building. The big-shot, however, found a "fall-guy" to plead guilty.

"Up to this time, no one, to my knowledge, had ever thought of using the science of finger-printing in connection with liquor violation. Captain O'Brien believed it was a good time to begin, so he asked me to examine the bottles. I did, and—fortunately for the Booze Squad—discovered numerous latent (hidden finger-prints) impressions of the big-shot. The wily O'Brien made no announcement of his discovery until the case came to court. He let the fall-guy receive sentence for ownership of the liquor, then he had the prosecutor question the big-shot—the real owner—as to whether or not he, the big shot, had ever seen the liquor. The latter solemnly swore he had never so much as entered the house. After that declaration, I was put on the stand. There was no way he could squirm out of the fact that the bottles were covered with his finger-prints, so he was found guilty! As we already had one man plead guilty, we caught, literally, two birds with one stone.

White was transferred to the Booze Squad under Captain Clyde "Cossack" Plummer. He did not enjoy "morals work."

I came to hate crawling through the muck and mud in the middle of a cold, rainy night to search for finger-prints on some stinking still in a lousy hen-house. (Why hen-houses seemed the favorite spot for stills is a mystery I never bothered to solve.)

When White offered to resign from the Booze Squad, he was transferred back to county bureau of investigation, which made him happy again.

"Prominent Citizens and the Business-bribe"

Ninety percent of our cases were petty offenses and as Prohibition was then considered almost a religion, liquor violation predominated. During office hours, we served papers, conducted investigations of various kinds, and handled the routine work of the office. Nights were reserved for liquor raids and sudden crimes. My enthusiasm was such that after a particularly tiring day, I would relax by going out in the evening and snagging a bootlegger. It was on these solo jaunts I made my first acquaintance with police graft.

As a deputy sheriff, I had police jurisdiction over the entire Ventura county. I cared nothing for the imaginary limits of town or village; I believed that any crime committed within the county was fair game. But the local constables and marshals began to squawk; they insisted I was poaching on their preserves. A compromise was reached only when I agreed to call them in any raids in their territory.

This attempted cooperation failed. Nearly every time we launched a raid, the offender had flown. For a long time this puzzled me. The local constable would sometimes suggest there must be a leak in our office. Finally I caught on—there could be no leak from our office because no one save myself knew anything about the proposed raid, but perhaps the local constable...

I resorted to my lone raids and the percentage of arrests picked up. Then occurred an incident which froze my ardor.

Neither Bill nor I could leave Ventura at the same time; we had to be constantly on call. If Bill wanted to attend a party or drive down to the city, I stayed uptown where I could be reached on a moment's notice. The usual hangout was the local cinema. We always loafed in the same seat after advising the usher and the local telephone operator. When anyone called for an officer, the telephone operator would ring the theater and I would dash out on the job.

Halfway through a very interesting show, I received a call reporting an accident on one of the lonely beach roads. One of the local news reporters

Mash vats raided at 1324 E. 12th St., Los Angeles. Building is still there. Photo courtesy Pomona City Library.

happened along as I bolted out of the show and he hopped into the squad car with me. We highballed for the beach.

There was always a thrill about a fast ride through the night. The long red-eye of the official spotlight reached through the low fog, like the tremulous feeler of some prehistoric beetle. There was no way of guessing what would be found at the termination of the ride. An accident often meant a corpse, a ghastly injury with its accompaniment of hysterics, and sometimes straight humor—we never knew.

This call had humor—but I wasn't prepared to accept it as such. We found a well-known local doctor huddled on the top of his roadster which lay on its side in the ditch. He was accompanied by a charming and willing brunette who was only slightly less plastered than he. They were unable to maintain a vertical stance, but their hospitality, like their thirst, was unquenchable. The doctor brandished a quart bottle of Scotch whiskey, two-thirds gone, and invited us to make a party of it.

I was inclined to be surly. The attitude of the authorities towards drunk-driving was very severe; it was on the statute books as a felony. Even when the offense was reduced to a misdemeanor, the local magistrate had been handing out sentences up to two hundred and fifty days in jail. I had made numerous arrests at this time, most of them among the Mexicans and poor whites, and the court had been uniformly drastic.

The doctor wanted us to pull his car back onto the road and then run along about our business. The brunette told us we were dears. I told the doctor that he was under arrest, a statement which brought gales of laughter from the brunette.

The reporter, however, was more experienced. He drew me aside and advised against arresting the doctor.

"Why in the hell shouldn't I?" was my demand. "It wasn't his fault he didn't drive another car into the ditch and kill someone!"

"Okay, okay," the reporter placated me. "Don't break out in hives about it! But I know this guy—and this dizzy wren isn't his spouse. He's got a wife and family who'll be hard hit if you cause a scandal."

"*Me* cause a scandal? Did *I* bring him down here with this dame? Did *I* make him turn his wagon upside down? The hell I did! I'm always sorry for the wives and kids, but what about the wives and kids of those Mexican hombres we've locked up for a year in jail."

"This guy is prominent!" the reporter warned me. "Why don't you do this...we'll pull his wreck back on the road and I'll drive him home. I don't think the car is damaged enough to prevent that. You talk to the sheriff in the morning, and if he says 'pinch him!', well, I'll testify for you. How's that?"

It was rotten, but logical. We finally succeeded in towing the machine back onto the road and the brunette wanted to kiss us both good-by. When we broke the news that their party was all over, in so far as the car was concerned, and that they had their choice of going home under the direction of the reporter or to jail under my care, hostilities broke out. The doctor swore he would get my job! He would have me "broke"! The brunette developed a remarkable vocabulary. Despite the verbal fireworks, I confiscated the remains of the Scotch, and stood in the middle of the road and watched the reporter drive away with the inebriated amorists.

Bright and early the following morning, the under-sheriff came into the office. He looked stern as he demanded to know whether I had taken a bottle of whiskey away from Doctor So-and-so.

I exhibited the bottle and explained the circumstances. I fully expected he would sanction my work. He shook his head.

"Sometimes, White," he growled, "you show lousy judgment! Young as you are, you ought to know better than to antagonize a prominent citizen like the doctor."

That took the wind out of me. "I don't give a damn about antagonizing him! Didn't he...?"

"Well, the office does," the under-sheriff snapped. "How long do you think we can stay in office if you go around alienating the real, worth-while citizens of the community. Now if you've got any sense, you'll call him up and apologize."

"Apologize for *what*?"

The Hypocrisy of the Volstead Act
by John Clausen, Victorville

The 18th Amendment to the Constitution of the United States became effective January 16, 1920. Political entities from the White House, Congress and the Foreign Diplomatic Corps served wine and spirits, at will, during the prohibition era. Also, the mansions of the Eastern seaboard were never short of the forbidden refreshments for entertaining or daily tippling, nor were the Hollywood, Beverly Hills or Bel Aire communities dry.

There occurred almost immediately a symbiosis between law breakers and law enforcement. The example set soon permeated all or almost all of society.

I was ten years of age in 1920 when the prohibition amendment became "effective" and almost 24 when the 21st Amendment repealed the 18th Amendment. My first eye-opener occurred when I was 12. My father, then a reporter at the *Los Angeles Times*, took me to visit a new Los Angeles Police Station near Los Angeles High School. The tour included a visit to the jail. Therein sat a newly arrested burglar, unhappy and dejected. As we were leaving, our guide, a uniformed officer showed us the drunk tank. This was a tall room about six feet square of cement. The only adornment was a drain in the middle of the floor, plus a high barred window. Added to these were at least a dozen cases of high-grade "booze" being held as evidence, presumably. Our guide took out a bottle and sold it to my father. I continued to believe my father intended this to be an educational trip for his 12-year-old son and it was. I vowed that I would never spend a night behind bars and I also learned that some policemen broke the law and so did my father. I soon learned that breaking the Volstead Act was common practice.

In 1923 I started working after school in a drugstore on Santa Monica Boulevard and Fairfax. My job was cleanup and delivery boy. Soon I observed reputable doctors signing medicinal whiskey prescription blanks and selling the entire book to the druggist, fifty to a book. These prescription blanks resembled banknotes and were issued by the U. S. Government. Each one entitled the "patient" to one pint of the finest bonded whiskey. I never knew the financial part of either transaction.

Each drugstore was allotted pure grain alcohol in quantities necessary for prescription preparation. It was delivered in shiny five gallons cans of 180 proof. Some druggists immediately cut it in half with distilled water to create 90 proof alcohol. The water was jokingly called "aldehyde alteration." From this was concocted "Bathtub Gin" using oil of orange and juniper and any other flavor deemed appropriate by the preparer. This furnished a steady income for the owner. How else could three drugstores survive in the same block of Santa Monica Blvd. at Fairfax Avenue.

The wineries of Southern California never shut down during this period. They furnished great quantities of sacramental wine and wine tonic. The wine tonic was required to be medicinal. A physic was to be added during manufacture. At one time some one at the Virginia Dare Winery left out the medication and substituted pungent spices. Word got around and sales boomed. The store where I worked could not keep enough on hand to meet the incredible demand. Stacks of cases of very attractive bottles in white boxes with a portrait of Virginia Dare on the label would be delivered one day and gone the next. Another bonanza until the Feds got wise.

Some ladies bought Lydia Pinkham's tonic, regularly. It was near 20 percent alcohol.

One notable drinker was a Hollywood cowboy—never got out of costume—who bought each day a bottle of Jamaica Ginger in the drugstore across the street, then walked to the store where I worked and bought a second 8-ounce bottle of the same Jamaica Ginger. He then asked to use the toilet. When he came out, he left behind the two empty bottles. Jamaica Ginger was hotter than cayenne pepper. I tasted it. But it was about 80 percent alcohol.

The Garden of Allah on Sunset Boulevard at Crescent Heights was a posh live-in party place. While in high school I took many deliveries of soda water siphons to the cottages that were scattered about the well kept grounds.

Someone else was delivering the booze. I found out later how the high-grade liquor got into the area, but never witnessed any delivery of the fine champagne and scotch whiskey that was being consumed by the leading citizens of the Hollywood community.

We high school youngsters thought we were big time until most of us got sick at the beach parties at Castle Rock (Malibu).

After leaving high school in 1926, I got a job in a drugstore in Sherman (now West Hollywood). The store was at the corner of Larrabe and Santa Monica Blvd. across from Pacific Electric's Sherman car barns. My job was behind the soda fountain, not on the drug side of the store, except to translate for the Mexican employees of the Pacific Electric who traded in the store. None of the druggists spoke Spanish.

Eventually, I came to know that the owner also had an interest in the fishing fleet at Santa Monica. These boats took fishermen out daily. At night they went to sea for bait. On most nights they detoured to merchant ships, hove to beyond the three-mile limit. From these they bought fine wine and spirits from Europe, landing it in a cove north of the present Malibu Colony. Incidentally, the boss did not like fish or fishing.

Most of this narrative is happening in Los Angeles County—an area from La Brea to Doheny (the Beverly Hills boundary). At La Brea, this area was about one-half mile wide on either side of Santa Monica Blvd. At Doheny it is wider. Known for years as the "Strip" it is now incorporated as West Hollywood.

The district attorney of the time period lived across from the Chateau Marmont Apartments, a posh movie people hangout. There was a Sherman Justice Court and a sheriff's substation in the "Strip." During this time both the Los Angeles City and County officials were more than tolerant of unlawful behavior of the prominent citizens, i.e., movie stars and executives. One of the most revealing examples of this tolerance was witnessed by myself at the corner of Santa Monica Boulevard and Gardner Street where I lived. On the south side of Santa Monica at Gardner there was a business in a two-story building. It was called "The House of Props." A rental business of exotic furniture and other movie set dressing materials that occupied the ground floor. I never witnessed any movement of the "Props" in the four years of living across the Boulevard.

One evening the owner of the gasoline station on this same corner asked me to go upstairs at "The House of Props" and get some change. There was a door at the top of the stairs with a little door at eye level. A man looked out and asked me what I wanted. I said, "Change" and held up some bills. He opened the door and let me in. What I saw surprised me more than anything I had so far experienced. I had heard that gambling was going on there, but was unprepared for what I saw. There were roulette wheels, blackjack tables and card tables, all green-felt topped. There were gamblers at all of them. There was a bar and a bank-type window where I got my change and the doorman urged me to get along. Now I understand why there were so many automobiles parked around the neighborhood.

Eventually the residents complained about the lack of parking spaces, loudly enough, apparently, because sometime later in one evening we heard multiple sirens coming from Los Angeles direction. Immediately, V16 Cadillac touring cars, paddy wagons, motorcycles and other official sheriff vehicles whipped into U-turns in from of the House of Props. Sheriffs jumped out and ran up the stairs and soon returned with men in custody. The men were loaded into the paddy wagons and other cars. They all U-turned again and headed for Sherman and the justice court. Mystery question: How did the justice court happen to be open that late at night? Other officers carried the gaming equipment down the stairs and loaded it into the Cadillac touring cars and headed east toward town. A friend and neighbor watching with me said, "Let's follow them." I asked, "Why?" He answered, "Come on, you'll see."

We went east on Santa Monica. The Cadillacs were long gone, or so I thought. I drove to La Brea and there were the sheriffs' cars. The men were already unloading the gaming equipment—up the stairs to the loft of the two-story structure. The next day the parking problems were in the neighborhood of La Brea and Santa Monica Blvd.

My neighbor had a shipping business on the ground floor of that building. He asked, "Now do you see?"

Sometime later I learned that the "gamblers" were shills picked up on skid row and set up at the gaming tables to wait for the "raid." They were each paid $20.00. The gambling was free. In the first and only night court in Sherman they were fined $10.00 each. The judge just happened to be working overtime that night.

LAPD Defends Itself

The Los Angeles Police Department responded to complaints of corruption, payoffs, bribery.[9] Division of Public Relations in 1929 published memorandums for news releases, such as, "...success in bringing the city's major crime rate per 100,000 of population to a level below that of any year..." Every traffic officer was a policeman, affirmed one report. This helped in the "persistent persecution of bootleggers, the constant vigilance to prevent successful formation and operation of 'gangs' such as have proved disastrous in several Eastern cities, development of a fingerprint service becoming nationally famous, and the increasing use of modern business methods and scientific aids in crime solution." Another memo published the fact that Los Angeles had only 70 murders for 1928, which was a 4.7% rate, whereas Chicago and Philadelphia had 498 and 182, which rated 15.8 and 8.8% respectively.

Periodically the public relations division published credits from the state, federal government or from other police departments. The memos, of course, being sent all over, helped elicit congratulations in the first place. Every memo had several examples of crimes solved. One example was the alert motorcycle traffic cop who was suspicious of a large southbound truck on Ventura Boulevard. "We stopped the truck and saw that it had been loaded with cordwood, stacked so evenly and solidly that it was impossible to see between the sticks of wood further than an inch or two at any point on the load." When the driver said it was eucalyptus from Santa Barbara, he added it was worth $15 a cord and there were two and one half cords.

The price didn't add up to a profit. The suspicious traffic officers found 100 cases of rare high priced liquors, still wet and sandy from being brought in from the rum boat. Value of the liquor was $10,000. There would have been profit in that cordwood after all.

Numerous other bragging rights filled the 1929 Memorandum: Chief of Detectives Clyde Plummer went out on a routine raid and came back with Stephen Musatti and 1,439 gallons of wine, retail value of $8,000. The court gave Musatti, a first time offender, his choice between paying $500 or serving 50 days in jail. Cooperation with the Feds brought in Ernesto Quirtino, Mike Collura and Rose Walker with two 200-gallon stills, mash and 85 gallons of 180 proof moonshine. A look at arrest records reveals much about the law and order problem in California: "Ernesto Quirtino, alias Ernest Mariano: on November 7, 1927, arrested for Wright Act possession and transportation; caught driving a Star coupe on Sunset Boulevard, had one gallon of wine in car—case dismissed. Arrested on August 6, 1928, Wright Act possession and transportation, $100 or 10 days on each charge. Arrested again on August 6, 1928, Wright Act, possession and manufacturing, Senate bill 814 (possession of a still, a felony), turned over to county authorities and released on $6,500 bail; arrested on December 14, 1928, Wright Act possession and sale, released on $1,300 bail. Mr. Quirtino is still at large and his cases are still "pending."

The city was pleased with a 15-week period where 321 arrests for selling showed 90% convictions. Of that number 16% drew suspended sentences; 12% drew jail time of 33 days average; 71% drew choices of jail or fine which averaged 31 days or $248.

The population of L. A. as of December 1927 was 1,300,326, with liquor arrests of 8,480 (652 per 100,000 people) and a conviction record of 85%, higher than Boston, Detroit, New York and Chicago. St. Louis, for example, had a half million smaller population, the same amount of arrests, but only 3.3% conviction rate.

The federal agents in the Southern District of California had 1,660 arrests in 17 counties for the same fiscal year of 1927. However the federal conviction rate was only 282, 16.98%. The LAPD tried hard to overcome its image of corruption [see Appendix].

Long Beach
Rumrunning and the Rich

Long Beach millionaire packer Alexander B. Stewart hosted several federal officials and a U. S. senator on a "jolly and very wet" cruise and this seemed to be the key to the "whole booze situation" in 1926-33 California, according to a local article by Max Stern. Stewart, under indictment and arrest for conspiracy of violating the Volstead law, had yet to be brought to trial. Many thought he would never be because of his influence in Washington. Stern said that the same influence caused the dismissal of California chief field agent Harold H. Dolley and his assistant C. A. Parker who caught Stewart and 18 of the "Dudry Gang" in the spring of 1923. Dolley and Parker "lost their official heads." After the cruise, the officials met a local politician in a mountain resort and said, "This Stewart appears to be a mighty good fellow."

Stewart was head of the Curtis Corporation, and was, until his arrest, President of the Long Beach Chamber of Commerce.

On the night of March 23, 1923, the watchman across from the Curtis plant in Long Beach saw a number of trucks drawn up on the Curtis dock. When he called the police, the police and the dry squad found Frank Nagai, a Japanese fisherman, unloading from his boat, the "Nagai," 80 cases of whiskey and found two trucks driven by well-known bootleggers, Oscar Lund and Jerry Knowlton. As the officers pulled up, they caught a big Studebaker sedan leaving the scene. Inside the sedan was Stewart and five cases of the same kind of whiskey Nagai was unloading. The officers arrested the above as well as the lookout, Walter Lord, and nearby Jack Miller, "a Canadian Jew, agent for the Consolidated Exporters, Ltd., the 'trust' of British Columbia."

The case Dolley and Parker worked out, before these agents were dismissed, revealed the complex conspiracy of huge proportions. In Miller's room in a Los Angeles hotel, agents found a manifest of Consolidated's chartered rumrunner, *Borealis*, from which Nagai obtained his cargo. Two middlemen, Larry Talbot and Claude Dudry, bought the cargo from Miller and sold it to Stewart. Dudry reportedly was the chief booze ring leader in Los Angeles. Talbot and Dudry paid Frank Kabota, "generalissimo of the Japanese fishing fleet," $4.00 a case, and he in turn hired Nagai to haul the booze at $2.00 per case. Lord, night lookout who took the regular night watchman's place, turned out to be Stewart's sales manager. Agents also indicted Jack Leary, general manager for Stewart. The night watchman who called the police that night affirmed that previous nights he had seen trucks at the Curtis dock.

Three months before Max Stern wrote this article, several agents raided Stewart's Ocean Boulevard mansion, arresting seven wealthy guests, in various stages of undress, for liquor possession and immoral conduct. Mrs. Stewart, the police said, tried to escape in her silk "undies," stockings and a tam o'shanter. "The police said they were there by invitation of the roistering Stewart." [police or the guests?]

Stewart vowed never to go to jail. Trial delays, scattering of witnesses and dismissal of Dolley and Parker made Stern feel that maybe Stewart was right.

Stewart was, indeed, right.

Case # 6552-m went to the Supreme Court in 1926, but in December 19, 1933, the case was dismissed. Prohibition had just ended, and so did the case against Stewart.[10]

Because You Voted for Hoover
by Eleanor Widolf, Laguna Beach

I was in the early grades of grammar school and, coming from a Republican family, voted in my class for Hoover, gave a speech for him. "If Roosevelt gets in, wine will flow down the gutters of the streets," I said, quoting from my father. Later, I asked Marguerita Avila, my classmate, to stop the foot-pedaled merry-go-round so I could get on.

She retorted, "No—you voted for Hoover!"

It was very sad for us when Hoover lost the election as he was our hero.

Homebrew was made one mile up from our ranch in San Juan Capistrano. When my husband was younger, he went where rumrunners hid their bottles in the sand on the beach and brought home hooch to his folks, the Carl Bensons of Laguna Beach in 1932.

Surprising What a Little Good Liquor Can Do
as told by Doug Perrin, Bud Watkins, Gladys Stein,
William Shields, Eleanor and Phil Widolf[11]

Doug Perrin and Bud Watkins went 16 miles to Tustin High School. After school, holidays, weekends, Doug used his boat for odd jobs, sometimes lobstering, not always too fussy about the size of the lobsters or the season.

He was an operator.

When he was 17, rumrunners asked if he wanted to earn some money running booze.

"How much?" he asked.

"Fifty cents a case."

"It's dangerous, could get caught," Doug answered.

"If you get caught, you'll be paid $50 a day, and you'll be out of jail within three days." He took the job.

Prohibition agent in escape tunnel two lots east of distillery at 1324 E. 12ᵗʰ St., Los Angeles. Later the house with the escape tunnel was torn down and the property became a Coca Cola plant. Photo courtesy of Pomona City Library.

A constable from Costa Mesa named Von, with one leg, helped out worthy causes by selling benefit raffle tickets to speeders and helped them out by not giving them citations. He benefacted rumrunners too by escorting their trucks along Coast Highway "for a ways." Smugglers bought tickets to many worthy causes.

Rumrunners along this part of the coast looked for a smooth cove where at high tide water covered the entrance high enough for dories to come right between the reefs. On the cliff by Boat Canyon (present Cliff Drive), local boatmen watched the whitecaps as the water broke over the reefs. When high tide covered the rocks sufficiently enough for dories to navigate in and out of the cove, the 45-65' rum boats and speedboats brought Canadian liquor from the mother ship, out past the 12-mile limit, to the entrance of the cove and either anchored or drifted. When dories rowed out, the boat gave them a load and the dories navigated to the beach. Fishermen like Doug Perrin received 50¢ a case for bringing it onto the shore. His dory carried maybe 20 cases. He and another young Tustin High School student earned a lot of spending money. Another dory rower was Oscar Farmin.

Rumrunners offered Jim Smith's folks $500 to go to the show one particular night. The Smiths owned a house overlooking Boat Canyon and the road that led up to the newly-paved Coast Highway, dedicated in 1927 by Mary Pickford cutting the ribbon across the highway and young Ruth Benson (La Porte) holding the ribbon.

Early one morning before dawn the Coast Guard chased a small boat, full of liquor, to Laguna Beach, firing a few rifle shots and a couple bursts of machine guns to make the boat surrender. Instead, to avoid capture, the boat clung close to the rocks at the southern part of the bay. The smugglers went too close to the rocks for that morning's tide and tore up the hull. Abandoning the sinking boat, crewmen swam to shore. Waves, rocks and current tossed the boat every which way, emptying its contents, gunny sacks of imported liquor, all over the beach and on the rocks below the popular Coast Inn—Canadian Club, Coon Hollow and White Label Scotch on the rocks!

With the early morning discovery by local men, word spread around town, and young men in their late teens and early twenties harvested the gems the ocean bore.

Keith Stein tightened his belt, stuffed his belt, shirt, pockets and arms with bottles of rum and assorted liquor. Stein had a time getting through town, without being seen by the police, to his Richfield Service Station on the corner at Coast Highway and Broadway. He kept most of the bottles at his station, but took a few home.

His service station became special as friends and good customers enjoyed their day at the expense of the unfortunate rumrunner who lost his boat and his cargo. One of the bottles is still in possession of Gladys Stein [see photo].

Doug Perrin found some bottles and took a couple to the Coast Guard men on the beach. "Care if we dive for some?"

"No, you won't find much, go ahead," they answered.

The boys found a lot.

The power of good alcohol in those dry years enabled Stein to have the road contractors blacktop from the new highway to his gas station and part of his property at state expense.

Doug Perrin made good use for his liquor beachcombing and diving. He didn't like school that well, especially since it took too much of his valuable time. Since he wasn't doing that well in PE, he brought one or two bottles on the bus in a small case and set it on the coach's desk. He did fine in PE after that.

William Shields said when the family awakened with the rifle and machine gun shots, his mother came into his room and said, "You get back in bed and stay there!" He said the scow dumped its load by Laguna Beach Hotel [now Hotel Laguna] in 1927-28. In 1930 another accident occurred on Victoria Beach, south of Coast Inn, where rumrunners ran a speedboat ashore and ran off.

One boat that was run ashore was the *Oakwood,* supposedly by CG 827, the confiscated *Diatome,* fhe fastest boat on the coast. [Since the *Diatome* was not captured until 1931, the *Oakwood* or the date 1927 may be wrong or it was driven on the rocks by another Coast Guard boat.]

According to Gladys Stein, smugglers used Laguna Beach and Emerald Bay, just north of Laguna Beach. At Emerald Bay on the road to the beach was the McKnight Campground. Booze went through there and from dory to truck it cost $3.00 a case each time. By a pier on the north side of the bay [Laguna Beach] there were metal tracks and a tackle shop, where fellows would drink Virginia Dare wine and medicinal wine and play cards. Liquor was usually at the dance halls, like Cabrillo Ballroom Dancing. Liquor was a big part of Laguna Beach life.

San Diego's Irrigation Committee

Everything was set. San Diego formed an "Irrigation Committee" to ensure an adequate supply of safe liquor for the 11th Annual American Legion Convention in August 1929—planned to be the best yet, especially honoring the famed Sunshine Division (40th). Planned activities: a special Midnight Frolic at the Fox Californian, visit to Camp Kearney, jaunt to Agua Caliente, stag smoker, pistol shoot, parade, day at the beach, day at the mission, a barbecue and tours. Local legionnaires did all they could to give the expected 20,000 veterans the best hospitality sunny southern California could provide, with plenty of irrigation for the thirsty throats of the Legionnaires. Besides having safe liquor, locals wanted to keep out L. A. and Tijuana bootleggers.

Something went wrong: The liquor was raided just before the convention started. Mayor Harry C. Clark of San Diego and Coroner Schuyler C. Kelly met with American Legion spokesman Clive Wayland in room 209 of the Grant Hotel. Wayland thought it was a shame the Seventh Street store was raided of $27,000 worth of liquor when everybody agreed not to molest the bootleggers in their distribution of liquor. Everything was fixed.

Supposedly Wayland had gone to Chief Hill before the convention explaining how they would have liquor at the convention. "Then Wayland said, the chief waved his hand and said, 'I won't see a thing.'"

Arrangements had been made with bootlegger Charles Mulock to be the sole provider of 3500-4000 gallons of liquor at $4.50 per bottle. Mulock thought all was "fixed." Mulock had several locations, hired a few helpers to mix, bottle and label. "The best laid plans of mice and men..."

Even independent brewer Fred Ivey, 767 Pigeon Street, was caught for selling beer again, being fined $250 on his previous arrest. If Ivey had planned to sell to legionnaires, the dry squad ruined his aspirations. Whatever the mix-up was, Mulock's plans and the Irrigation Committee's plans went awry. Coroner Kelly said, the mayor would try to gain possession of the confiscated liquor. He did not get it back, and the Legionnaires had a more sober convention. San Diego tried anyway.

From the beginning of prohibition to the end, from young and old, from observer to participant, all southern Californians who knew the corruption of local authorities, their willingness to look the other way or to take bribes and to be involved in part of the conspiracy to violate the law, helped defeat prohibition by being involved.

Imported bottles of liquor were found "on the rocks" by Keith Stein and young men in Laguna Beach one morning after the Coast Guard ran a shore boat onto the rocks. Good liquor like this helped Keith obtain free paving from the new state highway to his gas station. This bottle, owned by Gladys Stein, has been in the Stein family since 1929-30. Photographed by author.

CHAPTER 17

I REMEMBER ...

Hey, Moma, They're Drinking Daddy's Beer
as told by Celia Ortega Villegas, Barstow

My father, Juan Ortega, had a unique moonshining operation. Juan lived and worked in San Pedro as a blacksmith on Harbor Bou levard for a Mr. Smith. He hid his still in various houses in Wilmington. Juan rented a building out for a few months, had his operations established, then he'd move to another small building near Banning Park or Drum Barracks. Since the depression had started, most people were poor. They had wood stoves for cooking and heating. The few with gas stoves used gas sparingly. My father's gas bills to distill liquor would be so high someone might be suspicious so he'd move his still to another house. He might have had a still in San Pedro, Mexican Hollywood we called it, I don't know why.

He often had poor people work the still and live in the house for free rent. He supplied their food too. Juan always had plenty of food. He assumed the responsibility to feed anyone in the area who needed food.

He traded his whiskey to the Japanese farmers around Palos Verdes for vegetables. Then he went to the fish market on the pier, trading liquor for fish.

I remember two-three times a week the Helms bread man came to the house with his leftovers at the end of the day. He filled our big old oak dining room table with bread, cakes and rolls. My dad set a gallon of whiskey on the table and the barter was completed.

He fed his moonshiners and the poor in the neighborhood. We had one room all filled with food. Some of the Mexicans got free cans of corned beef. They didn't particularly like it and after awhile they'd bring it to my father's house and he'd buy it for ten cents a can or trade for it. We always had corned beef. I liked it myself. For us there was no depression. Though Juan was a bootlegger, drinker and carouser, he was very social minded, helping anyone. He lent people money to pay their bills, gave some down payments for homes, never turned down anyone at the door for food—a one-man welfare program.

He was caught selling alcohol, but his stills never got raided. I remember one time, I must have been six or seven years old, we had to go to jail in San Pedro to Daddy's trial or pay his bail. I looked down a small window of the basement of the jail, and I saw men opening bottles and drinking. I yelled to my mother, "Hey, Mama, they're drinking Daddy's beer!"

One time us kids were looking out the window and saw a big woman walk down the street and come to our house. As she got closer, it looked like a man.

It was a man! Dressed in a woman's coat and shoes. He was an alcoholic and his wife took all his clothes out of the house to dry him up. He needed a drink so bad he dressed up in his wife's clothes and came to our house.

Several years after prohibition ended in 1933, my father was arrested for drunk driving. It wasn't the first offense. So they took away his driver's license. He had to walk to San Pedro. From there he could not find a ride. The people whom he fed during the early depression, some he lent money to, passed him on the street without offering him a ride. This hurt my father a lot.

Bottle Fisherman
as told by Bat Falcone, San Pedro

We had quite a few "bottle fishermen" in San Pedro. These fishermen smuggled in bottles of Canadian and European whiskey, instead of catching fish. They would unload their stuff all over, never at the same spot unless somebody was paid off. I'm sure there were a lot of payoffs. One spot was the beach at Portuguese Bend, at the beach by 22nd Street before the army barracks were put up. Smokey Pringle lifted a few too many bottles of his own imports. As he brought his full load into the harbor, right to the wharf, he hit a barge, sinking his boat. He swam to shore, then sobered up at his loss.

Some of us young men hijacked stock from the smugglers. South of 22nd Street there was a big tunnel, a cave by the castorbean oil plant. We waited till dark when no one was around and relieved them of 5-10 cases of their load.

One bottle fisherman we called Cat Eyes, 'cause he looked at people like a cat does, never dried out or repaired his nets. He'd go out on his boat, *The Bear,* early in the morning, come in with his nets all dry, everything in place. We became suspicious and watched him. From his boat we stole 11-12 cases, as many as we could throw into our Buick touring car. We went back over to the wharf, saw Cat Eyes from the distance so stayed away.

We heard of some activity over at Portuguese Bend, went over there to see if we could steal some liquor. The Feds beat us to it. The rumrunners' timing was off. When the boat unloaded at the beach, no trucks came up to pick it up. Soon federal agents came down to the load on the beach. The boat hastened off. The Feds wanted the booze.

Always Fixed a Lot of Faucets
as told by Frank Hall, San Pedro

Al Forgie captained a boat, used to bring in booze but never touched the contraband. Forgie docked the boat in Long Beach and walked away. He returned the next day. The boat was cleaned up and emptied of booze. In the cabin, he always found an envelope filled with money. He smuggled but never touched the stuff.

Buster Hyder was a doryman. He ran the booze from the taxi boat to the shore with the utilitarian dory. One beach he used frequently was Haggarty's Cove at Redondo Beach. The doryman rowed as fast as he could to shore where the truck crew carried it from the dory to the awaiting truck.

Gene Larson was another smuggler, but he sure drank a lot of it. He's now retired in Hood Canal, Seattle, a retirement place.

My family owned some rentals at the time. One renter named Charlie bought some Canadian whiskey off the beach crew, then brought it to his rented house and diluted it in the bathtub. My grandfather liked booze too. He seemed to spend a lot of time over at Charlie's house fixing faucets and sipping Charlie's variant of Canadian import.

Some people used the excuse that the depression was the reason fishermen went into smuggling. "Fishermen never have a rough time if they're any good. They can always make a living."

My Baby Brother
as told by Louise Green, Wilmington

Louise Green was born in Los Angeles near 23rd and Central Street on March 11, 1908, but spent most of her life in Wilmington.

My father was a policeman in Wilmington but died from a beating by Mexicans in a bar in Wilmington in 1917. My husband started a career with the U. S. Post Office in 1926 and we were married in 1927.

Neither of us drank, nor did my mother so we just didn't become exposed to drinking. Since we were involved in church, our friends had no alcohol either.

Wilmington was a nice town, a safe place, safer than now. We could walk anywhere. There were speakeasies around the 800 block of Avalon Blvd. and 100 East Anaheim. The doors were black, sometimes the entire building black. In order to get in you had to be known. People were careful not to be seen around them for two reasons: not to be seen by bootleggers and not to be seen by other people in town. There was plenty of bootleg whiskey.

San Pedro was a terrible place, not like Wilmington!

The tragedy in our family was my baby brother. Elijiah Albert Jaggers was born 1913, and started drinking at high school age, even quitting school.

He became an incurable alcoholic. Mother worried about him so much that we let him move in with us in 1933. He came home drunk quite often. My husband never complained about him or to him. He was a wonderful husband.

Albert and our cousin, another alcoholic, were always in trouble. My cousin was worse. He needed the doctor's help to stop. He drank cologne, vanilla, and anything with alcohol. He too started drinking during prohibition times. He died young.

They had a good time—oh they had a **good** time! Another cousin of mine died at 42—alcoholism too.

My brother was married in 1934 and his wife and child lived with us but she kept on going out on him. His drinking didn't help. Several of his marriages ended in divorce. In World War II, 1942, he entered the navy, made a career out of it but could not cure his drinking so he was discharged after 17 years.

He died at age 61. Because of his alcohol drinking starting so young in the exciting prohibition days of the late 1920s, my baby brother had a very tragic life.

Fathers on Both Sides
as told by John Murello, Wilmington

John Murello was born on January 19, 1902, in Wilmington, his ancestors were settlers from San Juan Capistrano.

Wilmington had so much alcohol and prostitution it was called Goose Town by the old timers.

Many people made alcohol; even more made beer. To make the alcohol the people ground corn, added sugar or honey, let it ferment, then cooked it. Other places had beer and even women in houses doing bad things. Wilmington was wide open—all over making and selling booze. There was no drugs except marijuana. Most of those who sold the booze were Mexicans, especially aliens and other foreigners like Italians.

My real father was a policeman and my stepfather a bootlegger. The authorities caught my stepfather Celayo several times. He made both homebrew and whiskey. People called at home and either picked up the booze or he'd deliver it. He bought a very expensive still. He kept the door closed but I knew what he was doing. Three-four officers came in, took away all his equipment. He served a short sentence, got out and was caught again.

He accused me of turning him in. Although we never liked each other, I was not that type of person to turn him in. He didn't believe me until just before he died. He called me over to his home, said he was sorry he blamed me for things and sorry that we didn't get along. I forgave him, kissed him. He died a few months later.

Jackals of the Fog
by R. "Swede" Pedersen, Sausalito

You could call us "Jackals of the Fog" because that's the way it was! Like jackals we waited for the lions to bag the game, then we would glide in under cover of the coastal fog and pick up the pieces.

The fog coming in through the Golden Gate, the lions being the bootleggers, the game being bootleg whiskey and we kids being the jackals. The

Volstead Act made the nation a dry one! There was only one problem. You could lead a person to the dry trough, but you had a helluva time keeping him from seeking a drink! There were too many thirsty individuals objecting to the rules and regulations set down by the prohibitionists.

Like the old fox said when raiding the hen house: "It's not always the wanting of the hen, it's the fun of the hunt, the chase of the hounds plus the buckshot sailing overhead." The experiences related here during the prohibition era were almost the same as fulfilled by kids our age all through this country in the 1920s and early 1930s. Almost for the same reasons.

In comparison to youth today, there was more "man" and "management" in kids aged 10 to 16 in those days,

In order for kids to earn a piece of the pie during the depression, we had to wait our turns getting jobs. We could deliver newspapers, deliver groceries, chop wood or whatever job we could find. In Sausalito, we kids had several reasons for getting involved in bootleg roulette: Hard times, no money; Sausalito in the path of the Golden Gate and across from San Francisco; coastline with easy access to hidden harbors, coves and hideaways; the fog; the ferry boats between San Francisco and Sausalito; limited police; local fishing fleet and sailing crafts; an imitation of elders; adventure and "to raise hell and high water."

Learning to play bootlegger wasn't hard. We just watched our elders unobserved and borrowed a few bad habits from them. We returned the bad habits as we grew older.

Sausalito is a hill town with roads and stairways leading uphill to the top and back down to the waterfront. It is a rowboat away from the Golden Gate. Sausalito is sectioned into old town, downtown, new town and the Hill.

Old town, which was our territory or point of activities, housed the fishing fleet, adjoined Fort Baker and Fort Barry army reservations and has access to the beaches and coves ideal for the bootleg game.

Old town was also blessed with two old beer gardens of the 1890 era straight from the Barbary Coast days, the Walhalla and Castle-By-The-Sea, now the Jack London House. These two establishments were prominent in the bootlegging days.

The old town gang, consisting of 10 to 12 kids, had our headquarters in a well-built and secluded tree hut in Hurricane Gulch. (Real estate agents changed the name to Shelter Cove.) The tree huts were above the Main Street Creek which flowed straight down from the hills to the bay. It was here with the foghorns moaning in the background that we planned our early morning escapades.

In our days all deliveries of dairy products, bread and pies and newspapers to homes were done around 4:30 a.m. We had one of our gang promoted to delivering newspapers with delivering help from the rest of us. The newspapers were brought daily by tug from San Francisco.

Our system was easy. The kid living up hill had the delivery route. He would awaken and head down hill. Along the way he would stop at various houses, tug on a fishing cord hanging from a bedroom window tied to the toe of the sleeper. On awakening the kid would pull in the cord and hide it, then stealthily sneak out the house.

This system was continued down the hill until the majority of the gang was on hand. We would then proceed to our next venture since we were always earlier than the arrival of the newspaper tug. By this time the milkman had delivered his products to his customers' porches and the bread and pie man had delivered his wares in the large wooden bread box sitting alongside the grocery store.

We then silently approached the houses and would borrow a quart or so of milk, some butter and cream. We were very tactful borrowing only from houses with large orders and did not pursue the same homes too frequently.

While the milk-nappers did their job, the rest of the gang approached the bread box, borrowing a large loaf of milk bread, a loaf of dark bread and a pie.

We all met back at the tree houses and enjoyed our breakfast until paper delivery time. Of course we lit up our handrolled Bull Durham cigarettes along with some tailor-made snipes we found on the street and gave a sigh of contentment.

Later we thought it was best to lay low from this borrowing game until the milk company took down the $15 reward signs for information leading to the arrest and conviction...they had posted on the telephone poles too near our tree houses.

Our delivering papers gave us many advantages in watching how the other half lived during the early morning hours. Just as jackals, we learned that stealth and observation would be a benefit for better things. We watched the fishermen when they played their game of subterfuge with their illegal activities, especially where they hid their sacks of undersized crabs, etc. When we got caught raiding regular-sized and undersized crabs, we plea bargained to clean barnacles and seaweed off the bottom of the boats. The fishermen couldn't turn us in because of their undersized crabs.

We borrowed rowboats, rowed with fence posts to Fort Baker where the army dumped trash. We salvaged the brass, lead and copper and rowed back, sold our junk to the junkyard which made weights out of it for fishermen.

With such experience behind us we learned various hiding places used by fishermen. We learned how to enter the storm drain pipes at low tide into the army bunkers used by bootleggers. We learned the people, the timing and the fog.

At the beginning when bootlegging wended its way into the Sausalito area, everyone seemed to have gotten into the game. It was a natural! The natural coastal approaches, the multitude of fishing and pleasure crafts, the depression era and the lack of law enforcers to cover such a wide and isolated area, everyone had a try at bootlegging.

At the front of Main Street across the Walhalla tavern was Nunes Bros. Boatyard. Numerous boats were tied up to the docks. We would gain entrance to a boat and use the boat as an outpost. We would not take anything and were careful to leave the boat as it was when we left it.

Approximately 4:00 a.m. one foggy morning with numerous fog horns moaning in the background, our lookout heard noises. We all lent an ear and picked out the sounds of oars dripping and oar-locks protesting.

A large rowboat barely visible in the low fog was working toward the Walhalla beach. Being so close, we could hear voices quietly giving directions from the boat: "Head for the beach under the porch."

At this early hour and with such dense fog there were no problems being observed. We heard the keel of the rowboat beaching on the sand so we watched the unloading, which was quick and professional.

After watching the boat pull out and making sure no one else was around we crawled along the beach and under the boathouse ways to the beach side of the Walhalla.

The Walhalla porch area was on pilings with the basement area enclosed with planking down into the beach sand. The old driftwood door was padlocked as usual. We dug down into the sand along the plank for about four feet deep. We made sure we wouldn't have a cave-in, then all but one of us slid into the entrance and inside the basement.

With matches we located the booze cache. This wasn't local home-made product. Here were cases of first grade liquor wrapped in straw. Rum, scotch, bourbon, cognac and gin. We could tell rumrunners brought this load through the Golden Gate off the mother ship from Canada or South America.

We were smart enough not to touch this load. We dug under the sand and extracted a dozen bottles from broken cartons of a previous load.

After wrapping the bottles in our jackets to avoid any clinking noises we passed them up through the entrance hole. We smoothed and covered our tracks in the sand and got the hell out of the area.

We laid low for a few days getting the feel of things. No one was aware of our two-bit hijacking job!

Not knowing how to properly cash in on our possession we traded bottles to the movie operator at the Princess Theatre for free passes (in the back door) and for watermelons and other fruit from the produce man.

One day a town official saw us with a few bottles we had hidden under the yacht club pilings. That worried the hell out of us. I won the honor of going down to the town hall and giving the official a bottle of bourbon. My story was I found it under the Yacht Club.

Instead of blasting my head off with fire and brimstone, he said I had performed a fine civic duty. He handed me twenty-five cents and told me if I find any more bottles like this to bring it right down to him.

What a surprise! Here was our first steady customer. We both got the best bargain. Two-bits went a long way them days for us kids.

Well from then on we did our thing. It didn't take us long to stake out when and where a "drop" would be made. The rule of thumb was, "Check with the fog" and "see which way the local police was pointing."

By playing it cool and not trying to flood the market we didn't run into much trouble. Although we were just drops in a bucket full of water, we felt big!

It didn't take long before the syndicate entered the game. This was where we got off. The syndicate played rough and for keeps. It also scared off about 90% of the local citizens who didn't mind it when it was everyone's game to play.

My buddy and I overheard that a cache of booze (not imported) was under a carport garage foundation next to the Princess Theatre. We checked out the area and saw two gunnysacks below the garage floorboards.

This was a quick drop so we crawled under the narrow foundation opening. It was awkward trying to pull the one sack along the narrow passage.

We finally pulled the booze out into the open but we were looking up at a couple of mean, mad individuals at the same time.

We had no excuse, we were way off base. We knew better. They bruised us up plenty where it didn't show. Again we had to pay penance! Every so often we were given the word to deliver booze to local citizens. We had to wear overcoats which held two pint bottles in the pockets.

We would carry the booze to a certain place and then leave. Two pints was all we had—quarts were too obvious. After six months and an increase in volume the big boys took over.

While visiting up in new town, I was taken down in the basement of a home and shown a full working still by my school friend. While looking and sampling we heard cars stopping along side the house. By the startled look on my friend's face, I realized all was not well in this area.

As footsteps were pounding in our direction my friend pulled me by the belt and we both crawled into and behind a false-built wall near the retaining wall.

You guessed it! It was a raid! I was sweating behind that wall copying my friend giving Hail Mary's and anyone else's name who needed hailing as long as we wouldn't be discovered.

The still was smashed, the equipment knocked over. After, what seemed forever, the prohis left and we crawled out, not lingering long enough to inhale the potent fumes.

I found I wasn't built to get involved with the hard core crowd. I about had it.

I do recall having to round up several of the gang, dress up in scout uniforms or parts of, and head for Tennessee Cove or Pirates Cove on the coast and have a weenie roast and song fest so that our benefactors could load up the two touring cars with imported liquor. Silver dollars were the rewards for these trips. These outings would only last three or four times then discarded. As one of the benefactors stated, "Don't run a good thing into the ground."

Other times we would fill our lunch packs with several bottles of booze and wait for the hay trucks heading through Fort Baker, Fort Berry, and Point Bonita to get to Sam Silva's ranch and Jolly's ranch by the ocean. We would hop the hay truck on the last steep grade out of Sausalito. After settling on the bundles of hay we would slip the booze in the hay also. As we stopped enroute at various points, the soldiers, Coast Guard and ranch hands would claim their goodies. When pickings were scarce we would walk along the beaches gathering whiskey bottles floating in from passing ships and with the tides from San Francisco. Whiskey bottles being a premium, we were paid from two cents for a half pint to 25 cents for a gallon jug.

Bootlegging became a serious game. Floating dead in the bay, dead in a ditch or wasting away in a jail cell, these were the top choices. We all settled down to safer and better things like avoiding getting hit by a speeding car.

The most satisfying bootleg job we enjoyed happened in 1930. Across the street from the Walhalla, Nunes Bros. Boatyard contracted to build a schooner for Charles Templeton Crocker, a wealthy San Francisco hotel owner. He paid $450,000 to have an 118 foot, two-masted schooner named *Zaca* built in Sausalito for a world cruise.

On April 14, 1930, the movie actress Marie Dressler was to christen the yacht at the big launching festivities. It was an evening high tide for launching. Marie Dressler, bless her soul, had a few drinks too many. When she swung the bottle of champagne at the hull during the launching, she missed! The bottle landed on the beach at our feet.

Charles Templeton Crocker yelled to the crowd, "Twenty-five dollars to the person who brings me the bottle of champagne!"

Six of us jackals in bib overalls ran to the launching platform and handed the champagne to Crocker. We immediately were escorted back down from the platform without a thank you or twenty-five dollars! Our overalls evidently clashed with their evening wear.

Revenge is sweet! After *Zaca* was outfitted in Richmond, she was returned to Sausalito for incline tests and proper ballast installation. The *Zaca* was moored off shore from Captain Langer dock. On the captain's dock was stored ingots of lead weighing fifty and one hundred pounds to be brought out to the *Zaca* by tug boat. On the first night with the foghorns blowing, during the wee hours of the morn could be seen six forms (in bib overalls) pulling homemade wagons loaded with as many ingots as could be carried. The caravan silently wended its way in the fog to the junk yard where the ingots were destined to be melted into fishing weights and lures for the fishermen. With pure lead paying premium prices, the jackals of the fog smilingly counted their shares bidding Charles Templeton Crocker to enjoy his twenty-five dollars and his bottle of champagne and a rocky cruise.

College Life in the Roaring Twenties
as told by Bright [pseudonym], San Bernardino

While attending USC, I worked in the parking lot at May Company. Many college students worked there at night. We did have time to party. All the boys drank or at least tried "Alky," the white moonshine liquor. Perhaps 80 percent of the girls drank or would try a little of their date's drink. Kids weren't any different than now. They partied, had sex. I think maybe the girls were smarter in the prohibition days as at least less of them became pregnant.

The Walhalla, built in 1893, was a Sausalito speakeasy during prohibition. Supposedly Baby Face Nelson worked here for a while in 1932. Photo courtesy Jack Tracy and Sausalito Historical Society.

Before a party we'd see a druggist to buy 190 proof pure grain alcohol. We'd take a kettle, boil distilled water. We added an equal amount of alky to the boiled water and let it sit for a while. We poured it into our flask or small ½ pints and take it with us.

One of the best places for college students was the Venice Ballroom, across from Noah's Ark, a Disney-like park. The dance floor was square and flat but the place you stood on was at an angle so no matter were you stood you could see the girls or anybody else. We danced the Charleston and other dances— like what you call disco now. We did that in the thirties. I only finished two years at USC, cost too much and the depression had begun.

At the drugstore on 6th and Union [L. A.], we'd go in at the soda fountain and say, "Give me a limy." If he knew you, you'd have a drink of lime, plus a jigger of alky and soda water.

Former Jackal of the Fog Ralph "Swede" Pedersen, in 1984, looking over former tidal storage area of smuggled liquor at the Walhalla in Sausalito, where he and other Jackals dug into the sand to obtain booty. Photo by Len Beckett Jr., courtesy of Pedersen.

When I was in high school, San Fernando High School, about 33 percent of the boys drank or tried it occasionally, maybe 20 percent of the girls. The valley had little towns with farms and fields in between. Many Italians out in ranches bootlegged. One I remember as a high school student, an old man called Lawrence. He made Dago red out by Pacoima. Three of us went to his back door and knocked hard. There was no answer. We knocked again.

"What do you want?" he finally answered.

"We want a glass of wine."

"Who are you?" he asked.

"I'm Melvin, remember I came here with _____ last month?" I explained.

"Go to the cellar door."

He came out in his union suit, opened the cellar door. He poured three water glasses of wine for us, but just before he handed the glass, he said, "I want a little tastie first" and he took a drink of each of ours. He charged 25¢ for a glass of wine. I thought that was high but two of those glasses and we'd be walking on our heels.

College Days at Santa Ana J. C. and Losing a Good Job
by Carl Bergman, Lancaster

Times were tough in 1930 and I was on my own. Dad had a dairy farm in San Joaquin Valley but not able to send me much money. My favorite professor, Mr. Drake, arranged for me to work in a florist shop. The boss of the flower shop found out I could drive a model "T" and I was assigned the job of going to the Flower Market in L. A. I would get up at four o'clock in the morning, three times a week to pick up a panel-truck load of flowers. He was a very thoughtful man, he paid for my breakfast and told me not to handle the flowers that the people at the market would load the truck while I was eating my breakfast. Upon my return he would not let me unload the flowers; he personally would do that. Well and good—I had a soft job, and that I liked.

One foggy morning coming home on Telegraph Road, I hit one of those street corner bumpers and blew out a front tire. In the back and under the flowers were the tools as well as the spare tire, pump and two square five gallon cans. Unscrewing the lid I smelled the contents. Hooch. Boy was I scared: I knew that the cops would surely check my load, someday...so, I quit. And that's how I lost a good job.

Bakersfield and How I Got Started Picking Oranges
by Carl Bergman, Lancaster

Shortly after Alta and I were married and we were going to Tulare to visit my parents, we saw a sign on a little old service station in Bakersfield, "For Sale." The man wanted $200 dollars for the inventory and the lease that he owned. This was the day before motels; however, he had six small one-room cabins out behind the station. We went to Santa Ana and got Alta's dowry. Our first business venture.

The station did fairly well with me selling gasoline and Alta doing the maid work for the rooms. We got one dollar per night for the rooms and I made four cents profit on each gallon of gasoline sold when I kept the price up. I recall dropping a penny per gallon and lit the sign up with a flashing light. Soon I was criticized by the old-time station operators in the neighborhood and had to think of another method of increasing the income. One of our steady renters, Frank, came to the rescue. His idea was to run the station until midnight. He was to operate the evening shift for the rent of the cabin.

All went well and good, no shortages. I thought we had it made until one evening when Frank had the night off. At approximately nine o'clock in came a big Packard car inquiring for Frank. I said, "This is Frank's night off."

The Packard man opened the trunk and set off two square five gallon cans in a wooden box marked "Standard Oil Kerosene." I became worried and a little suspicious that Frank was supplying the local joints with hooch. These were the ones where you would go to the door and give the password thru a small door, eye height, before you could enter.

Next morning we sold the station lock stock and barrel to Frank for $250. Not bad profit or so I thought. We took the money and went to Lindsey where I got a job picking oranges.

Old Times in Stockton
as told by an old timer

I was a painter, made good money when I worked, but in winter I didn't have much work. I had a wife and two small children. In 1928-29 I hired on to help moonshiners at French Camp. Where the road came off the main road, one man acted as sheep herder. His job was to push this button when anybody came down who wasn't supposed to. The button shut off all the electricity in the place, stopping the still. The goddamn PG & E wondered what was happening to all the power (Who was using the power?). There was nothing down there. They looked all over, couldn't find it.

The sheriff was in on it and said, "You boys are too hot. You'd better move." That sheriff, Bill Riecks, was in office for years, finally was defeated. Got caught stuffing the ballot boxes.

The next day some people from San Francisco came with trucks and we moved everything near Valley Springs. While setting up the still I broke my goddamn foot. They took me to the Stockton hospital, put it in a cast for six weeks. The moonshiners paid my hospital and doctor bills and gave me one hundred dollars.

But in Valley Springs the sheriff wouldn't play the game—knocked the goddamn joint over before they made a drop. The only man they caught there took the rap, spent a year in jail. They paid him $1,000 not to talk. I made $5.00 a day then working for them. Goddamn good money in those days. We made it out of corn sugar, block rolls ? of it. Prohibition never did go over big. The Volstead Act—that's what they called it—was the most preposterous thing. Three or four judges after court would go out to a roadhouse, drink and get drunk—some goddamn law that was. How that son-a-bitch law was passed I don't know.

I was out of the army before it went into effect. We had local option law then. San Joaquin County was dry, Sacramento County wet. I and my army friends had to go to Sacramento to drink. After prohibition started, you could buy it here. We'd go up to a place for a drink—may buy Bevo, near beer, on tap—horrible stuff—or coke. To get a real drink, you'd say to the bartender, "You know me?"

"Sure," he would say.

"Well, this is my friend; he's all right."

"Sure. What'll you have?"

The funniest thing I remember. One Sunday morning I was walking on Weber Avenue between Central and El Dorado. This little pipsqueak deputy was cleaning out a bootlegging joint. Took everything, loaded it on a truck. This little-bittie some-bitch—how'd he get to be a deputy I'll never know. He's a mean some-bitch when he has a couple big cops around him. Well, when this deputy sheriff had the truck loaded and the driver was ready to leave, the deputy yelled, "Wait a minute!"

He went back into the speakeasy and brought out the goddamn broom too. That little bittie sheriff, no bigger than a racehorse jockey, cleared the whole goddamn place out including the broom. He cleaned it, everything 'cept the water pipes. The bootlegger didn't pay off. No pay, no play.

You better not put my name on this. I may end up with a dagger in me.

You could go to many ranches around Stockton and buy a gallon of whiskey for $6.00. It's mostly grappa, clear alcohol made from grapes. The Italians didn't need whiskey. They had their grappa—strong like jackass whiskey. They get up and have hot coffee and if they wanted a drink before they went to work, they'd pour it into the coffee.

Not too many places sold beer. It was too big to hide, hard to keep cool. You had to go out into the country usually to drink beer. Many people made it. You put the cap on and in the night the goddamn thing exploded. Some beer was bad. It smelled. We didn't drink much of it. If you drank some of it and blew on a candle, the candle exploded—boom! I'm sure they put ether in it. Jesus Christ, the next day my head would go round and around.

In bars we bought grappa or jackass whiskey.

My wife never touched a drop, never wanted me to either. How many times she ate my ass out for drinking!

Roosevelt ended prohibition. He put thousands back to work. That depression was a son-of-a-bitch. He closed the banks right away—straightened those bastards out. Best president we ever had.

When prohibition ended, the whole goddamn town went nuts. What celebration! No different than any other town, I'm sure. But they closed up at 2:00 a.m.—two to six it was closed, still is.

I had a wife and two kids; I'd work at anything, painting when I had a job during the depression. There was no welfare in those days. You could go to the Red Cross, they could help some. I went to the Red Cross for help and they turned me down; there were too many people who needed help. But at least people wouldn't hit you over the head then. You were safe 'cause they knew you didn't have anything.

Collegiate Prohibition Years
as told by Marian Isaacs, San Francisco

I entered University of California, Berkeley, in 1922 at the age of 16, receiving my A.B. in June 1926.

Everybody made booze: My father purchased good alcohol from a friendly druggist and added juniper flavoring to make gin, Italian friends made wine, many made homebrew. Everybody had connections with a bootlegger whom you could phone or meet on a street corner.

The speakeasies and clubs where you could buy liquor were numerous. The most famous in San Francisco was Izzy Gomez' on Pacific Street. Also Poppa Coppa's and Tate's At The Beach—always sold, seldom raided. But there were literally hundreds. I didn't know them because I was very young at the time, but the cabbies, newspapermen, etc. knew them all. One of my boyfriends, somewhat older, took me to a small home in a residential district where there was gambling at high stakes along with the liquor.

The better hotels sold "set-ups" or fruit punch and you added your own liquor. The beer sold in speakeasies was spiked beer, in order to raise the alcoholic content of legal beer.

My uncle signed a pledge before prohibition not to drink. He kept that pledge until he was 70 years old. But most of us did not feel unpatriotic by drinking. That was a rotten law to pass when our men were overseas. My father sometimes took the medicinal alcohol and added orange juice, "orange blossom" we called it, the predecessor of the screwdriver.

By mail order, one could order all types of booze-making kits. They even sold charred barrels in which alcohol and some flavorings will make "bourbon."

At U. C. Cal, the night before the big game with Stanford, I went danc- ing with a date at the Claremont Hotel. Afterwards we went back to my apart- ment, and with the girls who lived with me we drank orange blossom. My date asked me if I ever got drunk.

"No," I said.

"Let's try," he said.

That was the last time I ever got drunk. We almost missed the big game.

There was a complaint about the party we had and we girls were called before the dean of women at Cal.

My First Drink
as told by Ruth, Anchor Bay

Les and Jimmy wanted to go to a bootlegger. I went with them to pick up a pint. I was only 15, still in high school in San Francisco. The bootlegger lived in an old house, near a cemetery—lonely and spooky place. I didn't want to go in but I did. We bought a pint. The bootlegger gave us three shot glasses and a glass of water for a chaser for me.

The only thing I knew about drinking was what I knew from the mov- ies. You had to drink it all the way down at once. I did! It was god-awful stuff, burned, choked me but I hurried with the chaser as I was supposed to according to the movies.

With a burning throat, a hot stomach and tears in my eyes, I managed to say, "That's keen!"

That's what the movies told me to do.

Later, the only drink I ordered was whiskey sours. I learned that from the movies too.

My cousin's husband rented an apartment for a speakeasy right across from KFRC radio station on Van Ness. Al and Cal Pearce had a popular after- noon radio show. They frequented the speakeasy. It was so exciting there. I stayed with them whenever I could. My mother would have died if she knew. She didn't find out. I was only 15-16 at the time, graduating from high school in 1931, so it was before 1931. I took care of my cousin's children when my cousin was at the speakeasy. But I spent much time there at the speakeasy.

I often went with my cousin's husband to deliver. We drove in a big black limousine, like a gangster car. We drove right up to the front door of the big houses in Russian Hill or Nob Hill, I'd hop out and give the clients the bottle.

I delivered it because no one suspected a 16-year-old girl. God, those were the fun days. Everything is dull now.

Later I had cards to the best speakeasies. When we went to places like the St. Francis Hotel, we'd sneak in a bottle. We ordered ginger ale, I believe, pour our alcohol in under the table and drink it in the open.

What I Remember
by Nellie Breaum, Redwood City

I was very young and didn't smoke or drink in those days, so didn't like what went on. (My, I have really changed since those days, early 1930!)

Believe me, Clifford, it was all a big farce, the police knew what was going on but they never bothered anyone, only if they became too boisterous and caused a lot of trouble.

My father made his own beer, [I] remember helping him to cap it, my mother made us ginger beer. Budweiser Malt was used for beer. He also made apricot brandy in the tea kettle.

The priest at the mission in San Jose made real good wine and sold it for fifty cents a gallon. I also remember going to Mission San Jose with my father to get the wine.

Some had to have their drink stronger so they made a gin and called it bath tub gin, it was made from straight alcohol with a little flavoring and that was dynamite, they also made cordials, very sweet and sticky.

Half Moon Bay was where the smugglers came in with the real good stuff. We were over there one evening and saw it take place, but didn't really know what was going on at the time. Just a group of us having a beach party, we saw this boat giving signals, so we watched and kept very quiet and sure enough we saw them unloading cases on the beach. I wanted to go home and told the gang let's get going before someone comes to pick up those cases. We just got in our cars when a truck came with four men in it. Gosh I was scared.

Two of our friends did steal a case each but we didn't know this till we arrived home. It was scotch whiskey and gin. No police came around that evening to inspect the beach.

Saturday nights we would go dancing, often went to the Fairmont; the guys would have a flask and they kept it under the table. The hotel would serve ginger ale. Getting so many flashbacks about the good old days and the fun we had together.

CHAPTER 18

PUT A PADLOCK ON THAT REDWOOD TREE

Northwestern California had its unique bootlegging atmosphere. Churches were generally strong, supporting the Anti-Saloon League and the Woman's Christian Temperance Union (WCTU). Yet the towns were fairly wide open even up to the beginning of World War II.

From the Oregon border to northern Marin County, 300 miles of jagged coastline buttressed against the rugged Coast Range and Siskiyou Mountains, forming small inlets and dog holes, the latter being tiny isolated bays with sharp cliffs preventing easy road access. At many dog holes, lumber companies put A-frame structures to lower timber from the cliff down to the water where barges hauled them to San Francisco and San Pedro. During prohibition smugglers used the A-frames to lift liquid gold from the dog holes to the cliffs, where trucks raced it to the cities.

This coast had just a few harbors and bays like Humboldt Bay. Hundreds of miles of highways, usually two-lane windy roads, ran through the Coast Range, and between that range and the Siskiyous. Wild land. Wild mountains. Wild forests. Independent people—the kind who took care of their own problems and didn't look kindly to outsiders coming in to tell them what to do. Some families had been there from the 1850s, making up to four generations of independence, freedom and relative isolation.

Two main industries supported the economy of this part of the Pacific Northwest: fishing and lumber. Farming, tourism and transportation also brought money to the area.

Perhaps one can see a primitive subsurface to life in California's Northwest. What the lumber companies did to the forest and what lumbermen did to the individual trees, so did the businessmen do to the lumbermen: pick them out, isolate them, make them fall in a certain direction, drag them away and slice them up. The trees were well used and so were the men. The main job of the locals was to harvest money from lumbermen and fishermen—and to a lesser extent from tourists, farmers and travelers.

A lumberman coming into town could have a few drinks at bars, saloons, cabarets and whorehouses. Women could often be had at these houses; cabaret dancing ladies would sit and talk or dance for a price—profit for her and for the house. Thirsty fishermen or lumberjacks added to these profits by buying drinks for the ladies. Poker games allowed men to leave with lighter pockets. House shills maneuvered the lumberjack, used tricks to involve him into the game and get him deeper once he was in.

Some houses gave credit on the man's next paycheck. The "good guy" approach was carefully seeded with tokens, good for a drink or a dance or anything the light-pocketed man wanted.

When National Prohibition came, selling drinks became illegal. But that just made the cabaret owners more creative in order to liberate the farmer's son from his money—and not run afoul of the law!

Helping Tourists and Workers

Crescent City, like Eureka and other coastal towns in northern California, had some economic advantages over the industrial cities in the state. Fishing and hunting brought in tourists and vacationers—often men with the sporting urges in the fields, streams and oceans of the north country, and often men with sporting urges in the wild towns of the north coast.

With the advent of better cars, highways and affluence, the redwood forests became a place to visit, spending time camping or in a resort cabin. With the influx of visitors, came a market for liquid refreshments. Each resort area, and perhaps each filling station stop had a bootlegger. A family could drive its car through a *Sequoia sempervirens* and buy souvenirs at a redwood tree store. Supposedly one redwood tree got caught so many times selling moonshine, it had to be padlocked under the nuisance law.[1]

Commercial fishermen and the lumbermen brought in their paychecks and their hungry appetites into town. These hearty and healthy men waited for days off to satisfy this drive, and the businessmen of Crescent City were anxious to satisfy their wishes with good food, good drinks and "good" women—sometimes not-so-good drinks and often times definitely not good women. Entrepreneurs satisfied the workers' needs and lightened their pockets.

The ranchers and farmers suffered with the post World War decline for agricultural products. Many marginal farms struggled to keep pace with declining crop prices and rising expenses. Prohibition helped some ranchers and farmers in Del Norte County. Some leased out their farms to moonshiners from San Francisco. Others went into the moonshine distillery business themselves. Crescent City and Eureka needed more liquor, and the sparsely populated countryside had numerous suppliers of liquor and beer.

Tokens
as told by Norton Steenfott, Eureka

When a man entered a place, cabaret, you paid 25¢ admission. They gave you a ticket, good for a drink or a dance. You had to pay for each dance or for sitting in the booth with a girl. Every time the music stopped you had to buy a drink, two ounces of orange juice. During the week nights it was about a minute and a half; on Saturday or a busy night the dance might be only a minute long. The girl got a round token with a hole in it. She had these big horse

Northwestern California

blanket pins and pinned tokens on it. Every time you'd be in a booth you'd buy two drinks so she would receive two tokens for that. For a dance you'd turn the ticket in and she'd get the token for the dance. In other words she'd earn 12½¢ a dance and 25¢ for a booth drink, half of what you bought she earned. It was expensive, 50¢ for one or one and one-half minutes in a booth. If you bought several, a waitress might skip you for a dance or so. There was no alcohol in the orange juice—you had to bring your own. You didn't have to drink all that juice but you had to pay. You couldn't just stand around outside the booth either. You had to dance some of the dances or buy some drinks every time the music stopped. It cost from $5 to $25 an hour to stay in these cabarets. Though the cabaret received half the take, one woman said she saved as much as $400 a week. Men didn't let you sit and around much, especially Saturday nights.

Practically every logger was single. The train would bring you in every week or every two weeks. The men would then take the streetcar or walk a mile to town, get a shave, haircut and a bath and head for a card game, cabaret or speakeasy. They'd have a drink or so, maybe play cards until the games closed at 12:00, then went to a cabaret until it closed at 2:00 a.m.

All semi-legal.

On Sunday about 4:00 p.m. they had to catch the train back to the logging camp, otherwise they would have to walk.

Their checks would be gone. If they wanted to buy a shirt or something all the places were opened on Sunday for the guys. Many had to go to a place to borrow money. The next time in they'd go to the card room to cash their checks, pay back the $5 they borrowed the last time in town. Then the owner would give a signal for one of the shills to leave the game. The owner Tom gave him the money for his check and said, "We have a nice game over there. Oh, by golly, there's an empty seat too. You don't have to wait."
The logger would usually play because Tom was his friend and done him a favor, lent him money. Then he'd go to the cabaret, ending up the night with a big head and broke and have to borrow more money. That would continue over and over and over.

And it was the same way with the fishermen. Very few of them were married. They went out, made their catch, got paid and never went out until that money was gone. When the money was gone they'd go out. When they needed money or the rent piled up, or they needed a new motor for the boat, the fish company would buy them a new motor, take it out in payments from the fish they brought in. The companies often gave false weights, cheated them, but fishermen don't dare say anything 'cause he knows he has credit. If he brought in 2,000 pounds of fish, he may get cheated out of 200 pounds.
All his extra money went into the cabarets and bootlegging joints.
In this wide open town, tokens were popular. Five cents could buy a pound of hamburger or some milk or a loaf of bread. The tokens kept the name of the

place in one's mind—advertising! If you paid a bill or bought a lot, the store gave you a token for 5¢, 10¢, 12½¢ or 25¢. You'd go back to that store.

You could buy a glass of beer for maybe 5¢ or a shot for 10¢, a big 2-oz glass of whiskey. If a man buys the house a drink, there may be ten people at the bar. The bar isn't going to miss a chance so if a person has two drinks in front of him and someone buys the house a drink, the bartender gives the man a token in place of the drink. When a person wants a drink later he could use the token. But the money was in the cash register or in the owner's pocket.

Card game owners used tokens too—they might give everyone betting heavy a cigar. If a person didn't smoke, he received a token instead. That would encourage him to come back and lose more money or spend his token and more besides and be harvested again.

⌀

It didn't matter what year it was during bootlegging in California, Eureka folks seemed not to care. Local enforcement was scattered and mostly symbolic at best. When federal agents came up the coast, they found enough places to raid and enough easily obtainable evidence to make sorties into California's northwest profitable.

According to the January 23, 1923, issue of *Eureka's Humboldt Standard*, prohis netted many liquor violators. A raid on the old Charlie Jackson saloon at 525 Second Street caused the arrest of proprietor William Matthews. He had 11 gallons of wine in demijohns and two dozen eight-ounce bottles of a new kind of wine, wine of pepsin, which contained 20% alcohol by volume. Matthews pleaded not guilty because the small bottles, made in San Francisco, were for medicinal use, not for beverage.

Agents arrested William Verhein and Mrs. Justice Adams, in whose place at 233 H Street were four stills. Since Adams could not make the $1,000 bail, she spent time in the county jail. But when she obtained $1,000, she became the second donor of a grand to the county treasurer since the Wright Act started at the end of 1922.

Harry Henry, arrested for selling at a restaurant known as the "noodle joint" on lower Third Street, paid his bail. Abatement proceedings started for G. Celli and A. Massei for "conducting a nuisance, otherwise blind pigs," for selling and possessing wine at the Swiss-Italian Hotel. Demurrers were withdrawn and suspects were given 10 days to answer complaints. [The Feds arrested Dorothy Tschrifter, owner of Dorothy's Cafe on D Street, but released the cook Teddy Michelson.] For some reason officials had problems destroying evidence. Too many people in that area could not force themselves to dump 1,900 gallons of good Italian wine. The wine was part of 17,000-20,000 gallons held "under seal" by Massei, but 1,900 had been sneaked out and sold and confiscated. The county could not destroy the wine so the judge ordered the city court to do so. Massei countered and appealed to the California Superior Court. It just would not be right to spill good wine in the gutters of Eureka.

During the rest of prohibition, the raids continued in the north, but never stopped the selling or making of illegal liquor. A few examples from the *Crescent City American* of 1927 illustrate the business of the times. On January 20, the Dry Squad of Charles Smith, Schultz (Schulte?) and Deputy Sheriff Roy Plaisled raided the home of Walter Parish near Pacific Avenue. They confiscated a ten-gallon keg of jackass brandy and a one-quart jar of extract of gin. Parish pleaded guilty and paid a fine of $150.

That same month, District Attorney George W. Howe, deputies Schulte and Brown swooped down upon A. W. Studarns and Luigi Braido at the Ashley ranch near Fort Dick. This moonshine operation had been busy for three months. With 150 gallons of wine mash and 20 gallons of beer as evidence against them, both pleaded guilty before Judge C. A. Potter and were fined the going rate of $150. South of town, across the bridge, the dry squad caught Jack Evans with one gallon of jackass whiskey. He too was released after paying his $150. Just a few days later on February 3, William "Whittie" Snath on K Street had his third appearance before Judge Potter. This time, however, his jug of jackass cost him $500 or six months. Since he couldn't pay the fine, Potter told Snath that for the "next six months, at least, you are going to earn an honest living."

The Parish family did not have the best of luck that year. Mrs. Walter Parish, her car stranded on the beach, had to be pulled out. Ten days later the *Crescent City American* reported Chief of Police A. R. O'Leary arrested Walter Parish, an "old offender of the liquor laws," when he was "raising a disturbance" at Spann's barber shop on 2nd Street, but he ran from O'Leary, ran into someone and then surrendered. Between Saturday night and early Sunday morning, Parish crawled through an 8" by 12" vent, escaping and heading for better luck at Grants Pass, Oregon.

Not Getting Caught
as told by Norton Steenfott, Eureka

Some speakeasies used the old bars. Others just built a bar out of boards, real crude—anywhere to sell a drink. One fellow, just after prohibition started, rented a little hole in the wall in an alley in Seattle, like a little woodshed and he had a 50-gallon barrel, one shot glass in his pocket and a pint bottle of whiskey. He hid the whiskey. He just stood in, he said, and customers came in, laid down 50¢ on an empty barrel, he set the shot glass down, poured it full and they picked it up, drank it right down. Sometimes he had them lined up waiting for a drink. He made money that way. That was all he had for a bar. His wife had a rooming house upstairs and she was selling coffee royals for $1.00. With that they were able to buy a number of buildings, apartment houses to get their start. That's how fast the liquor sold. Then he moved to Eureka and bought a few buildings here.

A bar was sometimes a wooden counter and a sink. At the door there was usually a bell or buzzer. Another guy further away would see all the people coming. Like back of this building there was a gate. If he'd see somebody suspicious the man at the gate would give a signal with a buzzer "Be careful." Then he had another signal if a person was all right. Then the man opened the inside door.

Other places had a front, a cigar stand, soft drink parlor, then the back room was a speakeasy. It seldom sold in the open where somebody could walk into it. It was sold in the back room and the door was locked. See anybody could walk in sit down at a bar. The cigar stand was a fake; they didn't care if they sold a pack of cigarettes or not. The guy who was behind the cigar stand was the guy pressing the buzzer too. If the police are there—the police know what's going on but you don't let them in the back room and you don't let anyone leave. You're not going to let a bunch of guys leave when the police or dry squad are out there.

The men would stand around and talk. Anytime someone wanted a drink, he put the money on the bar, they poured him the drink and he drank it right down. It didn't sit there. In case the dry squad came in, they wanted no evidence sitting around.

Behind the bar, they had a big pitcher of water that was never touched, sitting right along side the sink. If something did happen, the whiskey they had—usually in a pitcher because it would pour out faster than a bottle—went into the sink. Right behind it went the water. Agents got smart. Many places in California, agents jumped right over the goshdarned counter, took the pipes apart, used the whiskey in the pea trap for evidence. Bootleggers learned that right fast and took the pea trap off the sink and used straight pipes. When raided, down went the whiskey, followed by the water. Like a straight shot of whiskey with a water chaser.[2]

There were a number of false rooms in the Bono Guasto, a gray colored building, now called the Eagle House, 2nd and C, where they are working on the back end of it now [1980]. It was a three-story rooming house. Found in there were old labels where they bottled gin.

In the Monte Carlo Hotel there was a wall tank, 1st and D Street, torn down for a parking lot. It was between the floor joist under the first floor, built under there and a long copper tank and the copper tube to a place in the wall where they could fill it. Then another spot where they came up with a pipe with a valve stem. They took a bicycle tire pump, attached to the valve stem, pumped enough air into it to force the whiskey up to the second floor where they had a little pipe and spigot. They were hard to find.

Like the one I found in this wall [pointing to the wall where the interview was held]. It had been in that wall for over 50 years and no one found it. I was cutting a new doorway through and found copper tubing. At first I thought it was a line for an oil stove. Then I thought, no, I took that out already. I followed the line and found two copper tanks and spigots coming out of a light plug.

Where Two Street Music Store is now, there was a copper tank on the second floor and a tube, where it was filled. Gravity let it run down to the first floor. The bootlegger had several ways he could hide his booze. Say there was a room with a light fixture with pipe going down an arm going out to the light on it. He'd rent the room above it, cut a hole out. Where that pipe comes down it's all hollow except for the wire. There's enough room for a small copper tube, right straight down into the light fixture and a spigot. They could just take a ladder and fill the bottle. Or the tubing could come out at the wall socket. Some people had a lever. You turn it one way for water and one way for whiskey. I've never seen one like that but I know they had them. Richie, a sheet-

Front of the Louvre on Eureka's notorious Second Street. Men could relax downstairs with soft drinks, playing pool or cards. Upstairs, an elaborate Cabaret welcomed lumbermen and fishermen with orange juice and dances with girls that lasted 1 ¾ minutes on a weekday and 1 ¼ minutes on the weekend—all costing 25¢. A lumberman could spend $1.25 in less than 5 minutes with one dance and four orange drinks in a booth with a lady. He paid with 25¢ tokens—the girl receiving half. The alcohol was normally smuggled in. Photo by author.

metal worker, put most of the tanks in around here. He was an Italian carpenter who made false walls and doors for anyone who wanted one. The thing is he never talked. Everyone would hire him because he never told anyone where he put anything.

Moonshining in Del Norte County
as told by Allen Lehman, Crescent City

I remember distinctly we had at least seven bootleggers in our county here at Del Norte. Three or four are still living. We kid about it all the time. One is my best friend, a man 88 years old, in fairly good health. He had a still in the Sand Hills. We called his moonshine "Sand Hills Whiskey." Down seven, eight miles on Highway 199, there was on old fellow from Kentucky named Dan London. He made whiskey back in Kentucky and they called it "London Whiskey," mostly 5-gallon kegs, 1-gallon jugs and flasks, but you could buy a whole gallon of Sand Hill or London Whiskey for $5.00.

We had parties and would have clear-color moonshine around. In those days, ha, ha, we never had sense enough to cut it or put it in a glass with water. With friends or family it was always in shot glasses. Shot glasses, not cocktail glasses. We never thought of ice, never gave it a second thought. I'm referring to the end of prohibition when the depression was quite prevalent too.

I remember one time the assistant district attorney in Eureka—he's long gone now, bless his old heart. He had the affliction of alcohol, a little bit more than he should have had and a lot more than the rest of us. Being an assistant district attorney, a lot of confiscated whiskey found its way other than the gutter, down the drain or down the toilet. He found his way to get a share of it. When we visited him there, he'd have a pitcher of orange juice. In those days there wasn't any frozen orange juice. You could buy cans but not too many people had freezers. He put a certain amount of moonshine in a big pitcher and put some orange juice in it. I've always given him credit, whether he deserves it or not, as being the originator of the screwdriver.

I went with some other people for a party or anniversary at his home. He gave us a bigger glass, kinda like cheese glasses. When he poured this orange juice in there, we joked and said, "My goodness, this is the kind of party it's going to be, an orange party."

"You just drink. It's not poison, won't make you blind."

I drank quite a bit of it and that's all it was, moonshine mixed with orange juice.

Moonshine was sold in all the whorehouses and bars. We called the bars blind pigs and speakeasies. Most of the places those days in Crescent City, Eureka and in San Francisco were in alleys. You know, you go down an alley and go in a door. Anyone could enter a blind pig here in Crescent City, but in San Francisco unless you were with somebody whom the bouncer knew or he knew you, you didn't get into those places. He had a little peephole in the door. You knocked on the door and the little thing would open up and if he knew you, fine—the door would come open right away and if he didn't know you, you just didn't get in.

Some of them became quite elaborate, once you got in. Most of them had one or two big bouncers, men—great big husky devils. If any rumpuses went on in there or any Feds—they called them Feds—came in to raid them, the bouncers protected the place. Most of those places in San Francisco and Eureka, according to the district attorney of Eureka, were bought off before they ever opened, speakeasies or cabarets they called them. They were bought off, but they went through periodical raids to supposedly satisfy the prohibitionists. They would submit to a raid and they'd go in, bust up a few bottles of booze, turn over a few tables, one thing or another and they'd leave. A day or two later they'd be back in business just the same as before.

The first year or two of prohibition was a little different, but as time went on, it was evident that the population wasn't behind prohibition. There were a few die-hard district attorneys and police chiefs who were a little on the prohi side themselves, I guess. You'd find a few of them in San Francisco and even in Eureka. We didn't have many raids in Crescent City. The fact of the matter is I knew lots of owners. We had maybe 10, 11 speakeasies or blind pigs in Crescent City at one time during prohibition. Somehow or other if we happened to have a sheriff that year that was on the prohi side and was going to make a name for himself, he put a raid together. Hell, all bootleggers and moonshiners and speakeasies knew about it and they got rid of all the booze. When they were raided there wasn't anything there.

If there was a complaint, they'd have to make a periodic raid and that satisfied the prohibitionists. But they were right back in business again in a few days. I remember one fellow, a big tall fellow, Tommy Thompson. He ran one of the better places here in Crescent City. He said once or twice after they had raided him, "Oh well, I needed a vacation anyway."

He'd close up for a couple of weeks, take off to the city or someplace. Several of them fellows who were in speakeasies are still in Crescent City. I knew them all. They're all pretty old, but they're still there, still going.

When my father came here in 1915, I was eleven years old and worked with my father. He was in the meat business, had a meat market, slaughter house and a sausage kitchen. In those days you didn't buy from Armour or Swift, you made it. You didn't buy bacon from any packing house, you made it. Hams, all your sausages, bologna, all that stuff. I can remember in one room there we had 15 barrels, wine barrels, or whiskey barrels. Whiskey was brought into Crescent City in those days legally, before prohibition, in barrels, 50-gallon barrels. Bulk wine, bulk whiskey, Yellowstone, Green....

My father bought these barrels from the saloon keepers to cure our hams and bacon. You put your hams and bacon in and cured your own meat and your sausage. It consisted of saltpeter, brown sugar and salt. That's your cure. It's still done today exactly the same way; every ham you eat, every wienie you eat and bacon is all kept with FLP, saltpeter. Anyway we'd buy these barrels and knock the head out and we'd put some coal oil, one-half gallon, swirl it around, set it on fire and char it and that got rid of the wine and whiskey that had soaked into the wood. On every damn one of those whiskey barrels was three or four plugs of chewing tobacco nailed to the bottom. I pulled many of them out. That's what gave the whiskey the brown color. That's what gave you red eye, or rot gut. That's what gave you rotten whiskey. You'd get so much of it, you'd burn up all those old guys, alcoholics would be just burned up. You know, all that tobacco juice in your system. One bootlegger took sugar and burned it a little bit and mixed it. That gave his whiskey a little brown.

In Eureka they had their troubles down there too. I remember one year, I can't even remember the sheriff's name. He was going to have everybody obey the law, period. He damn near got himself strung up two or three times. Oh, he raided and he raided, you know. There was no payoff with him, period. He was going to make sure prohibition worked, right in the middle of prohibition.

In the tail end of prohibition some of the speakeasies, like on Front Street in Crescent City there would be a bar in the typical speakeasy. But prior to that you'd just go into a room, a few chairs around, hardly anything else and you'd sit down, and the one selling the booze would come in. Ninety-nine percent of them would have it in their hip pocket. It was warm from their body. They'd give you a shot glass and you'd drink it. You just drink it. That's the way people drank moonshine. They just took the glass. Some of that was 90-100 proof. It would burn the living heck out of you.

There was one fellow, very prominent fellow, Bill Murphy, long dead. I don't think he has any relatives around here. Big fellow, big pouch. Bill Murphy ran a saloon prior to prohibition called Murphy's Corner. It was the most popular saloon in Crescent City in those days. I was 15-16 and I never indulged in alcohol. When prohibition came, he remodeled this saloon, making a poolhall out of it, sold some near beer which had only one-half of one percent. You'd have to drink two barrels to feel anything. When prohibition was on and I was 18-19, Bill went into the speakeasy business. He bought his moonshine from one of my very dear friends. I had dinner with him the night before last.

Bill kept the old bar selling near beer, soda pop and that kind of crap but he took on selling moonshine. He always wore a big black coat, enormous stomach on him and inside to this coat he carried a flat pint flask, of jackass. He'd sell you a drink of jackass for 4-bits, but you had to go into the potty, into the toilet in the back. There was room in the toilet for four or five people but you had to crowd like heck to get in there. He'd pull out this pint of whiskey and in another pocket he had the glasses. He only did it in the toilet. This was the period of time at the beginning of prohibition when they were all a little bit afraid. In the tail end of prohibition the places were almost as wide open as they are now. Then they built better speakeasies, a little more elaborate, tables and short bar. You could take girls there. Prior to that, women hardly ever went into a saloon, the old type saloon.

The reason he'd only sell in the toilet was that if the place were raided, he'd drop her in the toilet right now. I knew him very well. I asked him, "Bill, why in the world do we have to go into the potty to have a drink with you?"

He said, "If I'm raided I can get rid of the evidence that quick (snap of the fingers)."

All those places sold moonshine. I don't remember a one that sold Canadian whiskey. I personally don't remember anybody going blind but I remember hearing stories about bad bathtub gin. I remember some friends that drank poor moonshine (and) they would sit for three-four days, consistently

This was the old Charlie Jackson Saloon before prohibition went into effect. Located at 626 Second St. in Eureka, the new proprietor, William Matthews, tried to carry on the tradition of the saloon. He was arrested in January 1921. Before Norton Steenfott reached the age of 17, he washed dishes, bussed and cooked at this place and most of the other bootleg joints on Second Street. At 16 he drove a taxi and mixed his own "Canadian pints" for his customers. In the 1980s he owned this and many other buildings in Old Town, restoring places where he formerly washed dishes. Photo by author.

throw up, throw up, throw up till they had nothing to throw up. They call that the dry heaves. One time I became quite ill on Dago red, a dark red, heavy burgundy. We had quite a few Italians around here, they lived on that stuff. It was like coffee to us or water. They just drank it. I drank some of that one time on my young stomach and I became very, very ill. To this day I can't drink that. I can drink a little rosé, but wine is not my cup of tea.

That big Surf Hotel, now a derelict in town on Front Street, was at one time the center of sociability in Crescent City, the best dining room Crescent City ever had at that time. That's where the elite went. That was the time before motels. The hotel was the center and it was pretty much the same until the tidal wave here in 1964. The tidal wave wrecked the dining room. Actually I look at that old building today and I can't believe it: It was *the* center of all our social life, and anything that took place of any significance took place there. In those days prior to World War II our entire county had less than four thousand people

Tokens used in Eureka to entice lumbermen and fishermen to come back week after week and use the tokens. Once there, most spent their entire paycheck. Photo courtesy of Norton Steenfott and Ann Mendenhall.

in it. After the war and they started cutting all the timber, it got up to 21,000 people. Now it's down to 16,000-17,000. So you can see up until World War II, Del Norte County wasn't very prosperous until big lumber. A lot of people had trouble paying their taxes. I had a few problems, too.

Semi-legal Anyway
by Norton Steenfott, Eureka

I sold booze during prohibition as a teenager. I was driving taxi when I was 16-years old. Someone would ask me to get a bottle, I'd go get one, just like they'd ask me to get a pound of hamburger at the butcher shop. In those days it was semi-legal anyway. I would charge him his fare, fifty cents, buy the bottle for a dollar and charge him $1.50. A mickey, half pint, would cost about a dollar. We always would try to sell a short mickey if we could, 6-7 ounces instead of 8, or sell him a short pint, 11-13 ounces instead of 16. Everybody violated the law. People sat around and they knew the district attorney and detectives were running their own stills or they had somebody running places for 'em. All they were doing was the same as hijacking. When they went out and busted in a place and got booze, of course the guy got fined but officers took the booze. Everybody else did the same thing. If they found someone had some booze somewhere, they hijacked. What the hell could they do about it? Similar to one night over here, the building on the corner, a bootlegging joint, where the small park is now (2nd Street, 600 block). This fellow who was a special policeman and a door shaker, a beat cop who checked doors at night, and another fellow were going to hijack booze. There was a little breezeway between the buildings. One guy was going to go into the building when suddenly a flashlight turned on and this guy said, "What are you doing there?"

They looked up and here was a sergeant of the police. "What are you guys doing back there?" asked the sergeant.

The special police said, "Someone said there was a bunch of booze hidden underneath here and we were going to go hijack it."

"Oh, go ahead. I'll block the alley and watch out for you." So he watched the alley while they hijacked the guy. They used it for themselves. They'd have to go quick and look for someone to sell it to. That was done all over the county. Gangs did it too. If they found out there was a load coming through, they'd set up a roadblock. Sometimes the gangs just shot the drivers. There was a lot of hijacking on the Redwood Highway.

At the old courthouse occurred an interesting thing. A man was arrested and he had a whole keg of whiskey confiscated. The officials stored it on the floor of the old court house. But he looked through the window and could see where the liquor was stored. Either he or someone for him went under the building, took a brace and bit, drilled up through the floor of the courthouse and through the bottom of the barrel. The whiskey drained into his own container. When his court case came up, it had to be dismissed because of lack of evidence.

The corn liquor was just run through once, and drunk that way. It was good. Pure alcohol had to be diluted. It had to have water added to it or it would burn your throat. One goldamn guy gave me some and it goldamn burnt my throat out. I didn't know it was pure alcohol. We had a dance out at Lolita and we were drinking beer and he came up and said, "You want a shot?"
I said, "Yeah," I had a beer there. He hands me the goddamn bottle. I took a swig of it and holy Jesus, it was pure alcohol. And boy! I got it down and got the beer down fast! Well, not thinking about it when he comes back again said, "Have another one." I did. So when I went to take tickets at the door, that was fine. The people were coming up the ramp. I saw two of them, then three. They'd go this way and that way. Finally a guy came and said. "For Christ's sake, will you take care of this door?"

"I'll be right back," I said. I beat it I went outside to get some fresh air and went around the back of this big auditorium sitting way up on a hill at Lolita and I laid down back there. I woke up when everybody was leaving. They were looking for me and thought I went back into town. Holy gees, I was the sickest bugger there ever was. I had to go to work the next day.
My dad had a hog. My brother was working for a guy making wine. After, they had all the left-over pulp, it had an odor and if they dumped it someplace you could smell the dang thing. My brother said, "I know where you can get rid of it. It would be good for the hog." They dumped it and the goddamn hog devoured the goddamn stuff. Shortly after, the hog was laying on the ground squealing its godamn head off. It couldn't move. It just laid out, sprawled out and squealed and squealed and squealed. It tried to get up and fell back down.

County Didn't Want to Be That Dry
from Richard H. Walton, District Attorney
Humboldt County, Associated Press 1995

In District Attorney Richard H. Walton's investigation of a 70-year-old murder, Walton found that politics might have led a former district attorney, Stephen E. Metzler, to go after the wrong man. Said Walton: "It was Prohibition, and political intrigue was intensified by friction between the 'Wets' and the 'Drys.'

"District Attorney Arthur W. Hill had formed a 'Dry Squad' of police officers to smash illegal liquor operations. Their operations were not popular." Humboldt County did not want to be that dry!

"Later in 1926, Eureka attorney Stephen E. Metzler campaigned for district attorney on a platform of dissolving the Dry Squad and solving the Coyote Flat Murder. Having been elected, he dissolved the dry squad and solved the murder but may have accused the wrong man. Soon, however, he directed

Treehouse, at Piercy, on Redwood Highway, that served beer during prohibition. May have been the first tree "padlocked" after occupants were caught selling moonshine.

the largest bootlegging ring in the county right out of his district attorney's office"[3] [see Metzler, Chapter 26].

✆

Although Customs Service was separated from the prohibition activities except when liquor was smuggled or involved vessels, the Customs Collector at Eureka became immersed in local prohibition affairs in 1926-27. Most victories occurred in cooperation with Humboldt District Attorney Hill, before Metzler became the D. A. Prohibition accomplishments in the Redwood Country according to the Collector: raiding and destroying 28 stills and equipment, destroying 12,000 gallons of mash and 1,500 gallons of moonshine whiskey, collecting $4,600 in fines, giving 74 months of aggregate jail time, seizing nine autos with liquor, selling some cars for the county and receiving $3,000 fines; one boat seized in port with 738 quarts of liquor and fined $380, and another 600 gallons from coastal vessels and eight barrels of liquor from the Northwest Pacific Railroad, paying penalties of $2,100 to the county; some 21,000 gallons of wine either seized or taxes or penalties of $5,624 paid; and scores of bootlegging joints raided by local and federal agents.[4]

After D.A. Hill lost the election, Feds carried out raids but nothing like during 1925-26. An example, toward the end of prohibition, was Harry David Ball who spent two months in the Humboldt County jail for violation of the Jones-Stalker Act, selling alcohol at 1331 "M" Street in Eureka. He pleaded guilty to selling and had the nuisance and possession charges dismissed. Fred Beam, at the same location, had two of his charges dropped and served two months and paid $100 fine for selling. Del Norte County bootleggers did not stop selling. Tom Thompson pleaded guilty for violation of the Jones-Stalker Act in 1930 and spent three months in Del Norte County jail. Records of the Sacramento Docket covering northern California show that 97% of the 500 pages of cases were violations of the National Prohibition Act.[5] The 3% covered offenses like hunting migratory birds out of season. Indeed, the northwestern counties of California were active during the bootlegging years. After Metzler took over as D. A., it seems as if Humboldt County went back to the good-ol' boys style of law enforcement with the coastal towns being wide open, wide open until World War II.

324

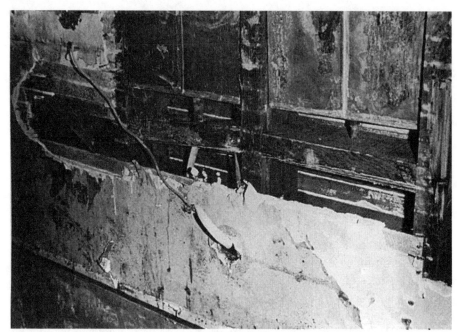

Two secret copper liquor tanks left over from the bootlegging days in a Eureka speakeasy. Copper tubes from the tanks went to a spigot in a wall socket. These were discovered by Norton Steenfott when he remodeled the old building in the late 1970s. A talented Italian carpenter and sheet-metal worker named Richie made most hidden devices like this and false walls and doors for anyone. He never told and was always busy. Photo courtesy of Norton Steenfott and Ann Mendenhall.

Three bottles of liquor purchased about 1932 from rumrunner Slim Kelsey of Crescent City. Three Star Hennessy, Bacardi Rum and French Ernest Irroy Champagne with its straw covering. Allen Lehman and four friends purchased ten cases from Kelsey.

CHAPTER 19

MEAN BULL—NO RESPONSIBILITY FOR INJURIES

Counties north of San Francisco and Sacramento did not support prohibition. Perhaps being so close to major cities that practically nullified the Volstead Act had an impact on these northern counties. Ethnic Italians and other southern and eastern Europeans had wine imbedded in their cultures. And this was wine country. Thousands made their legal 200 gallons of wine, and hundreds of these could not refrain from making a bit more or selling some of their home stash. Thousands of families made their living in the wineries and vineyards, directly or indirectly. They could not believe a country as great as the United States could make a law that selling or transporting wine was illegal. The Volstead concession to ethnic people who had wine as part of their culture softened the jolt of prohibition. But this concession led to loopholes and a common disregard for the law. Panic occurred as prohibition set in. Wineries closed, vineyardists plowed up vines, table grapes replaced wine grapes. But resilience and cleverness abounded as people found ways to survive their economic stresses. Wine and brandy from these counties found their way to anybody who wanted them, including hundreds of thousands of gallons ending up in Sacramento and San Francisco. With the advent of better roads and cheaper cars, resorts and tourist centers capitalized on city dwellers who escaped to vacation areas where county sheriffs and local constables had poor eyesight. Music, dances, great climate and hot springs allowed travelers to relax with copious quantities of liquid refreshments. The area not only survived prohibition but profited from it.

Very Mean Bull— No Trespassing

A mammoth distillery hidden away among the hills near Point Reyes about four miles from Tomales Bay did not elude detection by the dry squad. Federal raiders stated the plant had $200,000 worth of equipment and during the three years it was believed to be operating it made a profit in excess of $2,000,000 for the owners. Concealed from prying eyes by a thick forest, piping water from a mountain spring five miles away and guarded by a rifleman in a lookout tower, the distillery represented the most elaborate operation found in northern California in months.

Acting on a tip, prohibition agents George Neary, Tom O'Callahan and Harry Brickell searched the woods of Marin for hours until they came upon the sign: "Very Mean Bull—No Trespassing—Not Responsible for Injuries." The agents rushed the place, driving through the place for about a mile before coming to the distillery building. Here they arrested R. Lucchesi, owner of the farm about 1/8 mile down hill from the distillery.[1]

326

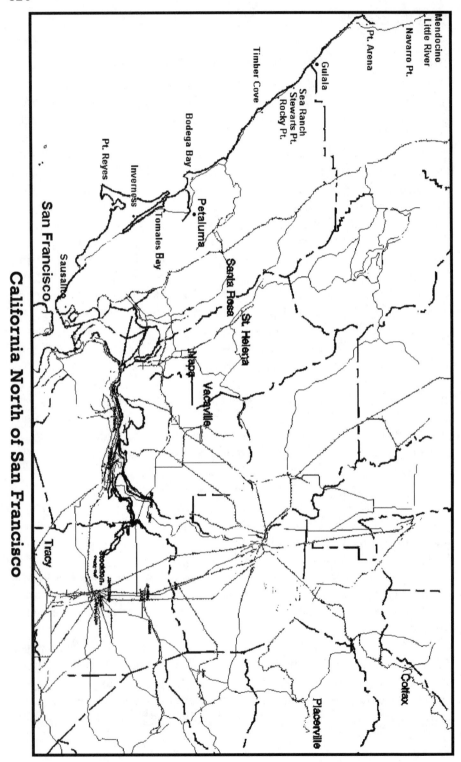

California North of San Francisco

Mendocino
Little River
Navarro Pt.
Pt. Arena
Gualala
Timber Cove
Sea Ranch
Stewarts Pt.
Rocky Pt.
Bodega Bay
Pt. Reyes
Inverness
Tomales Bay
Petaluma
Santa Rosa
St. Helena
Napa
Vacaville
San Francisco
Sausalito
Stockton
Tracy
Colfax
Placerville

✍

From the 1st Floor of the Donovan Building, Santa Rosa, C. C. Donovan, owner of C. C. Donovan Choices Hops, voiced the early concerns of central Californians. In March 1922, he predicted the downfall of the Republican Party if the party continued to support the Anti-Saloon League. In May he repeated his foreboding if the Republicans did not come out "flat footed" for 2 ¾ % beer "to relieve discontent and taxation."

He predicted defeat in the 1924 election. Wayne B. Wheeler had the government "hog-tied." An Illinois congressmen lost recently and so did Senator New. "Millions of us good old black Republicans who supported the administration are going to throw a monkey wrench into the workings of the Republican Party and the Anti-Saloon League. We are going to give the administration the same jolt that New got." Enforcement would take millions of dollars and a country of detectives, he said, and signed the threat "Respectfully yours."

The curt answer came on May 22, 1922, from Mabel Walker Willebrandt, Asst. Attorney General, "where you make certain predictions for the Republican Party, has been noted by the Attorney General."[2]

"...the woods are full of stills"

A letter from Robert A. Barker, a realtor from Berkeley and Brown's Valley, Yuba County, wrote to the Department of Justice in May 1923 about the woods around Brown's Valley being full of stills and negative people "that grow up on the stuff." A "neighbour" has fallen under the spell of "the Bootlegger and she is becoming notorious for drunken spells—an object of scorn and derision."[3]

They make it in the woods and peddle it around town in Marysville. "The Greeks are to be cleaned up; but the White folks will not be interfered with at all." "The authorities...are no good," since they raid the stills of the foreign Greeks, but not the stills or the selling of the white folks.

"Family Combine"—Barker called the old families who are related to every one else, including the officials and "they stand together." "Consequently, if any of their connections are under suspicion of Bootlegging or other delinquencies, it is always hushed up—Don't you know that the accused is a sister, a daughter, a widow of some Official and must not be touched."

In protecting their relatives, they dare not be too hard on others. Thus the decision to clean up the Greeks. Barker didn't know what to do, but said "[it]...does not need a Sherlock Holmes...but needs a person to get acquainted, look for land to buy to grow figs Kadota Figs! "They will open their hearts to a prospective Buyer."

"These Bootleggers have nothing but contempt for the law and the Constitution. Just an unscrupulous desire to make money regardless of man or maid or devil. They ought to be CRUSHED."

"Looking Back on Days of Prohibition"
by Eugene L. Gray, *Sutter County Historical Society News Bulletin,*

The sign at Cliff House Bar read "Last Chance" or "First Chance," depending on which side of the Feather River one was on. Yuba City was more law abiding with officials taking the law seriously.[4] Only a few places in Sutter County could one buy bootleg whiskey: Cotton Club was one, with palms and lush greenery, where one could dance and drink with discretion. On the other side of the river, Marysville, less discrimination was needed as one could "drink almost any place." One drinking place was located across from the police station. The Chief said, he thought there was a leak: when he got there the booze was gone. Some bartenders kept it in a pitcher so it could be dumped easily. On July 6, 1921, "Officer Allread, with the spryness of a cat, sprang over the bar and seized the evidence...." Even in the main channel of the Feather River, bootlegging went on. "Blind Pigger is again in the hands of the Law. W. H. Prather must again answer charges of selling liquor from his houseboat." The blind pigger at Knight's Landing and at Sutter City, Prather, claimed the Feather River was a navigable river, so the U. S. had jurisdiction, not the justice of peace. Because of the open violations of the law, once the county grand jury called the council and chief of police before it." Marysville's "Little Volstead passed 814 to 646 in 1922. But that did not mean too much.[4]

Be Careful, Else It Will Become Wine
You Wouldn't Want That, Would You?

Instructions on Grape Bricks, blocks of dehydrated wine grapes, told how to keep from making wine. Follow these instructions so grape juice from the grape bricks won't turn into wine. Now who would want to risk taking reconstituted grape juice and turning it into wine?

To make "Non-Alcoholic, Unfermented Grape Juice, (1) dissolve one grape brick into 3/4 gallons of warm water in an earthenware dish or crock, never using metal containers or iron utensils. For best results always make at least five gallons of grape juice." Then cleverly, Vino Sano Co., makers of Grape Bricks, explained to the reader: "If the juice is not intended to be consumed within five days, it will gradually turn to wine." [What a waste of good grape juice that would be!] The brochure further stated that to prevent fermentation, "Add 1/10% of Benzoate of Soda." (2) Let juice stand for five or six days, stirring at least once a day. Strain through cotton or linen cloth and place back in jug or keg. (3) Close jug to prevent impurities, using Vino Sano Glass Tube Cork or a cork with a "V" cut into it to allow the gases to escape. (4)

Sugar should be added for the consumer's taste: For port, sherry, tokay and malaga or all sweet types use 1½ - 2 pounds per gallon; for dryer "types," like rhine, champagne, burgundy, use ¾ - 1 pound of preferably corn-sugar. Using white cane sugar, boil it for five minutes and skim off the top. (5) To hasten clarification which will finish in three to four weeks, stir or shake the contents occasionally. Then the directions stated: "If BENZOATE of soda was not added in time, the liquid may now be in fermentation, and turn to wine."[5]

Fermentation, the manufacturers continued, is a natural process, by which yeast germs, which are everywhere in the air, convert two parts sugar to one part alcohol and one part carbonic gas. Of course, the added sugar increased the alcohol content.

In a further attempt to satisfy the law on how righteous the company was, it announced other ways to stop fermentation: Keep liquid in the refrigerator; sterilize by boiling before bottling; avoid using yeast.

These recipes were condensed from the U. S. Government publication on how to make grape juice for home use, the company stated. "We do not encourage the making of wines or other intoxicating beverages. If the beverage is consumed there is no need of sterilization. "It might be illegal to teach anyone how to make wine. We are instructing our consumers how they can prevent their fruit-juices from turning to wine. But after all, nobody can actually make wine. All a person can do is make fruit-juice and God, or Nature, or whatever we want to call it, makes either wine or vinegar out of it without our assistance at all, by the law of fermentation."

This company stressed how wine was healthy. More people lived to be over one hundred years old in unsanitary but wine-drinking countries like Bulgaria and "Servia," France and Spain than in the U. S. which only had three centenarians per million population, whereas Bulgaria has 400 per million, Servia 200, Spain 20 and France 5. Vino Sano praised itself for helping farmers sell the surplus grapes, and for doing Americans a favor by producing inexpensive and easily transported wine bricks.

The brochure ended with "... we condemn anything in excess...however to legislate what people should eat or drink in their homes is obnoxious to thinking people, which we have to admit, are rather in the minority of a people, which therefore is governed by the unthinking, ignorant majority."

The Wineries
AP, January 6, 1994, *The Times Herald Record*[6]

Foppiano Vineyards dumped 150,000 gallons of old wine out in the creek and road ? in 1926, under the watchful eye of two prohibition agents. The town's people of Healdsburg caught whatever they could in any containers they had.

The wine industry plunged from 51 million gallons in 1918 to three million in 1925. California lost hundreds of wineries, from 694 in 1922 to less than 200 by the end of prohibition.   Louis P. Martini of the Martini Winery said most vine grapes were uprooted and planted with a thicker-skinned grape, one that would ship better.

Thomas Pinney, Pomona College, said the grape-growing acreage doubled from 1920 to 1925 because of shipping grapes and the concentrated grape juice. Grape prices went up from $8 a ton to as high as $200—then in the later 1920s the market collapsed.

Aftermath of prohibition affected the wine industries. Since people were not used to drinking wine, they went for fortified dessert wines—a bigger jolt of alcohol "without a lot of quality."

Where Did All the Wine Go?

In bonded warehouses and bonded wineries in the United States, government records showed an inventory of 23,138,754 gallons of wine on July 1 of fiscal year 1929.[7]

Wineries produced 3,409,943 gallons of natural wine, ameliorated and fortified wine that year. Therefore the government had 26,548,698 gallons of wine to account for, 26.5 million gallons, mostly stored in the Golden State.

USE	AMT. IN GALLONS
Wine legally withdrawn and tax paid	2,513,333
Exported Wine	25,214
Manufacture of De-alcoholized Wine	2,100
For Distilling Material	1,801,141
For Manufacture of Vinegar	69,758
Used in Manufacturing of Champagne or Artificially Carbonated Wine	24,741
Total Legally Withdrawn	4,435,288

The losses "in storage" were 955,856 gallons—almost one million gallons in 1929! Some loss was wine spoilage, turning bad or turning into vinegar, breakage and accidents. Losses in transit (hijacking, pilfering, stolen, bookkeeping) were 5,092 gallons.

At the bottom of the report was a note: *Difference of 16,182 gallons between debit and credit items is due to excesses ascertained by inventory, quantities returned to bonded premises, differences in quantities in transit first and last of year.*

These were legal inventories, subject, of course, to much manipulation and creative bookkeeping: Illicit wine never inventoried, wine siphoned out of barrels and then filled with water again, barrels hidden behind false wall; grapes diverted to small sheds to be processed, and grapes delivered to private contractors to make wine. None of this counts the 200 gallons of wine any family could make legally or the extra couple hundred gallons made illegally. Millions of gallons of wine selling for $1 to $3 per gallon created a huge cash-flow in this wine country.

A Drop in the Wine Bucket

An example of wine filtered off, or a better word, "flowed," from legal wineries is Federal Case # 5005, where Guiseppe Sodini had 2,564 gallons of white wine in a small frame-structure barn, 30' by 30', located within 30 feet from Bonded Winery, No. 316, Healdsburg.

One vat contained 2,426 gallons, another puncheon, 140 gallons. Agent H. Z. Drew arrested Sodini who pleaded guilty to possession. The Federal District Court dropped other charges and only fined him $100.[8]

Supervising Agent in San Francisco and his staff had sought the source of large quantities of vinous liquors reported to have been making nightly deliveries into San Francisco. Deputies stationed on the highway by Santa Rosa stopped three suspicious trucks, two of which were seized and the one that fled away at full speed was caught two miles later. The largest truck carried seventeen 50-gallon barrels, and the two smaller trucks contained six barrels each. One truck wore a disguise of furniture and bedding on top of the casks. The $5,000 value would have been increased in San Francisco as this wine was intended to be distilled into brandy.

As a result of investigations, agents seized R. Martini Winery near Healdsburg, confiscating the entire stock, almost $1,000,000 worth in the winery and other secreted spots around Santa Rosa. Seven San Franciscans, caught in the net, were O. Sourentini, 1409 Greenwich Street, Vincent Conanti, 1120 Lombard Street, John del Pratto and E . Morello, both of 1745 Chestnut, Mario Lensini, 75 Van de Walter Street, P. Masoni, 533 Greenwich and Antonio Boldi, 837 Union Street. The raid did not catch the owners of the winery.

Those in the raiding party were Deputy Internal Revenue Collector Mark Chamberlin, J. H. Crawford, Deputy Sheriff Marvin Robinson of Sonoma County and Agent George W. Poultney.[9]

"Stolen" Wine
as told by Norton Steenfott, Eureka

Down in Sonoma County you had your federal warehouses where confiscated wine was stored. If you made a connection you could buy the wine for 10 ¢ a gallon. They would leave a door open for you. There would be a certain time you could get that wine. You had to buy at least 100 gallons but you could buy 500 or 1,000 gallons. The door would be unlocked, nobody around. You'd drive in, load up and take off. You had twelve hours. Then they reported that the place had been broken into.

Strange Deaths

by Clarence Magistretti, from "Funny Old World"

Mr. and Mrs. Pete Pelacio, living on the Scillacci Ranch, near Point Reyes, met strange deaths. Pete Pelacio moseyed out to a shed to check on the wine vat and fell in. A bit later Mrs. Pelacio wondered what had become of him. She too fell in. Both were found drowned. [Assumption is they were making much more than the 200 gallons the law allowed.][10]

Intoxicating Children Make Marin Clean Up

Not too far from the Presbyterian Seminary in quiet San Anselmo, teenagers were having a wild house party, but it was obvious they were running out of intoxicants. Eighteen-year-old Joe Willis, not realizing he already had too much and did not need any more, volunteered to drive to San Rafael to obtain reinforcements. Willis and three other youths made it to San Rafael but did not make it past Antone Lucchini's house. He tried to go through it or around it but did neither. He crashed into it.

Information from the young folks led to the arrest of Vincent Garratti [Garatti?], who later pleaded guilty to violating the Wright Act and fined $250 by Justice Herbert de la Montanya. Garatti was the father of Eleanor Garatti, the internationally known swimming champion. Probation Officer Thomas O'Connor and District Attorney Henry Greer said they had already planned to clean up sources of liquor for youngsters as well as go after juvenile offenders themselves. Said O'Connor: "Primarily we intend to make it hard for all minors to get drinks. We are also going after a gang of 'sheiks' who have been making their rendezvous within the county and making a practice of securing liquor, then, in companionship of girls 15 and 16 years of age, holding wild house parties in secluded houses."[11]

Rum Agents "Take" Town in Army Style

Fifteen officers in five cars surround and close in on places in San Rafael before alarm is sounded. At zero hour 8:30 Colonel Sam I. Johnson led agents Cal Ahein and Harold Charlton to 16 places, including Hotel Tamalpais, making 14 arrests. Hundreds of gallons of assorted whiskey, gin and wine were confiscated before the townspeople were aware a raid was taking place. At Hotel Tamalpais, Johnson himself led the charge and found a "fully-equipped and ultra-Bohemian wine cellar. A wild party was in progress, according to agents, many of the guests being young girls and men. The walls of the cellar were covered with caricatures and the rough topped tables were carved full of initials." The agents battered down the barred door and arrested Frank Uvaldi, said to be the bartender. Joe Ghirighelle, owner of the place, escaped out a back entrance.[12]

Two other hotels, the Terminal at Third and Tamalpais streets and the Carmel at 318 B Street, fell victim to the onslaught. At the former, agents arrested Louis Macchi and would file on the owners, E. Calette and Joe Bianchi, and confiscated a large quantity of jackass brandy. At the Carmel, agents arrested Ernest Bracckia and Pete Ostaggi. Vincent Garratti [Garatti] was arrested at 324 Second Street. In a pool hall at 327 B Street, raiders found a drunken brawl in progress. They took Sarah and Giuseppe Rossi, proprietors, into custody. At 400 B Street Ben Barbara was taken into custody and Mrs. Ethel Barbara was cited. Others arrested were as follows: A. H. Schmidt 436 B, Charles Vachaboski, Sebastiano Falco 434 B, Herman Ferraio 321 B, Felix Canade 224 B, and Guy Ferro? and F. Thomasini at a news stand.

Atop Mt. Tamalpais

What could be greater than to celebrate New Years at the Tamalpais Tavern on top of Marin's impressive peak. The problem was the party was raided by agents, led by Joe Campanoli and William Glynn. The bust came when most celebrants were dancing. Of course when the music stopped and doors were blocked, 200 dancers refused to go back to their tables under which were stashes of liquor.

Another problem was the club was filled with high school students from San Francisco, from secret fraternities of at least two high schools. Names were taken for future reference and investigations were to continue. It was against state law for high schools to have fraternities. Citations were issued to Mr. and Mrs. R. Prierd [?] of the Tavern and William Sell Jr., said to be connected with the Mt. Tamalpais railway upon which the booze was shipped up the mountain, and Miss Dorothy Perkins one of the participants at 428 Fourth Street [S.F.?]. The Feds planned to ascertain who gave the party and who supplied the liquor.[13]

B Street Raid (one of many)

A surprise raid on B Street, San Rafael, in December 1925, netted hotel keepers, bootblacks, barbers, and soft drink venders and quick justice disposed of the violators in the federal court in San Francisco.

Sebastian Falso [Falco, see below], a bootblack, received five months and $500. Falco, having a wife and four children, asked to be sentenced to the county jail in San Rafael, but the jail had too many federal prisoners already. Poor A. Schmidt, the barber who was just helping two strangers on a cold morning and who were going to Santa Rosa and wanted to know if Schmidt had something to warm them up. He only had his personal stuff but gave them a bottle. The strangers left $1.50 on the table as they left. He was just being neighborly "and out of the kindness of his heart...pulled out a bottle that did not contain bay rum." His attorney pleaded that he had an aged wife and the judge let him off with a $100 fine which Schmidt paid. The judge gave Felix Canopi six months and $500, Frank Ubaldi three months, Joe Ghingelli [Ghinghelli?] six months, and E. Netopanavoso dismissed because he was not at the location when liquor was sold. Others serving jail time were Guiseppi Rossi, Louis Milani, Fred Carrell and Ed Quinn.[14]

Falco [Falso] served six days of his six months and had yet to pay the $500 fine, when his wife and four children, ages 4-11, pleaded to Judge Partridge to release Falco for hardship reasons and so "Santa Claus can come to our home." Partridge released him and gave each of the children a $5 bill. Within two weeks he was brought before Commissioner Hayden on charges of transporting liquor from Sausalito to San Francisco. Agents Henry Sirard was just looking around in the ferry and found liquor in the car Falco was riding in and went up to the cigar stand upstairs, arresting Falco and Bochoboski. In court this time Falco showed that it was not his liquor and he was just riding into San Francisco to show Judge Partridge he was not a wealthy man. Bochoboski promised Falco's daughter a new hat if she just stayed in the car until they came back. The judge believed the wine was not his and released him. He won again in the judicial system of the State of California. The loser was Bochoboski and also the people who were to receive the gallons of wine for that New Year's Eve.[15]

Intolerable San Rafael

San Rafael continued with so much bootlegging that in 1930, William Walker, local prohibition administrator, threatened the local police force that if it did not clean up the intolerable conditions in San Rafael and if Walker received more complaints, he would station a prohibition headquarters in San Rafael. In one raid the Feds apprehended six bootleggers and distributors, and seized several truckloads of liquor. Twenty agents separated in squads and pounced on suspected places at one time.

Arrested and arraigned in a night session of the court were Charles Ghiringhelli, Henry Bechtold, Lois Machhl [Macnhl?], Phillip [—ddiso?], J. W. Tetford and C. Raider. Ghiringhelli, Bechtold and Tetford pleaded guilty and were released after paying $350 each. Raider's guilty plea cost him $500. The other two posted bail.[16]

On a ranch just seven miles west of San Rafael, Prohibition Administrator E. H. Bohner broke up a modern still site so cleverly hidden that one could walk within 75 feet before seeing it. This illicit still was a short distance from the plant of American Commercial Alcohol Corporation of California, the second largest commercial distillery in America.

With an 1,800-gallon still capacity, the operation used steam. Much equipment and liquor was destroyed. Those captured were Fred Clifford, Earl Murphy, Jack Davis, Martin Gruver, Thomas Russell, Allen Turner and William Andrews. Two months before these men were involved with another raided still in Petaluma. As always officials reported that the capture of this gang would break up the liquor ring in Marin County.[17]

With Tears in Their Eyes

Three husky inmates of Marin County jail had to do forced labor. They had to empty 700 gallons of sundry liquors, held in the county wine cellars which the sheriff had given orders to clean out. They dumped the liquor in the

The front of a blind pig or speakeasy in Sausalito. The back of this building faced the bay, had a garden, and had a two-way mirror to allow the owner to see if prohibition agents, prohis, were coming from patrol boats. Photo courtesy of Ralph "Swede" Pedersen.

View of Sausalito from the bay in the early 1900s, where "The only place you can't get liquor is the church." Photo courtesy of Ralph "Swede" Pedersen.

Confiscated alcohol being dumped from Muni Dock at old Sausalito Firehouse in the early 1930s. The dock is now the public pier next to Ondine and Trident Restaurant. L-R. Frank Mancelo, Charles Loriana, Judge W. Helmore, Councilman Manuel Ignacio, Jim McGown (later police chief), Chief of Police Manuel Menotti, Gladys and Francis Inkick. Photo may have been staged for show rather than dumping real alcohol—so say some old timers. Photo courtesy of Swede Pedersen.

creek. Tears of anguish must have run down their cheeks as the creek runneth over with liquor. The inmates were in jail for rumrunning.[18]

Double Envelopment

Using tactics from the World War, prohibition agents left their San Francisco offices for the annual 49ers Days in Sacramento in 1922, using a double envelopment on the route to the capital, sweeping in their paths numerous resorts and soft drink parlors. One group taking the northern route illustrated the type of illegal activities occurring north of San Francisco Bay, especially the resort area around Calistoga Hot Springs.

This squad headed for the "diggins" in Sacramento by going through Marin and Sonoma counties. They no sooner crossed the ferry, then hit a Sausalito place, operated by Ben Young and J. W. Scott, then raided Parente's Tavern, run by Louis Parente in El Verano. His place had been a toast among highway travelers for a generation, according to the *San Francisco Examiner* of May 25, 1922. Parente and his liquor were taken into custody. Ed Peters' place at Boyes Springs, known as Carlhnet's (?) French Resort; Clement's Hotel and Inn at Fetter's Springs and Mike's Inn on the Petaluma Highway were enveloped in rapid succession, arresting the three proprietors, Edward Peters, C. H. Clements and Michael Lawrence. The northern sortie through Marin and Sonoma netted five raids and six arrests.

The southern swing took the long way to Sacramento through San Jose with the following victories: Monterey Road Home, Dave and Maud Holt; 28-30 Fountain Street, San Jose, J. L. Chargin; 26 Fountain, Dan Haley and J. L. Perry; 77 Post Street, San Jose, Oeite Maggiore and Ed Wood; 65 West Santa Clara Street, San Jose, Louis Dossoo and S. ?. Zaro; 41 North Market Street, G. Flasch, A. Jassento [Jassente?] and Joe Bauman. After reports and evidence were sent to San Francisco, the squad headed for the 49er Days.[19]

If You Had Enough Nerve
as told by H. A. Jones, Carmel Valley

When the author was in Carmel Valley looking for information on bootlegging, someone suggested he go into this quaint little bar in town and ask for an old timer named Jones. When his eyes adjusted to the darkness inside the bar and the bartender pointed to Jones, the author approached Jones.

"I'd like to talk to you about bootlegging and rumrunning," I said.

Without hesitation, he responded, "Why? Do you have a warrant for my arrest?"

The following is Jones' story.

At Wright's Beach on the Russian River in Petaluma, one who wanted a family supply, or a liquor supply for resale, purchased excellent Italian grappa for six dollars a gallon for five gallons or more. Cheaper wine could be obtained for 65¢-75¢ per gallon. Stills were in the hills and ranches of Marin County.

For those who wished to make their own wine, excellent wine grapes could be purchased from the Dry Creek company for $125 a ton, with 21-22% sugar content.

At a winery in St. Helena one could help his anemia problems by buying Nervine, a medicinal wine made from port wine and iron herb. "If you had enough nerve you could drink Nervine. It wasn't bad if you had nothing else."

The popular drinks of the day served in the good speakeasies like the Four Winds in San Francisco were Golden Fizz and Silver Fizz, both made of gin.

I used to go to the Bar None bars, the bars that would bar none [see also Jones, Chapter 20].

∅

In the little towns in north central California, over the 14 years of prohibition, hundreds of bootleggers sold liquor, scores of moonshiners supplied the small towns with homebrew and "shine." Though most of these men were not caught, several hundred were arrested. Of these, many were not brought to trial, much less convicted. Perhaps a hundred or so had their day in the U. S. District Court. Prohibition agents like Elmer C. Pieper, John M. Burt, M. J. Buckley, D. E. Dawe, A. W. Morgue, H. Z. Drew, and N. D. Austin had to be sure, had to catch the bootlegger selling or possessing alcohol, being careful to have specific evidence, legally obtained evidence with proper search warrants.

The following cases are but a few brought before the U. S. District Court. At Healdsburg: After investigation, four prohibition agents raided 327 West Street, where agents made an arrest for possessing and selling; 441 East Street where they caught Agnes Buchignani for possessing 9 ½ gallons of red wine and 1/5 gallon of white wine. After pleading guilty, she only received a fine of $25. H. Z Drew caught Frank A. Buffi with a variety of whisky, gin, rum, beer, white wine, red wine in "The Inn." He pleaded guilty to a nuisance. Agents Austin and Burt arrested Fred Dinucci in the American Hotel, corner of East and Mason streets. Dinucci's possession of whisky, beer and wine cost him $250 when he pleaded guilty to nuisance. Agent Morgue caught Bret Dressen (alias Bert Dressere), at the Riverside Villa, east end of Mason Street, with small amounts of gin, whiskey and beer, making him $200 poorer. At Petuluma: At # 4 Washington Street (# 4998) Sidney Lehman pleaded guilty of a nuisance. A couple blocks east on Washington Street, the Feds caught Charlie Bianchi at the Yosemite Hotel with "3 bottles more or less of whiskey and wine." The court released him after he pleaded guilty to a nuisance and possession and paid his $250 fine.[20]

The counties north of San Francisco and Sacramento continued violating liquor laws as most counties did. They had their bootleggers, rumrunners and vintners that skirted the law and helped supply thirsty Californians with alcohol all during prohibition. Readers will soon see how these quiet counties had ties with organized crime in northern California.

CHAPTER 20

MACHINE GUNS TO FRISCO: BABY FACE NELSON AND ORGANIZED CRIME

On a December morning, at the Agricultural Inspection Station at Daggett on U. S. Hwy. 66, an inspector asked a truck driver what was in the back of his big canvas-covered truck.

"Supplies for the Firestone Tire Company in Los Angeles," answered the husky driver.

The inspector went to the back of the truck, untied the flap on the canvas covering the back, pulled it open, then gazed at two rough-looking men sitting on top of shiny new five-gallon cans—each man holding a Thompson submachine gun.

The inspector nodded, closed the flap, tied it securely and walked back up to the driver: "Looks like everything is fine."

The inspector kept one eye closed and was doubly rewarded the next week when a mysterious traveler left a package for Inspector Number 4. It contained four bottles of Canadian whiskey. The inspectors at Daggett and Yermo had a more joyous holiday that year.

In the bootlegging years, California had gangs—hundreds of them. Each gang was organized, of course, to various degrees—some employing a few men, other gangs dozens. Unlike in Chicago with Alfonse Capone, there was no great war for absolute control of the distribution of beer or for territories. The gangs of rumrunners bought from the Canadian exporters, making payment deposits to Canadian accounts in California banks. Anyone could buy. Indeed speedboats waited their turn in line by the mother ship along with fishing boats representing individuals and small gangs.

The stories of the rum war, the border war and the race to the city illustrated surface organizations of the prohibition underworld. Contacting the Canadian representatives, paying for the consignment, obtaining codes, contracting boats to meet the mother ships at key times and places, obtaining landing crews to unload the boats and load cars and trucks, arranging for storage depots and access through private ranches to and from the beach, hiring vehicles and escort cars to run the booze to the cities; and within the city having warehouses and distributing to clients—all show organization. Big gangs had a team of lawyers. In 1925-6 Parente-Stittmatter gang had $20,000 available bond money to help arrested members. And they had payoff men to encourage key people to look the other way: local sheriff, beat cop, judge, Coast Guard official or prohibition agent or many of these.

Then entered the hijackers. History does not leave good records of this activity. Hijacking was seldom reported. It was underworld business that stayed in the underworld. Hijackers were small groups of men who could save time and money by hijacking goods on the beach, on the highways or at the city warehouses.

Rumrunners protected themselves by adding hired gunmen, and their favorite weapon—the Thompson submachine-gun, a 45-caliber automatic, invented in the 1920s just in time for the late bootlegging days. Convoys, follow-up cars, shotgun riders all helped rumrunners protect themselves from prohibition agents and hijackers.

Hot Gangs Cool Off in Northern California
as told by Norton Steenfott, Eureka

Baby Face Nelson was here in Eureka. When he was in Eureka, in the town, he stayed in a house, gone now, but it was in the alley right on D Street between 3rd and 4th. When he first came into town he hid out on Freeze Avenue, a big house that sat way back. From there he was taken out to the mountains to an old ranch, him and his wife, and she had a little baby. Nelson was cooling off out there [hiding out]. He laid up there for awhile.

When he was going to pull out of the Eureka area, he and his wife hid one night in a whorehouse on D Street. They were going out of town. They had the car parked in the alley. His wife went up town to get something. When she came back one of the policemen saw her. Well, this guy happened to be always after the women. He would always see a good-looking woman and talk to her.

He had seen her going to this whorehouse and right away quick he figured a new girl had come into town. Just as she came into the alley he came around and stopped her. He asked her who she was and what she was doing working in the place.

"No, I'm just coming through and stopped in town to visit a friend of mine and going out," Nelson's wife said.

So he gave her a big line of how if she plans to work, go to the police department, they'd sign her in.

All this time Baby Face Nelson watched from the upstairs window, his machine gun at hand. If there had been a false move, the policeman could have had it right there because Nelson would have figured they had been spotted.

From there he went to Sausalito about 1933. A fellow was telling me there—he didn't know who he was since he had some phony name. He used to come play cards every night. He was a nice fellow; everybody liked him, got along with everyone. He was there about two-three weeks when someone came up and said he was wanted on the phone. He went to the phone, talked for a few minutes, went right out the door and they never saw him again. Within days the

FBI was all over the place and they were looking for this guy—showed the picture. It was Baby Face Nelson. He was killed in the Midwest right after that.

He was involved in everything, rumrunning included. Any of those guys, wherever they could make a buck, they would make it.

There was an incident one night here: A car pulled into a service station right across the street from the county jail in Eureka. Men were all sitting in the car; they got the gas and they were doing something else. The attendant slipped in and called the sheriff's office saying there was a suspicious looking bunch, to check them out. Then he goes back, puts in some oil.

Then a deputy sheriff came over, asked the guys to come over to the jail.

They no sooner got over to the county jail then the phone rang and they answered the phone. "This is the FBI. Turn those people loose: we are watching them. Turn them loose, do not do any more."

"Oh, you fellows look all right; you can go," said the deputy after a few minutes.

The FBI had been following them all over the United States. There were two bunches that the FBI was following. They were to have a meeting but the agents didn't know where the meeting was. The law was following this bunch to find the rest of the gang. They were involved in something in the east and split up and were supposed to meet and divide some money or something. They could pick these men up but the others would fly the coop.

A number of eastern gang members came out to San Francisco to cool off. The Marino family in San Francisco would send them out to different spots. Eureka was one location chosen to hide them out. They had it worked out with different people. They'd stay for a month or two on a ranch to cool off.

The Marino gang was called the "Tar Baby Family" in North Beach in San Francisco. They were pretty black Italians, nicknamed Tar Baby. They had hangouts here in California and speakeasies. They had connections to hide people back east too.

Baby Face Nelson
as told by G. William Puccinelli, San Mateo

Baby Face Nelson was a friend of the rumrunners and hired on to protect them from the hijackers. Tough kid. Worked for Johnny Mareno. [Marino?]

Al Capone tried to come into San Francisco to try to take some control, but the San Francisco police chief met him at Mills Field, now present-day San Francisco Airport. When he got off the plane he was told he wasn't wanted in San Franciso. He left. But he did have some control over the labels [labels that go on bottles] in San Francisco.

[Since Pucci was a land shark, delivering booze from the shore to his clients in the city, he would know much of what was happening in the under-

"BABY FACE NELSON"
ALIAS OF LESTER J. GILLIS

- MEMBER OF DILLINGER GANG.

- KILLER AND BANK ROBBER IN MIDWEST.

- DURING HIS CRIMINAL CAREER NELSON KILLED 3 FBI AGENTS.

- NELSON WAS KILLED IN A GUN BATTLE WITH FBI AGENTS ON NOVEMBER 27, 1934, AT BARRINGTON, ILLINOIS.

Taken from wanted circular for Lester J. Gillis, alias George Nelson and Baby Face Nelson, 1934. Gillis hid out in Sausalito, Crescent City, Eureka, Sonoma County and western Nevada in 1932 and 1934. In 1932 he and Johnny Paul Chase of Sausalito helped the Moreno gang smuggle liquor into California. See also Chapter 30.

world. Someone else said Capone tried to come into Los Angeles and was told by officials he was not wanted.]

Excerpts from Ten Thousand Public Enemies
by Courtney Ryley Cooper
Note: This excerpt must be taken with a grain of salt as this reflects romantic stories of the 1930s. [see also Nelson, Chapter 30]

Later, whether he liked it or not Dillinger was forced through fear to bow to Baby Face Nelson.

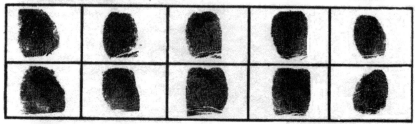

IDENTIFICATION ORDER NO. 1223
April 25, 1934.

DIVISION OF INVESTIGATION
U. S. DEPARTMENT OF JUSTICE
WASHINGTON, D. C.

Fingerprint Classification
18 5 Ra 16
19 Wa

WANTED

LESTER M. GILLIS, with aliases GEORGE NELSON, BABY FACE NELSON,
ALEX GILLIS, LESTER GILES; "BIG GEORGE" NELSON, "JIMMIE".

MURDER

DESCRIPTION

Age, 25 years
Height, 5 feet 4¾ inches
Weight, 133 pounds
Build, medium
Eyes, yellow and grey slate
Hair, light chestnut
Complexion, light
Occupation, oiler

RELATIVES:

Mrs. Mary Gillis, mother,
5516 South Marshfield St.,
Chicago, Ill.
Mrs. Helen Gillis, alias
Mrs. Helen Nelson, wife,
148 North Mayfield,
Chicago, Ill.
Mrs. Juliette Fitzsimmons, sister
5516 South Marshfield St.,
Chicago, Ill.

Photograph taken July 17, 1933.

George Nelson

CRIMINAL RECORD

As George Nelson, #5437, arrested
Police Department, Chicago,
Illinois, January 15, 1931;
charge, robbery; sentence,
1 year to life;
As George Nelson, #5437, received
State Penitentiary, Joliet,
Illinois, July 17, 1931; crime,
robbery; sentence, 1 year to
life; escaped February 17, 1932.

Lester M. Gillis is wanted for the murder of W. Carter Baum, Special Agent, Division of Investigation, U. S. Department of Justice, near Rhinelander, Wisconsin, on April 22, 1934.

Law enforcement agencies kindly transmit any additional information or criminal record to the nearest office of the Division of Investigation, U. S. Department of Justice.

If apprehended, please notify the Director, Division of Investigation, U. S. Department of Justice, Washington, D. C., or the Special Agent in Charge of the office of the Division of Investigation listed on the back hereof which is nearest your city.

(over)   Issued by: J. EDGAR HOOVER, DIRECTOR.

Years ago [from 1933], a tough boastful, cruel little boy played around the packing-house district of Chicago. In every game, he wanted to be the crook, and his extreme joy came when he could play at shooting cops. His name was Lester Gillis. It was not long before the police were warning him that he was under suspicion for petty thefts in the neighborhood.

This only made the boy more boastful. He joined a crowd of toughs that went for stealing automobiles, driving them for a few hours and abandoning them. About this time Lester Gillis achieved two things. He gained the name Baby Face and he became girl crazy. Whereupon he began selling what he stole, that he might gain the reputation of being a free spender. He was caught and sentenced to the St. Charles School for Boys.

From there he was paroled, a clemency for which he was twice returned on charges of violation. At last, free from reformatory, he got a job as a truck driver, which he quit to become a gunman. He now became George (Baby Face) Nelson. His first job was the robbery of a bank at Spring Grove, Illinois, followed by another at Hillside and still a third at Itaska, both cities in Illinois.

For the Hillside robbery he was sentenced to from one year to life, and while in Joliet Penitentiary he failed in an attempt to escape. That was about 1931. A year later he was taken to Itaska for trial and was sentenced to from one to twenty years. On the way back to prison he got away and was not retaken.

Shortly after this Nelson went west, where he engaged in bootlegging around Sausalito, California, and where, among other persons, he met a bootlegger named Johnny Paul Chase. He also met many other bootleggers and criminals, finally to become affiliated with the notorious Joe Parente crowd, operating from San Francisco all the way to Reno. Finally he came east again. He robbed a bank in October 1933, hid out in Texas with a gang and his wife Helen Gillis and their son Ronnie; robbed a bank with Dillinger and others in March 1934.

Then came a raid [by federal agents] at the Little Bohemia, north of Rhinelander, Wisconsin, where barking dogs heralded the approach of special agents and allowed Dillinger to escape. It was during this raid that Baby Face Nelson, true to his custom, did some cowardly shooting and killed W. Carter Baum of the division of investigation.

It was a grand, dishonorable crowd, and that included Baby Face Nelson. I implied that Dillinger was afraid of Baby Face. In that he was not alone. The entire gang was afraid of him, even to the women. Everyone looked upon him as a rat among men. After a bank robbery, they inevitably would give him the honor of dividing the spoils. In reality, this was a protective measure. They would engineer him into a position in the center of a room, and all the group about him, while he split the money. Otherwise, they lived in fear that if he was allowed to be on the outside of the group, he would machine-gun them all and take everything.

So after the Little Bohemia battle, where Baby Face killed his first federal man, there was little disposition on the part of the gang to harbor him. He was too hot. Baby Face then moved to his old hang-outs in California; the government says that on the way he was protected by seventeen persons in various parts of Montana, Nevada and California. These seventeen have all been indicted by a federal grand jury in San Francisco. At last [1934], with John Paul Chase, his old bootlegging friend, he started east again.

Agents rented a cottage in a resort near Chicago that Nelson liked and spotted Nelson, his wife and Chase. Nelson decided not to stop at the resort, but reinforcements sped up on Nelson, who stopped and turned his car around, parked on the side of the road. Nelson fired at agents H. E. Hollis and Samuel Cowley as they exited their car. Hollis fell fatally injured with a bullet through the head. But Cowley, though torn with bullets, lived long enough to sweep Baby Face Nelson with his machine-gun. Then he too fell.

Chase and Helen took the agents' car, sped away with Nelson who died that night in a bed. "His body was stripped and was thrown in a ditch [...two thousand dollars was taken from his money belt]."

These Were Professionals

The case below illustrated the sophisticated state of some liquor operations. Californians produced Canadian and European bottles, labels and fake "legal" strip stickers to make moonshine look like authentic Gordon's Gin. The case also showed the disarray of the court system.

San Francisco Special Agent R. A. Beman contemplated seizing Standard Bottle Supply Company's warehouse in L. A. This plant was the largest distributor of blown and labeled whiskey bottles, strip stamps, labels, corks and articles designed for manufacture of intoxicating liquors on the Pacific Coast. Having connections with Chicago and New York and "a gang of eastern racketeers," it was also connected with J. C. Millett Company, seized in San Francisco and presently in court.

Beman could not obtain permission to close down the operation in Los Angeles because of difficulty of seizure and because of the cost of six months to a year delay in bringing the case into congested federal courts in the Southern District of California.[1]

In San Francisco, case # 1704, June 1932, authorities arrested Charles C. Chamberlain and seized articles designed for manufacture of intoxicating liquor at a store at 567 Hayes Street, San Francisco. Although agents used no search warrant, only "sight violation," i.e., seeing the crime committed, they searched the premises and confiscated large quantities of bottles, assorted sizes and shapes, labels of assorted whiskey, gin and wine labels, 107 cardboard boxes containing assorted labels, corks, caps, foils, wrappers and cartons. One package had counterfeit Canadian strip stamps. Many were found in cartons marked "J. C. Millett Company 241 Clay Street, San Francisco" and some were marked "724 Montgomery Street."

Special Agent Richard H. Shaw, 311 Grant Blvd., San Francisco and Robert Bager, Prohibition Agent, were in charge of seizure. Other special agents making the raid were Frank A. Wegner, A. Clay Gaines, Earle E. Koehler and Thomas W. Goodwin. They caught defendant Chamberlain putting Gordon Gin labels on bottles. P. Rumburg, Special Agent, wanted to seize Southwest Specialty Co., 235 Aliso St., L. A. However Rumburg, too, could not obtain permission from the Attorney General's office.

That's Why They Called Him Baby Face
as told by H. A. Jones, Carmel Valley

Pure alcohol came from Mason's Distillery in Sausalito, five-gallon kerosene cans of 180 proof for $12.50. The gang had a regular route they'd take to San Francisco so you see the payoff that went on. They'd leave from the distillery or from Mason's Garage, take a certain ferry, at a certain time and they were never touched. They delivered it to that big bootlegger—oh, what's his name in San Francisco, the biggest one there, Italian name—anyway they'd take it over there and he'd distribute it to smaller places.

Two hijackers were Sal Carlo and his brother from Fetters Springs. One was running the Lark [a bootleg place in Fetters Springs] and came down to raid an apartment on Valencia Street in San Francisco, I'm pretty sure, and someone tipped 'em off and was waiting for them in the closet and shot them. One died right there, I think Sal, the other got out across the street by a school and tennis court below street level and died under a sign. Those were rough boys then.

I played ball with the Chase boys in Sausalito. Johnny Paul Chase later became a gang member of Baby Face Nelson. Howard Chase was in charge of an electric plant, I think, lived up by where Sally Stanford later had her place, the Valhalla [Sausalito]. Her real name, by the way, was Martha Owens, you know. Baby Face Nelson and his wife hid out up the hill above Caledonia Street, above the bootleg place The Four Winds. The house, his hideout, was across the street from Manuel Menotti, Sausalito policeman. Gillis (Baby Face Nelson) also hid out with Sal Carlo at the Lark at Fetters Springs. [Jones also said, "In Fetters Springs, Ma Fetter, an ex-madam, ran the Lark."] Gangsters held up there. Baby Face was a contract man. He had no set job but would do guard work for several gangs. I met him at Sal Carlo's place. My oldest boy sat on his lap. He was a nice-looking man—that's why they called him Baby Face, you know.

Baby Face was here in Carmel Valley. [Supposedly] he came to a Saturday dance and a couple of local toughs came up to him and asked, "You passing through or sticking around?"

"Just passing through," responded Baby Face.

One of the people he worked for was V.O. [Leo?] Burke, who had the largest chicken hatchery in Petaluma. Burke owned a fast yacht that was used to get booze from the mother ships on the ocean.

Another big runner was Rainard involved with a shooting, a hijacking deal, in Bodega Bay, and that was the owner of a big dry goods store in Petaluma.

I've known many men in the gangs in those days. Some tried to get out and couldn't. They were given concrete walking shoes and put in the ocean to walk their way to China, but the shoes kept them on the bottom of the ocean and they never made it. Pegleg Lucich shot [Nick] Sturtevant near Bodega. Pegleg couldn't run in the sand, it was said.

Parente's Gang

After the Moss Landing shootout in July 1925, in which Deputy Sheriff N. H. Rader was killed and Sheriff James Oyer was shot in the knee, federal agents intensified the search for the California gang responsible. Surprisingly, government investigators found a network of operators from Canada to both northern and southern California.

From the lips of a dying sailor, came the most incriminating evidence allowing officials to round up key gang members. Fatally burned when rum ship *Comet* blew up at Union Oil docks the first part of July 1925 was sailor Karl Wells. Using aliases Kirk Williams and L. M. Becletel, Wells stubbornly refusing to talk about his activities and his employers, inadvertently gave authorities the tip needed when he told a woman to tell someone else to go to a prestigious hotel in San Francisco and warn George or Ralph to be careful and that Kirk Williams was dying. The intercepted message led to the arrest of 85-year-old Ralph H. Omens, wealthy hotel owner from Los Angeles, and the issuing of federal warrants for a score more.

The group smuggled alcohol from the ship *Principio,* supposedly owned by Joe Parente who obtained liquor from Consolidated Exporters, Canadian shippers. Arrested conspirator Mayor J. H. Madden of Sausalito said, "I am at a loss as to explain this matter. Unless it is due to some work I have done for someone at my shipbuilding plant. I accept all work and can't examine the nature of every job. I am not involved and can establish my innocence." Madden went to San Pedro, doing some work on the rum-running mother ship, the 1910 German built *Principio.* Two weeks before his arrest, Madden signed a contract to recondition 10 Coast Guard vessels at his boat works in Sausalito. He had started to make the government boats faster so they could compete against the rum-running boats, which he also worked on. And these were racing from the mother ship *Principio* to shore all during 1924 and the early summer of 1925. For a while he had the best of two worlds—besides being mayor of Sausalito for four years.[2]

Others arrested on warrants were Tom Fay, financial agent to the *Principio*; A. and "JohnDoe" Peterson, tug boat and launch owners; Al Hamblin; George McAdam, reputed lieutenant to Parente; Frank Boullett; Louis Linehart; Charles Johnson; Hans Stittmatter; Jans J. Neilsen, Sausalito boatman.

San Francisco tailor, Joe Parente, had skillfully woven pieces of rum-running cloth together to create an intricate pattern. His gang even ran booze into southern California racing up the coast to supply his northern California operations. With two other indictments pending, Joe Parente turned himself in and was released on $50,000 bond, as was the mysterious "Ralph" Omens.

When bogus Northland Coffee Co. of Arcata received 30 huge 150-gallon drums of whiskey labeled "coffee," federal agents confiscated the whiskey and investigators found Hans Stittmatter involved. All 30 drums, 4,500 gallons of whiskey, disappeared but the Feds caught Stittmatter. The Prohibition Commissioner also accused him in the involvement of the rum-boat *Heron*.

Although Parente's gang was suspected of year-round smuggling, the government only charged members of conspiracy of two counts of bringing gin, whiskey and beer into California from the *Principio* in May and August of 1924.

Simon Bube, supposedly one of the hijacking machine gunners in the Moss Landing battle, avoided capture for six months by moving from the bay area to the Sierras and back to Redwood City.

Although Bube's room in Redwood City was a virtual arsenal with a Bergman machine gun, 1,000 rounds of ammunition, a loaded rifle and a dirk, he was tricked into capture before he could use the weapons. Warned that Bube was armed and dangerous, Redwood City Police Chief Collins sent a plumber and two deputies, disguised as plumber helpers, to inspect the house that Bube was working on as a carpenter. The trick worked and they cuffed Bube before he could use any of his weapons. The machine gun and rounds of ammo were the same type used at Moss Landing. Bube had a scar on his right leg from the wound he received at the rum fight in Moss Landing and had treated at an Oakland hospital.

When agents brought him to Salinas to face charges of murder, he admitted he was hired by hijackers but denied he was a machine gunner. Bube reportedly was in the employ of wealthy San Franciscan William Bowen. Arrested were Paul Brokaw, the "rum-running fashion plate"; and Ed Ferris, suspected ringleaders of the hijacking crew that participated.

Parente Tells a Good One
"Parente Reveals Rum War on Hijackers"
San Francisco Chronicle, June 12, 1927

The ship *Malahat* sailed from Papeete, Tahiti, with a load of liquid cargo for the coast of California. Since the Coast Guard knew it was off the coast of Half Moon Bay unloading cargo, it ordered Coast Guard cutter *Gaviota*, commanded by Captain W. H. Payne, to deter speedboats from unloading on shore. When Payne sighted a suspicious looking launch, just off-shore a few miles north of Santa Cruz, he ordered it to stop. Instead of obeying the order to heave to, it sped off toward the beach. Despite shots being fired across its bow, it headed for a secluded cove just four miles north of Monterey Bay where the rumrunners beached the boat. The crew abandoned the craft, A-287 out of Los Angeles, with 300 cases of scotch whiskey from the *Malahat*.

Federal agents patrolled roadways in the San Francisco Peninsula, looking for other cargoes that had reached the shore. Agents caught up with a caravan of vehicles with 250 cases on the Skyline Boulevard. Caught were notorious rumrunners Joe Parente and Frank Cuneo, driving one car that had no liquor but had two rifles and one revolver. Parente admitted to Assistant United States District Attorney Eugene Bennett that he was indeed a rumrunner but that he had declared war on hijackers and that was why he was on the Skyline looking for hijackers, not part of the liquor convoy that was picked up. Angelo Firori and Fred Mareno drove one car that had 10 cases of contraband. The truck, driven by Fred Olsen, had 240 cases—believed also to come from the *Malahat*. Another man escaped from the truck and disappeared into the woods.

When asked why Parente had the weapons with him, he told the reporters and Bennett the following story:

"All right it was like this. In the first place, I don't know these birds Firori, Mareno and Olsen. Never saw them before.

"Several nights ago I was driving up the coast with 280 cases when I was 'stuck up' by hijackers. Where? Well I don't care to say except it was in the southern part of the State.

"It was the second time in the last couple weeks I'd been hijacked out of a big load and I was good and sore.

"I was tipped off Thursday that the stuff they'd grabbed off me was coming through up this way. So I got hold of Frank Cuneo and he and I went out on the highway that night to lay for it. That's why we had the 'artillery' with us. We meant business.

"We stuck around all night and stopped half a dozen different cars with booze in them. None of them had the stuff we were looking for. Friday night we did the same.

"We'd just stopped the car with Mareno and Firori in it, looked it over and saw we didn't want them, when the big truck came up from behind and then the 'prohis' came down on us.

"I figured at first they were more hijackers and I was going to fight it out with them. When I saw who they were I didn't figure any reason for trying to get away because I didn't have any booze."

U.S. Commissioner Thomas E. Hayden arraigned Parente, who was already out on $50,000 bail waiting appeal on another case, gave him $20,000 more bail to make and each of the others $10,000. Evidently no one believed Parente's sincere and convincing story. They were all charged with violating the Volstead Act and the Tariff Act of 1923.

Rum-Running King Jumps Bail

While Joe Parente was on appeal and waiting in Fresno for a verdict, he heard he lost and was ordered to serve his two-year term at the federal pen at McNeil Island for his part of the *Principio* case in 1926. But when the U. S. Marshall went to pick him up in December 1927, he was gone. He had packed his suitcase and headed to Canada. Since he jumped the McDonough brothers' $64,000 bond, their detectives and federal agents were searching for the distinguished traveler. For almost a year he traveled with assumed names but with no disguises. He went across Canada to see the sites at Niagara Falls, New York and Atlantic City. Other places visited were Chicago, Seattle, Montreal, Detroit and Omaha. Later Vancouver immigration authorities caught him and had planned to turn him over to the United States. On a Canadian bond of $5,000, however, he jumped again. In November, he said he got "sort of lonesome for California. So I came down to Sacramento. Election night I listened to the radio in the Senator [Hotel] lobby." He returned to Vancouver where he was caught again after his "See America First," experience, said the *San Francisco Chronicle.*

Offering its Pacific Coast agent, Joe Parente, legal counsel, the Canadian liquor group helped him fight extradition, but the rum king decided to give up his 11-month flight. "I'm tired of dodging the law and it's a relief not to be in momentary fear of being touched on the shoulder," said Parente. "I'm through. I want to go home and get it all over with."

The bonding company, of course had to go to court to recover $20,000 from Parente and his wife Catherine, expenses for trying to retrieve Parente. Despite "wild rumors[,] he is not going to squeal." He kept the code of silence. The Feds, after listening to his astonishing tales of travel, allowed him a few escorted minutes with his wife before his trip to McNeil Island.[3]

The Story of Rumrunning
by Frank I. Hyman
Historic Writings Reminiscences: Biography of My Activities

In the fall of 1932, in San Francisco, there was on Columbus Avenue a not too frequented "speak-easy" or "bootleg" joint owned and conducted by a North Beach Italian by the name of Sal. He was a dark, heavy-set, determined person, with a commanding look in his eyes. He was conceded to be the best shot of the gang, with nerves of steel, and fit to cope with anyone.

He had been a second rate pugilist but abandoned this game to become a body guard for a Chicago beer baron.

He sat slouched down in a bar-room chair beside one of the poker tables. When he heard a knock on the door (code rap), Sal moved to the wicket in the side of the wall, piped the visitor, moved leisurely to the door and admitted a small middle-aged, smartly dressed man, who seemingly was a bit nervous.

This man had been a prosperous business man, later a big shot of the Pacific Coast rumrunning, and a one time loser.

"Hello, Tony, what brings you here and what's up?" asked Sal.

"Well, I'm out, and I'm not used to laying around, we've got to get going and do something. I've made a few millions in my time and it's plenty tough to be in this shape. If it hadn't been for that squealer and I had not paid so much money for protection, foolin' around with women, liquor and fast living I'd have plenty of jack left now and we're going to start over, see?" was Tony's little talk, as he pounded on the table top very emphatically.

"What do you want me to do on this job?" asked Sal.

"I'll tell you, you know that old method of handling booze is out, it's too old fashioned, too easy to get caught, I've a new wrinkle—but with the experience you've got you're the best man to handle our stuff on shore and dat's your job—shore boss," answered Tony.

"You know that the holidays are coming on and the supply of good liquor in this town is very low. There is a big demand for that Canadian stuff and we've got to get it down here if we want any of that business, you understand?"

"Okay with me, when do we start?" was Sal's reply.

The following day Sal and Barney met Red in his apartment. Red was a stout, redheaded, good natured Irish lad, a dependable truck driver, and wise to the many tricks of the hijacker. They were trying to figure out some plan to cope with the new Coast Guard boats—and the increased federal force. When Tony arrived accompanied by his wife and sister-in-law, feeling his wines, he greeted the boys heartily. "Boys, let's get down to business. We're going to the races, and I am playing Princess Belle to win."

"Well, boys, Sal and I are going back into the game. And we will run it again right thru the Golden Gate.'

Sal replied, "Don't talk foolish, that ain't being done any more, we can't afford to buy the Coast Guard and the federal forces. There are too many of them now, and we can't take any chances of getting caught. We're not in the money and can't stand the fines and compensation for the men while they are doing time."

"We might try our old spots at Half Moon Bay and Moss Landing," said Tony.

Then Barney speaks up. "They're hot too! Marino's gang has been working them and Tony, you sure haven't forgotten the fireworks at Moss Landing."

When Tony suggested that they work the Point Reyes and Bodega section, Barney spoke up. "They are burning! The Swedes have been working that territory, landing dope—the Feds are wise to them."

Looking discouraged, Tony hesitated..."The new agreement with Canada to extend the International Boundaries from 12 to 30 miles, or one hour steaming time, had made it impossible for Americans or slow boats to operate."

"Sal, you know I think the Canadians have it figured out right. A few weeks before I got out, a young Limer, who made the 'Big House' for running a fishing boat, told me that the Canadian 'big shot' was having built three cruiser type boats, 85 feet long, capable of carrying under deck 500 cases and powered with three motors, a diesel for cruising and two powerful engines, placed one on each side of the diesel for use in case of emergency. They are capable of 30 miles an hour. The boats will carry a crew of five men, including a wireless operator, and would be able to stay out to sea continuously. Their supplies would come from the mother ship and shore contacts.

[Tony went to Vancouver, leased a new boat, contracted for 10,000 cases of different brands for $8 to $12 per case, and made arrangements for the mother ship to move from off the coast of Monterey to west of Point Reyes.]

Tony said, "We will have to pay $4 a case more, for delivery to any spot we wish. All we have to do is wire their Vancouver office by code message.

"They have made arrangements with a wireless station to broadcast these messages twice daily, then the runners will know what to do at all times and with a few hours notice, can hit any spot. The federals will not be able to stop this round-about way of contacting the boats. They figured when they located the wireless plant of the Marino gang, that they had the runners whipped."

[Sal hired an old whaler and salmon fisherman Captain Beck to choose spots along the coast to land since he knew every inlet. They checked out Noyo River, Russian Gulch, Little River, Dark Gulch, Albion River, and Salmon Creek—all used in earlier days of rumrunning. They picked out a spot three miles north of Stewart's Point, which they called Cypress Cove because of the cypress trees leading from it. The first landing spot chosen was Salt Point, where they hired a rancher for $100 a load, plus $25 extra a night if he operated as watchman on the landing nights. Since this was a dog hole, it had a 50-foot cliff. He bought a hoist to operate from the jacked-up back end of his Buick Roadster, hauling up a sturdy wooden sled, holding 20 cases at a time.]

Tony continued: "While in Seattle, I met our old friend Captain Larson. You remember the rough Swede that used to smuggle Chinamen when he was Captain on the oil tanker by exchanging sailors in San Francisco as per instructions from the big shot of Chinatown? I promised him $150 a month salary [to be 'shore pilot' because the Canadians did not know the shore line], and a bonus of fifty cents per case for all cases he landed. He said he would show the limeys how to find the spots in the dark. I gave him fifty bucks and told him to be here on the 15th.

"The boat owners told me that they were going to work the bonus system with their crews and were paying the captains, engineers and wireless operator a salary of $250 a month and a bonus of 75¢ a case for all the cases landed. The balance of the crew $150 per month and a bonus of 50¢ per case. I think that is the best plan, the more cases landed, the more money for the crews and us."

[Tony found a friend in Sonoma County who had a summer resort to rent during the winter as a storage depot, north of San Francisco Bay.]

"Sal, you better buy a couple of speedy trucks, large enough to carry 200 cases each. Have solid sides and end gates made for them. Pay the smallest down payment possible and register them under the name Jones. You better also buy a couple used Cadillacs to distribute with in the city and we can haul our own crews around with them. You had better get another driver and couple of triggermen who know why we are furnishing them with 'gats.'"

[The next day] "I've hired these boys, Tony. Mac here says he can land a dory through any surf, Slim says he was city distributor up there [Seattle] and is used to driving in heavy traffic. He will be a good follow-up car driver and city delivery boy."

[They hired Lardo and Snipe, two small-time Italian gangsters from the slums of North Beach, and who were just off a job with the Marino Gang, and always ready to use a gun. Two men hiding out in San Francisco, two real gunmen, were hired: Jimmie who was Baby Face Nelson and Jack who was John Paul Chase, Nelson's gang member.]

Several days passed before Tony came rushing into Sal's speakeasy all excited, handing Sal a wire which read, "The boat is leaving-stop-located sixty miles west of Point Reyes,-stop-otherwise advise."

"I'm sending this sealed letter by Captain Larson to the captain of the *Kagome,* with instructions that the code names are to be changed on the first, tenth, and twentieth of each month."

[At the campsite back of Stewart's Point]

Sal spoke: "Boys, I want you all to agree to forget personal grievances. If there should be an argument I want you to remember I am the law while you are in this camp. If we should run afoul of the federals, it's every man for himself. If we should get scattered, make your way to DeQuesto's at Fort Bragg, or to San Francisco and wait there for instructions. Remember, no drinks until I or the man in charge pass them out."

Sal looked at Snipe, who was cleaning his fourteen shot forty-five automatic, "Snipe, you and Mac take the first watch. Get down there before dark. Look the place over carefully and see that no one is planted. Take the Ford, give the rancher this flashlight and tell him to watch the main road for any strange cars. And if the federals show up while we're working, have him flash four times at us."

Later that night Mac came up in the Ford, "She's in boys. Bring down the trucks and the cars."

By the time the trucks were backed into place and the drum attached to the wheel of the Buick, Captain Larson had landed with a dory load and handing Sal a letter said, "There is another dory out on the *Kagome* we can use."

In less than two hours, the five hundred cases were landed and loaded into the trucks and cars.

"Lardo, you leave first. Red, you leave next, stay a couple of miles behind. Snipe, you come with me, we will trail along behind. The rest of you boys better get back to camp, have the stew cooked, you can expect us back around ten tonight. Barney, you drive the Cadillac, and Fritz, you take the other one."

Day after day, the gang went through the same orderly routine, doing the chores, playing cards, lying around, trying to sleep. With the setting of the sun, the first pair of watchmen would take their positions, followed every three hours by a fresh pair. Three more loads were landed in a month. The spot was getting
hot. They worked the place too long. The federals had located them.

There were several delays out to sea, caused by bad weather and by Coast Guard boats who had located the mother ship and would not leave her. They proved too fast for the loaded *Kagome* which was forced to wait a week at a time for the fog to drift in so that she could slip away.

Then one night the *Kagome* landed at Salt Point and was about to unload, when the federals made their appearance. Fritz, Red, and Lardo, comprising the hoisting and loading crew upon the bank, were having trouble with the hoist and were lying down looking over the hoist-drum equipment and did not notice the flashes from the rancher who was posted at the entrance to the main road and before they knew what was up, the federals had them covered, and handcuffed Red to Lardo as they had only one pair and those two were the toughest looking of the three.

The gang on the beach were worried when the sled did not return down the bank, Sal ordered, "Snipe, you go up and see what the trouble is up there."

When Snipe climbed to the top of the bank, the federals noticed him and two of them ran toward him and shouted, "Stop or we will shoot!" Snipe scrambled down the bank giving the alarm.

The gang was making for the dory, when the federals opened up on them. Bullets were coming too close to be healthy, so they began returning fire, which made the federals run for cover.

Some of the bullets hit the deck of the *Kagome* and frightened the Canadians so much that they were having trouble getting their engines started. This was lucky since it gave the dory time enough to reach her side just as the first engine started. Olie missed the dory and started swimming to the boat, but was too late. He either had to swim back to the beach and into the hands of the federals, or swim around the rocky point and land in the next cove. He finally made the beach at day break. He climbed up the canyon and hid there until dark, and then started for Fort Bragg, where he arrived the following night.

The federals made a hurried survey of the cove and found that they had captured four men, two trucks, four cars and five hundred cases of scotch. One of the federals left for Santa Rosa to get help, while the remaining two took the prisoners up to the rancher's house, which they wanted to search.

On the high seas *Kagome* crewmen made things as comfortable as possible for the gang under the crowded conditions. Some were taking turns sleeping in the bunks, while others were lying on the floor of the rolling *Kagome*, seasick, anxious to get back to the shore. After rolling around for three days, they received a radio message, stating, "Hit the Noyo at 12 tonight, will use same signals."

Tony, the leader, was still in bed in San Francisco when he received the bad news. He hurriedly phoned his lawyer to go to Santa Rosa and see what he could do for the prisoners. He was able to secure the release of Lardo and Red on $5,000 bond each. He said he could get the trials postponed until spring. Regarding the rancher watchman, he advised Tony that they did not have enough evidence to hold him long.

Tony had two new trucks ready when Lardo and Red reported back to him in San Francisco.

"Well, Tony," said DeQuisto in Fort Bragg, "if you need another truck, I can get you the vegetable truck. I have an interest in it; he can haul right into the city, and no one will be the wiser."

At about twelve on that bright, starlit night, the long low *Kagome* came chugging up the narrow Noyo River, her dark hull invisible until she was right up to the fish dock. The gang had left her in the outer harbor, landing on the jetty and walked up, taking no unnecessary chances of getting caught.

The runner was soon unloaded, took her supplies on board [supplies of fresh vegetables and meat] and steamed out to sea. The trucks took a load out to new depot, returned, loaded up and left for the plant in Sonoma County, the cars following up their regular position.

The *Kagome* landed four more loads without any serious trouble on land, but the spot was getting hot. The gang members were staying undercover, but were going about the small country town to the pool rooms and shows as any tourist would.

The one night when Red was on his way down with his truck loaded with two hundred cases and followed by Slim and Baby Face Nelson, the latter spotted three federals parked at the foot of the Mountain House grade. Baby Face quickly trained his submachine gun on them and said to Slim, "Shall I let them have it?"

Slim replied, "No, not unless they try to stop us. We'll drive up a way to a side road and if they follow we'll have to give them the works."

The federals saw too many guns for them and did not follow. They showed good judgment this time.

Out on the wintry ocean, the runner had several long delays. One was on account of rough weather; another time she was trailed by the Coast Guard boat for eight days without a fog drifting in to give her a chance to sneak off. On Thanksgiving Day the crew of the *Kagome* were celebrating their feast with the Coast Guard still in sight, when Captain Larson announced, "We might as well let the boys on the Coast Guard boat get in on this." He climbed on the deck and signaled them to come over. When they were along side, the Captain yelled out, "Throw me your heaving line and I will send you over something to go with your turkey." They complied. He tied on a case of scotch and one of champagne and then they steamed off a short ways.

Just after sundown, the Coast Guard boat came back, pulled up close along side with the First Officer at the wheel (the only man in sight), and warned, "Boys, at nine o'clock, beat it."

Julius, the vegetable man's truck driver, was taking down a load each return trip [to San Francisco], but it was not long before the hijackers were wise to him hauling without protection. One night there were three of them waiting on a side road for him to come along, about ten miles up on Navarro highway. When Julius passed, they drove by him, up the road where they had some ties piled. When Julius came to a stop, one of the gang climbed into the car, poked a "gat" into the frightened truck driver's ribs, and ordered him, "Drive on down a few miles and turn up the first road to your left where we have our trucks parked."

They forced Julius to help load their truck and on leaving broke all the spark plugs, advising him that he had better stay there until morning.

[Next they landed at Shelter Cove in lower Humboldt County. They paid off Dick, the watchman at the wharf, $100 per load and $25 extra if he helped.]

The *Kagome* made the pier at eleven that night, unloaded and put out to sea at two with fresh meat and vegetables.

In Kansas City the federals were called to investigate two railroad cars which were leaking and did not smell like fish as per their invoices. They were found to be loaded with scotch, shipped from Eureka. This put the federals to work in this territory and one evening when Sal was returning from San Francisco, he noticed from the tracks in the snow that several cars had turned off into the side road a few miles from the spot. On investigating this, he found three of the cars loaded with federals, heavily armed, who were waiting for the *Kagome* to make a landing.

That night the gang left for the city where another conference was held. They decided to hit a spot once, as the federals were on the scene if they worked a place for any length of time.

They wired the *Kagome* to hit Rockport, a spot halfway between Fort Bragg and Shelter Cove, a harbor with a bad beach, where dories would have to be used. They had about four hundred cases landed, when a comber caught the dory, threw her end for end and the boys into the boiling surf, where they rolled around and finally washed up on the beach. The dory drifted out to sea where Captain Beck found her the next day, with 26 cases still lashed to her.

The next load was landed at Noyo, as they—and the dory men did not want any more of Rockport.

Winter was about over. The fast Coast Guard boats again were able to put out to sea. The gang had several more loads to land, before repeal [Congress made 3.2 beer "non-intoxicating" in April 1933.].

The Coast Guard set a trap for the *Kagome*, capturing her and one of her sister ships within the thirty mile limit. The other runner's crew saw the game was over for them, beached their boat and made a safe get-away.

At the trial of the *Kagome* the defense was that they were out more than one hour's steaming time when caught, and when she was taken out for a trial run, with her engines in bad shape and loaded down with five hundred cases of scotch she proved her point. She was found to be in international waters and was finally turned loose.

Two years later it was evident that crime did not pay for the notorious gang. Tony, the dressy leader, who made millions in the game, was about broke, and had failed to find a paying racket in the New Deal. He was still playing ponies, hoping some day to be in the money again.

Sal went back to his old game of operating a night club, and was getting along well until Lardo got into a tight spot and squealed on his old gang for harboring the Nation's Notorious Public Enemies [Baby Face Nelson and Johnny Paul Chase] and Sal received a jail sentence.

Booze on the Beach
by Richard Mason, Marin County

The bootleg years on Point Reyes were rowdy and romantic. Fortunes were made, but few reputations tarnished, for Point Reyes winked at the Volstead Act. The action took place on the ocean and Tomales Bay beaches, in the pine woods, along Inverness Ridge, on Sand Point, at Marshall and Millerton Point and on private wharves. Garages became storage sheds for booze. Trucks fled down local roads at midnight leaving teams of baffled federal agents far behind. Tommy guns sprayed bullets across the beaches. Vincent (Pegleg) Lucich tells of being shot while guarding a catch. Although wounded in the hand he fired back and routed what he supposed were federals. The liquor was choice stock, most of it down from Canada in ships that stood three miles off shore while it was unloaded on the beaches. The "stevedores" included many whose names are familiar on Point Reyes today. "There are a lot of skeletons in the Point Reyes area that have never been dug up," is the way Lucich puts it. The rum merchants paid good wages, and the occasional bottle of spirits a man could spirit home added incentive to the game.

Sacramento was headquarters for the liquor Mafia. Getting the booze from here to there without being caught was the game. The rules were simple: it was played mostly at night. Every road out of the area could be used by the players—and was. The idea was to decoy the federals. Leak word that a truck full of scotch was coming over the hill into Inverness Park at ten tonight; then—with the agents crouched along Drake Summit Road to make the pinch—divert your shipment across Pierce Point to Tomales Bay, thence by sailboat to Marshall and the waiting truck. Tomorrow night reverse the procedure. Being a liquor agent was frustrating and risky. The bootleggers traveled in droves, the prohis in pairs; it was hardly a fair match. More than one crept into the woods to make an arrest only to creep out again in fear of his life. The ranch owners did little to abet the law, some of them reportedly keeping silent for a share of the profits.

Two agents lived in a Point Reyes Station cottage. One carried a long rifle, the other a pistol. A white bulldog and several sets of handcuffs were in their arsenal. Tipped off one night that liquor was coming in on an Inverness wharf, they commandeered a local auto (theirs was out of commission) and forced its frightened owner to drive them at top speed to Inverness. Later the owner of the wharf (no longer with us) was shot at while running through the woods. He got off by turning state's evidence. Another celebrated case involves the *Queen*, the larger of Brock Schreiber's two Inverness excursion launches, whose hulk now rots on Children's Beach. One night the agents forced the *Queen* into service and with Schreiber's hired help at the wheel were taken to the mouth of the bay, only to find hijackers, with fake badges, had beaten them to the haul.

Most old-timers on Point Reyes gave their favorite prohibition memories. Beryl Schreiber Jesperson had hers: "I can remember a certain picnic of my family and two other families to Abbott's Lagoon. When we got to the beach area here was a huge box covered with shoe advertisements. On opening it we found 20 two-quart bottles of square-faced Holland gin, each wrapped in its straw package. I guess it was jettisoned because the prohis were hot on their trails. Mother hated liquor of any kind so she played Carrie Nation and broke every bottle on a driftwood log. All the men just about wept. The irony is that we went out several weeks later and one member of the party cut his foot badly. We happened to find one bottle partly intact and mother used the contents to sterilize the wound."

A couple of the federal men deserve no credit in history. They charged hundreds of dollars worth of guns, handcuffs and other items at local stores, then skipped town. One of them later became a bootlegger himself on the strength of what he had learned on Point Reyes. Justice of sorts was achieved when an employee of one of the markets helped a team of rumrunners lift their truck out of a ditch. He was rewarded with a case of good scotch which he brought into Point Reyes Station and sold for ten dollars a bottle.

The white beaches at the mouth of Tomales Bay seem to be those most often used by the nocturnal smugglers. Pegleg Lucich said it took a first class navigator to run the mouth of the bay through its 50-foot-wide channel. He did it by waiting for high tide and riding through on the "third wave"—a chance the federals refused to take. Cases of liquor were carted by horse and wagon across the dunes and transferred to trucks on the nearest road. Other cargoes were spirited as far as Chicken Ranch and Millerton Point by fishing craft. It was Lucich who made the biggest headlines during these years. On the night of May 21, 1930, he murdered handsome Nick Sturtevant as they sat together in an automobile parked along the road near Dillon Beach. Sturtevant was a hijacker who had been supplying Marin County millionaires with booze. Arrested by the federals, he won leniency by promising to squeal on his customers. Lucich, who claims he shot Sturtevant for revenge alone and not to protect the millionaires, was sent to San Quentin for life. He got out on parole in 1947.

Towards the end of the prohibition era the bootleggers, now more brazen, used a Navy-type launch painted black for night duty. Its cargo hold astern was roomy and its high-powered engine could be gunned to foil pursuit. The black hearse that made regular runs to San Francisco needed no protection: no one looking at the lugubrious driver would suspect him of transporting booze. Liquor of poorer quality was manufactured in stills by local folk indisposed to rumrunning. It was not unusual to see a truckload of sugar headed in their direction. The alcohol they distilled was served on A Street in Point Reyes Station and elsewhere. In one saloon periodically raided by the agents the bottles were stored under the floorboards behind the bar. As soon as the agents left, up came the floorboards and it was "What'll you have?" all over again. What you had was usually straight alcohol colored and flavored with Kitchen Bouquet. One of the larger stills, between Point Reyes Station and Bolinas, hired a man for 14 dollars a day to sit in a tree looking for prohis. This particular pad came to grief when its overconfident owners hung a ten dollar brass padlock on the gate. The federal men figured only a bootlegger could afford anything that fancy and knocked the still over.

None of these adventures, however, equals the one that I am told took place on the main street of Point Reyes Station. A Northwestern Pacific freight car stood on the siding. Word got around that it contained crates of hospital alcohol. Tempted beyond endurance, some of the local menfolk bored their way into the car and made off with the makings of the best vodka ever consumed in these parts.

Cornero's Gang—1925-26

Charles Barnett, sales agent representing Central American Shipping Company, Ltd., Vancouver, B. C., sold shipments of liquor to various gangs in southern California. One was Tony Cornero's gang, operating from San Luis

Obispo down to San Diego. Barnett took orders, collected money, sent it to Canada, sometimes delivering lists of orders to mother ships by way of speed-boats from California, arranging for buyers to pick up loads at designated points off the coast. Cornero used Captain Johnny McClusky to pick up the loads and bring them to Cornero's landing spots. During 1925-26, McClusky, alias "Red" or "Red Jew," operated three boats: *New Elmer, Bithulithic,* and a Japanese fish boat *Minato* which name later changed to *Mauritius.* He used Japanese crew-men, including Harry S. Kerata, the alleged owner of the boat. Tadashi Kimura was McClusky's cook

Meanwhile, Wilmington policeman J. W. Thomas arrested Tony Biena driving a Ford truck with 100 cases of imported liquor at Anaheim and Truck Boulevard. Biena was booked in San Pedro on possession and transporting. In the municipal court he pleaded guilty and paid $1,000 fine on each count. Biena was Tony Cornero. In early 1925, as Thomas and Officer Gillie H. Griffin pa-trolled the docks in Wilmington, they noticed a suspicious-looking boat. Later they found the boat by the San Pedro Lumber Company. Crawling through a hole in the fence, they found Officers Charles Wyckoff and Pruitt watching a crew unloading liquor from the fish boat into a Pierce Arrow truck. The names given by captured smugglers were Anthony McCann, Mike Sabatine, Bert Hanes, O. T. Olsen, T. Haido and N. Yanto, the latter two Japanese crewmen. Both officers recognized Anthony McCann as Tony Cornero and heard him say, "My God, Thomas, it seems to me you are giving me hell. I thought I was unloading out of your territory tonight. You knocked me off for a hundred that time on Anaheim Boulevard." They were taken to San Pedro where Cornero, alias McCann, alias Tony Biena, deposited $500 bail for himself and another for Sabatine and $250 for each of the other men. All this money was forfeited as none of these men showed up for their hearings.

In December 1925 the *Kuyakusmpt* from Vancouver sailed to Guadalupe Island, off Mexico, gave fuel and stores to the mothership *Lillehorn* and re-ceived 14,000 cases of whiskey and brandies. The *Kuyakusmpt* sailed north to the *Prince Albert,* receiving more liquor. Both the *Lillehorn* and the *Prince Albert* went back to Canada, leaving *Kuyakusmpt* as the replacement mother ship. All three vessels belonged to Central American Shipping. On January 29, 1926, at a point 45 minutes off of Santa Rosa [Island] a gray speedboat named *Skeedaddle,* out of Los Angeles, came to the *Kuyakusmpt* and picked up 500 cases. Shore agent Charles [Barnett] came out on the *Skeedaddle* and deliv-ered several orders for liquor and returned on the shore boat. On April 16 and 24, 1926, Captain McClusky went out and picked up 350 cases each day. Again on April 28, McClusky headed *Bithulithic* with a Japanese crew called, accord-ing to the government report, "Timid Jap" and "Jovial Jap." At rendezvous, McClusky picked up 400 cases for Cornero to distribute in southern California. McClusky took the *Mauritius* out twice, bringing back about 380 cases each time. The second trip he brought some Bull Durham tobacco for a rumrunner. Because of the capture of *Mauritius,* another captain brought out *S.N.S. (A-218)* and secured 400 cases. McClusky, the same day, came out with black seine boat *New Elmer (215406),* loading up 1100 cases for Cornero to distribute in southern California. McClusky told about his other boat being captured and his close call. He and his Japanese crewmen had to swim for it. On shore and wet, he was stopped by a policeman, but after telling a believable story, he was allowed to go home. Another May trip on the *New Elmer,* McClusky obtained 800 cases. Within a couple months *Kuyakusmpt* was empty and headed back to Vancouver.

The story here turned bizarre and complicated. Since the large yacht *Donosarrie* had been for sale for quite awhile, James L. Gunliffe, a ship broker in the area, had permission to take prospective buyers for a demonstration cruise by Captain Gudman Grimstad, who lived in San Pedro. On July 20, 1926, about 5:00 p.m., Gunliffe brought over a Mr. Thompson to look at the boat to buy. Thompson seemed pleased and asked the skipper Grimstad pertinent questions: use of oil, gas use. "Was there enough gas and oil to take a cruise out into the Pacific?" When Grimstad answered that there was enough for a normal test run, Thompson gave him some money, saying to fill it up that night and they would take it out the next morning.

The next morning Thompson arrived at the boat with his so-called partner and a sailor. "By direction of Thompson the boat was headed for San Clemente but stopped at Avalon to get lubricating oil. Because of the roughness of the water the boat was tied up at Avalon when Thompson told them to leave." When the captain objected, Thompson opened a handbag, pulled out a big gun, put it in his pocket and said, "You had better go down and get ready and do as I tell you." Grimstad did as he was told. They proceeded to a large vessel, a rum boat. Because of rough seas, Grimstad did not want to tie up to the boat, so they anchored 100 yards apart. They transferred 1,100 cases of liquor by rowboats.

When the *Donosarri* came back from its trial run, it docked on 7th Street landing dock. The others left the boat after warning Grimstad not to "try any funny stunts" because he was being watched.

Grimstad went to his home and fell exhausted in bed, telling his wife to tell anyone who wanted him that he was buying parts for the yacht. One owner of the boat came over and stated there were strange men on the boat. The wife drove down to the boat and came back and woke her husband. Grimstad drove to the boat. Upon passing a cannery, he noticed Thompson and another man at the cannery. He walked over to him but Thompson disappeared, according to Grimstad. But when he walked toward the boat, Thompson reappeared and told him not to go to the boat or he'd be arrested. He told another man to take Grimstad "someplace" so he would not be arrested. They drove in the country for an hour, going through side roads near Compton, and held him in a shack for almost two days, with nothing to eat except a bottle of milk and some bread. Finally when he was released by this "strange man," he wanted to see his wife and the owners of the boat, but was arrested by the police at his house. Despite his close contact with the strange man, Thompson and the two crewmen, he could not, or would not, identify anyone, and couldn't find the shack or even recognize whether the rum boat was the *Kiltuish* or the *Chassina*, a ship with some of Cornero's booze on it.

In the meantime the owners found the boat in Long Beach Harbor, messy and locked up. From the skylight, they saw the booze and called the Long Beach police who seized the liquor and ordered the arrest of Grimstad.

The police saw a Chrysler roadster parked near French and Company—with a good view of the police unloading the *Donosarri.* When the police checked the man, who said his name was Louis Donalds, was from the Chrysler dealership and was returning the car for a customer who worked in the plant there. A good story, filled with details. It was Tony Cornero. He was held for awhile at gun point while his story was checked out. The tale was "all wet." Thrice he offered a bribe of $500 to let him go or $1,000 to take him to Los Angeles. Thrice policemen turned it down. At the police station, he was identified as Cornero. Other officers recognized him as Paul Kent or Tony Bieno—depending on which alias he used when arrested.

In October 1925 and June 1926, A. Strallo helped load the *Chassina* in Vancouver with 5,000 to 6,000 cases of liquor assigned to A. Strallo in San Blas, Mexico. James H. McLaughlin, Customs officer in Canada, said he knew A. Strallo and he did help load the rum ship. He told Strallo that since his sister lived in Los Angeles, he would like to visit her there. Strallo said to look him up and he'd show him a good time and wrote in McLaughlin's notebook: "Tony Cornero, 322 South Witner Street, Los Angeles."[4]

One conspiracy case from the Federal Archives was the epitome of gang organization. The Federal Grand Jury in Southern District of California brought charges against well-known southern Californian rumrunner Frank Cornero and seven conspirators, including northern California rumrunner Joe Parenti [Parente].

During the summer of 1925, Cornero made arrangements with Eddie Jones to unload liquor from the *Coal Harbor* onto beaches by Laguna Beach. The constable of Laguna Beach and Traffic Officer Frank E. Howell received $1.00 a case, to be split with L. V. Murphy, Justice of the Peace. The gang agreed to pay Austin J. Allen, owner of Green Bay Auto Court at Green Bay, sometimes called Emerald Bay, north of Laguna Beach, 25¢ per case for permission to land booze on his beach. Jack Wilson paid Allen his share. Officer Howell attended the landings in uniform at Green Bay, Laguna Beach and Salt Creek, south of Laguna. Smuggler Eddie Richards paid Howell several times and at least once for unloading liquor with Joe Parenti [Parente]. In 1925 and 1926 Howell received about $10,000.

When federal investigators broke the case, they received much information from Eddie Jones, who hid out in Big Bear. Cornero sent Eddie Richards up to Big Bear with Cornero's Chrysler to tell Jones to come see Cornero in Los Angeles or "else." Richards conveyed the threat and scared Jones who wondered why Cornero would want to "bump him off." Jones went to the Federal Building in Los Angeles, confessed, pleaded guilty to conspiracy charges and testified against Cornero. In 1927, when Cornero thought he might be found guilty, he said he hoped Jones was in San Quentin the same time because Cornero would "kill the son of a bitch."

Richards also broke. Constable Howell fled Laguna Beach, going to Missouri, Stockton and San Bernardino. The Howells bought Shady Brook Auto Camp in San Bernardino. Then Howell, himself, fled to Canada so he would be safe [from prosecution and perhaps from Cornero]. He crossed the border with a 1928 Whippet Sedan and $3,000 in cash.

Through the Judge, Verne Murphy and his wife, Betty, Mrs. Howell received $800 to be taken care of and for money so Mrs. Howell could also "leave the country," i.e., go to Canada with her children. She decided not to go up north. She turned herself into the federal authorities.[5]

L. A. Wineries Under Prohibition
as told by George Edward Giardina, Yermo

George Giardina, long retired in the Mojave Desert from the winery business in Los Angeles, on advice of his lawyer, would not be tape-recorded, but candidly gave inside information of the winery business during prohibition.

Even before prohibition went into effect, Los Angeles was a rough town. Can you imagine some elementary students having to check their pistols to the principal of Avenue 21 School in Lincoln Heights each day before they went into class? That's what we did. Although my father was a top Italian in the Los Angeles area, our house was bombed twice because he would not give into the Black Handers. "They're Dagos like me. Why should I give them $5,000?" my father said about 1913-14. The Black Handers was an Italian fraternal organization that tried to control all Italians around Los Angeles. They were civic minded in that they helped out widows, orphans and families that needed food or shoes or a job. They came up to Italians with money and stated, "We need to help the ____ family. Your share is $200. We'll collect it next Tuesday." They would pay for fear of their lives. [At this point in the interview George tapped the table hard three times.] My family never joined the Black Handers but helped them out on a voluntary basis. Black Handers came from southern Italy, basically Sicily. Their techniques of using fear came with the Italian immigrants before the turn of the century. Especially powerful in New York and Chicago, they tried to take over Los Angeles before prohibition. The bombings, the messages with a dagger, or a black-inked imprint of the hand on the bottom (of the message) victimized their compatriots, usually *cafoni*, ignorant southern Italian peasants. Depending on the area and the style of that particular society, they might hit up a laborer for a dollar a week or a wine maker for several hundred dollars.

About 1917-18, seventy-or-so Italians came to Los Angeles to take over all of California: San Francisco, Los Angeles and San Diego—again mostly Sicilians, the Mafiosi. They did not control California but they overshadowed the Black Hand Society. They did not have the welfare of a poor widow in mind, only the welfare of their organization.

Then prohibition came in 1920. My father closed his saloon near 20th Avenue and concentrated on the winery. The government officials tried to control the winery. We always tried to have 1,000 gallons extra. We'd sell 10 barrels and put down 15, or make more than we said we made. We didn't report all the money we took in. The rabbis came in periodically and blessed some of the muscatel, angelica and port. They would buy extra—we did not care what they did with it. The angelica, the best in California, was popular from 1920-1925. We delivered grape juice to people who had permits ($3.50-5.00 per permit) to make 200 gallons for the family's use. But they couldn't keep the juice over a week or it would ferment within ten days. We took care of it at their places for 90 days for $75-100 for a 50-gallon barrel. We delivered a lot on the hills (to the houses) with no permit. The family with a permit could not take the wine from the house or sell it. James Cruze, director of the 1923 classic *Covered Wagons*, made 200 gallons for himself and 200 gallons for his niece.

Once we delivered wine to Santa Barbara, right next to a winery, but the buyers didn't want to use local places. We delivered 50 gallons of sauterne to Bel Aire for a police party of a hundred people. Because of hijacking, we had a motorcade of four motorcycle policemen, followed by four cops in a car, then our truck, with a police car bringing up the rear. We donated it. I received a call from Consonares [not sure of spelling or reference to him other than this interview] who controlled north of Broadway, while I sold south of Broadway, asking why I was selling in his district. We made an agreement. Broadway was the dividing line. When I told him it was just a donation to the police, he did not get angry.

We also sold champagne from France that came in through San Pedro, six bottles for $35 a bottle.

In a corner at Little Joe's Restaurant on North Broadway, ¼ mile north of Temple, I had a table where I was specially treated. I could send a couple people there and they received special food and drinks just like I would. That was my office.

Al Capone came to Los Angeles and hid out in my winery. He wore overalls and worked like one of the boys. Alphonso (Alphonse Capone) was a good guy. He stayed for three weeks, a good worker.

Depth of Involvement—We'll Never Know

Sometimes gang members were involved in other affairs whereby one did not know what occurred as a result of liquor problems and what was unrelated. In 1931, 35-year-old Frank Hugo was being investigated "for recent asserted liquor activities" in the Southland when he was charged with the double murder of his wife Rina Hugo, age 22, and her friend Louis White. It was purported that the two were lovers. Frank Hugo went home with his nephew and killed both White and Rina Hugo as they came out the house. However, others suspected the "pair might have been killed to seal their lips."[6]

Hijacking the Hijackers

Earl A. Withrow, a pasty faced youth of 22, surrendered to police in 1929 to answer charges of shooting and seriously wounding Robert Murphy and James Le Gros, two alleged hijackers, on a busy L.A. intersection on a Friday afternoon.[7]

Withrow was to have gone to federal prison to serve an 11-month sentence with James O. Lail, well-known auto rental agent, on a liquor ring conviction. Investigators took Withrow to the police hospital ward, where Murphy and Le Gros had been held while recovering from being shot down. Supposedly Withrow shot them as he took liquor away from their automobile. Hijacked the hijackers!

Both men stoically refused to identify Withrow. But Murphy turned and said to Withrow, "You sure didn't give a guy a chance. What did you want to plug me for?"

♉

In southern Los Angeles Phillip Rubino, 30, owned a bottle supply shop. He came home about midnight, August 26, 1928, drove his car in the driveway along side his house, exited the car into a volley of bullets from five men hiding in his back yard, shotgun pellets tearing through his body. He left a widow and three children. Police told reporters that gangs of bootleggers were warring each other in Los Angeles.[8]

Ferndale Enterprise reported that Mrs. N. O. Dunning of Holmes, found the body of a stranger at Dyerville, his head beaten with a club until it was almost jelly. Someone repeatedly stabbed him. Either wound would have caused death. Local authorities suspected he was a hijacking victim. Whoever he was, whoever killed him certainly was unhappy with him.[9]

In Reprisal for Killing a Hijacker

On a peaceful farm road two miles south of Fair Oaks, east of Sacramento, two bodies of San Francisco men were found still warm but riddled with bullets. On a dirt road, near the abandoned Citrus Hotel, where Fair Oaks and Folsom roads came together, the two Sicilian gangsters met their execution deaths.

Investigators identified one man as Alfredo Cearisso, wanted in the Bay Area for the murder of Gerry Ferri, reputed Mafia leader and hijacker. Detectives surmised the hits were Mafia, black-hand reprisals for Ferri's murder November 24. Also found with the bodies were two newspapers, one in Italian, both with headlines of the Ferri murder. A "letter in Italian script" gave evidence of a "Black Hand Plot." The other man remained unidentified.[10]

✆

Bodies were found all over California, many may have been attributed to gang rivalry, internal gang disputes, hijacking, witnesses disappearing, and revenge. Most stayed on the books as John Does. For example, a 38-45 year old man, part bald, sandy red hair was found near El Centro with a bullet hole in his heart. Someone did not want him identified as he was left nude and acid had been put on his fingertips to hinder identification.[11]

In Los Angeles, late in 1929, Byrant Vauchelet of Hollywood told his landlady. "I guess somebody double-crossed me. I'm poisoned." Then he fell down writhing. The police surgeons and a private doctor could not determine the type of poison which caused his death. Although he didn't appear to be employed, he drove an expensive car and frequently had big rolls of money. He may have been in the liquor business.

In a remote desert spring by Hesperia, the dry squad investigated a moonshine operation in May 1931 and found what appeared to be graves. Joseph Taylor, Chief of Detectives of Los Angeles Police Department, and Captain George Contraras of the "gangster squad" of the San Bernardino Sheriff Department came out to the desert to see if these could be the graves of two men who disappeared. Frank Baumgartner [actually Frank Baumgarteker], a prominent Cucamonga winery operator and Los Angeles distillery owner, disappeared in November 1929. Although his car was found in a San Diego parking lot, Baumgarteker had not been seen since he went to lunch with his partner in Los Angeles. The other one "taken for a ride" was Joseph Newman of San Bernardino who went on a one-way trip in 1930. Newman was supposedly a noted bootlegger.

Since the abandoned still site had mounds that looked like graves, detectives ordered machinery to excavate. They found no bodies. Newman and Baumgarteker continued to be listed as missing persons.[12]

Well-known liquor smuggler, Frank Cornero, later owner of the gambling ship Rex, put out of business by the government in 1946, answered the door of his Beverly Hills home in 1948 and was shot. Though he almost died, he recovered and died in Las Vegas in 1955 before opening a casino on the strip. Courtesy of Los Angeles Examiner Hearst Newspaper Collection, Dept. of Special Collections, University of Southern California Library.

Never Returned from Lunch

When the "six Italians from Chicago" told Frank Baumgarteker to relinquish control of Bonded Winery No. 1 and be a rich man, or be eliminated, he kept this threat from his wife, and life-long friend, Mary Quint Baumgarteker. She knew, however, something was wrong. She sensed a problem. He finally told her about the threat, gave her the list of the six Italians and told her if he did not come home some night, turn these names over to the district attorney Buron Fitts. He did not come home the afternoon of November 25, 1929, after a luncheon appointment with his partner, Robert Demateis, and a couple businessmen at 8th and Spring Street [see Chapter 1]. That morning was the last time Mary and son Herbert saw him. The papers reported that Frank Baumgarteker, 43, L.A. "capitalist," disappeared.

San Diego police found his car in a parking lot. Frank's billfold, with four corners torn off, and his keys were in the car. There were no signs of violence, no blood anywhere. The jack and a wrench were in the back seat. The car, covered with red dust, looked as if it had been in the Julian area. On December 2, the *Los Angeles Times* had the heading "Wine Man Hunt Extended."

His partner, Robert Demateis, said that at the luncheon meeting in Los Angeles, they discussed Demateis' contract to remove 40,000 gallons of wine from the Cucamonga Winery to a local wine tonic establishment. The government-supervised contract was still on Baumgarteker's desk. Los Angeles assigned Captain E. Raymond Cato, Detective Captain W. C. Allen, Head of Missing Persons, Detective L. Condaffer and Detective Lieutenant O. E. A. Nord to work the case.

Detectives drove Baumgarteker's dark blue phaeton-type auto to trace the possible route from 8th Street in Los Angeles to the San Diego parking lot. They used Valley Boulevard as a shortcut to San Diego, wanting to see if anyone remembered Baumgarteker, who, on the day he disappeared, wore a leather jacket, khaki trousers and riding boots.

Baumgarteker owned Union Motor Transport Co., 2320 State Street, was half owner of Western Grape Products, Bonded Winery #1, a distillery at Avenue 19 and Humboldt Street capable of producing $50,000 per day and owned a winery at Cucamonga, the Western Medicinal Wine Co. At the Western Grape Products, they sold sherry, distilled alcohol and shipped thousands of five-gallon cans of grape syrup with directions: do not open or add water or it will ferment and cause wine. His business affairs were in order and there were no family problems. The Austrian-born immigrant built up a large trucking firm, hauling between Los Angeles and Bakersfield. He later bought the Cucamonga Winery and the distillery, across from Lincoln Heights Police Department. He married his first love from Austria. In fact, he would joke that he slept with Mary Quint when they were babies. They were often placed in the same crib by their families in Austria. Frank and Mary had one son, Herbert, sixteen years old when his father disappeared. Frank was a devoted husband, the home-every-night type.[13]

One good friend was an old Italian named Demateis, who owned San Gabriel Winery, east of Olvera St., and with Guasti, planted hundreds of acres of grapes in San Gabriel and San Bernardino valleys. Demateis had two sons, according to an interview with Herbert Baumgarteker, who were "as different as two sons could be": Charles from his first wife was dark complected, respectable, honest; Robert A. Demateis, from his second wife, was blond, handsome, sneaky and dishonest, "would rather make 50 cents illegally than $1.00 legally." He was a lover, a playboy, always needing money for his girls and boats, said Herbert Baumgarteker. When Robert's father went back to the old country, Robert bootlegged over $40,000 worth of liquor from his own father's bonded winery. As a favor to his elder friend, Frank took Robert Demateis as a junior partner. The father thought it would help Robert. Herbert always felt Robert was behind his father's disappearance. Alcohol and wine strangely came up short. Back doors of storage rooms had been pried open. All caused federal agents to investigate Baumgarteker's business. Frank had received no satisfaction from federal agents and told Mary, "I've got to go to Washington," and "we have everything sewed up." Herbert could only assume, years later, that these mysterious comments had something to do with his father's elimination. After Frank had been missing for awhile, Mary asked prohibition agents to watch the distillery, especially the back entrances.

Herbert said Robert let it slip out that Frank may have had a blond girlfriend and probably ran off with her. District Attorney Buran Fitts, supported the assertion when he said Baumgarteker was "free, white and twenty-one, probably took off with a blond." Fitts was a "creep!" said Herbert fifty years afterwards. The investigations turned up nothing: the Italian names were fictitious, no body found, and, of course, no blond.

Said Herbert: We were in difficulty: we received only $150 per month from the trustee who took over the businesses, we had to rent out the family home and live in the servants' quarters, we could not pay the bills, and Metropolitan Life would not pay because he wasn't legally dead. Mary hired a flamboyant lawyer who told her, "The next bag of bones found in the desert, we'll identify him as your husband and collect on the insurance." Mary felt that was "fraud of the first water" and "quit" that lawyer. The insurance company extended the time needed to wait and even then tried to deny the claim because the premiums had not been paid after Frank disappeared. Mary finally won her claim, but had to go to court to do it. In 1933, Mary got some of her businesses and property back—Sheriff Ernest Shay, San Bernardino County, sold her the property in that county—as the highest bidder. Vai Brothers received permission to buy the Bonded Winery #1, just in time for repeal. The popular Padre wine sold well. Herbert stated there were suspicious dealings as Vai brothers were on the "fringe of gangster," and not the most reputable or even the lowest of the bidders, yet were authorized to buy it. Officer Nord became Mary's friend, but was "pushed aside." The police even followed the private detective Mary hired. Nothing came of the investigation. One reporter kept on the case, kept pushing, and was also a friend, but later was killed when a bomb exploded on his front porch. Herbert did not remember his name or dates, yet thought there might be a connection. Although he may have worked for the *Times*, the author did not find any information from the newspaper and has not pursued it further. Most of this story is left untold and the murderers left unpunished. Frank Baumgarteker would not give in and as promised was eliminated.

The whole experience was a nightmare, said Herbert, with reporters, police, accusations, legal problems, insurance and loss of his father and devastation of his mother.

How Organized Were the Gangs?

Hundreds of pages of FBI files on Lester Gillis (Baby Face Nelson) and John Paul Chase revealed connections between Chicago gangs, Reno and northern California smuggling gangs. Hans Leon Stittmatter, Sausalito, and Joseph Parente headed a smuggling gang in northern California, of which John Paul Chase was a member in 1932. After Baby Face Nelson escaped from custody in Illinois State Penitentiary in February, 1932, he arrived in Reno in March, receiving refuge from two heads of the Reno underworld, William Graham and James C. McKay. These men sent Gillis to James J. Griffin, at the Andromeda Café, 155 Columbus Avenue, San Francisco. Gillis at this time, using the alias Jimmy Burnett and Jimmy Burnell, joined the Stittmatter and Parente gang, which consisted of, among others, the following members: Anthony "Soap" Morino (Moreno), Louis Tambini, Nippy Constantine, Louis Leonhart, Castro Aversen, Red Kennedy and Joseph Ray Negri. Stittmatter, who owned the Bridge Cigar Company, Sausalito, introduced Gillis to Chase who introduced him around Sausalito as Chase's half brother. For about two months Gillis and Chase were involved in coastal smuggling and rumrunning, residing at the Mohn Apartments. Later his wife Helen lived with him. Chase listed his address as The Oasis, 922 Water Street, Sausalito.[14]

Gillis lived some of 1932 in Reno at 126 Caliente Street. When his wife needed medical help, the Gillises moved to Vallejo, living in Casa de Vallejo Hotel, and Helen was treated at Vallejo General Hospital, with Gillis visiting her every day. Thomas C. Williams helped harbor the Gillises in this area "known to be a rendezvous for some of the most notorious gangsters," according to the FBI files. The Gillises went back to Reno until May 1933, then traveled back to Chicago.

FBI agents suspected Baby Face was linked to the disappearance of Roy J. Frisch, Reno bank teller who was supposedly taken for a ride. Frisch went to the movies in March of 1934 and never returned. He was to have testified in New York on a nation-wide bunco ring. McKay and Graham, ones who hid Nelson in Reno, were to go on trial for being part of ring. Rumors were that Frisch retired at the bottom of Lake Tahoe [see Chapter 30].

These stories and others aver to the complicated organizations of gangs and the power that some of the underworld had. It was truly an underground world and the depth and intricacies will forever remain underground.

Frank Cornero, brother of Tony Cornero, owner of the gambling ship Rex, being handcuffed by officers. Handcuffed to Cornero is Ralph Owen, said to be only a "passenger" on the Rex, but probably the same Ralph H. Owen[s], Ralph Omens [?], Los Angeles hotel owner involved in liquor smuggling in the 1920s and 1930s.
Courtesy of Los Angeles Examiner Hearst Newspaper Collection, Dept. of Special Collections, University of Southern California Library.

CHAPTER 21

SAN FRANCISCO—AS WET AS THE PACIFIC OCEAN—BUT DON'T WASTE IT

Federal Agent William R. Paget caused quite a turmoil at Bush and Steiner Streets in San Francisco when his dry squad raided a flat in possession of Joseph E. (Eddie) Marron, in November 1927. Marron, former California assemblyman, was at the time under sentence of two years for liquor violation conspiracy.

When Paget's men carried out $15,000 worth of imported scotch and French liquor and began breaking the valued bottles, neighbors of 2021 Steiner Street lost control—trying to salvage the liquor. Thirsty San Franciscans probably had heart palpitations and undoubtedly shed more than a few tears as hatchets broke into cases and imported and expensive liquor flowed out. So many people crowded around, blocking the house and the streets, that the Feds sent a message to the Bush police precinct for help.

As liquor drained from the back yard to the gutter, citizens practiced some of their Puritan ethics of thriftiness— waste not; some no doubt practiced their Italian ethics—don't waste good liquor! Besides that, November days and nights can get mighty chilly in San Francisco. And what a horrible thing to waste something that could warm the inner soul.

Typically in incidents like this, the crowd pushed to pick up broken bottles with some contents remaining. Men sent their wives or children to bring back a Mason jar or a pot. Dozens used hands to scoop liquor out of newly-formed puddles; others soaked scarves, handkerchiefs and desperate ones even used socks to sop up 80 proof moisture—waste not, want not was the motto of San Franciscans that day.

The flat, stated Paget, was headquarters for one of the rum-running rings. The phone directory listed Mrs. Joseph Marron as the resident, but inside were bills and orders of liquor for Marron, one being a bill for five-gallon cans of alcohol and for labels to make the not-so-genuine alcohol look more genuine. "Most of this batch was genuine," said Paget.

And that night many Bush Street neighbors enjoyed the evening and slept well, affirming that it was the real stuff.[1]

In her master's thesis at U. C. Berkeley, *The Enforcement of Prohibition in San Francisco*, Elizabeth A. Brown analyzed San Francisco's attitude toward prohibition. Whether the rest of the country voted for it or not, whether California voted for it or whether prohibition was part of the constitution—none of this mattered much, not to most San Franciscans. They just didn't want it, Marron, as an example, ran his rumrunning and bootlegging within a half

374

block of the Bush precinct, a station with over 100 officers in it. Both Marron and his partner, Birdsal, had brothers-in-law as San Francisco police sergeants.

In fact, in Marron's books, dozens of officers were mentioned. According to Brown, many Bush officers were transferred to other stations. Payoffs of $5 were noted next to Patrolman Kissane 32 times. Sgt. Gorham received $90 from Birdsal.[2]

People from the "City," as San Francisco Bay Area residents affectionately called San Francisco, ignored the law, closed eyes to violations, participated in violating prohibition or a few became totally frustrated with crime. Basically San Francisco practiced nullification of the 18th amendment. A police study showed over 1,500 places in the City where folks could buy liquor. And boots paid well for their right to sell in the City. In fact, in the middle of the 1920s, a group of boots complained to the Internal Revenue that they had to pay from $60 to $600 per month to the police. In these few pages one can see how from Mayor Jimmy Rolph down to the patrolman on the beat, San Franciscans either ignored the law or profited from it.

In 1922, for example, Sgt. William Fennessey, Patrolmen George Becky and Ellis M. Miller of the North End defended themselves against charges that they did not report knowledge of a robbery planned at 154 Filbert St. on January 20, 1922. These officers allegedly knew of the plot to steal $250,000 worth of liquor from the Filbert St. warehouse. They denied anyone approached them

New Year's Eve, 1915, at famed Poodle Dog Café. Raided several times by federal agents during prohibition and finally closed its doors in the mid 1920s. Photo from advertising postcard.

with information. They stood on their good records and part of their defense was that the charges were all "hearsay." Their attorneys attacked the character of the witness William C. "Chick" Speiss. Through the trial came the repeated cry: certain San Francisco police are fixed.[3]

At the end of a Customs report on the Pacific Coast, a paragraph compared San Francisco and Los Angeles in 1929: "Enforcement varied, for example, in an comparison of Los Angeles and San Francisco. In the latter the police are of little help, due in main to a decided wet sentiment. In the other, local police help on smaller cases, but high character [cases are not enforced by L.A. police] as in the wet city. There always are, of course, other determining factors, for example, that Los Angeles had the denatured alcohol problem and San Francisco illicit stills."[4]

Wet as the Pacific Ocean:
An Informal History of Prohibition in San Francisco[5]
by Merritt S. Barnes, Foster City

At the Palace Hotel in San Francisco, a few minutes before prohibition went into effect, Harry Annan walked into the middle of the dining room and with a "Hear ye, hear ye" solemnly announced the passing of the old era. The Palace Hotel, whose legendary bar had been an obligatory stop for "old time San Francisco *bon vivants*" who made the daily pilgrimage along the famous cocktail route when Andrew J. Volstead was the comparatively obscure attorney of Yellow Medicine County, Minnesota, was a fitting place for the announcement. The hotel was an institution in San Francisco so that the news that its cozily paneled bar with the famous Maxfield Parrish mural would become a soda fountain provoked the *Chronicle* to headline "PALACE BAR TO BE ICE CREAM SHOP, YE GODS!" But most San Franciscans, however, had learned long before that as Ring Lardner wryly said, prohibition was better than no liquor at all.[6]

San Francisco's pragmatic accommodation to the Eighteenth Amendment was succinctly expressed by prohibition agents who reportedly admonished New Year's Eve celebrants in 1925 to "keep your liquor under the table!"[7] In interests of keeping their liquor under the table San Franciscans were scrupulously dry at official public gatherings. When French World War I hero Marshal Ferdinand Foch visited the city in 1921, he was given a tumultuous welcome including a formal banquet at the Palace Hotel accompanied by numerous toasts from glasses containing nothing stronger that California's finest ice water. To commemorate the launching of the first scheduled air service between San Francisco and Los Angeles, Imelda Shannon, daughter of a San Francisco Supervisor and a passenger on the first flight, smashed a bottle of grape juice over the propeller to christen the plane.[8] A number of the city's most notorious restaurants, including the Poodle Dog which dated from gold rush days, closed their doors early in prohibition.[9] A superficial glance at the city might have indicated that prohibition had brought about fundamental changes in San Francisco's social life. In 1926, the progressive editor Chester Rowell advised a gathering of San Franciscans to "look around among your friends and see for yourself. You see among your friends less drunkenness. It isn't done. The thing is pretty well enforced."[10]

Apparently Rowell spoke for the 15 percent of the population he associated with because Assistant United States Attorney General Mabel Willebrandt said that San Francisco was "85 percent wet" and estimated that between $5,000 and $20,000 worth of illegal liquor was smuggled into the city nightly.[11] The Anti-Saloon League characterized San Francisco as ranking with New York as "the wettest city in the United States."[12] Liquor was available throughout the city, albeit at inflated prices, from the earliest days of prohibition. The city's newspapers reported that bootleg whiskey was selling at well-known San Francisco cafes like Coppa's Neptune Palace as early as March, 1920, for $12.50 per pint.[13] By mid-1926 New York *Times* informed its readers that in San Francisco: "...raw Scotch, selling for $60 per case, delivered anywhere in the city is imported from Canada..."[14] "Real Scotch, Bourbon and Cognac find their way in through 'Rum Row' from Havana and the orient. The genuine article ranges in price from $90 to $125 per case..."

One year after passage of the Wright Act, California's prohibition enforcement measure, San Francisco Police Chief Daniel O'Brien asked his men to report all establishments in the city where illegal liquor was sold. The list he received stretched to 1,492 locations.[15] So ineffective was prohibition in San Francisco that the city's 1922 Grand Jury called the Volstead Act "a farce."[16] The attitude of San Francisco toward prohibition was captured in the newspaper of the Association Against the Prohibition Amendment [AAPA] which boldly asserted, "We may see a few cargoes of booze seized and a few pigs closed up, but San Franciscans will continue to drink their liquor, questionable of origin though it may be."[17]

Sodom and San Francisco

The dry Governor of Colorado scaled the height of hyperbole in warning that if the *Bible* were re-written in 1922, it would read "Sodom and San Francisco,"[18] according to AAPA.

A full decade before the passage of the Eighteenth Amendment the entire San Francisco delegation to the State Legislature voted against a local option bill. When any measure regulating liquor appeared before Congress, the state legislature, or the voters, the city was uniformly opposed, with a single exception. The exception, State Senator Edwin Grant, in 1914 not only voted for local option, but also proposed that the Panama-Pacific International Exposition to be held in San Francisco the following year be dry. The voters acted immediately to remove this blot on their record by recalling Senator Grant within the year. When given the chance to express themselves directly, San Francisco voters resoundingly defeated a proposal for statewide prohibition by 104,817 to 22,024.[19]

Local newspapers gleefully reported in 1922, resolutions from the Chamber of Commerce, Board of Supervisors and Grand Jury petitioning Congress to modify the Volstead Act in favor of beer and wine. The same year San Francisco's two representatives, John I. Nolan and Florence Kahn, were the only representatives west of St. Louis to support a bill legalizing beer. By mid-decade the *Examiner* criticized efforts at enforcement as "official snooping." By 1929, San Francisco Bar Association added its voice for repeal by releasing "the strongest pro-repeal statement of any bar association in the country."[20]

While forthrightly seeking modification or repeal, San Francisco was completely intransigent concerning enforcement. Within 30 days of the passage of wartime prohibition, the Board of Supervisors, with the concurrence of Mayor James Rolph Jr., repealed the two blind-pig ordinances which had previously been used to regulate unlicensed sale of liquor. "As if to give emphasis to this official friendliness toward bootlegging," the Board reprimanded Police Captains Charles Goff and Arthur Layne who had accepted small federal court fees in connection with prohibition enforcement cases. Although based on a technicality the message was not lost on San Francisco's Police Department. The captains were censured because "they were active in raiding blind pigs with federal warrants and federal help. The city's police courts proved "so hostile to the state dry laws that during the first six months of 1923 these four courts dismissed 532 cases; 833 bootleggers were fined an average of $32.12." By 1926 the Board of Supervisors voted unanimously to oppose the use of local police "on any basis" to enforce prohibition. Fabled San Franciscan Sally Stanford, operator of the city's most elegant house of prostitution, explained, "All this was done pretty much out in the open with God and Jimmy Rolph looking on."[21]

Mayor Sunny Jim developed a healthy ability to avoid controversy, displaying a "complex against crusaders" because they intrude into a society which should be perfectly happy. Will Rogers offered, when Rolph was moving into the Governor's mansion: "Thank goodness we won't be reformed during his administration."[22]

There was no doubt of Rolph's personal view of the dry laws: He ignored them. Some went so far as to say he was an alcoholic during the last ten years of his life. A reporter recalled a parade in which "he was so drunk he got on one side of the horse and fell off the other." A Yellow Cab official remembered that Rolph was intoxicated during a ceremonial appearance at a building near city hall which was part of a civil paint and cleanup drive. He emerged from the mayor's limousine in full formal dress, supported by an aide. Sunny

Jim said a few words, turned and was handed a paint brush, thrust it into the paint up to his white-gloved wrist, withdrew it, and slapped the paint onto the building.[23]

During the 1920 Democratic National Convention, when a few reporters remarked how boring [the convention was], Rolph wanted to show them his city was, indeed, "The city that knows how." He invited them to wine and dine at his house, "poured illegal but authentic liquor into us—until I, at least, was ready for a two week cure," said one reporter. Then Rolph put on a cockfight on his Persian rug in his living room.[24]

His answers to complaints of reformers was "the world has never succeeded in eliminating human weakness," then asserting that San Francisco was superior to other American and European cities "in the matter of regulating and controlling that amount of vice which could not be eliminated."[25]

District Attorney Matthew Brady was popular enough to be reelected as the city's chief law-enforcement officer six times between 1920 and 1944 and to earn a reputation as one of San Francisco's "most beloved" public officials. But he became a favorite target of prohibitionist broadsides. The difference between the mayor and the district attorney was that Rolph could quietly ignore the dry laws, but Brady was "an extremely uninhibited man" who, through word and deed, flaunted his staunch opposition to enforce sobriety. He served as vice president of the California Association Against the Prohibition Amendment, and even told a reporter, "Prohibition should be left up to the federals. They are responsible for the law. Now let them enforce it." Anti-Saloon League head A. H. Briggs fumed impotently, "Brady heads a force of two thousand policemen and...is doing absolutely nothing to stop the booze smuggling conspiracy."[26]

When Brady's longtime friend Jim Griffin was convicted on a federal charge of bootlegging and incarcerated in the Alameda County Jail, Brady led a party which included a mandolin and an accordion player on a Thanksgiving visit to the jail to serenade Griffin with a few rounds of "Sweet Adeline." Brady committed an even more blatant affront to enforcement of the law at a New Year's Eve party where he was present "as a guest enjoying entertainment at a notorious bootlegging resort" when it was raided by federal authorities.[27]

Sally Stanford explained, while discussing the many years of "permissiveness" in San Francisco that "Nothing lasts that long unless the people are willing that it should."[28]

Foremost guardians of local bootlegging interest were two Irish brothers, Pete and Tom McDonough, who began as saloon keepers and branched out by establishing the nation's first bailbond firm around the turn of the century. By the 1920s the McDonoughs had built up a fantastic network of political influence among local officials which gave them nearly complete control of the city's police and courts. Their bailbond office was later described as "the fountainhead of corruption." Their power was so complete that a local attorney was convinced "Tammany never ran New York City as completely as the McDonoughs ran the right to break the law in San Francisco."[29]

McDonoughs were active bootleggers themselves. They operated their own bar known as "The Corner" across the street from the Hall of Justice, had an interest in the popular Coppa's Neptune Palace and were financial backers on numerous soft drink parlors which dispensed bootleg whiskey. Pete McDonough was reputed to own several distilleries and have four boats smuggling illegal Canadian liquor into the Bay Area.[30]

Samuel Rutter, chief of federal prohibition enforcement in San Francisco, was convinced "the McDonough brothers are the main source of supply" for illegal alcohol and he launched a determined campaign to put them out of business.

Rutter believed he had succeeded when his agents arrested Pete and Tom McDonough and their nephew Harry Rice for violation of the Volstead Act in April 1923. Although agents had seized $5,000 worth of liquor from Rice's garage which they described as a retail depot and they purchased several drinks at The Corner, Pete McDonough was undaunted. Telling reporters, "I was tipped off three days before the arrest direct from the prohibition office," McDonough boasted, "I will give $100,000 to any charitable institution in San Francisco if Sam Rutter or any of his agents can prove that I sold a drop of whiskey..."[31]

[Said Rutter: McDonoughs were] "Kings of financiers in arranging bail for practically all bootleggers and since the prohibition law went into effect they have cleaned up in the neighborhood of $600,000." One agent explained that each San Francisco agent had at least six bootleggers paying him off.[32]

Federal prosecutor Kenneth Green assessed the situation accurately when he said, "McDonough is up against a prosecution he cannot corrupt." Indeed, he could not, and on May 15, 1923, Pete McDonough was sentenced to 15 months in the Alameda County jail. [People thought "King" McDonough was dead. When appeals failed, his lawyers tried executive clemency.] On November 22, 1924, a petition requesting a pardon was presented to President Calvin Coolidge by former Governor James N. Gillett. The petition was signed by more than 300 leading citizens of San Francisco: Mayor Rolph, three congressmen, police commissioner, judge of appellate court, 11 superior court judges, two justices of the peace, city clerk, auditor, District Attorney Brady, four assistant district attorneys and the president of Bank of Italy. Although insufficient to keep him out of jail, it undoubtedly helped him gain a parole after serving eight months, making him the first bootlegger to be paroled in California.[33]

While no longer active as bootleggers after Pete's jail term, the McDonoughs were able to provide virtual immunity to others engaging in illegal activity.

It was clear that San Francisco's judicial system reached its nadir in 1928 when a jury was itself put on trial for drinking up the evidence in a prohibition case. The McDonough organization was clearly responsible in a large measure for this deterioration of the local justice system to the point where "nullification of prohibition" was virtually complete in San Francisco.[34]

Another strong organization was a gang known as "The Forty Strong." The Forty reportedly dominated the lucrative Italian bootlegging in the city's North Beach District. They relied upon force and intimidation to maintain control. On one occasion the gang buried a suspected hijacker up to his neck and stood over him with a shovel until he divulged the location of the missing liquor. In another instance The Forty Strong took a victim to Ocean Beach, poured gasoline over him and flicked lighted matches dangerously close until he talked. These were not standard practices however.[35]

Other bootleggers tried to evade the system of *de facto* licenses through protection payoffs by considerably more ingenious methods. Shanty Malone, "a crazy Irishman whose only idols were athletes," sometimes seemed to own "half the speakeasies in town." Rather than pay off officials, Malone simply moved from one Tenderloin location to another each time he was raided. His customers followed, and Malone, regardless of his address, was able to maintain his reputation as operating San Francisco's finest sports bar. Indeed, it was often possible to find a large contingent from each of the local college football teams at Shanty Malone's on Saturday night recalling their exploits in the day's game.[36]

The Hotel d'Oloron continued to serve illegal liquor by resorting to an even more colorful scheme. Located at the apex of a triangular block formed by two alleys near the intersection of Columbus Avenue and Broadway, the hotel was frequently raided by federal officials. After each raid the courts ordered the premises at the hotel's address shut down. Business continued, however, without loss of a day's drinking when the proprietor summoned a carpenter to build a new door into one of the alleys so that the hotel could register a new business address. The Hotel d'Oloron eventually possessed a long string of front doors with a matching string of addresses.[37]

The amicable relations between operators and authorities were maintained even when "the heat was on" and police had to raid a few speakeasies to placate the reform element. This cordiality was demonstrated when Rex Glissman's Golden Fan was raided. The Chinese bartender, Charlie Ting Gan, was arrested. As the patrol wagon rolled through Chinatown, Charlie asked his captors to stop at his Grant Avenue home. They did, and Charlie went in unescorted to get his overcoat because he might get cold in jail without it.

Indeed, with the mild sentences customary in San Francisco courts, it was easier to take one's punishment than to go to the trouble of escaping.[38]

Authorities made no attempt to cut off the source of supply. In 1926 when an explosion occurred in the basement of the International Hotel on Kearney Street, 200 yards from Central Police Station and two blocks from prohibition headquarters, and within sight of the Hall of Justice, the blast brought authorities to "the largest distilling plant uncovered in San Francisco since the inception of prohibition." The basement contained two stills with a 750-gallon capacity, 10,000 gallons of wine, and all kinds of bar equipment valued at $75,000. Subsequent investigation was abandoned after finding only that the basement had been leased for three years to "persons unknown."[39]

San Franciscans frequented well-known drinking establishments and made only the barest gesture toward discretion. Officials of the city's Recreation Park, where the Seals of the Pacific Coast League played baseball, had to change their policy of selling tickets for a special screened-in section running from first to third base which entitled buyers to redeem their stubs for a shot of whiskey or two bottles of beer. After the Eighteenth was enacted, a ham and cheese sandwich and a soft drink were substituted for the liquor, but the use of whiskey or gin from pocket flasks to season the soft drinks was so prevalent that few fans found it necessary to stop referring to the section as the "Booze Cage."[40] The Palace Hotel closed its bars, but most patrons knew that a request for flowers would bring the waiter back to their table carrying a flower box containing a bottle of liquor. Italian restaurants in North Beach continued to serve wine and even retained hard liquor for especially trusted friends, but the illegal beverages were brought to tables in coffee cups to avoid suspicion. Spider Kelly's at Mason and Ellis made its only concession to legal propriety with a house rule that all liquor should be served from the floor beneath the customer's table. The numerous soft drink parlors in the Tenderloin avoided embarrassing discoveries in the event of a search by law enforcement officers by keeping no liquor on their premises. When patrons ordered, they were served soft drinks, and they waited while a man stationed outside the door carried in a bottle of liquor to pour into their glasses, then returned to his post on the sidewalk.[41]

A number of speakeasies were exclusively liquor dispensaries. Anyone could walk into establishments like Firecracker Jim Griffin's Saloon on the old Barbary Coast, Dutch White's on Eddy Street, Philosophers Inn across the alley from the Hall of Justice, Star Bar a little further up Kearney Street, or the Inferno Cafe operated by Joe Parente, described as "the biggest of the independent" bootleggers. Other clubs like the Swastika Club on Maiden Lane, Town Club on Hyde Street, Chapeau Rouge on Powell Street or the Royal Camel on Filbert Street required patrons to display membership cards.

Certain places became identified with specific professions; for example, Breen's at Third and Market became a hangout for newspapermen. The House of Shields across New Montgomery Street from the Palace Hotel became a favorite watering hole for people in the financial district. A few resorts gained notoriety for things other than the liquor they served. Amelio's on Powell served food which made it a culinary landmark. In 1931 "Bimbo" Guintoli and "Monk" Young opened the 365 Club at Market and Fremont, featuring the "Girl In The Fishbowl," the product of a projection system which produced the image of a live mermaid seemingly swimming around nude in a hexagonal glass tank. The 365 Club became one of the city's leading nightclubs in the years after prohibition.[42]

Two speakeasies in particular came to be celebrated as uniquely San Franciscan in atmosphere. They were Coffee Dan's, housed in a basement on O'Farrell Street just off Powell, and Izzy Gomez's at 848 Pacific Avenue. Coffee Dan's allowed patrons to make a spectacular entry by way of a steep slide or a more sedate one by way of the stairs along side. The combination bar and restaurant served food and liquor on wooden plank tables reputed to be of pre-earthquake vintage. Dan's featured the vocals and piano of Frankie Shaw and Lee Poe whose sometimes ribald lyrics were accompanied by customers banging on the plank tables with wooden mallets they had been given with their silverware. Known as a hangout for gamblers Coffee Dan's became a favorite spot in the downtown area. Izzy Gomez's, located where North Beach met the old Barbary Coast, possessed a different kind of fascination. Housed in a dilapidated loft, Gomez's saloon had been described as "infinitely more colorful than sanitary." What attracted crowds was Gomez himself, a remarkable enough figure to become a celebrity in a city renowned for its characters. A large Portuguese with penchant for a black fedora, he reportedly once won a bet that he could smoke a cigar in a shower, but refused to remove his hat. Gomez was noted for his generous hospitality. Regular customers remembered sometimes "he seemed positively embarrassed at the act of picking up your money off the bar. 'Aw, go on,' he would mumble, shoving it back at you. 'You my friend.'"[43]

Like Izzy Gomez, San Francisco continued to be noted for its generous hospitality. The City knew how to entertain and make tourists feel welcome. A silly law like the Volstead Act certainly would not stop "The city that knows how." The City just nullified that law.

Min and Hattie's Bohemian Rendezvous
by Bernice Scharlach, Lafayette

"A salon in time—risky, frisky, minus the whisky…for those of the artistic world which finds itself at midnight all dressed up and no place to go"—that's how a writer on the old *San Francisco Call and Post* described San Francisco's first night club. It opened in 1925, during the height of the prohibition era. It was run by two sisters, Hattie and Minnie Mooser. If they had any talent at all, it was for cooking and making a fuss over celebrities.

The club had a ridiculous name. As ridiculous as the whole idea of prohibition in a city known as the drinking capital of America: Aladdin Studio and Tiffin Room. Min said, "The Aladdin Studio part was from the days when Hat founded the Children's Theatre in San Francisco and rehearsals were held in a loft on 220 Post Street. The Tiffin Room came in 1921 when we began serving lunch—Hat was a divine cook—to parents and onlookers. Well, pretty soon the restaurant part became so successful we had to look for larger quarters. In 1923, we heard about a new building going up on Sutter Street. They offered us the entire second floor. It was enormous. In order to make expenses, we stayed open for dinner." And then for midnight supper.

Vaudeville was going strong in San Francisco then. There were headliners at the Granada, Pantages, Alcazar, Columbia, Orpheum, California and the Warfield. When the shows closed at midnight, there were a lot of hungry people. The Moosers described their establishment as a "Bohemian rendezvous for polite society, professional men and women and visiting celebrities."

Celebrities came, all right. A quick flip through one or two of the worn pages of the Aladdin's guest book is proof enough: Francis X. Bushman, Gus Edwards, Norma Shearer, Al Jolson, Lon Chaney, Olsen and Johnson, Leo Carillo, Fannie Brice, the Duncan Sisters, the Marx Brothers....

Ken Murray, in an interview recalling the old days, once said the club was "the theatrical headquarters of the west....We always felt at home here. It

California's attitude about ending prohibition: San Francisco car with "Repeal 18th Amendment" tag in 1932. Photo courtesy of S.F. Public Library.

was a place with heart." A heart yes, but why Bohemian? While most night spots during prohibition consisted of a peephole at the door and a whistle to let patrons know when the place was about to be raided, the Aladdin's trademark was the Family Table, reserved for the most noted guests, and presided over by Mama and Papa Mooser, who ate their dinner there every night. It had elaborate Oriental decor, Chinese waitresses, a German cook, a Latin orchestra, and Hattie's famous Italian spaghetti. And it could boast that it was never raided.

"That's because we never served," said Min.

But that is not to say that liquor didn't flow freely. There was the bootlegger, Joe Finocchio, who made a small fortune running back and forth from his headquarters across the street selling gin in the Aladdin's men's room. How could the girls keep track of what was going on in there?

"Once we hired a couple of private police, but they were absolutely smashed before the night was out," said Min.

A primary source of supply was the guests themselves; they brought in their own. "We supplied the ice. Lots of ice." The girls were acting on the advice of Capt. Laine [Layne?], head of the police prohibition squad. "We told him we weren't going to serve, but we had to admit that people would bring in their own liquor and we didn't know what to do about it. He told us, 'If you don't let them bring it in, you might as well close the door. They'll just go somewhere else. But you keep your nose clean and we'll protect you.'"

The only run-in with the law the girls had was with District Attorney Matt Brady. "We couldn't get him to go home. He'd stay until three or four in the morning, and we liked to start closing about one. He'd keep sending out for more and more liquor—all the stuff they had been confiscating. How could you tell the DA to go home?"

But Min wants to talk about "my Rudi." In her apartment in Daly City, she settles back in an ornately carved Chinese armchair. It's a relic of the Aladdin days. Her frail hands hold firmly onto the dragon claws. Her eyes are misty. She transports us back to the days when Mah Jongg lessons were taught every afternoon at the Club; when George Milliner would design clothes for society matrons who came to lunch to have their fortunes told, and when Fontella La Pierre gave Charleston lessons during the day and starred in the Club's floor show at night.

"It was a quiet Thursday night about 10:30, February 25, 1926. I was in the foyer talking to Polly the hatcheck girl. Four people were coming up the stairs. Polly said, 'That man looks like Valentino.' I glanced up and said, 'Yes, he does.' We went on talking and I did a double take. 'My God, it is Valentino.'"

With him were movie director Douglas Gerrard and two local socialites.

Min rushed forward with greetings and profuse apologies because it was so quiet.

"Valentino was delighted. 'That's just how I like it—quiet,' he said."

Min seated him and his entourage at the Family Table. They watched the floor show which featured a brother and sister dance team doing the Charleston, the dance that was the current rage.

Valentino summoned Min over—she was never very far away. "I must learn to do that dance before I return to Hollywood. Could you arrange a private lesson for me tomorrow morning?"

Min was ecstatic. Not only would the brother and sister team be there, but Fontella also and the full orchestra.

When she got home that night, she woke Hattie to tell her.

"You don't really think he'll come, do you?"

In the foyer at the Aladdin Studio Tiffin Room, a popular after-theatre night club at 363 Sutter, claiming to be San Francisco's first nightclub, Chinese waitresses greet customers. Because Hattie and Minnie refused to turn the club into a speakeasy, the nightclub eventually closed. "How much money can you make on ice?" asked Minnie. Photo courtesy of Bernice Scharlach, Lafayette.

"Of course I do. He wouldn't let me make all those arrangements for nothing."

"He won't even remember tomorrow morning."

Nevertheless, the whole Mooser family arrived early the next morning. Newspapermen began drifting in. The rumor had gotten around.

By 10:15, Valentino still hadn't arrived. Min was nervously peering through the front window for a glimpse of the Isotta Fraschini. At 10:30, she felt someone reach for her hand. "I'm so sorry I am late. Would you forgive me?"

"It was my Rudi. I wanted to put my arms around him and hug him. I'd gotten a crush on him. You couldn't help it. He was so sweet."

Min shepherded him through the crush of reporters and on to the stage. Fontella was waiting. The curtains were drawn. Only Mama Mooser was allowed behind it. At Valentino's insistence.

He put his arms around Mother and kissed her and said, "I just left my mother in Europe. You remind me so much of her."

"When the lesson was over, he came out in shirt sleeves. He looked so handsome in his waistcoat with a gold watchchain. My, he wore a lot of chains and link bracelets! He graciously consented to be interviewed. Somebody asked him if he were engaged to Pola Negri. He said, 'I'm engaged to no one. I've been married twice and I'm very glad to have my freedom for a while and I don't intend to get married to anybody.'

"He said he'd be back for dinner. He did come back with Douglas Gerrard. They were supposed to leave at nine o'clock because he had to be in Los Angeles the next day and they were driving. But he developed quite a case on Fontella. She was a beautiful little girl. He didn't leave until after one."

Three hours later, Valentino , a notoriously reckless driver, wrapped the Isotta around a telegraph pole, narrowly missing death.

"So that's how we met, and from then on, he never came to San Francisco that he didn't come to the Aladdin. But always without prior notice. Once I chided him for that. I said, 'I wish you'd let me know in advance so I could advertise and have a huge Valentino party.' He said, 'I am going to New York now and when I come back, you can have that party. I promise.' Well, he never did come back. My dear Rudi! He died so unnecessarily of that ruptured appendix."

She removed her glasses to dab at her eyes with a Kleenex.

If Rudi was Min's, then Houdini was Hat's. Their friendship went all the way back to the fire and earthquake. It was their brother Leon who lent the magician a tuxedo for his first stage appearance. Hattie cherished a picture Harry inscribed to her. And the page in the Aladdin guest book, written in Houdini's bold flourish, proclaiming: "Houdini, March 15, 1923, wish to go on record as to his high esteem of the Mooser family."

When he played locally at the Orpheum, he always gave a plug to the Aladdin. Al Rhine, a contemporary of Min and Hattie's, and one-time president of the Golden Gate chapter of the Society of American Magicians, remembered how Houdini pulled off that trick.

"As part of his act, he would swallow a needle and thread, and he held up a glass of water saying, 'See this glass? I stole it from the Aladdin Studio. Anybody who wants to see me after the show can find me at the Aladdin.'"

"Once Harry took Hat for a ride to Half Moon Bay. There was a landing place for bootleggers. She thought it was just an outing, but it was more than that. When they got down there, Harry started unwrapping all this para-phernalia and told her he was going to do a little investigating for the Treasury Department. She had to sit in the car all alone and ready to blow the horn if anyone came by, while Harry slipped under the water looking for liquor caches."

With their close friends they would laugh at such incidents as the time the gold Buddha in the foyer was stolen by the visiting University of Washing-ton football players after they lost a game to the UC Bears, and how the papers raised such a furor that Mayor Sunny Jim Rolph wrote to Seattle's Mayor Edwin Brown officially demanding the safe return of the Buddha.

What made us have to close was the bootleggers. Min and Hattie re-fused to turn the place into and out-and-out speakeasy. "How much money can you make on ice?" asked Min, shaking her head sadly. "Even the rubbing of the wonderful lamp could not save Aladdin and bring in the shekels to keep the sheriff from the door," wrote one newspaper columnist when the Moosers closed their door in January of 1929.

"Just a little bit of the savor of San Francisco died last night when the Aladdin Studio and Tiffin Room dimmed its light for the last time."

⌀

Through ferries, fishing boats, beaches, cars and trucks—every day in every way liquor came into San Francisco. On one Hyde Street ferry three out of three vehicles inspected had liquor destined for the City. The third inspec-tion ended in the death of the liquor agent.

Liquor Runner Kills Dry Agent
Clinging to Car

William S. Grubb, veteran prohibition agent, was killed on March 31 while clinging on the side of a liquor-laden automobile. He was crushed be-tween the car and a telephone pole which the swerving car hit. H. E. Meyer, on the other runningboard, forced driver James Curran, 27, to stop and arrested him for murder.[44]

Meyer and Grubb had been watching the Hyde Street ferry for "deliv-ery" cars. Two other cars had contained 40 cases of whiskey coming into San Francisco. Curran, whose real name was Firman Deiro, said officers did not show badges and he thought they were bandits. When Curran refused to open his car, the agents jumped on the runningboard. As soon as the ferry ramp dropped, Curran sped away, even before the wooden blocks were removed. Trying to get away, he swerved into the pole, killing Grubb. It was just an accident, Curran protested. Already being indicted on liquor running activi-ties, Curran carried 72 pints of whiskey in canvas sacks and certainly did not want another charge. Now he would be tried for murder.

A Bootlegger Defended his Constitutional Rights

Manuel Perry was a slight Portuguese, only 5'5", 135 pounds, dark hair, dark eyes, about 35 years old. Not very imposing. When federal agents raided his soft drink parlor at 30 Jackson Street, San Francisco, on February 28, 1925, they thought they had him. However this Portuguese man fought back, fought for his rights as an immigrant in a freedom-loving country.[45]

Agent Carl W. Ahlin knew Perry's soft drink parlor had been a bootleg joint for perhaps four years. But in order to shut it down he had to have proof. He and agent George H. Hard, on February 12, 1925, met a stevedore on the Embarcadero and offered to buy him a drink at Perry's. With a working stevedore to disguise their plan, Ahlin bought three drinks of jackass brandy for 25¢ a shot. When Ahlin tried to buy another drink, Perry refused to sell him any more. Maybe the "Portagee" was a little smarter than Ahlin thought and had become suspicious. A week or so later Ahlin and Hard tried to make another buy but again Perry refused. On February 28, Ahlin signed an affidavit requesting a search warrant from Prohibition Commissioner Thomas E. Hayden to search Perry's soft drink establishment.

Armed with a federal warrant Ahlin and agents Hard, Rinckel, Taylor and Paget entered Perry's. No one was there. They searched all over, finding an old coffee percolator, a few soft drinks, some evidence the place once served sandwiches. Finally they found a trapdoor under a carpet, which led to a basement. When an agent discovered a lever behind the bar which unlatched the secret door, Hard entered the basement and soon found six pints of jackass in the rafters. Ahlin then found five more. After awhile Perry came in and admitted he was the proprietor. He denied he sold liquor on the 12th or that the hidden stashes were his.

Perry's lawyer, Edward A. O'Dea, interposed a demurrer to exclude evidence, but the court overruled him, and Perry decided to fight by pleading not guilty. He petitioned the court to quash the search warrant used at the Jackson Street business and exclude the evidence seized because of violation of his rights under the Fourth and Fifth Amendments. District Court Judge A. F. St. Sure denied the petition. During the subsequent trail, O'Dea failed again to negate the evidence. He said no probable cause existed for issuing the search warrant: No probable cause to suspect intoxicating liquor on the premises. Of course there was liquor, but with no probable cause, the search warrant should have been invalid and the evidence suppressed. The jury convicted Perry, sentencing him to one year in the San Francisco County jail and fining him $1,000. Again O'Dea filed a complaint that the court erred in its rulings, one frivolous argument being the agent's affidavit was not firmly attached to the search warrant, but "loosely joined to same." More relevant was the search warrant did not specify a description of property to be seized and therefore the warrant was simply a writ of assistance (a blanket search warrant). Another point reiterated since there was no probable cause stated or shown, the U.S. Commissioner issuing the warrant had no reason for "believing that intoxicating liquor was kept, sold, possessed and bartered on said premises"; when the place was raided, no liquor was in view. No crime had been committed in the presence of the agents since Perry was not there during the first part of the raid. O'Dea further asserted that Ahlin had "every reason to believe at that time that intoxicating liquor was not being sold, kept, possessed and bartered there for the reason that after the buy of February 12, he attempted to purchase intoxicating liquor...but was unable to do so." On cross-examination, Ahlin confirmed he bought three drinks for the agents and a stevedore. He admitted trying to buy another round but Perry refused to sell them more. Hard agreed they failed to make a purchase a later day. Since the agents tried to make another buy and could not, Ahlin suppressed evidence when he neglected to tell Commissioner Hayden they could not buy more liquor.

Since the evidence seized violated Perry's constitutional rights, O'Dea objected before and after each agent testified and the evidence was entered. Seventy-three pages of documentation, listing and arguing for 12 Assignment(s) in Error, went to Circuit Court of Appeals for Manuel Perry, Plaintiff in Error. Said O'Dea: "There are no exceptions or reservations set forth in the (Fourth) amendment; and that no person, house, business, papers, effects or place, suspected or unsuspected, good or bad, is denied the protection of its salutary provisions...the amendment does not discriminate. A soft drink parlor, a legitimate business, duly licensed to operate as such, by the laws of a great city of one of the sovereign states" is protected, especially the private recesses not open to the public and reserved for the running of the business.

The brief cited many cases, two from California, showing evidence obtained through improper search warrants were not allowed by the Ninth Circuit Court [Marron vs. U.S., 2F (2nd) 251]. Congress sharpened laws of search and seizure in 1917 by stressing probable cause, responsibilities of the judge or commissioner and officers who served warrants to bring them back to court promptly. Part of the warrant to Agent Ahlin stipulated: "That affiant on or about the 12th day of February, 1925, visited the above and foregoing mentioned and described premises and purchased...3 drinks jackass brandy for the sum of 25 cents per drink, purchased from Perry. On cross-examination, Ahlin affirmed he made no additional buy after February 12; and in fact, he "'attempted to purchase liquor but didn't make any purchase.'" Agent Hard, under cross examination admitted the same.

In the case of Dumbra v. United States, the Supreme Court held: "In determining what is probable cause, we are not called upon to determine whether the offense charged has in fact been committed. We are concerned only with the question whether the affiant had reasonable grounds at the time of his affidavit and the issuance of the warrant for the belief that the law was being violated on the premises to be searched...that a reasonably discreet and prudent man would be led to believe that there was a commission of the offense charged, there is probable cause justifying the issuance of a warrant. The Act of 1917 also stated a search [warrant] must be executed and returned to the judge within 10 days, otherwise it was void." Since 10 days kept an officer from abusing his power and Ahlin negated the "at the time of the affidavit and issuance," O'Dea argued that when Ahlin waited 16 days to obtain the warrant, the delay made it inconsistent with the time the crime was committed. Ahlin illegally kept secret that a crime had not been committed within 10 days, and in fact his later attempt to buy showed that within the 16 days, to their knowledge, a crime had not been committed. Judge Kerrigan in the Northern District of California, in 1924, said the "passing of 11 days would be sufficient to invalidate the warrant." Kerrigan's decision in 1924 supported Perry's case: "...in the absence of special circumstances a search warrant should not be issued solely on the strength of a sale of intoxicating liquor, where more than ten days elapsed between the sale and the making of the affidavit."

Not even a scintilla of evidence, said O'Dea, proved a search warrant should have been issued. The indiscriminate use of the search warrant in the colonial days, he said, was a cause of the American Revolution. James Otis argued against the British Writ of Assistance: "Their menial servants may enter, may even break locks, bars and everything in their way." Just as Otis did before the American Revolution, the diminutive Perry in San Francisco defended the rights of all Americans by resisting this encroachment on his constitutional right.

ɤ

Police officers like Captains Layne, Charlie Goff and Christenson were honest, but being honest became a handicap in San Francisco. Goff went after the Howard Street gangsters and bootleggers. Once when a hood said, "Take off your badge," Goff did and "bamb, bamb!" out went the challenger! According to former lawyer from San Francisco, Jack Derham, of the Bush Street Station, the policy was "no dough" and you're closed Friday, Saturday and Sunday. Goff played a different game than the city wanted and was forced out in 1925. A criminal lawyer, Jake Erlick, said a criminal lawyer's job was easy in those days with so much evidence being quashed. "Take handcuffs off the police and put them back on the criminals," said Erlick. Prosecution was difficult in San Francisco.[46]

From the beginning of the decade when San Franciscans voted against all prohibition proposals and the Board of Supervisors gave the Democratic Party 50 barrels of whiskey to entertain delegates to the 1920 Democratic National Convention, to the reprimanding of clean energetic officers like Goff and Layne for too much enforcement, San Franciscans ignored the federal and state prohibition laws. A *Literary Digest* survey of 3,000 city dwellers proved what prohibitionists and federal agents already knew: San Franciscans, over two-thirds of them, were for repeal, and with the help of city and county officials, they nullified the 18th Amendment. This city had been voted the best-dressed city in the nation several times. During all these bootlegging years, they wore their displeasure with prohibition openly and proudly for all to see.

CHAPTER 22

THE MOUNTAIN FOLK

The Wright Act was California's version of the federal Volstead Act. It made federal prohibition laws state laws, requiring local, county and state enforcement. As with so many laws, the burden was put on the local government without extra funds to carry out the enforcement of those laws.

A typical reaction to the Wright Act came from the popular sheriff of Siskiyou County, A. S. Calkins. He said the act will be rigidly enforced. He would stake out buildings where liquor was sold. Calkins affirmed in the November 30, 1922, *Siskiyou News*, that buildings can be closed as nuisances for a year, thus encouraging owners to oust suspected sellers. The new law was to go into effect on December 20, 1922, but Calkins could not hire extra deputies, "We can work a little overtime if necessary," he said. "We will enforce the law." The penalty for violation of the Volstead Act applied to the Wright Act: first conviction $1,000 maximum and six months in the county jail; second conviction $2,000 and a maximum of five years.

The mountainous area of northeastern California contained fiercely independent, generally conservative, very patriotic, and some deeply religious people. Perhaps they could be called Mind-Your-Own-Business people.

A strong WCTU and conservative church groups pushed for prohibition from the turn of the century on. In 1909 one writer from Old Taylorsville said he "would rather be full of 'buttermilk' than full of whisky."

Professor Burke of Berkeley and an official of the Anti-Saloon League gave a speech in Montague, Siskiyou County "pleading for a 'dry' Siskiyou and for the sake of the boys and girls." An article in the Plumas County Museum, with no date, but around 1910, had a satiric open letter to the "Honraable" Board of Supervisors of Booze County, State of Debauchery. The spoof told about opening a saloon in the town of Corruption. The owners really cared nothing about the Fourth of July but only for "money for me." In 1911 the Native Sons of the Golden West voted down using malt and spirituous liquors at their conventions.

Yet with all the pro-prohibition sentiment, one could look back and see signs of times to come. Plumas County voted in prohibition and a year later voted it out. In 1909 Patrick O'Connor, Supervisor for Siskiyou, kept disturbing prohibition meetings "with frequent interruption."

No sooner did prohibition go into effect, than did these mountaineers see that something was wrong: Prohibition was not working. Notice the essence of this perceptive editorial in February 3, 1921, *The Plumas National*

Bulletin. "Of all the laws made by Congress...the prohibition act is the most lamentable failure in-so-far as enforcement is concerned." Some people believed in the law as long as it was on the books—even if they wanted a little "nip." For these [people] prohibition prohibits. Others were law abiding except for liquor. "With them prohibition does not always prohibit, for many of them wink one or both eyes when there is an opportunity to 'put a little joy into life.'" There are others for whom the law is just an "odious restraint"; they are becoming rich from the illicit traffic. Some are slave to drink and would sell their souls for a pint. "If they continue to guzzle the wood alcohol and other poisonous stuff that is sold for whiskey they will soon have no souls left to

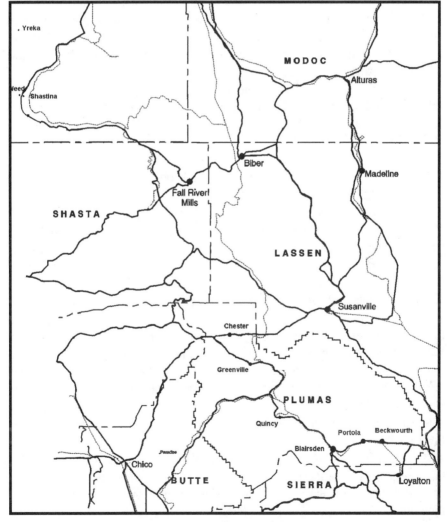

Northeastern California

barter." People are wondering if they were right in supporting the cause. Enforcers are conniving "at its violation—for graft." District attorneys are suspected "of suddenly becoming blind" when men with political influence are involved. Municipal authorities are slow to prosecute saloon keepers as they continue to sell at sky-high prices. The courts seem to be covered with a thin veneer.

"Does Prohibition Prohibit? Superfluous," said the editor who was not in support of prohibition or against it—"It is simply a cold statement of facts." With all the resources of Congress, the law was not enforced. The opponents were jubilant. The people in the middle of the two camps were weary of the whole thing: "To them it is a national joke."

The irony of the dilemma showed up in the humor of the *Plumas National Bulletin* 1 January 1920: "If all the booze in the country could be frozen into blocks—well, you know, there is no law against selling ice" and "A bootlegger certainly occupies a peculiar place in this old world. One half the people want to hang him and the other half want to send him to Congress."

When League of Nations members wanted to limit the number of warships, an item appeared in the same paper: "What is the use of the League of Nations prohibiting battleships when some wicked nation will come along and start bootleggin' 'em?"

The Great Weed Raid

from 1926 testimony statement by ex-agent Hess to George Horner,
Special Agent, Justice Department.[1]

The amount of liquor that came into Weed in Siskiyou County was trivial (compared to the rest of California). Some, mostly gin or alcohol, came up from Sacramento and some from San Francisco. Distillation occurred in the mountains—"It is all mountainous—it is nearly impossible to get around there. You go five miles off the railway and you are in the same country the '49ers were in—you are right into the heart of the Rocky Mountains [*sic*]. People who live there are not highly educated types, except in the small towns. The town of Weed is company owned—owned by the lumber company. There isn't any town there. They have a company store, a railroad station and a hotel, a small moving picture place, and of course there is a lot of people live around there. But there is no downtown district. And right next to it is Shastina. There is where the law violation takes place. You walk from one into the other. The town of Shastina—I don't think there is more than a thousand people live in it all together. The business blocks—I think there are four blocks of so-called businesses. They are the types of places you ordinarily find in a frontier town, or a boom town. It is made up of places where men of low type come and spend their time.

There was a lumber strike there in, I think, 1921. At that time the lumber company attempted to break the strike, or did break the strike, by importing a lot of Negroes. Those Negroes are still there. At the same time they brought in a lot of Greeks and Armenians and Servians [Serbians] and they are still there. There is where your so-called "Klan" first got its birth, in that district.

And then there was some trouble between that faction known as the Klan and the Sheriff of the County. The Sheriff was protecting the lumber plant at the time of the strike in 1921 or 1922. When the company brought in these Negroes to break the strike they organized the Klan to scare them (Negroes) out of town and they paraded the streets of Weed with sheets on and in their paraphernalia. The Sheriff of the County heard of it, came down from Yreka and stopped the parade, stating that while he was not in favor of the Negro strike breakers, at the same time it was against the law and they must stop it. At this time this group stated they're going to get the sheriff. It is one of the things that is the real basis of this argument.

Charlie Miller was the head of the Klan; another prominent man is Jack Miller, "Nigger" Miller, a locomotive engineer or fireman. Jack Miller was an agitator, a troublemaker during the strike. "He was one of the men when we were going up there that we ought to watch out for."

Kern was a little wrong in the head. He thought he was a detective. "It was a mania with him." He told me that he broke into the Justice of Peace Bradley's office to get his records.

Another deeper problem in the community was the People's Store in Shastina. It was started by Charles Miller and E. Rosa and a few Italian investors who thought they were being cheated by the company store of the Weed Lumber Company. Miller ran the store but when it started losing money, Rosa and the investors kicked Miller out. They put in $1,500.00 more money and reorganized the store. Miller was furious and swore to "get Rosa."

When the federal agents raided the community of Shastina, Charles Miller assigned himself the Savoy, premises of Rosa. This is where most of the damages occurred. "Mr. Miller was working out his own animus."

Another man in the raid was Kern. Someone drove 35 miles to fetch Kern because they heard he was a good man (meaning anti-sheriff). Fred Starr, commonly known as General Custer because this "two-gun man" had spent most of his life in the army, was a civilian raider. Another citizen was a man named Small, a city fireman of the Long Bell Company.

Charlie Miller helped raid the Savoy Grill, owned by E. Rosa, the grill being operated by Pete Goldman. Padgett [Paget] was in charge of the whole raid. Agent Taylor was the agent in charge of the group who raided the Savoy. Dr. Himes, of Dunsmuir, was also in this group.

Before the raid Paget did not swear them in and he said to a civilian, Mr. Gilstrap, "No, you are assigned to assist these officers and you go and assist them." These were the only instructions received. Miller rode with Taylor in Miller's car.

Raiders discovered customers drinking in curtained booths, wine coming out of a soda flavor dispenser, but instead of strawberry flavor coming out, out came a sharp Dago red. They found a false room where wine was pumped into a barrel and pumped out into the flavor pump. The basement was full of empty barrels and kegs. When Taylor took Rosa to jail, the civilian deputies knocked over the bar, used a meat cleaver to scar the bar top, and used an axe to knock out some booth partitions. They did much damage.

These raiders (agents and posse men) did so much damage that Rosa sued for damages. He won in a Sacramento court with four of the civilians fined $400 each for the damages. This so offended prohibitionists, when government assistants could be held responsible for damages while doing their civic duty, that letters poured into Washington, D. C. from all over the country. One letter came from Arthur H. Briggs, San Francisco.

The Siskiyou Boys
After the trial, partisans rallied around the Siskiyou "boys" to complain about their treatment in court. Arthur H. Briggs of the California Anti-Saloon League wrote to Mabel Willebrandt at the Department of Justice in February 1927, saying it was "pretty tough to have the Siskiyou boys made to suffer for helping to enforce the federal law. They have lost so much time and been at so much cost that one of them is afraid that he will lose his home.... "Briggs wanted to know if the government could reimburse these men. He also wrote to Senator Wayne Wheeler and California Senator Shortridge.

In his letter to Wheeler, Briggs accused many of perjured testimony at the trial. "The District Attorney, the Sheriff, and the Justice of Peace swore that they would not believe the posse men under oath. During the trial the District Attorney was in San Francisco drunk."[2]

"The story of Weed is worse than what went on in Sodom and Gomorrah," said Briggs. The three main law enforcers in that county are bootleggers, he wrote. A Greek bootlegger with a gun kept a game warden away from a hill where the Greek had a still. "Weed is in a state of insolent rebellion against the United States Government." Briggs ended his letter with the following: "There is not a drop of my blood that is not tingling at the outrage which a drunk, brutal bootlegger was permitted to put over on honest, clean citizens of this state who did nothing more than serve the Federal government, when asked to do so by Federal officers."

Briggs did not know local politics, the "animus" toward the sheriff, the move by wealthy Brown to get Calkins, do anything to get him, even hire a woman to entice the sheriff into some act since they knew Calkins liked the ladies and the Klan's hostility toward Negroes and Greeks. Brown used the

Law Enforcement League and its investigator to obtain evidence against Rosa and other bootleggers. Ironically they were against Reed Lumber Company for breaking the strike. Miller was against Rosa who was keeping People's Market strong to curtail the lumber company town's monopoly. It was a mess. Thus it seemed obvious that federal agents making the raid did their jobs, not realizing they were in the middle of serious political and social factions in Weed and in the county. They stepped in the middle of it, as California farmers often said.

Despite the internal Siskiyou politics, letters of complaints arrived from Washington, D.C. about Sheriff Calkins and constables frequenting Almonti and Black and other bootleg places. Rumor had it that Calkins had an interest in stills gambling, drinking and "sporting houses" [brothels].

Old $500 or 500 Days
as told by John Orr, Quincy

John Orr was a Special Deputy for Prohibition and former Deputy Sheriff of Plumas County. He was nephew of Sheriff L. A. Braden, who had a 32-year reign as head Plumas County law enforcer.

At 21 years old I became a special deputy used for prohibition enforcement. My pay was $10.00 a raid, $10 for each place knocked over. Sheriff L. A. Braden called me up to go on a raid. The federal agents out of Reno notified me to meet them someplace.

Braden would usually hit the places 3-4 times a year to keep things in hand. We had a judge, Vic Miller, at that time—the only thing he gave was $500 or 500 days. When we knocked over a place, Judge Miller would ask the alleged how he pleaded. Usually he pleaded guilty; then "old $500 of 500 days" passed his sentence. The bootlegger generally pulled out a roll of greenbacks, sometimes rolls 2" thick. Why he'd just peel off $500 worth, pay up and be in business again the next day, sometimes the same night, knowing he probably wouldn't be raided again for maybe three months.

When we went on raids, Braden gathered many of us, deputies and local constables. We divided and hit two-four places a night at the same time. Otherwise the word went out like wildfire if only one town was knocked over at a time. Around 1930, I became a deputy sheriff for $75 a month, on call 24 hours a day. Soon after that the depression started and the trend against prohibition went the other way. We did not hit as many places.

I was never offered a bribe and I never took one—wouldn't have to work as hard as I did all my life if I had (ha). As far as I know Sheriff Braden was honest. We never made enemies with the bootleggers or the moonshiners. They knew the law and they knew our job. If I were to see John Egbert the next day after knocking him over at his Main Street place, now the Plumas Club in Quincy, we'd greet each other and we're still friends. Most of these fellows were fine people. We had respect for each other; each had a job to do.

I disliked going on raids with federal agents. They had no respect for the people as individuals. We'd raid with them, say a still in the hills or a bootlegger in a house, why they'd smash up everything afterwards, dishes, tables, walls, the whole place. There was no sense to that but they did it. They were rough.

I have remained friends with these people over the years because we respected each other. My wife and I have had many a laugh with Nellie Marshbanks in Portola. A few years ago we were with Nellie and had another good laugh. Back in those old days, Gene Mercer, of the Plumas County Fish and Game Department, called on me to make a raid, as he had on several occasions, but this time it was Nellie's little restaurant in Portola where she served a little wine and some moonshine. Mercer was an excellent officer—he knew who was poaching, would really catch the poachers. Nellie was supposed to have shot a deer so he sent me to the front door while he went around back. Nellie saw Mercer heading around the back and saw me in the front. Suddenly the front door flew open before I even knocked. A big plate filled with steaks was thrust into my arms.

"Here, take these quick," she spurted out.

She thought I was someone else, one of her friends from Portola. The steaks were venison. She handed me the evidence.

We did have a rough time knocking over one bootlegger who also ran a house of prostitution at Storrie. There was no road down there, only the Western Pacific Train. P.G.& E. was building a power plant there, lots of workers. The sheriff took the train at least once to raid the place for bootlegging. But the word reached the house before Braden did. The prostitution was left alone in the county as long as the ladies had checkups once a month.

This bootlegger was in cahoots with Western Pacific employees. He bought his liquor kegs around Oroville, and they loaded the 25-gallon keg on the front of the train on the tender and unloaded it at Storrie.

Braden and I sneaked on the train and rode the "blinds" between the cars, to three-four miles outside of town. We jumped off and waited around until morning and knocked over the place. We took the bootlegger back to Quincy. "$500 or 500 days," said Judge Miller.

The owner went back, bought more moonshine and was in business again. But we'd hit him again—another $500. Then the prohis out of Reno hit him—$500 or 500 days. After many raids like this he went broke, left for a more profitable part of California. The girls left also.

The moonshiners created very good moonshine in these mountains in Plumas County. John Egbert made it at Nelson Point and brought it into his Main Street business. He had a trap door on the floor behind the bar that's still there. It's about six feet deep, need a ladder to get down there. It's about seven by ten feet wide with dirt floors. The place where the Moon Cafe is now sold illicit liquor. Chinese ran it. Butterfly Valley had very good jackass brandy. Beckwith [also know as Beckwourth, named after mulatto trapper James Beckwourth] ranchers supplied the mountains with wine. At Beckwith Taverns, Blackie sold 120 proof almost pure alcohol. Indian Valley made beer—wild beer. You'd knock the head off the bottle and it'll go all over the place. In Portola, H. M. & J. Bar on Main Street across from the bank sold the area's fine liquor, some of it better than you buy in stores today.

Bootlegger J. W. Egbert ran for Plumas County sheriff but

These were rough people who lived around the hills in those days. We had no trouble arresting bootleggers but had quite a bit of trouble from some drinkers—railroad workers at Indian Valley, miners like the Czech miners at the Walker Mine (copper). They were so rough they'd get rid of a foreman they didn't like. They'd let him walk in an area that was about to be blown up.

Plumas Club, site of a speakeasy in Quincy, across from the county offices of Sheriff Braden and District Attorney S. C. Young. The dirt basement that once had a trap door is still supposed to be there. Photo by author.

Quincy, county seat of Plumas County, during prohibition years, was the center of moonshining and bootlegging for the mountain folks. Post card courtesy of Plumas County Museum.

⌀

The *Plumas National Bulletin* of 1926 showed the variety of bootlegging activities in the northern Sierras. Most of the news of these mountain people centered around the snow, forest fire fighting, lumber, mining and the Western Pacific Railroad.

The Feds from Reno made sorties into Plumas County. In Portola they arrested John K. Adams and David Kassar for possession and selling. Both pleaded guilty before Justice Nels Feirl, who fined them $500 or 500 days. Both paid their $500, but the justice held Kassar for attempted bribery. Kassar tried to give Justice Feirl $50 in greenbacks before the trial.

A prohi from Reno, F. S. Perise, came into the county for a raid on Mr. and Mrs. M. E. Fouts and netted a big cache of illegal booze: 20 gallons of distilled whiskey and 275 gallons of assorted wines and cordials, most bottled goods bearing bonded labels from the U. S. Commissioner. Ironically but not altogether uncommon, Mr. Fouts' brother-in-law Roy Bowers made the complaint when he witnessed Mrs. Fouts selling seven bottles to three men. The judge in 1926 let the Fouts' out with a $1,500 bond.

Federal agents caught John K. Adams again at Portola three months after his last arrest. This time Adams pleaded not guilty and posted the bail of $1,500 to walk away. Others arrested were J. Calles, Henry McGowan, and Harry Koenig, all pleading guilty and paying $400 in fines. Sammuel Hantes pleaded not guilty and since he could not come up with the $1500 bail, he went to jail.

Just a week later Al Koenig went to jail when he could not pay the $500 part of the $500 or 500 days. Daisy Williams, Cecil Brown, and Fred Miller of Beckwourth paid their $500. The *Bulletin* mentioned that Jack Beall of Cromberg had also been arrested for dispensing liquor. Agents Du Bois and Brown raided the Clyde Ball house, but only found one bottle under a seat. He received a fine of $25. Judge H. G. Hilton fined Billy Martin of Beckwourth $400 for possession.

A strange case appeared before Judge Hilton. Sheriff Braden arrested former sheriff of Yolo County, P. H. Griffin of Woodland, for selling at Chester. Griffin's son paid his $400 fine and escorted his father back to Woodland. This was Griffin's fourth arrest. At Yolo he was convicted once and had the charges dismissed twice.

Patriotic citizens of the county celebrated Independence Day in 1926. Bootleggers helped with the festivities—but got caught. On July 4, the law arrested six bootleggers for possessing and dispensing intoxicating celebration liquor. Two acknowledged the correctness to the charges, pleaded guilty and were fined or sentenced. Four others were charged with possession: W. T. Schneider, Charles Stallard, A. T. Burlon and Steve Woods, Stallard and Burlon also being charged with selling.

Again in 1926, Michael Ryan and two friends with too much of the "cup that cheers" wanted to "clean up Main." When Sheriff Braden objected and arrested the three, Ryan "swung" at Braden, scraping his head near his eyes. Braden sent Ryan sailing head-over-heels into a lobby. Justice V. A. Miller gave Ryan a comfortable compartment at county expense for six months.

Braden used fine detective work in catching Hugh Porter Hall of Quincy with the goods. After watching Hall for a long time, he caught him with his friend Grace Malone, landlady of a resort in American Valley's restricted district. Hall and Malone drove to the old O'Neil house on Indian Valley Road, obtained a 12-gallon keg, put it in their car and were arrested with the goods. Officials let Malone go but Judge Miller gave Hall, yes, you guessed it, $500 or 500 days.

Valentine Urez, a 1926 manufacturer of liquor and a peddler from Portola, had 12 gallons of his moonshine dumped into the street. He was fined $400 and paid it promptly, "Sadder but wiser."

Federal prohis out of Reno continued making liquor buys in Plumas County and raiding the county. In 1926 Feds arrested 22 in a series of hits. In or near Quincy officers arrested John Bresciani, Myrtle Hall, Sherley Voal, Jessie Clark, Maurice Williams, Louise Morgan, J. P. Kielly and William Byrne. Greenville and Crescent Mills contributed Lillian Campbell, Loony Baker, Loui DeCoser, B. C. Johnson, Irene Sherwood, Bernice Foster, Tom Goodfellow, Lou Lowther and Joe Palazza. At Blairsden and Johnsville the raiders captured B. Walker, Bert Turko, Avaristo Arcorta, Angelo Guadaguini and A. Tachella. Johnson and DeCoser went to federal court in San Francisco. A few were freed after paying their $400-500 fines, while most occupied jail space until paid.[3]

Another raid followed this in October 1926. American Valley arrests were Jessie Clark, Myrtle Hall, Bessie Wayne and Jessie Park, all keepers of "questionable resorts" and all charged for possession and selling. Each girl was fined either $500 or $400. At Greenville, "Mother" Campbell, probably "Lillian Campbell," this time receiving the wrath of the Feds was remanded to the federal court. Also received by the federal court was George Bacher of Beckwourth. Al Cumbly was arrested at Beckwourth and released. Fined $400 each were W. S. McAllister and Amelia Lee of Crescent Mills. Receiving visitors from the prohibition department were Lou Blakesley, bartender at Quincy's Grand Central Cafe, and Goon Moon, an investor in a restaurant and soft drink parlor in Quincy—both held on $1,500 bond for the federal court.[4]

The *Bulletin* showed a little humor in 1926 with a joke: "Plumasites will drink anything in the way of booze, but they raise an awful row if someone puts a little water in their milk."

Liquor often caused more serious crimes. Harrison Wells shot E. K. Knight in the chest. Wells came to buy liquor from Knight, but Wells' credit

Beckwourth Store—Owned by "Blackie" Tucker on Main Street, Beckwourth, where Tucker was not afraid to sell a little liquor to farmers, miners and rails, and where the Portola-Beckwourth area was called "27"—nine bars, nine brothels and nine churches. Photo by author.

In 1932, "Blackie" Tucker built his Beckwith Tavern next to the new highway. This former speakeasy still carries its speakeasy name. Tucker also "ran" a few ladies for the pleasure of the hundreds of single men in the area. Photo by author.

was worthless. Knight kept the dollar Wells had proffered and said, "It's now 50¢ you owe me." Wells came back and shot Knight.[5]

Butterfly Valley in Plumas County had its habitual bootlegger. The *Bulletin* on January 6, 1927, stated that at Quincy Sheriff Braden and Constable Carlton arrested Byron "Toad" Smith of Butterfly Valley. Scott Lawson of the Plumas County Museum related a story he heard many years ago of "Toad" Smith of Butterfly Valley. A prohi came into Quincy to investigate all the moonshine operations in the surrounding valleys. He kept getting turned down in finding someone to show him around the county. A Quincy citizen pointed out a man and said, "Why don't you ask that man over there. He's been in the county most his life and really knows the county." The prohi did and spent all day checking out the county for moonshiners and bootleggers. They found none. When the two returned to Quincy, the agent was really discouraged. He said to the citizen he met in the morning that he didn't locate "Toad" Smith or any other moonshiners.

"Why that's 'Toad' Smith there, the one you were driving around with all day."

Once when the booze squad arrested Hugh Porter Hall with Smith in Butterfly Valley, Hall came running into his house saying he needed things to sell for the bail. He sold his wife's diamond ring to Arch Braden, the county sheriff.

Inez Nelson revealed much about the wild town of Beckwourth in the late 1920s and early 30s. She worked at the post office and knew all the people in town. Her first experience with the town came as her new husband brought her to their house. She was pleased to see some near neighbors. Her husband said, "We will be doing no neighboring with them." Her neighbor was the Sage Brush Inn, a Beckwourth brothel.[6]

When Nelson worked at the post office, she found out one prostitute might receive mail under her real name but quite frequently had given the post office a list of five or six aliases the post office should have in order to place all her letters in her box.

She knew "Blackie" Tucker who owned a place on Main Street that is now a store and town post office [in 1993]. In about 1932, he started building a new building where the road and traffic went. The ex-speakeasy is still called Beckwith Tavern. Tucker also had women either in his place or at another house he had an interest in.

In those days, the town was busy. The largest valley in the Sierra Nevada produced excellent dairy products to supply California and northern Nevada. Some mines, like the Walker Mine, had at times 500 miners and maybe 2,000 people around the mine. Railroad workers and their families mixed with farmers and ranchers. The place was busy. When these miners, ranchers and railroad workers came into town, the town was roaring, especially on Saturday nights.

One brothel was called the Green Lantern; another house was at Willow Glen, near where Jim Beckwourth's cabin is now located; another called the Pump House was by the airport. In Portola two popular houses were the Seven Steps and the Last Chance.

Moonshiners made booze all around the mountains; Greeks and others made their legal 200 gallons of wine, but a few made too much, some of it getting into the retail market. A farmer named Tam had a still in the mountains. He would come to the post office smelling of wine and garlic. His breath was awful. "I had to keep backing up," said Nelson. One rancher came into the post office, crying, "My vino gone; my vino gone." The prohis smashed his barrels and dumped his wine in the street. Some of the locals called the wine "Vinegar Red." Whenever one visited a farmer who made wine, it was customary to offer guests wine. "I insulted one family when I turned down wine because I did not drink. The son [or husband] said, "Would you have a cup of coffee?" When Nelson said she would, he graciously started a fire in the stove and brewed up a cup. Later, people accepted the fact she did not drink. Local people were very hospitable.

Once a prostitute drove her car down the street from Grizzly or Willow Glen to town, screeching her tires and yelling: "Prohis are coming! Prohis are coming!"

"The rocks were flying," Inez Nelson said. The word got out and usually spread faster than the prohis could make a raid. Sheriff Braden periodically made raids but usually had slight effect on the local sale of booze. He often arrested the bartender but not the owner. For example, in Portola authorities arrested John Adams, who took the fall for Jack Hoxie, Henry McGowen, Jack Martin and Harry Jones, owners of the H. M. & J. Club.

When M. E. Fouts owned the Beckwith Tavern, in September 1932, two men came in a car and bombed the tavern, leaving a mystery known only to a few. Other incidents made for exciting reading. When Judge Long of Portola sentenced L. D. Miller to 30 days in jail for drunkenness, Constable McIntosh reported the next day the jail was "literally wrecked." Miller ruined the interior and threw a chair through the window. Evidently, he sobered up mean. Another Constable, Neil Merrill ordered lumber camp employee Bob Thompson to go home and sober up from a drunken orgy at the Westwood Club. He was crazed with moonshine, however, and shot at Merrill, nearly severing his arm and killed A. E. Hinshaw. Constable Jim Snall disarmed Thompson and arrested him.[7]

As with Siskiyou County, a few pleaded for help in making the northeastern part of California more law abiding. E. J. Wallace of Quincy wrote to Mabel Willebrandt, Assistant Attorney General, begging for dependable agents to come up and investigate the "bad bunch" of bootleggers in Plumas County. Said Wallace: "Some of the bootleggers at Greenville have been selling whiskey to the high school students and in fact openly plying their trade in defiance of the law, and one of the ones engaged in such at Quincy, conducts his place of business directly across the street in front of the court house in plain view of the office of S. C. Young, District Attorney of Plumas County, and [*sic*] there is a general distrust of both S. C. Young and L. A. Braden, Sheriff. bothe whome [sic]are under suspision [sic]of being implicated with the bootleggers, though there is no proof or evidence sufficient to indict either of them." Wallace did not want his name given out because some engaged in this business "are dangerous carecters [sic] and would stop at nothing short of arson or murder."

He listed the names that should be investigated: Harvey W. Egbert, and Jake A. Stephan, Quincy; J. E. Bannister, Steve Sorsoli, Crescent Mills; Lillian Campbell, and Abram Landon, Greenville; and Rafel E. Lozano.

Willebrandt wrote right back, thanking Wallace and stating that since this enforcement come under the Treasury Department, she forwarded to Commissioner of prohibition James M. Doran.[8]

"27"

Manit's father moved the family from Loyalton to Portola when he bought the Liberty Club.[9] Hap Manit, a life-long resident of the valley, confirmed what others suggested about the payoffs that were made to the local officials. He had no doubt Sheriff Braden was on the take and divided the money with other authorities. "Constables got paid off too."

Manit called the area "27." Portola and Beckwourth had nine bars, nine churches and nine red-light houses—therefore "27." Some clubs he remembered were Pete's Club, gone now; National Club; Whiskers; Bank Club, which is still on Commerce Street across from the bank and next to the Masonic Lodge; Liberty Club, which Manit's father owned and is now a vacant lot on the other side of the Masonic building; Past Time Club; H. M. & J. Club, across from the Masonic building was one of the biggest, maybe 75' long. This bar had a peephole at the entrance. It had H. M. & J. tokens, 5¢, 10¢ and 25¢, good for purchases. These places were "behind-the-curtain places." The front had pool tables and card tables and sold soda pop. Sometimes in the back, men four-five deep were lined up at the bar which sold liquor openly.

His dad paid off periodically and officials probably divided with each other. Portola was lively and wild, said Manit. On Saturday nights when the miners came in from Grayeagle and Walker and other mines, sidewalks were full. They came for the Saturday night dances held at the at the Odd Fellows' Hall across from the H. M. & J. Drinks were not sold at the dance—but thirsty miners could buy across the street or at the Bank Club or Liberty Club on both sides of the Odd Fellows. If one wanted to go home he had to walk in the center of the street, there were so many people. Fights broke out all over, in bars and out in the streets. It was a wild town.

Jones, one of the owners of the H. M. & J., hid some of his liquor under the community church. He lived across the street from the church; even the minister did not know. Jones also went on some raids with liquor officials, said Manit.

The "Hook Shops," brothels, sold shots of liquor for about 25¢; the charge for girls was about $2.00. Two main houses were the Seven Steps and Last Chance.

After the St. Valentine's Day Massacre in Chicago, Al Capone came to Reno. Manit's father bought some alcohol from Lake Street in Reno, supposedly involving Al Capone. Local bars received it in five-gallon cans and "ran it through again" to make it into gin or whatever type of booze they wanted. Each bar had a still to do this.

As young teens, Manit and a few friends collected bottles and sold them to the H. M. & J. for 5¢ each. When the bottles were placed in the back, they took them and sold them to Pete's Club. Sometimes they sold the same bottles several times. They made their school spending money that way.

When the depression started a dollar was a lot of money; one could get by on $1.00 a day. The depression made money more dear for the Plumas County mountain folk, for in 1933 before prohibition ended, the sheriff ordered raids in the county. Manit said not for the law but for the money—the county treasury needed the money. These mountain folks became more austere, had picnics, went to Saturday night dances and survived as best they could.

☙

Every spring the paper announced the opening of Buck's Road, from Oroville to Quincy by way of Buck's Ranch after being closed for six or six and a half months. During 1932, *Feather River Bulletin* had a cartoon showing that hoarded money was needed for the prosperity wagon, urging citizens to buy, spend their money. Over and over came taxes and anti-taxes editorials. "I am a taxpayer..." started many letters by those mountain folks. Elsewhere, American naval forces practiced the annual war games in Hawaii, using landing boats. Also editorials and news about Japanese invasion of China, possible U.S. intervention and maybe even a war with Japan. Anti-Japanese editorials seemed to be a distraction to the financially hard times. Always in the news: farm loans, bank loans and railroad jobs and businesses going broke. In 1932 the Walker Copper Mine closed down. The county cut wages of employees and stopped hiring. Fifty cents a day was cut off the pay of the road workers. The county urged all to volunteer to take a 10 percent pay cut. When Supervisor O'Rourke was asked if he would cut his salary 10%, he responded, "The people hired me at $1,000 a year. If they think this is too much, it's up to them to say so." Sheriff Braden said he would take a cut if others including supervisors would. He probably knew O'Rourke's attitude about his own pay cut. These mountaineers kept their humor. A joke appeared in the 1932 paper: "Mr. Swallow married Miss Beers. And in this prohibition country!"[10]

Dr. A. H. Briggs of the Anti-Saloon League wrote in urging donations to fight the referendum to abolish the Wright Act in 1932. He said "the forces of disorder are financed." The newspaper editor responded: "Quite true, dear doctor, they are financed by prohibition itself. These senseless legislations have created a set of conditions that make it easy for gangsters and bootleggers to make money...if you come down to earth...there might be some hope to promote the cause of Temperance. If you keep on hacking your nose to spite your face, you will eventually bleed to death."

Beckwourth continued with its problems with the law. Delleker was arrested in the spring of 1932 with equipment and property leased from M. (Joe) Mastelloto. Some of the equipment was evidently stolen and Joe Mastelloto was arrested for grand theft. Fifteen months earlier Joe had been caught with 24 pints of beer, two quarts of whiskey and two quarts of wine at the Beckwith Hotel. He pleaded guilty to having a nuisance and for possession and his selling charge was dismissed. The guilty pleas only netted the county $200 combined.[11]

Lumberjack Jim Pool was arrested for selling to Indians, two miles north of Quincy. Under-Sheriff Fred Cook had warned him to stay away from the Indians, but Pool came back and was caught with whiskey in his car. The judge fined him $150 and 60 days. He could get out after he paid the fine and the judge would suspend the 60 days if he left the county. During the fourteen years of prohibition, these independent mountaineers did pretty much what they wanted to do. They never stopped drinking it, or making it or selling it.

Bars changed to soft drink parlors and poolhalls, sometimes in name only. Jack's Place (The H.M. & J. Co.) was the most popular speakeasy in Portola, Plumas County. During the last two years of prohibition it was practically an open bar. Photo by author.

Pass Your
Leisure Hours *at*

Jack's Place
H. M. & J . Co.

Portola, Calif.

Recreation Center

for Men

Pool *and* Billiards

Ice Cream, Soft Drinks
Candy, Cigars, Tobaccos

Coffee, Pies, Sandwiches

Office building in 1993, site of popular H. M. & J. Club [speakeasy] in Portola, conveniently located across from the Odd Fellows, where weekend dances brought in hundreds of the miners and railroad workers. Photo by author.

CHAPTER 23

I DIDN'T KNOW HE WAS MAKING IT ON MY FARM
On Ranches All over the State

The favorite place for stills was the ranches and farms of California. The National Archives has hundreds of federal court cases for the manufac ture of liquor on farms. In the 1920s most of California was rural; towns were rural villages with farms located a couple blocks from the main street. With the exception of San Francisco, farms surrounded cities like Stockton, San Jose, Modesto, Redding and San Diego—many farms being within city boundaries. The great valleys of Sacramento and San Joaquin and the deserts of Mojave and Colorado (Imperial County), the smaller valleys of San Bernardino and Riverside counties were basically rural, all areas of potential still sites—isolated, sparsely populated with look-the-other-way sheriff departments. With a farmers' depression after the Great War, hundreds of farmers could not make mortgage payments. When the depression hit in the 1930s, drastic means had to be taken for families to survive. Rural valleys of California runneth over with moonshiners and bootleggers.

A few examples will suffice to show use of farms during prohibition: File number 23-11-341: October 7, 1930, a raid on the Paul Pacheco Ranch four miles southwest of Novato in Marin County, arresting Tom Beliganis of San Francisco, Tom Haliotis of Petaluma and Manuel Dias of Navato. Haliotis had been involved operating a still on Harry Rodger's Ranch near El Verano in the spring of 1930. The still and vats were used at both places.

File 23-11-343: December 8, 1930, apprehension of Joe Barca and Anthony Cassio on the Joe Bares Ranch, south of Bay Creek near Roseville.

File 23-11-259: On the Lister Ranch, 5 miles south of Stockton, prohibition agents apprehended three men with a 700-gallon still, 36,000 gallons of mash, and about 1,000 gallons of whiskey, plus the other equipment for this large operation.

File 23-11-274: June 1, 1929, in a case against Aladdin, Bertolucci and John Torei, where the officials found a large operation on the Fred C. Dollar place on Zayanti Lakes Road about one mile from Mt. Herman with two stills, 300 gallons of 190 proof alcohol per day capacity, eight mash vats, 16,000 gallons of mash, two kegs of whiskey, 100 pounds of yeast and more.

File 23-11-291: October 1929, four men were caught running a still at Herbert Henry Ranch about five miles southeast of Vallejo. Someone hired Mamie Dwyer for $30 a month to cook for the men.[1]

Moonshine in Meadowbrook (Riverside County)
from Bill Cox, *Moonshiners in Meadowbrook*[2]

At an old goat farm in Meadowbrook, between Perris and Elsinore, Los Angeles Prohibition Agent William Clemens (Clement?) completed his scouting and investigating, went for a search warrant and came back and raided a huge haystack on the farm. The stack was 15 feet high. Inside it had three levels with stairs between the levels: The main room was 600 square feet with 14 huge vats, the second floor with a 20-foot boiler, a high capacity cooker full of finished mash; the third floor was dug into the ground like a cesspool to catch the dross (dregs or impurities) from the cooker.

According to author Bill Cox, the owner of the farm was working on the farm but said he had no idea the haystack was a distillery capable of producing an estimated 5,000-10,000 gallons a day.

Helping the investigation were George A. Sweet for the Treasury Department and Riverside County Sheriff Clem Sweeters. The dry squad also raided sites in Riverside, Nuevo and Menifee Valley—all in January 1930. They arrested four men at the goat farm. One was Elsinore miner Herman "Kid" Quirin, who received 21 months in San Quentin. Captured later was Peter Connley, who had 18 priors in Chicago and was the son of a Chicago policeman. The court gave him six years. The jury went out to look at the haystack distillery, seeing the buzzer system connecting the house and the haystack, seeing the boiler from Kelly's Boilerworks of L.A. and examining the cooling system as the elaborate condensing coils went through tanks of cold water. This case was tied in some way with the case of a gangland slaying in Los Angeles and another in Chicago.

Much to the frustration of the prohibitionists, the county sold the distillery equipment at an auction for $100.

San Diego County

San Diego County was mostly rural and was typical of the rest of California country. In one raid in Escondido officials apprehended five Italians and fined them for operating a still and possessing liquor: A.W. Vienna, Joe Besco, Andrew Giuffre, Joe Buccolo and John Batista. On an abandoned ranch in Otay, officers found a quantity of liquor but no owner.[3] East of Vista, Oceanside Constable Fred M. Sickler, searching for a stolen car, found a full-fledged distillery, a large still and a barrel of grape brandy. Not finding the owner, Stickler believed him to be a Mexican who had been bootlegging for quite some time. Stickler also found Frank Reynolds of Gopher Canyon with a still hidden in the creek bed, two barrels of mash in the process of becoming corn liquor and a little whiskey already made. During the raid, Stickler saw black smoke coming from the house. Mrs. Reynolds was burning dresses that may have been stolen from Mrs. C. T. McKeehan of Oceanside. Reynolds went to the county jail while his wife went to Los Angeles.

It looks just like a regular haystack on this "Old Goat Farm" in Meadowbrook, southwest of Perris in Riverside County. But it was three levels underground with the 15-foot haystack cleverly disguising the smokestack and the top of the still. One room had 14 fermenting tanks to keep a ready supply for constant distillation. Photos from National Archives, Laguna Niguel. See article by Bill Cox in this chapter and "The 10th Anniversary..." in Chapter 27.

On closer examination, the haystack hides an elaborate $100,000 still, the biggest in Riverside County up to 1930.

John Bragadello, released from jail for possession of a still in 1927, was arrested on a ranch northeast of San Diego in Jamacha, a ranch owned by George Bourass, who was blown out of his bed by the explosion of a still. Investigating officers found the still in Bragadello's home.[4]

∅

Six were arrested on a ranch leased by the Alameda Gun and Rifle Club between Petaluma and Marshall but agents were assured the still and alcohol plant had no connection with the gun club. While returning from investigating a rumrunning incident involving a machine gun, agents smelled mash. They arrested Manuel Topani, W. D. Carey, M. J. Sturtevant, M. J. Pimental, J.[?]E. Martin and Walter Anderson. The operation had a capacity of producing 300 gallons a day.[5]

More Than Just Water On the Rowland Ranch

From March 1929 to 1931 a group of men violated prohibition laws as the District Court said they did "knowingly, willfully, unlawfully and corruptly and feloniously conspire, combine, confederate, arrange and agree together and with each other." Harry Kessler, alias Harry Harris negotiated the rental of office space in the Star Truck and Warehouse Company building, 1855 Industrial Street, Los Angeles. Then defendants Jack Zuker, alias Jack Jacobson, and James D. Conner, aliases Frank Martin and James D. Gavagan, in San Gabriel leased Rowland Mineral Water Works on the Rowland Ranch near Puente. Frank E. Howard, alias Frank Smith, and Conner operated a 500-gallon still there "against the peace and dignity of the United States of America." All, along with Marvin Hart and Lawrence K. Morrison, alias L. E. Morris, were caught and found guilty. Conner and Morrison received 12-month suspended sentences, Hart had to serve 18 months at McNeil Island and pay a $1,000 fine, Zuker received 12 months in the L. A. County jail with six months suspended and a fine of $500.[6]

Central Valley

From Redding to Bakersfield, the Great Central Valley of California stretches over 500 miles and nearly 100 miles wide. Between the majestic Sierra Nevada Mountains and the wide but lower Coast Range lies this geological "bathtub."

On the floor of this valley sit impressive cities like Sacramento, Stockton, Fresno and Bakersfield. And hundreds of smaller cities and towns dot the valley, along roadways, highways, along rivers, each with a history of its own development. Some, like Visalia, evolved as an early mining supply route, sending mule caravans over an old Indian trail to the Owens Valley. Taft developed as the center of oil fields. Fresno county had more acres in grapes than any county in the United States. Each area proud, chauvinistic and resilient—sur-

414

Seizure made on the Freitas Ranch, five miles NE of Newman, Stanislaus County, arresting L. V. Palmer and William Larson. The daily capacity of this still was, 2,000 gallons. Agents William P. Goggin and John M. Burt dumped 96,000 gallons of mash, destroyed two 40 h.p. engines and confiscated one automobile and 875 gallons of alcohol. [Case 25606, November 17, 1933, Dept. of Justice, Alcohol Beverage Unit, S. F.]

viving and evolving into the electric and automotive age of the 20th century. Each town and each county handled prohibition differently.

Even in the Nicest Hotels (in Stockton)
Excerpts from *Prohibition in Stockton During the 1920s*
by Susan C. Ratliff

Stockton was wide open during the 1920s, with bootlegging accepted in the entire county, prostitutes even in the nicest hotels and with Chinese running gambling.[7]

Thirsty folks made beer in basements, harmless fun defying the law, said Carmen Piccardo in 1974, made mostly for the family and friends. "We always had a lot of company in the days of prohibition. My parents' friends came from San Francisco, brought empty bottles labeled 'Pure Old Panther Piss.' We would fill them up with my father's home brew." Piccardo's father made brandy with a stove still, watching out for visitors who could be stool pigeons. "Everybody was doing it."

Bootlegging was different; it was done for a profit, and occasionally rot gut made people violently ill. "Some people were known to die, lose their eyesight or spit up blood because of poisoned alcohol," said Ratliff.

Having a daily capacity of 1,500 gallons of 190 proof, this molasses still was shut down a few days before prohibition ended in 1933. Agents arrested seven men on the Cowell Cement Co. Ranch near Hopetown in Merced County, destroyed 84,000 gallons mash and confiscated 2,525 gallons of alcohol. Notice mash bubbling (working) in two huge vats in picture below. [Case 25609, November 28, 1933, Dept. of Justice, Alcohol Beverage Unit, S. F.]

Covello said people sold "mickies" [half pints] of "jackass booze," straight whiskey for $1 or $2. No checks were used, only $20 gold pieces.

Oscar and Angie, two bootleggers from a ranch near Stockton, said moonshine whiskey usually cost $1.25 a gallon to make and sold for whatever the traffic would bear. Oscar and Angie diluted it. They kept their stash under their chicken coop. About 4:30 in the morning, a woman driving a Hudson coach delivered the moonshine to us, five ten-gallon barrels. Two armed guards, "goons" who carried guns, meanest looking devils, stood out on the street looking both ways to make sure they weren't followed.

The police were paid off—$500 on Monday morning: "The police were all crooked, especially Sheriff Riecks," said Angie. Oscar enjoyed those times, "never had so much fun in my life," he said.

Covello also confirmed the police and sheriff payoffs. Speakeasy owners worked out a schedule for raids, bartenders knowing about the raid and warning patrons to leave, rounding up some bums to have people to put in the paddy wagons. Owners paid the fines the next day. Clamping down sometimes in the city, sometimes in the county, officials made a pretense at enforcement.

Proprietors had black limousines pick up patrons, owners hired B-Girls, "come-on" girls, to dance with customers and to get customers to buy them drinks, colored tea that only looked like whiskey. Bars had a steel rod by a drain, and on a raid, the jug was broken on the rod and the evidence flowed down the drain. Bea's place had a lounge with couches and a pleasant atmosphere.

Another informant, Glenn Kennedy said there was a moral code: forget you were ever there, ever saw anyone there.[8]

Justus Wardell, 1919, Collector of Internal Revenue at the port in Stockton said: "As far as the district is concerned, I shall endeavor to discharge the duty as vigorously as lies my direction."

Fines came into the city and county almost every day, letting both profit. Bootleggers paid their fines and kept on selling. When critics complained, one official answered "... moral tone had never been better in the history of Stockton."

When Riecks contended he did not have forces to shut down 30-40 speakeasies, District Attorney Guard Darrah conducted raids. He used three men Riecks refused to deputize: H. H. Clark, Andrew Margher and Vernon Smith and surprised roadhouses, raiding 12 speakeasies in one night, arresting 11. One raid was the Tavern on Waterloo Road where Mike Campidonmico was arrested for resisting arrest and Ralph Tullis for selling. A big scandal evolved as accusations flew about against Vernon Smith, alias Frank Neff, for soliciting bribes, accepting bribes and changing testimonies. Smith went to San Quentin, ending Darrah's raiders and his efforts to clean up the county. Sheriff Riecks was in charge and he knew how things should be run. He knew people wanted some enforcement but not to find influential people in speak-easies and not to close down the county.

In order to wean the drinkers from their habits, WCTU and Anti-Saloon League opened Waterfront Coffee Club right in the middle of the old saloon district. This coffee shop was to become a substitute for the bars, a social place where the drinker could hang out and talk. Reformers worked hard to stop the evils of alcohol. Crusaders like Reverend Maddox of the First Baptist Church said, "Remember, when a woman begins to booze, it is but a step to the brothel."[9]

See-No-Evil Sheriff

Eleventh Edition of *Byron Times Development Edition 1928-29* glowed in its praises of William Riecks, Sheriff of San Joaquin. He was well-liked, "one of California's ablest officers" and "the people of San Joaquin are justly proud of their sheriff"—electing him five times. "His fearlessness and justness to all and his rugged honesty are among his chief characteristics."[10]

Yet one who knew him said he was a "see-no-evil" sheriff. Sheriff Riecks knew how to keep one eye closed. He did not quit imbibing. According to an interview with Teresa Rivara (1889-1983), she and her husband Venansio were bootleggers and were warned by Riecks about a planned raid, maybe to protect his source, "because he was a regular customer." The Feds found an empty barn.[11]

Excerpts from It Happened in Stockton
1900-1925, Vol. 3
by Glenn A. Kennedy, Stockton

Glenn A. Kennedy performed a valuable service for the history of San Joaquin County when he catalogued 25 years of newspapers from Stockton. Here are some entries and his personal recollections.[12]

1/16/20 18th Amendment goes into effect.

I recall one experience of a young fellow who took upon himself to drink a quart of zinfandel wine from a many times used bottle. Half crushed rotted grapes fogged up the liquid content. Within an hour he was completely overcome, violently sick. He vomited until blood came, as he sat there in agony with a piercing diarrhea. We could do nothing except to stand there and watch him in his agony. Fortunately he survived from this poisoning. This was just one of thousands of examples of the "rot-gut" being peddled at a high price.

8/6/20 Feds swooped down on some moonshiners at 917 South Madison.

12/3/20 Two barrels of whiskey had been taken from San Joaquin County jail in September, word leaked out in December. The best grade whiskey was stored after a truck wreck. The sheriffs claimed whiskey leaked out and loss due to evaporation. [Looked like Stockton had a leakage problem.] All hushed up but

418

*County Captures—Display of liquors taken at San Joaquin County Court House, ca. 1928.
Photo courtesy of San Joaquin County Museum, Lodi.*

not well enough. Plymouth Rock (Old Heidelberg) was raided but someone also leaked that out too. The place was clean. Savoy Dance Hall license revoked after several problems. [Day after day, according to Kennedy, these raid notices appeared—only the names and locations changed.]

In November 1922 California voted on the Wright Act, the "little Volstead Act." Then in December Stockton voted on a little, little Volstead Act.

Death threats came to Sheriff in 1923 with this demand: "Stop raiding bootleggers."

12/18/23   Abatement proceeding began against French Camp Lodge, Mariposa Inn, Tavern on French Camp Turnpike, Washington House, Travelers Inn, the Chateau, Waldo place on Linden Road near the diverting canal, Armburst place on West Lane. The Chateau at French Camp ordered closed for one year.

10/16/24   A city ordinance was passed against slot machines. It was about this time that I became acquainted with a young Italian fellow who took care of slot machines for the biggest operator of this equipment in the city. His job was to call at the many blind pigs to adjust machines that paid too much, that paid too little, or were broken. He was on twenty-four hour call, with most calls after dark. It was my privilege to make many calls as his guest—with the understanding that I was to talk to no one and keep out of the way, in other words, just look and listen. It was a liberal education. I was not to recognize anyone, nor to mention the name of anyone I might see.

✍

On one ranch near Manteca in 1932, a bootlegger, arrested several times, killed his brother with an axe. July 6, Joe Floda, 40, allegedly murdered his brother Gene Floda, 35. Said Guard C. Darrah, District Attorney of San Joaquin County, the principal witness will be a neighbor who heard them arguing. Gene Floda was a shell-shocked war veteran.[13]

Toward the end of prohibition, when 3.2 (percent alcohol) beer became legal, farmers in California celebrated. But a few valley residents had little to celebrate. The Federal Court in Fresno had a busy schedule in the early summer of 1933. Two Los Angeles residents, Herman Miller and Angelo Bacci, sold their supposed influence to federal prisoners in the San Joaquin Valley, promising to fix liquor cases. Ten Merced County men wished they could have had some influence. A big liquor plant near Los Banos was raided with arrests and federal charges going to the following: Herman Miller, William Goldman, John Bianchi, Sam Miano, Gino Parve, Antonio Catania, John Ferrero, Dominic Mori, A. Gambi and E. B. Taylor. Nick Pennetti paid Herman Miller for "influence," but never received it and later became a government witness against the above gentlemen. Federal Judge Paul J. McCormick sentenced Nick Pennetti, William Golding, a Merced businessman, and Bianchi and Catania, two Bay Area liquor runners when the four pleaded to operating a huge still near Los Banos and another one that was raided three years earlier. Charges against Miano, Parve, Ferrero, Gambi, and Taylor were dismissed. Miller collected large sums of protection money, claiming he was paying off Federal Agent W. G. Whitfield and others. Miller, himself, was a victim of extortion threats of $1,000 in Bakersfield and moved to Merced County to avoid extortion. He set up the conspiracy and received bribe money from his own hirelings.[14]

Another Los Banos still operator had little to celebrate when Judge McCormick sentenced him to two years in prison, five years probation and a $350 fine. The federal court deliberated five hours over the charges against Louis Toscano. Prohi Whitfield arrested him on conspiracy charges when a still on his ranch exploded. Toscano claimed he didn't know what the lessee of his ranch was doing. He said he had no interest in the products produced on his land. When the mid-August, 1932, explosion and fire on the Toscano Ranch near Los Banos destroyed thousands of gallons of booze, Whitfield contacted Toscano, in Santa Cruz at the time, who agreed to come to Fresno for the investigation. The side-line business had machinery and nine 3,000-gallon still capacity.

The transient nature of California society showed itself in prohibition cases. People disappeared. The District Court of the United States Northern Division, case 4996, tried to prosecute George H. Hull for selling out of a garage on Vail and Sergeant Avenue, one mile from the Stockton city limits. When he did not show up for the charge, a bench warrant was issued for his arrest. Unable to find him from December 1930 to May 1931, the court ended the case with "gone to Idaho." Hull's selling of "large quantities of whiskey, gin, alcohol, wine and Anisette" went unpunished. He had one of California's first "garage sales" before he left.

Joy Ostrander received a sentence of three months in the county jail and a $100 fine for violation of section 3258, possession of an unregistered still on the S & O Ranch, 15 miles from San Andreas, Calaveras County. Upon conviction, she was transferred to Solana County Jail in April 1931.

Dos Palos Star
July 1927

Dos Palos, especially South Dos Palos, never settled down during the prohibition years.[15] Firebaugh was another wild town that kept constables and federal dry agents busy trying to end crime. Once Officers Mike Jones and Claude O'Banion raided Nick Trainer's place in Firebaugh. While the officers were in charge of the place, several cash customers came in and wanted to spread their money out on the bar in exchange for whatever it was Nick is said to have been selling. The officers turned down a chance to make some extra money.

In the summer of 1927, the H. C. Dryden family went on two weeks vacation. While they were gone burglars broke in and had a party with the Drydens' music and liquor stash.

Once in a while raids had to be made. Constable Campbell raided drinking and gambling places in South Dos Palos, confiscating 25 illegal slot machines and many punchboards.

Napa

In Napa, Judge L. A. Maynard fined Lewis Rossi $200 and destroyed 1,300 gallons of wine and liquors at the Rossi place, fined Ann Carrow Rutherford and Dixie Wallace, $200 and $250 respectively for wine and jackass liquor found at their premise, and the Feds arrested and released on bail Felix Frellone of St. Helena.[16]

No Installment Plan

Superior Court in Stockton sentenced Dominic Bertolli with a fine of $750 or two years for having a still in 1931. Although he offered the court installment payments, the judge turned him down, saying he would have to spend one day in jail for each $2 of fine not paid.[17]

Liquor Raids in Sacramento Hit 48

During December 1-18, 1928, police and federal flying squadron of the prohibition department hit 48 establishments in Sacramento and the imme-

Reo Speedwagon truck, confiscated while unloading sugar at barn distillery at Buttonwillow. Lic. # P/C G 5132, 1933. Prohibition agents' modus operandi: "Follow the sugar shipment" worked in this case. Photo courtesy Pomona City Library.

diate vicinity, arrested 27 on charges of possession in violation of the Wright Act, majority of arrests being made by Detective Sergeant E. L. Roberts and Detective E. W. Gapen of the dry squad. The last three arrested were John Smith at 1016 Sixth Street, George Ostega [Ortega?] at 1105 Fifth Street and William Lean 1018 ½ J Street. The raiders attested to a quantity of liquor taken at each establishment.[18]

Captured Elephant and Deer in Beer Raid

Quite a quandary existed for federal agents when they raided a bootlegging establishment owned by Jerry Andrews, of Sacramento, who was selling high-proof beer. The atmosphere of the beer parlor at 1213 J Street was enhanced by a menagerie of stuffed animals. Agents legally seized a taxidermal elephant, deer, snipes and other animals as part of the decor, valued in excess of $5,000. This was a first in prohibition history, putting the district court in a quandary whether to start the condemnation proceedings and then what to do with them. In the meantime, the prohibition agents had to store buckets, barrels, glasses, pitchers and a collection of stuffed animals.

Two other places, 610 M Street and 1015 Fifth, netted more high proof beer with the arrest of Theodore Jones and George Robertson. In these places the only animals seen were beer guzzler types; a little stiff but not stuffed.[19]

A Terrible Menace to the City

The latter part of the "Roaring Twenties" in Sacramento continued as wet as some of its famous floods. At the end of January 1929, Detectives E. L. Roberts and E. W. Gapen closed two bootleg joints suspected of catering to youths. Complaints about young high school and junior high age students going to 1904 K Street, operated by Ray Johnson. At the time of the raid there were no customers and Johnson answered the door but refused to let the officers in. They crashed the door and found a large quantity of wine, jackass brandy and gin cached in the building. Wine, shot and "Tom and Jerry" glasses and mugs were found on an improvised bar in the kitchen.[20]

The two detectives hit another bootleg establishment at noon at 2675 Sacramento Boulevard, two blocks from Sacramento High School. This establishment was also purported to sell to young people. Five youths, two only 16 years old, were playing pool, but denied ever buying liquor there. These raids ruined the plans of bootleggers to start the year on a prosperous note. Chief of Police William M. Hallanan commented, as long as "I am chief of police I intend to continue the drive on bootleggers, but particular attention will be paid to persons suspected on providing juveniles with intoxicants." The owner, C. K. Glover, arrested before of Wright Act violations, faced two more counts, possession and allowing juveniles to play pool in a poolroom. These places are "a terrible menace to the city," said the chief.[21]

Every few months the federal dry squads hit Sacramento and environs. This time government officials started abatement proceedings against seven places, seeking to close them in the valley. Location and violators: Sacramento, 2420 Nineteenth Street, Joe Marin, Harry Richard, Mike Montaldo; 1126 Seventh Street, Jack Cramer, Frank Brian, the Capital National Bank and Tony Nero; 1015 Fifth Street, Dick Kennon, George Roberts, Angelo Benomi, Teressa Benomi; 731 J Street, Alfred Rouse, A. Piazza, Edward Evans and Capital National Bank. Stockton, 20 South Center, Alexander Govoni, Pete Varney and G. B. Gianelli estate; Truckee, The Club, Gus Brown, Walter Dolly, Jack McKelvey, Larry McKelvey, Edward Brown; Bieber, Lassen County, The Smoke House, Lee Metcalf, Gail Parker, Tex Carter, John Todina.[22]

For deliveries one Sacramento boot used codes, such as "two whites and one dark" meaning two gins and one whiskey. A few drinkers squeezed canned heat through cheesecloth for a desperate drink. Farmhands were reported in the valley to drink lemon extract. Sacramento reporter Edward H. Dickson said "a Sacramentan who cannot get a drink fell into the description of what Ring Lardner termed a '12 wit' [dumber than a half-wit]."[23]

∅

Leland Edwards poignantly narrates the story of widower Thomas C. Wrinkle, near Porterville, who raised his motherless children alone on his farm. Though he had a brush or two with the law in 1920 and spent some months in jail, he was respected by folks in the neighborhood as hard working and honest—a moonshiner but an okay guy.

But federal agent Maurice Tice employed an undercover detective in the Visalia area, who reported to Tice that Wrinkle had a still in his barn. Armed with a warrant, the raiding party split, a couple going to the farm house and Tice going to the barn to search for the still. Wrinkle, who was eating a late lunch with the owner of the farm, a mortgage holder from Los Angeles, asked the two agents who entered his house if he could finish his lunch first. No problem.

But when he finished, he calmly went to the cabinet and pulled out a rifle and covered the officers. When Tice discovered the still and 300 gallons of mash, he walked into the house, not knowing of the standoff. The outnumbered Wrinkle fired and wounded Tice. The shootout that followed left Winkle dead and two officers wounded. Though hard working and respected, moonshiner Wrinkle gave up his life for what probably would have only been a fine or a six-months' sentence at the most—an extreme case among thousands of farm and ranch moonshining.[24]

∅

These few samples of prohibition violations in the huge interior valleys of California, their major cities including the Capitol, and on farms throughout the state show the magnitude of California's lack of regard for the 18th Amendment.

424

A trash-littered hole is all that is left of the new "dairy" on the Sandoz Ranch in Hinkley, northwest of Barstow. Men from L. A. rented the ranch to make a dairy and secretly built the biggest distillery found in that part of the desert. The hole allowed trucks to back in with their beds level with the loading dock. A pump sent the spent mash to a reservoir, creating drunk ducks and desert animals. Photo by author.

CHAPTER 24

THE PEACEFUL PENINSULA

The San Francisco Peninsula, south of San Francisco, was quiet after the Great War when Camp Fremont closed. Wounded, gassed and shell shocked veterans recovered in the beautiful oak-covered hospital grounds by Willow Avenue in Menlo Park. The Peninsula was a peaceful rural setting with small towns, separating the cities of San Jose and San Francisco. Large live oaks forested much of the rolling foothills that sank at the San Andreas fault, then blended with pines and redwoods of the Coast Range. In the winter and spring, fields of rich green grass, wild oats and mustard covered open areas between groves of oaks. On the bay side black adobe soil stretched to the mud and salt flats of San Francisco Bay. El Camino Real, State Highway, later U.S. 101, linked the small towns, four-five miles apart from San Francisco to San Jose, small towns that had been slowly taking over farms and orchards. And most afternoons, especially after May when the grasses were tall and brown, an ocean breeze blew down the Peninsula cities, keeping the weather mild, and clouds of fog rolled over the rounded Coast Range from San Bruno to Santa Clara and the fog looked like slow motion ocean foam over rocks. And everywhere one looked, it was beautiful and the weather mild year round. A pleasant and serene place to live and raise a family. People fell in love with it and soon their relatives and friends came, making this beautiful place their home too, encroaching a little more on the pastoral scene.

Daily, workers commuted to "The City" on the Southern Pacific Railroad. Quite a few citizens were wealthy enough that they didn't have to commute anymore, multi-millionaires in Hillsborough, Atherton, and Portola. Most citizens, however, were middle class, working middle class, developing skills to work for the Southern Pacific Railroad, P.G.& E., Frank's Tannery, the salt works, automobile support services and canneries. Many, migrating from rural settings in the mid-west and from Europe, planted fruit trees, raised chickens and sometimes rabbits in their back yards, saving a little money and keeping some of their rural roots. A large minority of people were simple working class people, struggling with lower paying jobs as servants, gardeners, farm help, laborers in the above industries and store workers. The ethnic makeup of the Peninsula dwellers was diversified with Italian, Mexican, Irish, Scots and English and Chinese—mixed in with a few blacks, Eastern Europeans, Filipinos, Japanese and some of everything else. They worked hard, enjoyed leisure living, were law abiding, supported schools, followed Stanford's football team and Sequoia High School teams.

Many, especially bachelors, drank in saloons, with enough saloons to choose from in each town, except those communities that went dry under local option. Menlo Park, in the 1910s, had numerous saloon owners: A. Burk, A. Carlton, W. A. Maloney, Charles Meyers, Frank Roach and William Warren, to name a few. John Beltramo, on Greenwood Avenue, and John H. O'Keefe, on State Highway, were liquor dealers.[1]

Prohibitionists were pleased that Redwood City and several other towns voted themselves dry in 1917-18. Before voting to become dry, Redwood had an average of 25 drunks a month in jail. In 1919, it averaged only one. "Now that the national prohibition is in force there is no one in Sheriff Sheehan's boarding house." Jailor Will Hogan guarded a big empty old building.[2]

When War Prohibition went into effect July 1, 1919, the people of the Peninsula expected to go into a dry era. A few days before, an announcement appeared in the *Times Gazette*, heading "Last Wet Dance of the Season at Woodruff Inn," near La Honda. "Practically the last wet dance to take place at La Honda," said the newspaper, for on July 1, the country would go dry and Californians made plans where they would spend their last wet day. They could partake of the wine supper given by Henri Devere, the popular Woodruff proprietor, noted for his dinners. The ball would be under the auspices of returning soldiers giving the dance for La Honda, who earlier had a reception for the returning soldiers. Dancers from all over the county would be there, the reporter predicted.

Woodruff Inn had a wet dance but it was not its last. Activities all summer summoned city folks to come to this mountain country to celebrate— celebrate anything: 500 Hibernians from San Francisco converged on La Honda waving their Irish banners; Bastille dance in July at Bonzagni's with $1.00 chicken dinners and a five-piece jazz orchestra; in August it was the annual Knights of Columbus picnic; and another big dance at Sears Hall put on by La Honda Social Club. Also in August Woodruff Inn held "Uncle Ben's" grand opening, with a grand march led by Uncle Sam and Miss La Belle France in character costume. Uncle Ben is a natural born caterer who knew how to provide for the inner man—in other words he provided food and drink!

With all this activity word soon spread that the mountain resorts of San Mateo County did not go dry socially. They stayed wet all during the dry years. One could drink unmolested at stores surrounded by pines, oaks and redwoods, ferns and creeks, and with the sweet smell of humus and conifers in the air, a person could forget city life and conflicts of the world.[3]

The six months of War Prohibition, followed by months of National Prohibition, would indicate that prohibition was working—except, of course, at the mountain resorts. Despite many robbin' hoods raiding the rich estates and liquor warehouses, there were few arrests, few drunks on the streets, few prisoners in the jails. It must have been like boxers feeling each other out.

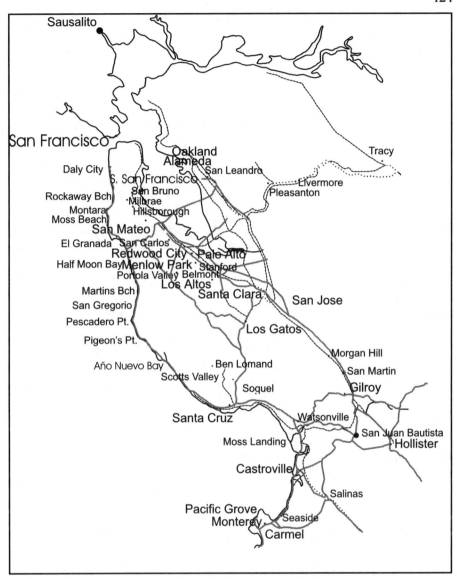

California Bay Area and Peninsula

Perhaps bootleggers were overly cautious the first few months of 1920. Or maybe the officers gave a little transition time to get rid of stock and to change over from bars to soft drink parlors. More likely, officials looked the other way in the resorts of the Coast Range.

Then in April 1920, three ex-soldiers strolled away from the Veterans Base Hospital, taking a weekend off from their care and incarceration. They found their way to La Honda. They probably heard that Uncle Ben was such a good cook and perhaps they were tired of Base Hospital food. Uncle Ben, probably being patriotic and wanting to help the vets, sold them more than a dinner: two quarts of whiskey for $15 a quart. Remember he knew "how to provide for the inner man." They were found intoxicated at Woodside. This incident incensed the good citizens, seemingly always paternalistic toward veterans at the hospital. The high price of the liquor, especially for bottles of moonshine, offended officers. Judge Ray Griffin issued search warrants for the Woodruff Inn and had Ben Curtiss arrested.[4]

Prohibitionists complained about illegal sales on the Peninsula and a few arrests had been made, but bootlegging became an established part of California life, and especially in Redwood City and Menlo Park. In 1921, Mayor Mark E. Ryan said, "Redwood City was the center of 'Booze Joints.'" He said, one drink of "grappo" could damage one's health and recommended the city revoke licenses of those operating blind pigs and that dances be allowed only till 1:00 a.m. instead of 3:00 a.m.

Saddle Rock Restaurant, near the Court House in Redwood City, lost its license in February 1921 for selling liquor. Owner A. Baradat also owned 16 Mile House in San Bruno. A witness and supposedly a friend testified that after lunch he called for "some good whiskey" and the waiter brought some. "It smelled like good stuff," said the witness. The waiter said it "was 105 proof and they reduced it to 100 proof." The witness called for two drinks and paid $2.40. Baradat and his manager D. S. Wright denied knowing about any liquor sold. Baradat was only opened six weeks and had spent over $5,000 to fix the place. The board listened to an appeal by Baradat and Trustee Kreiss was in favor of giving him another chance. When Mayor Ryan said that Baradat planned to use the restaurant for selling liquor and the board could be bought for $10, the trustees denied the appeal. In March Baradat sold out to Lucien Ducuing of San Francisco and thanked the people of Redwood for their patronage and hoped they would support Ducuing.[5] Others should be punished besides the Saddle Rock, said the editor of *Times Gazette* "It is hardly fair to make flesh out of one and fish of another." There were 16 blind pigs in town every day breaking the law. "It is alleged that they [owners] are foreigners who do not speak the languages and are not citizens."

In the spring of 1921, D. A. De Giovanni, Redwood City; Jack Everson, Beresford; Carl Nelson and Ben Race of Portola Valley were caught selling grappa out of their houses. Harold Johnson, after drinking some grappa, brought suit against the Portola Valley folks because of temporary loss of eyesight.[6] The bail for each, set by Judge Buck, was only $100.

Every town on the Peninsula had its bootleggers. A routine settled in as the second year of prohibition went into the third (1922). Three soft drink parlors and one restaurant were raided for violations of the Volstead Act: Joe Deluchi arrested at 1325 El Camino, Joseph [Edward?] Bennett on the corner of Washington (Broadway)? and Hamilton, J. A. Genochio at 207 Main Street, and L. Ducuing, proprietor of the Saddle Rock Restaurant at Broadway and Washington—all in Redwood City, the county seat of San Mateo County. Chief of Police C. L. Collins used detectives from San Francisco to buy drinks from these operators. Since each pleaded guilty, Judge Albert Mansfield fined them $200. Bennett had already been fined and was on parole for selling booze to a Palo Alto youth in a Woodside soft drink parlor. It was not a good year for Bennett. Bootlegger Bennett seemed to have an affinity with making the wrong decisions in Redwood City. His place on Broadway was across from the county building and by the Redwood City Central School. Redwood City revoked his business license for selling "booze to school boys," namely 19-year-old Robert Tucker, son of a Broadway furniture dealer. Tucker and three other boys obtained liquor from Bennett. Bennett evidently liked doing business with youngsters. He was convicted of buying liquor from a San Mateo youth who confessed to stealing booze from a well-stocked liquor cellar. Thus Bennett bought from a young robbin' hood. Even Mayor Ryan produced evidence against Bennett and other operators.

A big contention in 1921 was whether the cities and county should approve the weekend dances. The Forresters and other legitimate groups wanted to hold dances as they had before, but many kids attended and there was too much bootlegging going on at the Saturday night dances. Mayor Ryan said liquor was sold at restaurants near or at the dance halls. One Sunday he discovered liquor "sold in small coffee pots and the reason so many out-of-town people attended dances was that liquor was so easily obtained here." A delegation from the Congregational Church, because of the "evil of the dance hall," asked city hall to close the dances earlier than midnight. Kids went to the dance until it closed, then went out to procure liquor, they said. Sometime young people were found passed out on the lawn.[7] The counter argument was that the dances were not evil, only the bootleggers. Dances remained open until 1:00 a.m.

One Tuesday evening in March, 1922, officials hit three bootlegging joints: New Travotore Hotel (formerly Europa Hotel) at 402 Arguello St., Fly Trap Inn at Five Points (Redwood City) and a grocery store at 1228 Main Street in Five Points. A few days later Redwood City Chief of Police Collins arrested Joe Gaffanti, proprietor of the Verde Hotel and restaurant at 1304 El Camino Real. After pleading guilty, Gaffanti paid a $200 fine. In less than three weeks, Redwood City's coffers increased by $1,600 with prohibition fines.

The month of April saw more arrests in the small community of Belmont. Caught loading six 50-gallon barrels of whiskey at the Belmont Casino were J. N. Costa and Manuel Caubet, who claimed they didn't know the ownership of the booze.

One of the biggest fines up to 1922 went to John Beltramo of Menlo Park, owner of Beltramo's resort. He pleaded guilty before Judge Frank H. Rudkin in the U. S. District Court in San Francisco. Because he got caught selling to Stanford students, Rudkin fined Beltramo $400.

Beltramo's resort was typical of many scattered through the Peninsula. Since the Peninsula was close to San Francisco, it became a favorite place for weekend trips to shaded oak, pine or redwood forests for picnicking and camping resorts during the Roaring Twenties. Picnic grounds with tables and shade and cooking pits and usually a dance pavilion, a store and of course some place to dispense food and drinks. All legal—until liquor was dispensed. Children played in the forests and caught polliwogs in the creeks, while older folks relaxed and forgot their city world by sipping on a cold beer or tall, icy Tom Collins.

Lost Babylon

As with the ancient city of Pompeii, everything was just the way it was when people departed from Babylon, San Mateo County. When disaster struck, people fled leaving food on the stoves and tables, half empty glasses with liquor, a dance floor covered with bright sparkling paper and paper imitation "teddy bears" left strewn about the debris.

Disaster came not from billowing ash from a volcano but in the form of Rutter, chief prohibition enforcement agent in northern California, said the *Examiner*. "The law was not respected in that barbaric age and such gatherings were generally under suspicion of officials, for human beings that were accustomed to stimulating themselves by taking a chemical preparation called alcohol." Several hundred were celebrating the end of the year 1922 and issuing in the new year when disaster struck. The owner of the property, George Hensley of Los Altos, announced to the hosts of the celebrants that the lease was up and closed the place down. But unlike Pompeii this archaeological site will not be preserved to the age when the "race was emerging from an alcoholic wilderness."[8]

The editor of *Redwood City Standard* picked up on an Oregon editorial when he wrote that patrons of the bootleggers were not the poor, because they could not afford $10 a quart. "Rich men encourage rumrunning, smuggling and violations of the law by buying $100 cases of whiskey. They make themselves confidants of the lowest class of criminals."[9] enforcement

The biggest Peninsula raid since Amendment 18 occurred in January 1923, netting Redwood City $6,000. Chief Collins and Officer Ed McAuliffe hit the Fly Trap Inn at Five Points, finding 360 quarts of home beer, 182 quarts wine and one bottle whiskey. Also hit were the Rainbow Inn on State Highway and California Market on Main near Maple. Arrested were Joe Garfoli, proprietor of Fly Trap Inn, Peter Benozzio, waiter, Charles Constantino, cook and

Charles Gonzales; arrested at the Rainbow were G. Deluchi, proprietor, R. Pergollo and C. Perzollo (may be Charles Persello?), waiters; California Market, Albert Caruso, owner with wine and moonshine as evidence. At the Monte Verde Grocery ("The White Rat") on lower Main Street, caught were Steve Monteverde, owner, and Antone Monteverde, his nephew, with 500 gallons wine, 250 gallons moonshine whiskey, hidden in a false chicken house at rear of the store.[10]

A citizen's complaint against San Francisco cigar merchant August Faisst led to Faisst's arrest, but also the arrest of the citizen. Pietro Carmani complained to Judge George H. Buck that Faisst, pretending he was a prohibition agent, tried to extort $1,200 from Carmani for a still somewhere in La Honda. Faisst pleaded guilty to extortion and was fined $100. Then in June 1923, Sheriff Lampkin and Deputy Sheriff Pete J. Larrecou and city policeman Elgin Kreiss spent hours "over hill and down dale and came across the nicest looking outdoor manufacturing plant one would want to see." On Old Langley ranch, along Woodruff Creek, eight miles from La Honda, in an isolated spot at the bottom of a deep gulch was the hidden distillery operated by Carmani, G. Preimo, Barney Bonzagni and, officers claimed, Ralph Dickinson, well-known Woodside man. Carmani and Preimo surrendered but the other two men escaped amid a hail of bullets. Warrants went out for their arrest. The still worth $5,000 was destroyed, 3,500 gallons of mash dumped and 100 gallons of moonshine dumped in the Woodruff Creek. Carmani and Preimo pleaded guilty to possessing a still and paid $300, then pleaded guilty to operating a still, with a fine of $800 each. Preimo paid his fine but since Carmani did not have enough money, he sat in the county jail. It just wasn't right to be extorted. That was a dishonest thing to do. He stuck to his principles.[11]

Another strange case occurred in South San Francisco, which had gambling dens, booze joints and vice dens. Andrew J. Kane, Detective Agent, and 11 prohibitionist detectives, acting like vigilantes, wanted to clean up South City in the summer of 1923. Constable James C. Wallace tried to stop the detectives and gathered up a handful of hastily assembled deputies, but was himself arrested by the cleanup detectives. Feelings ran high in South City as people expected "some little fireworks" with a street battle between the two groups. Upon Wallace's request, Justice Ed Farrell issued a warrant for Kane who was arrested with his 11 deputies for disturbing the peace. Eight employees of Kane were discharged with only a judge's reprimand and comment, "It's a wonder you weren't all mobbed by indignant citizens." Three were convicted of impersonating an officer: Charles Coffman, Joe Moreno and J. Y. Walker and fined $20 or 10 days, while William Nelson was found guilty of battery. People were tired of seeing little attempt at stopping bootlegging and were trying to clean up South San Francisco. Court testimony showed that Kane and his sleuths were secretly and hastily employed by some city council members and a local notary public.

The same summer people were still enjoying La Honda and other mountain areas for vacations and weekend retreats. About 50 people were guests at the Woodruff Inn when it burned, causing $30,000 damage. It had been leased by F. Richardson, B. Wright and B. Collins. Rumors were that a still blew up.[12]

Two more manufacturing outfits were put out of commission late that summer: A barn on the Phelps estate along Marsh Road in Belmont held a miniature brewery, containing 40 cases of beer, four dozen bottles, 15 large vats, two corking machines and a large quantity of malt, hops and sugar. But no brewers! A mystery. The other was a distillery at Jules Louchere's place at 224 Olive Ave, Redwood, operated by Louchere and Joseph Bloise of Mill Valley. At 2:30 p.m. "all Roosevelt Avenue was rocked by a terrific blast and fire when the still blew up. Chief Ryan found Louchere trying to put out the fire and confiscated a quantity of moonshine. The house was destroyed by flames." The moral, said the *Redwood City Standard*, was never try to operate a still when the thermometer reached the 95 degree mark. Louchere's defense was he was just renting the building to Bloise and didn't know if it was being used or not. A $300 fine anyway.[13]

San Mateo's Coastal Communities

Three men enjoying a friendly abalone dinner at Petroni's roadhouse at Hotel Princeton in Half Moon Bay ended up with too much to drink. Robert Bianchi, Duilo Benedetti and A. Michele ate their abalone but had an argument about who should pay for the dinner. Perhaps Bianchi was too slow to come out with his wallet and Benedetti shot and killed him. Benedetti surrendered to the county authorities a week or so later and was exonerated. Pressure on the county sheriff, however, caused a crackdown on the open vice in Half Moon Bay.

San Mateo County's District Attorney Frank Swart closed the Princeton Hotel, near Miramar, under the Redlight Abatement Act. He arrested R. Flowers, M. H. Root, Red Claire, P. Nannini and E. Caleno. Swart announced: "Places like this on the bay solicit men and boys to come there and participate in acts of ill-fame, women and booze." These places weren't just selling Napa Soda Ginger Ale. The sheriff arrested Antonio Vannucci of Miramar for contributing to the delinquency of a minor and William Cunho, son of Manuel Cunho. Vannucchi sold his holdings in the county and disappeared. He gave up his $500 cash bail. Red Claire and Pete Ninnini, lessors of the Princeton Hotel, pleaded not guilty to contributing to the delinquency of a minor but guilty of operating a "disorderly house." The judge suspended the $150 fine on the condition that they leave the county.

A father of a 17-year-old Oakland girl complained to the prohibition commission that his daughter was "plied with liquor" (poison liquor) in the

Rockaway Beach resort Rockaway Inn, then she was dragged from her escort to an inner room and there assaulted, first by the proprietor, and then by the other men. Upon investigation, the owner Herbert Bazinetti denied selling "poisoned liquor" at his place and assaulting the girl. Dry squad forces arrested two other proprietors at Rockaway Beach. Officials confiscated liquor at all three places. U. S. Commissioner Thomas E. Hayes [Haynes?] set $1,000 bond for Bazinetti's release.

Convicting Dr. Rinehart Allen of contributing to the delinquency of a minor, along with Dr. Galin Hickok, at the "Castle of Mystery," Salada Beach, the court gave Allen a $2,000 fine and two years in jail.

The Biglieri brothers, Angelo and Louis, received a year each for prohibition violations from Federal Judge Lauderback's court in San Francisco. The judge acquitted Sebastiano Belli, a worker for the brothers. The attorneys pleaded for the sentences to be consecutive so that one could serve his year and the other work at their business, then the other would serve his time. Judge Lauderback denied the request. Lauderback gave some small fines too. In 1930 he sentenced Alfredo Angeli of Half Moon Bay only 10 days in the county jail and no fine at all.[14]

In April, 1928, Sheriff James J. McGrath led a raid on Gray's Resort at Salada Beach. Two ladies, "inmates of the establishment," received free trips back over the hill to the county jail in Redwood City: Miss Lorraine Hill, 25, manicurist, and Miss Anna Briengan, stenographer, along with a customer John Ferrero, 30, a tile setter by trade. The manager of the place, not being a very good host, escaped by means of a secret door and disappeared.[15]

Throughout prohibition the coast from Montara down to Pescadero was not only a landing center for rumrunners coming from the mother ships 12-40 miles off the coast, but was also a moonshine haven. Tiny beaches and inlets, fed by small creeks in narrow canyons and valleys coming out of forested mountains all contributed to this isolation and privacy that made the area great for moonshining. Yet, it was fairly near a large population center—San Francisco.

Sheriff H.W. Lampkin and Half Moon Bay Constable Fred Simmons located three stills in the summer of 1923. They confiscated five sacks of sugar, two boxes of prunes, 10 gallons of moonshine whiskey and a demijohn of liquor. Since a large quantity was manufactured on the coast the county dry squad planned to make more thorough searches from Colma to Half Moon Bay.[16]

A moonshine tragedy hit Half Moon Bay in March, 1922, when Gerald Marsh burned to death at a still accident. Sheriff McGrath, deputies Ed Farrell and Leland Quinlan found evidence of a still burner, hydrometer and cans of sugar which they turned over to District Attorney Franklin Swart.[17]

Moonshining activities resulted in the seizure of two stills in the summer of 1930 where the dry squad arrested Gircilano Girclani and Daniel Duli for having a 500-gallon still, 200 gallons of liquor and 15,000 gallons of mash at the Ernest Consani ranch near Half Moon Bay. On the same raid they found a 300-gallon still at Miramar, but no one was around and they made no arrests.

Fourteen years of raids into the backlands produced few results. Tipoffs were common. Charles Steele of Pescadero, a San Mateo County traffic squad member, was accused of warning a roadhouse proprietor about a planned federal raid. Some suspected that he might have given warnings about raids into Woodside and La Honda.

The Alpine Inn, Portola Valley

Historic Alpine Inn in Portola Valley, 3915 Alpine Road, has existed since about 1851, the only saloon on California's historic registry. During the turn of the century the saloon was called "The Wanderer." During prohibition, Julius Schenkel operated it as Schenkel's Picnic Park. This popular resort had partitions to form small back rooms. Being away from the sheriff of San Mateo County, it became a favorite for weekenders from San Francisco and, of course, Stanford students.

In the 1950s, it was called Rossotti's—and still a place for Stanford undergrads to forget their exams for a few hours—some collegians might be third or even fourth generation Stanford Indians [Cardinals now] to enjoy cold ones at the Alpine.

Apple Jack Inn, La Honda
as told by Armand Zanoni, La Honda

I was born in La Honda in 1896, living in this mountain area between Palo Alto and the Pacific Coast all my life. I knew all the bootleggers in this area. My brother Louie Zanoni, a good Irish name, ran the Peek-A-Boo Inn in San Gregorio.

Weatherby was a bootlegger in the Apple Jack in La Honda. He rented the building for $10-15 a month to park his car. Those double doors opened and he parked his car right in the middle of the building (Historic site 102, site of the first building in La Honda, originally a blacksmith shop). He served beer and burgundy wine on tables around the car at times or at the picnic area in back, beer 15¢ a glass and whiskey 25¢ a shot, wine 10¢ a glass.

The prohis never arrested anyone. At my brother's place and other places in San Gregorio the sheriffs used to drink with 'em, pour 'em a shot of whiskey. They never got knocked over and I don't think they paid anyone off.

Local people bought grapes over the hill and made wine here. It sold for 75¢ a gallon as I remember.

Apple Jacks, famed bootlegging resort in La Honda, on the San Francisco Peninsula, built by Apple Jack Gabriella and later run by a man named Wetherby. In this former blacksmith shop, Wetherby sold beer at tables around his car and at tables in the back, 15 cents [use cents sign] 25 cents per shot of moonshine whiskey, and 10 cents for a glass of wine. Photo by author.

The Boots and Saddle used to be a speakeasy. The first building was called Manzani Lodge. Alec Manzani ran it.

The Woodruff, three miles to the east of La Honda, blew up one night and burned down. It was a beautiful place, a garage and dance hall. A man named Weeks owned it, who had a still there which exploded.

Apple Jack Gabriella, another good Irish name, built Apple Jack's in 1919, but within a year prohibition came into effect, making an open bar too conspicuous. It used to be a blacksmith shop. I helped tear down the first building.

Apple Jack had many customers. The competition from across the street had none. He (the competitor) spread the word that the prohis were coming in to raid the Apple Jack. The customers went across the street to the safer establishment. Along the coast, oh there was nothing but speakeasies, Half Moon Bay, Pescadero and San Gregorio.

Might Be More Abalones Toward the North
as told by Pat Bell, San Gregorio

All the beaches and inlets were used for smuggling on the coast side of the peninsula. La Gaza Creek at Pescadero was prominent. A man named

Pinkham worked that area as did Elodino Bertalucci. Lobitas Creek, the cove north of Martin's Beach, was also a favorite spot.

The smugglers needed manpower. They hired men for $25 a night to pull the sleds of alcohol up the beach and load the trucks. Drivers might receive more.

One day a friend of mine was diving for abalone south of Pigeon Point. He decided to try the next beach south. After walking to the beach, he met an armed man standing guard. The guard said to my friend, "I don't think you have any reason to go on this beach."

The abalone diver didn't think so either: perhaps "abaloning" would be better back toward the north.

These people were mean, rough. They even used machine guns. Hijackers and rumrunners constantly fought. I was working in Salinas when Moss Landing battle took place, 1925. Afterwards I saw a power pole [like a telephone pole] with many machine gun bullet holes.

All places in San Gregorio sold booze at one time or another, depending on the owner. Bertalucci sold it at The Stage Stop.

They didn't make it in San Gregorio but in the more remote areas. They were never raided. If the prohis came to Half Moon Bay, the word spread all along the coast.

Good Corn Whiskey Never Hurt Anyone

Year after year the same names appeared as bootleggers or moonshiners or the same places seemed to get raided every six months or so. The idealism of the progressive movement had diminished by the mid 1920s. In 1924 prohibitionists felt the government was not doing its job stopping bootlegging, gambling and prostitution. Claims of payoffs, officers drinking at bootleg joints, and tip-offs circulated but few scandals surfaced. It seemed everyone in Menlo Park knew John "Jack" Doyle bootlegged at the Palms Hotel on Oak Grove. People liked John, liked his sense of humor. When he guaranteed every customer a free coat hanger and cigarette lighter, he handed him a match and a nail. He wired up a tray so that customers picking up their change would receive a little electric shock. Doyle owned a saloon before prohibition and evidently just could not stop the habit of selling. He must have been arrested seven-eight times, always getting off or receiving such a light sentence he just went right back to selling until do-gooders reported him again and he could not be ignored.[18]

"Little Tia Juana," or Five Points also had raids every six months or so. One of these raids was late in February 1924, when agents hit the Blue Bird, a soft drink parlor. Fined $300 were Lawrence Marin and John Olivera for selling cream soda—except that the bottles of cream soda contained whiskey. The Dew Drop Inn saw Lorenzo Perez, Joe Marquez, Antonio Vertodes arrested for liquor violations and M. Olson for gambling. In May officers caught Charles Tognoli, owner of Fly Trap Inn. The end of the year, another raid by Officers Kreiss, Wood, Roza, McAuliffe and Thorpe caught Henry Lomello for having a still behind the Fly Trap Inn, two large stills in fact. From the basement came so much booze that it took two trucks to carry the liquor away: wine, jackass brandy, several barrels of mash, approximately 900 gallons of contraband. Lomello received one of the heaviest fines in the city so far, $1,000 or 500 days. Sam De Gregorio, another Five Points merchant, lost $1,000 bail money when he was caught the second time in a month or so.

Santa Cruz Avenue in Menlo Park had its share of repeats and drinking areas. Daniel Red, in a little resort on the southeast corner of Santa Cruz Avenue and University Avenue, sold to minors who confessed to buying there. Larrecou, Chief Collins of Redwood and McAuliffe raided Red, whereupon he pleaded guilty but not to selling to youths. The judge fined him $500. Another Menlo rancher Serifin Mangini, experienced bootlegger, topped other bails in Menlo Park with $1,500, given to him by Judge Ray Griffin.

The Genochio family made the news periodically. In May, Albert Genochio played Mr. Ingoldsby, one of the lead roles in the play "The Trysting Place." The same paper had the news of John Genochio of Jack's Liquor, 207 Main Street, Redwood, and George Genochio, Peninsula Restaurant, 153 Main, caught bootlegging. Carl Schmidt of Del Monte Hotel, 250 Main, suffered from the dry squad. Pasquales Bialo, City Boarding House of Phelps, lost his freedom for awhile, as did A. Bertolucchi, Hotel de Redwood man, when he was remanded to the federal court with $1,000 bail. Ben Race was fined $500 for liquor finding its way into his Portola soft drink parlor. Portola's Ed Johnson and Roy Peterson also made the trip to the county seat in handcuffs. In Belmont, Mrs. Philomene Baradat was fined $250. When her lawyer pleaded hardship, saying she was sole support of her children, federal agents countered with evidence she had $15,000 in the bank and $15,000 worth of property.

Raids subsided a bit until October 1924. Then too much was too much. Barbara Romero, a mother of three, went to jail when she could not pay her $500. The court then had a change of heart as they recommended she be released from custody with the strict provision she leave the city. Albert Elmette, 1104 Main Street, made the mistake of selling too much whiskey to youths.

That same October the Redwood City police and Sheriff T. C. McGovern raided another place on Santa Cruz Avenue in Menlo Park, netting 36, including five minors, some from Stanford and a couple from Sequoia High School. At the Kavanaugh place, Edward Kavanaugh and Fred Egli, hosted a merry party, with a large fireplace and everyone enjoying highballs and other drinks. When the raiders hit, people flew out every exit, finding most blocked. One youth dived out a window, badly cutting himself. Two women "inmates," Edna Calvin, 23, and Edna Lewis, 33, pleaded not guilty. The boys were charged with visiting a house of ill fame and fined $10 or $25 cash bail. The women and owners Kavanaugh and Egli were charged with running a disorderly place, Wright Act violations and contributing to delinquency of minors. Judge Griffin fined both $500, but the case was flawed and most charges were dropped thanks to a good lawyer, J. J. Bullock. He proved the illegal sale should be dropped because the undercover agents bought liquor improperly and strangely two witnesses didn't show up.

Peninsula citizens were furious. They had meetings from South San Francisco to Santa Clara and formed the Veterans and Citizens Protective League (V and C Protective League). Newspapers listed names of citizens from each town who pledged to fight crime and abide by the laws of the land. A crusade spirit took place in the Peninsula as complaints went to both San Mateo and Santa Clara officials and this pressure made both more active: In Palo Alto and College City (Stanford), Police Chief H. H. Kink and Sheriff George W. Lyle of San Jose caught Dominico and Rino (Reno) Bettini, 921 Em (Emerson ?); Joe Ferioli, 926 Ramona; Theodore I. Glasnow and William J. Morrison at College Bowling Alley; Fran Sargent, 627 Fulton.

December 1924 raids nabbed the following in Redwood City: Henry Crowhurst, 132 Spruce; Joe (G.?) Deluchi, Rainbow Inn, State Highway; Fred A. Leavitt, 126 Spruce; Tony Bertolucci, Hotel de Redwood; Joe Basso (Bosso) and Joe Garfoli, Fly Trap Inn; Charles Tagnoli, State highway; P. Besozzi, waiter at Fly Trap, dismissed; Jack Genochio; Joe, Frank and Charles Ferrando, 122 Whipple, the latter two dismissed when brother Joe took all the blame; and Sam Buffa, 31 Oak Street.

The League members expressed their pleasure when bootleggers were caught, especially around schools and the veterans hospital. The American Legion complained that the following men sold to veterans: Menlo Park: John Doyle, Palm Hotel; August Buchman, service station and resort on the corner of State Highway and Valpariso; Serifino Mangini, Isabel Avenue and Camino a las Cerros; Andy Monte, Luis Arman, Paul Franceschini owner of resort formerly operated by Daniel Red, corner of Santa Cruz and University; Woodside, Carl Nelson and August Krieps; Redwood City, Sam De Gregorio, Albino Merlet, George Brooks. Properties of five of the above were temporarily abated in December; several cases went to district court.[19] Perhaps because of pressure from the V and C Protective league, Bud Thorpe captured a seller of liquor to patients at Base Hospital. He had been sought for a month, but had been illusive, having a "saloon on wheels" like a lunch wagon. Thorpe caught J. McGuire, alias D. M. Lawrence, at one in the morning on Main Street and charged him with possession and transportation. McGuire had "a high-powered sedan, completely equipped for mixing cocktails" and contained two gallons sweet wine, a gallon of gin, three gallons whiskey, several kinds of flavoring extract. "The owner was apparently used to mixing wet goods."

When Prohibition Agent Charles Goff moved against sellers to veterans and students, he caught Menlo Park Ice Cream Parlor owner Roy Peterson and Ida Murray; Thomas E. Fitzgibbons on Railroad Avenue; and Frank R. Maloney, store keeper at a billiards place by Pine and Oak Grove. Maloney posted $2,000 bail.

Conversely when courts gave too lenient sentences, the group publicized it and complained, especially about Judge George M. Bourquin's attitude and light sentences. Doyle, Buckman and Mangini pleaded guilty and received $40 and 125 days, $30 and 100 days and 30 and 100 days respectively. The Veterans and Citizens Protective League said that 30 days is better than a fine. But Doyle and Mangini "are old offenders" having been convicted of illicit selling many times. At least this time they received jail time. "Doyle has shown adroitness in escaping with light fines...now part of his hotel is closed under abatement proceedings." Mangini's house was also closed by federal abatement orders. "In the case of August Buchman much pressure and influence were used on the Federal prosecutors to 'go easy' ... that Buchman was being persecuted, framed , etc. For this reason his out-and-out confession of guilt leaves his 'influential friends' out on the end of a limb." When Judge Bourquin said, "The Volstead law has driven the liquor dealers so under cover that a decent man cannot go to a decent place under decent circumstances and buy a decent drink at a decent price," prohibitionists seethed.

Again the League was offended when a jury could not come to a verdict against black bootlegger Pinky Hall, known to have sold to veterans. Judge Buck chastised three women on the jury for disregarding the law, evidence and judge's instructions. One of the women was heard to say after the hung jury: "Good corn liquor never hurt anybody." No matter how offensive her words were to League members, it was obvious that her sentiments were more universal than everybody thought.[20]

Though County District Attorney Swart said the Wright Act gave them the duty to enforce the law without the machinery to do so, he would do his best. But he said, "...we are not going to be intimidated by self-constituted committees, either for so-called good or so-called bad."

Nevertheless this reform movement helped for awhile. People were caught and given more jail time in 1925. The league felt definite progress had been made. August Fabbro was caught again at El Travotore, Joe Garfoli, at State Highway and Roosevelt; Jimmie Pasut and Ed Fruzi, moonshining in North Atherton; Angelo and Mani Turco in Millbrae; The Blue Bird, alias The Dew Drop Inn and Joe Basso in Five Points again; Tony G. Ferrari, a Redwood garbage man, Pasquale Bailo, two times; Ruth Miller, Juan Russell, Cecile Paulson at Tanforan Hotel in San Bruno. When one threw the evidence down the sink, Sheriff McGovern unscrewed the drain and retrieved half a bottle of booze for evidence.[21]

✍

In order to control illegal alcohol selling in San Mateo County, an ordinance requiring resorts and roadhouses to have licenses from the board of supervisors took effect in 1925. Sheriff McGovern with the aid of deputies and constables swooped up to the northern Peninsula and closed a number of soft drink parlors and cabarets and arrested proprietors. Officials charged John Bonimini, owner of The Box in Colma, for selling liquor and operating a roadhouse without a permit. Raiders gained entrance as the girl entertainers and their escorts entered through a secret door. They arrested T. Borgni, who ran Colma Poolroom, charging him with allowing minors in a poolroom and operating slot machines. Mrs. Adele Dussetto was held in the county jail in lieu of $500 bail because of selling soft drinks and having a dance hall without a license in the Sixteen-Mile House in San Bruno. Borgni also sat in jail for not paying $1,000 bail. The trio was taken before Justice of Peace Bird of Burlingame.[22]

The year 1927—a bad year for the Peninsula: a bad year as far as bootleggers were concerned, a bad year for county and local officials trying to curtail the flow of booze. Prohis from San Francisco sent down gumshoes, amateur detectives, to investigate and buy liquor and inform prohibition officers. Dry squad teams swooped down the Peninsula, armed with informants' information and search warrants, raided the whole year. They received several complaints about Alex Beltramo, but could obtain no buys and thus no search warrant. On a Sunday evening in March, hijackers evidently broke into Beltramo's garage and liquor warehouse (barn?) in North Fair Oaks, leaving the door ajar. When the sheriff received word of the break-in, he sent an officer to investigate. After viewing the vast stores of booze, he obtained a warrant and a raid followed. On Monday, the sheriffs arrested Beltramo who was released on $500 bail by Justice Ray Griffin. Deputies spent most of the afternoon moving the cache from Atherton to the county jail: 75 barrels of wine, two barrels of high-grade whiskey and a dismantled still.

The jury freed Alex Beltramo at the end of the month. Beltramo's barn full of liquor was not sufficient evidence of ownership after the alleged break-in and robbery of part of the wet goods. Attorney Joseph J. Bullock represented Beltramo against Assistant District Attorney Ed Scott. The court, however, ordered the liquor destroyed.[23]

The same month saw agents clean up Belmont and Beresford resorts, arresting two women and four men: Tom Johnson, 52, pioneer confectioner of San Mateo who had moved to Beresford with a soft drink parlor; Mrs. Anne Coste, 18, proprietor of Belmont Casino; Mrs. Elsie Smuck, 28, in charge of an establishment west of the state highway; William Yount, 49, and John Klos, 47, both of Belmont. One group of raiders turned its attention to Redwood City where they found a cleverly constructed trapdoor on the floor of Rainbow Inn. When a raid was imminent, a spring was pushed and down went the liquor into the basement. Chief Collins, involved in the raid, discovered the trick, or knew about it beforehand, and before it could be triggered he seized the controlling device and saved the liquor. He found a small compartment beneath the floor that would catch the disappearing liquor. Joseph Deluchi, the alleged proprietor, walked after paying a $500 bail.

A $1,000 Bail for Helping Federal Agents

At Frank D. Roach's residence, opposite Menlo Military School, two men came to the door wanting to come in. They were refused, but pleaded they had been "out for a time" and "simply had to have a drink."

"In that case I know you are all right, come right in," answered Roach.

The men purchased two drinks and arrested Roach. As they were ready to leave with their prisoner, young Frank Roach Jr., 19, drove up with a quantity of liquor. He too was arrested. The two men in need were, of course, federal agents. The court transferred his case over to the federal court. The elder Roach was the village blacksmith in Menlo Park, a saloon owner, then an auto mechanic, finally a nurseryman. As a former constable of Menlo Park, he should have known better to be so trusting: He unsuccessfully ran for county sheriff three times.

At 1836 El Camino Real, 22-year-old cook James Buffa's bootlegging activities brought him a bail of $1,000, fixed by Commissioner Hayden.[24]

As the weather warmed the mild Peninsula, more citizens ventured to resorts or went out for a night of drinking. Gumshoes were also out making buys in May and June, and up went the income of many communities in the Peninsula with almost $5,000 in fines for violating the Wright Act: Angel Simonini, Menlo Park, slot machines; Angel Luvisatt, Lawndale; Roy Peterson, Portola; Bill O'Keefe, Beresford, slots; William Real and John Pera from Colma; Louie Bergamaschi, 12-Mile House; Tony Marquis; Mike Milia, San Mateo; George Switzer, Milbrae; Joe Berrone, San Bruno; and Louis Marlini for operating a soft drink resort without a license. Later in June: Francis Guiterrez, 30, Redwood City, for selling out of his home on Hemlock Street; Victor Masotti, San Carlos; Rito Peris, laborer, jail time for being drunk and not able to pay $10. Others who did jail time because they could not pay fines were Mrs. Mary Gibson, 25, and Grace Jones, 36, for operating a disorderly house, $250 fine each. For Wright Act violations were Charles Ward, 48, car washer, August Fabro (Fabbro), 39, merchant; Pasquale Bailo, 39, merchant, Phelps Street; "Jimmie the Greek" Jimmie Caracudas, 34, tanner at 116 Maple Street; A. Gemiginani, 39, Pescadero hotel man; Madro Mangini, 39, lineman, Woodside.[25]

In September a spectacular raid caught five men at the Davis ranch on La Honda Summit near Skyline Boulevard. Confiscated were a $100,000 still operation, 100 pigs to eat the spent mash and two tons of sugar. Built in a deep void, the still was entirely hidden by trees, perfectly camouflaged until one came within 10 feet of the big shed that held the machinery. For weeks Sheriff McGrath tried to locate the still. Moonshiners had two lookouts on the outskirts of the ranch. Succeeding in evading guards, officers got past the "lines" and surprised the distillery. The posse caught workers attempting to escape. Sentries, in the meantime, found the hidden officers' autos and ran to warn the moonshiners. Instead they ran right into officers Larrecou and Meeks. Captured were Joe Pardini, 20, F. Zolanis, 40?, R. F. Winter, 22, W. Ratson, 20, and O. Moriti.[26]

Gun Fight at Simonini's Place

Under-sheriff Pierre "Pete" Larrecou and Traffic Officer Elgin Kreiss, using crutches for a broken leg, entered the "eating establishment" and bootleg joint of Angelo Simonini, on El Camino Real, south of Atherton about 9:00 p.m. After finishing dinner they "were in the act of leaving shortly after 10 o'clock when there was a knock on the front door. The proprietor opened the door and as he did so two men stepped in. Each carried a gun and each had a handkerchief over his face. The first of the pair to enter was Caines P. Miller, who pressed a gun against Simonini backing him into a corner. Miller then rushed to the back of the restaurant, leaving his companion at the door. Entering the kitchen, Miller came face to face with Larrecou and Kreiss. Knocking Kreiss' crutches from beneath him, causing him to partially fall to the floor, the bandit sprang at Larrecou and before the latter could make a move pressed his pistol against the officer's abdomen and shot.

"Larrecou, though in agony, pulled his gun from his pocket. Three times it barked and each time it found its mark in the body of the bandit. It was a duel to the death, Miller returning shot for shot. Larrecou crumpled to the floor dead. The bandit, mortally wounded, reeled toward the door, but a bullet from the gun of Officer Kreiss stopped him in his tracks. He died instantly, the bullet piercing his brain...."

The other bandit escaped. And the search and investigation started.

Pete Larrecou, raised in Menlo Park, joined the army during the war and became a fireman at Camp Fremont. He worked his way from a Redwood City policeman, to deputy sheriff and was appointed under-sheriff by T. C. McGovern who had recently passed away. A member of 109 IOOF, Eagles, Elks and Native Sons of the Golden West, Larrecou was sadly laid to rest in Holy Cross cemetery in Menlo Park.[27]

After a resurgence of complaints as an aftermath of the shootout, and newspapers objecting to the continual crime after years of enforcement, county officials reacted with a new crusade on crime.

Peninsula's Second Reform (1927)

After years of being enforcement head in San Mateo County, District Attorney Franklin Swart and Sheriff James J. McGrath pushed for a determined and cooperative end to county bootlegging and vice resorts. Swart wrote a personal letter to all constables, chiefs of police and traffic officers about doing their duties. McGrath followed with an endorsement of hardy support: "When officials of a county or community closely cooperate with each other in stamping out violators of the law, crime and vice can hardly exist....He will certainly get the co-operation of myself and my office. I am sure every police chief and every police officer...will follow Mr. Swart's instructions faithfully—as faithfully as my office will." Chairman of the board of supervisors, John W. Poole, said he would "go to bat" to put down vice and disorder.

Prompted by the death of Larrecou in a bootlegging joint, Swart warned the "very few officers" who frequent such bootleg joints that they cannot survive here. He complained about the ordinary gumshoe man. The tramp gumshoe who went from county to county was undesirable and unnecessary. They come into an area, buy some drinks and report to the prohis [good way for one to make a living and have all the drinks he wants].

Swart recommended each office make an official visit, not a social one, to each establishment once a week. The officers will be able to tell if there was vice at the resort, cigar shop, soft drink parlor. Drunks in parking lots gave a good indication, said the sheriff, "and if there is anything unlawful there, you have the power to arrest without the necessity of a search warrant. You don't need a search warrant to grab a glass of liquor being served to a patron." By doing their duty, the county could eliminate these bad joints and the need for gumshoe men.

He congratulated officers for eliminating the graft-producing slot machines. Compared to Yolo County, "I am proud." He also recommended the sheriff appoint a good, clean officer to check on suspected vice places once a month. Praising the new constable in the third district, Menlo Park, of proceeding in a "very nice, quiet way" and producing wonderful results, he said, "Personally, I believe much in the effectiveness of consistent and persistent work rather than spurts in periods of newspaper excitement. Just now we have criticism directed at officers of this county and at certain alleged resorts based upon alleged facts stated in an anonymous letter. Most pathetic anonymous letters are often written by competitive bootleggers and it is very unfortunate that unjust criticism should be directed at people from such sources." Ironically the constable for Township 3, Menlo Park, in 1928 was Frank P. Roach, a bootlegger.[28]

Calm on the Peninsula for Awhile

Not many raids hit the newspapers. Evidently bootleggers took a little vacation for a month or so. When someone was caught he received harsh treatment. Federal Judge Partridge of San Francisco showed little mercy in his court to A. F. Monte for selling in the vicinity of the Veterans Hospital in Menlo Park and for selling to Stanford students: six months jail time and a fine besides. A plasterer named Bert McManus, 37, battered his wife one Saturday night in December. Obviously very drunk, he admitted buying from Joe Ferrando, owner of a soft drink establishment in Menlo Park. Deputy Tom Malone and Constable F. B. Grill arrested him, whereupon Justice Ed McAuliffe gave him a fine of $500. Collins and a posse raided Five Points, ending with $500 fines for Bernard Romero, 37, George F. Raiser, 37, and Prudencio Lopez, 32. For only $50 bail the court held Elisio Guerra, 27, Priscillans Cepela, 38, and R. A. Pickel, 32, Domenico De Laura, 35, Inocensio Guterrez (?), Andrew Kokhou (or Kokhors?), 35, Francinio Naurguis, 21, Refugio Huerta, 23.

The same day, as a gesture of the Christmas spirit or to make more room in the county jail, the parole board of McGrath, Swart and Collins gave a model prisoner parole for Antonio Lafricola, a 40-year-old cook from South San Francisco; Eugene Howeth, 28, switchman and a Negro, Charles Ward, 48.[29]

Raids and arrests continued: B. Servetto and Michael Martini of Colma; Bill Yount of Belmont and Jack Resta of Beresford; Rinaldo Polono, a Colma rancher; John Oliver, Villa Hotel, Lawndale; and Angelo Martini, proprietor of a soft drink parlor in Millbrae—all spent time in jail or paid a fine. Hotel man Lino Fabbro, 53, enjoyed time in the jail after a raid on Il Travatore Hotel on Arguello Street, Redwood City. After a quantity of liquor was found by officers Thorpe, Mengal and Fleishman, Judge Albert Mansfield gave him a $500 cash bail. August Fabbro, 40-year-old laborer, also lost $500 to Judge Mansfield, along with hotel keeper George F. Raiser. At Las Lomitas farmer Frank Maybell pleaded guilty to operating slot machines and his liquor charge was dropped.

Was there a letdown in the amount of drinking and selling? Seemed not to be. Things got back to normal with more arrests in April 1928, some of the same people or their relatives enriched the treasuries of the county and communities: Nina Castagnoli (Castignoli?) a Colma druggist, $500; Nello Simonalli, Redwood City inn keeper on State Highway; George Fabbro, 46, cement worker on Redwood Avenue, $1,000 each for Redwood City; John Cornolo, 36, cement worker from Milbrae, Charles Bacigalupi, 41, cook from San Mateo; Jack Resta, 49, San Mateo; Albert Swanson, 60, Portola; A. Firenzi, 33, Lawndale.

A moonshining operation lost its business on San Benito Avenue, near Middlefield Road in Redwood City, when McGrath, Undersheriff Edward Farrell, Deputies Joseph Meeks and Thomas Maloney sneaked up on the miniature brewery in June. They captured "enough beer to quench thirst of South half of the county": 160 cases of beer, 200 gallons in crocks, 5 cases in the car ready for delivery. When Al Leahy, 35, pleaded guilty to possession, he only received a fine of $150.

A grass fire led to Frank Ferrando's arrest again. When a fire on his Lincoln Avenue home in Redwood spread to his raspberry bushes, then to a shed, Chief Ryan put out the blaze and discovered the shed contained 2,000 gallons of wine. Another $500 for Ferrando. Five Points was hit again when Guiseppe Faitanini (Faitinni?) pleaded guilty of possession and paid $300, Mae De Knight's case was dismissed and G. W. Knapp was given $1,000 bail by Judge McAuliffe. Harry Nicoden, 45, at the Woodside Inn paid the same amount when agents found wine and whiskey. The county hit an Atherton roadhouse, belonging to Frank Maybell, 35, on Alameda de las Pulgas where agents had bought drinks. This time Maybell did not have enough bail and did jail time. Guiseppe Faitinni (Faitaninni), 40, Menlo Park, had barrels with government warehouse labels in his garage. Bail, $2,000. Other raids in June netted Jack Rosenstein at Beresford and Louis Belcamphell [Beltramo?] of Menlo Park, both arrested by Ed Farrell and had bail set at $500 after the judge saw the wet evidence.[30]

Juries seemed more willing to convict after Larrecou's death. In August the jury took less than five minutes to convict Frank Ferrando and kept his $500 bail. A jury found Fred Rosenstein guilty in October. Most cases were handled immediately as officers obtained enough evidence; bootleggers pleaded guilty, were fined and free to enter into any entrepreneur pursuits they wanted, including, of course, bootlegging again.

A. Bartolucci, 264 Main Street, Redwood City, just accepted his fine for possessing wine. Officers Thorpe and Douglass hit the City Limits Boarding House on Middlefield Road, finding wine and whiskey—another $500 bail from the proprietor.[31]

John Colombo picked the wrong time to move to Redwood City and open a pool parlor at 1104 Main Street. Chief Collins arrested him on October 12, 1928, and the judge hit him with $500 bail. On October 22, another raid netted the city $500 more from Colombo.

Under Guard in San Jose
as told by Norton Steenfott, Eureka

There was a case in San Jose, a warehouse loaded with whiskey, no guard, just a warehouse with whiskey, leased with a phony name. The federal officials left a 24-hour guard on the alcohol to see who would come and get it. They waited and waited and waited. Finally in a month nobody showed. They said we'd better get the goddamned stuff out. There was nothing in the place.

Gone! It was loaded before. While it was under guard, it all disappeared. Nobody knew what happened.

There was a place I worked for. The same guy did this too. In San Jose, a woman was working for this man and she got mad at him so she went to San Francisco and told the authorities where they kept the liquor. It was after repeal and most places were still selling bootleg whiskey. It was a great big 4-car garage, plus storage place. At one end of the garage they had a dog, a Pomeranian dog in a dog house. You move the dog house aside and there was a stairway and that's where all the booze was stored. She told and prohis came in, moved the goddamned dog house, went downstairs and there was 5,500 gallons of whiskey. They hauled it out. Here's cars in the garage, trucks, a couple thousand gallons of tomato puree and tomatoes, everything.

They haul the goddamn stuff up to San Francisco, put it into the State Building in the basement. That's fine. This man has all these charges against him. One night I was cooking in his place in San Jose. The chef told me they were going to have a big party over his house, a big Spanish house. We cooked frog legs, everything special, put it in five-gallon cans to haul it over there.

"What's going on?" I asked.

"Oh, Christ, U.S. Marshals, US Attorneys, all goddamn bunch, all coming over."

They had a hell of a big party over there that night, all the food and all the booze and everything. The man comes up for trial. They go get the evidence. No evidence. Gone! The same old story happening in the other warehouse. Stolen out of the State Building on McAllister Street in San Francisco.

He pleaded guilty to a tax charge. He had to pay. In the meantime everything was switched around in his wife's name or someone else's name. He didn't have to pay a goddamned thing. He got out of the tax problem. Then he got a year and was sent to San Mateo County jail.

Some of the fellows and I went up to visit him. We took some salami and cheese and other stuff for him. We asked where he was. The guard said, "Oh, just go on up the stairs, the first door on the right. You'll find him there." We get up there and I said, "This isn't the place, Jesus, there's carpet on the floor. Let's go down a little further."

Then he comes out, "Hey, hey." We gave him the stuff we brought and he says, "Oh, come on down my room. That was his room. No locks on the door or nothing else.

A U.S. attorney came down with papers for him to sign. Couldn't find him. He was down in San Bernardino County. The federal officials got hold of him, transferred him to the San Bruno jail. That showed what happened in those days. The laws were made for somebody to violate them, for somebody to make money.

"Worst Goddamn Piece of Legislation
Congress Ever Made"

Alex Beltramo said, "We were in the liquor business before prohibition took effect. That was the "worst goddamn piece of legislation Congress ever made," he said. They [?] spent thousands of dollars bringing over European grapes and growers and then they pass prohibition. We had 20 acres of Slavic grapes planted by Ringwood Avenue in Menlo Park. "My father would not sell a thing, 'the hell with it!' he said." He closed his liquor store. "I did carpentry work," said Beltramo. "We made our 200 gallons [of wine] a year."

He bought this old Army building on Santa Cruz Avenue and moved it to the El Camino, just north of the creek, in San Mateo County. It was a garage during prohibition. In 1933 he opened the Oasis, a most popular beer tavern with locals and Stanford students. In 1934 Alex Beltramo opened a liquor store one mile from the county line and it became one of the best liquor stores on the Peninsula. Since it was over a mile from Stanford University property, it could sell wet goods.

Two long-time Menlo residents said Beltramo had a big yellow building, a car garage, set off the highway and when one drove up, he placed his liquor order by way of what he wanted done to his car. Then he waited at the other end for his car to be driven out. As the car owner drove the car away it had the bottles he had paid for. When told that Alex said they did not sell liquor during prohibition, this old-timer said, "Beltramo is a good liar," and then folded his arms and said, "I am not saying any more."[32]

The Fill-the-Hole Club
from John V. Young
Santa Clara Valley Memoirs[33]

Journalists from Santa Clara Valley and Monterey Bay, during the early depression and the last years of prohibition, had to fill in empty spaces left on the ad pages of the newspapers. Several clever writers filled spaces by using announcements of a factitious club called "Fill-the-Hole Club," derived from their job of filling void spaces in the paper. The club had no dues, by-laws or officers. Journalists put in club notices of parties, picnics, meetings—which did not exist. These men enthusiastically excelled in their job of filling space in the papers. When the depression struck, they answered the challenge of fewer ads and more gaps to close.

Father Riker also announced his events at Holy City near Los Gatos in the Santa Cruz Mountains, using the papers to promote his "Holy" City, which wasn't particularly holy, being somewhat a utopian white supremacy and prohibition group. The "City," a small community with housing, a store, a gas station—quite a tourist attraction, handling busloads of visitors. Riker had his own local radio station KFQU. Something intrigued Riker about the advertisements for the Fill-the-Hole Club whose fascinating ads were often close to his. Perhaps he wanted to join this group that had so many activities. He invited them to a party, wrote columnist John V. Young, and the club accepted, even the hard-drinking pressmen who usually did not associate with the reporters.

Thirty newsmen and pressmen showed up ready to enjoy the night's festivities. Mother Riker brought out punch that "had all the authority of a W.C.T.U. afternoon tea."

The newspapermen conferred quickly, contributed to a kitty and sent two delegates to a nearby bootlegger to repair the punch. While the group diverted Riker's attention, they spiked the punch with two gallons of white mule.

All partook of the new punch and enjoyed it, but soon Mother Riker excused herself and left. Father Riker, after numerous "chug-a-lug toasts," "floated" to the couch. It must have been the mountain air but the printers had their appetites whetted and the food continued to be brought out.

The radio was broadcasting and some men sang ribald songs on KFQU. While relieving themselves, pressmen noticed the long line of urinals conveniently placed for tourists. A sign above the urinals read "STAND CLOSER PLEASE" and soon these words became a slogan for the amateur radiomen as they stepped up to the mike to perform. While exploring further, they found flush toilets with handles that had the word "PRESS" printed on them. Since these handles could be unscrewed, they were becoming badges for the club members.

Club members never heard from Father Riker after the party. He probably changed his mind about joining the Fill-the-Hole Club. Holy City's paper, *Holy City Hurrah,* never printed anything about the party or the moonshine-spiked punch served at Holy City one evening.

After several reforms, the liquor situation was no better. Men still sold and citizens of the San Francisco Peninsula bought. Bootleggers plied their trade, paid their fines when caught and usually started again. Fines ended up being like a license that bootleggers had to pay periodically, some more than others. In the enumeration of those arrested, most seem to be just common folk, most with steady jobs or a least a trade. Influential citizens had their names in the paper for trips they took, visitors they had, parties they gave, country clubs they attended. That affluent Peninsula society was a different world. They did not get caught or at least arrested and they drank better liquor.

The peaceful-looking Domby Ranch on Olive Street, Menlo Park, near old Camp Fremont hid the still (next page). Agents William P. Groggin, Keith DeKalb and George L. Edman destroyed still and arrested Joe Siaroni, 27, Nello Monticelli, 41, and Gime Fugia, 45. His neighbors smelled the rotting mash dumped in trenches between Domby's pear trees. [Case CN-499, Dept. of Justice, Alcohol Beverage Unit, S. F.]

CHAPTER 25

THE LAST STAND

The last half of the Roaring Twenties was an exciting period of California history. Advancements in industry, business and entertainment added a sophisticated zest to California life. With better and more plentiful cars, and more paved roads being added to the Golden State, and new money seemingly everywhere, Californians made certain areas vacation resorts. Auto courts, filling stations, and auto repair shops aided the new hobby of driving. People traveled to places they read about in the paper or saw in the movies—now a man could pack up his family and see the sights at San Diego, Mount Shasta, Russian River, Big Bear Lake and on and on, for week-end trips or two-week vacations. It was a good life in California.

In 1928 a Buick Beauty set customers back $1,195, but could be handled by time payments. A Chevrolet Roadster cost $495. Up north, the Crescent City Garage sold Runabouts for $476.93 and Touring cars for $497 in 1927.

As more people entered the state, thousands each year, business flourished, new folks needed cars and homes and appliances. The population of Tracy, for example, was up to 5,330, Alhambra 30,000, Pomona 25,000, Los Angeles rising fast to 1,338,266, San Diego 150,000. California reached over five million people.[1]

Fascination with the good life came with the radio and daily programming being well established by 1928.

Newspapers continued as a source of entertainment and news. Comics read in California: "Boots and Her Buddies," "Boots in Shanghai" and "Freckles and His Friends." "The Prowler" articles became a feature for years to come in the *Palo Alto Times.* Not a lot of news came from Washington. President Coolidge added to his reputation as "Silent Cal" by being unobtrusive and having a *laissez-faire* policy about government interference with Americans. Yet he was so popular, papers predicted in 1927 that if he chose to run again he would win.

Becoming more sophisticated, clever and subtle, producers created films like Clara Bow in "Get Your Man" at the Grand Theatre, Victor Hugo's "Les Miserables," and "Ben Hur" at the San Mateo Theatre and in practically every town in the state.

Local baseball helped people entertain themselves. Every town, no matter how small, had a baseball team. Tracy Tigers played Modesto and Trona played Randsburg for pride of the hometown. This love of hometown baseball continued to World War II. In fact, in Trona during the depression when one couldn't buy a job, a cousin from Oklahoma got a job at Trona. He was an outstanding ball player and Trona needed a shortstop. Favorite discussions centered on sports, Ernie Nevers of Stanford versus the Four Horsemen of Notre Dame. A news item in Palo Alto was La Honda resident Armond Zanone [Zanoni] attended fights in San Francisco. The City continued to be the place to go for a night out.

Growing fascination with the airplane made a town without an airport, or at least a landing strip, a town that hadn't come into the 20th century. Comic strip flying hero "Tailspin Tommy" excited California newspaper readers. Reality did not hinder enthusiasm for the airplane. A student pilot did a tailspin in San Francisco Bay and died—that type of news was common the last half of the decade. Daredevil Jack Schalk would hang by his teeth from a rope from an airplane at Tracy Aviation. The winners of the 1929 air races "Used Union Gasoline." In the daytime, planes made their routes by following roads and railroads. Lt. Jimmy H. Doolittle flew into North Island, San Diego from Florida, breaking a cross-country record with his 21 hours and 19 minutes. As an aid to the growing popularity of night flying, the government announced beacons were to be set up at Las Vegas, Jean, Baker, Barstow, Victorville and San Bernardino. At Merced Hills, San Luis Obispo and Los Angeles 75' towers were built. These beacons helped make night flying safer.

Prices remained steady. A 24½ pound sack of Sperry flour cost San Joaquin Valley residents $1.00, potatoes 50 pounds for $1.35, only 39¢ a pint for Wrights Mayonnaise, Crisco 3 pounds for 68¢. In the spring of 1928, sugar was 100 pounds for $5.73, brown sugar 5 pounds for 5¢, Easter ham 26¢ per pound, bacon 22¢, lettuce two heads for 7¢. Eggs, two dozen for 49¢, Hills coffee also 49¢. Lehman & Son's Bay Market, on 2nd Street in Crescent City, had prompt deliveries for ice, meats, fruits. J. C. Penney's put on a 25th anniversary sale, featuring silk hose for $1.49.[2] Stocks continued to rise. On September 5, 1929, General Electric reached $380, down 1; General Motors, 74¾, up 3 1/8; General Mills, 71¼ down ¾.

Citizens kept up with state news. For example, the southern campus of the University of California searched for a name since "Southern Branch" was not satisfactory. The name settled on was, of course, University of California at Los Angeles, i.e., UCLA. Always in the news from 1922 on was Aimee Semple McPherson sometimes three times a week. She turned a poor church in Los Angeles into the richest and the largest. A few citizens become conscious of the environment as Californians read an article about their condors being in danger of extinction: only 50 pair left in the U. S. Natural disasters reported in papers kept Californians aware and informed about their country: "Horrible" Tennessee-Mississippi flood, Sacco and Vanzetti, convicted in 1921, denied a new trial and set to die. Many citizens saw world events as ominous danger signs: Communists fought in China, attempting to spread Marxism throughout China, and Mussolini warred against the Blackhands of Sicily.

Overshadowing most current events was the prevailing concern of prohibition. L. C. Andrews, Assistant Secretary of Treasury in charge of prohibition under Coolidge, tightened one loophole by limiting sacramental wine to one gallon per year per person, no more than five gallons per year per family. A rabbi or minister could make application to purchase religious wine, but had to keep a list of members of his congregation and the quantity of wine distributed to each during the year. Though Andrews tried to close this loophole, drys knew this "religious" wine helped the bodies as well as souls of the congregations. Five gallons per family a year helped keep a few poor sinners like grandpa from drying out. Andrews withdrew 12 Coast Guard cutters from the east coast. Although this act saved money, it came at the same time corruption surfaced with the Coast Guard in New York. "Coast Guard in Pay of Rum Ring," a report said. Investigation by new commander Captain W. B. E. Jacobs searched for truth of scandal rumors. He was unable to uncover evidence of signals between rum ships and Coast Guard vessels indicating areas where rumrunners were free to land. Alleged:14 or 15 rumchasers were involved in payoffs, but Jacobs could not cut through the subterfuge.[3]

With so many scandals hitting the newspapers, and so much empirical evidence that prohibition was not being enforced, believers in prohibition looked for people to blame. Secretary of Treasury Mellon and President Coolidge received vitriolic blows as frustrated prohibitionists and rabid extremists laid the blame on these two leaders. Episcopalians and the United Committee for Prohibition Enforcement attacked the administration. More moderate Methodists became angry at the unfair blaming of Coolidge and Mellon. Anti-Saloon Leaguers met to see which side to take and luckily for the dry cause, moderates implored the radicals not to blame the administration. A "peace conference," so to speak, was held in Washington between Methodist and Episcopal leaders to analyze how to obtain better enforcement and to remind each other who the enemy was. They would all drink to that.

Poor Mellon, with all the world affairs to worry about, especially collecting war debts from former allies and enemies alike, Coast Guard scandals, wets agitating for repeal, "everyone hurling unsolicited advice in all directions" and criticism from people who were his supporters, the Secretary was, as one journalist said, "...showing signs of [being] shell shocked!"[4]

For years prohibition agents had been some of the most dedicated and professional men in the service of the United States. Yet some were the worst of scoundrels.[5] Prohibition agents had a difficult job in California. Many were political appointees and thus not well trained in law enforcement. Relations with apathetic or even hostile local officials were sometimes estranged. Agents, considered by locals as outsiders, were not always trusted. Conversely federal agents did not know the county politics, the good-old-boy structure, and officers who could be trusted. All agents got burned when they confided in the wrong person and found a federal raid had been tipped off. Besides being betrayed, Feds were tempted and bribed.

Nationwide over 1,300 agents were suspended for cause—only four in California, though multitudes in California accepted bribes, joined bootlegger gangs, resigned before action would be taken or before being caught. Frank B. Becker, San Francisco prohibition agent, lost his job during his probation period. He went over to Oakland, indulged in a few too many drinks stronger than the law allowed and was arrested for intoxication. When he pleaded guilty, his supervisor let him go. Ernie J. Kreuger received a suspension for his extortion efforts in Los Angeles. Two southern California agents, Leroy E. Schermerhorn and Sanborn R. Short, really got into their jobs. With two female informants, they went undercover in San Bernardino, really undercover. They rented rooms as Mr. and Mrs. and had a little "excessive use of liquor" that they bought as evidence and perhaps partied more than duty called for. Their dedication to their work wasn't appreciated by the Los Angeles headquarters. When a citizen informed on them, they were charged with intoxication and misconduct. Both resigned with prejudice.[6]

Because of complaints, Coolidge put the Prohibition Bureau under the Civil Service and after 1927 federal agents improved. Civil Service set pay in 1927 at $1,860 a year for Junior Prohibition Agents, $2,400 for Prohibition Agents, $2,400 for Junior Prohibition Investigators, and $3,000 for Investigators. The average salary for prohibition agents on December 1, 1929 was $1,800, with individual annual salaries as follows: Field Division $1,800, Mail clerk $1,620. That wage equaled $120 to $150 per month, $40 per week, not a bad salary for the late 1920s, but appearances and reality were often different. The 21st District in California, for example, wanted more compensation for their prohibition warehouse watchmen. They had an average salary of $40 per week, but they were working sometimes 56 hours per week. In 1921 a watchman received $145 per month. In 1929 under Civil Service, with retirement taken out, he only received $106 per month. For a job with many hours and many more temptations, $26 per week was not much money.

Civil Service tests screened out weak prospects. In fact, when tests for beginners were given to experienced agents, most failed. Three-fourths received a score that would have precluded an applicant from taking further steps to become an agent[7] [see Appendix C].

California assistant administrators fared well as the following grades showed: Receiving B's from San Francisco were Quincy J. Boone, George H. Seaver, Assistant Chemist Wilson D. Wade; A grades: Chemist Ray F. Love. From Los Angeles receiving B's were Walter Peters, Jesse E. Flanders, Special Inspector George S. Taylor and Assistant Chemist Clifford E. Hubach; passing with A's were Chemist Fred D. Stribbling, W. W. Anderson and Special Agent R. R. Read. An evaluation of 227 incumbent agents showed problems with the quality of the agents. Forty-seven only had a grammar school education, though many had business school training. Although 123 had gone to high school, only 44 graduated. Again some high school dropouts and graduates had attended business schools. Fifty-seven had some college but only 19 graduated.

With Civil Service screening prospective federal agents, the quality of agents improved after 1928 as the following figures indicate:

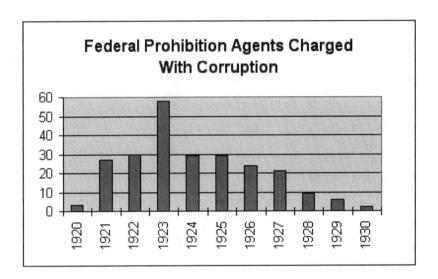

As of March 31, 1930, those agents receiving convictions were 50, jail sentences 34, fines only 19, sentence deferred 5, paroled 109, acquitted 60, not processed 32, dismissal 38, fugitive from justice 4 and pending 5. The total was 245.[8]

On April 8, 1928, the court decided it was legal for prohibition agents to drink alcohol "When it is absolutely necessary to obtain evidence of sale that will stand in court," said Assistant Secretary Andrews. The next week, April 15, ironically, the *Times* reported one agent dead, another dying, five other federals ill as result of drinking bad liquor in Bay Cities. Dave Mahoney, 56, died and Hugh Morgan seriously ill. Federal Chief E. R. Bohner wanted insurance on his agents working in California, but no insurance company in the country would take an undercover agent as a risk. With just average pay, local animosity, many temptations, much risk to body, stomach and eyes, the life of a prohibition agent was difficult.

Only Three Killed

During the first ten years of prohibition, with thousands of federal raids, it is remarkable that only 154 citizens and aliens were shot by agents. Most victims were from Kentucky, South Carolina, Virginia, West Virginia and other southern states. Federal agents killed only three civilians in California.

The first man killed was, strangely enough, a state fish and game ranger. On October 17,1923, Agent John H. Vail had local help in raiding Shasta View Hotel at Castella. Deputy Fish and Game Warden James S. White entered the room, drew his gun, pointed it at the raiding party and defied them to pull their guns. A fight ensued between Vail and White. White fired two shots, both taking effect in Vail's body. Vail managed to return the fire, shot three rounds at White, with two of them hitting and killing White. On a 16-3 vote, Shasta County Grand Jury decided not to indict Vail, exonerating him of murder charges. However one year later, the owner of the hotel filed a charge of manslaughter against Vail. When the case moved to the federal court, the verdict was not guilty on December 31, 1926.

Another victim of an agent's gun was Jose Villegas. Villegas had already been arrested and found guilty of selling in San Luis Obispo and Santa Barbara, but was still a prominent alcohol dealer in the area. Agent Robert L. Knight, with informer Pete Cook, went to Santa Maria and made arrangements with a Mexican dealer living near Guadulupe [Guadalupe] to deliver 20 gallons of whiskey to a spot north of Nipomo, about 12 miles north of Santa Maria—the Mexican: Jose Villegas.

Villegas's stepson Gomez dropped off Villegas and the whiskey at the designated spot and pulled down the road and parked. When Knight arrested Villegas, Villegas ran to the car and yelled in Spanish. Gomez then threw a shotgun to Villegas, who turned to face Knight. When Knight ordered him to drop the shotgun and he refused, Knight fired. They took Villegas to the hospital in Santa Maria where doctors operated, but he died that night.

Knight turned himself in to Chief of Police W. E. Feland who refused to place him under arrest. Knight acted in "performance of his duty when he fired the fatal shot."

California's third victim of agents' shootings was a runner caught by Agents George H. Wentworth and D. D. Magnan, caught for transporting liquor into Berkeley on November 23, 1926. Agents arrested Burrell Morris, placed him in the middle of the front seat between driver Wentworth and Magnan on the outside. After driving some distance toward the police station, Morris placed a gun on Wentworth's ribs, commanding him to stop. When Wentworth did not stop, Morris shot him through the side. Morris and Magnan grappled and as the car pulled to a stop, all exited. Wentworth pulled his gun and shot Morris through the heart. Wentworth died of his wounds the next day, "died in the performance of his duty." [9]

Overcrowded state and federal courts created a serious problem. Dismissals and plea bargains became a necessity. California's Jones Act made it a felony to own or operate a still and added teeth to the prohibition laws. Possessing a still could get the owner some time in San Quentin, which further cluttered state courts. Flooded with prohibition cases in the federal courts in the Southern District of California, U. S. Attorney S. W. McNabb of Los Angeles met with the district attorney of Los Angeles, senior judge of the federal court, city prosecutor and presiding judges of the municipal courts. All agreed minor cases would go to state courts, 800-1,000 per year, thus unclogging federal courts, alleviating the need to accept minimum plea-bargains just to get on with the day's calendar. Although this agreement helped, all the courts were still awash with liquor cases.[10]

Liquor law was making crime, said an article in the *Daily Palo Alto Times,* April 19,1927. As many already surmised a couple years earlier, instead of liquor laws preventing crime, these laws created crime. Attempts to prevent crimes caused by alcohol created more crimes than were originally generated from the liquor.

Liquor criminals became more adept at using the law to help escape prosecution. A large Yolo County liquor case, involving a conspiracy involving 15 persons from Sacramento and San Francisco, was thrown out by Federal Judge George M. Bourquin. The prosecution star witness L. C. Blaney had disappeared. No witness, no case.[11]

From "A Tale of Christmas Spirits, Shattered"
by Jerry MacMullen
San Diego Union, December 22, 1968

A collection of tramp steamers and a schooner anchored off Cape Colnet kept the sauce flowing in San Diego. A sailor or traveler could buy Bacardi Rum for $4.50 a jug on the wharf in Cuba. Sailors often made spending money by selling Cuban rum in California ports. One day before the holidays in the later prohibition period, as a crane lifted a heavy box on a cargo board out of No. 2 Hold, the hatch tender waggled his upheld thumb, the electric winch whined, and the load surged upward through the hatch toward the end of the cargo boom and down toward the wharf—Crash! Tinkle, tinkle, tinkle! And gurgle. The crate was labeled "Washing Machine" but the sound was unmistakably broken bottles, and the odor was the heavy bouquet of Cuban rum. The winch-driver lowered away too fast. A washing machine would have taken it but not two dozen glass jugs.

"Ho, ho, ho!" and everyone looked around to see where Santa Claus had come from. A man in khaki, with a "U. S. Customs" badge, hustled over to investigate. The ship was fined. No one on shore or on board knew anything about the liquid "washing machine."

"The mayor [whom people suspected of ordering the rum] had to settle for some of that fine imported Scotch, assembled by Jose MackIntosh on a schooner off the Mexican coast."

WCTU—Frustrated But Hopeful

Mrs. Louise James, President of the Palo Alto WCTU, attended the Santa Clara County Convention at Gilroy in April 1927. The club had seven new members. Despite discouragement for lack of enforcement, these ladies kept the faith.

The WCTU celebrated the eighth anniversary of National Prohibition in January 1928. *The Corona Daily Independent* reported that at the Corona WCTU meeting, officials proclaimed "One million lives saved in the United States since Uncle Sam mounted the water wagon," announced WCTU information. Fifty percent more children are in school, 187 percent more students in universities and colleges, 1,130 more people added to the Protestant churches every day during the past year. Even: "We have paid one third of our war debts with prohibition in six years."[12]

Later that month: "The U. S. is riding on unequaled prosperity and no economist of standing has denied that prohibition is more or less responsible." To the WCTU, the solution was clear and simple. The *Union Signal,* February 25, 1928, commanded: "Let us pull together—you catch the little fellow, punish him quickly and drastically, and then hold the federal government responsible if it does not...dam up the sources of illicit wholesale supply." This organization cannot be faulted for lack of effort. They continued meeting, recruiting, singing and selling posters, 15¢ each, 12 for $1.50, such as "Beer for Bluffers" and "Alcohol Hinders Success in Business." Prohibitionists maintained power in Congress. In a vote in Congress in July 1928 for the wet Lihthicum Amendment, only three Californian representatives (Florence P. Kahn, San Francisco; Richard J. Welch, San Francisco; and Harry L. Englebright, Nevada City) voted for the amendment. The above WCTU magazine said, "Let's see what they do in November 1928 [election time]," showing their use of clout, political power and intimidation. However, since Kahn and Welch were from San Francisco, a wet vote guaranteed their election. The drys won that amendment vote by 251 to 61, with 89 not voting.[13]

Despite claims prohibition was working, it wasn't. Riverside County news pointed to people drinking, buying, making and transporting alcohol. Riverside County Sheriff Clem Sweeters announced he entertained 925 guests in the county jail the previous year (1927). Of those prisoners, 198 were for Wright Act violations. Four-fifths of this total were Mexicans, fifty-nine of whom were jailed for driving under the influence. Inference here is not that Mexicans were drinking and selling more but perhaps, as with much of the state at this time, a double standard attitude existed toward minorities whereby one eye was closed more often with non-minorities. Whites were not as apt to be arrested, not as apt to be prosecuted and certainly not as apt to serve jail time.

The new year continued the same trend. January's *Corona Daily Independent* listed numerous county Wright Act violations. E. Vasquez, Refugio Lopez and Samuel Feliz of Corona had a trial for selling. The trial ended with an 11-1 hung jury. To avoid another trial Felix and Lopez pleaded guilty and Judge George R. Freemann fined them $500 and six months on the county road gang. The court gave truck driver Rufus Bali $200 or 100 days. County sheriffs charged E. H. Hall, Ralph Ferris and Tom Powers for selling in Palo Verde. I. Stevenson received $100 fine or 50 days for drunk driving. Three drunks had small fines of $20.00 or 10 days. Paula Bergstrom of Norco pleaded guilty to drunk driving after hitting another car.

In Hemet eight men and two women visited the county jail for selling and using counterfeit whiskey "Imported" or "bottled-in-bond" labels. This group made moonshine bottles look like pre-prohibition bottles. Searchers found evidence at the Bradford Cafe and the owner's home in Hemet, arresting Charles Miller and his wife, 123 N. Ramona St. Others caught were Jack Flynn, 24; Roy Mayben, a 27-year-old laborer; James Anderson, a 35-year-old Negro porter; Russell Brock, 28; Francis Lom, 21; Frank Bowen, 41; and Mr. and Mrs. Bacon.

One of the county's saddest cases was that of J. L. Smith, a 37-year-old auto salesman, who had a few drinks and crashed into a stalled truck near Banning. Killed in the accident was his passenger and good friend O. R. Hale. His defense was that he only had "two or three drinks" but was in control of his car. When he was taken to the Banning Sanitarium because of slight injuries, a patient gave him a few drinks to "quiet his nerves." Dr. A. L. Bramkamp examined him, and testified that Smith was intoxicated when he arrived in the hospital.

Superior Court Judge W. H. Ellis found him guilty of drunk driving, rather than manslaughter, giving him one year in San Quentin. Though allowing him to visit his wife and 12-year-old daughter before being escorted to prison, the court turned down probation because of mixing gas and booze. Saying sad good-byes at the end of the month, Smith kissed his bitterly weeping wife and daughter, who had hoped "they'd let daddy loose."

Tracy typified the state in 1928. She continued to prosper as did the rest of the state with a new hotel called the Tracy Inn in 1927. She made pretenses of obeying the prohibition laws (as well as gambling and prostitution), yet looked the other way. The Waldorf ad in Tracy read: "Try a bottle of Valley Brew Steam [near beer] and a sandwich." Near beer was certainly available but so were regular beer and other drinks.[14] San Joaquin County Sheriff William H. Riecks gave the appearance of stopping illegal activities in the county. News articles came out with his periodic raids, such as "Sheriff Rieck's dragnet landed two southsiders" [south Tracy bootleggers] in a liquor raid. Deputy Cassidy and Bernard got one quart of "so-called whiskey" and 565 gallons of wine. Nick Deni pleaded guilty and Justice Albert C. Parker gave him a $250 fine; the other defendant was out on $1,000 bond. A facade made it appear the county, state and country tried to win the war for drys.

Age of Republicanism

Republicanism dominated politics in California in the 1920s. In 1924 only seven of the 120 seats in the state legislature were Democratic, and barely 22 percent of registered voters were Democrats. State Democrats won only nine of 66 seats in the House of Representatives during six elections of the decade. The *L. A. Times, S. F. Chronicle* and the *Oakland Tribune* practically ignored Democrats. California's cross-filing system allowed candidates to file in both parties, and as a result Republicans often won both sides of primary elections.

For governor, William D. Stephens succeeded Hiram Johnson in 1917 and was elected on his own in 1918, continuing progressivism. He reorganized state government, making it more efficient. Friend William Richardson defeated Stephens in 1922, cut 13 million dollars off Stephens' budget, cut education costs, gave fewer pardons and stressed law and order. In turn, Lt. Gov. Clement Calhoun Young defeated him in the primaries in 1926—all Republican governors since 1899! More and more demand came for Jimmy Rolph for governor, the affable mayor of San Francisco—also Republican, a wet one.[15]

Nationally, Republicans were riding high and expecting to elect their third president in as many elections. Coolidge could have won the presidency again if he had chosen to run. But party strife pulled the party apart like the San Andreas Fault. Two prominent Republicans debated the issue of prohibition. Borah of Idaho led the dry Republicans and Dr. Nicoholas Murray Butler, President of Columbia University, argued for the wets. Hoover remained conspicuously silent and vague on the subject. Mayor La Guardia of New York City pushed for a realistic Republican platform because the 18th Amendment caused "enforcement impossibility and the breakdown of the law." The party refused his suggestion and put an enforcement policy in the Republican platform. Moderates who wanted a modified Volstead Act lost to avid prohibitionists.

Despite the Democratic platform also having an enforcement clause in it, Governor Al Smith openly opposed prohibition, but was for temperance. No doubt where Democrat Smith stood.

Hoover stampeded the Republican Convention, but tiptoed around prohibition conflicts, keeping both wets and drys happy; few knew where he stood, but each thought he was on their side of prohibition. His political leaders suggested Assistant Attorney General Mabel Walker Willebrant, in charge of prohibition enforcement, give the talk on the prohibition and enforcement plank. Thus she became the focus of prohibition, not Hoover. Hoover distanced himself from the issue except to say the Constitution would be enforced.

An editorial in the *Ontario Herald* said the following about the Republican convention: "Mr. Work, chairman of the Republican National Committee, gave out orders right after the Kansas City Convention to 'refer to liquor only in a whisper.'" Republicans echoed Hoover's don't-bring-it-up policy.[16]

The hard workers, who for years devoted their energies and lives to passing prohibition, watched with a growing hopeless feeling as year after year the law was enforced haphazardly, or not at all, the guilty getting off on technicalities, loopholes, lost evidence, improper search, improper seizure, absconding or disappearing witnesses, bribery, plea-bargaining, eyes closed and eyes red.

Election of 1928

The election year 1928 set so many forces against each other that even 60 years after the election, historians are still not able to determine what forces created winners and which were responsible for losers. Smith being a Catholic was a great factor. Except for farmers, post-war America flourished. Industrialization and electrification spurred so many inventions, so much prosperity that the stock market never seemed to quit going up, breaking one record after another.

As soon as the country elected Herbert Hoover, defenders of prohibition took heart. After all Hoover received over 21 million votes, 5,500,000 more than wet Al Smith—that was a victory![17] Drys felt that soon they would have a doer in the White House—finally! After the election frustrated supporters of prohibition wrote to President-elect Hoover and to Assistant Attorney General Willebrandt to congratulate them on the election and to suggest how they can start correcting the prohibition mess. A secretive complaint letter about California bootlegging came from Canton, Mississippi, written on December 10, 1928, by Mrs. G. E. Smith who said she would sign her name as I.Z.X., reminding history buffs of the "XYZ Affair" with the French at the end of the 18th century. "Please destroy this letter too," she said.

When she lived in California in the mid 1920s, she informed prohibition agents in San Francisco about violations. Mrs. I.Z.X. was pleased as she "saw place after place closed by these faithful men to whom I had confided my suspicion."

Since Monterey policeman Darling threatened her because she reported that Monterey cops furnished her husband with alcohol, she feared the consequences if someone found out she informed. Her husband too would make trouble. The agents could write her if they used another envelope addressed to Mrs. Irene Adams and no Internal Revenue return address.

Included in the letter were four automobile license numbers and names of prohibition laws offenders:

Clark Emory, 1927 License no. 630 440, Monterey

Mrs. C. Fitzgerald, 42nd Ave., Oakland, Phone Fruitvale 8207

Rogers' Drug Store, Pacific Grove, protected, they say, by

Frank B. Wilcoxsen, Chief of Police [constable of Pacific Grove]

Barber Shop [Goldsteins, or something like that] near the La Mar Hotel, Pacific Grove

Chief of Police of Monterey, Bill Oyer, Monterey

Policeman Darling (the one who threatened me), Monterey

She ended with this note: Please make a special effort to get Floyd Rogers at Rogers' Drug Store at Pacific Grove (corner Lighthouse and Forest) because he has been getting away with it a long time now. Signed I.Z.X.[18]

Californians protested and expressed their cynicism. One such writer was George M. Veile, from Inglewood, on December 6, 1928, saying the elections showed the prohibition sentiment in the "good old U. S. A. Now let's have an honest, sincere prohibition law...abolish the private cellars of our super wealthy class." Volstead law equals the "rottenest piece of hypocritical bunk ever put over on the people," making the rich man's vices respectable. He wanted "real prohibition or nothing. No class privilege." The "p.s." said: "There are those who say that dry talkers but wet drinkers back the Anti-Saloon League. Is this true?"[20]

Since the 1928 Annual Jumping Frog Contest in Calaveras County had quite a celebration with "all the salloons [sic] run wide open and there was hundred [sic] of men and women drunk...and the sheriff was the Marshall of the day," J. E. King, of San Andreas, wrote to Mabel Willebrandt to help prevent the same outrage in the 1929 celebration in Angels Camp. He blamed local officials who take an oath to enforce the law and then violate that same law. The only time the sheriff or the district attorney deviated from his pretense to arrest a bootlegger was when a liquor dealer came in from the outside and began to infringe on the local fellow. King said, it hurts to hear bootleggers say there are no honest officers, "all we have to do is pay their price, now my friend [,] I appeal to you for a change of affairs in this county."[20]

An article in the *San Francisco Examiner* on George Washington's birthday, explained how the first president was fond of his wine and how he had large liquor bills and served his guests fine liquor. Another article entitled "U. S. in Legal Chaos Over Dry Laws, Says Ex-official." Hearst newspapers held a nationwide contest, called The Hearst Temperance Contest, with $25,000 first prize for anyone who came up with a proposal for a "practicable plan as a substitute for prohibition."[21]

A December newspaper from San Francisco, sent to the Prohibition Office in Washington, D.C., illustrated a foreboding attitude if one were a "dry" reader. The headline "Mind Volstead Law at New Year" can also be interpreted that the law will not be strongly enforced over the holidays. "Deal lightly with offenders" and "impossibility of enforcement" made sub-headlines as did "officials will lay off during the celebration." The paper said that "common sense" and "relief in sight" for modification of the Volstead Law was coming. "Eight years of trial" have shown frustration in enforcement. "Even church members and reformers were admitting to the impossibility of enforcement." The writer of the article expected modification to come in 1929. He didn't expect repeal: "To remove the eighteenth amendment from the Constitution of the United States another war will be necessary or a great panic will be the means of removing this incubus from the shoulders of the people."

How ironic—"great panic" used less than a year before the stock market crash in 1929. The paper stated people wanted permission for use of beverages of 3 to 10 percent, relieving the grape growers and stopping the waste of thousands of tons of grapes. Bankers, the paper said, have gotten behind grape growers and these bankers have influence with President-elect Hoover. "Manufacturers all over the country (except for Henry Ford because of his 'billicky' condition) leaned toward modification. Every record in the United States goes to show that the Volstead law has been a burden on the people."[22]

By the end of 1928 people were becoming increasingly aware that enforcement was not working. Coolidge was the lame-duck president. Al Smith lost the election of 1928, but he lost partly because he was a Catholic, not that he was a wet. Republicans ran on the wet and dry side, both believing what they wanted to believe. Moderates felt Hoover would support modifying the Volstead Act. Drys knew they won the election because Hoover won. A change was coming now that strong Hoover would soon be in charge of the country and in charge of national enforcement. At last prohibition would be effective and the country would be truly dry.

Assistant Attorney General Mabel Walker Willebrandt, appointed by President Harding as a young lawyer from Los Angeles, she served three presidents as Department of Justice head of prohibition enforcement. In 1928 she was used by Republicans and Hoover to take pressure off candidates by presenting the prohibition platform at the Republican Convention. She supported Hoover until she resigned in1929. In 30 years as a lawyer arguing 69 cases before the Supreme Court, she lost only two! Photo taken by author from Willebrandt File, Library of Congress.

CHAPTER 26

THE WICKERSHAM LETTERS

Hoover won the election. The Republican Platform and Hoover's acceptance speech made enforcement a policy of the Republican Party. The sound thrashing of wet Democrat Al Smith delighted prohibitionists everywhere. Churches, Anti-Saloon League branches, and the WCTU celebrated with tea, coffee and soft drinks, of course, and anxiously waited for the anticipated fruits of the election. They waited for real, no-nonsense enforcement. Said Hoover: Prohibition is "The dominant issue before the American people."

Willebrandt Supports Hoover

Hoover would be the third president Mabel Walker Willebrandt would work for. She remembered the day seven years before when she had come all the way from California to be interviewed by the new President, Warren Harding, who in 1921 was appointing his staff to handle the enforcement of the 18th Amendment. When she came into his office and was told to sit down, Harding took a long look at this young lady sitting in front of him and finally said with his good-old-boy mentality, "You look so young and inexperienced. Thirty-two is not very old."

Mabel Walker Willebrandt stared right back into his eyes, leaned forward a bit and pleaded guilty to being young, "But," she said, "I promise to grow out of it."

Harding hired her as Assistant Attorney General in charge of prohibition. He got himself quite an experienced lawyer in 1921. She had been legal advisor to the draft board, legislative chair and president of Professional Women's Club of Los Angeles, one of the largest women's club in the nation. .She had been active in the Republican Party. The *Woman's Viewpoint* of Houston, Texas, said Willebrandt was "Our greatest woman lawyer...most fearless and the straightest woman I know." When attending USC Law School, she toiled night and day as a student, a school teacher and a principal. She worked 14-18 hours a day making a name for herself in southern California. She continued to work tirelessly for the Justice Department for Harding and Coolidge and soon for Hoover. The first two presidents were lukewarm about backing enforcement. Many people thought she had been made a "goat" to take blame from the presidents. Since she admired Hoover's efficiency and kindness, she knew he would "go forward with better enforcement with less waste and friction in the legal use of men and money." She disliked that prohibition agents were earning the reputation of being gunmen. She also disliked the nickname she obtained: "Prohibition Portia" in 1927 [Portia being the wife of Julius Caesar], "America's Portia" said the *New York Herald Tribune* on July 1, 1928, and "That Prohibition Portia," said Democrat Al Smith.[1]

On her way to try a case in San Francisco, she visited Hoover's home in Palo Alto. She was an active feminine Republican leader in the '28 campaign. Hoover's campaign chiefs asked her to present the Republican stance on prohibition in the Republican Convention in 1928. She defended prohibition, while most Republican candidates avoided the subject.

Now that he was elected, she was pleased. "Real prohibition," she told San Francisco reporters after the election, "is a slow proposition. Active enforcement takes time and requires public sympathy." Under Hoover, "what benefits have been gained will be preserved and many of the present abuses will be eliminated." His election would mean "for the nation a clean, orderly, constructive and efficient enforcement of all laws, including prohibition." She said, "As bad as conditions appear to local eyes, conditions are better throughout the country as a whole." Of course, she was talking to San Francisco reporters, and San Francisco was still as wet as the Pacific Ocean.

While waiting to take the oath of office, Hoover made his plans. Willebrandt and others expected this new tough president and his Republican Congress to close loopholes, deal swiftly with criminals, end political graft and corruption, and lead America into a new age of morality. Most drys assumed Hoover was dry, but had no proof. When wets chatted with the president in 1928, they walked away feeling Hoover was not against repeal or at least not against letting the citizens vote again to change the Constitution. Few knew Herbert Hoover's position on prohibition. People joked about the reason for naming bridges after Hoover: "A Hoover Bridge is dry on top, wet underneath and straddles both sides."

Hoover's inaugural address announced to the American people: "But a large responsibility rests directly upon our citizens. There would be little traffic in illegal liquor if only criminals patronized it. We must awake to the fact that this patronage from large numbers of law-abiding citizens is supplying the rewards and stimulating crime. If citizens do not like a law, their duty as honest men and women is to discourage its violation."[2]

President Herbert Clark Hoover acted less than decisively. Hoover's plans were almost no plans. At the new President's request, Congress passed an act forming the National Commission on Law Observance and Enforcement, known as the Wickersham Commission, to study and investigate crime and enforcement of the Eighteenth Amendment. His plan was **to study the question.** For over a year and a half the commission investigated whether the 18th was being enforced and could be enforced, investigated causes of crime, apathy and corruption in general in the United States. The commission took it upon itself to decide whether the 18th should be repealed, retained or revised.

Twelve commissioners studied the faulty Volstead Act and Amendment 18. They studied what most people knew already: Prohibition was not working, people and many officials disregarded the law, young people perpetrated most crimes, foreigners committed a good percentage of crimes, and big crooks were seldom prosecuted, while little guys served hard time.

For six months the Wickersham Commission sent letters to governors, sheriffs, chiefs of police and judges, requesting information and opinions on more than just prohibition. It elicited responses on anything to do with law and order, such as juveniles, foreigners, criminals and court systems. The commission invited the public to respond.

And respond they did. These letters candidly expressed thoughts and concerns of that generation of Californians. Some quite succinctly analyzed prohibition and law and order problems and came up with solutions that were relevant to problems of the Roaring Twenties. So incisive were hundreds of these letters that they are still relevant to concerns of Californians in the 1990s. A few letters also showed a bit of what California was becoming known for—a land with some fruits, flakes and nuts.

Governor C. C. Young's secretary answered his, saying the governor was too busy at the time but would answer later. He never did answer. Many district attorneys, however, responded, some in great detail. W. E. Wright, District Attorney, Nevada County, November 7, 1929, attested that constables were of little value in law enforcement, and along with townships, were products of the horse and buggy days. Wright responded negatively about the question of "foreign born," affirming they presented a real problem in crime and cost of crime. "I would say that not less than 75 [%], and this very conservative, of the crimes which reach trials are committed by those who are foreign born....this [was a] civic disease." About prohibition, Wright said, after considerable experience, intoxicating liquors should be sold under the supervision of the government until such time as a great majority of the people will be in favor of strict prohibition.

"The present procedure of enforcing prohibition is cumbersome, inefficient and ineffective, especially by reason of public opinion of the law. It reduces the federal courts to the level of an inferior court, and elevates inferior courts to the level of federal courts. In other words, a justice's court has the power to sentence a liquor violator to pay a fine of $500 or serve 500 days in the county jail; for the same offense the Superior Court may fine him $1,000 but can only confine him to the county jail for six months, and oftentimes our federal courts, for the same offense, will impose a fine all the way from $5 up to $500 without any imprisonment whatsoever. Heretofore, citizens feared and respected federal courts—now they neither fear nor respect federal courts or any courts."[3]

George H. Johnson, District Attorney, San Bernardino County, November 23, 1929, summarized problems as follows: people get off of serving on juries; criminals expect to get off for their first offense, even though they may have been committing that crime for a number of years; prisons are disgustingly overcrowded.

Orrin J. Lowell, District Attorney, Placer County, November 13, 1929, stated the problems as "police were not courteous, competent, faithful nor loyal—I mean all enforcement officers." Private people had second class help with court, rich and criminals hired the best. Penal institutions seldom built up the inmate's character, and frequently destroyed it. Our newer "moral laws" received less respect from the police than from the public. More policemen were former bartenders than any other occupation. They should be "ambassadors of our country at home. They are the one point of contact for the ordinary person between the sovereignty of his government and himself."

Wallace Rutherford, District Attorney, Napa County, November 22, 1929, warned the Wickersham Commission: "...if we are going to have a mass of reports which will be uninteresting to 80% of the people, then the time and money expended by your commission will be wasted; if your report is going to result in more laws to be violated, then you are only going to have more criminals and a greater percentage of law violators. Prohibition has added so many different crimes that it is almost impossible to enumerate them, without voluminous statistics." Rutherford made a comparison to the 20 to 50 new criminal laws that have resulted from the advent of the automobile.

S. E. Metzler, District Attorney, Humboldt County, October 26, 1929, enumerated 12 reasons for crime in an eight-page, single-spaced letter. He said, based on his experiences with thousands of criminals, criminals ranged from those born with that predilection to those who lust for wealth without labor. Suggesting the 18th was a reason law-abiding citizens committed crimes: "The United States Congress, and state legislatures sought to legislate the American people into the path of righteousness. This cannot be done. We cannot legislate an evil thought out of the human mind, nor cleanse an evil heart by statutes" [see Metzler, Chapter 18].

Later he became more specific. He said, "prohibition made extant a great class of criminals. All the millions the government can use to enforce and even with the army and navy, prohibition won't be enforced. ...no good is accomplished by trying to deceive ourselves. It never has nor will be enforced. The moonshiner, the importer of illicit liquor, and the bootlegger, are more firmly entrenched today than they have been at any time since the enactment of the Eighteenth Amendment." The demand for liquor will always exist. "Therefore, it is time, if we are to save our self-respect among nations of the earth, and the respect of our own people, to drop the mask of hypocrisy, and repeal or amend the Eighteenth Amendment and the subsequent enforcement laws, so the American people...can have respect for the Federal District Court, which by reason of the law, has degenerated to the level of merely a Police Court, passing judgment on bootleggers, prostitutes, pimps, and dope peddlers. Men, especially Americans, resent statutory control of his natural, domestic, relative, political and industrial life, to the extent that it becomes a burden and he has a right to resent it..." He said, "The best government was one with the fewest laws."

Interesting comments on the foreign born: Most foreigners, he said, were law abiding. The Irish drank and engaged in fist fights, mostly among themselves—"a sort of Irish pastime." The Greek was a "white-slaver by nature...a sexual pervert, and a knife wielder." But the greatest liquor violators were the Italians, the most successful who bribed officials and corrupted juries if possible. When Italians got out of jail, they went right into the business again.[4]

Judges at all levels responded to the Commission's request for information. Judge Edwin F. Hahn, Superior Court, Los Angeles, November 14, 1929, wrote "Undoubtedly the attitude of many respected citizens in openly flaunting and ridiculing some of our laws has done more than any one thing to inculcate in the minds of our citizenry the feeling that there is no reflection upon a citizen if he disregards or disobeys any law which does not please him.[5]

"Unquestionably the prospect of large profits to be derived from the illicit sale of liquor had induced many people to move from the class of law-abiding citizens to the class of law violators." The country needed penalties for buyers, said the judge.

Federal judge Edward J. Henning, Federal Court, Los Angeles, September 12, 1929, urged a separation of first offenders from the habitual criminal and not cramming them like sardines. Said Henning: "Half the states need to throw out their rules of evidence in criminal cases and rules on appeal into the scrap heap."

"...75% of the heinous crimes [were] perpetrated in America by young folks from 15 to 25...[from] wrecked homes or homes worse than no home at all." There were too many "Thou shalt nots" on the "statute books of our state—yea, of our nation also." We had "...statutes which don't reflect the moral sense of the great majority whom the statute affects, is without sanction of law, is unenforceable, and will not be respected. "Some legislatures felt that people were made for their pet statutes, instead of statutes being made for the people. When there were only four people on earth, we had a 25% murder rate. We are surely doing better than that today. The crimes classified as 'malum per se' are based upon the weakness of human nature and will always be with us. The crimes designated 'malum prohibitum' are often as much the result of statutes out of harmony with the philosophy of a great majority of the people affected and offer a tremendous field for your commission."

From Frank H. Kerrigan, Judge, U.S. District Court, July 31, 1929, affirmed the federal court was too packed with prohibition cases that should be in state and local courts. Probation was given on the condition that the guilty would not go into the bootlegging business again. Some criminals preferred to take their sentence and go back into the business. The Jones-Stalker Act put "teeth" into the law and some crooks wanted to get out of the business. Many cases resulted in a permanent rehabilitation which would be extremely doubtful following a penitentiary term.

Judge Charles W. Fricke, Superior Court Judge, Los Angeles, November 7, 1929, gave his recommendations to solve law and order problems: we needed police academies, we're 25 years behind times, prosecutors were "insufficiently equipped as to learning and experience to properly present...[cases]"; courts gave inconsistent penalties, no time or fine for a narcotics pusher, yet six months for a petty crime.

Robert B. Lambert, Judge of the Superior Court of Kern County, November 5, 1929, proposed vigorous and honest prosecution charged therewith. In criminal cases a verdict of three-fourths of the jury in all but capital cases should be sufficient. The state should form a prohibition court or at least have more judges to handle prohibition cases. "...there is nothing that deters the commission of crime so much as the thought of swift and certain punishment."

Showing faith in common people being informed, George A. Sturtevant, Associate Justice, District Court of Appeals, San Francisco, October 28, 1929, said: "The prohibition amendment and some statutes enacted trespassed on our personal liberty. In the west, objections to these laws were growing rapidly and included fifty percent of more of the electorate. Laymen recognize the imposition. Anyone who thought the laymen did not know wherein their rights are being trespassed upon need do no more than attend a labor union or similar assembly and listen to the speakers a very few minutes. The laymen in our country have the intelligence to read, study and debate these matters. Feeling as they do regarding the impositions, it is idle to talk to them about obeying such laws."

Raymond I. Turney, Presiding Judge, L. A. Municipal Court, November 19, 1929, felt the court needed to educate people about respect for the law, eliminate the system whereby lawyers and their clubs have difficulty investigating their own scoundrel lawyers; judges and lawyers show timid apathy to stop "these creatures."[6] Yes, he said, prohibition could be enforced, 12,000 murders a year in U. S. not enforced: depends on public sentiment; substantial jail time with absolute impartiality was needed. Fines for this class of offense is laughed at. "When I first was assigned to a division of the L. A. Municipal Court handling liquor cases, I found that everyone was accustomed to the fine or license system and that all the scoundrels in the community, prominent among the shyster attorneys, crooked bail bondsmen, politicians and the like, thought they were entitled to tell the judge of the court what policy to follow. I did away with that sort of thing by simply refusing to see or talk with anyone respecting cases and by imposing jail sentences upon seller and manufacturers of liquor regardless of their wealth or power in the community. During the first few weeks numerous threats were made against me but when it became apparent that the law was being honestly enforced and no distinction was being made between the rich and the poor, public sentiment rapidly crystallized in my support and I had no further difficulties of any magnitude. ...I was not opposed for a second term."

C. E. Tovee, Chief of Police, Chico, October 11, 1929, said the causes for crime and disrespect for the law were lack of enforcement, small percentage of apprehensions, difficulty in obtaining conviction, ease in obtaining paroles and often paroles given for the wrong reasons, unjust and too severe punishment, mobility of the criminal and loss of religion. His last sentence: "We could also prevent much crime by finding a substitute for Prohibition that would take the profit out of liquor."[7]

Chief James E. Davis, Los Angeles, August 24, 1929, said his office was interested in all the points of Wickersham's request and wished the commission could meet in L. A. where people could give their opinions. Davis used this opportunity to send the commission twelve pages of reports on the L. A. Police Department, showing arrests of drunken drivers and the percentages of convictions of various crimes.

From W. T. Stanford, Chief of Police, City of Vallejo, August 31, 1929, came a list of causes of crime: idleness, poverty, influences of early environment, illiteracy, lack of inculcation of moral restraint and the sense of right and wrong in early youth, false standard of living, "together with the multiplicity of inhibition and laws regulating minor matters, thereby obscuring and creating a disregard for the laws governing the vital conduct of the more important and essential affairs of the commonwealth." To ameliorate the problems, said Stanford, the country needed a "co-operative system of law enforcement, with prompt and diligent prosecution of law violators and jail sentences for habitual criminals...perform[ing] some useful and gainful labor during their incarceration."

"Modify or repeal all unenforceable and fanatical blue laws and establish closer confidential and co-operative relations between Federal Prohibition Enforcement Officers and Peace Officers...deport all habitual alien criminals, abolish probation for felony cases." Separate first offenders from hardened criminals.

Hundreds of Californians responded to Wickersham's invitation for ideas. A letter from J. T. Baker, Schilling, urged the use of martial law to stop people in open rebellion to the U.S., confiscate all corn syrup, malt syrup and other paraphernalia used for moonshining. Since the recent election of Hoover was a plebiscite for prohibition, Baker said, the country did not need another convention. Educate people, suspend writ of *habeas corpus* as "the time for rebellion is almost here." He said, "Distillers, brewers, bootleggers, hi-jackers and gangsters, with their bombs, rifles and machine guns, together with all who aid and abet them, must be gathered up and put out of business...mild form of martial law."

From Arthur R. Boyden of R. K. O. Studios, Hollywood, August 5, 1929, came this: "Idle men and women are like idle machines, a liability rather than an asset. Unlike machines, idle men must eat and sleep." He suggested every employer hire more workers "every man they could," therefore stimulate buying.

Edgar L. Bishop, Attorney, 3605 McClintok Ave., L. A., compared jail time given with the rates of prohibition crimes and alcoholic poisoning. He quoted Chief Davis: "Of those convicted only 11% received straight jail sentences; 78% received choice of jail sentence or fine, paid the fine and returned to do business until caught again. Because a limited number of officers can be detailed to work on securing the conclusive evidence required to convict a bootlegger, L. A. cannot hope to do more than curtail the business so long as the fine-license system is in vogue." "Fine-license" referred to the bootlegger receiving a small fine and going back to bootleg again, thus amounting to no more than a license to bootleg. A fine was like a fee to operate.[8]

Dr. A. L. Brown, Riverside, recommended cutting down crime by unsexing all major criminals, castrate the men and take out the women's ovaries.

Benjamin F. Bledsoe, Attorney, L. A. , October 11, 1930, wrote two letters urging the government to "prevent the criminal from being made an habitual criminal"—better to prevent him from becoming a criminal at all: "imbue him with the idea that substantial punishment, not to his liking, will follow violation of the law...done by unyieldingly firm, yet withal moderately mild, punishment, is my profound belief born of enlightening experience." The country has two choices: "...surrender out of sheer weakness or else going forward with complete firmness. I am truly hopeful that the work of the Commission will not make it necessary to adopt the first alternative."

Lawyer Chalmers S. Baird, San Francisco, November 25, 1930, asked for a yes or no answer to: "Has Congress authority now, without any change in the Constitution, to enact a liquor law whereby the federal government would dispense intoxicating beverages, without private profit in states that have no Volstead enforcement acts?"

Answered Wickershsham's Chairman: "NO, no one can make or sell, not even the government."

Herbert E. Bonham, Oakland, May 2, 1931, said we need to change word "prohibit" to "Protect"—protection from evils of alcohol. "[One] can't lead a bull out of a garden by grabbing his tail, must rope his horns and use force ...therefore take the law by horns and force it."

From J. L. Campbell, 64 Pine St., San Francisco, June 1929: "Criminal law is now protection to criminals rather than to society." Campbell sent a newspaper article about 350 gallons of evidence thrown out in Eastbay—Filipelli-Ratto liquor ring. Judge Harold Lauterback threw out liquor evidence in court because it was seized without warrants entitling them to enter the basement of 433 Taylor Street, Alameda, thus ruining the case against 14 major and 38 minor defendants, including John Filipelli, bail bond operator and supposed leader of ring and G. B. Ratto, partner in widespread bootlegging in Oakland and Alameda. A raid on Filipelli's 510 Fifteenth St. property brought indictments which also named several police, one Capt. Thorvald Brown. But the case was thwarted because of technicalities.

Dr. M. Morgan Cloud, a lawyer from L. A., October 26, 1929, wanted to have public defenders assigned to criminals, eliminating the criminal's lawyer. "The criminal lawyer being eliminated, there would not be jury bribing, jury fixing and perjury as under the present system."

R. A. Zehnder, Los Gatos, May 5, 1930, wrote to President Hoover because he wanted to hear what Hoover intended to do about violators of the prohibition law, "...wet, or other law violators are always busy over radio and in print and berate you and the government in no uncertain terms." The large number of "violators who get free or out on probation, especially those who happen to get the right attorney, is appalling."

"I know of a case where several men were before the judge charged of driving while drunk, everyone was found [fined] $300, except one, who was let out on probation, mark you why, because he had a certain political attorney to defend himself; this attorney rules the District Attorney and a certain judge, it is said. In my humble opinion the law is inadequate if it punishes only ones who sell liquor, and not the ones for possession of same. I know someone who used to be on the Federal Grand Jury, who never helped convict a heavy drinker, etc. because he was a heavy drinker himself. I know of a police judge who is the worst kind of boozer. In and around San Francisco (and for that matter all over the State), clubs and associations go to picnics indoors and outdoors, and the drinking that's carried on by many thousands and under the very eyes of the police is astonishing, men & women walking about drunk. I have reported people to Prohibition administer (*sic*) in S. F., having strong evidence, but nothing was ever done about it, because it is common knowledge that agents take money to be quiet about it."

It is "...disheartening ...if President after President was weak & could find no solution to the ruination of the coming generation. A partnership of weak men does not add strength, weakness multiplied by weakness equals naught."

Mrs. Sina Walsh, S. F., June 21, 1929, asked the Wickersham Commission to allow light wines in place of hard liquors. "Fines, jails, judges have allied to control the acts or sentiments of the low-grade multitudes included in our population, more particularly the foreign element."

Someone sent a 1929 clipping about Paul A. Paulson, a Chico teacher, whom the Chico School Board investigated, not for teaching atheism but inquiring into charges "he uses alcohol."[9]

Carl Webber, S. F., on July 2, 1929, wrote that "prohibition is the beginning of real civilization." Webber said, "Too much sex plays in the motion pictures and youth feel they can "get some easy job by pull or drag"—these are the causes of lack of law and order, not prohibition."

From Maxwell J. Welch: "arrange to give us a national referendum in 1932 for the following confusing question: The present 18th...shall not be prohibited because of their alcoholic content." Welch sent a clipping about Superior Court Judge Emmet Wilson who sentenced a pregnant 22-year-old woman, Mrs. Thelma Holland, to San Quentin, and the "uproar maternal love of a nation arose in protest." Because of the clamor, he allowed her to change her plea to not guilty. While her husband was in jail, she tried to take care of her six step children at home the best way she could. Citizens donated the bail, allowing her to await trial at home. Judge Wilson backed down quickly when faced with the wrath of hostile protest.

"The eyes of the nation are on you, Mr. Hoover!" wrote Mary Florence Wirth, L. A., 6241 Marmion Way, on June 13, 1929, only a few months after Hoover took office. "We hear much about the breaking down of the law and the lack of respect for government. Causes: late war, still paying for it, high taxes, high assessments for roads, make us lose our houses."[10]

"We all know that rich men are constantly breaking the 18th amendment and getting by with it and many public officials are guilty of breaking it while the little fellow is usually fined or imprisoned. I believe we should obey the law as long as there is law, but it is asking a great deal of intelligent people to try to force respect for a thing which is not respectable. Laws should be fewer, simpler and more understandable. We...are controlled by special interests."

Edward Walker, of Ben Loman, read the *Santa Cruz Sentinel*, March 5, 1930, and fired off a letter to Washington the same day. The acquittal of Norman Costella, a Garibaldi Hotel man, incensed Walker. The raid, made by Constable William Horstman and Deputy Constables A. J. Meagher, John Capitanich, E. F. Mattocks, on December 7, followed the next day with a raid on the Lloyd Groat place near Soquel. Jurors were released from jury because they were either for or against prohibition. Walker sent another article on January 6, 1930, showing the court ordered the evidence to be given back, including cappers, electric ager, rifle, ammo, dagger, siphon tubes, 16 bundles and packages of various labels, beer caps, and assorted liquors. "The search warrants used...in the raid on the Lloyd Groat place and Hotel Garibaldi were insufficient and void..." Much of the evidence couldn't be found, presumed to be taken when in the hands of Uncle Sam.

From Charles W. Wallace, Santa Monica, November 21, 1930, an ex-officer in the World War: "Put cities like L. A., if it should be corrupt on martial law and clean it up like in the war, have 1,000 trained police like in the army."

E. L. Wentworth, S. F., November 27, 1930, complained that the Wickersham Commission allowed liquor interests to speak before the group, and should permit prohibition supporters to plead their case: "...it is time to give Prohibition a show."

From Henry Wagner, L. A., October 2, 1930: "There is an awful howl of the ati [sic] saloon league and other prohibition societies about the violation of the law, of the law that was violated in its passage. Robberies, murder and crime is [sic] worse then it was when we had saloons. I don't think it would be any worse if we get saloons back...employment to thousands of men and would be a benefit to the farmers...."

Dr. H. B. Weiper of Lower Lake wrote in June and again in August 1930, about the liquor business growing luxuriantly; take profits away. Give it another ten years? Damage would do incalculable harm to youth, even if "...let us suppose for a moment that with a large army of Federal officers or soldiers with bayonets, machine and other guns etc. prohibition would in a half way manner be enforced...[at a cost of] millions of dollars." Repeal and educate. The majority of Lake County favor repeal, said Weiper.

K. C. Wells, Hollywood, July 19, 1930, confirmed that the images of Hoover shown in southern California were still good: "We feel that the enforcement of this wonderful 18th amendment lies close to his [Hoover's] heart and that he is striving to do all in his power to put down the evil of liquor."

Another view came from Gardena a few miles away, from Dr. Daniel Woods, January 3, 1930. Woods sent his plan based on the Declaration of Independence: Register everybody so he could be contacted within 24 hours, "thereby minimizing crime," expose those who traffic in Dope, white slavery and bootleg, place the issue of Prohibition to a vote of the people; "[this] will not alter our Country's Liberty, which our Forefathers fought for; let us preserve it. No body of men should have undertaken to add this 18th Amendment to our Constitution, therefore, to preserve our Liberty it must be recalled." Then he added: most traffic is by foreigners.

"Little children have been known to refuse their milk bottle and hold their fathers bottle of mash and sucking it," said Woods.

"Popes and Catholics fault," was the dogmatic answer why the country had a law and order problem, wrote Dr. M. M. Yates, Santa Barbara, October 3, 1929.

Mr. Sarden Smith, San Diego, October 14, 1930: "Since prohibition began we hear of crime it caused. I verily believe that the Eighteenth amendment was the worst crime ever inflicted on the American Republic. Prohibition never has, and never can be enforced in free America. [It] proves ALL MEN ARE LIARS [referring to] Phil D. Swing, Congressman."

From Hayward, U. S. Saeger, wrote on February 12, 1930, "I have a method to stop the crime here in this U S....What is it worth to you? If you are interested, send your Representative to call on me."

Preston W. Search, Carmel-by-the-Sea, January 25, 1931, supported prohibition: "The people as a whole will not endorse repeal, modification would satisfy no one, government vending unthinkable, nullification would be secession. Must enforce prohibition. It will win in time," said Search.

M. Vaygouny, Research Lab, Berkeley, May 29,1929, said: "As a free man to the leader of Free Men[:] A strictly religious law has wedged in the pages of civil Constitution...[I] have not had the predilection for alcohol, still the presence of that foreign substance, so wanton thirst in the sacred and otherwise perfect body politic, grieves me. And it grieves me because the liberty of my fellow man to ferment, boil, cook, distill, yes, and to carry, 'possess,' eat or drink what ever he wishes of his own free choice and will in his own free home, is trampled upon." Making, transporting, drinking doesn't involve civil. Selling involves civil law, the Berkeley man said. "Jesus went out of his way to make wine out of water" and people have put religious law inside our most noble book—the Constitution.

Earl F. Van Luven, wrote from Colton, November 11, 1930: Conditions at Seattle and other cities of the U. S. are not satisfactory under our prohibition law but I am sure they are not worse than government control.

Another letter came from Sarden Smith of San Diego, via Congressman Swing: "I am not a prohibitionist and never was, and I do not believe in it, and will not support it. My candid opinion of it is: That it is unconstitutional and cant [sic] be driven down any good American throat."

Homer W. Payne, Berkeley, November 16, 1930, wrote a three-page letter analyzing how making liquor legal will harm the economy. He signed "Yours for prohibition and prosperity."

Kernan Robson, S. F., October 10, 1929, said succinctly: making it illegal to buy is important like morphine—the purchase is illegal.

George Evans, L. A., May 23, 1929, laid the blame on moving pictures, with gangsters and crime and "flood of underworld stuff....the very nonchalance with which murder is flung in the faces of moving picture audiences."[11]

Albert Elliston of L. A. and later of Hollywood, wrote he had a plan but it would take three months to write it out and he would need financial help during the time. He'd do it for his country free, but "I am penniless." He sent another letter from Long Beach, offering his help to solve the nation's problems with law and order.

A workingman from Los Angeles, June 9, 1929, before the depression, wrote he was a day laborer, receiving $24.00 per week for 8-10 hours plus having to pay bus fare, said, he had "no overtime when I work on Sunday. If I get sick...," he has nothing. He pleaded, "...if I could save a little against old age." People will find a way to get bread for their children—that is what causes crime. "Let our government abolish Prohibition and take charge of the manufacture and distribution of licker [*sic*] on a permit plan to the users and stricter laws about drunken Driving and enforce said laws to the fullest extent."[12]

Elizabeth P. Pike, Los Angeles, September 1930, said, "Without our consent the 18th was put in. Now, after nine years of futile efforts to enforce it, it is a matter of RIGHT that the...people be given a chance to express their wishes." She urged the commission to recommend Congress start the repeal amendment process. "[Prohibition]...can never be enforced as long as good citizens refuse to regard the moderate consumption of alcohol as a crime." Dr. Charles D. Koch, Maryville, Missouri, sent the same letter. That basic letter, perhaps 700 of them, came from Rhode Island, New York, Missouri, Massachusetts, New Jersey. Mrs. Roy Pike, from Livermore, used the letter as did several people from San Francisco.

After the stock market crash occurred in 1929 and the vast unemployment started in the early 1930s, the letters changed to stress economic factors in crime. An example about the homeless and the unemployed arrived in November 1930, saying crimes were done by the unemployed and gangsters. The gangsters were not living in the riverbed, they were in the "swellest hotels." The writer sent a clipping about L. A. Police and District Attorney Buran A. Fitts and sheriffs department having a meeting with the L. A. Chamber of Commerce about the unemployed. Editorial: we don't want to arrest unemployed as vagrants. And we don't want to give "work tests" for those who apply for aid.[13]

In the late 1930s, clippings came from all over, not about prohibition but about unemployment, homeless, stealing rather than begging. H. C. Nennetch from Venice, October 14, 1930, wrote: "Hey diddle, diddle! The cat and the fiddle! Prohibition and Crime! The cow jumped over the moon!" Some interesting points: without references and recommendation plus experience, it is difficult to get a job. "Most convicts were born without references, recommendations or experience. The fabled fox said to the farmer, "Feed me like your dog and I will not steal your chickens." Most people admired a criminal who dared to rob a bank more than they admired an honest beggar. "How about E. T. Earl of Los Angeles, who was running church politics and the underworld at the same time?" "When a man spends 25 years of his life building roads or going from mining camp to camp in the Rockies, what country does he belong to in his old age?" [paraphrased]

"The National Government is only a 'white-wash' on crime investigation as long as it evades its responsibility on the *vagrancies* [*sic*]and pauper problem," said Nennetch.

"When policeman Costello was shot in L. A., I heard a fellow remark that he had laughed until he cried in glee" because "he was arrested by Costello four times...poor fellow [the shooter] and only one arm and was probably in the bootleg business." A job as a waiter may be a step to obtaining a bootleg job. If a man were hired, said Nennetch, as a restaurant waiter, and the bootlegger found him "o k," he transferred him to another place and raised his wages. If he were risky the bootlegger fired him in a few days. Bootleggers found it easy to hire men even to take responsibility for bootlegging and going to jail. When he got out of jail, the crook provided for him. Some cafes and restaurants were recruiting stations for bootleggers. A job in a candy store won't pay the rent. "Along the boulevards in California are chicken dinner signs. The number of customers would not pay taxes and assessments out of the profits of chicken dinners...husband probably worked, the wife cooked chicken dinners. "Usually the husband had a commission job that don't [*sic*] average over two dollars a day and the wife makes home brew." "In the Coolidge Prosperity, the criminals, gangsters, corporate employees, and overtime employees had a high standard of living while millions lived with second hand rubbish for clothing and furniture and a swill of pancakes and bread and coffee and oleo for food."

Samuel Z. Wwiss, L. A., April 17, 1930, said prohibition is blamed for unemployment. "...responsible to a large degree for the present unemployment of so many thousands." The bootleggers, he asserted, are hiding every dollar they make, instead of putting it in circulation which is one big reason why money is scarce at the present time."[14]

"Will you please handle this letter confidentially as I am working on some very important matters."

A typical letter of anti-prohibition sentiment came from William Hoffman, 6403 Dana Street, Oakland. This 50-year-old man affirmed that more harm came from the drugstores than from the saloons. Hoffman ended with "I do not like the 18th amendment, in fact I hate it. I am not going to tattle on those who do violate and I am not going to insist that it be enforced, in fact I am going to help this fall to repeal our state enforcement law [Wright Act] and rest assured it will be repealed. Californians are disgusted with the entrapment idea and the country's hiring a lot of cheap detectives and the splitting of fines [dividing fines between federal and local coffers].[15]

Wickersham Report

Wickersham made a preliminary report in January 1930, recommending more money for enforcement. California newspapers, such as the *Riverside Daily Press,* November 24, 1930, reported the country anxiously awaiting the

Wickersham Commission report. "Both sides watching," said the paper as the Commission had to present its report to Hoover by January 1, 1931, after over 18 months of study. Before the report, the Methodist National Convention in Washington, D. C. and the Anti-Saloon League Convention hoped to have some influence on the report and on President Hoover. Wets pushed their side by firing off letters and telegrams asking for a national vote on prohibition, and "if people vote dry, let's enforce it. But let's allow the people to decide."[16]

The *Christian Century* feared the Wickersham report would be wet or at least "moist." They were wondering what actually Hoover was, wet or dry. Said the *Century:* The great issue is Democracy versus the Liquor Traffic. A wet report, confessing the inability of democracy to enforce its own laws and therefore making concessions to the liquor traffic, will weaken democracy. A dry report will strengthen democracy....[17]

The Commission reported to Hoover that some improvement in enforcement occurred since 1927, but the present enforcement is inadequate. The report opposed repeal, opposed reestablishing the saloon or having the federal government or state go into the liquor business and opposed modifying the sale of wine and beer.

They recommended restricting the medical professional, appropriating more money, eliminating some restrictions on fruit juices and cider, hiring more agents, tracing denatured alcohol, codifying prohibition laws such as prosecuting petty offenses in federal courts, and creating more effective padlock laws.

The written report came several months later. One of the commissioners, Newton D. Baker, read the report, signed it, then in a separate paper stated he was in favor of repeal and leaving the liquor problem to the states. Henry W. Anderson and a few other commissioners proposed repeal and letting states operate liquor stores under licenses. The liquor could not be consumed on the premises. This proposal would end the saloon.

In essence, Wickersham Commission recommended keeping prohibition.

From New York came this poem:
>Prohibition is an awful flop.
>We like it.
>It can't stop what it's meant to stop.
>We like it.
>It's left a trail of graft and slime,
>It's filled our land with vice and crime.
>It don't prohibit worth a dime,
>Nevertheless we're for it.
>   Franklin P Adams, *New York World*[18]

480

According to Fletcher Dobyns in *The Amazing Story of Repeal*, the enforcement lawyers said the greatest obstacles to enforcement had been the loopholes, technicalities and restrictions of the Volstead Act and the Wickersham Report. The wet press garbled from that report all the statements that tended to discredit prohibition and gave them daily and universal circulation. From that time on (1930), Dobyns said, the attitude of the people became increasingly indifferent or hostile, and juries let bootleggers go regardless of the evidence.[19]

Hoover's policy on National Prohibition was to continue enforcing it, studying it for almost two years, delaying major decisions. The reorganization in 1930 helped do a better job of enforcement. But it was too late for "more of the same," because another factor forced itself in the middle of the prohibition struggle: **The Great Depression had started.**

Sarcastic political cartoon showing how the country felt about the Wickersham Commission, after thousands of hours of studying law enforcement and prohibition, coming up with no recommendation to end prohibition or even modify it. It was a Wicker SHAM which made the bootleggers and the gangsters happy.

CHAPTER 27

DAMPENING THE DRYS

A ll the time the Wickersham Commission studied problems of prohibition and law and order in the United States, Californians still faced prohibition with one eye closed. Enforcement had improved with the civil service tests given to prohibition agent applicants. However, as the federal government improved, so did moonshiners, rumrunners and bootleggers. Frustration and anger enveloped both sides of prohibition as hypocrisy continued, as absurdities appeared in newspapers and as wets rapidly eroded Amendment 18. And when the effects of the Crash of '29 and its subsequent depression affected the mass of Americans, the war was basically decided, but the battles were not over.

Wineries started another loophole in southern California by producing wine tonics. Add some oregano or tarragon to wine, according to old country recipes, and sell the bottles for anemia or whatever. Wine tonics in San Bernardino, Los Angeles and Riverside counties started a brisk sale in the late 1920s and immediately ended in court or on city council agendas. San Bernardino County limited sales of wine tonics at drugstores only and then just one pint per person every three days. In 1928 Chief H. J. Henry of Chino arrested J. Sandoval, who was delivering cases of wine tonics from the Vida Nueva Company of L. A., and released him on $200 bail allowing him to plead at another date. Even though Vida Nueva had a government permit, this was thought to be a test case pushed by Chino and the Anti-Saloon League. L. A. County had a similar law which was also immediately tested in court. Pomona drug-store manager Samuel Nason, 362 West 2nd Street, sold two bottles to the same person under different names three days in a row. Riverside County Supervisors voted the strongest wine tonic ban, making it a penalty of $500 or six months to "possess, sell, serve or give away" tonics capable of being used as a beverage. The county's new law required manufacturers to put 30 percent soluble solids in the tonics. One supervisor said, "...make the stuff so disagreeable a dog wouldn't drink it." There was no reason to have the tonics in the car: "Let them doctor themselves at home." Loophole: Druggists could sell what was in stock.[1]

After eight years of being in charge of enforcement of prohibition as Assistant Attorney General of the United States, Mabel Walker Willebrandt, perhaps disappointed in Hoover's inaction, resigned in the spring of 1929. Hoover accepted her resignation. She took on a client in her new Los Angeles law office, a strange client—Fruit Industries, Ltd., a California corporation of vineyards.[2]

When Willebrandt received a public commitment from the new Prohibition Director Amos W. W. Woodcock, "not to molest her client," the California company felt safe selling Wine-Glo. California's surplus grapes, made into grape juice, could be sold nationwide. If barrels of wine accidentally fermented, that was not the company's fault. Essentially, light wine became legal as long as it was called grape juice. Prohibition, therefore, eroded more. As one reporter looked at the change, he said "along came Mabel," a parody of a Roaring Twenties song and a reference to Mabel Walker Willebrandt.

Former Prohibition Director Doran actually helped the wineries before Woodcock. Doran went to California to straighten out the wine industry. He came back to Washington, announcing that the wine industry "assured him the grapes would not fall into evil hands." He, therefore, would cooperate in helping market its crops. The government stopped bothering home wine makers, as it had stopped bothering family homebrew makers when it allowed malt syrup, used for homebrew, to be sold. During Doran's administration, the Bureau permitted grape juice to be delivered to homes. One company had in its instructions to telephone the company after the wine sat for 21 days, and the wine company said, "Today is the day it comes off." In other words, wine making directions were given over the phone. Under the Volstead Act, if non-intoxicating grape juice were not used immediately, it must be sealed to prevent fermentation. Of course, a lot of people just forgot.[3]

The next year Fruit Industries placed full-page ads in major papers. The *Evening Star* [Washington, D.C.] had an ad for Wine-Glo: "Our plan is to take a product that has always been available on the farm and place it within the reach of the city dweller...." They did not contrive to put more alcohol into the country, the ad stated, because if all the surplus juice were in homes and allowed to ferment, that would only be 560,000 gallons, 22/100 of one percent of the estimated 249,000,000 gallons of illegal alcohol in the country. "Our aim is to find an outlet for surplus grapes in California."[4]

Washington, D. C. representatives for Wine-Glo took orders for five-gallon kegs for $16.50, ten-gallons for $29.50 and 25 gallons for $65—choice of varieties: port, Virginia Dare, tokay, muscatel, claret, riesling, burgundy and sauterne. In the shadow of the Capitol, California grape growers found a market for their surplus grapes. And the spirit of prohibition weakened further.

ℬ

A Los Angeles criminologist, Nick Harris, told a gathering of Ontario realtors that the cause of 50 percent of all crimes was related to prohibition. He contradicted the dry forces' claim that crime is just a post-war condition and not alcohol related. Only one percent of arrested criminals were veterans. "The great majority of the criminals range in age from 17 to 21 years," he asserted.

Two solutions were evident to Harris: Educate the people to stop drinking or have the government take control of sale and distribution of liquor, such as what is done in Canada.[5]

The Annual Report of the Division of Criminal Identification and Investigation, State Department of Penology showed the growth in arrests for the twelve years of the prohibition amendment, not counting local arrests under the Wright Act. Fiscal Years: 1921-2 none; 1922-3 none; 1923-4 546; 1924-5 1272; 1925-26 1707; 1926-7 2,065; 1927-28 4,762; 1928-29 10,509; 1929-30 8,662; 1930-31 6,157; 1931-2 5,074.[6]

With continued discussion about the Wickersham Commission and its tentative findings, California newspapers voiced their opinions of possible solutions to prohibition and law and order.

Shotgun Prohibition
San Francisco Examiner, December 1, 1929

The *Washington Herald*, a Hearst newspaper, perhaps growing impatient with the Wickersham Commission, researched the ten years of prohibition. *San Francisco Examiner* picked up the article, used yellow-journalism-type headlines to sell papers and prove prohibition was not working: "1360 KILLED IN DRY ENFORCEMENT."[7] Coupled with that headline was a quarter-page cartoon, with a government leader, pistol in his hand, yelling directions to government men, wearing Lincoln-type hats and carrying shoulder guns: "YOU SLAY IN A RIGHTEOUS CAUSE! FOR ONCE ENDS JUSTIFY THE MEANS!! GO FORTH WITH YOUR GUNS AND DRY THE NATION!!!"

Los Angeles led the counties in body count, the *Herald* said. Of the prohibition killings in California, L. A. had seven. San Francisco had five: Basil Artuffo, killed by agent Thomas Warren; Ariel C. Eggers, alleged hijacker, killed by John Donnelly, U.S. Deputy Marshall; Low Jew, aged Chinese who took his own life when police raided his room; John O'Toole, agent who was killed by a fall from an automobile during a liquor chase; James W. Horton, policeman killed by someone unknown. San Luis Obispo County lost one, Jose Villegas, alleged bootlegger, killed by prohibition agent Robert L. Knight; Shasta County had its one loss in a game warden, James S. White, killed by agent John Vail; T. C. Wrinkle, rancher, was the only death in Tulare County when agent Paul Shannon killed him.

The *Herald* gathered data for five and a half months, from county officials throughout the states. Responses came from sending out 10,000 letters to 3,075 county sheriffs, coroners and clerks—92 percent responded. The results showed deaths five times higher than was read into the *Congressional Record*, June 1929, and the figure was seven times higher than the latest compilation made public by Commissioner Doran in November 1929.

Modern Tower of Babel
from a full page cartoon and editorial
San Francisco Examiner, July 14, 1929

"Foolish people in ancient times tried to build a tower that would reach the sky.

"Foolish people of our day try to construct a PROHIBITION TOWER that will reach the heaven of perfect righteous, and the confusion already existing is 'worse confounded.'[8]

"Legislation that was to stop deaths from drinking alcohol has IN-CREASED deaths from alcohol.

"Legislation that was to do away with secret drinking behind closed doors has given us, in our biggest city, New York, 32,000 hidden speakeasies in place of ten or twelve thousand saloons that, BAD, AND VILE AS THEY WERE, were at least open to police supervision.

"The old Tower of Babel has crumbled and gone. How long is this modern imitation to stand with its crime, bootlegging, hijacking and general villainy?"

A Federal Grand Jury was told by some industrialists, bankers and others: "Yes, we dealt with this bootlegger, found his goods reliable, think well of him." The new law said in essence "Make the laws for the little people, but don't bother us."

The editorial said, "...the absolute pathetic helplessness of the government in the face of a problem with which it cannot deal."

The *Examiner* quoted Thomas Jefferson several times referring to the benefits of beer and light wine in comparison to the destructiveness of whiskey. The *Examiner* purported that prohibition forced the common people to drink vile whiskey, suggesting that the government make light beer and wine legal.

Liquor on the Hip—Money Gone
by W. M. Hallanan, Chief of Police, Sacramento

Contrast if you will the home life of even ten years ago where the vast majority of our homes were still homes—not mere houses.[9]

Homes where the motherheart and motherlove guided the destiny of the child. Homes where fathers understandingly applied their wisdom of the world—and where Dad led the way bravely—wisely—well.

Contrast the old-fashioned mother of but ten or twelve years ago to the flapper mother of forty-five of today trying to outflapper and outdance, and outdrink, and outsmoke, her twenty year old flapper daughter.

The cigarett[e] smoking mother and cigarett[e] smoking sister, the can opener, the hip pocket flask, cards, cabarets and Jazz. Joyriding youths, three or four boys sixteen to nineteen years old and as many girls, first in Dad's auto, then cramped into any old auto found footloose.

Liquor on the hip—money gone—service stations or isolated stores easy prey to supply the needed coin—and a group of young hold-up men are in the making, timid at first at the touch of the pistol.

Twelve pages of a letter covered a gamut of subjects: politics interfering with justice; dishonest lawyers who use wit to confound witnesses for the state; criminals escaping hundreds of miles with the auto; crime still resulting from the late war; echoes of the Volstead Act; movies that incite shallow brains; influx of Japanese, Hindus, Filipino laborers displacing American workers; addicts of canned heat; evils of divorce and problems of step-parents; young boy or girl taken in tow by the "lecherous Asiatic" or one from the Mediterranean; miscarriage of justice by women jurors, who can't vote to hang that boy even though he was a killer; too much delay between arrest and imprisonment; prison too lenient; parole too easy; poor work training in prison; and criminals who have a protective association so they can be bailed out in a matter of hours.

He berated Judge Bourquin for fining a habitual narcotics peddler only $25.

ᘓ

A moonshiner or bootlegger was not held in contempt but the gangster, the corrupt policeman and the growing violent acts were contemptuous to the normal law-abiding Americans. Most major newspapers in California carried the story of Harry Daudson, a special prohi agent in the Cleveland area. When he quit his federal job, his reported wealth exceeded $2,000,000. He owned his own island on the Canadian side of Lake Erie.

On a more local level, offending agents disturbed the public. When a car full of border patrolmen crashed in Chula Vista, in March 1932, officers who came to the scene of the accident, picked up bottles from the car and hid them to protect the officers. Although two were in a drunken stupor, rescuing officers suggested to the witnesses that it would be better not to say anything.[10]

Al Capone stories amazed the relaxed Californians month after month, yet violence in California occurred daily, much of it laid on the growing gangsterism of prohibition. William T. Wilson, a rancher from Bloomington, for example, was taken for a ride, beaten, stabbed and thrown from a car on Colton Avenue outside San Bernardino. He recovered but told the police he knew nothing, remembered nothing.

In Los Angeles the same month, a hunter who lived in the hills near San Fernando sauntered about looking for something to shoot with his small rifle. He found a decapitated body that had been there for months. The canyon was named "Bootlegger Canyon" because the local residents said it was a hiding place for rum-runners' caches.

When Congress received a preliminary report of the Wickersham Commission with its recommendations, the nation and Congress responded. Wickersham did not recommend repeal or modification of the Volstead Act, but stronger enforcement and funds to fight crime. The editorial of *The San Diego Union*, January 15, 1930, said, "The wets need not repine." Renewed appeal to "put teeth into" the dry laws, showed a need for facts in the case not the doctrines of extremists. The "glad outcry of the drys that Wickersham Commission found ways to make prohibition work; remember we have heard these glad outcries before," said the editor sarcastically. The House of Representatives discussed spending $200,000,000 on enforcement. January 15, 1930, the House concentrated on ways to implement Hoover's recommendation. Wets offered their own solution to prohibition: repeal the 18th.

News of Hoover's recommendation came out within a day or so of the 10th anniversary of the start of prohibition. And the debate continued in the tenth year of the "Noble Experiment." Anti-Saloon Leagues celebrated 10 years of prohibition with the slogan "We mean business!"[11]

"The 10th Anniversary of Prohibition in Wet Riverside County"
by Clifford J. Walker
Country Life, January 1980

The Hemet Woman's Christian Temperance Union started the new year of 1930 as optimistically as it had been for the last five-six years. Since January 1930 was the 10th Anniversary of National Prohibition, the Hemet Union held its meeting on January 7. At the local Baptist Church, ladies listened to a guest speaker praising the progress and state of "World Prohibition." The WCTU declared January 16, as Victory Day throughout the United States, to be celebrated with ringing bells, parades and mass meetings. Locally, one guest speaker was Mrs. Pearl Kendall Hess, National Director of Medical Temperance. Women received recipes for "loyalty cocktails," non-alcoholic drinks served New Year's Day at the state WCTU headquarters at 301 North Broadway in Los Angeles. The Union had much to celebrate: ten years of prohibition, election of Hoover and the first ten months of his term. Some members still smiled when they thought of how soundly Herbert Hoover beat the wet Al Smith.

More and more alcohol violators were arrested, it seemed, than ever before, showing that Riverside County officials were suppressing county drinking, bootlegging and moonshining. Riverside County Jailer Bailey and Sheriff Sweeters released their annual reports for 1929. The county jailed 1,867 people that year on 100 different charges, more for liquor violations than for any other crime. Jailed at the Riverside County jail were 150 Wright-Act violators and at Indio 49 more. The County hosted 165 people for drunk driving, 143 at Riverside city jail and 22 at Indio. As a comparison to these liquor violations, there were only 33 jailed for grand theft, 15 for forgery and 29 for vagrancy. About one-third of the 81 prisoners at the County Work Camp sobered up at 35 cents an hour, building the new county road from Idyllwild to Palm Springs. WCTU felt that surely with these results the county and perhaps the state would dry up soon, maybe even by the end of that year, 1930!

The fallacy of their thinking was not obvious to them. More arrests, bigger busts and more violators in jail did not translate into a war that was close to being won. The county did need to dry up. Every small community supported one or two bootleggers. Every canyon with running water and every desert spring were potential moonshine sites. Liquor was available everywhere in Riverside County. Hemet's Chief of Police, Berg, for example, was called to the front of the Hemet Theater because three men were disturbing the peace. Berg arrested J. W. Dodson, T. E. and Roy Lissenbee for drunkenness. After being examined by Dr. Henry, only Dodson was found to be intoxicated and so charged, while the Lissenbee brothers were held for disturbing the peace—six months sentence to the County Road Camp was suspended.

Hemet News gave Victory Day fine coverage for the WCTU. The ladies had more to cheer due to the efforts of Elsinore's Chief of Police A. G. Barber. Barber watched suspicious actions on a goat ranch at the old Sill place between Perris and Elsinore—truckloads of sugar entering and mysteriously-covered trucks leaving for Los Angeles at 2-4 o'clock in the morning. When Barber informed federal prohibition agents, local officials with agent Walter L. Peters and others from Los Angeles, raided the goat ranch on January 22, 1930, confiscating and destroying a $100,000 to $125,000 alcohol plant, able to produce 5,000 gallons of grain alcohol a day. The operation had 1,500 gallons of finished liquor, huge vats containing 10,000 gallons of mash, a 25-horsepower boiler, an underground series of rooms. The agents planned to dynamite the plant except what would be used for evidence.

Elsinore Constable Tom Boyle arrested Nick Bruno who rented the Sill place, adjacent to the Inland Highway, three miles from Elsinore. Bruno's "goat ranch" was evidently the front for the largest still operation busted up to this time in southern California. Others arrested at the still were Joe Verda, alias Ortega, 58; Harry Corwin, alias Herman Quinn, 36, both of Elsinore; Peter Connelly, alias George Walker, 35, a Los Angeles carpenter, all booked on possession of a still and then taken to Los Angeles on federal charges. Local authorities looked for three men who escaped the raid.

Hemet News editor said the raid should dry up sources of San Jacinto and Hemet liquor. Although informants said the still had been operating for quite awhile, most of the equipment was new. Probably both were correct; it had been operating for some time and new equipment had been added to upgrade this successful operation.

488

Did the raid help dry up Riverside County or the Los Angeles Basin? Not a chance. The next month twelve more Riverside County residents were invited guests of the county jail for Wright-Act violations or fined for drunkenness. On February 28, 1930, the *Hemet News* reported five bootleggers caught in a sheriff's net: Tom McCracken, a 33-year-old San Jacinto cafe owner arrested for bootlegging; Ray Dosheir, 22, Frank Duhamel, 20, Frank Milligan, 22, all of San Jacinto for possession; and Fred Moffit, 18, of Hemet, for possession. McCracken, who sold to undercover agents, was released on $1,000 bond. Moffit, Dosheir, Milligan and Duhamel were arrested at Romoland, alleged to have 20 gallons of whiskey in their possession. Moffit and Duhamel pleaded guilty before Judge Garner of Highgrove, who fined Moffit $500, $300 of which was suspended and fined Duhamel $500 or six months. Milligan had been fined $200 when caught with a load of liquor on St. John's grade.

The flow did not stop in 1930, nor in '31 or '32. Annual reports of Sheriff Sweeters evinced a continued stream of Wright-Act violators. The insidious part of looking at all these arrests and thinking prohibition was working, as the WCTU was doing in Riverside County, was that arrests were, as the cliché goes, only a drop in the moonshine bucket. Victory Day celebrations must have sounded as hollow as an empty whiskey barrel to all who knew the reality of the 10th Anniversary of National Prohibition.[12]

∅

While celebrations occurred throughout the state, life went on despite repercussions from the October stock market crash. In January 1930, new Chevrolet sixes were on the market. Ford advertised new bodies for various models. Although the impact of the October stock market crash hadn't hit hard yet, there were several signs of foreboding. Southern Californians bought 13,317 new cars in October 1929; but only 9,154 in November; 6,680 in December.

Most folks were still prosperous. Over fifty area residents felt the social and cultural need to pledge $100 each to the 1930 Ramona Pageant.

The United States also remembered her veterans that year. Invalid vets of the World War thanked the Hemet VFW Auxiliary for the Christmas gifts they received. Nationally the government paid pensions to 11 widows of veterans of the War of 1812, 75 widows of the Mexican War, 5,557 soldiers and widows of the Indian Wars and 59,066 soldiers and 180,323 widows of the Civil War.

Material progress proliferated with growing electrification. For example, the radio, a toy and hobby in the early 1920s, had scheduled programs and networks by 1930. Hoover Dam and the Golden Gate Bridge were becoming more than just dreams and plans.

The "moving pictures" were almost all "talkies" by 1930, with new stars appearing: Eddie Buzzell and Alice Day in "Little Johnny Jones," Warner

Baxter in "Romance of the Rio," Ken Maynard and Little Jack Hanlon in the classic "The Wagon Master" and dozens of stars in Florenz Ziegfeld's "Rio Rita."

Prices at the dawn of the depression weren't much different from those in the 1920s. Pork roasts sold for 19¢ a pound, 18 pounds of sugar for $1.00, a dozen eggs 27¢, Ben Hur "Drip" coffee 40¢ a pound and Idaho Russet potatoes 3¢ a pound. For the City of Hemet, the entire budget for 1929 was $16,972, in receipts and $15,995 in disbursements—a budget with a surplus. That was the beginning of the new decade, the 10th Anniversary of the Noble Experiment, a time for renewed hope that soon the dreaded curse of John Barleycorn would end.

That spring, the crash proved to be more than an economic crisis. Countless effects spread throughout the United States, hitting every part of society. The panic, decisions not to buy new cars, radios, refrigerators and sewing machines, full warehouses, lay-offs, insolvent businesses, over-speculation at home and in business, declining sales, defaulting banks, lost savings, even fewer sales, more lay-offs, delinquent taxes, county and state budgets in the red, and more lay-offs, foreclosures—these were some of the effects of the Crash of '29 and a sick economy. Behind all these were millions of personal tragedies and immeasurable tears and sorrows. Thousands lost their homes, moved to riverbeds, to the warmer deserts, anywhere they could find or make shelter. Gathering of hoboes or destitute families lived together in Hoovervilles. Men took to the parks and covered themselves with Hoover blankets—newspapers. News items of local events illustrated the depth of the depression. In San Joaquin County, for example: a 1932 Bankrupt Sale, Central Bazaar Quits, merchandise at cost or below, we must have cash. The Stockton paper printed a delinquent tax list ten pages long, for unpaid taxes of 1931 to 1932. These tax lists did not capture the feelings, the hurt of the individual families. A couple examples might suffice to show what happened throughout the state. John Pierucci, a hardworking Italian in the Stockton area, worked once a week for the county chipping wood, pulling weeds and digging ditches in return for groceries. Food that wasn't "fit for hogs," said Pierucci, bacon fat, not meat, canned mutton, mostly spoiled. As a veteran of the World War he received a special 50-pound sack of flour once in a great while. He raised chickens, sold eggs to pay for feed, worked for public works for $15 a week (30 hours). "Even they tried to cheat you when it came to pay day." In 1933-4 his family had to scrounge for the family's next bite. He helped at the dock, offering to load and unload freight and take goods to the market, not for wages but for a handout of food.[13]

"The salaries of our winery workers varied over the years," according to George Edward Giardino, winery owner, "showing the effects of the depression on labor. In 1919, men received $.65 an hour; 1929, the same; 1930 $.50 an hour; 1931, $2.50 per day; 1932 $.50 per day plus board and room; and

1933, room and board only. Men came in and offered to work for free to get started."

In Menlo Park, Gladys L. Mahan worked for the August Buchman family, businessman and former bootlegger, cooking, cleaning and taking care of the two Buchman children. Her pay: $20 a month including food and room. She paid $20 a month to have her son, George Clifford Mahan, later changed to Clifford James Walker, taken care of. Clothing came from people's hand-me-downs. The Menlo Park Fire Department provided the Christmas with a big tricycle (at least to a small boy, it seemed to be a giant tricycle).

Usually jovial, Governor Jimmy Rolph became more pessimistic. In response to Hoover's pledge that prosperity is just around the corner, Rolph announced to farmers at the Barbara Worth Hotel in Calexico: "I don't know what corner prosperity is behind." Sunny Jim's smiles were a bit cloudy, said the *Imperial Valley Farmer.*[14]

Hoover kept promising and hoping prosperity would come back. In March 1931, Henry Ford said the United States was "prosperous and doesn't know it...the dollar buys 50 percent more," therefore urging support for Hoover's second term.[15]

These economic problems buried the moral issue of prohibition. As happened before and since, the administration in office during a recession or depression received blame for that event. The government in charge received condemnation for the lawlessness, corruption and lack of enforcement of the Volstead Acts. According to common thought, bootleggers, moonshiners, rumrunners and drinkers were not as culpable as politicians or as prohibition itself. How ironic that the law itself was faulted, not the violators, the drinkers who created the demand, or thousands of Californians who looked the other way. Prohibition became the evil. To some, prohibition was the reason the state treasury was so low and counties bankrupt. Taxes should have been coming from bars, nightclubs, breweries, wineries and distilleries, filling depleting state and local treasuries. Illegal bootleggers and moonshiners made millions of dollars and paid no taxes from their ill-gotten gain, while legitimate businessmen lost their businesses and they, in turn, laid off honest workers. The demand for repeal grew with each bank that defaulted, with each speakeasy that siphoned off money from the legal cash flow of the state, and with each worker who lost his job. Economic issues became powerful and inseparable from prohibition issues.

In the summer of 1932, the brewers association promised to spend money to help the economy if beer became legalized.[16]

Prices were still falling in the markets: MJB coffee 35¢ a lb., 2 lbs. 67¢, butter 9¢, Bisquik 35¢/box, cheese 13¢ a pound, bacon $1.09 lb., ham 10¢, and a French lunch at the popular El Cortez Hotel, only $1.00. In Plumas County S & W Coffee fell to 2 pounds for 56¢, potatoes 2¢ a pound. With low funds local governments cut services and cut cost, some going into bankruptcy. Tax rates dropped along with property devaluation of 20 percent.

When drys were pushing for prohibition in 1917-19, their arguments purposely confused patriotism with prohibition. Now at the fight to end prohibition, after the layoffs started in the 1930s, wets used America's economic problems to sway Americans to the side of the repeal. It was not difficult to do—wets learned from the prohibition masters of 1917-1919. Prohibition became the antagonist to economic recovery.

With economic hardships paramount, more Californians noticed the absurdities in the world of prohibition. Instead of talk about rising stock markets, as in 1928-29, talk in 1930-1932 concerned the wrongs in society, the opportunities for jobs and the ridiculous happenings that incensed citizens.

The Bartender's Art

Pleasure boats and cruises offered opportunities for dry Californians to have a little liquid nourishment on occasion. The *S.S. La Playa*, a "palatial Panama pleasure liner," provided southern Californians a chance to take a six-hour cruise to "nowhere." In the summer of '32, the sponsoring company advertised the "thrilling" experience of watching the bartender mix an inexhaustible number of tempting concoctions. "This affable dispenser of liquid boasts of his ability to prepare any drink that a passenger can name." Passengers affirmed his boasts.[17] The bartender practiced his artistry as soon as the ship left the harbor of San Pedro, thus violating state and federal laws. Clarence H. Lee of Palos Verdes wrote to Attorney General William D. Mitchell, that these nightly trips to "nowhere" served liquor and thus must have the illegal alcohol on board in the harbor—a violation of possession. Reminding Mitchell that he recently said the liquor laws would be strictly enforced, Lee asked Mitchell: "Will it not be possible to take action as will avoid this scandal?"

San Francisco Chronicle, December 19, 1932, showed Californians that off-shore partying was a common occurrence for the affluent: The four-masted schooner *James Tuft*, anchored off Venice pier, became the object of a coordinated raid by 65 officers, including police, Coast Guard, and federal agents as a pleasure craft with gambling, drinking and lewd "performance" in the hold of the former fishing barge.

Fifteen young women "hostesses" and perhaps a couple key people evidently became suspicious or were warned and left the boat just before the raid. A thick fog and heavy swells impeded the raiders, most of whom came from a Coast Guard cutter. Thirteen officers boarded earlier disguised as pleasure seekers and when the raid started, fights broke out between the infiltrators and the boat operators. Nineteen men and four women were taken off to jail.

∅

The dry squads were often inept in catching big bootlegging fish, but displayed skill in catching little fry. Clever sleuths caught Stephen Abosonia of Belvedere Gardens, Los Angeles. Two women, operatives of the dry squad, one posing as a sick pregnant lady, came to the house of 91-year-old "Dad" Abosonia. They asked the aged man for a little wine needed for her condition.

"I told them," Abosonia explained to the *Los Angeles Examiner*, "I never sold wine. But the younger woman put her arms around my neck and sobbed as she pleaded with me to sell her some wine for the mother-to-be. I filled a small bottle and gave it to the younger woman. She took a dollar bill from her pocketbook. I would not take it. Then she put the bill in my pocket, explaining it was not for the wine but just a present so I could buy some tobacco."

A half an hour later a constable arrived, left a card for him to appear before Judge E. P. Wood at Belvedere Gardens the next morning. About an hour later four deputy sheriffs arrived in two cars, drank the rest of the wine and took him to jail on a possession charge. The dry squad caught their man, their desperate criminal.

One incensed reader of the story sent a copy to Washington, D. C. Stories like this inflamed Californians and continually reminded them of the hypocrisy of the law.[18]

The Wrong House?

Sometimes prohibition raiders made mistakes. Informers made mistakes, and even federal investigators. Evidently one such mistake occurred at the Bovard house on 1127 E. 65th Street, Inglewood. On February 28, 1931, federal agents raided John K. Bovard's rented house and caused such wanton destruction that his wife became sick and died from a heart attack. After she died Bovard sent a telegram to the Department of Justice complaining. Assistant U. S. District Attorney G. A. Youngquist answered immediately and turned it over to the Director of Prohibition to investigate.[19]

Bootlegging horror stories continued to occupy the press. In Alameda County, an enraged bootlegging prisoner A. S. Brown, 65, attacked agents with an axe. He thrust an ice pick into the stomach of Agent L. C. Jestes, penetrating clothing but stopping at his heavy gun belt.[20]

And tragedies continued and the people had enough! Toward the end of prohibition, teenagers became involved in one way or the other with liquor. Two atypical teen involvements follow; nevertheless these two stories showed what was happening to some of California's younger generation—each with different results.

An incensed citizen sent this photo and article to Wickersham Commission, repulsed at the way agents trapped this old man, Steven Abosonia, to make an arrest. Said Arthur W. Fisher of 836 South Ardmore, L. A.: Incidents like this "make one ashamed of his country." Copied from RG 10, National Archives.

Sixteen Years Old with Wheels and Money
as told by Andy Hollenstein, Carmel Valley

Several of us boys, at 16 years old, pitched in a couple dollars each, bought Puritan Dark Brown Malt, added three pounds of sugar for five gallons, yeast and let it work until it stopped fermenting. Usually we made 15 gallons at a time. We got brown bottles, added ½ teaspoon of sugar per quart just before we capped it. That would make 4 percent beer for ours and our friends' use. We could use five pounds of dark malt per five gallons and that would make strong ale, strong enough that after a couple bottles we could walk up "to a five-foot fence and step over it!" Two of the kids were _____ (inaudible) Nelson and our brewmaster Woodrow ____ (sounds like "Hydro").

Also when I was 16, I drove bottled liquor from a plant in South San Francisco to Red Bishop in Salinas. Two of us kids drove, got $90 each per trip, two trips a week. I bought a brand-new Hudson for $1,600 in 1931, a two-door brougham with overload springs. The plant was a modern cutting factory, where pure alcohol was cut, flavored with juniper flavor and sugar for gin or caramel flavor and brown sugar for whiskey, then bottled with Canadian Club, Gordon's Gin, Burnett's White Satin and other labels. This factory was a large, old brick building, a clean place, workers wearing laboratory white smocks. A high-powered operation. The bottles were put in burlap sacks just as if they came off of a rum boat.

We were given a Thompson sub-machinegun to carry under the dashboard in case of hijackers. When we arrived in Salinas, we delivered it to Red Bishop, walked into the office, got paid our $90 each and by that time the 24 cases, worth $800-900, were unloaded. He sold it. High-class stuff, got the high prices. And I would then go to high school. The other kid was a butcher for Espinoza, earning $18-20 a week. This bootleg whiskey was great stuff. The girls at Salinas High School loved it, and so did the teachers. I had wheels and money at a young age.

We were just getting going good, then the idiots elected Roosevelt. He legalized booze and put us out of business.

People went to the end of Vicente Canyon, bought whiskey for a buck-and-a-half and went to the country dances. Country dances were all over the place, Grange halls, like the Prunedale Grange, churches, dances local at Carmel Valley and down the coast past Big Sur. We paid $1.00, $1.50. The bands usually played older music, and we danced to that, not the Charleston. People brought their liquor in cars as they did after prohibition was over. Bootleggers also sold out of their cars, usually short pints or short half pints (mickeys), with 12 ounces in the pints instead of 16 and 6-7 ounces in the half pints (instead of eight).

Moonshine operations [were] at Buena Vista, on River Road at Daugherty's place. He leased it out, I don't know the arrangements, but sugar was brought in there by the truckload and the trailerload, and whiskey came out by the truckload, in five gallon cans.

Green Mansions out on Old San Juan Grade Road, where Crazy Horse Canyon crosses, was a whorehouse during prohibition times, which bought bootleg liquor and sold it for 50¢ a shot, normal would be 25¢ a shot. Wine $1.50 a gallon for good stuff. Bodogie sold it for years and years. Later Joe and his brother Carl Bodogie (?) opened a store after prohibition. Fernando Espinosa [Frank's father?] was a bootlegger. And across the street Berryessa sold beer, 15¢. Moonshiners used charcoal to get the fusel oils out. Take a shot glass and you can see the fusel oil on top around the edges. Fusel oil is present in all alcohol but it was filtered out of the best. It caused vision problems. Darn good grain alcohol was produced and was filtered and run through a couple of times. That's what they made "imported whiskey out of" [like the liquor made in the South San Francisco plant].

Lower class moonshine was available in the hills. Some people made lower-class beer, beer that was aged with a electric light bulb inside the beer to speed fermentation. It was sold before it aged.

Other means of getting whiskey, you realize this? Ol' Rollen Reeves, our family doctor, used to give my father a prescription regularly of Sandy McDonald. My dad had a lingering malady and old Doc Reeves prescribed Sandy McDonald. This kid Fred McDerr ?, still alive in 1980, visited me quite often. Fred and I would take swallows of my old man's scotch, mark the level with our thumb and fill it up to the original level with water in the bathroom. We had done this several times. My old man didn't drink much, but occasionally he wanted a shot of this bottle. One time we were sitting at the kitchen table at our farm. The door was open and it was a foggy day. My father came in, wanted a shot of it, got it out of the cabinet, took a big swig and "sppuuuthththt"— he spit it out!

"Now God dammit, listen. If you're going to drink my whiskey, that's one thing, but don't ever put water in my whiskey."

All the adults drank and the younger ones drank and the people who had any brains made money out of it. Absolute exercise in futility. Anytime you had laws or regulations that a big percentage of population wanted to disregard, that nullified the law. That was what happened. Never in the history of the world had a law been so disregarded. Anything that was illegal, the profits were high and channeled into a different direction.

"False Gaiety, Wild Parties and Search for Thrills, Blamed for Girl's Death"
by Byrd Weyler Kellogg

As a sordid, unvoiced indictment against existing conditions the body of pretty, vivacious Grace Carrell lies on a local undertaker's slab waiting for the coroner's verdict and a brusque, hushed internment.[20]

Unofficially the verdict now is acute alcoholism, but it does not matter what it is to the dead girl. The cold earth will receive her broken body unquestioning and without discriminating against her.

It does not matter to Mother Earth how her children return to her. With the dazed, helpless mother of Grace Carrell it is different. She cares. She sits in her lonely home, turning over in her anguished mind the things done and the things undone that might have brought a happy ending to her child's life. The mother's tired, protesting body shakes with heartbreaking sobs when she thinks of others' daughters following paths of false gaiety—riding the bottle to death!

Grace Carrell's mother knows the anxious nights, the undisciplined days that swept her own cherished, foolish little girl into the maelstrom of destruction. She fought against it, but was powerless against the great destructive forces that seemed to have rein.

Now she sobs over and over again, "Give them a chance, give the other girls a chance." As she thinks of her friends' daughters and her daughter's friends, she pictures them following the footprints of her own Grace.

She struggled to keep her daughter—her far too pretty daughter—from the corroding influences of today. Now her memory is turning back to the days when her black-haired, willful girl was a tiny baby, a rosebud baby with warm, clinging fingers. These warm little fingers are cold in death, and there is no peace in them now.

The tragedies—the wicked waste of life's promises! This mother knows them all. Her daughter died—died alone in a drunken stupor, because she didn't have a chance, and nobody cared very much.

Who is there to dispute the statement that nobody cared? Certainly not the fathers and mothers of girls whose pastimes lead them to questionable places and absolutely not the parents who can be found in the same places when they know their children are in other quarters.

Grace Carrell was a happy girl, just a girl who liked a good time. Her teachers and friends describe her thus. She would have made good if she had been given a fair chance. Those who knew her best make this assertion in no uncertain terms. They say she was striking looking, and had black hair, black eyes and a strong will. This is the girl who is now gone.

She is dead. She died alone. Her lips must have trembled at the last and she must have cried out in fear, perhaps in loneliness just before her lustrous eyes closed.

To die alone! Mothers whose daughters' feet are straying—she died alone without even a friend to shield her dead body from the eyes of the curious and the morbid.

Never in life did this misguided, unprotected girl know justice, but swift leering death will give it to her. She will sleep in the same earth that covers the pure in heart and the sinner, the rich and the poor.

That, fathers and mothers, will be your only comfort when your sons and daughters round the corner to physical decay. Then they, too, will meet justice in a cold grave.

This poor girl, un-coffined—her simple finery done up in a neat package for her family to claim—lies in the morgue, and she is not the last one who will lie there, sacrificed to a good time.

As long as shiftless parents turn aside from their irrevocable obligations to youth there will be more Grace Carrells—and more, and more.

A simple black dress, a green scarf, a blue coat and decent underwear do not sound like the wardrobe of an habituate of the primrose path, but these are the garments Grace Carrell wore to her last dance.

There is a lust abroad in the land, seeking only the fairest marks—and the harvest will be great unless the death of Grace Carrell awakens this and other communities into a realization that youth must be saved.

A laugh, and drink—and then another—afterward a cold gray slab for a couch!

Is it worth the good time you bluster about, you men and women? It may be to you, but the young folks should have a chance to find out for themselves after they have reached a discriminating age. They may have better wits than you—and a backbone!

Aside from the humanitarian aspect—if people are no longer their brother's keepers—youth has a monetary value. It costs $10,000 to give a child a public school education. Grace Carrell had finished up to the two grades in the high school and was last in school at the part-time high school.

A wasted life and wasted efforts of countless teachers!

Forgive us, Grace Carrell, that we point to you, but death levels all things, and in your narrow tomb you must become a goad to drive selfish, thoughtless men and women back to the safety and sanity of home life.

You will sleep sweeter when illicit liquor rots in its own vats, and no longer robs youth of its opportunity to fashion a world after its own mind.

But those who have helped destroy you and others like you will never find peace here—nor will they ever die with decency.

More Press Pressures

Women's Organization for National Prohibition Reform (WONPR) had formed to add some feminine muscle to the wet cause for reform or repeal of the liquor laws. These women, led by Mrs. Charles Sabin, were some of the richest and most influential in the country. Sabin herself was one of the founders of National Women's Republican Club. WONPR joined the Association Against Prohibition Amendment (AAPA), formed early in 1919 to stop the War Prohibition Act, ameliorate damage done by Amendment 18 and to repeal it.[22] By 1930 these two organizations had clout. For example, they petitioned Congress not to put more money into enforcement of prohibition as the Wickersham Commission recommended. They put money behind candidates who were for repeal. When Franklin D. Roosevelt and the democratic party platform came out for repeal in the spring of 1932, the executive council of WONPR, led again by Sabin, passed the following resolution, 55-22: "We urge the members of our organization to support in the coming election candidates...who are committed to repeal. We, therefore, urge the members of this organization, because they are committed to the cause of repeal, whether they be Republicans or whether they be Democrats, to give their support to the nominee of that party which favors the repeal of the Eighteenth Amendment, Franklin Delano Roosevelt."

That took much for some of the Republican women leaders to do; in fact, a few could not go that far—not enough to cast a vote for a Democrat.

Headlines in the *San Diego Union* reflected the work of WONPA: "1,000,000 women in both parties back Roosevelt in Repeal Fight".[23]

Specious Arguments

Counter arguments for prohibition groups condemned "untruthful and misleading propaganda financed by the liquor interests, which floods the country through...the wet metropolitan press...."[24] The drys ridiculed each new wet voice: the Democratic party spokesmen not really speaking for all Democrats, the American Medical Association being unscientific in attributing any benefits to alcohol as a beverage, even some California Republican County Councils urging repeal and a poll showing lawyers favored repeal. All these were irrelevant [and irreverent] hollow voices.

Said a dry spokesman: "...specious arguing that beer would bring lower taxes, cause crime waves to disappear, fill empty dinner pails, and change us all into angelic, law-abiding prosperous citizens is a modern example of unconscious humor."

Hoover and his Republican advisors used evasive techniques for the wet-dry issue in 1932. It worked in 1928—wets thinking Hoover would not object to changes in the Volstead, drys thinking his stand on enforcing the law and obeying the Constitution meant his support of prohibition, yet few knew how he stood. There was no doubt how Franklin Delano Roosevelt stood. Prohibition repeal would be submitted to the states to vote on; the Volstead Act would be modified immediately. Wet Republicans knew better than to think Hoover was really wet. They moved to the Democratic party by the thousands. Drys had no choice but to try to elect Hoover again. Churches, Anti-Saloon League members and the WCTU kept the faith, hoping faith and right would overcome the evils of alcohol and the horrible economic situation.

Theme Song: "Me"—Call to Arms

At weekly meetings of the WCTU, the ladies kept hope in the face of growing discontent with prohibition. For example, on November 30, 1931, at the Holtville WCTU meeting, the speaker for the program said, "The Present Law Best Way." The wets claimed prohibition cost $213,000,000 in nine years. The WCTU countered that the collection of fines amounted to $460,000,000, and prohibition "was building a new civilization." Before, alcohol consumption was 22 gallons per person a year, down to seven gallons now. The wets claimed liquor taxes would add $400 million in new revenue to the local and federal treasury but auto taxes according to the WCTU were $799 million. The liquor spokesmen claimed liquor industries might employ more. The WCTU said 86,916 more people would, indeed, be employed, but the wool industry employed 364,021. This logic is, of course, *non sequitur*. Assumption here may be that so what if liquor would employ 86,916 more people. Since the wool industry employs over four times as many people, the liquor would be just a minor help to the economy.[25]

WCTU continued holding meetings up and down the state. The Anti-Saloon League in the Barstow area had a party in the hills—a shanty party. It was sponsored by the League and the Four Hundred Club—featuring fried chicken, roasts, refreshments (non intoxicating of course), music and boxing. One might wonder just how this little group of Anti-Saloon Leaguers were going to fight the national trend toward ending prohibition—by boxing them?

In 1931-32 California wets, however, obtained enough signatures to place Proposition 1 and 2 on the November 8, 1932, ballot, abolishing the Wright Act and modifying prohibition laws respectively. Signatures were easy to obtain. Although gangsterism had been around for 40 years, Californians put the blame for the rise in crime on prohibition. A girl in trouble, a death from an automobile accident, open violations of the law, alcohol deaths, political pay-offs—all were caused by prohibition, people said. Because of the depression, California voters went Democratic and most Democrats were wet. The anti-prohibition plank highlighted the Democratic platform for the 1932 presidential campaign.

On November 8, Californians voted 2-1 to abolish the Wright Act, California's enforcement act for the Prohibition Amendment, 1,308,428 to 730,522. Despite *Feather River Bulletin* recommending no votes on Prop. 1 and 2, Plumas County citizens repealed the Wright Act 1828-355, and Prop. 2, 1,614 yes and 538 no. The Jones Act, making possessing a still a felony, was not part of the Wright Act, therefore was on the books. Several other laws were still valid: selling within a mile of Stanford and University of California, selling to minors, selling on election day, selling on school grounds, and nuisance places being able to be abated.[26] As a result of the election, wet Governor Jimmy Rolph stated he was going to let liquor violators out of prison when the Wright Act came off the books at midnight December 18. Governor Rolph kept his word. He went to bed on the 18th planning to sign the pardon certificates in the morning. Rolph, always known for his spontaneity, changed his mind, got out of bed, had his secretary meet him in the Capitol with the pardons and signed them in the wee hours of the morning. Therefore 123 men and six women walked free on the 19th. Since no state liquor violator languished in the San Francisco County jails, he pardoned no one from the city and county of San

Francisco. Most came from Los Angeles County, others coming from San Joaquin, Orange, San Bernardino, Ventura and San Diego counties[27] [see Appendix E].

Editors, before and after the election of 1932, wrote about the high cost of enforcement, taxes spent, windfall profits of illegal breweries and breweries not having to pay taxes on these profits.

The pressure from editors came from all over the state in the fall of 1932. Roosevelt had won the election. Plumas County voters, for example, turned to the Democrats: 1,846 for Roosevelt, 540 for Hoover. With Hoover a lame duck president and the depression worsening each week, the country was ready to end the Noble Experiment.

COME ON, YOU SANTA CLAUS!

This plea appeared in the *San Francisco Chronicle*, December 11, 1932, over a political cartoon, showing Santa Claus, labeled "Congress," carrying a tray of three foaming draught beers. The *Chronicle* asked Congress to give the American people beer for Christmas: HURRY UP, CONGRESS, and pass that beer bill before Christmas.[28]

"No good can possibly come from obstruction. If the present Congress does not give the people beer, the next Congress will.

"Congress cannot make a mistake about the November mandate. The people voted for BEER and asked for it BEFORE CHRISTMAS.

"Beer may not prove a panacea for all our economic ills, but it will at least remove a prohibition that for twelve years has been a source of grave discontent and confusion among the people.

"Millions want to drink an honest glass of beer without hiding behind a bush.

"Congress should pass the best bill it knows how. The President should sign it. That done, arguing over any fine constitutional points raised can be left for the United States Supreme Court.

"Then take up the wine bill after Christmas."

The state already pushed for legalizing wine. Roosevelt had not even been sworn in yet when, in January 1933, Assembly Resolution No. 3 passed the legislature and was sent to Congress, the president-elect and to anyone with power, requesting the right to produce and sell light wines at restaurants and authorized stores. The need for jobs and tax revenue was a major thrust of this resolution.[29]

Another vociferous editor hammered the public in the small desert town of Barstow to cut out the bootlegger. "No more unlicensed distilleries and boot-leggers will be tolerated," said T. G. Nicklin of the Barstow *Printer*, "throwing taxes and other expenses on farmers and businessmen." The next week he predicted legalized beer will end racketeering. Editor Nicklin, pleased with economic prospects with the election of Roosevelt and the probable end to prohibition, said San Bernardino and Kern counties and others now producing grapes will produce more wine and ship the same economically to the east and drink wine at home as in former years. Thousands of farmers in California will appreciate the relief. This will put an end to bootlegging and distilleries and pay the license fee into the public treasury to relieve the taxpayers. "Thousands of political liquor agents and snoopers can seek other employment." Again he wrote, the production of wine and beer will mean industry and millions of dollars to California. "Large stocks are now in storage awaiting legal action which will put bootleggers out of business and pay a fair share of the taxes."[30]

On December 29, 1932, Nicklin had a 3-inch article on liquor taxes going to the towns and cities, giving encouragement to the people. The last four months of 1932 saw a deepening of the depression. More hoboes walking the streets and more riding the Union Pacific and the Santa Fe through Barstow and hoboing in the trees along the dry Mojave River bed. Nicklin said that millions of hoboes who did not vote in the November election must now find winter homes.

Prices dropped further: onions almost a penny a pound, grapes were less than 3¢ a pound, cabbage 1½¢ a pound. At Pendleton's Market one could buy 15 pounds of potatoes for 25¢, a three pound can of Crisco 57¢. Nearby a desert resident could buy a used 1929 Chevrolet for only $200. At Milletts Dining Room in Daggett, one could buy a leg of pork dinner with apples and sweet potatoes for 50¢, a chicken dinner for 65¢. One restaurant offered a Thanksgiving dinner for 40¢.

An advantage to the desert towns along the new Route 66 and Route 91 was the increase in tourists and travelers into California. Over 49,000 cars came into California in July, almost 40,000 in August. Auto courts opened and survived along with restaurants and filling stations.

As in the rest of the state, life went on that fall. Barstow Union High School had its first football team. Clubs met, churches helped feed the poor. Hinkley, northwest of Barstow, remained dry. The WCTU still proclaimed the goodness of prohibition, yet clandestine moonshiners operated in Lucerne Valley, along the Mojave River, at springs and in and around Harper Lake—west of the dry ladies of Hinkley.

Nicklin continued his pressure to effect a change in the laws the next three months. But the drys hadn't given up. The January 26, 1933, *Printer* printed an article from *The California Liberator*, describing the upcoming dry fight in a battle metaphor: "In the recent election they [drys] suffered another defeat. The wet attack was made on the front line holding the advance outpost—Prohibition. This line was broken in many places from coast to coast." By popular votes California, Oregon, Washington, Michigan and Arizona repealed state enforcement acts. The next Congress was probably wet. The next president was.

"It is likely that an article repealing the Eighteenth Amendment will be submitted to the states by the incoming Congress. A major battle is ahead for the drys and the immediate concern is to get ready for it."

President-elect Roosevelt recommended repeal of Amendment 18. The lame duck Congress passed the first step to repeal: it proposed the repeal amendment calling for state conventions to ratify Amendment 21. The new amendment must now be ratified by 36 states. "Machinery is now in motion to put liquor on the tax list, and cut out the bootlegger," said Editor Nicklin of the *Barstow Printer*. He also reported that the county dry raiders put three more moonshine operations out of the distillery business. At the same time a legal one started as the Pacific Brewery and Malting Co. of San Francisco incorporated for $2,000,000. One director said, "We are sure that legalized beer will become a reality by June 1." He was right.

Again this editor told of the battle strategy of the drys. Although it may appear anticlimactic, the drys would concentrate on 20 traditional dry states to block repeal. California was not one of these. It was over in California. Prohibitionists agreed the wets were organized better than before—money, leadership, literature and speakers. Drys had less money and fewer leaders like the late Wayne B. Wheeler who by sheer force of his personality and political acumen drove the Eighteenth Amendment through Congress fourteen years before.

William Borah of Idaho argued the moral strength will "pick up speed as the campaign proceeds....So as the state legislatures pass legislation providing for conventions in several states, the battle is on." Some drys planned to stop states from having a convention.

COME ON, YOU SANTA CLAUS!   —   By Arg

"Come on, You Santa Claus!"—The election of 1932 insured a wet Congress and President, Roosevelt, would take office in 1933. California and several other states repealed their liquor enforcement acts and demanded that 3.2 beer and light wine be legal. San Francisco Chronicle, December 11, 1932.

Their efforts were nugatory.

Michigan did not wait long. The state held the first repeal convention, voting overwhelmingly for repeal—99-1.

Within two weeks after Roosevelt took office on March 4, he gave the shortest presidential message recorded—only 72 words—urging Congress to amend the Volstead Act:

"I recommend to the Congress the passage of legislation for the immediate modification of the Volstead Act in order to legalize the manufacture and sale of beer and other beverages of such alcoholic content as is permissible under the Constitution; and to provide through such manufacture and sale, by substantial taxes, a proper and much needed revenue for the government. I deem action at this time to be of the highest importance."

The new House of Representatives immediately passed a bill allowing 3.2 percent beer by volume. The House dubiously, of course, considered this the highest limit they could allow as not legally being intoxicating. The Senate wanted 3.02 percent using a British Commission report that 3.02 was the legal non-intoxicating limit, but the Senate compromised by accepting 3.2. The Senate also wanted wine legalized and a law prohibiting sale to 16-year-olds. A compromise bill omitted both Senate proposals. The federal government placed $5.00 a barrel tax on beer and a brewery license fee of $1,000 a year. Revenue of $5.00 a barrel helped the treasury with an additional $125,000,000. The bill passed by a non-partisan vote, with 238 Democrats for and 58 against; 72 Republicans for, 39 against, and 5 Farmer-Labor members for. Twenty members did not vote. Forty-three senators voted for, 30 against, again non-partisan. The bill became effective 15 days after the President signed it. Therefore in early April 1933, beer became non-intoxicating. It was then up to the states to allow or not allow this new non-intoxicating beer. The states could choose to accept the 1933 miracle of Congress.

The vote for repeal was the reverse of 1918-19, a David and Goliath struggle but in this case instead of bone-dry forces being the giant, it was the wets. The drys had lost, lost years before with eroded laws, open loopholes, hypocrisy of law makers and law enforcers, opportunity for making money, and in some cases for surviving hard times, the market in California for any kind of liquor, and finally apathy of those who did not drink but kept quiet and looked the other way.

CHAPTER 28

HAPPY DAYS ARE HERE AGAIN

Dos Palos Prepared for Some Legal Cold Ones

Spring 1933, the school board in Dos Palos had assured the parents that there was enough money to pay teachers for the rest of the school term. Almost weekly, news hit the papers on problems of Europe and then about a hitherto unknown person in Germany: Adolph Hitler. Since Americans voted Hoover out of office, these suffering American people waited to see what miracles President Franklin Roosevelt and the new Congress could achieve. Upon Roosevelt's recommendation Congress created a miracle—like in the New Testament when Jesus changed water into wine. Congress outdid the miracle makers of old. It changed alcoholic beer into a non-alcoholic beverage. John Barleycorn became a soft drink.

After Congress made 3.2 beer non-intoxicating, the jobless lawyers should be kept busy, according to Mac McLeese, in his weekly column "Just Between Friends," in the *Dos Palos Star.* Now that 3.2 is not intoxicating, therefore not illegal, why does the same federal law prohibit "its sale or transportation within dry territories, indicating that it is intoxicating, else it should have free sale the same as other soft drinks." It's the same drink as before when "so many went 'to the mat.'" Said McLeese: "How come a license tax to sell this 'soft' drink, when Coca Cola flows so freely? But why worry? With plenty of good canal water and a dependable ice plant, we'll pull through the summer, somehow, beer or no beer."

The beer came. On April 7, 1933, the state received its tax of 62¢ a barrel. The annual license for hotels and eating establishments to serve beer was $50.00, and $10.00 for off-premises sale. No one under 19 years old was allowed to buy the new beer. No one under 19 could buy the new soft drink? Dos Palos Drug Store, Moore Drug Store, Dos Palos Recreation Parlor were well stocked with bottles of beer. Most sold it for 25¢ a pint for mid-western, like Schlitz and Pabst, and 15¢ for California brew. Brewers already packed the beer in cases to be sold for home consumption.

A sad state of affairs existed however: **THE TOWN WAS OUT OF PRETZELS!** Some places had no beer, but had pretzels; Dos Palos had the reverse. Three major pretzel factories were going in the United States. Since the election of Franklin Roosevelt, these factories did their patriotic duty to meet the demand, but the orders kept coming in. Not since the Great War did they work so hard, worked around the clock for such a great cause. America's industrial potential manifested itself in this crisis.

G. H. Kinney received the first truckload of legalized beer into town. He went to El Dorado Brewing Company at Stockton, early to avoid traffic, yet he got himself hemmed in for 12 minutes. April 7 was a day for celebration for the breweries with mayors, stockholders, official beer tasters and bathing beauties—all there to give beer a proper send off!

Mac McLeese said he heard that "Adeline" bands, pretzels, bartenders with mustache wax have been taken out of the attic to give the pre-Volstead boys a realistic setting. The lads of '33 put Uncle Sam on its feet by switching from Coca Cola to 3.2 lager. These boys were raised on jazz, Jamaica gin and TNT, so 3.2 beer and tunes like "Sweet Adeline" will be as invigorating as a funeral march. McLeese thought that the Boys of '33 will hold their noses and gurgle as much as their stomach can take on "New Beer's Day." After all it is the patriotic thing to do—to keep Uncle Sam from going to the poor house.

Constable Campbell reacted rapidly after the first day or so of legal, non-intoxicating 3.2 beer. He had to arrest Tom Ervine and Joe Barlot at the Saturday night celebration at the Dos Palos Park Pavilion. Perhaps they just wanted to test to see whether beer was really non-intoxicating. They found out something they probably didn't know before: The government did not tell the truth. It wasn't the pretzels, that's for sure.

"I will not tolerate drunkenness or rowdyism on public streets, at dances or in public places," said Campbell. "Those who violate this edict will be forthwith locked up."

The *Star* and other papers urged citizens to register to vote on the June 6 repeal election. Perhaps enough Californians had their fill of moonshine and soon good liquor could be legal. The fight in California for repeal commenced.

Fort Bragg had beer on April 7. Ward Reis became a local distributor. He paid $50 a year for a wholesale license and $20 per year for retail. He paid the Custom House in San Francisco, and bought his beer from the California Brewing Association. The beer was released from San Francisco brewers. Reis sold wholesale beer in cases only. Home Restaurant in Fort Bragg announced it had beer and all kinds of sandwiches for 10¢, regular lunch specials for 40¢ and ham and eggs for 35¢. They had "Private Booths for Ladies and Gentlemen."

One city that wasn't so lucky was Modesto. The dry ordinances of that city prevented the sale of the amber fluid in Modesto. Festoons of black crepe from which hung empty bottles adorned the north and south entries to the city. But generous citizens and officials from Stockton and Merced extended hearty invitations to "Modestians to come and quench their parched throats."[1] Los Gatos, guided by a long prohibition tradition like Pasadena, took no action to legalize beer. Ceres, Carmel and Pacific Grove, Berkeley, Riverside and Palo Alto voted no beer. Since Palo Alto remained dry, the *San Jose Mercury* said, "Menlo [Menlo Park] will be a beer oasis for Stanford Folk." And the old pre-prohibition saying would apply once more to a new generation of Stanford students: "Here's the road to Menlo as plain as can be..." Menlo Park planned to ignore the one and one/half mile from Stanford rule since 3.2 beer was voted non-intoxicating by Congress. Menlo usually ignored the law during prohibition anyway.[2] Most northern California cities, however, received their beer. Saratoga had legal beer for the first time in 40 years. Gilroy made sure it did not have saloons and the ones owning licenses had to be citizens of Gilroy for a year. Licenses varied but were $150 a year for wholesale and $100 retail in Gilroy; San Jose required $200 a year for 10 wholesalers and 65 retailers with on-sale permits for restaurants and hotels serving meals. For off-sale, package stores, $100 per year and 37 received their permits.

At 12:01 a.m. on April 7, beer left breweries all over the state. Trains loaded with beer in San Francisco headed north to Oregon and 111 carloads of beer took the Southern Pacific south toward southern California and Arizona, called "The Midnight Ride of Legal Beer!" One California brewer dispatched a case of beer to the governors of Oregon, Washington and Arizona.[3] A few cities made legislative mistakes. Though beer became legal at 12:01, it was not legal in San Jose until 1:00 a.m. Perhaps a few San Joseans thought about impeachment charges against the councilmen. But they probably forgot about it when they heard about San Franciscans' faux pax; they made it legal at 6:00 a.m. So much for the planned midnight legal beer parties. A few parties went on anyway, as citizens from the City never went without. They had beer for an early breakfast.

One-half million cases flowed out of Los Angeles for beaches, mountains, deserts and Arizona. Unfortunately L. A. didn't authorize beer for themselves until the end of the month. Hundreds of Angelinos were employed so could now afford to drink beer—but had to go out of the city to do so. Prohibition agents were kept busy making sure beer did not leave the breweries early. Frothy brew was illegal in Long Beach but flowed anyway—into the gutters as police caught a truckload trying to sneak into Long Beach. An actor in Hollywood was to use near beer in his movie scene of drinking, but since there was no near beer around, directors forced him to drink real beer, well 3.2 beer anyway. "Tough, tough," responded the actor as he smiled.[4]

The capital became "bone dry" on the second day. Sacramento drank its supply and all the reserve the first day beer was legal. Drinking the "foamy flood" for breakfast, dinner and supper and in between times. The demand was ten times the supply. Appeals to local overworked brewers met with little results.

And the breweries were overworked. The three large San Francisco breweries could not supply the demand that came from the west coast states, including Nevada and Arizona. Some cities were bone dry before noon. Some breweries barred their door, despite the pounding of demanding customers with empty trucks waiting in vain. A near draught existed, but the workers had to obtain some sleep. It was "beyond endurance," said one brewmaster. Some took a brewer's holiday.[5] Brewery orders were well beyond their "wildest dreams," said a spokesman for Rainier Brewing. They planned to enlarge so they could produce 500,000 kegs.

U. S. Attorney General Webb announced to the country: "In the absence of any state legislation on the subject there is no reason why beer cannot be sold in the cities and counties." If a state later changes, he said, the state law superseded local law if there is a conflict.[6]

Ending Imperial County Prohibition

When the federal government took off the restrictions to 3.2 beer, Holtville City Attorney D. B. Roberts announced in the *Holtville Tribune*, "City Law on Liquor Still Is Effective" although "under the program of the national congress alcoholic beverages of 3.2% was legalized throughout the nation...."[7]

Besides Imperial County having strict liquor ordinances, patterned after the Volstead Act, many towns like Holtville had liquor restrictions on the deeds, even with a forfeiture clause such as George Chaffey had required when he subdivided Etiwanda and Ontario as well as part of the Imperial Valley. Roberts announced the city council wouldn't act without a petition and suggested that the State of California repeal its "local option laws" which would automatically eliminate local liquor ordinances.

The next week both sides were active. WCTU had a spirited meeting, singing a poem "Bring Them Back," put to the tune of "My Bonnie Lies Over the Ocean." Anti-prohibitionists had circulated a petition obtaining signatures of 80 percent of the Holtville voters to make Holtville competitive with El Centro and other valley towns that were allowing 3.2 beer. On Wednesday, April 5, 1933, the city allowed beer to be sold, corresponding with Assembly Bill 2336, governing beer traffic. The *Tribune* announced Friday: "City Allows Beer Sale Today" and in smaller print: "still no sign of drunkenness." On-sale—off-sale licenses were to be issued, but since no provision had been made at the time, sales that week were made without licenses. Perhaps Holtville broke the record from petition to downing legal beer in just a little over a week. City fathers were either super efficient or they were just chauvinistic enough not to let Imperial beat them out of a sell—or perhaps just thirsty, very thirsty.

"Beer Is Just A Drink Now" was the headline on April 14, 1933. The understated story showed how quickly the beer restrictions ended after the 14-year drought—and for Holtville an end to prohibition they had since it was founded.

"Beer...ceased to be a novelty by yesterday and was being accorded its place among beverages without the big ado of last weekend. Practically all seasoned drinkers had at least a nip of it yesterday; many not so 'hardened' had sipped just a tiny bit, and those selling it admitted even some of the church members had looked at the bottle a little trustfully but were reluctant to disclose names."

That first week, ten cases arrived for Holtville drinkers. The small town sold their allotment in less than two hours when reinforcements had to be obtained from El Centro—ten more cases. These also disappeared down the thirsty throats. From eleven o'clock on the town was as dry as it was for the previous 25 years. Saturday, however, found several places selling and rationing beer to help quench the thirst accumulated over the years (legally speaking). There was no rowdyism, only one arrest, a celebrant having had more than the 3.2 volume percentage allowed by law. Perhaps he was just seeing if the beer was really non-intoxicating.

In less than two months after Roosevelt took office, Holtville issued licenses to selected stores and restaurants—public eating places with tables. Violators would face a 90-day county jail sentence or a $300 fine or both. The city taxed sellers $6 a quarter for on-sale, drinking on the premises and $10 per year for-off sale.

Each week the *Tribune* had ads from El Centro and Holtville. For example: "Tacoma Beer: The Best in the West; call 1470—will deliver 480 Main St., El Centro." Maggio Brothers announced they were going to build a brewery for Imperial Valley, a branch of Maier Brewery Co. from Los Angeles. Fifty thousand dollars were to be expended to build and equip the new facility. By July 14, Maggio Brothers distributed Maier Beer, draft and bottled. July 21, Acme Beer came to Holtville at Nell's Drive-In Market, 225 Fifth Street. A one-third page ad for Eastside Beer announced a 600,000 gallon output by August 15. They claimed aging for months, promising not to hurry the process. By August, Nell's Drive-In had 24 hour service to help Eastside sell a share of the annual production. The desert town also did its share to help the national economy. Beer on ice sold for 14¢ a bottle, no tax, 20 varieties to choose from at $2.90 a case.

By September 1, the 1,700 citizens of Holtville had the following brands: Kings, Edelweiss, Tacoma, Tavern Pale, Golden State, Pickwick Ale, Acme, Eastside, Pilsner and Rainier. Ellis Pool Hall, 484 Holt Avenue, promoted a free barbecue with, "ABC pitcher beer in the Beer Garden."

WCTU had certainly lost the war but kept its good works by encouraging Christian living. Members had pot lucks, elections of officers, lectures, such as "Old Fashion Christian Home," dinners honoring mothers and reports of Mrs. Grace Walker on child welfare. On May 26, 60 attended the WCTU Mothers and Babies program.

From the other side of the border came a quick reaction to California beer sales. On July 7, Mexicali counterattacked: "We serve 6% beer (not 3.2). The line [border] is open all night. At the Owl Club in Mexicali—Bock beer 5¢

a glass and 'a quart of beer every 10 minutes to those on the lucky seat." In September the Owl had a one-third page ad in the *Tribune* stressing 6% beer and a new feature: "Pretty girls, Beautiful girls, Gorgeous girls." Quarts of beer sold for 40¢, later reduced to 35¢, Bock for 5¢ and cocktails 35¢. By November legal beer in California caused ghost towns along the border: Algadones virtually deserted, a reporter announced; 58 bars closed in Tijuana on Friday, April 7.

Non-intoxicating beer helped California's economy. Director of San Francisco relief, C. M. Wollenberg, praised the work provided by legalizing 3.2 beer: "Since beer came back, a total of 5,025 [unemployed] have been able to leave the city's relief rolls." Farmers also improved their lot. The price of hops, for example, soared to a high of 50 ¢. The California breweries planned to use surplus corn, rice and barley. Another benefit from the legal sale of beer: Someone estimated the U. S. Government made $10,000,000 in beer revenue the first part of April.[8] Two Lodi wineries received permission to make 3.2 wine, increasing to four wineries with that right.

In May, the freighter *"American"* unloaded in San Pedro 21 tons of roller skates from New York and 35 tons of Boston Beer. Just in time for thirsty Southlanders. Pretzels were still in demand. Libraries were emptied of all books that had pretzel recipes.

Fort Bragg Advocate had an article in May 31,1933, from Major A. V. Dalrymple, National Prohibition Director, that estimated 50,000 speakeasies were driven out of business. Dalrymple reorganized his department by putting alcohol, drugs and related industries under one official.[9]

Los Angeles City Council was a little slow in eliminating the "Little Volstead Act." They did not put it up to vote until May 2, 1933. Therefore they had legal beer about 30 days after the more aggressive cities in California.[10]

In Quincy, the "action on beer" was deferred for a Thursday, April 6, 1933. In the meantime Plumas County supervisors repealed unanimously the "little Volstead Act." A burden was taken off of the desk of the county District Attorney S.C. Young.[11]

In the same paper the PTA had a milk fund drive for undernourished children in the county. The economic problems of the whole country manifested itself in these little counties of California. The sale of beer would improve some of the depression mood and would improve the economics of the county and the coffer of the Plumas County treasury.

On May 4 and May 11, the *Feather River Bulletin* announced the Beer Ordinance for Plumas County. Off-sale licenses sold for $20 per year, good for one year; on-sale permit for restaurants, hotels and clubs was $50 per year. The ordinance stipulated that no one convicted of a felony or convicted of violating a liquor law and no wholesaler or brewer could have a retail liquor license. The brewer's fee was $100, with a tax of $.62 on a barrel. The on-sale beer could only be sold in eating establishments, thus placating the Anti-Saloon people. No one under the age of 19 could buy the beer.

Hotel Quincy Company announced that it was the distributor of Schlitz Beer in April. Telephone Quincy 100 for orders over the telephone. By June, the early summer season, the beer was flowing. "Join the Crowd!" went one ad for the dances with music every Saturday at Happy Hollow. "Ice Cold Beer on Draught," announced the ad. The Globe Brewing Company of 1401 Sansome Street, San Francisco, advertised in Quincy for a beer distributor who was financially able and capable to serve the county efficiently.

On-sale licenses were held by C. L. Gandy of the Quincy Hotel; Tom Niclas, Peter Niclas, P. Brombal, Capital Pool Hall; Ray Ferguson, C. E. Walter, Coffee Shop; R. E. Lozano and the California Fruit Exchange. The county issued off sale permits to Pyper and Rowse, Minnie Lee West (Vest?), J. C. Cloman, T. F. Trusty, Coykenail and Morgenthaler, F. M. Waite, Damon and Hamilton, W. E. Frick, G. R. Sobrio, Hamilton Meat Market and E. I. Lane.

"National drinkers will now pay some of the taxes this spring and summer, easing the burden from the farmer and other property owners," said Nicklin, vocal editor of the *Printer* in Barstow. The *Printer* of April 13, 1933, announced: **"IT IS HERE. SOMETHING YOU'VE BEEN WAITING FOR, FOR THE PAST FOURTEEN YEARS. REAL BEER,"** at Julian Smith's Pool Hall, 104 East Main St., Barstow.[12] Then Honolulu Jim's announced "Virginia Baked Ham and Beer." The Do Drop Inn on Main Street advertised: "Yes, We Have Beer—15¢." A week later Milletts put in a small ad: "We serve beer."

California and thirteen other states had beer by April 7, and five others okayed it before July 1.

But in a way, one could feel something was going on that was right. Legal businesses were prospering by selling beer. They would be paying taxes, hiring a few more people and the money would be doing some good for the economy. It was as if putting down a few beers a week was the patriotic thing to do. The citizens of the Mojave Desert were, indeed, patriotic. And still are.

Most people had to scramble for jobs and ways to obtain food during these deep depression days. Conversations centered on the crashing of the Navy's dirigible *Akron*, with only four of 77 surviving. Ruth Judd murder case was a topic. That spring, movie theaters competed for fewer dollars in circulation. Spencer Tracy and Joan Bennett starred in "Me and My Gal," James Cagney in "Hard to Handle," and Bela Lugosi in "White Zombie."

Carrots fell to 1¢ a bunch, Swift Ham 17¢, butter 19¢, eggs 25¢ for two dozen, 16 oz. cans of pork and beans for only 4¢. Rexall drug stores started its one cent sale, one item and one cent for a second item.

Let's Try Some of These
as told by Allen Lehman, Crescent City

Joe Smith, the owner and the cook [of the Surf Hotel] ran the dining room. Smith and I had an experience with the first legal beer in 1933. Beer came in town and a friend of mine Andrew Rozia, Italian Swiss, came in 1933 and talked me into taking out for almost nothing an off-sell liquor license for beer and wine. We were all struggling in those days. I took over my father's meat market and little grocery store. Rozia took on the wholesaleship of selling Schenley's and Budweiser Beer and the wine from a couple wineries. He became very wealthy at it.

Our store wasn't a very big store then. The "off-sell" meant you couldn't drink it on the place naturally. So I took it out right at the beginning. When I sold my business seven years ago I sold that with it. Twelve-fourteen thousand bucks was added to the price because of that license.

This Joe Smith came over when I got my first shipment. He was a good customer of ours, bought all his meat from us. When it first came out, every brewery tried to make as strong a drink as possible. Some of it got up to 18 per cent. Even though 3.2. per cent was the limit, it was 18.2 or 18.3. It didn't take more than two or three bottles to put you away.

"Joe, goddammit, here's a case of some kind of beer, let's try it."

Joe and I went out the back room where we had our groceries. I put a few cases in our refrigerator, walk-in box where we kept our meat. We sat down on some boxes of groceries. I brought out a couple of bottles of that beer. Hell, before I got rid of that first bottle I could feel it. I knew I had a drink. Anyway we ended up he and I drinking three or four bottles.

He never cooked the meal at the hotel that night. His wife ended up cooking the dinner menu. She wasn't too happy with him.

When Joe left I went up stairs in the little office there. I had a cot in it. I laid down on the cot. It took me two or three hours to get up. My cousin, my manager, kept the place open and later closed up.

ꙮ

The state approved 3.2 beer officially on April 27, 1933 with state on-sale permits costing $50 per year and off sale consumption $10 a year. Manufacturing licenses were $100, and tax was $.62 for every barrel not over 32 gallons. The on-sale license had a feature that affected Californians for decades to come. Consumption on premises meant that only bona fide restaurants and eating places, hotels, clubs and boarding houses could serve liquor. This ended saloons as Californians had known them. Clubs, which looked like saloons or bars, had to be food-serving places, "to be consumed only with meals furnished in good faith at regular public tables, or at eating counters at which said guests and patrons are seated." Therefore, no bar or saloon *per se.*

The act allowed local option for cities and counties. The same legislature also required no liquor be sold within one mile of a university and one and one half mile from a veterans home.[13]

State Convention for Repeal

The June 27, 1933, election called for a repeal convention within 40 days and chose 22 convention delegates to vote for or against repeal of the 18th Amendment. Electors picked one delegate from each congressional district either for or against repeal. Two were chosen from the state at large. The repeal convention was held on July 24 in the Senate Chamber. It could have been completed in half the time as one delegate later said. It was very ceremonial, with speeches of lofty goals and high responsibilities. The 22 delegates had comic relief with Will Rogers and discussed taxes which had nothing to do with repeal. The voting just took a few minutes and repeal passed overwhelmingly, 22 for and 0 against. The *Sacramento Union* said on July 27, 1933: "The things men do are bigger than they are. We forget the actors in life's drama but the play lingers long in memory." Imogene G. Hook of Victorville was one of the delegates and was chairman of the Committee on Credentials—at least one delegate will be remembered. California voted to change the Constitution and waited for the rest of the 36 states needed for repeal.

At 3:04 p.m. the same day California's Secretary of State Frank C. Jordan mailed the results to Cordell Hull, President Roosevelt's Secretary of State. Californians reacted with their eyes open this time and voiced their opinions on the fourteen years of the "Noble Experiment."[14]

Reaction to the number of states voting for repeal encouraged businessmen to plan for opening liquor dealerships, bars and saloons and clubs. Many invested early to be ready when liquor became legal. In order to avoid unnecessary loss by exuberant liquor dealers, California's Board of Equalization clarified the law. State voters abolished the Wright Act in November 1932, but the vote strictly prohibited "public saloons, bars or drinking places where intoxicating liquors are sold. "Even light liquors, wine or beer, consumed on premises must conduct a regularly established restaurant or eating place."[15] In November of 1933, the state took up tax measures of 3.2 beer. All beer over 3.2 sold would be reported to the federal agents. During the previous two months 6,444,425 gallons of taxable beer had been sold to thirsty Californians.[15]

Wineries and grape producers prepared themselves in anticipation of producing legal wine. In September, in San Francisco they held the biggest wine and grape industry conference in 14 years. The conferees had to be pleased with the results of the legalized 3.2 beer. National news pleased the members also. Vermont and Maine, two Protestant strongholds, swung toward repeal. Maryland, Colorado and Minnesota had just voted for repeal. Their activities of buying new machinery, repairing old machinery and buildings, hiring new

514

workers, helped the depressed area in Humboldt County: in Ukiah—Mansueto Guidi and California Grape Products; Capella—Fornasero Bros. and Peter Rovera—Yorkville, Albert J. Gianoli, Ed Zina—Gualala, Charles Ciapusci.[16]

State news took over the headlines of December 1, 1933, when a mob of angry people caravaned down El Camino Real from San Francisco, gathering more people as it passed through Peninsula towns. The mob, incensed over the kidnapping and killing of 22-year-old Brooks Hart, took killers Homes and Thurmond out of the San Jose jail and lynched them. Supposedly Governor Rolph knew the plans and refused to do anything. Soon he was nicknamed Governor Lynch. This diversion from the depression imbedded itself into the minds of Peninsula people for years to come. The author remembered in the early 1940s people recounting what they remember about that day.

And by the time the lynching excitement ended, Utah became the 36th state to ratify the 21st Amendment. Roosevelt announced on the morning of December 5, 1933, that prohibition was over. Drinking or not drinking was now up to the states.

Vai Brothers preparing Padre Wine for the end of prohibition in 1933. Via won the right to buy Baumgarteker's Cucamonga Winery several years after he disappeared in November 1929 for not turning his winery and distillery over to bootleggers. According to son Herbert Baumgarteker other "less-shady" wineries should have been able to buy it. Courtesy of National Archives, # 306-NT-727-25.

CHAPTER 29

A WOODEN SANDWICH MAKES A DRINK LEGAL

A Ford V-8 traveled up the El Camino Real from Los Angeles to San Francisco, 442 miles, in just 6 hours, 41 minutes. Austin E. Elmore raced at an average of 66.134 miles per hour. From then on little California kids could ride their tricycles on the sidewalks, yelling "Going like sixty!"[1] Speeding children used that expression for years to come.[1]

Depression prices dropped further as sugar fell to ten pounds for 46 cents, bacon 15¢ a pound, ham 10¢ per pound, bread 12¢ for a large Langendorf loaf.

At Ft. Bragg the Red Cross distributed clothes on Franklin Street to needy citizens. Californians had already voted for repeal in the summer and were just waiting for the 36th state to ratify the repeal amendment.

State after state ratified the 21st . When Ohio, Pennsylvania and Utah were ready to vote for repeal, *Fort Bragg Advocate* said in November 1933, repeal was "just around the corner...The liquor-ring racketeer and his henchmen will have to take to the want ads, or pawn shops, for few of them are said to have saved their ill-gotten gains during our noble experiment." According to *Stockton Record*, December 4, 1933, $100,000 liquor supply awaited dry repeal in Stockton stores. Prices of bootleg liquor dropped as Stockton readied for another celebration. When Utah, the 36th state, voted for repeal, prohibition ended, on December 5, 1933. On that day, in 1 ½" headlines the *Stockton Record* announced: NATION GOES "WET." "In some of the 18 states that will be able to drink tonight, some people will have to stand, in some states the drinker has to sit and in others he has to take it home and drink it. In California he must take it home but can have beer or wine by the glass at restaurants. The *Dos Palos Star* announced "Whiskey Flows Legally after 13 Years." No unusual hilarity, said the *Star.*[2]

On December 6, the editor of the *Advocate,* in Fort Bragg, calmly announced liquor "became legal yesterday." People can drink a different drink than they were used to with the so-called prohibition. Repeal would help government finances. "Large hip pockets will go out of style," the editor said. The man with a hip flask will not be trusted; before they were known as "smart, a man who knew how to put it over."[3]

The State Board Of Equalization asserted it was responsible for liquor enforcement, but actually the prodigious job required that it be handled by local authorities. "Liquor may be drunk in the streets, in hotel rooms, in any place except the place of sale or in public dining rooms. Wine

516

and beer may be sold by hotels and restaurants having license and served with meals, but not so with hard liquor."

Of course, the relaxed enforcement and interpretation of the law varied. Boiled eggs, pickled eggs, sausages, pretzels, peanuts are all food but were not meals by state definition. Neither was the wooden sandwich one bar had that the owner would set on the bar and say, "Yes, we have food, see here, I'm legal," and the crowd laughed as he pointed to the wooden sandwich.

Last Prohibition Arrest in San Francisco

Anton Friscovich had the honor of being the "last man to be arrested under prohibition club." He ran a rooming house where "agents found his personal supply of personally made brew for personal use" and confiscated it. The U. S. Prohibition Commissioner refused to prosecute him under the Volstead act. At the time he was arrested in the morning of December 5, there was a Volstead Act, but by the time he had his hearing Utah had already passed the repeal amendment and prohibition was over.[4]

President Franklin Roosevelt announced the end of prohibition with the following words of faith: "I trust the good sense of the American people that they will not bring themselves the curse of excessive use of intoxicating liquors to the detriment of health, morals and social integrity."

Celebration Time

One would think the nation would celebrate December 5, 1933, when prohibition ended—the first legal time to drink hard liquor in 14 years. The nation would be like a boy saying, "Wait till my 21st birthday. I'm really

Celebration of Repeal of the 18th Amendment December 5, 1933, at San Francisco's famed Palace Hotel. Photo courtesy S. F. Public Library.

going to tie one on!" This was not the case, especially in San Francisco, where booze had been available any time during prohibition.

Dorothy and Wayne Rossiter hired a baby sitter for their son Gary, went to San Francisco to see how wild the City would become. They expected a celebration like the one that ended the World War. Not so. Crowds were just a little larger than normal. The celebration subdued—a dinner, order of wine or brandy or legal Canadian whiskey.[5]

Los Angeles bar ready for legal drinks on December 5, 1933, the end of National Prohibition. Courtesy of National Archives, # 306-NT-727-4. Looks as if the man in the foreground was getting a head start.

When prohibition ended, said William Genini of San Francisco, there was some rejoicing by some people, more because I believe the great promise of all the jobs this would create during the depression, than because of the idea of legally being able to get booze, because booze of every sort was always available during prohibition.[7] Many went to their former speakeasies, walked in and ordered their favorite drink, just as they were doing in San Franciso several months before. In fact, a little of the excitement had been taken away with the end of prohibition. The *Sacramento Bee* reported,

518

"Sacramento arose from bed and shook its head and discovered her day-after-repeal hangover was no worse than the usual one."

In January, when the law of supply and demand leveled off, the prices of fortified wine were $1.00 for a fifth, $1.25 quart, $3.00 gallon. Whiskey sold for $.85-3.50 for full pints, 65¢ for half pints. A two-ounce bottle of bottled cocktail cost 20¢.[7]

The Repeal from "The Era of Prohibition"
by Ernest D. Wichels, Vallejo

The ratification of the 21st Amendment (Repeal) had been anticipated and many taverns and dealers had previously mailed in their applications to Sacramento. Most were in business on December 6, 1933—but the merchandise seemed hardly different from the "quality" served by the speakeasies. It would take time to restore business as usual.

The *Vallejo Evening Chronicle* seemed unaffected by the repeal. It was hardly mentioned.

But there was other news on that December 6, 1933, date—such as the Rotary Club's banquet honoring Bill Corbus, the All-American from Vallejo; Director Kenneth Dick announcing the final rehearsal of his Vallejo Choral Society of 80 voices; Dr. John W. Green's election to head the Solano

Typical downtown Los Angeles Liquor Store on/off sale the day of repeal, December 5, 1933. Photo courtesy National Archives, 306-NT-727-1.

County Medical Society; Mare Island's award to build two new destroyers, the Smith and the Preston.

Oh, yes—the grocery ads: two heads of lettuce for 5¢; catsup, 9¢; 60 pounds of potatoes for 67¢; hamburger 10¢ a pound.

And the depression was also with us, in that year of 1933.

After prohibition ended on December 5, 1933, some people continued to make moonshine, smuggle and bootleg alcohol. The main reason was, of course, financial. In 1933-34 the depth of the depression, sometimes 13 million people were unemployed. Thousands had become skilled in making moonshine or diluting it and creating gin and bourbon and scotch that it was natural to continue or start up again. They needed money. They had a market in some of the local bars or with the wholesale distributors who could pocket the money that was now supposed to be paid in taxes. Others, like Italian families, continued to make family wine that was legal. But most knew how to make grappa, the distilled moonshine from wine, and they had their little stove stills. Though it violated the law, they continued to make grappa for their family use. But that avoided taxes, federal and state license fees, possessed a still and distilled liquor—all against the law. Most operations were small time and did not sell; however, a few sold to make big money.

Mrs. Antoinette Schultz, on Sanford Avenue, Wilmington said she sold three or four pints because her husband, Fred Schultz, was sick, had heart trouble. She sold for the purpose of "trying to save her home" and "go get something to eat." However, she sold to a federal agent. She had nine and one-half gallons of liquor. She lost her home anyway. A year later, 1936, she borrowed $18 from friends and offered it to the government to end the case.[8]

Frank Joseph offered $25 in September, 1939, "in compromise of liability by the above violation" which was in June 1936 for having 66 ½ gallons of anisette brandy, plus stove, still and 50 gallons of mash. While the agent was looking for the still dome and coils, May Joseph took an axe and started breaking the containers of brandy to destroy the evidence. She only destroyed nine before she was stopped. In 1939, agent M. M. Kelly recommended leniency because the Josephs already paid $138.53 in taxes and penalties, did not own the premises where the violations took place and had no financial resources. Said Kelly: He "had a broken shoulder and rather than go on county relief he resorted to the manufacture and sale of liquor in order to make a few dollars on which to live." The government accepted the $25 and closed the case. Chris A. Tasulis of Culver City had a beer license after repeal, but sneaked a little selling of "un-tax-paid" wine to sell at Chris Market, 8634 Washington Blvd., in 1935. He was arrested for manufacturing, selling, and having a 50-gallon still. He paid a small fine and offered a $10 compromise in 1936 and the government gladly accepted the small amount and closed the case rather than prosecute him.[9]

Quiet Mexicali, the elegant ABW Club, the Owl, had almost a depression atmosphere after prohibition ended in California on December 5, 1933. Noted Imperial County bootlegger and smuggler Bob Davis owned an interest in this night club. Photo courtesy of Imperial County Historical Society, Imperial.

B. Aatti, on a ranch just outside of Holtville, a ranch owned by James Grossman of El Centro, made 40 gallons over his 200 gallons of wine allowed. The government accepted his compromise offer of $8.00 in 1936 for possession of "un-tax-paid" wine. Somewhere in San Bernardino County, Constable C. Oliver and Deputy Sheriff Caster seized 25 gallons of grape brandy and 400 gallons of wine belonging to M. H. Bundincich. This case was dismissed in 1937.[10]

Two Los Angeles residents went into the liquor business in 1936. Earl E. Blunder sold liquor in a grocery store at 1210 W. 112th St. He was drunk when arrested, empty pints and full jugs in his closet. When he sent $10 to the government in April 1936 and another $10 in August, both were rejected and in October of that year the court sent $20 back to him, but accepted his $40 that he sent early in 1937. His defense was: "I had the liquor for a party and did not know a tax was due on it."[11] Robert D. Elder, 1026 W. 22, St., used his car to deliver and pick up liquor. The agents arrested him picking up supplies "to replenish his stock" at 229 E. 5th St. He said he was in the "trucking and transfer business." His previous car had partitions with racks for hauling gallon bottles. He lost his new car, a Chrysler coup which he put $412 down and owed $880. The government accepted his $25, "submitted in compromise of criminal liability" but refused to give his car back in a decision that ended the case in June, 1939.

Hundreds of cases of post-repeal bootlegging occurred in California: Nicolas L. Cruz of Lompoc, William Peters of Pasadena, Michael Petrelli and Otto Pupillo of Los Angeles, and Rocco Torres of San Diego.

The government needed money during the depression, but it turned down $75 from radio entertainer Lillian M. Zielke in 1936. The Feds had confiscated 17 gallons of moonshine, diluted with water and colored and flavored for taste, just like in the prohibition days. They sent the money back to her, which she promptly spent. The government then changed its mind, said they would accept it. She didn't have it then and had moved to San Diego for her career. She did not respond to official letters, and the case lies in the National Archives unclosed. She beat the system out of $75, but did lose her 1935 Terraplane coach which had been forfeited.[12]

A Lot of Headaches in That Stuff
by Norton Steenfott, Eureka

The first whiskey that came in after repeal was just rectified whiskey—nothing more than straight alcohol, flavoring and coloring. Some of it was horrible; some of the first to come out was called Green River. I don't know where they got that but they sure got a lot of headaches they stuck in that stuff. That was for one year after repeal. Then the distilleries got going. They had one-year-old stuff; it couldn't come out of the distillery until it was a year old. Here in Eureka they rectified whiskey down on C Street.

Moved the Moonshine Operation

When half the states had already voted for repeal, informants tipped off federal authorities that a distillery was being constructed on the Wolfskill Ranch near San Jacinto. Hugh Van Dusen had rented part of Wolfskill's property and sub-leased it in October 1933 to Sam Bruno for $100 per month and was paid $10 a day—great wages for 1933—for repairing the road to the still site. Tony Bruno came each Sunday to check the progress of the still, until John Wolfskill ordered Van Dusen to have the still removed. Sam Bruno was doing that when the still site was raided. The owners of the still were also tipped off and abandoned the site before the raid. During the raid, thinking these men would come back and rescue their equipment, the Feds recorded serial numbers of the large machinery.

The operators moved the equipment to Charles L. Wright's Ranch, 12 miles east of Yermo on the banks of the Mojave River bed and two miles from the Barstow-Las Vegas road. The still was up and running when investigator Sweet heard about three carloads of sugar being surreptitiously routed around the state and dropped off at the tiny depot at Nipton, just inside the California border. The circuitous route from the Spreckles Sugar Company, Manteca, used Western Pacific, Tidewater and Southern, Santa Fe and Union Pacific to reach Nipton. Sweet planned to have a rider on the next sugar shipment, but the San Bernardino County sheriffs raided before Sweet put his plan in effect.

Confiscated on the raid, on December 21, 1933, about two weeks after repeal, were a large 250 gallon still, 500 gallons of distillate, 100,000 gallons fermenting sugar mash, 16 massive 9,000-gallon mash vats—a big operation! Arrested were Charles L. Wright, John Manes, Sam Ferra (Fera, Fira), Bill Jordon, Lewis Tanzino. Upon investigation of the conspiracy it appeared Sam Bruno had supervised the construction at the Wolfskill Ranch; that he and Joe (Giuseppe)(Jack) Parrino had arranged for the purchase of a truck used in hauling sugar and supplies to the still; that William H. Jordon and John Caccicoppo hauled sugar from Nipton to Wright's Ranch; that Gaetano and his Uddo Taormina Corporation were involved and authorized the release of the carloads of sugar; and that the owner of the ranch Charles Wright was a knowing participant, the still being 400 yards west of the house.

When one sugar truck broke down, son Chauncey Wright helped transfer the load to his father's Ford truck, brought it to the still and used the ranch tractor to tow the damaged truck to the barn for repairs. Chauncey admitted his part and that his father knew of the still and even housed six-eight workers in a shack until they could live in the still barn. The government's case was solid, but dragged on until the middle of the depression when a $5,000 compromise payment took care of the tax liability in 1935. Finally in 1936, conspirators, Charles Wright, Parrino, Cacciocoppo, Manes, Jordon and Uddo offered $500 to settle the criminal liability of the case, which the government accepted.[13]

The depth of the depression, the stills probably already set up, state liquor laws in limbo, profit beckoning, and high unemployment—the temptation was just too great for some. After prohibition ended in December 1933, hundreds of stills continued to operate. Revenue men were busy and effective. Just in northern California alone over a hundred stills were raided and destroyed.[14] Below are a few of them:

DATE & CASE #—ADDRESS—PERSONS ARRESTED—COMMENTS

August 29, 1934, CN-33—Dunn Ranch, 11 miles east of Gilroy on San Felipe-Hollister Road, San Benito Co.—Jim Belli, Ital., 40; Tom Nolan, Amer., 22.—750-gal. daily capacity, 75,000 gal. mash dumped.

January 7, 1935—CN-123SF—Gospednetick Ranch, Fairview Dist., Hollister—A. Gospednetick—1200 gal. daily capacity; 50,000 gal. mash destroyed.

February 12, 1935, CN-145—40 acre ranch belonging to Kiyota Sunahara, 3 miles east of Florin, Sac. Co.—John Hague, Amer., 39; Oliver Neuman, Amer., 33; Edward J. Allen, Amer. 31.—1,000-gal. daily capacity; dumped 40,000 gal. mash.

April 25, 1935, CN-313—Home Dairy Ranch, 1 ½ miles south of Pacheco on Walnut Creek Rd.—Louis Steiner, Swiss, 37.—250-gal. daily capacity; 7,500 gal. mash destroyed.

May 13, 1935, CN-335—Sparrow Ranch, Concord.—John Rosso, Amer., 36; Johnny Morse, Amer., 18; E. R. Sparrow, Amer., 51.—250-gal. daily capacity; 60 gal. spirits seized.

June 3, 1935, CN-349—Old River Rd., 12 miles SW of Salinas, Rt. 1.— Frank A. Daugherty (Dougherty), Amer., 50; Angelo Rodni, Swiss-Ital., 28; Dante Brunza, Ital., 31; Giuseppe Guinto, Ital., 28; George Harrison, Amer., 32.—750-gal daily capacity; 25,000 gals. mash dumped; one truck seized.

August 13, 1935, CN-436—515 Lewis St. (rear of 1600 5th St., Oakland— Manuel de Silva (Manuel Silva), Portugese, 43; Joaquin F. Lucus, Portugese-Amer., 37.—making wine, malt liquor and spirits.

September 12, 1935, CN-469—Warrington St. near SW corner of Alameda, South of Redwood City.—Lee Kelly, alias Guido Reggi, Ital., 33; Gino Moretto, Ital., 34; Mario Moffatti, Ital., 33; Emilio Bedini, Ital., 38; Giovannia Togonotti—250-gal. daily capacity; 18,000 gal. mash dumped; Plymouth and DeSoto cars seized.

524

October 25, 1935, CN-499—Domby Ranch, west side of Olive St., Menlo Park.—Joe Siaroni, Amer., 27; Nello Monticelli, naturalized Amer., 41; Gime Fugio, Ital.,45.—700-gal. daily capacity; 24,000 gal. mash dumped.

November 26, 1935, CN-522—721 Quintara, S.F.—Blasei Rampuli, Italian, 44—300 gal. capacity, three story still. See Ch.30.

December 2, 1935, CN-533—Tash Ranch, ½ mile NW of Old Mission, Soledad—Giovanni Boneti, Ital., 53; Frank Rossi, Amer., 22, Benardino Venditti, Ital., 33.—1,000-gal. daily capacity; dumped 35,000 gal. mash.

One of the biggest cases after prohibition took 14 years to conclude In 1946 Jack I. Dragma, with a $1,000 compromise, ended his fight with the law. Dragma and many other fellows continued their gang after prohibition ended. They operated two distilleries, one seven miles north of Las Vegas next to the Rains Ranch and another 25 miles north of Las Vegas next to a ranch owned by C. B. Richardson. These stills had an output of over 1,000 gallons daily, from November to December 11, 1934, when it was seized. These men used public transportation shipping cartons camouflaged by labels saying "Utah Mineral Water." Strong mineral water!

These Los Angeles men spent $173,315 from March to December setting up a first class operation. R. L. Russell, a parolee for murder, operated the headquarters at 274 Tonopah Boulevard in North Las Vegas. He lived at 317 Carson Street, Las Vegas. Much was shipped to Dean's Liquor Store at 2000 N. Broadway, L. A. and Universal Wine and Liquor Store (L. A.?). Agents arrested over 100 people in this syndicated operation.[15]

Since nightclub and restaurant owners could not resist buying untaxed alcohol and serving it as house liquor, sometimes even pouring it into bottles that said "FEDERAL LAW FORBIDS SALE OR RE-USE OF THIS BOTTLE," post-prohibition moonshiners had a market for their liquor. After 14 years of choosing which federal laws to obey and which to nullify, hundreds chose to ensure higher profits by substituting California moonshine for taxed liquor. And after a few years, even with taxes, liquor became fairly inexpensive and moonshining stopped.

During the 1930s, America kept both eyes open to the depression and attempts to ameliorate it, and crises in Europe and Asia soon embroiled the world in a war of such magnitude that historians changed the names The Great War or World War into World War I. Despite these sobering events after prohibition making Americans forget prohibition, the effects of those bootlegging years were innumerable.

Before-and-after photo of raid of April 1935, almost 1½ years after prohibition ended. On the old "Home Dairy Ranch," 1½ miles south of Pacheco on Walnut Creek Road, Louis Steiner lost his post-repeal still. [Case NC-313, Dept. of Justice, Alcohol Beverage Unit, S. F.]

Notice ax imbedded in center of still, east of Gilroy on the Dunn Ranch, on San Felipe-Hollister Road, San Benito County. After arresting Jim Belli, 40, and Tom Nolan, 22, agents dumped 75,000 gallons of mash. [Case CN-33, Dept. of Justice, Alcohol Beverage Unit, S. F.]

Blasei Rampuli, arrested at 721 Quintara Street, S. F., when agents Sam Byrd and John M. Burt destroyed the 300-gallon daily capacity still two years after repeal. The huge still went through the floors from basement to the attic. The building is still there though an addition has been added. [Case CN-522, Dept. of Justice, Alcohol Beverage Unit, S. F.]

A. Gospedetich had a warrant for his arrest for his 1,200-gallon per-day still on his ranch in the Fairview District, Hollister, San Benito County. Agents seized 650 gallons of 160-proof alcohol and dumped 50,000 gallons of mash in January 1935. [Case CN-123, Dept. of Justice, Alcohol Beverage Unit, S. F.]

528

Long-time illegal distillery finally got caught after prohibition, June 1935, Arrested on Old River Road, 12 miles south of Salinas, were Frank A. Daugherty (also Dougherty), 50; Angelo Rodni, 28; Dante Brunza, 31; Giuseppi Guinto, 28; George Harrison, 32. A "confidential" informant led to the successful raid which destroyed 25,000 gallons of molasses mash, seized 550 gallons of liquor, and taken into custody one V-8 Ford truck, loaded with 15 58-gallon drums of molasses. One can see the energy expended by federal agents in destroying the stills.[Case CN-349, Dept. of Justice, Alcohol Beverage Unit, S. F.]

CHAPTER 30

THE LEGACY

The Desert Fox, Dan Murphy, went into mining after prohibition. His friend Glen Settle said he didn't know how long he kept his homestead east of the dry lake where he operated the large distilleries. He was around Rosamond for awhile and then went over to Las Vegas. Settle said one casino had a picture of him holding two large gold nuggets. He might have settled down in Pahrump, northwest of Las Vegas. Supposedly he promoted investments in gold mines. The last Settle saw of Murphy, he must have weighed 300 pounds and his dark hair had turned white.

After prohibition, Pucci, G. William Puccinelli, the Land Shark, developed some alley restaurants and bars in San Francisco. Belden (alley) Street was renamed Pucci's Alley. "I liked alleys," he said. He bought some property on the Peninsula. When the Atherton Commission, investigated crime in U. S. cities, Puccinelli testified. Later he said, "I lied for weeks to the Kefauver Commission. The cops coached me, told me what to say and how to answer." He had a loyal group of followers who enjoyed his clubs. Seemingly for spite, he opened on election day in San Francisco—against the law, but a knock on the door and one could drink with Pucci and discuss the election.

Still spry and mentally sharp, "Pucci" Puccinelli set up the bar at his daughter's restaurant on Skyline Boulevard in 1980. Photo by author.

At 80 years old in 1980, he could be found every Sunday on Skyline Boulevard at his restaurant and bar, which his daughter ran. He prepared the bar by slicing lemons and limes, setting out the olives and cherries, cussing, "Where the hell's the martini glasses?" He was still full of life and mentally sharp as he reminisced about "the best years of my life." He was still a little bitter toward the corruption of the Coast Guard: "You couldn't get a case of booze ashore unless the Coast Guard knew about it. They wouldn't allow it. They were hungry, really hungry. Of all the groups in my book, they were the hungriest. They wouldn't come to the Palace Hotel themselves. Their payoffs would go through two, three different hands before they'd get it. They were protected by the middlemen. They made more money than the smugglers." And Pucci was even more bitter toward the government. "They are the worst thieves of all, the way they tax us for everything. There's more bootlegging now to avoid taxes. This bottle of Early Times," he said as his lips got tight, his mostly gray mustache stretched out a bit and his sharp nose accented the point, "more of this stuff is sold without invoice, places that sell a lot of booze, they take it off the top. They buy a carload of this and there's no invoice."

For Pucci's 75th birthday, a lawyer friend wrote the following poem:

Poem to Guido Guillermo Puccinelli on the Occasion of his 75th Birthday

Buon Natale Signor Puccinelli
Rosy of cheeks—firm of belly—
Raconteur and world-wide Rambler
Gourmet Chef and Cold Eyed Gambler
Friend of the Poor—Pal of the Great
Like Angelo, Joe, Jake, Low and Nate
He—that the Police were a Private Patrol
Paid by a C-note—Coffee and Roll
He knew where so many bodies were buried
He—once with the Grand Jury
Thrust and parried—
His philosophy of Law, stated in brief:
Show me a lawyer and I'll show you a thief
So you can have Paoli, Bulgers and Gucci—
With glasses raised High!
Let's hear it for Pucci— 12/7/75

For this "land shark" those exciting days were fond memories.

The Water Shark

Jack Hale, Napoleon K. Hale, learned to deep sea dive as a result of retrieving liquor loads that had to be dropped over the side because of pursuit.

He took that trade to New York and worked on the *Normandy* when she was sabotaged at the dock during WW II. He became a plumber in the Peninsula and lived a long life, remaining friends with Puccinelli, the Land Shark.[1]

℘

Buster Hyder, the doryman who rowed booze from the motorboats to the shore, retired and settled down on a small ranch in New Cuyama. He and his sister spent ten years or so of their childhood with their father on Santa Barbara Island from 1911 to about 1922. In 1994 the beautiful Hyder family had a reunion on Santa Barbara Island. It was shown on KCET-LA Huell Houser's *California's Gold* program. Three generations of Hyders were there. Buster Hyder was 94 years old at the time.

With a Cool Head
by Bob Morgan, Palo Alto

Approximately two years after prohibition had ended, my mother and father were having a cocktail party in their Berkeley home. At the height of the party the doorbell rang. My father went to the door only to find a policeman at the door wanting some information about a street location.

My mother happened to be walking past the front door and to her horror noticed the "jauntier" confronting my father. Alarmed, she quickly retreated to the kitchen and expertly poured all the bourbon down the drain.

After my father finished conversing with the officer, he came out to the kitchen to freshen up some of the guests' highballs. There he discovered my mother who informed him that with a cool head she cleverly got rid of the evidence, pouring the liquor down the sink as was done in the bootleg days. My father, of course, aghast and in disbelief, ended the very legal cocktail party.

Now Owns the Places

After Norton Steenfott's experiences as a 16-year-old taxi driver and bootlegger, he became a huge asset to Eureka. He loved researching county history. He had a collection of hundreds of old newspapers since the town's founding. He researched old maps and charters. He owned many of the buildings where he used to wash dishes, bus and cook during the prohibition days. Most of these building were houses of prostitution, cabarets or speakeasies in those wild bootlegging years. The magnificence of Old Town Eureka today owes much to Steenfott's efforts of restoring the elegance to these buildings—working even into his seventies.

℘

A kingpin in the Canada-to-California rumrunning, Charles Hudson, the designer and builder of *Kagome*, retired as a wealthy man from his smuggling business. His experiences and leadership enabled him to serve his country well in the Canadian Navy in World War II. He offered John Schnarr, the *Kagome* engineer who almost died of seasickness off southern California, a naval job as an instructor in naval speedboats. Schnarr declined because of his lack of education (and maybe not wanting to go out into the rough Pacific again!). When prohibition ended, it was sad in a way as prohibition was "good for me ...made a very good income," said Schnarr. He had to get rid of the *Revuocnav*, too expensive with two 600-gallon tanks to feed two 860 horsepower engines. He had $10,000 in the bank which was a good piece of money in 1933. He retired in 1969, fishing most of that time since he stopped smuggling. "Fishing was not as exciting as rumrunning but I was still my own boss and it was good, healthy work. Never had a problem with seasickness while I was fishing." Someone else offered Schnarr $25,000 to smuggle drugs. He turned it down. Schnarr showed an ingenious ability with motors . Marion Parker and Robert Tyrol featured his life in an excellent book, *Rumrunner—The Life and Times of Johnny Schnarr.*

Poor Tom Colley never recovered from his bout of gangrene when he mangled his foot on the *Kagome.* His left foot was amputated in a San Francisco hospital where he was taken to shore after the accident. Though the amputation saved his life, he had to have parts of his leg amputated almost each year and even part of his other leg. In 1940 in Canada, he died of a heart attack during a card game, being only 50 years old.

Frenchy's Attempt to Become Legal
by John Clausen, Victorville

Frenchy worked as a serviceman for the Western Electric Company in 1929. He made excellent wine illegally in his winery under his large hillside house near where the Dodger Stadium is now. He made good wine for the company executives and swept the floor of the shop some.

At repeal he tried to legalize his winery. The Feds refused to give him a permit and raided it almost instantly. After that he did not work at the Western Electric, perhaps getting fired.

Cases Dragged On

The case involving Regal Drug Corporation vs. IRS closed in 1940. Since the liquor problem happened in 1923 at the Regal Drug, 1110 Market Street, S. F., it took 17 years to resolve.[2]

℘

In 1979 the owners of Apple Jack's in La Honda, Mr. & Mrs. Bill McMill, who have created a friendly atmosphere, traditional to the old days, purchased a rocking chair just for Armand Zanoni. Zanoni could stay as long as he wanted, greeting his friends of old.

San Bernardino Prostitutes
by S. Bright, San Bernardino

Prostitution was accepted as a service needed, a service performed. The federal government in World War II closed up the prostitutes in San Bernardino, ordered the city to clean up the town, but the girls just scattered out into the hotels and out-of-town areas.[3]

I met one ex-prostitute introduced to me by a former judge. She lives in Yucaipa, a delightful old lady. Now she hobnobs with Palm Springs people. She made so much money then; 'course they don't know her past.

She was knocked over once outside of Vegas. Served time.

Others became quite respectable too. At one time, seven doctors in the San Bernardino area had ex-prostitutes for wives.

$\mathcal{C}\!\mathcal{S}$

Scars and memories faded over the years. As with the Civil War veterans after the 1880s, the wounds healed but the fading memories became more personal. Some participants told friends, relatives and bartenders. One old man, according to Jill Morrow, secretary for the Brewers Union in 1969 Mission District, San Francisco, frequently came into the offices and social hall of the union. He was fairly well dressed, clean looking, but was an "old character." One barely noticed his limp as a result of losing his leg some way in rumrunning during the bootlegging days. He carried a clipping he sometimes showed, a story about him and his smuggling misfortune. He did some time. Morrow did not remember his name [in 1995] but said he visited other unions like the Teamsters, telling his story of how he got "his leg shot off."[4]

Carl Eifler and Lee Echols

Lee Echols stayed in law enforcement until he retired. In the mid 1930s, he and Aaron Quick went to Puerto Rico to organize the Customs Border Patrol there. During World War II, Carl Eifler and Echols helped organize the Office of Secret Service (OSS) and then went into the CIA. Echols had wild experiences in various Latin American countries with CIA operations in the Cold War. Echols also had a long service as Yuma County Sheriff in Arizona. Eifler co-authored a book written about his life called *The Deadliest Colonel*. He retired in Salinas and Echols in Chula Vista—both proud of their lives committed to honest police work and public service.

534

A Little Justice

With years of making untold profits off Californians' need for imported liquor, one Treasury Department agent, Chester A. Emerick, made some progress in obtaining a bit of compensation for the wealth Canadians funneled out of California, Washington and Oregon.[5] Emerick, according to author Don Whitehead, was a big, young easygoing agent who investigated west coast smuggling operations toward the end of prohibition. Canadian liquor interests formed the Pacific Forwarding Company of British Columbia. One ruse was to ship a consignment of liquor to Papeete, Tahiti, where the customs bond was can-

Two former Customs Officers who tried to stop the flow of liquor from Mexico during prohibition, Lee Echols (left) and Carl Eifler (right). They became life-long friends and both helped form the OSS in WWII and joined the CIA after the war. Photo taken about 1976, courtesy of Lee Echols.

celed and shippers were not required to pay taxes on the exported liquor. Shipments then went to Rum Row off the coast of California or Washington. Their network of salesmen in Los Angeles and San Francisco and Seattle guaranteed quality, quantity and price. Salesmen deposited the money in California banks to the credit of Gulf Investment Company, owned and controlled by Canadian liquor interests.

After prohibition was over, Emerick doggedly followed through, pressing for federal prosecution. Secretly he obtained warrants for the arrest of conspirators George and Henry Reifel of Canada. When the two arrived in Seattle for business, federal marshals arrested the brothers.

While federal authorities proceeded with the case, Canadian liquor interests agreed to pay United States government $3 million to settle all liabilities. The government dismissed the case against the Reifel brothers.

Must Have Been In His Blood

A few people could not resist trying to beat the government out of liquor taxes. Jay Baker sold moonshine in 1934 and so did "Pucci" Puccinelli and numerous others. Some moonshiners continued to operate and newly-established liquor stores did not mind avoiding taxes or slipping customers bathtub gin instead of imported. J. D. Cannizzaro, 2734 Taylor Street, San Francisco, was called a "big shot" by *San Francisco Chronicle*, January 18, 1936, when he was indicted and later jailed two years for moonshining. The judge refused to lower the bail from $5,000 to $2,500 from the still raid at 721 Quintara Street. Also indicted was Biagi Rampoldi who pleaded guilty to evading $672 of taxes for $19,000 income from still operations in 1929. Like Al Capone, he got caught on tax evasion.

While in jail, serving his two years, J. D. Cannizzaro induced his nephew Angelo Cannizzaro, 20, to install another still at 721 Quintara. He was caught and put on probation. The bungalow was wrecked, said the *Chronicle*, but on which raid was not clear.[6] [The house at 721 is still there, only in 1998 it's a rental and not a distillery.]

Wad Oates

Flora Valensuela, Wad's beautiful Mexican wife, was from a very well-thought-of family in Calexico, according to Lee Echols. After repeal, she divorced Oates, went to San Diego and worked as a cocktail waitress for a Jewish man who opened a semi-private club, the Studio Club, in a large home on 6th Avenue. When Echols was a Special Agent in Laredo in 1941, Oates was on his way to Mexico where he had a good job with an oil company. Oates went over to Echols' house, had a couple of drinks and talked over old times in Calexico, smiling and laughing at those exciting days. Said Echols: "After he got out of prison the second time, he went to Saudi Arabia as an arc-welder for several years, sending all his savings to his mother who put it in cattle for him. I think she owned a cow ranch in west Texas" [see Appendix F].

WCTU—After the Battle
as told by Gladys Ferguson, Holtville

In 1932 when California repealed the Wright Act, and after 1933, most Imperial County towns modified their "non-alcoholic charters and sold liquor legally for the first time since it was formed in 1908. Many of our Woman's Christian Temperance Union members became discouraged and were ready to give up the work. When our state president came to the county and with the help of the county president, Mrs. Angie Miller, they reorganized, assisting the weaker unions.

The post-prohibition WCTU stressed education and youth, as the schools in our county were favorable to the teaching of total abstinence. We were allowed to place speakers and materials in all of our county schools. Our films were used continually in the school film libraries.

Essay and poster contests are held each year in the public schools. WCTU materials are placed in the school libraries. A number of teachers have attended the Narcotic Education course at Redlands University.

The county YTC (Youth Temperance Council) secretary had sent youths to summer camps and helped teach LTL (Loyal Temperance Legions, ages 8-12).

We had a food booth, a "Milk Bar," at the California Mid-winter Fair in Imperial for 16 years, featuring milk products and homemade pies and cakes. All the unions shared in the project. We kept the WCTU before the public.

Beginning with World War II the El Centro Union opened a reading room for the servicemen until the USO became active in the city.

In 1957 the Imperial County Unions celebrated their 50th anniversary at Imperial. We had six unions and 153 active members. The county had its share of liquor licenses but we protested where we had a legal right, and some licenses had been refused or have gone out of business due to the faithfulness and prayers of our members.

In 1934 I became president of the Holtville Union and in 1938 the Imperial County president.

Fraser Miles

The young Canadian radioman Fraser Miles got into the rumrunning business in 1932 by accident. He just finished Sprout-Shaw Wireless School in Vancouver and couldn't find work. Needing a job, he took someone else's job for the day, loading the fish packer *Ruth B.* A crewman did not show up and neither did the radioman. Mills became the radio operator and assistant engineer. The fish packer was clean—no fish smell. *Ruth B* was a rumrunner.

Miles earned enough money from his trips on rum row off the California coast to pay for college, later becoming an engineer. Ironically he spent his ill-gotten money at Tri-State College in Angola, Indiana. Money obtained from the hard-drinking Americans recycled back into the United States during the depression. With this fine education, Miles for many years was Assistant General Manager of British Columbia Hydro and Power Authority. During World War II, he and four of his boyhood friends went to war. Only two came back. He wrote a fine book, *Slow Boat on Rum Row*, about his rumrunning days, and he dedicated the book to his three friends who gave up their lives in the war.[7]

∅

Charley W. Petersen, the San Pedro smuggler, went into the real estate business after prohibition ended. He went belly-up in a subdivision investment in 1934, took his old Chrysler coupe, a borrowed tent, went up north and panned for gold in the Mother Lode Country to survive. He did some construction work in Placerville, then full-time in Tahoe, being successful in several businesses, retiring three times. He died on a fishing trip by Vancouver Island in Canada in the early 1970s. Young Charley E. Petersen, the boy who went on his father's smuggling boat, later worked in construction with his father, went to University of California at Berkeley, then enlisted before World War II started, surviving in Europe in a tank-destroyer unit. He went into the resort and ranching business, and in the 1990s traveled in his motorhome and in his own boat, 70 years after his exciting boating experience with his father.[8]

Recycled *Diatome*
Sometime after 1934 the Coast Guard burned or auctioned surplus boats used to curtail but never stopping rumrunners off the California coast. Ernie Judd picked up the *Diatome* and used it to ferry tourists back and forth to Catalina. Remember when it was a rumrunner? She was faster than any Coast Guard boat, and of course she became the fastest Coast Guard boat on the coast, CG 827. Judd advertised he'd get you to Catalina in less than an hour or there would be no charge. Judd took one of the three powerful Liberty (World War I) airplane engines out of it and replaced it with a smaller cruising motor.[9]

Capone's Friend
George Giardino left the Lincoln Heights area of East Los Angeles, left the winery business, bought property in Carson and became the "gerkin and tomato king of Carson" on property he owned since 1942, the south side of Carson Street between Alameda and Wilmington. Active in Rotary International, he set a record for perfect attendance, even into his 70s. At 71 he was Rural-Urban Relations Chairman. In the 1970s he started developing a beautiful ranch in Yermo, California, planting a vineyard. He applied for a permit to

produce wine, but was turned down by the government. Although candid with the author in two interviews in the 1980s, his lawyer advised him not to be tape-recorded. He became upset during the second interview when the author brought a still to his ranch hoping he would explain some concepts about it. Since it was illegal to possess a still, he made sure it stayed in the car. His granddaughter Tammy Stoner was one of the writer's former high school students.[10]

☙

Robbin' Hood Charles Schmitz, Customs Broker for the Port of San Francisco, 28th U. S. Collection District, was sentenced to 18 months, charged with Agnes A. Crees and Daniel J. Cottrell for conspiracy to forging documents and allowing tons of liquor to leave H. B. Thomas & Co., a bonded federal warehouse. After serving his time at McNeil Island, he was released on parole in 1931, discharged from custody in March 1932 and in October of that year, pardoned by President Herbert Hoover, because "...since his release, has conducted himself in a law-abiding manner." On January 1936 the Treasury Department dropped all charges against Schmitz and he continued to work at 510 Battery St., the H. B. Thomas & Co. warehouse.[11]

☙

After repeal, Needles bootlegger Joe Collins could not obtain a liquor license since he had been convicted of a felony liquor violation. He went into the liquor business with Bill Cooper and Delores Nelson. They had a successful business for years.

The popular, easygoing Needles Constable Frank Bland, later became a most popular sheriff of San Bernardino County.

"Baby Face" Nelson

In August 1934, George "Baby Face" Nelson headed supposedly for Los Angeles, robbing a gas station in Utah on the way. However, he spent the summer months in northern California, between San Francisco, Sausalito, Sonoma County and Reno, sometimes one tip-off ahead of Bureau of Investigation [later FBI] traps.

When Nelson was hiding in Sausalito in 1932, he frequented Mrs. John Carlisle's restaurant, eating there sometimes three times a day. Mrs. Gillis, Nelson's wife, and their two-year-old son Ronnie also ate there along with San Rafael High School graduate Johnny Paul Chase, known bootlegger and smuggler. Mrs. Carlisle said, "They...were unassuming fellows, quiet in manner, and nothing was known against them except that they were rumrunners." A patron told Mrs. Carlisle that he had seen the two together during the summer of 1934, but he didn't say anything because Chase knew him and he feared reprisals.

They hid out in 1932 just a few doors from officer Manuel Menotti's home. Locals assumed Chase just operated in northern California until officers found a "hot" car registered to Chase in the mid-west after a Dillinger Gang bank robbery.[12]

November 27, 1934, was the last day for the young Nelson. A chance meeting with a G-man at Nelson's friend's house, a call for help from two agents who had been looking for Nelson, and another chance meeting on a roadside in Barrington, Illinois, sparked an instant machinegun shootout between Nelson and Chase against Agents Samuel Cowley and Herman Hollis, resulting in the deaths of both Cowley and Hollis and the mortal wounding of Nelson.

When Nelson was buried, only a few attended, no prayers except one by the undertaker. Nelson's mother, Mary, sobbed. Quite a contrast to the huge funerals of Cowley and Hollis.

Helen (Nelson) Gillis told the following story of Nelson's death: "The federal men's fire knocked out our gas supply and we took to a field.

"Les [Lester Gillis] yelled at me to duck into a ditch. I did and I kept my head down in fear it would be blown off, but I was able to see Les fire back at those men who were trying to kill him.

"I saw Les jump and grasp his side. I knew then that was the end.

"I stayed there in the ditch until the firing stopped. I could see one of them—I don't know whether it was Les or not—go over to where the Federal men lay. Then they went to the government car.

"Les took the wheel and they called to me. They picked me up. Les tried to drive but couldn't make it. I knew it was no use trying to get a doctor."

She and her male companion (Chase) found a house near Chicago, took off Nelson's bullet-torn clothes and placed him on a bed. He died in her arms, Helen Gillis said, at 7:35 p.m., four hours after the gun battle. They carried him to the car.

"We didn't dump him in the ditch like they said. During the ride I sat in the back seat, holding him as if he were alive. We put him down comfortably on the grass by the road and I got the blanket and covered him up."[13]

For her part, especially for breaking parole by associating with her husband, the court sentenced her to a year and a day. Afterwards the diminutive, 23-year-old widow of former Public Enemy No. 1, heard the judge say, "Today the Department of Justice has convinced you and others that there is only one end to that kind of life—prison or death. It ought to teach a lesson to you and those who are inclined to be criminals." She served a year, but the G-men brought her to San Francisco to face charges of harboring her husband. She loved Lester Gillis, stuck by him, said he never cheated on her and she didn't want him killed: "He was her man," said the *Chronicle*. When sister-in-law Leona McMahon brought Helen's son Ronnie, 6, to see his mother in prison for the first time in over a year, he asked, "How long are you going to be in the hospital, Mama?"[14]

"She is guilty of being a good wife to a bad husband," said her attorney Richard H. Fuidge, in December in 1935. She married George Gillis when she was 15. "He dominated her, as he dominated all in his gang." Helen left school in the 7th grade to care for a family of nine. In a soft voice, in a plain black dress with a white collar, carrying a rabbit's foot a Negro woman in the county jail gave her, she pleaded guilty. She received mercy from the San Francisco judge. U. S. District Attorney said, "The Dillinger-Nelson gang is wiped out." The federal court placed her on probation, and she moved to Long Beach to raise her child and live with Leona McMahon, the sister of Baby Face. For Helen, gone forever were the machinegun days of the Dillinger-Nelson gang.

Back in Chicago Federal agents were peeved, not only of the loss of two of their men, but the leisurely way Nelson "toured" California and rested safely in San Francisco both in 1932 and the summer of 1934. Said West Coast federal investigative head, E. P. Guinane, "We hope to get a lot of those babies (who helped Nelson)." The federal sleuths worked hard to obtain a list of 19-20 "big shots" who aided Nelson and Chase. One person known to have harbored Nelson was San Rafael underworld member "Fatso" Joseph Ray Negri, alias Rinaldo, alias Passerino, "but better known among the old Barbary Coast associates as 'Fatso.'" He had been a "chum" of Baby Face in rumrunning along the Sonoma and Marin county coasts. Earlier in 1932 he had been sentenced to serve six months in the Sonoma County jail after being captured aboard a truck which was followed by a car carrying a machine gun.[15]

After Barrington, agents figured Chase would come back to familiar territory to hide out. All known haunts of Chase and Nelson were under surveillance. FBI agents watched Johnny's brother, Frank Chase, and his house and even broke in and "ripped opened a mattress, and offered me $5,000 to go around the country looking for my brother," said Frank Chase in the *San Francisco Chronicle*.

Broke, down and out, unarmed, the 31-year-old Sausalito bootlegger and former baseball player, Johnny Paul Chase, lost his freedom at Mt. Shasta, Shasta County. Chase did head for California, hitch-hiking across Montana, to Seattle and headed down to Mt. Shasta where local officers were warned to keep a lookout since Chase had worked at Mt. Shasta Fish Hatchery six— seven years before.

When stopped on a street in Mt. Shasta by Police Chief Roberts, Chase gave his name as "Mr. Elmer Rockwell," former Californian returning as a tourist. He had identification to prove it. Five agents flew up to Mt. Shasta with Sausalito Chief Manuel Menotti. who had known Chase since boyhood. When Chase saw Menotti, he admitted his identity and his knowing Gillis and Dillinger, but not to any crime.

Surreptitiously, the United States government moved Chase to Chicago by train in a special prison car, with Chase wearing an "Oregon boot," a hobbling device. Frank Chase tried in vain to see his brother, hired a lawyer and traveled back to Chicago to offer help.

The Federal Grand Jury had to decide if Mario De Paoli, alias "Buck Kelly," bouncer at Spider Kelly's on the Barbary Coast, should be tried. He had just been arrested after a gun battle with justice men in December. Accused Reno men were also brought to San Francisco to answer to the charge of helping Nelson. Three more arrested in January were Thomas C. "Tobe" Williams, part owner and manager of Vallejo General Hospital, accused of harboring Helen Gillis and for treating wounded criminals; Anthony "Soap" Moreno and Louis Tambrini, taxi driver and both bartenders at the Bank Buffet, 3286 Twenty-second Street. Moreno was picked up on the steamship *Santa Rosa* at Los Angeles. The three prisoners were nonchalant, said the *San Francisco Chronicle*, of January 14, 1935. These three had a "pipe line" to Nelson when he was around San Francisco's Mission District, Vallejo and Reno.

Others arrested were Ralph A. Rizzo, alias "Scabootch," bail bond broker at 833 Kearny, alleged to have cashed a $700 check for Baby Face; and William Schivo, 1525 Larkin Street, box manufacturer at 517 Davis Street, suspected gangster with a murder record. Judge St. Sure allowed a lower bail for the "small fry," but not for Moreno and Thomas Williams, whose alias was "Gonif (Yiddish for *thief*) from Galway." This "moniker" was obtained from "Gloomy Gus Schaefer", Sacramento post office robber and member of the Touhy gang." San Rafael filling station man Eugene Mazet was arrested. In Reno, Frank Cochran, Fatso Negri and Nelson removed weapons from a Hudson car and stored them in Cochran's basement: Thompson sub-machinegun, Browning Automatic Rifle, .22 cal. rifle, bolt action 30.06 rifle, three bulletproof vests and one suitcase of ammunition.[16]

In the meantime Charles Chase also went to help his brother in Chicago. Johnny Paul Chase offered no alibi, admitting being at the death duel in Barrington. Although Chase was a known California bootlegger, his record was clean.[17]

Californians who went to Chicago to testify against Chase as government witnesses were Sally Backman, Chase's girlfriend; Jim Griffin, fight promoter, 155 Columbus Avenue; Louis Parente, 2195 Pacific Avenue; Joseph Parente, 731 Fourteenth Avenue; Policeman David Dillon, who was almost shot by Nelson at the failed trap set for Nelson at El Verano; nurses and doctors at Vallejo General Hospital. When pretty Sally Backman took the stand, she corroborated the testimony of Fatso Negri, key witness against the defendants, Louis Tambini and others. The judge allowed a motion to free two San Francisco bartenders Frankie Fields and Vince Markovich. Mazet admitted selling a pair of auto license plates to the Nelson gang for $500 which were later found

Sausalito Police Officer Manuel Menotti, later Chief—helped capture John Paul Chase, a member of Baby Face Nelson's rum-running gang. Earlier, Nelson hid out in a house in Sausalito—across from Officer Menotti's home. One hiding place was the Sylva Mansion (a boarding house in the 1930s) on Turney Street, and supposedly for a while he worked in the Walhalla. Photo courtesy Ralph "Swede" Pedersen. Size: 10" x 12 ¼".

after the shootout at Little Bohemia, Wisconsin, where Nelson and Dillinger escaped and an agent was killed. He also said he guarded a truck, received from Chase $10,000 which he presented to Helen Gillis, when she handed him a card with Chase's secret "gang code number—62." Williams was found guilty of treating wounded confederates in Vallejo, sentenced to serve 18 months and pay a fine of $5,000. Cochran received a year and a day and fine of $2,000. Anthony "Soap" Moreno was found guilty of harboring Nelson.[18]

The federal court convicted Chase of the shooting deaths of agents Hollis and Cowley on March 27, 1935, the same gun battle where Nelson received mortal wounds. When the court gave him a life sentence, Chase said, "I think I'd rather dangle." Arriving secretly in Alcatraz, the new federal "escape proof" prison, on March 31, 1935, Chase spent 26 years in Alcatraz. He was only a rifle shot away from his home town of Sausalito, where as a petty bootlegger and rumrunner, "man-about-town," said the *Chronicle*, he rose to become Public Enemy No. 1 and ended up within sight of his old home.

In prison he became an accomplished shoemaker and even spent his own money to make shoes for handicapped people. Also becoming a good painter, Chase had many of his paintings on the walls of Bay Area houses. Chase made the *Guinness Book of World Records* for being in Alcatraz for 26 years. When Alcatraz closed, the government sent him to Leavenworth. President John F. Kennedy pardoned him and he spent the remainder of his years in seclusion as a custodian at St. Joseph College in Mt. View Catholic Seminary.

When Chase gave speeches to school classes on the theme crime did not pay, FBI Chief J. Edgar Hoover stopped him in order not to glorify crime, not to be admired for his rehabilitation but to hold the mark of scorn all his life. Chase died at 71 years at Stanford Hospital in 1973 and gave his body to the University of California.

Menotti remained Chief of Police of Sausalito, a much milder town than during the bootlegging days when Sausalito was the northern funnel of smuggled liquor flowing into San Francisco. Sally Backman, Chase's girlfriend for a time when Chase was on the run, testified in the federal trial and lived out her days in Sausalito.[19]

"All That Glitters"..., and Sally Knows
Editorial in March 1935 *San Rafael Independent Journal*

A pretty, black-eyed cigarette stand sales girl who "graduated" from a little "back woods" town on the bleak Mendocino Coast to the glittering white lights of the ferry-railroad terminal of Sausalito that she might "see more life" tearfully revealed her past yesterday as a gangster's "moll."

There was no romance in Sally Backman's story of her several months' association with John Paul Chase, "Baby Face" Nelson, Jack Perkins, "Fatso" Negri, Tamino Marcovich and Helen Gillis, wife of John Dillinger's first lieutenant. Nothing of the adventure and excitement that Sally craved as eyes heavy with tears, she told of the mad flight of the gang around California and Nevada, in and out of hotels as one by one they became "too hot" when G-men closed in.

What a precious crew it was, that Sally teamed up with. For what did the pretty young girl sacrifice her security of a good job in the concession at the Golden Gate ferry ticket office in Sausalito?

For a brief few minutes on a dark highway with her lover, Chase, contacting others of the gang by blinking automobile headlights on Valley of the Moon Highway—for an hour with her sweetheart in a cheap south of Market Street hotel room which they were forced to flee as the G-men closed in...a hurried return to her Sausalito room to pack her clothes...another dash into the mountains via Sonora to catch up with Chase and Negri.

"I wanted to go with Johnny...[to] the Nevada desert." "Baby Face" was desperately trying to get away. The Perkins and Gillis babies crying...nights spent along the highway...or eating uncooked food beside the road because "Baby Face" was afraid to go to a restaurant...fear...fear...newspaper headlines...echo of machine guns...then Sally came home alone.

Why she left Johnny, she didn't tell, nor was she asked.

She quit the "mob," probably when the glamour that she anticipated was found missing. Perhaps Sally came to realize that one by one every one of the nation's outlaws, craven cowards they were, when the crucial test came was being "picked" off by the G-men as the Department of Justice agents are known to gangland. And, unless she quit in time, she too might stop a federal officer's bullets, or find herself where Mrs. "Baby Face" Nelson is today.

But today, Sally Backman, like "Fatso" Negri is afraid. Her eyes, her very demeanor depict fear. Sally doesn't want to die yet, but she knows just as Negri knows, that she has talked too much.

℘

Despite a guilty verdict for Anthony "Soap" Moreno in the Baby Face Nelson conspiracy charge, U. S. Attorney H. H. Pike planned to prosecute Moreno for the shooting of Agent Norman D. "Doc" Austin, near Stewart's Point, on October 28, 1933. The fight on the rugged Mendocino Coast occurred when government forces surprised a liquor smuggling party landing at Bowens Landing, near Fort Ross. Agents watched the party unload 100 cases of smuggled liquor. Austin nearly died and almost had his arm amputated and laid in the Santa Rosa Hospital for weeks. Agent Sam Byrd was also shot. McPike filed the charges at Sacramento based on information by Fatso Negri.

℘

Swede Pederson, a jackal in the fog, retired as Captain in the Sausalito Fire Department and became the town historian of Sausalito, generously contributing to *One Eye Closed, the Other Red.*

℘

By January 1935, the State Board of Equalization, defined the policy of serving alcohol with food, met with city police departments to have a consistent policy. The Board of Equalization ordered the following: check with all licensed liquor dealers to see if they were obeying rules of bona fide eating places; hot dog and hamburger stands were not allowed to sell hard liquor by the drink—obviously wooden sandwiches didn't count as a bona fide restaurant fare; police were not allowed to raid just to maintain control of liquor establishments; old-time swinging-door saloons were out; and wine and 3.2 beer parlors had better equip themselves as eating places.[20]

To make sure Californians did not go back to the despicable saloons and bars, the state legislated that the name "bar," "saloon," "cocktail lounge" or "tavern" would not be used. Since "grog shop" or "gin mill" did not seem appropriate, the state amended the law allowing "cocktail lounge" and "tavern." About 1970, Assemblyman John T. Knox, of Richmond, introduced a bill to allow both "bar" and "saloon." Columnist Ellis L. Spackman said "a saloon by any other name..." but the ban in 1933-34 was a concession, a token, to those prohibitionists who fought for over 75 years to end the horror of the saloon. These drys lost the battle in 1933, but could at least say "We now have no bars or saloons in California." In the 1970s bars and saloons came back. Prohibition was truly over.[21]

A 1978 federal law allowed Americans to make homebrew, 100 gallons per adult per year, maximum of 200 gallons a household. Of course Californians made illegal homebrew during and after 1933, but in 1978, they could make it legally. In the 1990s thousands made homebrew as a hobby. When microbreweries were allowed to serve their products to the public, Californians took on a new love of beer for fun and taste and a new social respect, replacing the stigma of "the beer joint" and the saloon.[22]

Too Close to the Church
as told by Dick Devlon, Barstow

One ruling from the post-prohibition laws stipulated how close a church could be to a liquor store. A church could move next to a bar or liquor store, but a liquor establishment could not move within 500 feet of a church.

The Empire Hotel on McAllister in San Francisco was owned by (built by?) a religious group. They put a church on one end and opened a nightclub at the other but had to stop the selling of liquor in the nightclub—too close to their own church! A church official measured the distance from the church to the top floor of the Empire Hotel—500 and some odd feet! The hotel opened a nightclub on the top floor. This lounge became successful, making money while the hotel lost money in the depression. The Mark Hopkins Hotel liked the idea of a nightclub so well it evicted the penthouse/top floor residents and started what became the "Top of the Mark."

The Claremont Hotel had its problems in Berkeley. Part of the Claremont was right at the legal one-mile mark away from the University of California. Part of the hotel was outside the boundary so could sell drinks, but the rest of the hotel was within the one-mile exclusion zone. A line was drawn on the floor to show the legal side, and people carrying drinks around periodically had to be reminded that in this part of the hotel they are too close the Golden Bears' campus.

The owner of the Sage Inn profited by being over one mile from Claremont College in San Bernardino County. Montclair, a nearby town, benefited from its location near Claremont as the boys from Claremont and Harvey-Mudd could enjoy a few beers in Montclair between classes.

Menlo Park, being over a mile from Stanford University, enjoyed the Stanford students who wanted to celebrate their big games with Cal. These Indians, now Cardinals, just drove across San Francisquito Creek and made the Oasis a successful beer joint for forty plus years. The north end of Menlo Park was over a mile from the San Francisquito Creek which divided San Mateo and Santa Clara counties and the northern boundary of land owned by Stanford. Beltramo opened up his liquor store in north Menlo and made himself lots of money. Nightclubs opened nearby in Menlo and Atherton which could sell hard liquor since these did not violate the state constitution which prohibits liquor being sold near this private university.

Moss Landing Battle Participants

Deputies Carl Abbott and Alex Bordges both later became Monterey County sheriffs. Traffic Officer Henry Livingston became a supervising inspector in the California Highway Patrol before he retired. The hayfield battlefield became the location of Kaiser Refractories. Sausalito Mayor Madden, sent to Federal Prison McNeil Island in 1926 for two years for helping the Parente gang make faster rum-running boats, came back and lived a peaceful life in Sausalito.[23] He became mayor again in the 1930s.

∅

Mary Q. Baumgarteker never found out what happened to her husband, Frank Baumgarteker, after the business luncheon in November 1929. Though his car appeared on a 6th Street San Diego parking lot with red dust on it, his body was never found. Mary had a difficult time because her husband's disappearance was not cleared up. She could not collect insurance to pay her bills since he was not declared legally dead for years. His Metropolitan insurance company did not want to pay since he was not proven to be dead. After he was officially declared dead, the company still did not want to pay because she had stopped paying premiums after 1929. A court suit forced the insurance company to fulfill its obligations. As her distillery was under investigation and tied up in court, she had to petition the court for money to live, pay bills and raise her nine-year-old son Herbert. She lost the distillery and the trucking company. The winery was purchased from the court by Vai Company which made Padre Wine after prohibition. In the late 1980s Herbert Baumgarteker donated and sold part of the vineyard to the city of Rancho Cucamonga for a park. He still believes that Frank's junior partner Robert Demateis was in collusion with those mysterious Chicago Italians who demanded Baumgarteker release control of the distillery to them. He did not. He was eliminated as promised.[24]

ℬ

Sally Stanford never retired. She opened the Valhalla [?] in Sausalito and later became mayor of Sausalito. When she died in 1982, a fountain was placed in honor of Sally so that people could have a "drink on Sally" and on another level for animals to have a drink on Leland, her dog.[25]

The beer industry promised to help communities financially and kept its promise during the depression. For example, Eastside Beer presented a weekly half-hour musical program called "Ship of Harmony," with aboard-ship atmosphere. California radio stations broadcasting it were KFI, KGO, KOMO and KHQ.

The downside of repeal was an increase of drunk driving and driving fatalities involving liquor. Chief E. Raymond Cato, California Highway Patrol, reported in March 1934 that fatalities increased more than 11 percent in just January of 1934 compared to January 1933. For the entire year 1933, when beer was allowed in April and prohibition ended on December 5, fatalities involving alcohol increased 40 percent and all alcohol related accidents increased

Ralph "Swede" Pedersen, with white beard left, with friends in Sausalito. Pedersen retired as a captain in the Sausalito Fire Department, became a local historian and a great contributor to this book. Photo by author 1979.

by 26 percent. Counties increased penalties for drunk driving. Merced County made it a misdemeanor punishable by both fine and imprisonment.[26]

In October 1925, a young district attorney from Alameda County used his deputies to hit the town of Alvarado, 17 miles south of Oakland, raiding eight saloons and gambling houses. Four women were held for vagrancy. "Vagrancy" was often a euphemism for prostitution or for being a bar fly, a B girl. The young D. A. was Earl Warren, later two-term California governor and Chief Justice of the United States.[27]

And the Rest Is History

In 1933 beer had come back to make it seem as if happy days were here again even in the midst of America's worst depression. Wine would be openly sold soon and by the end of the year prohibition would be over. In Modesto two brothers found wine recipes in the basement of the McHenry Library. They rented an old building at Eleventh and D for $60 per month. The building had a grape crusher, press and tanks. The boys made wine. One brother took charge of the wine production, the other, sales and marketing. "How much can you sell?" asked the young vintner. The sales brother answered, "I'll sell all you can make." And Julio answered, "I'll make all you can sell." And they did.

In 1940 their names appeared on their bottles: Ernest and Julio Gallo![28]

The Secret Boss of California

In 1935, Arthur Samish represented California State Brewers Association. During the next 20 years, the tax on beer never raised; other taxes rose but beer remained 62¢ a barrel. Bills to raise taxes on beer somehow in committees went as flat as day-old brew.

Samish talked brewers into keeping beer at 3.2 percent alcohol. Because Congress had declared in 1933 that 3.2 beer was non-intoxicating, licenses sold for only $10.00, giving California a virtual monopoly on beer. Every shipment of eastern beer, always over 3.2, coming into the Golden State required a new license and was taxed appropriately. Up to the early 1950s, one ordered either "Eastern," like *Pabst Blue Ribbon* or "Western"—the latter beer was California beer like *Acme*, being 10-15 ¢ cheaper. The Supreme Court affirmed the state beers laws.

When Coors tried to market six-ounce bottled beer, Samish had the state legislature pass a law stipulating that the minimum "size of a beer bottle in the state was eleven ounces. Goodbye Coors," said Samish.

Later in the 1950s, eastern companies bought California breweries or built plants in the state.

The brewers paid Samish $30,000 a year as a beer lobbyist, and five cents for every barrel sold was put into "an educational fund to be used as I saw fit." That was $150,000 a year at his disposal.

Frank X. Flynn represented the California Liquor Dealers Association and the wholesale dealers of northern and southern California. Flynn and Samish often worked together. That represented 50,000 businesses, their families and workers—half-million votes as a basis of power. Liquor manufacturers also controlled 4,000 billboards.

The state regulated unfair competition laws. For example, Samish convinced enough key people that it was unfair for Thrifty Drugs to use its wholesale liquor license and its retail outlet too. The state took away Thrifty's right to use its own wholesale license by a 1937 law which made "unfair trade practices for any alcoholic beverage." We stabilized the industry, said Samish and smiled that good old boy smile.

Although the drys lost in 1932-33, they hadn't quit yet. In 1936 when they tried for local option control over liquor in a state initiative, Samish proposed counter propositions to defeat the opponent's initiative or "at least confuse " the voters. It worked then and again in 1948, where Samish used ads and billboards with a pretty mother in a gingham dress, holding a broom and saying, "Let's clean them out—vote yes on number two." Said Samish: "It had not a damned thing to do with the proposition but attracted a lot of sympathy." Even in the 1990s, businesses and interest groups confuse California voters with initiatives and counter initiatives. Most Californians need two or three bottles of more than 3.2 beer to understand some of the state propositions.

"I put through the fair-trade laws to protect wholesalers, distributors, and retailers. I kept the taxes so low that illegal stills became as rare as Hollywood virgins." If anyone wanted something passed or voted against, he saw Samish, "The Secret Boss of California," the man who controlled the state legislature from 1935 to 1955.[29]

Prohibition Portia

After President Hoover accepted Mabel Walker Willebrandt's resignation as Assistant Attorney General, she wrote a series of articles on prohibition. She opened up law offices on Sunset Boulevard by the Hollywood Hills and in Washington, D. C. Practicing law for over 30 more years, Willebrandt ended up arguing 69 cases before the Supreme Court, only a third being prohibition cases. Though she argued against some of the best lawyers in the country, she lost only two cases in the Supreme Court.

She became counselor for Aviation Corporation, pioneering transcontinental travel. To show her faith in the company, she made the cross-country trip by plane and train from New York to Los Angeles, delivering a thermos of water from the New York mayor to Los Angeles Mayor Cryer. She divorced her husband after World War II.

In 1961, she told a reporter from the *St. Louis Post-Dispatch*, in a rare interview, "I never wanted to be known as a 'woman lawyer,' just as a lawyer." Then she said, "'Prohibition Portia'—that's a terrible name."[30]

Who Can Measure?

Tragic family losses permeated every county of the state: Reputations ruined, children embarrassed, divorced parents, unemployment, education stopped. Although the author's father Jim Walker went through those years being a very light drinker, his brothers Dave and Bill had difficulty stopping. Bill's wife died of too much alcohol. Bill also died of alcohol related illness. Dave stopped his drinking and was able to continue a successful brick contracting business.

The young members of the most prominent family in Barstow had a serious problem with alcoholism. The daughter became an alcoholic in San Bernardino, a "tramp" according to one relative. One brother died of alcohol— his life ruined doing the vogue thing in the 1920s, i.e., drink. He and another young businessman made constant hunting and fishing trips to places like Big Bear Lake—weekends of drinking. Another had business problems later because of his drinking. The youngest son was a renegade: He did not drink.

These simple examples show the long-time effects of the California bootlegging years.

Stockton historian, Glenn A. Kennedy, thought the book *How Dry We Were* epitomized the prohibition period. "No doubt, we wandered in the experiment in an almost childish spirit of unrealistic idealism, but as the realities dawned we extricated ourselves democratically, peacefully, with ballots alone. When drys fell, we did not turn the axes on them, nor did they sulk in the caves plotting a counter *putsch*. Prohibition shows that, loud as we sometimes are, we are civilized. It was a test of national character. We survived it."[31]

Two California editors predicted this national American character in 1919. In the *Contra Costa Gazette*, the editor said Americans "are patient to a fault and charitable even to criminal politicians and crazy people...[but] one of these days the majority will have something to say again." The other editor, from *Mountain Democrat* (Placerville), portended that after Americans "give expression in a dignified way to their real sentiment...in a republic the will of the majority must prevail."

Indeed the bootlegging years was a test of national character. The nation changed the Constitution in 1919 and changed it again in 1933, changed it peacefully and democratically. We learned about ourselves: that though patient, once we feel wronged we act in our own ways to change what wronged us. Changing sometimes takes a long time. We are now more cautious about legislating morality and legislating aspects of people's private lives. We struggled with deep moral and political issues, such as obeying laws we did not believe in. These lessons from the bootlegging days carried through the crises and horrors of the depression, World War II, Cold War and the rest of the great events in the 20th century.

APPENDIX A

PROHIBITION CHRONOLOGY

November 1874—National Woman's Christian Temperance Union (WCTU)formed.
   1876, 1880, 1887—Constitutional amendments submitted to Congress—defeated
1893—The Anti-Saloon League of Ohio formed
1895—The Anti-Saloon League formed.
1907—Georgia, Oklahoma, Mississippi, and North Carolina legislated themselves
   dry.
November 1913—Webb-Kenyon Bill passed over President Taft's veto prohibit
   transporting alcohol into dry
states.
August 1914—World War I began in Europe.
1914-1917—The Anti-Saloon League linked the German-Austrian Alliance with
   American brewers, using German war atrocities for anti-beer campaign; the
   League used patriotism and food conservation to prohibit food stuff from being
   made into beer, distilled liquors and wine.
April 6, 1917—Congress declared war against Germany.
August 1917—Senate approved 65-20 to submit 18th Amendment to the states.
September 1917—Congress prohibited the manufacture of alcohol. They banned
   alcohol sales to servicemen.
December 18, 1917—Congress voted to submit prohibition amendment to the states.
January-December 1918—State legislatures debated ratification of 18th Amendment.
November 18—Congress passed the War Prohibition Act—after the war was over. It
   went into effect July 1, 1919.This bill was sneaked into an agricultural appropria-
   tions act by a California representative
January 16, 1919—Nebraska was the 36th state to ratify the 18th Amendment.
July 1, 1919—War Time Prohibition went into effect.
October 28,1919—Congress passed the Volstead Act, The National Prohibition Act,
   passed over President Wilson's veto. The administration of the law was under the
   Bureau of Internal Revenue, which is under the Treasury Department. John F.
   Kramer was appointed the first Commissioner of Prohibition.
January 16, 1919—The 36th state ratified Amendment 18, with certification on
   January 29, 1919.
January 16, 1920—The 18th Amendment went into effect.
1920—Californians proposed Proposition 1& 2 to delay passing California's
   enforcement act to the Volstead Act. This action delayed the bill until November
   1922 when both propositions passed. Therefore the Wright Act became
   California's Volstead enforcement act.
—Association Against the Prohibition Amendment (AAPA) started to fight the
   Volstead Act, to work for repeal and to amend the Volstead.
1920s—Drys stop several attempts to modify the 18th.
November 1928—Republican Herbert Hoover soundly defeats wet Al Smith.
   Prohibitionists are hopeful that finally a strong president will enforce dry laws.

1929—Hoover appointed the National Commission on Law Observance and Enforcement, the Wickersham Commission, to study lawlessness in American and violations of prohibition.

October 1929—Stock market crash. Reaction to the market spreads as panics, layoffs, large inventories, calls for more money on loans, banks collapsing, more layoffs on and on.

January 1930—Hoover presented a preliminary report of Wickersham Commission, requesting more money for enforcement. Bureau of Prohibition was moved from the Treasury Department to the Justice Department. Tenth anniversary of the prohibition.

January 1931—The final report of the Wickersham Commission, not recommending repeal or modification.

Spring of 1932—Republicans nominate Hoover again as full depression overtakes the country. Democrats nominate Franklin Roosevelt, with a pledge to submit a repeal amendment to Congress to be submitted to state conventions for ratification.

November 1932—Country elects Democrat Franklin D. Roosevelt for President by over 2-1 in California. Also California disavows the Wright Act, the Little Volstead Act.

December 1932—Governor Jimmy Rolph pardons over 160 state prisoners, including four women for Wright Act violations.

March 1933—Congress makes 3.2 beer non-intoxicating, and by April most California cities have beer, but tragedy struck—most towns ran out of pretzels.

June 1933—Californians vote for a repeal slate for the repeal convention to be held in July.

July 1933—California ratifies Amendment 21, the repeal amendment.

December 5, 1933—Prohibition ends with states making their own drinking laws.

1934-Smuggling pretty much stops but large illegal distillery plants continue to operate or start up operations again to 1936.

1978—Federal law allowed Americans to make homebrew, 100 gallons per adult per year, maximum of 200 gallons a household.

APPENDIX B

ALIASES

Antunez, Sam—Frank Kramer
Azarow, Louis—L. Schaeffer, Johnny Fogarty
Bedini, Emilio—Giovanni Tognotti
Cacioppo, John—Frank Gusto
Chase, Johnny Paul—Ed Burns, John Scott, John Madison, T. Coduz? Cody, John Powers, Addie James, Earl Butler, William Chase, R. Huf, Johnnie Chase, Elmer Rockwood, Elmer Jones, Ray Mead, Roy Meade [FBI File #26-5685], Edward Flynn.
Companelli, Guiseppe—Joe Campanelli
Connelly, Peter—George Walker
Conner, James D.—Frank Martin, James Gavagan.
Cornero, Anthony—Tony Cornero, Anthony McCann, Paul Kent, Tony Biena?, Louis Donalds,Note: Records before 1928 show Cornero as the real name; after 1928 Anthony Strallo as the real name and Cornero as one of the aliases. See Strallo. Black Tony?
Cornero, Pico—Jack Hammer, See above. Younger brother of Tony.
Corwin, Harry—Herman Quinn
Crank, Lewis A.—Howard Lowe
Curran, James—Firman Deiro
Dahlstrom, Henry—Henry Dalton.
Davis, Claude A—Jud Purdue, W. E. Horton.
Delcamo, Tony—Joe Dallas
DePaoli, Mario—Buck Kelly, bouncer at "Spider" Kelly's.
Dressen, Bert—Bert Dressero
Eads, Homer—Homer Hearst.
Ford, George—F. R. Forsyth.
Gillis, Helen—Marion Virginia Marr, Mrs. Joseph J. Marr, Mrs. Jimmy Williams, Mrs. Lester M. Gillis, Mrs. Helen Burnett, Mrs. Helen Nelson, Mrs. Helen Williams
Gillis, Lester M.—George Nelson, George "Baby Face " Nelson, Baby Face Nelson, Alex Gillis, Lester Giles, "Big George" Nelson, Jimmie, Jimmy Burnell [Dept. of Justice, Identification Order No. 1223, April 25, 1934].
Hale, Napoleon K. —Jack Hall, Jack Hale.
Herata, Harry S.—Timid Jap
Howard, Frank F.—Frank Smith.
Hupp, Clyde—Clyde Hudson and A. B. Figueroa.
Kelly, Lee—Guido Reggi.

Kessler, Harry—Harry Harris.

Kimura, Tadoshi—Harry, Jovial Jap

Knowlton, W. E.—Jerry Knowland

Martin, M. M.—Happy Martin.

McClusky, John—Red Jew, Red

McGuire, J.—D.M. Lawrence

Mazet, Eugene—"Blondie" Mazet, Frenchie Mazet, Gene Mazet.

Moreno, Anthony—"Soap" Moreno, Tony Moreno, Frank Moreno, Anthony Morino [sometimes spelled "Morino"], "Soap" Morino, Joe Soap, Joe Pasquale, George Grazio.

Morley, Ralph R.—R. J. Williams.

Morrison, Lawrence K.—L. E. Morris.

Negri, Joseph Raymond—Fatso Negri, Fatso, Rinaldo Negri [*San Francisco Chronicle*, December to April 1935], Joe Pasquale, George Pero, Joseph Passerino, Joe Pasarine, John Novo, J. J. Ghie, Joe Barty, Leonardo Negri, Dago Joe, James Jackson.

Nelson, E.—Axel Bjork

Pagamassino—"Black Tony."

Parente, Joseph—Joe Parenti

Parker, J. W.—Emmet C. Perkins, F. E. Patton.

Phelps, John—John Glore.

Quintino, Ernesto—Ernest Mariano

Rasmussen, Victor—Victor Read.

Richards, Eddie—Eddie Wilson.

Rinckel, Algernath S.—Ralph E. Jones

Rizzo, Ralph R.—"Skibootch," Scabootch, Bill Scabootch

Ross, George—William Ross

Schouweiler, Marvin E.—Dr. Ross

Smith, Vernon—Frank Neff

South, Walter—Walter Southland, Walter Oats

Strallo, Anthony—Tony Cornero—Louis Donalds, Thompson

Strallo, Madeline—Esther Cornero, Mrs. Esther Crank

Sugarman, Maurice—Jack Schwartz, Eddie the Jew, Jack Gordon

Tambini, Louis—"Doc Bones" Tambini, [*San Francisco Chronicle,*March 26, 1935], "Doc" Moore.

Verda, Joe—Ortega

Wells, Kirk—Kirk Williams, L. M. Becletel

Westman, J. B.—Harry D. MacDonald

Williams, George—George Wilson, Paul Davis

Williams, Thomas C.—Tobe Williams, Big Tobe, Gunnif (Gonif) From Galway, Tove Williams, Cohn.

Zuker, Jack—Jack Jacobson

APPENDIX C
U.S. Civil Service Exam

United States Civil Service Commission Examination (Page 1) for Prohibition Agents. Started 1927 by President Coolidge to obtain better qualified agents. National Archives, RG 10.

Confidential

Series No. 1 June, 1927	UNITED STATES CIVIL SERVICE COMMISSION	**Sheet 3**

JUNIOR PROHIBITION AGENT	PROHIBITION INVESTIGATOR	
PROHIBITION AGENT	JUNIOR ALCOHOL AND BREWERY INSPECTOR	**EXAMINATION**
JUNIOR PROHIBITION INVESTIGATOR	ALCOHOL AND BREWERY INSPECTOR	

FIRST SUBJECT—Practical Mental Tests—Concluded

Place of Examination _____ Examination No._____

Date _____ (City or town) (State) Time commenced _____ Time finished _____

You will be allowed 2 hours to study the directions and samples and answer all the items in this booklet.

When you understand the directions and samples, turn the page and continue with the test without waiting for a signal.

Do not spend more than 15 minutes on the directions and samples.

RATING
(Sheet 3 only)

DIRECTIONS AND SAMPLE QUESTIONS

This part of the examination is made up of questions of three types: (1) Questions which are based on cases of law violation such as a Federal prohibition agent might have to deal with in his regular work, or on problems of judgment like those met by prohibition agents; (2) questions which are based on short paragraphs and which require you to interpret the meaning of the paragraphs; (3) questions which test your understanding of words which are used in regulations and orders, and which a prohibition officer must be able to interpret.

For every question in this part of the examination there are five suggested answers. From these five suggestions you are to select the one BEST answer and to write its number on the answer line.

Do not write out the answers to these questions; for each of the questions, you write only ONE NUMBER—the NUMBER indicating the best answer.

In answering questions based on cases of law violation, you are to assume that the only facts or clues which are known in the case are those given in the question. You are to indicate in which of the suggested actions you, as a prohibition agent, would take in order to meet the situation or solve the problem.

SAMPLE 1. An inspector of a bonded winery discovers that, on a large number of casks of wine which were sealed for storage, the seals have been cut and glued together again. Which of the following is the BEST action for the inspector to take? (1) Have the seals examined to find out whether or not they are genuine. (2) Take a sample of the contents for a chemical test and then reseal the casks. (3) Weigh the casks to discover whether part of their contents has been removed. (4) Open the casks and, if they are full, have them resealed in his presence. (5) Open the casks and, if they are not full, have them destroyed. . . . .

This question is based on a case which is typical of those with which the prohibition officer must deal. If you were the inspector, ought you to do (1) or (2) or (3) or (4) or (5)? You know that the seals have been cut and, therefore, that the casks have probably been opened. If a cask was opened, the contents may have been diluted or changed. The only way you can determine positively whether this has been done is by having a chemical test made. So (2) is the only correct answer. Write "2" on the line at the right.

You are also to assume, in answering questions of this type, that the events upon which the questions are based occur in a state where a *licensed physician is permitted to issue prescriptions for intoxicating liquor and to have in his office a certain amount of liquor for medicinal use. Drug stores may secure permits to make legal sales of liquor to persons presenting either doctors' prescriptions or permits to buy.*

SAMPLE 2. A Federal prohibition agent, who is passing a car which is parked near the curb while the owner is changing a tire, notices a half-emptied flask lying on the seat of the car. The flask is partially covered by the man's coat, but the whisky label on it is plainly visible. The agent sees no prescription label on the flask. He questions the man, who claims that he obtained the liquor on prescription from a near-by drug store which he names. Which of the following actions would it be BEST for the agent to take first? (1) Accompany the man to the drug store to see whether the druggist has a record of the prescription. (2) Destroy the bottle and its contents in the presence of the owner. (3) Use the testimony of the man in order to convict the accused druggist. (4) Arrest the doctor who issued the prescription. (5) Arrest the man and seize his automobile.

(2) is not the best action for the agent to take first, because unless the man's statement is false he possesses the liquor legally. Neither should the agent do (4) without securing further evidence, because a physician has a legal right to issue prescriptions for liquor. If the liquor was sold on prescription, there is no evidence that the druggist has done anything wrong, so (3) is not an answer. The agent ought not to do (5) until he is sure that the law has been violated. (1) is the correct answer, for if the man has secured the liquor legally, he can prove it, and if he has not, the agent can then arrest him. Write "1" on the line at the right.

SAMPLE 3. Which one of the five following suggestions is the BEST reason why fingerprints are a means of identification of criminals? (1) Fingerprints are easily obtained. (2) Fingerprints indicate the character of the individual. (3) Fingerprints are easily filed. (4) No two fingerprints are exactly alike. (5) Fingerprints may be obtained without the knowledge of the criminal. . . . .

Fingerprints may be easily obtained, but that does not make them a means of identification, so (1) is not the answer. (2) is not the answer, because fingerprints do *not* indicate the *character* of the individual and could not be used as a means of *identification* even if they did. The fact that fingerprints are easily filed does not make them a means of identification, so (3) is not the answer. Fingerprints are sometimes obtained without the knowledge of the criminal, but that fact does not make them a means of identification, so (5) is not the answer. The answer is (4)—fingerprints are a means of identifying criminals *because no two fingerprints are alike*. Write "4" on the line at the right.

Questions of the second type are based on statements which must be interpreted. *You are to base your answer to each question only upon the information that is contained in the statement before the question.*

SAMPLE 4. "The padlock law is intended to punish the particular establishment guilty of violation of the prohibition law—be it a cigar store, a cabaret, or a prominent hotel—rather than the individual waiter, clerk, or bartender who happens to be engaged in passing out the liquor at the time the place is raided."

According to this statement, which of the following is true with regard to the padlock law? (1) It is aimed at the person buying liquor, not at the person selling it. (2) It is used to prosecute a guilty proprietor instead of his employee. (3) It protects the rights of property owners. (4) It prevents the necessity of taking court action. (5) It is aimed only at those large establishments which disregard all laws. . . . .

If you read the statement carefully you will see that, of the suggested answers, (2) is the only one that is indicated in the statement. Therefore, (2) is the only possible answer. Write "2" on the line at the right.

SAMPLE 5. The word "individual," as used in line 4 of Sample 4, means most nearly (1) guilty (2) hired (3) suspected (4) foreign (5) particular. . . . .

Items like the one above are used to test your understanding of the words used in regulations and orders. *Particular* is the only word which has the same meaning as *individual* has in the statement. Write "5" on the line at the right.

TURN THE PAGE AND CONTINUE WITHOUT WAITING FOR A SIGNAL

APPENDIX D
BEING KIND TO THE LAPD

Editorial from a Los Angeles paper sent to the Wickersham Commision berating Police Chief Davis and Mayor George E. Cryer for either not knowing what is going on in their city or "double-crossing the public." National Archives, RG 10, Box 72.

BEING KIND

"EITHER Chief of Police Davis doesn't know what is going on in his city, or he is double-crossing the public," Councilman Carl I. Jacobson told the Presbyterian Ministers Association Monday.

That was a kindly way to put the matter.

The writer wishes that he could be kind enough to attribute the Chief's public attitude to ignorance, but unfortunately he cannot.

If it were only an occasional gambling joint or house of prostitution or instance of grafting that came to one's notice one might allow kindness to supercede intelligence and express an opinion that such things doubtless escape the Chief's attention in the midst of many law violations.

But none but an ignoramus occupying the Chief's position could fail to have full knowledge of the wholesale law violations and corruptions that have existed during the regime of Chief Davis and Mayor George E. Cryer.

For instance, none can believe for one moment that the big liquor parties that are staged in connection with certain public banquets are not known to the Chief of Police, for they are known to practically every business man in the community.

Few there are who have not walked into a banquet setting to find in a convenient location a bar operating under the very eyes of Chief Davis' men and in fact with Chief Davis' men indulging in the liquors that were freely dispensed.

Present in the gatherings on such occasions have often been not only many citizens of prominence but members of the police commission, of the Sheriff's force, commissioned officers of the police department, prosecutors, judges and other public officials.

Thus to the public is announced that not only is the law not being enforced but that its violation is being encouraged.

In the face of such conditions, for Chief Davis and Mayor Cryer to go about telling the people of the honesty of their law enforcement is more than "double-crossing." It is just about as serious a crime against their government as men can commit.

And thinking people see beyond the immediate effects of such protection of law violation.

Thinking people know that such open law violation takes away the foundations of all law enforcement.

They know that if the bootleggers who provide liquors for such occasions can secure full protection from the officers of the law at one time they can secure it under all conditions that they desire.

They know that whatever "pull" or "influence" that is necessary to secure sanction for the providing of liquors for big occasions can secure sanction for any other occasion.

They know that when the Chief boasts of the number of little fellows who are entrapped for minor violations of the law, he is covering up and protecting the big fellows who carry on their enormous activities undisturbed.

Let's be done with mockery.

Let's be done with hypocrisy.

Let's be done with claiming that we stand for good government when we uphold the protection of criminals, of corruptionists, of all the vicious forces that are the cause of bad government.

The Chief of Police or the Mayor or the Police Commissioners cannot provide liquors for assemblies of men of prominence and maintain themselves in a position where they can secure any appreciable degree of law enforcement or honest and efficient government.

If we want honest government we must make a contribution toward honest government.

We cannot secure honest government through lending whole-hearted support to the factors of dishonest government.

APPENDIX E

LIST OF PROHIBITION PARDONS BY GOVERNOR ROLPH

After Californians voted to abolish the state prohibition act, the Wright Act in the November 1932 election, Governor Rolph pardoned dry law violators languishing in prisons. Notice the absence of people from San Francisco County because San Francisco City and County arrested few offenders on liquor laws; therefore none sat in prison on state Wright Act charges [see Chapter 27]. The following is a list of those pardons, which includes six women:

ALAMEDA COUNTY—Richard K. Osborne

BUTTE COUNTY—Albert L. Mullins and Carl Edwards

GLENN COUNTY—Lee Pawley

KINGS COUNTY—J. F. Barcroft

LOS ANGELES—Maria Rodriquez, Kate Smith, Bill Glosson, Frank L. Cleminons, Ray W. Morgan, Lloyd 0. Beard, Philip E. Garvin, Lee J. O'Neil, William C. LeBec?, Wilburn Kincheloe, John D. Kelley, Jess F. Rutherford, Williams H. Cushine, Ted W. Downey, Paul Robinson, Frand H. Lopez, John Dinwiddle, Walter Hamilton, Manuel Chavez, Louis Schwartz, Joe Barrakan, Walter F. Grief, Claude Faggard, Violet Gilbertson, John Mulraney, George W. Corrigan, Eugene D. Carroll, John A. Miller, John W. Bacon, John H. Dunn, Lance L. Gleason, Christ J. Albert, Alexamder Puerto (?), Jack Skinner, Arthur C. Kendall, Wallace E. Alexander, Bill M. Patterson, Darrell Lee Moore, Herman W. Asher, Refugio ChavaHa, Herbert M. Smith, Thomas H. Metz, Paul McGee, Beltom Holder, Walter L. Murry, Bessie Kent, William A. Bonner, Salvador Aguire, Charles C. Harris, Carlos Ayala, A. F. Nfiller, William A. Tatum, Marvey A. Emory, Fred B. Kirk, Ray Gonnan, Earl Wilson, Harry Wilson, Henry Thomston, Fred D'Angelo, W. Roy Beeson, Andrew F. Johnson, Efijenio Meza, Ed Williams, George R. McNaurht (?), Gilbert H. Verdugo, John C. Waterhouse

NAPA COUNTY—Tony Beeler

ORANGE COUNTY—Mary Reilly, Howard Hobbs, Joseph Corcoles, Elmer Cota, Francisco Duarte, Joseph B. Trammull, Clarence E. McCord, Harvey Rice, James A. Armour, Vernon M. Pee

SAN BERNARDINO COUNTY—Wiley Livingston, C. H. Gaston, R. S. Shinn, Janaro Robeldo, Anastacio Palomino, Bert Shdtz, George Kieffer, James Stubbs, Goldie Jackson

SAN DIEGO COUNTY—Francisco Vega, Elmer Bell, Ralph H. Emerson, Vincenzo di Babbo, Jess Nolan Miller, Joseph James

SAN JOAQUIN COUNTY—Ed Dunnagan, John Cottis, Jose Olivarez (?), Peter Antoni, Jules Doneux, John Escobar, Frank Green, J. W. Graves, Newton D. Brannon

SAN LUIS OBISPO COUNTY—A. A. Hamilton

SANTA CLARA COUNTY—Phillip de Bello, Guy Petroni, Leo Garcia

STANISLAUS COUNTY—John Nfirandette

TULARE COUNTY—A. E. Shaw, Lester E. McConnick, W. C. Billingslea, Thomas V. Taylor, Charles Dolan, Fred Russell

VENTURA COUNTY—Jose Jesus Verdin, Domingo Perez, William J. Sharkey, Frederick G. Naso, Lesaro Ponce, Fred Nichhoefer, W. M. Cox

YUBA COUNTY—Martin Montgomery

APPENDIX F
LETTER FROM A. B. "Wad" Oates

Typed copy from original handwritten note from National Archives, Laguna Nigel.

Los Angeles, Calif.

Dec. 14 - 1937

Hon. Ralph E. Jenny
U. S. Federal Judge
Federal Bldg. Los Angeles, Calif.

My Dear Sir:

In the morning, Wed. Dec. 15, 1937 I am to appear before your Court for sentence on a charge of conspiracy to pass counterfeit coins.
On account of a certain amount of stage fright that one experiences in appearing before a Court and forgetting some important facts that one would benefit from were they known I am taking this means of placing a few facts before the court by which I believe I would benefit and at the same time give the Court a better idea of the person whom is being judged.

For the past two years I have been a very honest and hard worker. Have worked on W.P.A. digging ditches, in vegetable packing sheds, steel tank building, janitor and store room keeper, auto assemblyman, iron and steel shops, and finally to steel construction which I received from $8 to $10 per day. That has been recently. I have done any and every thing that has come my way in order to have an honest living and to avoid trouble. I have had a little trouble in [?] And I know what it means. For that reason I have tried more hard to keep my self clean.

At the time I entered into this conspiracy to dispose of some coins being made it was for the sole purpose of supplying my self and some one I love with a few groceries to carry us over until my job was open again, which had been closed down on account of shortage of steel here and a strike in the east in the steel mills. And had I not been trying to get a job I would have not become indicted. It was through a promise of a paint job that I contacted Mr. Campbell.

This was my first experience in Counterfit [sic] and by no means did I intend to follow any such line for a livelihood.

In asking mercy from the Court I would like for you to consider my working record and the endeavor I have made to do what is right. In all honesty I say I have not violated a law—I ask the Court to please give me the leash [sic] possible amount of time that it can under these circumstances so that I will not be taken away from my working connections so long that they will be (?) which has taken me so long to establish, and more so because of the circumstances under which I had to build myself up.

I would like to ask the Court to please consider the conditions under which a working man has to struggle, especially so with labor conditions as unsettled as they are today.

In closing I want to again ask the Court to be as merciful as possible and to consider my case on one who has done their best to do the right thing.

May I have the privilege of applying for probation?

Please pardon the pencil as it is all we have available.

Very Respectfully yours

[signed] A. B. Oates

Los Angeles Calif
Dec. 14 - 1937.

Hon. Ralph E. Jenny.
U.S. Federal Judge.
Federal Bldg. Los Angeles, Calif.

My Dear Sir:
In the morning, Wed. Dec 15, 1937 I am to appear before your Court for sentence on a charge of conspiracy to pass counterfeit coins.
On account of a certain amount of stage fright that one experiences in appearing before a court and forgetting some important facts that one would benefit from were they known, I am taking this means of placing a few facts before the Court by which I believe I would benefit and

END NOTES

When a reference is specified in the text, it is not usually cited in the end notes.

Abbreviations used:

Asst.—Assistant
Att.—Attorney
CA—California
Comm.---Commander
Dept. of Justice—Department of Justice
Gen.—General
L.A.—Los Angeles
ms—manuscript
NA—National Archives, Washington, D.C.
NA Laguna Niguel—National Archives,Laguna Niguel
NA San Bruno—National Archives, San Bruno
na—no author
nd—no date
np—no publisher listed
RG—Record Group in National Archives
S.F.—San Francisco
Univ.—university
WDC—Washington, D.C.

INTRODUCTION

1. American Business Men's Prohibition Foundation, Chicago, nd, National Commissions on Law   Observance and Enforcement, known as Wickersham Commission, RG 10, NA.
2. *Fletcher Dobyns, The Amazing Story of Repeal: An Exposé of the Power of Propaganda (Chicago: Willett, Clark & Co.,1940), 238.*

Chapter 1
THE BOOZE IS BEHIND THE TOILET

1. Don Beard, interview, San Bernardino, 1977. This story is about Beard's Aunt Jane, Armilda Jane James, an aspiring actress, and ex-chorus girl, who went to Palm Springs as a maid during prohibition.
2. *Edward H. Dickson, Sacramento Bee, 18 January 1970; Dickson said, "Sacramento lived through prohibition with one eye closed, the other red." The author modified Dickson's quotation for the title of this book.*
3. *Herbert Baumgarteker, interview, Lake Arrowhead, 29 May 1978; 12 April 1979; 10 April 1980. San Bernardino Sun, 29 November 1929, Los Angeles Times, 1-3 December 1929, 25 February 1930. He was the son of Frank who disappeared in November 1929.*
4. San Francisco Chronicle, 7, 10 July 1925.
5. San Bernardino Sun, 9 November 1929
6. William Genini, interview, S.F., 7 July 1980.
7. Anonymous.
8. Sausalito News, ca. 1925-26.
9. Sausalito News, 6 November 1925; 16 November 1928; San Francisco Chronicle, 10 July 1925, 6 November 1925; Jack Tracy, Sausalito Moments in Time: A Pictorial History of Sausalito's First One Hundred Years (Sausalito: 1983).
10.San Bernardino Sun, 14 September, 8, 9 November 1929; Redlands Daily Facts, 1, 7 November 1929.

Chapter 2
BONE DRY OR DAMP: THE WAR YEARS AND PROHIBITION

1. San Diego Union, 25-27 May, July, 13 August, 2, 11, 28 September, 22 October 1917; 9 October 1918.
2. Barstow Printer, 1918, 1919.
3. Sonoma Index-Tribune, 13 April 1918.
4. Inyo Independent, 14 December 1917.
5. San Diego Union, 21 October 1917; Barstow Printer 1918; Mountain Democrat (Placerville), 15 February 1919.

6. Sonoma Index-Tribune, *1918*.
7. Inyo Independent, *1918*.
8. Susan C. Ratliff, *"Prohibition in Stockton During the 1920's,"* The Study of History, *vol. II, ed. Delmar M. McComb (Stockton: San Joaquin Delta College, Spring 1974)*.
9. Congress, 65th Congress, 82.
10. Anti-Saloon League bulletin.
11. The Liberal Leader, The Official Organ of the Bartenders' Union Local 41 *(1 September 1917; 15 August 1916)*.
12. William Von Krakou, "Physiology and Hygiene Versus the Folly of Alcohol Prohibition" (S.F.: The Manufacturing Chemists and Pharmacists, ca. 1918).
13. "Final Calendar of Legislative Business," 42nd Session, Sacramento: 1917.
14. Sonoma Index-Tribune.
15. Mountain Democrat *(Placerville), 11 January 1919.*
16. Contra Costa Gazette, *1 February 1919; San Mateo News-leader.*
17. Sonoma Index, *7 March 1918.*
18. Sonoma Index, *January, 9 March, July 1918.*
19. Victor Valley News-Herald, *6 July 1918.*
20. Stanislaus Stepping Stones, *Fall 1983.*
21. Stepping Stones.
22. Susan C. Ratliff, "Interview of Leonard Covello, Stockton," 16 April 1974, ms., Holt-Atherton Dept. of Special Collections, Univ. of Pacific Library, 2.
23. Contra Costa Gazette, *25 January 1919.*
24. Gazette, June 1919.
25. Barstow Printer, November 1918.
26. Mountain Democrat, *4 January, 21 June 1918.*
27. Mountain Democrat; Paul Salopek, illustrations, Barstow 1977.
28. Contra Costa Gazette, *18 January, 1 February 1919.*
29. San Mateo News-Leader, *25 January 1919.*
30. Contra Costa Gazette, *11 January 1919.*
31. Mountain Democrat, *5 July 1919.*
32. Joseph A. McGowan, History of the Sacramento Valley *(New York: Lewis Publishing Co., 1961), 228-229.*
33. Contra Costa Gazette, *July 1919.*
34. Glenn A. Kennedy, "It Happened in Stockton, 1900-1925," vol. 3 (Stockton: 1967), Holt-Atherton Dept. of Special Collections, Univ. of Pacific Library.
35. Congress, 66th Congress, 306-312.
36. National Commission on Law Observance and Enforcement, known as Wickersham Commission, Box 202, RG 10, NA.

Chapter 3
ROBBIN' HOODS

1. San Mateo News-Leader, *2 January-31 July 1920. Most information in Chapter 3 came from seven months of the* News-Leader.
2. Redwood City Standard, *23 March 1922.*
3. Ann Mendenhall, ed., "Ann's Humboldt Scrapbook," excerpts from Humboldt Standard *(Eureka), 5 April 1923.*
4. Prohibition Circular, *11 June 1923, Treasury Dept., Box 11, RG 58, NA; San Bernardino Sun, 13 September 1929.*
5. San Diego Union, *14 September 1930.*
6. Millie Robbins, "Sausalito Salty Days," San Francisco Chronicle, *27 May 1966.*
7. Fraser Miles, Slow Boat on Rum Row *(Madeira Park, B. C.: Harbour Publishing, 1992).*

Chapter 4
ADD SEVEN DROPS OF CREOSOTE AND LET IT AGE FOR THREE HOURS

1. Howard Williams, Home Made Wine and Beer: A Neatly Compiled and Arranged Collection of Formula, *np, 1919, courtesy of Stewart J. Rogers, Apple Valley, 1 December 1979.*
2. Plumas National Bulletin, *17 March 1921.*
3. Pat Lulhman, "Atolia Pat," interview, Atolia , 29 September 1977.
4. Ontario Weekly Herald, *1928.*
5. Leonard Brock, interview, Deer Creek, 24 August 1977.

Chapter 5
PICKLED PIGS

1. Ray Conaway, interview, Barstow, 1978, 1980.
2. Harry Jennings Sr., interview, Santa Monica, 1978.
3. Ralph Kerr, interview, Mendocino County, July 1979. Kerr was born in Lake Tahoe.
4. Rolan Lyttle, interview, Barstow, 1978, 1979.
5. Ralph "Swede" Pedersen, interview, Sausalito, 1978, 1979, 1980.
6. Norton Steenfott, interview, Eureka, July 1979, 1981.
7. Artie Williams, interview, Dos Palos, 20 August 1977.

Chapter 6
DRYING UP THE STATE

1. San Francisco Chronicle, *23 May 1922.*
2. "Wineries in the Greater Lodi Area," Holt-Atherton Dept. of Special Collections, Univ. of Pacific Library, nd, 4-6; the Wright Act was approved on May 7, 1921, by the 44th Session, State Legislature, Ch. 80, p.79, and was to go into effect on July 29, 1921. It was delayed by a referendum until November 1922.
3. Dept. of Justice, 23-11-239, RG 60, NA.
4. Emerson E. Hunt, Chief, G.P.A., 13 August 1923, L.A., to Hon. E. C. Yellowley, Treasury Dept., IRS, RG 58; Hunt to Yellowley, 16 October 1923; Yellowley to Mabel Walker Willebrandt, WDC, 30 October 1923, Dept. of Justice, 23-12-130-1, RG 60, NA.
5. San Francisco Examiner, *8 November 1924; Case #s 4311, 4203, 4208, 4210, Department of Justice 23-11-301, RG 60, NA.*
6. Rutter, Director, S.F., 19 May 1924, to John P. Michieli; John P. Michieli, S.F., 26 May 1924, to Dept. of Justice, WDC; Willebrandt, WDC, to Michieli, 3 June 1924, Dept. of Justice, 23-11-56-1, RG 60, NA.
7. Criminal Case # 16812, District Court of CA, Northern District, NA San Bruno.
8. California Observer, *1 January 1921, 28-30, 33.*
9. California Observer, *1 January 1921, 33.*
10. Criminal Case # 16842, District Court of CA, Northern District, NA San Bruno.
11. California Observer, *1 January 1921, 27.*
12. Holtville Tribune, *January 1925.*
13. Solano County Currier, *5 January 1924;* Ferndale Enterprise, *1 January 1926.*
14. Edwin E. Grant, S.F., 4 march 1924, to Rutter, Prohibition Director, Dept. of Justice, 23-11-344, RG 60, NA.
15. H. W. Hess, interview by George L. Horner, Special Agent, S.F.,11 February 1926, Dept. of Justice, 23-11-?, RG 60, NA.
16. Victor Valley News-Herald, *11 April 1924, article from Arlene Kalenberger, Victorville historian.*
17. Los Angeles Examiner, *8 November 1924.*

Chapter 7
THE DRY DESERT MOISTENS LOS ANGELES

1. Descendant of the Sandoz family, interview, Hinkley, 1993.
2. Penny Morrow, interview, Oro Grande, 26 September 1977 and in 1978; Maggie Langley, interview, Oro Grande, 26 September 1977.
3. Thelma Gwin, interview, Barstow, 1980.
4. Edwin E. Grant, S.F., to Grand Jury of San Bernardino County, 1925. Grant, former state senator from S.F. who was voted out of office because of his prohibition stand, was president of the Sate Enforcement League.
5. Victor Valley News-Herald, *6 September 1929. Courtesy of Arlene Kallenberger.*
6. Barstow Printer, *6, 15 February 1923; 29 January 1925.*
7. Needles Nugget, *1928-1931;* Ehrma Watkins, interview, Needles, *18 March 1994;* Maggie McShan, interview, Needles, *17, 18 March 1994.*
8. Inyo Independent, *11, 25 May 1917.*
9. Independent, *5 April 1918.*
10. Independent, *15, 18 February 1918.*
11. Independent, *22 March 1918.*
12. Independent, *11 November 1922.*
13. Independent, *8 February 1917.*
14. Independent, *19 May 1923; see Chapter 8.*
15. Independent, *19 May 1923.*
16. Trona Pot-Ash, *1925; 6 August 1927; 28 February 1928; 1929; 1930; 29 August 1931; 2 January 1933; George Pipkin, "Trona Memories," Chapter XXXII, 22 June 1977; Chapter XXXIV, 27 July 1977; Chapter XLIV, 22 March 1978, The Trona Argonaut.*

Chapter 8
BOOTLEGGERS

1. San Bernardino Sun, *18 September 1929; 14 January 1930; Penny Morrow, interview, Oro Grande, 26 September 1977, 1978.*
2. William Puccinelli, interview, San Mateo & San Francisco, 25 July 1980 and 1981; Barbara (Puccinelli) Oswald and Ralph Oswald, interview, Menlo Park, 3 August 1998. Oswalds are the daughter and son-in-law of William Puccinelli.
3. Sausalito News, *23 November 1925; Oswalds, interview, Menlo Park, 3 August 1998; video tape of 1932 film, made by Jack Hale, courtesy of Ralph and Barbara Oswald.*
4. Inyo Independent, *7 July 1923.*
5. Willoughby, Malcolm F., *Rum War at Sea (WDC: Gov. Printing Office, 1964); page 168 lists a Julia, captured and turned into CG-940, used as a patrol boat, then destroyed.*
6. San Francisco Examiner, *6 November 1924.*
7. Case 15828-S, Dept. of Justice, 23-11-86-4, RG 60, NA.

Chapter 9
THOSE MINERS WILL TAKE ANYTHING—PROSTITUTION

1. Humboldt Standard, 22 May 1922.
2. Linzy Hudson, "A History of Prostitution in Jackson, California," ed. Delmar M. McComb, The Story of History (Stockton: San Joaquin Delta College, May 1976). Hudson interviewed several working girls of Jackson.
3. George Sparkie, "George Sparkie Knew Flora," ms, Salinas Library, Salinas, nd; George Robinson, interview of Jimmy Costello, ms, Salinas Library, Salinas, nd.

Chapter 10
DRY HUMOR (no end notes)
Chapter 11
BY SEA—THE RUM WAR

1. BC (pseud.), interview, north of Guala, July 1979.
2. Mellon, Andrew, "Regulations of Internal Revenue (T.D. 3601), 7 June 1924, WDC, Treasury Dept., 51-5.
3. Alf Oftedal, S.F., 4 November 1926, to Chief Intelligence Unit, WDC, Treasury Dept., RG 60, NA.
4. Case # 4287-c, 23-100-905, RG 60; Report of the U.S. Att. to Att. Gen. WDC, 8 July 1931; Malcolm F. Willoughby, Rum War at Sea (WDC: Gov. Printing Office, 1964), 166.
5. Criminal Case # 10686, May 1933, 23-12-351, RG 60, NA.
6. Charles Walker, Comm. Coast Guard Station, Humboldt, 16 November 1924, to Superintendent 12th District, NA.
7. _____, 8 March 1926.
8. Customs Information Bulletin No. 127, December 1932, Bulletin No. 128, Coast Guard, Treasury Dept., RG 60, NA.
9. Report Letter, 9 June 1932, Treasury Dept. NA.
10. San Francisco Chronicle, December 1930.
11. Ernest D. Wichels, "Prohibition Days," Times-Herald (Vallejo) from "The Story of the Hawk," from Wood Young, "The Saga of the Hawk," The Daily Republic (Fairfield), 3 April 1962, excerpts courtesy of Bertram Hughes, Vacaville.
12. Comm. Gabe Zimmerman, 24 March 1932, to Comm., Section Base 17, San Pedro, RG 60, NA.
13. "Report of a Customs Official on the West Coast," to Wickersham Commission, 21 July 1930, Box 200, RG NA
14. Case #15828-S, 23-11-86-4, RG 60, NA
15. Testimony of Capt. Eugene Blake Jr., 1 March 1933, Case # 21376-L, U. S. District Court Northern Division of CA, Admiralty Case Files, 1850-1934, Box 170, RG 21, NA San Bruno.
16. Marion Parker and Robert Tyrrell, Rumrunner—The Life and Times of Johnny Schnarr (Seattle: Ocra Books, 1988).
17. Fraser Miles, Slow Boat on Rum Row (Madeira Park, BC: Harbour Publishing, 1992).

Chapter 12
BY LAND—THE BORDER WAR

1. Don Whitehead, Border Guard (New York: Avon Books, 1963), 27-29, 39-40.
2. "Chinese Aliens and Booze Had Priority of First Patrol," Valley Grove ____ [?], vol. 6, no. 24. The rest of the title is missing; the press address was 419 Sweetwater Road, Spring Valley, now another business. No author or date was listed in copy provided the author.
3. "Customs Report," Wickersham Commission, Box 200, 17-18, RG 10, NA.
4. Wickersham Commission, Box 202, RG 10, NA.
5. Cornelius, Special Agent, Intelligence Unit, L.A., to Chief J. M. Doran, Intelligence Unit, WDC, 27 November 1927, S1-5435, N 23-12-197, NA; Charles L. Cass, Agent to Cornelius, Intelligence Unit, San Diego, 21 January 1927, numerous documents, Dept. of Justice, 23-12-197, RG 60, NA.
6. Carl Eifler, interview, Salinas, 1978; Thomas N. Moon and Carl F. Eifler, The Deadliest Colonel (New York: Vantage Press, 1974); for more on Carl Eifler, see R. Harris Smith, OSS: The Secret History of America's First Central Intelligence Agent (Berkeley: Univ. of CA Press, 1972), 243, 244, 246-48, 258, 265, 287.
7. Imperial Valley Farmer, 7 January-14 July, 1932.

Chapter 13
BY AIR—SMUGGLERS FLY IT IN

1. Dept. of Justice, 23-12-377, RG 60, NA; 99 US 584, 23-12-377, NA.
2. Dept. of Justice, 23-12-374, RG 60, NA.
3. San Diego Union, 13 August 1929.
4. San Diego Union, 6, 7, 8 July 1932.

Chapter 14
RACE TO THE CITY

1. Redwood City Standard, 29 May 1929; Redwood City Tribune, 2 July 1924.
2. Kearney, Tom, phone interview, Menlo Park, summer 1978.
3. Ralph Douglass, interview, Menlo Park, summer 1978.
4. San Francisco Chronicle, 19 May 1922.
5. May Hinds [pseud.], interview, Quincy, 21 July 1980.
6. Leslie White T., Me, Detective (New York: Harcourt, Brace and Company, 1936).
7. Redwood City Standard, 13 November 1924.

8. San Francisco Examiner, *9 March 1929.*
9. San Francisco Examiner, *22 ? 1925*
10.San Francisco Chronicle, *? 1925.*
11.Barstow Printer, *1931*
12.San Francisco Chronicle, *10 July 1925.*

Chapter 15
THE WET IMPERIAL VALLEY

1. Herbert Hughes, "What Volstead Started and Gillett Stopped," Hughes Collection, Imperial County Historical Society, nd.
2. _____, "Sheriff Puts Finishing Touch to Illicit Still," Hughes Collection, Imperial County Historical Society. Although not labeled, author was probably Herbert Hughes.
3. San Diego Union, *1931.*

Chapter 16
A PEANUT EXPOSES THE LAPD

1. *Thomas N. Moon and Carl F. Eifler,* The Deadliest Colonel *(New York: Vantage Press, 1974); Carl Eifler, interview, Salinas, 1978.*
2. Edwin Grant, "Report to San Bernardino County Grand Jury of Vice and Liquor Situation," 12 June 1924, Dept. of Justice 23-11-76, RG 60, NA.
3. Fred E. Wassen, L.A., to Prohibition Dept., WDC (received 20 January 1925), Dept. of Justice, 23-11-76, RG 60, NA.
4. Penny Morrow, interview, Oro Grande, 26 September 1977.
5. *Leslie T. White,* Me, Detective *(N. Y.: Harcourt, Brace & Company,1936).*
6. San Bernardino Sun, *24 September 1929.*
7. Sun, *5-6 September 1929.*
8. Criminal Case # 8591 & 8660H, U. S. District Court, Southern Division, NA Laguna Niguel.
9. "Memorandum," Division of Public Relations, L.A. Police Dept., 1929.
10.Criminal Case # 6552-m, Box 84, U. S. District Court, Southern Division, NA Laguna Niguel.
11.Gladys Stein, interview, Victorville, 1980; Doug Perrin, Bud Watkins, William Shields, Elinor and Phil Widolf, interviews, Laguna Beach, 20, 21 August 1980.

Chapter 17
I REMEMBER (no end notes)
Chapter 18
PUT A PADLOCK ON THAT REDWOOD TREE

1. *Anonymous;* Crescent City American *and* Humboldt Standard, *various issues.*
2. Al Bush, interview, Victorville, 5 December 1994, quoted after he heard this story of straight sink pipes.
3. *Walton, Richard H.,* San Bernardino Sun, *15 July 1995. Walton was district attorney of Humboldt County investigating an unsolved murder during prohibition where DA Stephen E. Metzler may have prosecuted the wrong man for political reasons.*
4. McGrath, Deputy Collector, Eureka, 7 April 1927 to Collector of Customs, S.F., 34-20, Box 88, Bureau of Customs, Treasury Dept., RG 36, NA.
5. Criminal Case # 4885, U. S. District Court, Northern District of CA, 30 December 1930 to 12 September 1932.

Chapter 19
MEAN BULL—NO RESPONSIBILITY FOR INJURIES

1. San Francisco Examiner, *24 June 1924.*
2. Donovan, Santa Rosa, to Asst. Att. Gen. Mabel Walker Willebrant; Willebrandt to Donovan, 22 May 1922, Dept. of Justice, 23-11-40, RG 60, NA
3. Robert A. Barker, Berkeley, May 1923, to Dept. of Justice, 23-11-52, RG 60,NA.
4. *Eugene L. Gray, Looking Back on Days of Prohibition,* Sutter County Historical Society News Bulletin, vol. XVII, no. 1 (January 1979), 13, 15.
5. Vino Sano Company (brochure), Dept. of Justice 23-11-?, RG 60, NA.
6. Times Herald Record, *6 January 1994.*
7. Wine Report, Wickersham Commission, Box 207, RG 10, NA.
8. Criminal Case 5005, U.S. District Court, Northern District of CA, November 1930, NA   San Bruno.
9. Article from Ralph "Swede" Pedersen, Sausalito, nd, np.
10.*Clarence Magistretti, "Funny Old World,"* Point Reyes Historian (fall 1978), courtesy of Richard Mason.
11.San Francisco Chronicle, *19 July 1925.?*
12.San Francisco Examiner, *25 October 1925.*
13.Examiner, *2 January 1926.*
14.Marin Journal, *17 December 1925.*
15.Journal, *31 December 1925.*
16.San Francisco Examiner, *15 January, 18 April 1930.*
17.Examiner, *30 May 1929.*

18.Examiner, *13 August 1928.*

19.Examiner, *25 May 1922.*

20.Criminal Cases 4989, 4990, 4991, 4994, U.S. District Court, Northern CA, NA San Bruno.

Chapter 20
MACHINE GUNS TO FRISCO: BABY FACE NELSON AND ORGANIZED CRIME

1. R. A. Beman, Special Agent in Charge, S.F., 14 March 1932, to Director of Prohibition, WDC, Dept. of Justice, 23-12-341 to 369, RG 60, NA; Criminal Case # 1704, U.S. District Court, Northern District of CA, NA San Bruno.

2. San Francisco Examiner, *8 July 1925, and various July* Examiners; San Francisco Chronicle, *7, 10 July 1925;* Redwood City Standard, *1926;* Sausalito News, *6 November 1925, 15 November 1928.*

3. San Francisco Chronicle, 11, 17, 22 November 1928.

4. John A. Conwell, Intelligence Unit, L.A., to Hon. Samuel McNabb, U.S. Att., L.A., 20 November 1926, Dept. of Justice, 23-12-192, RG 60, NA.

5. Criminal Case 8582-H, U.S. District Court, Southern District of CA, NA Laguna Niguel.

6. *San Luis Obispo* Daily Telegram, *5 January 1931.*

7. San Bernardino Sun, *29 November 1929.*

8. *San Francisco* Chronicle, *27 August 1928.*

9. Ferndale Enterprise, *21 May 1926.*

10.Sacramento Bee, *19 December 1928.*

11.Imperial Valley Farmer, *21 January 1932.*

12.Barstow Printer, *14 May 1931.*

13.Herbert Baumgarteker, interview, Lake Arrowhead, 29 May 1978; 12 April 1979; 10 April 1980; Los Angeles Times, *1-3 December 1929;* San Bernardino Sun, *29 November 1929; A Missing Person, Case # 109741, L.A. County, 25 February 1930; Sheriff's Deed of Execution, San Bernardino County, 30 August 1933, for Mary Q. Baumgarteker's purchase of California Medicinal Wine Company for $12,000 from her own estate.*

14.Case 95-57-8, Sections 7 and 8, Federal Bureau of Investigation, NA; Reno Evening Gazette, *15, 19 March 1935*

Chapter 21
AS WET AS THE PACIFIC OCEAN—SAN FRANCISCO

1. San Francisco Chronicle, *4 November 1927; Dept. of Justice, 23-11-189-11, RG 60, NA.*

2. *Elizabeth A. Brown,* The Enforcement of Prohibition in San Francisco, *MA thesis Univ. of CA, Berkeley, 1945.*

3. San Francisco Chronicle, *18 May 1822.*

4. "Pacific Data," 23, Wickersham Commission, Box 230, RG 10, NA.

5. **Merritt S. Barnes, "Wet As the Pacific Ocean: An Informal History of Prohibition in San Francisco," ms., Foster City, circa 1978. The title came from San Francisco Supervisor Richard Welch's description of his attitude toward dry laws, 25 May 1926. NOTE: End notes for Merritt Barnes' manuscript are 6 through 43.**

6. San Francisco Chronicle, *7 August 1930;* San Francisco Examiner, *17 January 1920; David Siefkin,* The City at the End of the Rainbow—San Francisco and Its Grand Hotels *(New York: G. P. Putnam's Sons, 1976), 115-116.*

7. San Francisco Chronicle, *1 January 1926.*

8. *Siefkin,* The City at the End of the Rainbow, *115-116.*

9. New York Times, *23 January 1921; 15 April 1922.*

10.Gilman Ostrander, The Prohibition Movement in California 1848-1933 *(Berkeley: Univ. of CA Press, 1957), 170.*

11.Brown, The Enforcement of Prohibition in San Francisco, *19-20.*

12.Ostrander, The Prohibition Movement in California 1848-1933, *150.*

13.The San Francisco Call, *25 March 1920.*

14.New York Times, *22 March 1926.*

15.The California Liberator, *January 1923.*

16.San Francisco Resolution quoted in The California Liberator, *October 1922.*

17.The California Minute Man, *November 1925.*

18.The California Liberator, *April 1922.*

19.Franklin Hichborn, Story of the Session of the California Legislature of 1909 *(S.F.: James H. Barry Co., 1909), 184;* Searchlight, *November 1914; George Mowry,* The California Progressives *(Chicago: Quandrangle Books, 1951), 217; Liston Sabraw,* Mayor James Rolph Jr. And the End pf the Barbary Coast, *MA Thesis, San Francisco State Univ., 1960, 177-178.*

20.The California Liberator, *April, July 1922; October 1926; Ostrander,* The Prohibition Movement in California, *192.*

21.The California Liberator, *April 1922; June 1924; Sally Stanford,* The Lady of the House—The Autobiography of Sally Stanford *(New York: G.P. Putnam's Sons, 1966) 46-47.*

22.Will Rogers, from Clementina Marie Fisher, quoted from Newsweek, *18 March 1932,* James Rolph Jr. 1869-1934: An Estimate of His Influence on San Francisco's History, *MA Thesis, Univ. of San Francisco, 1965, 107.*

23.Letter from Stanton Delaplane to author [Barnes], 6 February 1977; John Brooke, interview, 8 December 1977. He was former Yellow Cab Company official; Sabraw, Rolph and the End of the Barbary Coast, *95.*

24.Charles Metz, "The Crusader Starts," Outlook and Independent, *15 October 1930, 78, quoted in George Mowry,* The Twenties Fords, Flappers and Fanatics *(Englewood Cliffs: Prentice Hall Incorporated, 1963), 186; Stanford,* The Lady of the House—The Autobiography of Sally Stanford, *77;* San Francisco Bulletin, *20 June 1920.*

25.Rolph to Reverend J. C. Westenberg, 9 August 1913, in Rolph Papers.

26.Herb Caen, Bagdad by the Bay *(Garden City: Doubleday & Co., 1949), 69; Erlick,* A Life in My Hands, *135; Ostrander,* The Prohibition Movement in California 1848-1933, *172;* The California Liberator, *June 1926;* San Francisco Chronicle, *25 May 1926;* San Francisco News, 23 December 1924; San Francisco Examiner, *26 May 1926.*

27.San Francisco Call, *27 November 1924;* The California Liberator, *December 1924; June 1926.*

28.*Stanford,* The Lady of the House, *47.*

29.*Stanton Delaplane, "Pete McDonough,"* San Francisco Chronicle, *10 July 1947; "Atherton Graft Report,"* San Francisco Chronicle, *17 March 1937; Erlick,* A Life in My Hands, *87.*

30.San Francisco Chronicle, *25, 26 1923;* San Francisco Call, *25 April 1923.*

31.San Francisco Call, *25, 26 April 1923;* San Francisco Chronicle; *25, 26 April 1923.*

32.San Francisco Examiner, *25, 26 April 1923; "Atherton Graft Report,"* San Francisco Chronicle, *17 March 1937; Brown,* The Enforcement of Prohibition in San Francisco, *32; Harvey Wing, interview by Merritt Barnes, 27 February 1978. Wing was a former reporter of both the* Examiner *and the* News.

33.San Francisco Call, *5, 15 May 1923; 19 November 1924;* San Francisco Chronicle, *23 November 1924*; San Francisco News, *27 August 1925.*

34.*Ostrander,* The Prohibition Movement in California 1848-1933, *150, 173.*

35.*Herb Caen,* Don't Call It Frisco *(Garden City: Doubleday & Co., 1953), 63.*

36.*Stanford,* The Lady of the House, *66-67; Jerry Flamm,* San Francisco's 20's, 30's—Good Life in Bad Times *(San Francisco: Chronicle Books, 1976), 21.*

37.*Flamm,* San Francisco's—Good Life in Bad Times, *62-63.*

38.*Caen,* Don't Call It Frisco, *256.*

39.San Francisco Examiner, *26 May 1926;* San Francisco Examiner, *26 May 1926.*

40.*Flamm,* San Francisco's—Good Life in Bad Times, *62-63.*

41.*Caen,* Don't Call It Frisco, *131-132; Flamm,* San Francisco's—Good Life in Bad Times, *50; Stanford,* The Lady of the House, *66-67;* The California Liberator, *February 1923.*

42.*Herb Caen,* Herb Caen's San Francisco *(Garden City: Doubleday & Co., 1957), 70; Flamm,* San Francisco's—Good Life in Bad Times, *21; Stanford,* The Lady of the House, *66-67; Caen,* Don't Call It Frisco, *131-32.*

43.*Flamm,* San Francisco's—Good Life in Bad Times, *19-21; Stanford,* The Lady of the House, *66-67; T. H. Watkins and R. R. Olmstead,* Mirror of the Dream, An Illustrated History of San Francisco *(San Francisco: Scrimshaw Press, 1976), 264; Herb Caen,* Bagdad by the Bay, *174-175.*

44.*San Jose Mercury Herald, 1 April 1933.*

45.Perry vs. United States of America, case 4803, U.S. Circuit Court of Appeals for the Ninth Circuit. NA San Bruno.

46.Jack K. Derham, interview, Atherton, 19 June 1993.

Chapter 22
MOUNTAIN FOLK

1. H. W. Hess, statement made to George L. Horner, Special Agent, Dept. of Justice, 11 February, 1927, 23-11-?, RG 60, NA.
2. Arthur H. Briggs, S.F., to Mabel Willebrandt, Asst. Att. Gen., WDC; Briggs to Wheeler, S.F., 2 February 1927, Dept. of Justice, 23-11-?, RG 60, NA.
3. Feather River Bulletin, *February 1926.*
4. Bulletin, *October 1926.*
5. National Plumas Bulletin, *19 March 1931.*
6. Inez Nelson, interview, Beckwourth, also known as Beckwith, 24 June 1993.
7. Feather River Bulletin, *18 August, 8 September 1932.*
8. Wallace, Quincy, 24 April 1929 to Mabel Willebrandt, WDC; Willebrandt to Wallace, 1 May 1929, Dept. of Justice, 32-11-0-343, RG 60, NA.
9. Hap Manit, interview, Portola, 24 June 1993.
10.Feather River Bulletin, *January to December 1932.*
11.Bulletin, *15 June 1930; 31 March, 12 May 1932.*

Chapter 23
I DIDN'T KNOW HE WAS MAKING IT ON MY FARM

1. Case Files 23-11-341, 23-11-343, 23-11-259, 23-11-274, 23-11-291, Dept. of Justice, RG 60, NA; Ralph "Swede" Pedersen interview, Sausalito.
2. Bill Cox, Moonshiners in Meadowbrook, *High Country No. 2, Riverside: 1967.*
3. Oceanside Blade, *12, 17, 24 June 1924.*
4. San Diego Union, *15 January 1930.*
5. San Francisco Examiner, *9 March 1929.*
6. Criminal Case 10379 M, U.S. District Court, Southern Division of CA, NA Laguna Niguel.
7. Susan C. Ratliff, "Even in the Nicest Hotels" from Prohibition in Stockton During the 1920s, *ed. Delmar M. McComb,* The Study of History, *vol. II (Stockton: San Joaquin Delta College, May 1974).*
8. Ratliff, 17.
9. Ratliff, 22.
10.Byron Times Development Edition 1928-29, *Eleventh Edition (Contra Costa & San Joaquin Counties: 1928).*
11.Donald L. Rivara, The Goins Murders of 1926 *(Stockton: 15 November 1987), Holt-Atherton Dept. of Special Collections, Univ. of Pacific Library. 15 November 1987.*

12.Glenn A. Kennedy, It Happened in Stockton, 1900-1925, *vol. 3 (Stockton:1967), Holt-Atherton Dept. of Special Collections, Univ. of Pacific Library, 109-10, 310.*
13.San Diego Union, *7 July 1932.*
14.Dos Palos Star, *April-August 1933.*
15.Dos Palos Star, *July 1927.*
16.Sacramento Bee, *29 January 1929.*
17.Stockton Daily Independent, *4 August 1931.*
18.Sacramento Bee, *19 December 1928.*
19.Sacramento Bee, *1 June 1932.*
20.Sacramento Bee, *26 January 1929.*
21.Sacramento Bee, *31 January 1929.*
22.Sacramento Bee *3 June 1932.*
23.Edward H. Dickson, Sacramento Bee, *18 January 1970.*
24.Leland Edwards, "A Deadly Confrontation," Los Tulares, *Tulare County Historical Society, Visalia (March 1996).*

Chapter 24
THE PEACEFUL PENINSULA

1. Richard N. Schelleni, Menlo Park History: From Contemporary Newspaper Accounts *(Redwood City: 1974), 202, 208.*
2. Times Gazette *(Redwood City), 28 June 1919, 24 January 1920.*
3. Times Gazette, *28 June, 12, 19, July, 2, 16, August, 1919.*
4. Redwood City Standard, *1 April 1920.*
5. Standard, *10, 17 February 1921;* Times Gazette, *12, 19 February, 21 March 1921.*
6. Standard, *17 March, 14 April 1921.*
7. Times Gazette, *12, 19 February 1923.*
8. San Francisco Examiner, *January 1923.*
9. Redwood City Standard, *16 February 1922.*
10.Standard, *1, 8 February 1923.*
11.Standard,, *28 June 1923.*
12.Standard, *12 July, 2, 9, 16 August 1923.*
13.Standard, *30 August, 13 September 1923.*
14.Standard, *February, 1929; 13 May 1930.*
15.Standard, *12 April 1928.*
16.Standard, *2 August 1923.*
17.Standard, *22 March 1928.*
18.Tom Kearney, telephone interview, Menlo Park, 1978; Redwood City Standard, *28 February, 15 May, 9, 24, October, 11 December 1924.*
19.Standard, *30 October, 4, 18 December 1924; 12-15 February 1925.*
20.Standard, *4 December 1924; 1 January 1925.*
21.Standard, *26 March, 2, 9, 23 April, 3 July, 29 October, 10, 14, 31 December 1925.*
22.San Francisco Chronicle, *21 March 1925.*
23.Redwood City Standard, *3, 31 March 1927.*
24.Standard, *5 May 1927; Redwood City Tribune, 11 May 1927.*
25.Standard, *9, June 1927;* Tribune, *30 June 1927.*
26.Standard, *8 September 1927.*
27.Standard, *9 September 27;* Schelleni, "Menlo Park History," 202.
28.Standard, *3 November 1927;* California Blue Book 1928.
29.Standard, *15, 22 December 1927; 19 January, 21 February, 6, 29 March, 5 April 1928.*
30.Standard, *12, 19, 26 April, 7, 14, 28 June 1928.*
31.Standard, *2, 20 August, 1 November 1928.*
32.Hazel Ator Sommers, Menlo Park, interview, 26 December 1976; Alec Beltramo, Menlo Park, interview, 22 August 1977; Dave Walker, interview, Anderson, 24 August 1977; anonymous, interview, Menlo Park, August 1977.
33.John V. Young, Santa Clara Memoirs *(Santa Cruz: Western Tanager Press), 1980, 38-41.*

Chapter 25
THE LAST STAND

1. California Blue Book or State Roster 1928 *(Sacramento: State Printing Office, 1928).*
2. Crescent City American, *1 December 1926;* Tracy Press *(Semi-Weekly)1926-1928;* Daily Palo Alto Times, *1928;* Feather River Bulletin, *24 November 1927;* San Bernardino Sun, *5 September 1929.*
3. San Diego Independent, *2, 11 December 1926.*
4. San Diego Independent, *2-5 December 1925.*
5. Internal Revenue, Treasury Dept., Box 6, RG 58, NA.
6. Wickersham Commission, Box 206, RG 10, NA.
7. Wickersham Commission, Box 201, RG 10, NA.
8. Anslinger, 31 March 1930, to H. Jones, Esquire, Dept. of Justice, Treasury Dept., Box 6, RG 58, NA.
9. "List of Persons Killed or Fatally Injured by Officers of Bureau of Prohibition," ms, 14 October 1929, Box 199, RG

10, NA;

10.Hayden, S.F., to Att. Gen., Internal Revenue, Treasury Dept., Box 6, RG 58, NA; Senator H. C. Jones, 13 April 1927.

11.Daily Palo Alto Times, *19 April 1927;* Corona Daily Independent, *January 1928.*

12.Daily Palo Alto Times, *April 1927.*

13.Willebrandt File, *82-5961, Library of Congress;* Union Signal, *15 February 1928;* Corona Daily Independent *1927.*

14.Tracy Press (Semi-Weekly), *14 January 1927-30 May 1928.*

15.Daily Palo Alto Times, *9 April 1927.*

16.Ontario Herald, *26 July 1928.*

17.American Business Men's Prohibition Foundation (Chicago: nd), RG 10, NA.

18.E. Smith, Canton, Mississippi, 10 December 1928, to Willebrandt, WDC, Dept. of Justice, 23-11-0, RG 60, NA.

19.George M. Veile, Inglewood, to Pres.-Elect Hoover, Dept. of Justice., 23-11-0-343. RG 60, NA.

20.E. King, San Andreas, to Willebrandt, 23-11-0-343, RG 60, NA.

21.San Francisco Examiner, *22 February 1929.*

22.Dept. of Justice, 23-12-7-?, RG 60. NA.

Chapter 26
THE WICKERSHAM COMMISSION

1. San Francisco Chronicle, 15 November 1928.
2. Wickersham Commission, Box 206, RG 10 NA.
3. Wickersham Commission, Box 66.
4. Wickersham Commission, Box 66; see Metzler, Chapter 18 for the irony of his letter.
5. Wickersham Commission, Box 70. (Copied 12 pages.)
6. Wickersham Commission, Box 69.
7. Wickersham Commission, Box 70.
8. Wickersham Commission, Box 73.
9. Wickersham Commission, Box 85.
10.Wickersham Commission, Box 85.
11.Wickersham Commission, Box 75.
12.Wickersham Commission, Box 88, 89.
13.Wickersham Commission, Box 73.
14.Wickersham Commission, Box 85.
15.William Hoffman, L.A., to Wickersham Commission, 19 April 1930.
16.Riverside Daily Press, 24 November 1930.
17.Christian Century, nd.
18.Franklin P. Adams, New York World in Don Whitehead, Border War (NY: Avon Books, 1963), 84.
19.Fletcher Dobyns, The Amazing Story of Repeal: An Expose of the Power of Propaganda (Chicago: Willett, Clark & Co., 1940).

Chapter 27
DAMPENING THE DRYS

1. Ontario Herald, 5 November 1929?
2. Willebrandt Manuscript, File 8259618, Library of Congress.
3. Washington Post, 2 October 1930.
4. Evening Star (Washington, D. C.), 11 March 1931.
5. Ontario Herald, 5 November 1929.
6. Annual Report of the Division of Criminal Identification and Investigation (Sacramento: State Department of Penology, 1932).
7. San Francisco Examiner, 1 December 1929, Wickersham Commission, RG 10, NA.
8. Examiner, 14 July 1929, Wickersham Commission, RG 10, NA.
9. M. Hallanan, Chief of Police, Sacramento, 20 September 1929, to Wickersham Commission, RG 10, NA.
10.Chula Vista Star, March 1932.
11.San Diego Union, 15, 17 January 1930.
12.Clifford J. Walker, "The 10th Anniversary of Prohibition in Wet Riverside County," Country Life (Riverside), vol. 2, no. 1, 6-7 (January 1980).
13.Donald K Adams, "The Great Depression Years in Stockton (1929-1932)," ed. Delmar M. McComb, The Study of History, vol. II (Stockton: San Joaquin Delta College, 1974), 7, 11.
14.Imperial Valley Farmer, 11 February 1932.
15. San Francisco Chronicle, 14 March 1931.
16. San Diego Union, July 1932.
17. Clarence H. Lee, Palos Verdes Estates, 18 August 1932, to Att. Gen. William D. Mitchell, Dept. of Justice, 23-12-348, RG 60, NA.
18. Clipping of L. A. Examiner, nd, anonymous, 1932, to Dept. of Justice, RG 60, NA.
19. John K. Bovard, telegram, Inglewood, March 1931, to Asst. U.S. District Att. Gen. A. Youngquist, WDC, 23-11-350, NA.
20. Fort Bragg Advocate, 25 January 1933.
21. Byrd Weyler Kellogg, Santa Rosa Press Democrat, reprinted in the Fort Bragg Advocate, 15 February 1933.

570

22. Women's Organization for National Prohibition Reform (WONPR), MMC 1618, Library of Congress; Fletcher Dobyns, The Amazing Story of Repeal: An Expose of the Power of Propaganda, Chicago: Willett, Clark and Company, 1940, 105ff.
23. San Diego Union, 8 July 1932.
24. Holtville Tribune, 16 October 1931.
25. Tribune, 30 November 1931.
26. Feather River Bulletin, 20 October, 20 November 1932; Marin Journal, 18 September 1933.
27. San Francisco Chronicle, 19-20 December 1932; Sacramento Bee, 19 December 1932.
28. Chronicle, 11 December 1932.
29. Assembly Joint Resolution No. 3, January 1933.
30. Barstow Printer, September 1932-February 1933.

Chapter 28
HAPPY DAYS ARE HERE AGAIN

1. Fort Bragg Advocate, 12 April 1933.
2. San Jose Mercury, 2, 4, 6, 8, 9 April 1933.
3. San Jose Mercury, 6 April 1933.
4. San Jose Mercury, 7 April 1933.
5. San Jose Mercury, 8 April 1933.
6. Fort Bragg Advocate, April 1933.
7. Holtville Tribune, April, May 1933.
8. San Jose Mercury, 9 April 1933.
9. San Jose Mercury, 2 April 1933.
10. Dos Palos Star, 14 April 1933.
11. Feather River Bulletin, 6 April 1933.
12. Barstow Printer, 13 April 1933.
13. Fiftieth Session, Ch. 178, pp. 625, 2942? Ch. 26; 2516, Ch. 1023; 1697 Ch. 657.
14. Statutes of California, Section 7, Ch.149, 588ff; Sacramento Union, 27 July 1933.
15. Marin Journal, 28 September 1933.
16. Fort Bragg Advocate, 13 September, 11 October, 1 November 1933.

Chapter 29
A WOODEN SANDWICH MAKES A DRINK LEGAL

1. Fort Bragg Advocate, 1 November 1933.
2. Stockton Record, 4 December 1933; Dos Palos Star, 6-8 December 1933.
3. Fort Bragg Advocate, 29 November, December 1933.
4. Stockton Record, 6 December 1933.
5. Wayne Rossiter, interview, Menlo Park, 21-22 August 1977.
6. William Genini, interview, S.F., 7 July 1980; Sacramento Bee, 6 December 1933.
7. Dos Palos Star, 1 January 1934.
8. Dept. of Justice, 23-12-526, RG 60, NA.
9. Dept. of Justice, 23-12-51.
10. Dept. of Justice, 23-12-520; 23-12-533.
11. Dept. of Justice, 23-12-533.
12. Dept. of Justice, 23-12-529.
13. Dept. of Justice, 23-12-386.
14. Cases: CN 123 SF; CN 522; CN 145; CN 533; CN 436; CN 469; CN 499; CN 33; NC 313; CN335; CB 349 Dept. of Justice, Bureau of Prohibition, S.F., in possession of author.

Chapter 30
THE LEGACY

1. Ralph and Barbara Puccinelli Oswald, interview Menlo Park, 3 August 1998.
2. Dept. of Justice, 23-11-9, RG 60, NA.
3. Bright [pseud.], interview, San Bernardino, ca 1980.
4. Jill Morrow, interview, Las Vegas, 1995.
5. Don Whitehead, Border Guard (New York: Avon Books, 1963), 92-94.
6. San Francisco Chronicle, 18 January, 26 July 1936.
7. Fraser Miles, Slow Boat on Rum Row (Madeira Park, BC: Harbour Publishing, 1992).
8. Charley E. Petersen, interview, Barstow, 1996.
9. Bill _____ [last name unknown, member of the Mendocino County Historical Society], interview, Barstow, 1996.
10. Tammy Stoner, interview, Barstow 1996.
11. Unknown source at press time.
12. San Francisco Chronicle, 1, 3 December 1934; Dept. of Justice, Section B, 95-57-8, Lester Gillis [Baby Face Nelson] case.
13. Chronicle, 6, 8 December 1934.
14. Chronicle, 1 October, 7-8,10-11, 14 November 1935.
15. Chronicle, 1-2, 4 December 1934; 3 January 1935.

16. Chronicle, *30-31 December 1934; 1, 3, 16-17 January, 3 April 1935.*

17. Chronicle, *5 January 1935.*

18. Chronicle, *21, 28, 31 March, 2-3, 6 April 1935.*

19. Chronicle, *27 March, 1 April 4 June 1935; Ambrose Chase, interviewed by Ralph "Swede" Pedersen, ca. 1980; Ralph "Swede" Pedersen and Doris Berdahl, "Sausalito's Bootlegging Days,"* Marine Scope, *8-14 February 1972.*

20. Chronicle, *16 January, 31 March 1935.*

21. *Ellis L. Spackman, San Bernardino Sun, nd.*

22. *Patrick Baker,* The New Brewer's Handbook *(Westport, MA: Crosby & Baker Books, 1994).*

23. *Doug Baldwin,* Centennial Edition, *Salinas, 11 October 1971.*

24. Herbert Baumgarteker, interview, Lake Arrowhead, 29 May 1978, 12 April 1979, 10 April 1980.

25. Marin Scope, *23-29 October 1984.*

26. Unknown newspaper clipping, January 1934.

27. San Francisco Examiner, *15 October 1925.*

28. Stanislaus Stepping Stones, *vol. 7, no. 3 (fall 1983), 384-388.*

29. *Arthur H. Samish and Bob Thomas,* The Secret Boss of California: The Life and High Times of Art Samish *(New York: Crown Publishers, 1971), 63-69, 98.*

30. Willebrandt Manuscript, File 82-59618, Library of Congress.

31. *Glenn A. Kennedy,* It Happened in Stockton, 1900-1925, *vol. 3, mss 2, R618, Holt-Atherton Dept. of Special Collections, Univ. of Pacific Library; Stockton Index, 5 December 1933; Contra Costa Gazette, 1 February 1919; Mountain Democrat (Placerville), 5 July 1919.*

GLOSSARY

AAPA—Association Against the Prohibition Movement.

Abatement—Closing a house or business because of unlawful activity, sometimes called padlock law.

Age—to mature whiskey or to fake aging so that liquor will taste similar to bonded whiskey.

Alky Cookers—Stills

Alky—Alcohol, city made liquor generally with high sugar, instead of grain based.

Anti-Saloon League—Political force behind the prohibition movement.

Beads—Bubbles formed on liquor when shaken in jars, an indicator of alcohol proof.

Beer—Fermented cereal or fruit filled with alcohol, non-distilled alcohol, usually 3.0 -8.0 percent alcohol.

B-girls—bar girls, used to entice patrons to buy drinks.

Blind Pig—Speakeasy, an alky bootleg joint, "blind tiger" in the Eastern U.S., not used much in California.

Boil off—heating fermented mash until the alcohol turns to vapor.

Boiling—Mash is working, that is fermenting.

Bonded—Money put up to guarantee that whiskey will not be used for illegal purposes, e.g., bonded winery, bonded shipment of liquor, bonded alcohol plant.

Bond—Money or security put up to guarantee security or promise.

Bootlegger—One who makes illegal liquor; one who sells illegal liquor.

Bootleg—Illegal liquor of any kind, originally from old American meaning an Indian trader who hid liquor in his boot.

Booze—Any alcohol; boozer—one who drinks excessively from ME, Middle Danish busen, to drink heavily, boozehound, a big drinker.

Brandy—Distilled, fermented fruit juices, see jackass brandy and grappa.

Bureau of Prohibition Act—Act of 1927 reorganizing the Prohibition Department.

Charred barrels—Barrels burned on the inside to store whiskey and stimulate aging and encourage a brown color.

Coil—The condenser, usually made of curved copper pipe, going into water to turn the alcohol steam into a liquid; unscrupulous moonshiners used radiators which often created poison.

Cooker—The still or pot used for distilling liquor.

Cooperage—Bulk wine barrels made of oak for aging wine.

Corn—Corn whiskey, more traditional moonshine as compared to sugar whiskey.

Customs Office—In charge of the licensing of industrial alcohol, smuggling and border patrols. In charge is Customs Collector.

Dago red—Red wine, naturally fermented grapes with skins on, dinner wine, Italian house wine, dry like burgundy, usually made zinfandel grapes.

Demijohn—A narrow necked bottle, usually one to five gallons enclosed in a wicker covering.

Demurrer—A legal term meaning an objection or challenge.

Denaturing products—Methyl salicylate, oil of cassia, red mercuric iodide, phenol, quinine sulphate and 70+ more chemicals and or ingredients.

Denaturing—Process of rendering alcohol unfit for human consumption, approximately 60 formulas, giving it a disagreeable taste or smell. Most common was 10% wood alcohol and some benzine (benzene?) to 100 parts alcohol . In 1907, U.S. took the tax off of denatured alcohol.

Distill—To boil off the beer to separate the alcohol; the alcohol goes into vapor, then is cooled in a coil (condenser) to form liquid alcohol.

Dog hole—A small bay with little beach and no road down to the beach. Loggers used A-frames on top of the cliffs to lower logs down to the water and float them to San Francisco and San Pedro. The rumrunners reversed the process by using A-frames to bring liquor to the top of the cliffs.

Dory—A flat-bottomed rowboat used to haul liquor from a boat through the surf onto the shore; doryman, an experienced rower of a dory.

Dross-scum—Overflow from stills or from mash fermenting tanks, dregs, impurities.

Ethanol—Spirits of wine, etc., boils at 173.3 degrees.

Ethyl alcohol—From sugar by fermentation of water, sugar and yeast.

Feds—Federal prohibition agents.

Fifth—Standard American wine bottle contains 4/5th of a quart.

Fizzes—Drink made with egg whites for silver fizz, egg yolk for golden fizz, royal fizz with whole egg, plus juice of ½ lemon, shaved ice and shake long and hard. Serve in a 10 oz. glass, a fizz glass.

Gauger—Position hired by government to test wine and liquor in breweries and wineries.

Gin—Originally distilled from malt or other grains and afterwards rectified or flavored with juniper berries. Bathtub gin is slang for bootleg gin made from raw alcohol and flavored with juniper berries.

Glycerin—Glycol

Grappa—Italian distilled wine, clear grape brandy, sometimes called jackass brandy.

Gumshoe—Detective, usually someone hired by a government to do detective work by buying liquor from a bootlegger, paid for his buys and information, often employed by federal prohibition agents, not usually appreciated by local authorities.

Hijacking—Stealing someone's shipment of liquor.

Hijack—To take someone's property, namely liquor, maybe from wild west as hoboes robbed farm workers after payday, they said "Hi, Jack, how are you?"

Hooch—Homebrew, moonshine, sometimes bad liquor, liquor made from liquid of sourdough starter, said to have come from Hoochino Indians. Sometimes spelled 'hootch'.

Indictment—A formal charge in court.

Industrial alcohol—Alcohol used for making paints, inks, varnish, solvents.

International waters—Three miles accepted by most countries, then changed to 12 miles. Finally in the mid 1920s an agreement between Great Britain and the United States agreed to one hour's steaming time from shore.

Jackass—Jackass brandy—called by Italians if made out of wine, depending on the area, this was another word for liquor, brandy made from fermenting fruit juice (grapes, apricots) then distilled, that "kicks like a mule, bites like a horse."

Jake's leg—A disease from drinking bad Jamaica ginger, crippling the walking of the victim.

Jamaica ginger—Sometimes causing paralysis cases, especially in Kentucky, Ohio and Kansas, sometimes caused by using imitation fluid extract of ginger.

John Barleycorn—symbol or personification of malt beer, sometimes used for any liquor.

Malt—Grain, usually barley, steeped in water and fermented, by which the starch of the grain is converted saccharine matter, dried in a kiln, and then used in brewing ale, stout, beer or porter and in distilling whiskey.

Mash—Grain mixture of malt and yeast to turn starch into sugar and then into alcohol and carbon dioxide.

Methane—CH_4

Methyl—Wood alcohol, CH_3OH, poisonous and used to denature drinking alcohol.

Moon—Moonshine, illegally made alcohol.

Moonshine—Illegally made alcohol; moonshining—making illegal liquor.

Mother ship—A Canadian or other country ship off the coast of California to supply the fishing boats and launches that run the smuggled alcohol to the beaches and harbors.

Mula—Mexican slang for moonshine, potatoes and fruit fermented and distilled, "kicks like a *mula* (mule)."

Must—Crushed grapes with juice and skins.

Neat—Taking a drink straight. I'll take my whiskey neat, slang for great.

Neutral spirits—non-flavored alcohol, 80 proof or more.

Nuisance—A legal term referring to a bootleg joint or a brothel, i.e., "conducting a nuisance."

Off-sale—liquor license for selling liquor to be drunk off the premises.

On-sale—liquor license for selling liquor to be drunk on the premises.

Prohi—Prohis—federal prohibition agents.

Proof—Twice the percentage of alcohol in an alcoholic beverage, thus 80 proof whiskey is 40% alcohol.

Quash—Legal term to suppress, nullify, squash a search warrant or indictment.

Racking—Process of draining clear wine from barrel, leaving the sediment on the bottom.

Rap guys—Men, usually single or lackeys, who took the fall or rap for a boss.

Rectify—turn denatured alcohol into drinkable liquor; turn neutral spirits, raw, alcohol, into gin or whiskey.

Red eye—Another name for strong moonshine or alcohol "...brewing their own beer and the popular concoction know as 'red eye.'" From Astoia Mayor F.C. Farley about prohibition in Oregon in SI, April 13, 1918, moonshine that gave the drinkers red eyes the next day.

Resort—not necessarily a recreation facility, could be a store, restaurant and cabins; a picnic or camping area; sometimes forerunner of the motel.

Rotgut—Bad moonshine, sometimes just slang for moonshine.

Rum boat—A boat used to haul illegal liquor.

Rum row—A line of alcohol ships, mother ships, off the coast to supply the shore boats with whiskey.

Rummy—An alcoholic, a rumrunner.

Rumrunners—People who brought alcohol into the state or dry area by cars, airplanes or boats; boats used for smuggling liquor.

Rumrunning—act or process of bringing illegal liquor into an area.

Run off—to produce a batch of alcohol; to distill.

Run—run liquor onto a beach, smuggle, distill a batch of booze with a still.

Seine boat—fishing boat using nets.

Sheik—Used in 1925-6 for young men who provide alcohol to underage girls in Sacramento, Stockton and Marin County.

Sour mash—Aged mash from which grain alcohol is made—generally a more traditional way of moonshining.

Sugar alcohol—Made after 1911 with corn sugar or regular sugar and yeast, instead of grain and

Thump keg—"thumper" in the Appalachia, a tank or barrel where alcohol steam enters, separating excess water before going through the coils, making a stronger liquor.

Volstead Act—Act by Congress in forcing National Prohibition Act and the 18th Amendment, passed by Congress in October 1919, vetoed by President Wilson, passed right over his head within two days.

WCTU—Woman's Christian Temperance Union, dominant force for passing prohibition.

Whiskey—American spelling of whisky and generally refers to bourbon, scotch, Irish, Canadian or bootleg moonshine.

Whisky—See Whiskey—Scots spelling of whiskey, sometimes used in the United States.

White lightning—Moonshine made of grain alcohol.

White mule—Another term for grain alcohol, untreated, uncolored alcohol.

Wickersham Commission—Commission on law enforcement, initiated by President Hoover in the spring of 1929, deferring decisions to be made about law enforcement problems, repeal or modification of the 18ᵗʰ Amendment. It worked for over two years, making a report in June 1931.

Woman's Organization for National Prohibition Reform—WONPR, for prohibition reform or repeal.

Wood alcohol—One of the denaturants, methyl alcohol, poisonous, made from wood heated in a vacuum.

Worm—the coils used to cool distillate.

Wright Act—Called California's "Little Volstead Act", made to enforce the 18ᵗʰ Amendment; voted out in 1932.

Writ of Assistance—blanket search warrant, illegal in U.S., used by England against American colonists, ability to search anywhere, anytime for anything. Legal warrants must be specific.

yeast.

WORKS CITED

UNPUBLISHED MANUSCRIPTS

Baltz, Monica. "Sausalito's Prohibition." Sausalito, 23 May 1983. Mostly secondary material.

Barnes, Merritt S. *Wet As the Pacific Ocean: An Informal History of Prohibition in San Francisco.* Foster City, 1978. See Miscellaneous for works cited used by Barnes.

Bergman, Carl. "Antelope Valley Bootlegging." Antelope Valley, 1991.

_____. "Bakersfield and How I Got Started Picking Oranges." Antelope Valley, 1991.

_____. "College Days at Santa Ana J. C. and Losing a Good Job." Antelope Valley, 1991.

Breaum, Nellie. "Remembrances of Joseph Catalano of San Francisco." Redwood City, 1980.

Brown, Elizabeth A. *The Enforcement of Prohibition in San Francisco.* MA thesis, University of California, Berkeley, 1945.

Clausen, John. "The Hypocrisy of the Volstead Act." Victorville, 1985.

Dallara, Lou. "Typical Italian Family." Fairfax, 1978.

Echols, Lee E. "Badge, Pistol, Clock and Dagger." Chula Vista, 1978. Echols, an excellent writer, wrote several accounts of his Border Patrol days and generously allowed me to use them in this book.

_____."Capturing the Yukantravel." 1977.

_____. "Jiggers, The Cops." 1977.

_____."Smuggling Across the Border." 1978.

Fairchild, Donna. "Boron Bootlegging." Boron, ca.1980.

Hughes, Herbert. "Moonshining in Picacho." Holtville, nd.

_____. "Sheriff Puts Finishing Touch to Illicit Still," Hughes Collection, Imperial County Historical Society. Although not labeled, author was probably Herbert Hughes.

_____."What Volstead Started and Gillett Stopped," Hughes Collection, Imperial County Historical Society, nd.

Kallenberger, Arlene. "Around Victorville." Victorville, 1994.

"Patterson Place (Poeville)." na, nd, probably written by George Pipkin, given to the author by Margaret Brush, Trona, May 1995.

Pedersen, Ralph K. "Swede." "High Lights—Bootlegging." Sausalito, 25 July 1980.

_____. "Jackals in the Fog." Sausalito, 15 August 1980. Pedersen worked hard to research the Sausalito area and Baby Face Nelson for this book. Pedersen later published this in *Marin Scope,* 16-22 October 1984.

Ratliff, Susan. "Interview of Leonard Covello." Stockton, 16 April 1974. Holt-Atherton Dept. of Special Collections, University of Pacific Library.

Reese, Larry L. "Copper Bootlegging Tank." Victorville: 1999.

Rivara, Donald L. *The Goins Murders of 1926.* Stockton, 15 November 1987, Holt-Atherton Dept. Special Collections, University of Pacific Library.

Robinson, George. "Interview with Jimmy Castello." MS., Salinas Library, nd.

Scharlach, Bernice. "Min and Hattie's Bohemian Rendezvous." Lafayette, ca. 1978.

Schelleni, Richard N. "Menlo Park History: From Contemporary Newspaper Accounts." Menlo Park Historical Society, 1974, 202, 208.

Sparkie, George. "George Sparkie Knew Flora." MS., Salinas Library, nd.

Stearn, Fred. *Newberry Springs—Recollections of Its Early Days.* Newberry Springs: May 1987.

Stephens, Derrick. "Bootlegging." Ms., Sausalito, 1974.

Triepke, Jiggs. "A Boy's View of the Roaring Twenties in Culver City." Barstow: August 1995.

Wilhelm, Walt. "Desert Bootleggers." Yermo: 1978.

Willebrandt Manuscript, File 82-59618. Library of Congress.

BOOKS

Adams, Donald K. "The Great Depression Years in Stockton (1929-1932)." *The Study of History.* Vol. II. Edited by Delmar M. McComb. Stockton: San Joaquin Delta College, Spring 1974.

Altschul, Ira D. *Drinks As They Were Made Before Prohibition.* Santa Barbara: Schauerr Printing Studio, 1934. Copy courtesy of Joe Brown, Helendale, 1964.

Ames, Robert E. "Canada Whiskey," *I Remember.* San Bernardino: 1969.

_____. "Desert Whiskey Stills," *I Remember.* San Bernardino:1969.

_____. "Early Times in Las Vegas and Searchlight, Nevada," *I Remember.* San Bernardino: 1969.

_____. "My Story of Whiskey Pete and Death Valley Jack," *I Remember.* San Bernardino: 1969.

Baker, Patrick. *The New Brewer's Handbook.* Westport: Crosby & Baker Books, 1994.

*Bryon Times Development Edition 1928-29,*Contra Costa and San Joaquin Counties, 1928.

Byron Times Development Edition 1930-31, 156; 1932-33, 113; 1934-35, 107.

Carr, Jess. *The Second Oldest Profession: An Informal History of Moonshining in America.* Englewood Cliffs: Prentice-Hall, Inc., 1972.

Cooper, C. R. *Ten Thousand Public Enemies.* Boston: Little Brown & Co., 1935, 302-323.

Dobyns, Fletcher. *The Amazing Story of Repeal: An Expose of the Power of Propaganda.* Chicago: Willett, Clark & Company, 1940.

Gates, Dorothy L. and Jane H. Bailey. *Morro Bay's Yesterdays; Vignettes of Our City's Lives and Times.* Morro Bay: El Moro Publications, 1982, 70-71.

Hudson, Linzy. "A History of Prostitution in Jackson, California," *The Study of History.* Vol. IV. Edited by Delmar M. McComb. Stockton: San Joaquin Delta College, May 1976.

Kennedy, Glenn A. *It Happened in Stockton, 1900-1925.* Vol. 3. Stockton: 1967, Holt-Atherton Dept. of Special Collections, University of Pacific Library.

Lynch, Robert M. *The Sonoma Valley Story: Pages through the Ages.* Sonoma: The Sonoma Index-Tribune, Inc., 1997.

Mackrell, Lynn Holt. "The Disputed San Joaquin County Sheriff's Election of 1934 'The Hole in the Wall.'" *The Study of History.* Vol. IV. Edited by Delmar M. McComb. Stockton: San Joaquin Delta College, May 1976.

McGowan, Joseph A. *History of the Sacramento Valley.* Vol.II. New York: Lewis Publishing Co., 1961, 227-28, 231, 259, 285.

Miles, Fraser. *Slow Boat on Rum Row.* Madeira Park, BC: Harbour Publishing, 1992. Miles was a Canadian teenage rumrunner for the last two years of prohibition.

Moon, Thomas N. and Carl F. Eifler. *The Deadliest Colonel.* New York: Vantage Press, 1974; for more on Carl Eifler, see R. Harris Smith, *OSS: The Secret History of America's First Central Intelligence Agent.* Berkeley: University of California Press, 1972, 243, 244, 246-48,258, 265, 287.

Ostrander, Gilman M. *The Prohibition Movement in California, 1848-1933.* Berkeley: U. C. Press, 1957.

Parker, Marion and Robert Tyrrell. *Rumrunner—The Life and Times of Johnny Schnarr.* Seattle: Orca Books, 1988.

Pipkin, George C. *Pete Aguereberry: Death Valley Prospector and Gold Miner.* Morongo Valley: Sagebrush Press, 1982.

Ratliff, Susan C. "Prohibition in Stockton During the 1920's." *The Study of History,* Vol. II. Edited by Delmar M. McComb. Stockton: San Joaquin Delta College, Spring 1974.

Samish, Arthur H. and Bob Thomas. *The Secret Boss of California: The Life and High Times of Art Samish.* New York: Crown Publishers, 1971.

Smith, R. Harris. *OSS: The Secret History of America's First Central Intelligence Agency.* Berkeley: University of California Press, 1972.

Smith, Ron. "The Key Years of Stockton's El Dorado Brewery." *The Study of History,* Vol. V. Edited by Delmar M. McComb. Stockton: San Joaquin Delta College, 1977.

Starr, Raymond G. *San Diego: A Pictorial History.* Norfolk: The Donning Co., 1937.

Sullivan, E. Q. "Turtle Juice," *Reminiscences by E. Q. Sullivan, Former District Engineer.* Chapter XXVI of *Profiles.* Sacramento: September 1961.Courtesy of Cal Trans.

Tracy, Jack. *Sausalito Moments in Time: A Pictorial History of Sausalito's First One Hundred Years: 1850-1950.* Edited by Wayne Bonnett. Sausalito: 1983.

Union Title-Trust Topics. Vol. VIII, No. 5, Sept-October, 1953, 50th Anniversary Edition. San Diego.

White, Leslie T. *Me, Detective.* New York: Harcourt, Brace and Company, 1936.

Whitehead, Don. *Border Guard.* New York: Avon Books, 1963, 27-29, 39-40.

Williams, George F. *Home Made Wines for Family and Medicinal Use.* New Philadelphia (Ohio): George F. Williams, 1915. Given to author by Ruth Theodus, Apple Valley 1997.

Williams, Howard. *Home Made Wine and Beer: A Neatly Compiled and Arranged Collection of Formula.* 1919. Courtesy of Stewart J. Rogers, Apple Valley, 1 December 1979.

Willoughby, Malcolm F. *Rum War at Sea.* WDC: U.S. Gov. Printing Office, 1964.

Wineries in the Lodi Area. ND, np, na,.

Wortley, Ken. *Adventures with the Misfits.* Visalia: American Yearbook: nd. This 106-page book is excellent for Indian Wells Valley, South Owens Valley and Kern River area from 1921 to 1930 with characters who lived their own Roaring Twenties in a wild west way.

Young, John V. *Santa Clara Valley Memoirs.* Santa Cruz: Western Tanager Press, 1980.

UNITED STATES GOVERNMENT
U. S. CONGRESS
65th Congress, 82
66th Congress, 306-312

DEPARTMENT OF JUSTICE
Record Group (RG) 60 NA

Barker, Robert A. Berkeley, 1 May 1923, to Dept of Justice, 23-11-52.

Beman, R. A. Special Agent in Charge, S. F., 14 March 1932, to Director of Prohibition, WDC, 23-12-341-369.

Bovard, John K. Inglewood (telegram), March 1931, to Assistant U. S. District Att. G. A. Youngquist, WDC, 23-11-350.

Briggs, Arthur H., S. F., to Mabel Walker Willebrandt, Ast. Att. Gen., WDC; Briggs, S.F., 2 February 1927, to Wheeler, 23-11-0.

Conwell, John A., Intelligence Unit, to Hon. Samuel McNabb, U. S. Att., L.A. 20 November 1926, 23-12-192.

Cornelius, W. A., Special Agent, Intelligence Unit, L.A., to Chief J. M. Doran, Intelligence Unit, WDC, 27 November 1927, S1-5435; Charles L. Cass, Agent to Cornelius, Intelligence Unit, San Diego, 21 January 1927, Numerous Documents, 23-12-197.

Donovan, C. C., Santa Rosa, to Willebrandt; Willebrandt to Donovan, 22 May 1922, 23-11-40.

Grant, Edwin E. "Report to San Bernardino County Grand Jury on Vice and liquor Situation," 12 June 1924, 23-11-76.

Grant, Edwin E., S.F., 4 March 1924, to Rutter, Prohibition Director, 23-11-344.

Hess, H. W. Statement Made to George L. Horner, Special Agent, U. S. Dept.of Justice, S. F., 11 February 1927, 23-11-?.

Hunt, Emerson E. Chief, G.P.A., 10, 13 August 1923, L.A., to Hon. E. C. Yellowley, Treasury Dept., IRS, RG 58; Hunt to Yellowley, 16 October 1923; Yellowley to Willebrandt, WDC, 30 October 1923, 23-12-130-1.

King, J. E. San Andreas, ca. 1929, to Willebrant, 23-11-?.

Lee, Clarence H., Palos Verdes Estates, 18 August 1932, to Att. Gen. William D. Mitchell, Dept. of Justice, 23-12-348.

Report of the U. S. Att. to Att. Gen., WDC. 8 July 1931.

Rutter, S. F., Director, S.F., 19 May 1924, to John P. Michieli, S.F.; Michieli, 26 May 1924, to Willebrant, Dept. of Justice, WDC; Willebrandt, 3 June 1924, to Michieli, 23-11-56-1.

Veile, George M. Inglewood, to Pres.-elect Herbert Hoover, 23-11-?.

Wallace, E. J., Quincy, 24 April 1929, to Willebrandt; Willebrandt to E. J. Wallace, 1 May 1929. 23-11-0-343.

Wasson, Fred. E. L. A., to Prohibition Dept., WDC, Dept. of Justice, (received) 20 January 1925, 23-11-76.

Case Files 4203, 4210, 4311, 23-11-301.

Case Files 15828-S, 23-11-86-4, 23-11-9, 23-11-239, 23-11-259, 23-11-274, 23-11-321, 341, 23-11-342, 343.

Case Files 10686, May 1933, 23-12-35, 23-12-?, 23-12-51, 23-12-233, 23-12-374, 23-12-77; (99 US 584), 23-12-386, 23-12-520, 23-12-524, 23-12-526, 23-12-529, 23-12-533

Civil No 5301-BH, 23-12-534.

ADMIRALTY CASES 1859-1934. U.S. District Court, Northern District of CA, RG 21, NA San Bruno.
"Testimony by Capt. Eugene Blake Jr.," 1 March 1933. Case 21376-L, Box 170.

U.S. DISTRICT COURT NORTHERN DISTRICT. Criminal Docket. RG 21, NA, San Bruno.
Cases 1704; 4885; 4989, 4990, 4991, 4994; 5010, 5012, Box 289; 16842

U.S. DISTRICT COURT NORTHERN DISTRICT, Sacramento Docket, December 30, 1930-September 12, 1932, RG 21,NA, San Bruno.
Case 4585, Box 289.

U.S. CIRCUIT COURT OF APPEALS FOR THE NINTH CIRCUIT.
Perry vs. United States of America, No.4803.

U. S. DISTRICT COURT, SOUTHERN DIVISION. Laguna Niguel
Criminal Cases 8591 & 8660H; 6552-M, Box 84; 8582-H; 10379-M

BUREAU OF PROHIBITION
"Possible Production of Illegal Liquors in the United States for the Fiscal Year Ending June 1930." Report to Wickersham Commission, September 1930, RG 10, box 202, p. 6, NA.
"Prohibition Circular, 11 June 1923." Box 11 RG 58, NA
Cases CN-123 SF; CN 522; CN 145; CN 533; CN 436; CN 469; CN 499; CN 33; NC 313; CN 335; CN 349. In possession of author.

FEDERAL BUREAU OF INVESTIGATION(formerly Bureau of Investigation)
Case 95-57-8, Section 8. Lester Gillis (Baby Face Nelson and John Paul Chase cases); 26-5685; 25287, Joseph Ray Negri.
Memorandum, RE: Lester M. Gillis, with Aliases. 28 November 1934. 95-57-8.
Reno Evening Gazette. 19 March 1935 to 15 May 1935, various issues in Case file 95-57-8,   Section 7.

TREASURY DEPARTMENT
U. S. COAST GUARD
Bulletin No. 127, 128, S.F., 23, 30 December 1932.
Case 4287-C, 23-100-905, RG 60, NA.
Walker, Charles, Commander, Coast Guard Station, Humboldt Bay 16 November 1924, to Superintendent,12ᵗʰ District.
_____. 8 March 1926.
Zimmerman, Commander Gabe, to Commander, Base 17 (San Pedro).
U.S. CUSTOMS SERVICE, San Francisco. Box 89, 90, RG 36, NA San Bruno.
"Customs Report," and "Report of a Customs Official on the West Coast." to Wickersham Commission, 21 July 1930, Box 200, 17-18, Box 202, RG 10, NA.
Irby, Jonathan S., Surveyor of Customs, S.F., series of letters warning various agencies about boats leaving Vancouver with loads of liquor, December 1920 to June 1923, and letters clarifying the policy of Customs locking and sealing

liquor aboard ships coming into California ports, Box 333, NA San Bruno.

McGrath, H. F., Deputy Collector, Eureka, 7 April 1927, to Collector of Customs, S.F., 34-20, Box 88, RG 36, NA San Bruno.

INTERNAL REVENUE SERVICE, RG 58, NA.

Anslinger, 31 March 1930, to H. Jones, Esquire, Dept. of Justice, Treasury Dept., Box 6.

Hayden, S.F.to Att. Gen., Box 6.

Memorandum Re: Lester M. Gillis. With Aliases. 28 November 1934. 95-57-8.

Oftedal, Alf to Chief Intelligence Unit, IRS WDC November 4, 1926.

Mellon, A. W. "Regulations of Internal Revenue (T.D. 3601)." 7 June 1924, 51-55, WDC. Box 6.

NATIONAL COMMISSION OF LAW OBSERVANCE AND LAW ENFORCEMENT, known as the Wickersham Commission, RG 10, NA

Hallanan, W. M., Chief of Police, Sacramento, 20 September1929, to Wickersham Commission.

"List of Persons Killed of Fatally Insured by officers of Bureau of Prohibition." Ms., Box 6.

"Pacific Data." Box 230

Hoffman, William. L.A., 19 April 1930, to Wickersham.

"Wine Report." Box 207.

　　Boxes cited: 66, 69, 70, 72, 72, 75, 85, 88, 89, 200, 201, 202, 206

STATE OF CALIFORNIA

California Blue Book or State Roster 1928. Sacramento: CA State Printing Office, 1928.

Fiftieth Session, Ch. 178, 625, 2942; Ch. 26, 2516; Ch.1923, 1697 ? Ch. 657 ?

"Final Calendar of Legislative Business." 42nd Session, Sacramento 1917.

Sacramento Criminal Docket, 30 December 1930—12 September 1931; *Annual Report of the Division of Criminal Identification and Investigation.* Sacramento: State Department of Penology, 1932.

Senate Joint Resolution No. 4. 43rd Session, 6 January 1919, 1363-64 [Ratification of 18th Amendment].

Statement of Vote, 2 November 1886 to 2 November 1926, showing defeat of Initiative Act 1 and 22 by California voters, 1918, 33 and 43.

Statutes of California, Section 7, Ch. 149, 558ff.

Wright Act. California State Legislature, 44th Session, Ch. 80, 7 May 1921, 79. But this was delayed until referendum in 7 November 1922; repealed by initiative approved 8 November 1932.

COUNTY OF LOS ANGELES

Missing Person, Case of Frank Baumgarteker, L.A. County, 25 February 1930.

COUNTY OF SAN BERNARDINO

Sheriff's Deed of Execution, San Bernardino County, 30 August 1933, for Mary Q. Baumgarteker's purchase of California Medicinal Wine Company for $12,000 from her own estate.

CITY OF LOS ANGELES

"Memorandum," Division of Public Relations. Los Angeles: L.A. Police Dept., 1929.

PERIODICALS

"Chinese Aliens and Booze Had Priority of First Patrol." *Valley Grove* ___ [?]. vol. 6, no. 24. The rest of the title of the periodical is missing and magazine is no longer published, but the press address was 419 Sweetwater Road, Lemon Grove, which is now another business. No author or date was listed in copy provided the author.

Anti-Saloon League Bulletin. Nd.

California Industries and Prohibition. S.F: United California Industries (1916).

California Liberator. San Francisco (February 1926).

California Observer. (1 January 1921): 27-30, 33.

Christian Century (June 1930).

Cox, Bill. "Moonshiners in Meadowbrook Valley." *High Country,* no. 2 (autumn 1967): 17-22.

Edwards, Leland. "A Deadly Confrontation." *Los Tulares* Quarterly Bulletin, Tulare Historical Society, Visalia (March 1996).

Gray, Eugene L. "Looking Back on Days of Prohibition." *Sutter County Historical Society News Bulletin,* vol. XVII, no. 1 (January 1979): 13, 15.

Jaeger, Edmund C. "The Ghost that Refuses to Die." *Desert Magazine* (August 1954), excerpt from Al Bush, Apple Valley, 1995.

Liberal Leader: The Official Organ of the Bartenders' Union, Local 41 (September 1917; 15 August 1916).

Literary Digest. XXV, no. 5. New York: 4 November 1922.

Magistretti, Clarence. "Funny Old World." *Point Reyes Historian* (fall 1978).

Mason, Richard. "Booze on the Beach." Article courtesy of Richard Mason, Inverness, Marin historian.

580

Pedersen, Ralph "Swede." "The Highlights of Bootlegging." *Sausalito Historical* Quarterly Sausalito Historical Society, vol. 2, no. 1 (fall 1980).

Stanislaus Stepping Stones, vol. 7, no. 3 (fall 1983): 384-388.

The Wanderer, vol. 1, no. 1 (Los Angeles: May 1922).

Union Signal. WCTU publication (15 February 1928). Found in Willebrandt File, 82-59618, Library of Congress.

Von Krakou, William Eslers. "Phsiology [*sic*] and Hygiene Versus the Folly of Alcohol Prohibition." *The Liberal Leader* (San Francisco: 15 August 1916- 1 September 1917).

Walker, Clifford J. "The 10th Anniversary of Prohibition in Wet Riverside County." *Country Life*, vol. 2, no.1 (January 1980): 6-7.

NEWSPAPERS

"'All That Glitters'. .., and Sally Knows." Editorial. *Sausalito Independent Journal*, March 1935.

"Interview with John and Nellie Egbert." *Green Mountain Gazette, 13 February 1979*

Baldwin, Doug. *Centennial Edition. Salinas, Californian*, 11 October 1971,

Barstow Printer, 1917-1919; 6, 15 February 1923; 29 January 1925; 1 April 1926; 4 August 1927; March-December 1931; July1932-December 1933.

Berdahl, Doris. "Sausalito's Bootlegging Days." *Marine Scope*, 8-14 February 1972, with background by Sausalito's resident historian Ralph "Swede" Pedersen.

Chico Enterprise, 8 June 1928.

Chula Vista Star, 1 January 1931-1 July 1932. Not much in this paper on prohibition, except drunks and drunk driving.

Contra Costa Gazette (Martinez), 11, 18, 25 January, 1 February-July 1919.

Corona Daily Independent, January 1927—January 1928.

Craig, Pat. "When Tracy Was Called 'Poker City.'" *Tracy Press Centennial Edition, 6* September 1978.

Crescent City American, 1 December 1926; 20 January, 20 February 1927 (various issues).

Daily Palo Alto Times, 9-29 April 1927.

Daily Telegram (San Luis Obispo), 3, 5, 6, 12, 18 January 1931.

Del Norte Triplicate, 10 February-5 May 1933.

Dickson, Edward H. *Sacramento Bee, 18* January 1970. Dickson said, "Sacramento lived through prohibition with one eye closed, the other red," and the author used this phrase for part for his book title.

Dos Palos Star, 1 July 1932-November 1933; 1 January 1934.

Evening Star (Washington), 11 March 1931, found in Willebrandt Manuscript, File 82-59618. Library of Congress.

Feather River Bulletin, February-October 1926; 15 June 1930; 1 January 1931; January-December 1932; January-30 June 1933.

Ferndale Enterprise, 1 January-August 1926.

Fort Bragg Advocate and News, January-31 May, August, 31 October, 1-30 November, December 1933.

Healdsburg Tribune, 26 December 1918.

Holtville Tribune, January 1925; 16 October, 30 November 1930.

Humboldt Standard (Eureka), January-December 1922-January 1923.

Imperial County Farmer (El Centro), 7 January-12 February 1932; 30 June-14 July 1932.

Inyo Independent, January-December 1917; January-April 1918; 1922-1924, selected issues. Inyo County Library.

Journal-News (San Diego), 7 September 1932-10 April 1933.

Kellogg, Byrd Weyler. "False Gayety, Wild Parties and Search for Thrill, Blamed for Girl's Death." Reprinted in *The Fort Bragg Advocate and News*, 15 February 1933, from the *Santa Rosa Democrat*, 15 February 1933.

Livermore Herald, 21 September 1918; 1924; January 1925.

Livermore Journal, 25 May 1927.

Los Angeles Examiner, 8 November 1924.

Los Angeles Times, 1-3 December 1929.

Marin Journal, 28 September 1918; 17, 31 December 1925.

Marin Scope, 8-14 February 1972; 16-22, 23-29 October 1984.

Mendenhall, Ann, editor. *Ann's Humboldt Scrapbook*. Excerpts from *Humboldt Standard* (Eureka), 5 April 1923.

Menlo Park Recorder, 1 October-31 December 1933.

Morrall, Jane. "When Rumrunners Ruled," *San Mateo County Times*, 14 November 1997.

Mountain Democrat (Placerville), 14 December 1918-15 February 1919; 21 June-5 July 1919.

National Plumas Bulletin, 19 March 1931.

Needles Nugget, selected issues 1928-31.

Oakland Tribune, 13 July 1931, from "Christian Endeavor World Scrapbook."

Oceanside Blade, 6 December 1923; 17, 24 January, 12 June, 25 September 1924; 2 August1927.

Ontario Weekly Herald, January-December 1928; 5 November 1929; January-13 November, 11, 18, 25 December 1930.

Pedersen, Ralph "Swede" and Doris Berdahl. "Sausalito's Bootlegging Days." *Marin Scope*, 8-14 February 1972.

Pipkin, George. "The Owl, the Silver Dollar and the Monkey House," nd, perhaps from *Trona Argonaut*. Copy courtesy of Margaret Brush, Trona.

_____. "Trona Memories," Chapter XLIV. *Trona Argonaut*, 22 June 1977.

_____. "Trona Memories," Chapter XXXII. *Trona Argonaut*,22 July 1977.

_____. "Trona Memories," Chapter XXXIV, *The Trona Argonaut*,22 March 1978.

Placerville Republican, 3 January-5 February 1927.

Plumas National Bulletin, 1 January 1920; 6, 13, 27 January, 3, 10, 17 February, 17 March, 4 April 1921; 1926; 6
January 1927; 19 March 1931?; 20 July 1933.
Redlands Daily Facts, 1, 7 November 1929.
Redwood City Standard, January-July 1920; 10, 17 February, 17 March, 4 April 1921; January-June 1922; 1, 8 February,
28 June, 2 August 1923; 30 October,13 November, 4, 18 December 1924; November 1924; 1926; 3 March, June
1927; 22 March, 12 April, November 1928; February, 29 May 1929; 13 May 1930; 12-15 February 1925.
Redwood City Tribune, 2 July 1924; 11 May, 30 June 1927.
Reno Evening Gazette, 19 March-15 May 1935, various issues in Case 95-57-8, Section 7 (Lester Gillis case), Federal
Bureau of Investigation, NA.
Riverside Daily Press, 1 November-8 December 1930.
Robbins, Millie. "Sausalito's Salty Bootleg Days." *San Francisco Chronicle*, 27 May 1966.
Sacramento Bee, 19 December 1928; 1-30 June 1932; 6 December 1933; 18 January 1970.
Sacramento Union, 27 July 1933.
Salinas Californian, Californian's Centennial Edition,1971. Reprint of Moss Landing battle.
San Bernardino Daily Sun, 1-29 September, 20 November-December 1929; 14 January 1930.
San Diego Independent, 2 December 1925.
San Diego Union, 25-27 May, July, 13 August, 2, 11, 28 September, 21-22 October 1917; 1-17 August 1929; 15, 16
January, 14 September, 16-17 November 1930; 1931; 1, 6-9 July 1932; 22 December 1968; 9 October 1988.
San Francisco Call, 13 July 1931, found in "Christian Endeavor World Scrapbook."
San Francisco Chronicle, 4 October 1921; 18-19, 23 May 1922; 25 June 1924; 7-8, 10 July, 10, 25 October, November
1925; 2 January 1926; 12 June 1927;13, 27 August, 11, 15, 17, 22 November 1928; 22 February, 9 March, 30 May
1929; 15 January, 18 April 1930; December 1930;11 March, 15 July 1931; 11, 19 December 1932; 7-8, 10-11, 14
November, 1-4, 6-8, 30-31 December 1934; 1-5, 16-18 January, 27, 31 March, 1 April 1935; 4 June 1935; 18
January, 26 July 1936; 3 May 1937; 14 ? 1972.
San Francisco Examiner, 22 May 1922; January 1923; 24 June, 6, 8 November 1924; 6, 8 July, 22 [?], 25 October 1925;
2 January 1926; 13 August, 15 November 1928; 27 February; 9 March, 30 May; 14 July, 1 December 1929; 15
January, 18 April 1930; 15 July 1931; 31 March, 1 April 1935;15 October 1995.
San Jose Mercury. 1-9 April 1933
San Mateo News-Leader, 25, 29 January 1919; January-July 1920.
San Rafael Weekly Independent, January 1919.
Sausalito Independent Journal, 17 December 1925; March 1935.
Sausalito News, 6, 23 November 1925; 1926; 16 November 1928; 4, 11, 18, 25 January 1929.
Siskiyou News, 30 November 1922.
Solano County Currier (Suisun), 3, 5 January 1924.
Sonoma Index Tribune, 1917; January-February, 7, 9 March, 13 April, July 1918.
Spackman, Ellis L. "'Saloons' Are Gone Forever." *San Bernardino Sun*, nd.
Stockton Independence, 4 August 1931.
Stockton Index, 1-5 December 1933.
Stockton Record, November-December 1933.
Svanevik, Michael and Shirley Burgett. "Prohibition Simply Failed to Prohibit in San Mateo County." *Inquirer Bulletin*
(San Carlos), 28 June 1997.
The Tracy Press (Semi Weekly), 14 January 1927-30 May 1928.
Times Gazette (Redwood City), 28 June, 12, 19 July, 2, 16 August 1919; 24 January 1920; 12, 19 February, 21 March
1921; 12, 19 February 1923.
Times Herald Record,6 January 1994.
Trona Pot-Ash, 1925; 6 August 1927; 2 January, 28 February 1928; 1929; 8, 22 March, 19 April, 10 May, 14 June, 30
August 1930; 1931, 1933.
Victor Valley News-Herald, 6 July 1917; 11 April 1924; 1926; 6 September 1929. Copies courtesy of Arlene Kallenberger,
Victorville.
Walton, Richard H. "Investigator Seeks Posthumous Pardon in 70-year-old Murder." *The San Bernardino Sun*, 14 July
1995. This article referred to District Attorney Stephen E. Metzler, Humboldt County, who may have prosecuted, for
political reasons, an innocent man in the prohibition days.
Washington Post, ca 1930, found in Willebrandt Manuscript, File 82-59618. Library of Congress.
Wichels, Ernest D. "Inland Rum-running," from "Prohibition Days."*Times-Herald* (Vallejo) 18 February 1979, from
Wood Young, The Story of the Hawk." *The Daily Republic* (Fairfield), 3 April 1962.
_____."The Repeal," from "The Era of Prohibition." *Times-Herald*, 16 January 1972.
_____."Vallejo--Wet and Dry." *Times-Herald*, 8 August 1965.
Wood, Barbara. "Bill Miramontes Remembers Coastside Bootlegging Years." *Times Tribune* (Palo Alto/Redwood City), 1
September 1985.
Young, Wood. Excerpts from "The Saga of the *Hawk.*" *The Daily Republic* (Fairfield), 3 April 1962. Excerpts courtesy of
Bertram Hughes, Vacaville.

INTERVIEWS

All interviews, unless stated otherwise, were done by the author.
"Diamond George." Los Angeles, 18 February 1978.

Alf, Gertrude. Daggett, 25 September 1977.

Alf, Larry. Barstow, 1977.

Anderholt, Joe. Imperial, 19 September 1994.

Anonymous. "Doubling Profits." San Francisco, August 1978.

Anonymous. "Old Times in Stockton." Stockton, August 1982.

Anonymous. "Sally's Place." July 1979

Baker, Jay. Humboldt County, July 1979.

Barbereno, Ray. Redondo Beach, 16 August 1977.

Baumgarteker, Herbert. Lake Arrowhead, 29 May 1978; 12 April 1979; 10 April 1980. He was the son of Frank who disappeared in 1929.

BC [pseud.]. North of Gulala, July 1979.

Beard, Don. San Bernardino, 1977. Story "The Booze Is Behind the Toilet" is about his Aunt Jane, Armilda Jane James, former chorus girl in Hollywood during prohibition, who went to Palm Springs as a maid.

Bell, Pat. San Gregorio. 10 July 1978?.

Beltramo, Alex. Menlo Park, 21 & 23 August 1977.

Boggio, Joe. Winnemucca, 28 August 1977.

Bonjo, Josie. Menlo Park, 1978.

Bright [pseud.] San Bernardino, 1980.

Brock, Leonard. Deer Creek, 24 August 1977.

Calloni, Al. Redwood City, 21 August 1977.

Calloni, Valia. Redwood City, 21 August 1977. Mother of Al.

Campanelli, Joe. Redwood City, 19 August1978.

Carroll, Bill. Telephone conversation from San Marcos, 26 December 1995.

Chase, Ambrose. Interview by Ralph "Swede" Pedersen, San Rafael, ca. 1980. Ambrose was the younger brother of Johnny Paul Chase.

Conaway, Ray. Barstow, 1978 and 1980.

Conner, David. Saddle Tramp Saloon, Fern Fall, 10-11 September 1977.

Cullen, William. San Mateo, 1979-1980. He sang the 1919 song "Prohibition Blues."

Derham, Jack K. Atherton, 19 June 1993. Former lawyer in San Francisco.

Devlin, Dick. Barstow, 19 February 1994.

Douglass, Ralph. Menlo Park, August 1978.

Duckett [first name unknown]. Sonoma County, July 1979.

Echols, Lee E. Chula Vista, 1978 and 1979.

Eifler, Carl F. Salinas, 1978 and 1981.

Falcone, Bat. San Pedro, 3 August 1981.

Ferguson, Gladys. Holtville, 1979. She was a leader in the Imperial County WCTU from 1923 to 1970s.

Genini, William. San Francisco, August 1978.

Giardino, George Edward. Yermo, 1980.

Gillett, Harold. Citrus Heights, 1978.

Gillett, Paul. El Centro, 1978.

Green, Louise. Wilmington, 3 August 1981.

Gunn, David. Boron, 1978 and 1979.

Gwin, Thelma. Barstow, 1980.

Haensal, Arda. San Bernardino, September 1978.

Hall, Frank. San Pedro, 3 August 1981.

Hinds, May [pseud.]. Quincy, 21 July 1980.

Hollenstein, Andy. Carmel Valley, 26 July 1979.

Hyder, Denton O. "Buster." New Cuyama, September 1981.

Isaacs, Marian. San Francisco, 13 September 1978.

James, Henry. Barstow, 1977.

Jay, Henry. Helendale, 20 June 1994

Jennings, Harry Sr. Santa Monica, 1978.

Jensen, Ralph. Dos Palos, 20 August 1977.

Jones, H. A. Carmel Valley, 27 July 1979.

Kearney, Tom. Phone conversation. Menlo Park, summer 1978.

Kerr, Ralph. Mendocino County, July 1979.

Langley, Maggie. Oro Grande, 26 September 1977.

Larson, Burt. Menlo Park, 22 August 1977.

Lawson, Scott. Quincy, 23 June 1993. Lawson is historian at Plumas County Museum.

Lehman, Allen. Crescent City, July 1979.

Lehman, William. Moss Landing, 26 July 1979.

Leon [last name unknown]. Clark Hotel, Los Angeles, 19 February 1978.

Luhmann, Pat "Atolia Pat." Atolia, 29 September 1977.

Lyttle, Rolan. Paradise Springs, 1978 and 1979.

Manit, Max. Portola, 24 June 1993. Manit was son of a bar owner during the latter part of prohibition in Portola.

Mason, Jack. Inverness, 14 July 1979.

McNeil, Henry "Mac." Escondido, 19 July ?; 3 October 1977.

McShan, Maggie. Needles, 18 March 1994.

Morrow, Jill. Las Vegas, NV., 31 January1995. Morrow worked for the Brewers Union in the Mission District in San Francisco in 1969. She knew an old character who had his leg shot off in his rum-running activities.

Morrow, Penny. Oro Grande, 26 September 1977 and 1978.

Mortz, Charles J. Barstow, 31 July 1977.

Murello, John. Wilmington, August 1977.

Nelson, Inez. Beckwourth, 24 June 1993.

O'Leary, Jim. Fern Fall, 11-12 September 1977.

Orr, John. Quincy, 21 July 1980.

Oswald, Barbara (Puccinelli). Menlo Park, 3 August 1998. She is the daughter of William Puccinelli.

Oswald, Ralph. Menlo Park, 3 August 1998.

Pedersen, Ralph "Swede." Sausalito, 1978, 1979, 1980.

Perrin, Doug. Laguna Beach, 20 August 1980.

Petersen, Charley E. Barstow, April 1995.

Pollard, Helen. Dos Palos, 20 August 1977.

Pollard, Mike. Dos Palos, 20 August 1977.

Prendiville, Father Richard. Fairfax, 1978.

Puccinelli, G. William. San Mateo, 24, 25 July 1980 and 1981.

Reddick, Harry. Dos Palos, 20 August 1977.

Reese, Larry L. Victorville, 2 March 1999.

Rice, Francis. Holtville, 1978.

Rodriquez, Mike. Barstow, 30 August 1995.

Rossiter, Wayne. Menlo Park, 21-22 August 1977.

Ruiz, Ray. Hollywood,15 August 1977.

Ruth _____. Anchor Bay, 15 July 1979

Sandoz family descendant. Hinkley, 1989.

Settle, Glen. Lancaster, 21 June 1996.

Shields, William. Laguna Beach, 21 August 1980.

Silvestre, Ellsworth. Victorville, 26 September 1977.

Steenfott, Norton. Eureka, July 1979 and 1981.

Stein, Gladys. Victorville, 1980.

Stoner, Tammy. Barstow, 24 November 1995.

Stroud, John. Menlo Park, 21 August 1977.

Thorpe, Bud. Redwood City, 14 July 1980.

Van Luven, Judge Donald Earl. San Bernardino, 1977.

Villegas, Celia Ortega. Barstow, 1981.

Walker, Dave. Anderson, 24 August 1977.

Watkins, Bud. Laguna Beach, 21 August 1980

Watkins, Ehrma. Needles, 18 March 1994.

Wichels, Ernie. Vallejo, 1980.

Widolf, Eleanor. Laguna Beach, 20 August 1980.

Widolf, Phil. Laguna Beach, 20 August 1980.

Wilhelm, Walt. Yermo, 21 September 1977.

Wilkins, Ralph. Boron, 1978, 1979, 16 October 1983 (89 years old in 1983).

Williams, Artie. Dos Palos, 20 August 1977.

Williams, Robert. Phone conversation. 29 September 1977.

Zanoni, Armand. La Honda, 10 July 1978.

LETTERS

Breaum, Nellie. Redwood City, 20 April 1979 to author.

Cotton, Nan Hauser. Pollock Pines, 26 June 1996 to author.

Echols, Lee E. Chula Vista, 1 August 1981 to author. Reference about Wad Oates, Aaron Quick, Charley Gray and Chinese smuggling.

Hyder, Denton O. "Buster" New Cuyugas to author, 29 September 1981.

Morgan, Bob. Palo Alto, 15 October 1994 to author.

MISCELLANEOUS

Adams, Franklin P. "We Like It," New York World in Don Whitehead, Border War. New York: Avon Books, 1963, 84.

American Business Men's Prohibition Foundation. Information sheet. Chicago 1929, RG 10, NA.

Christian Endeavor World Scrapbook, 1931.

Crusaders, The. Membership Form and Pledge. New York: ca.1928.

Hale, Jack. Video tape (1998) of old film of Jack Hale's rumboat Zeitgeist, picking up a load of whiskey from a small mother boat, ca 1932. Courtesy of Ralph Oswald, Menlo Park, 3 August 1998.

Henderson, Tracey. Imperial Valley. San Diego: Neyenesch Printers, 1968. Small monograph.

Salopek, Paul. Original illustrations. Barstow, 1977.

"Prohibition Blues." Lyrics by Ring Lardner, music by Nora Bayer, sung in *Ladies First.* Copyright 1919. Words sung by William Cullen, 1978.

Warshaw Collection of Business Americana. Smithsonian Institution. Washington, D. C. This collection had hundreds of signed and validated prescriptions for whiskey for just one drugstore in New York.

Women's Organization for National Prohibition Reform. MMC 1618. Library of Congress.

WORKS CITED FOR MERRITT BARNES' "Wet as the Pacific Ocean,"
Chapter 21, from end notes 6 through 43.

NEWSPAPERS AND PERIODICALS
The California Liberator, April, July, October 1922, January, February 1923; June, December 1924; June, October 1926.

The California Minute Man, November 1925.

New York Times, 23 January 1921; 15 April 1922. March 1926

San Francisco Bulletin, 20 June 1920.

San Francisco Call, 25 March 1920; 26 April, 5-15 May 1923; 19, 27 November 1924.

San Francisco Chronicle, 25, 26 April 1923; 23 November 1924; 1 January 1926; 7 August 1930

San Francisco Examiner, 17 January 1920; 25 April 1923; 26 May 1926.

San Francisco News, 23 December 1924; 27 August 1925.

Searchlight, November 1914.

BOOKS
Brown, Elizabeth A. *The Enforcement of Prohibition in San Francisco,* 19-20, 32.

Caen, Herb. *Bagdad by the Bay.* Garden City: Doubleday & Co., 1949, 69, 174-75.

_____. *Don't Call It Frisco.* Garden City: Doubleday & Co., 1953, 63, 131-32, 256.

_____. *Herb Caen's San Francisco.* Garden City: Doubleday & Co., 1957, 70

Erlick, *A Life in My Hands,* 135.

Flamm, Jerry. *San Francisco's 20's, 30's—Good Life in Bad Times.* San Francisco: Chronicle Books, 1976, 19-21, 50, 62-63.

Hichborn, Franklin. *Story of the Session of the California Legislature of 1909.* San Francisco: James H. Barry Company, 1909, 184.

Metz, Charles. "The Crusader Starts," *Outlook and Independent,* 15 October 1930, 78, quoted in George Mowry, *The Twenties Fords, Flappers and Fanatics.* Englewood Cliffs: Prentice Hall Incorporated, 1963, 186.

Ostrander, Gilman. *The Prohibition Movement in California 1848-1933.* Berkeley: University of California Press, 1957, 150, 173, 179.

Mowry, George. *The California Progressives.* Chicago: Quandrangle Books, 1951, 217.

Rogers, Will. *Newsweek,* 18 March 1932, quoted in Clementina Marie Fisher, *James Rolph Jr. 1869-1934: An Estimate of His Influence on San Francisco's History.* Master's thesis, University of San Francisco, 1965, 107.

Sabraw, Liston. *Mayor James Rolph Jr. And the End of the Barbary Coast.* Master's thesis, San Francisco State University, 1960, 177-78.

Siefkin, David. *The City at the End of the Rainbow—San Francisco and Its Grand Hotels.* New York: G. P. Putnam's Sons, 1976, 115-16.

Stanford, Sally. *The Lady of the House—The Autobiography of Sally Stanford.* New York: G. P. Putnam's Sons, 1966, 46-47, 66-67.

Watkins, T. H. and R. R. Olmstead, *Mirror of the Dream, An Illustrated History of San Francisco.* San Francisco: Scrimshaw Press, 1976, 264.

MISCELLANEOUS
"Atherton Graft Report." *San Francisco Chronicle,* 17 March 1937.

Brooke, John. Interview by Barnes, 8 December 1977. He was former Yellow Cab Company official.

Delaplane, Stanyon. Letter to author [Barnes], 6 February 1977.

_____. "Pete McDonough," *San Francisco Chronicle,* 10 July 1947.

Rolph, Jimmy. Letter to Reverend J. C. Westenberg, 9 August 1913, in Rolph Papers.

Wing, Harvey. Interview by Barnes, 27 February 1978. Wing was a former reporter of both the *Examiner* and the *News.*

Index

Symbols

588

X

Y

Z